Postcolonial Studies *and Beyond*

Postcolonial Studies *and Beyond*

Edited by

ANIA LOOMBA,

SUVIR KAUL,

MATTI BUNZL,

ANTOINETTE BURTON,

and JED ESTY

Duke University Press

DURHAM AND LONDON

2005

2nd Printing, 2006

© 2005 Duke University Press

All rights reserved

Printed in the United States of America on acid-free paper ∞

Designed by Erin Kirk New

Typeset in Sabon by Tseng Information Systems, Inc.

Library of Congress Cataloging-in-Publication Data appear on the last printed page of this book.

Neil Lazarus's essay, "The Politics of Postcolonial Modernism," was originally published in *The European Legacy* 7, no. 6 (2002): 771–82, http://www.tadf.co.uk.journals.

Contents

Acknowledgments

This volume has been developed out of the "Postcolonial Studies and Beyond" conference held at the University of Illinois, Urbana-Champaign, April 25–28, 2002. The editors of this volume, who also organized the conference, would like to thank the many people, too numerous to be individually acknowledged, who sustained this entire venture. We are particularly grateful to Professor Jesse Delia, the Dean of Liberal Arts and Sciences, who offered a state-of-the-art conference grant. Peter Garrett, then director of the Unit for Criticism and Interpretive Theory, was quick to offer the programmatic, logistical, and financial resources of the unit, and Dennis Baron, then head of the Department of English, joined in making possible the major funding for the conference. For generous sponsorship we are also grateful to Christine Catanzarite, the associate director of the Illinois Program for Research in the Humanities (whose expertise we also drew on at each stage of planning) and Masumi Iriye, the associate director of the Center for Advanced Study. Several colleagues helped prepare the intellectual grounds for this event, and we would like particularly to thank David Prochaska, Tony Ballantyne, Bill Kelleher, Martin Manalansan, Adlai Murdoch, Dara Goldman, Jean-Phillipe Mathy, Elena Delgado, Simona Sawhney, Zsuzsa Gille, William Munro, Andy Orta, Eve-Lynn Jagoe, Kwaku Korang, Alejandro Lugo, Bob Parker, Adam Sutcliffe, and Michael Rothberg. Thanks also to Rob Henn, Boatema Boateng, and Dan Vukovich at the Unit for Criticism and Interpretive Theory, to Cathy Harney and Christine Clark of the Department of English, and to Scott Paceley of the University of Illinois Printing Services, all of whom proved vital to the planning and smooth functioning of the conference. While we have not been able to include all the papers originally presented, we would like to thank all the participants (including several members of the audience) who contributed to the conversations and exchanges that took place at the original event and that have shaped this book in numerous ways.

Our emphasis on the future directions of postcolonial studies locates this volume within a local genealogy, that of two major conferences previously organized at the University of Illinois, Urbana-Champaign, and of the volumes they produced—*Marxism and the Interpretation of Culture* (1988) and *Cultural Studies* (1992). Cary Nelson, who had an important role to play in both of those conferences and volumes, was always available for advice as we put together our conference. Even as we took such earlier ground-clearing enterprises as models, we also recognized that, in a sense, the moment for monumental interdisciplinary intervention has passed. But this is not by any means to subscribe to premature and exaggerated accounts of the "death of theory," nor to strike an elegiac pose toward postcolonial studies itself. Indeed, we undertook this project not so much in order to define or defend a specific intellectual territory according to its institutional origins, its decisive crises, and its ultimate destiny, but to try to locate the most exciting and fresh examples of the interdisciplinary, theoretical, and critical work currently redefining the meaning of postcolonial studies. A project like this requires the cooperation of many individuals and institutions, and we cannot list them all here; suffice it to say that the work of a great many people enabled this volume. Of them, no one was more gracious and efficient than Miriam Angress, our editor at Duke University Press. Finally, we wish to acknowledge the three anonymous readers at Duke University Press who offered valuable perspectives on the project.

Beyond What? An Introduction

ⓔ ⓔ ⓔ

ANIA LOOMBA, SUVIR KAUL, MATTI BUNZL,

ANTOINETTE BURTON, JED ESTY

The shadow the 2003 US invasion of Iraq casts on the twenty-first century makes it more absurd than ever to speak of ours as a postcolonial world. On the other hand, the signs of galloping US imperialism make the agenda of postcolonial studies more necessary than ever. In a context of rapidly proliferating defenses of empire (not simply de facto but de jure) by policy makers and intellectuals alike, the projects of making visible the long history of empire, of learning from those who have opposed it, and of identifying the contemporary sites of resistance and oppression that have defined postcolonial studies have, arguably, never been more urgent. In many ways, the new global reality has made the analysis of imperialism, in all its historical variants, more pressing, but also more difficult, than ever before. What, then, do we propose to move "beyond"?

We will address this question under a number of rubrics in this introduction, as will, in very different ways, each of the essays assembled here. This volume (and the conference "Postcolonial Studies and Beyond," held at the University of Illinois, Urbana-Champaign, April 25–28, 2002, at which the essays that follow were first presented as papers) was conceived before September 11, 2001, and before US president George Bush's so-called war on terror had catalyzed the new imperial situation. While no one could have foretold the exact sequence and pace of events that were to unfold, international relations across the globe were already marked by all the material and ideological tensions and inequities that fed into these later events, as the essays collected here make evident. When we conceived the conference, we had wanted to scrutinize whether postcolonial studies had proved important to the task of analyzing, with intellectual power and political clarity, both the colonial past and the new empires of our own times. Or did we have to go beyond the paradigms and analytical methods developed under this rubric to find answers? Our questions were in part dictated by the sense that most ideas, methods, and movements tend to have a distinct and bounded life span, after which it becomes clear that they have outlived their critical or political usefulness.

We emphatically did not want to rehash the controversies with which postcolonial studies or postcolonial theory have been riven from their formal beginnings in the Western academy, and for the most part we have not done so in this volume. Both the appropriateness of the *post* in *postcolonial* and the persistence of the *colonial* in helping us understand the past or the contemporary dynamics of our world have been debated at great (and, some would argue, unnecessary) length. The relationship of postcolonial studies to anticolonial nationalisms and struggles on the one hand, and to poststructuralist theory and the so-called linguistic turn, on the other, have resulted in particularly contentious debates about the place of the Western academy and Western-educated intellectuals from once-colonized countries in the institutionalization of the subject the world over. But these (and many other) earlier debates that regularly questioned the validity, contours, and future of postcolonial studies have now been reshaped by newer developments, the most urgent of which is globalization, at once an extension of the world-systems of modern capitalism and colonialism and a newer network that presents a complicated picture of national and transnational agents, capital and labor, suppliers and markets, NGOs and multilateral agencies. Some scholars view postcolonial methods and vocabularies as out of step with an intellectual scene increasingly carved up by such rubrics as the information age (the so-called digital divide), transnational capital, globalization, and alternative modernities. What, then, is the value of postcolonial studies in our globalizing world, and does it have a viable future beyond its existing life span, identified by Vilashini Cooppan in this volume as the period from Edward Said's *Orientalism* (1978) to Michael Hardt and Antonio Negri's *Empire* (2000)?[1]

We wanted to arrive at answers by asking scholars from a variety of disciplines and locations to consider the ways in which colonial discourse studies and postcolonial modes of thought have shaped intellectual, political, and methodological agendas both within their disciplines and among and beyond them. Thus we invited participants to reflect on the most crucial issues for the study of past colonialisms and the contemporary world. One consistent response from many of those we had invited was that they would not define themselves as postcolonialists. But that, in part, was precisely our point. Even among the five of us organizing the event, we could not always agree about who a "postcolonialist" might be. As Tim Brennan put it in his remarks at the conference:

> In spite of being clearly marked (if not segregated) within individual academic departments, postcolonial studies is a porous entity rather than a discrete field. It arose in the form of a political metaphorics rather than a bordered space, either "field" or "discipline." In disciplines like history and anthropology, postcolonial studies came into being under other names and without any claim to being a distinct subspecialty or field, as it did in English departments.

Postcolonial studies thus finds itself in a peculiar situation, one somewhat analogous to that of theory. It means different things to different people; it is housed in different disciplines yet widely associated with a few; it is viewed either as enormously radical or as the latest ideological offspring of Western capitalism; it is firmly entrenched in Anglo-US universities, yet its disciplinary status remains in question; it seeks to address the non-Western world yet is often received with hostility there.

Given this situation, we found it productive to move beyond narrow definitions of postcolonial studies and, frankly, beyond the usual suspects. Contributors address topics and issues that have had a transformative power in their disciplines, and in doing so, they remind readers that the project of postcolonial studies is a much larger and more variegated set of intellectual enterprises than we might have presumed so far. Very different kinds of scholarly inquiry now seem in fact postcolonial (even when their practitioners shy away from such identification).[2] Our belief is that this volume will serve as a powerful reminder of the different critical postcolonial practices that have been developing within, and are in turn rejuvenating, a variety of scholarly agendas and disciplines. We want in this way to signpost the expanded arenas of intellectual activity influenced by, and now constituting, postcolonial studies.

Of course, it is possible to argue that the term *postcolonial studies* has outlived its utility precisely because of this expansion of subject matter, analytical method, and historical scope. So one central question is: Does the work that we all agree is still relevant, perhaps more relevant than ever, proceed under the name *postcolonial studies* or not? One answer—the one we tend to gravitate toward—comes from Peter Hulme's contribution:

> If there is one particular stance I take with respect to the current state of postcolonial studies, it is that we are still discovering, slowly, perhaps, and unmethodically, but—as far as I am concerned—with a continuing sense of excitement, the dimensions of the field. What I mean by this is both that the field

is getting bigger as the characteristic language and thematic concerns of post-colonial studies spread across many disciplines and that at the same time we are unearthing a lot of earlier anticolonial work, often neglected at its time of writing, that is allowing us to piece together a fuller history of the development of postcolonial studies. So one of the fundamental "beyonds" suggested by my title is an encouragement to strip off the straitjacket of those accounts and definitions of postcolonial studies that simplify and narrow its range to the work of a handful of theorists and a handful of novelists. In the past, some of those who work within the field, or have a productive relationship to it, have even accepted that oversimplified picture of postcolonial studies. Fortunately, as this volume suggests, the picture is now beginning to broaden.

Thus, the *beyond* in the title of this volume is not meant to indicate a facile hope for a transformative shift in the practices loosely clustered round the affiliation postcolonial studies, nor does it mean to point to a wholly new mode of understanding the links between the critical study of empires and the neo-imperial structures of global inequality (although the volume does indicate significant new directions for future work). Rather, it charts a path between utopianism and "hip defeatism," as much by renewing engagements with analytical models developed by older anticolonial thinkers as by positing new forms of critique that will address the ideological and material dimensions of contemporary neo-imperialism.[3]

To that extent, one important theme running through the volume is the need to recapture a history of transoceanic and transcontinental trade, travel, and conquest so as to avoid a shallow embrace of the contemporary notion of the global. In the process, various essays suggest the new shape of an area studies whose contours include, for instance, unbeaten paths through the locally specific archives of Latin America and the rediscovered poetics of a truly *African* Black Atlantic. Equally important in the historical and geographical range of the essays is their ability to think beyond the West-rest binary and the legacy of Eurocentrism that continues to bedevil even its most ardent critics. The essays gathered here do not simply dispense with that old problematic, but they do trace unexpected and uneven developments before, during, and after colonial modernity. Rather than ritualistically rehearse the theoretical problem of Eurocentrism, they tend to point to a series of disciplinary and interdisciplinary practices that have already begun to gather outside its increasingly pale shadow.

Another crucial aspect of this volume is detailed in several different demonstrations of both the limits and the usefulness of disciplinary thinking in the field of postcolonial studies. Some essays offer broad reflections on the two-way influence between postcolonial thought and established university disciplines such as literary criticism and history, while others forge ahead into some vital if nascent areas for postcolonial research: media studies, environmental studies, religious studies, linguistic and semantic analysis, auto-ethnography, and the sociology of global cinema. At the same time, the volume presents several critical takes on the problematic intersections between the assumptions and practices associated with the term *multiculturalism* and those associated with the term *postcolonial*. Such discussion will be of interest to scholars concerned with the potential for postcolonial analysis as applied to the problem of multiethnic societies like Britain and the United States—especially with respect to the latter, where Jenny Sharpe's question, "Is the United States Postcolonial?" seems as self-evident as it is belated.[4]

Postcolonial studies has been at various times and in various ways inter-twined not just with multiculturalism and ethnic studies but also with an array of area studies, each with a differing sense of its place within (or angle of remove from) the prevailing conceptions of the postcolonial. The time seemed right to assess whether or not postcolonial studies was still offer-ing new intellectual resources to those fields or, indeed, as some of its most stringent critics have asserted, had begun instead to divert attention from the concrete particulars and current agendas associated with specific regions or subdisciplines.[5] As it turns out, some of our contributors do sense that post-colonial studies—once a provocative and illuminating new way to approach problems in their fields—has become staid or inert so that it now requires, in its turn, a revivifying influx from those intellectual quarters that once benefited from its paradigm-shifting energies. Although the volume reflects a range of views and attitudes, many of its contributors find common cause by reasserting the importance of the oppositional political energies that origi-nally animated decolonizing intellectuals the world over in the twentieth cen-tury. Several ask provocative questions about what has been lost in the in-stitutionalization of postcolonial studies as a cultural discipline dedicated to the analysis of discourse, and in the very important problematization of such central—and centrally imperial—Enlightenment concepts as "development" and "modernity." A keynote of the conference and of the volume, then, is the reassertion of a certain historical urgency that may have been leached from postcolonial studies during its period of theoretical refinement and in-stitutional consolidation.

The current effort to redefine and reassess (or, indeed, to elegize) post-colonial studies reflects a layered, complex history in which both anticolo-nial nationalists and, subsequently, postcolonial intellectuals generated dis-tinct and sometimes antithetical approaches to the legacy of colonialism both in the once-colonized zones, and, more recently, within the metropolitan academy. Moreover, in Britain, the old departments of Oriental and African studies—like state-sponsored area studies programs in the cold war United States—established and institutionalized influential divisions of academic labor, with the effect that Africanists (for example) have generally developed different understandings of postcolonial studies from those held by (say) Latin Americanists or South Asianists.

Indeed, the various legacies of modern colonialism across the globe have given rise not just to separate historical trajectories of conquest and resistance on the ground but to diverse traditions of postcolonial critique. Although, for example, postcolonial studies as such gained its footholds in the metropolitan universities through its rethinking of Anglophone and Francophone colonial legacies (due in no small part to the Anglo-French orientation of pioneering works like Said's *Orientalism*), the field has now been profoundly engaged by Latin American studies (among other area-studies fields that have remade themselves in the past fifteen years). The case of Latin America triangulates older models of West-rest geography and usefully reanimates the debate around alternative modernities, not just by pressing the claims of a historically salient semiperiphery but also by redressing the entire legacy of core-periphery thinking. Along these lines, Walter Mignolo has proposed a shift in orientation from "post-colonial" to "post-Occidental" reason, using the specific experiences and discourses of Latin America to come to fresh terms with what he calls the "modern/colonial world system."[6] Mignolo's work also pays close and due attention to the languages of colonial and postcolonial knowledge: he notes, for example, that "scholarly production in French, English, or German" has often displaced and overshadowed "intellectual genealogies in Spanish and Portuguese."[7] The encounter between postcolonial and Latin American studies means more than just recognizing new linguistic or geographic territory; it means a continual and reciprocal reshaping of key concepts, of intellectual practices reinflected by the thought of, say, José Martí and Roberto Fernandez Retamar, rather than Aimé Césaire and Frantz Fanon, or W. E. B. Du Bois and C. L. R. James. Scholars like Mignolo and Alberto Moreiras have sustained a serious argument about the translation and transformation of subaltern studies methodology into and by various settings in Latin America, with Mignolo's concept of "border gnosis" and Moreiras's resignification of "subalternism" offering theoretical elaborations and revisions of the original insights of subaltern historiography.[8]

The intellectual concerns and priorities that animate the intellectual borderlands between Latin Amerian studies and postcolonial studies differ again from those foregrounded by students of so-called minority discourses within Europe and North America, from those whose approaches derive from the study of colonialisms elsewhere and, perhaps most problematically of all, from those who produce postcolonial scholarship in indigenous or noncolonial languages. Instead of glossing over (or endlessly belaboring) such historical differences, we wanted to ask how the study of colonialism had shaped various scholarly domains and disciplinary genealogies. Conversely, how had the study of colonialism and of postcolonial societies evolved in conformity with or reaction to the institutional protocols of different subdisciplines or geographical "schools"?[9]

To pursue these questions systematically, we discussed them in biweekly seminars for a year leading up to the conference. Under the aegis of the Unit for Criticism and Interpretive Theory at the University of Illinois, we asked scholars in a range of fields—these could be disciplines such as anthropology or sociology, or interdisciplinary fields such as Caribbean studies or women's studies—to select and discuss seminal readings that addressed the reciprocal relations between postcolonial studies and their area of inquiry over the past decade. It goes without saying that even a yearlong seminar could not cover every geographic area or discipline, and we realized that this would hold even more true of a conference or a volume. While there have been very productive discussions about the relationship of postcolonial studies in relation to different histories and geographies (and scholarly languages), at this point we did not feel it to be intellectually useful to stage conversations that had as their main focus the differences between various colonial histories and postcolonial situations.[10] These intensive seminars confirmed for us that a more productive way of addressing some of the lacunae in postcolonial studies—such as the widely bemoaned lack of specificity and historical engagement of its "theoretical" components or the perceived centrality of an Anglophone model—would be to move to scholars who might not call themselves postcolonial at all, but whose work engages with and simultaneously ranges further than the recognizable paradigms and debates in the field. Conversely, scholarly practices in a number of fields, including those that do not announce themselves as postcolonial, share—have derived intellectual energy from—postcolonial critical projects and political priorities. Thus we wanted to focus on work that seemed to retain what was most valuable in postcolonial critique. These questions about methods, commitments, and objects of analysis in postcolonial studies have become even more important in the time that has elapsed since those seminars were first conceived. The rapid pace at which globalization is revealing its imperialist structure and ideologies throws our past debates into new relief, reminding us anew why we need to go beyond a certain kind of postcolonial studies, and also why we must reassert the value of many of the questions that it has examined so far.

Globalization and the Postcolonial Eclipse

Many commentators have recently observed that the debate around globalization—understood both as the structural transformation of geopolitical conditions and the academic study of that transformation—has in crucial sectors displaced postcolonial studies as the rubric under which interdisciplinary critique is produced in the academy today. This apparent eclipse of postcolonial studies by globalization studies works as perhaps the central galvanizing event shaping this volume. The key question addressed here is whether postcolonial studies can assert a specific method, interest, or political insight that can illuminate issues either ignored, marginalized, or depoliticized within the discussion of globalization.

Like most of our contributors, we think of postcolonial studies as a critical strain posed within and against, as well as antecedent to, dominant notions of globalization. As Simon Gikandi has recently noted, the shift from postcolonialism to globalization indicates the widespread belief that the explanatory, political, or intellectual power of the "narrative of decolonization" has collapsed.[11] Some take the eclipse of that narrative as a timely and progressive recognition that new answers and solutions must be posed to the problem of global social relations now, answers that no longer refer backward to the history of modern colonialism or to its legacies of core-periphery binarisms. But this, too, can function as an alibi for ignoring the persistent inequities and residual effects of colonially organized geopolitics. In the spirit of many contributors to this volume, Gikandi emphasizes a different orientation for postcolonial studies—one that does not prematurely overleap the nation, nor simply wish away Eurocentrism, nor accede to the image of a syncretic global village or to the neoliberal idea of a rising tide lifting all boats in the global economy.

Along similar lines, Susie O'Brien and Imre Szeman observe that "globalization may be the name for a false conceptual rapprochement between postmodernism and postcolonialism that eliminates all the worries expressed about the blind Eurocentrism of postmodernism through a spatio-temporal leveling of the globe." O'Brien and Szeman, like several of our contributors, stake a claim for the importance of postcolonial studies as a critical wedge against the superficial allure of that rapprochement, noting that "no other critical practice has foregrounded the links between cultural forms and geopolitics to the degree that postcolonial studies has over the past four decades."[12] Many of the most creative practitioners of postcolonial studies now, eager to avoid the assumption that difference is itself an outmoded concept in the era of globalization, have been seeking new models for describing the relationship between local, national, and transnational forces. In this volume, both Peter Hulme and Ali Behdad contend that postcolonial studies, in its insistence on the structural links between colonial and neocolonial forms of global hierarchy, has only now begun—in the age of globalization—to find its real critical vocation. Both present historically deep pictures of globalization—pictures, that is, of the embryonic and sometimes forgotten world-systems that have shaped the planet's social spaces for centuries and that redress the more superficial models of globalization that have come to prominence in the past five to ten years. Hulme's deft genealogy of the global image itself—the various techniques and technologies for representing planetary space and rendering planetary consciousness—gives a strong indication of how postcolonial studies might inflect or redirect the study of globalization. In particular, Hulme wonders what it might mean or whether it is indeed possible to imagine the globe without invoking imperial prospects and privileges. What he, following Denis Cosgrove, calls the Apollonian eye, that visual faculty powerful enough to generate an overview of the globe, seems almost always to require another kind of power that we call imperialism. In other words, Hulme's skepticism about globalization stems from a postcolonial humanist's insight into oversight: the way that the very vantage point necessary to enunciate the global implies an allegory of universal knowledge that cannot be ignored.

In this sense, Hulme provides precisely the kind of critical and postcolonial genealogy that Behdad calls for in his skeptic's tour of the discourse of globalization. Behdad notes that the global escapes most attempts to theorize or describe it, especially those using the terms of globalization discourse itself. One way, he suggests, to resist such occlusion is to detail the continuities—and indeed the innovations—between today's neo-imperialism and older systems of colonial capitalism. Like many in this volume, from different perspectives, Behdad envisions a vocation for postcolonial studies as, in a sense, the historical conscience—and consciousness—of the discourse of globalization. Behdad's postcolonial studies must insist on viewing the antecedent structural and epistemological conditions leading up to this particular moment in the history of global relations.

Of course the deep, even ancient, roots of contemporary globalization can also be mobilized for very different rhetorical and political purposes. As Vilashini Cooppan notes, both apologists for and critics of US hegemony have taken to resuscitating a Roman analogy to describe the shape of superpowerdom in the very epoch of globalization. Offering a brief reading of the blockbuster film *Gladiator* as a way to investigate and understand the United States' neo-imperial self-image in the flattering, silver-screened light of a Hollywood Pax Romana, she also marks the presence of such analogies in Hardt and Negri's *Empire*, which suggests (in Cooppan's paraphrase) that "the United States is closer to ancient Rome—with its expansionist republicanism, networked power, and syncretic, englobing culture—than to the territorial sovereignty, linear ambitions, and differentialist logic of the modern imperial European nation-state." Cooppan warns that if we follow "the implications of Hardt and Negri's analogizing of the United States and Rome as mirror republican empires, it becomes impossible to name, analyze, and contest the simple fact of US imperialism here and now." She sees the future task of postcolonial studies as more fully to address US power, to read that power as both an inner force and outer face of globalization.

It is not surprising that as the defense of the new empire becomes more unabashed in certain quarters, the Roman and British Empires, and particularly their fraudulent self-images, the Pax Romana and the Pax Britannica, are openly invoked by advocates of American hegemony. As the new imperial order shapes itself in the image of earlier empires, postcolonial studies must reshape itself to address that rhetorical effort and to redress the lost histories of colonialism obscured in the scramble for globalization's patina of universal progress. A large number of policy makers and academics in Britain and the United States are openly advocating the need for a Western, particularly US empire. They argue that the earlier wave of decolonization, not to mention the end of the cold war, has left a power vacuum that requires bold leadership on the world stage. Despite the fact that their essays were written before the events of 2003 had unfolded, and despite their methodological and philosophical disagreements and different assessments of postcolonial theory, our contributors agree that (to use Cooppan's words) "without an account of US imperialism in its various political, economic, military-industrial, and cultural guises, . . . we cannot hope to move postcolonial studies into the space of the beyond."

There will be no beyond, though, if we are held in thrall by the practice and the imagination of modern empires, especially given the remarkable speed with which US power is extended across the globe, threatening to outpace any description or analysis of it postcolonial critics might offer. As the writer-activist Arundhati Roy told a Harlem audience in May 2003, we live in a time when "we have to race to keep abreast of the speed at which our freedoms are being snatched from us, and when few can afford the luxury of retreating from the streets for a while in order to return with an exquisite, fully formed political thesis replete with footnotes and references . . . we have to think on our feet."[13] It is entirely the case that we must respond with speed and urgency to ongoing events, and true, too, that we need the conviction and simplicity of Césaire or Gandhi's pronouncements about the indefensibility, immorality, and brutality of imperial domination. However, as intellectuals and scholars, we cannot afford to choose between political responsibility and footnotes. The rapidly proliferating defenses of empire in the mainstream media and in the academy are today mounted precisely by ignoring the rich and varied scholarship of decolonization that has documented the complexity of the imperial past in order not only to make visible its continuing legacies but also to indicate its possible future forms.[14] Neo-imperialists have recently produced sound bites about the achievements of past empires and possibilities of future ones only by denying or distorting this scholarship. The destructive, even genocidal histories of modern empires are being whitewashed in order to rehabilitate the ideal of Western domination as an appropriate ideological cover for Anglo-American adventurism across the globe.

At this point, we should note how many postcolonial scholars (as illustrated in this volume) now take it as a central part of their work to come to terms afresh — analytically and critically — with the nature of US power in the contemporary world. Postcolonial scholarship thus has already shifted to consider more squarely the way US power has begun to absorb models of imperial might and rightness from the past. Since the invasion of Iraq, this agenda has become even more urgent in the face of historical claims such as this one from Niall Ferguson:

> The British Empire has had a pretty lousy press from a generation of "postcolonial" historians anachronistically affronted by its racism. But the reality is that the British were significantly more successful at establishing market economies, the rule of law and the transition to representative government than the majority of postcolonial governments have been. The policy "mix" favored by Victorian imperialists reads like something just published by the International Monetary Fund, if not the World Bank: free trade, balanced budgets, sound money, the common law, incorrupt administration and investment in infrastructure financed by international loans. These are precisely the things the world needs right now.[15]

Ferguson wants the US empire to do what Rudyard Kipling did, which is to "dare" to "speak its own name" and to act on its imperial convictions.[16] Thus the new imperial project appropriates the language of opposition. Ferguson's efforts at populist journalism are, if anything, a watered-down version of the pronouncements of that other holy warrior of Anglo-American expansionism, Paul Johnson, whose contribution to recent debate around Iraq also features the vocabulary and iconography of the British Empire:

> The US should put its trust in the seas and oceans, which offer a home and a friendly environment to its forces and do not change with the treacherous winds of opinion. The military lessons to be learned from the lead-up to the Iraq operation are profound, and all point in the same direction: America should always have the means to act alone. . . . it must also cultivate the will. Fate, or Divine Providence, has placed America at this time in the position of sole superpower, with the consequent duty to uphold global order and to punish, or prevent, the great crimes of the world. . . . It must continue to engage the task imposed upon it, not in any spirit of hubris but in the full and certain knowledge that it is serving the best and widest interests of humanity.[17]

Both Johnson's crusading zeal and Ferguson's more pragmatic Realpolitik are derived from imperial worldviews developed in the past three centuries. Both writers arrive at their neo-imperialism only by ignoring the murderous record of colonial history in favor of an emphasis on the failure to thrive, in the past three to five decades, of many decolonized nation-states.[18] Ferguson's nostalgia for Victorian imperialism stems from his belief that its leaders strove to implement "free trade, balanced budgets, sound money, the common law, incorrupt administration." But as Mike Davis has written in *Late Victorian Holocausts*, "If the history of British rule in India were to be condensed into a single fact, it is this: there was no increase in India's per capita income from 1757 to 1947. Indeed, in the last half of the nineteenth century, income probably declined by more than 50 percent."[19] Further, during the "age of Kipling, that 'glorious imperial half century' from 1872 to 1921, the life expectancy of ordinary Indians fell by a staggering 20 percent."[20] Davis goes on to explore several paradoxes that have an enormous relevance for our globalizing world today: "Where were the fruits of modernization, of the thousands of miles of railroad track and canal?" he asks.

> And where were the profits of the great export booms that transformed the subcontinent's agriculture in the second half of the nineteenth century? Here, if anywhere in rural Asia, integration into the world market should have resulted in significant local increases in local agricultural productivity and profitability. . . . Yet, as macroeconomic statistics demonstrate, such prosperity was usually ephemeral and quickly reabsorbed into the huge inertia of rural poverty. Peasant agriculture, even in the most dynamic cash crop sectors, remained radically undercapitalized. Only moneylenders, absentee landlords, urban merchants and a handful of indigenous industrialists seemed to have benefited con-

sistently from India's renewed importance in world trade. "Modernization" and commercialization were accompanied by pauperization.[21]

All this, and more, directly resulted from the imposition after 1857 in India of what the Victorians thought of as free trade. None of this makes for particularly new information: indeed, both colonial and anticolonial historians and political commentators from the late nineteenth century on argued about these agricultural and landownership policies, and postcolonial work has been assiduous in documenting the collaboration between local elites and the British government in the creation of systemic poverty and human misery.

Imperialism hijacked millions of people across the world away from local processes and into a world in which capitalist Europe pioneered the single coercive script of historical transformation, but the historical record is also replete with coruscating instances of alternative visions for human and social betterment. These are the visions that postcolonial historians must also pay attention to as we analyze the material and ideological foundations of imperial power. Indeed, this constitutes the most significant challenge facing democratic thought: what visions of a postcolonial world can we as humanists offer that will interrogate, perhaps even interrupt, the forms of globalization now dictated by politicians, military strategists, captains of finance and industry, fundamentalist preachers and theologians, terrorists of the body and the spirit, in short, by the masters of our contemporary universe?

Despite their other differences, contributors to this volume agree that our intellectual priorities must respond not only to the search for historical clarity about the making of the modern empires but also to the continuing and bloody ambition of neo-imperialism. As postcolonial intellectuals, we have to be responsible also to the cultural and political struggles that define the social being of once-colonized nations today. Faced with these circumstances, we see postcolonial studies reasserting its vocation in coming to terms with the contemporary shape of neoliberal global institutions, as well as with the wide ideological and intellectual spectrum that has begun—very recently—to align itself with the global juggernaut. Postcolonial studies cannot abandon, and must raise with new urgency, the epistemological questions that have animated the field from its inception: questions about the shifting and often interrelated forms of dominance and resistance; about the constitution of the colonial archive; about the search for alternative traces of social being; about the interdependent play of race and class; about the significance of gender and sexuality; about the complex forms in which subjectivities are experienced and collectivities mobilized; about representation itself; and about the ethnographic translation of cultures. These have to be seen not as distractions from "real problems," but as integral to our coming to terms with globalization as a new epoch nonetheless substantially organized by familiar and baleful structures of power. Writing the histories of unsuccessful or successful colonization, of anticolonial nationalisms, and of the state of nations after independence—the history of empire and its aftermath—requires an awareness of the struggles that define the present as much as of those that characterized the past. It is important, then, that we make explicit why we write, and to what institutional and ideological purposes, in the same way that Ferguson unabashedly writes on behalf of what he calls "Anglobalization" (and what Amitav Ghosh bluntly identifies as the "Anglophone imperium").[22]

As a corollary to the critique of US power, postcolonial studies has to maintain its historical awareness of imperialism and not too quickly to hail the now decentered mechanisms of empire. Thus postcolonial studies must add to its fields of analysis and explanatory reference not only the distant past but also the rapidly mutating present, thus, in a sense, trying to anticipate the future. Today, activists and public intellectuals in once-colonized countries not only recognize the new global situation as imperial but believe that this puts a special burden of responsibility on them. For example, in a recent request to Amnesty International to lead the international human rights community against US war crimes in Iraq, South Asian peace activists have expressed their conviction that

> the lead has to come from the people of the once colonized countries, while the support of anti-war activists from the countries of the West and the examples set by them remain valuable and as inspiring as ever. . . . This war, more than any other in recent times, has shown the difference between the colonisers and the colonised and the semi-colonised. . . . It is we, the people of the once colonised and semi-colonised countries, who have witnessed the manipulation of our history, denigration of our culture, destruction and looting of our heritage, wealth and resources.[23]

Others, however, have appealed to US citizens, saying that they have a pivotal role to play in the battle against empire.[24] While we cannot gloss over the real differences between our various locations across the globe, and between the histories and realities we analyze, it is equally important to forge connections between the differently positioned subjects of the new empire.

Several essays here address the question of how current academic disciplines and theories, especially those that think about globalization, can avoid the problem of being in thrall to the cultural kaleidoscope of contemporary world capitalism. How can scholars best distinguish the "Babel" (a term

Jean Comaroff deploys) of contemporary thinking on postcolonial history, economics, and culture from the atomized and consumer-oriented datascape of neoliberal capitalism? In his essay, Timothy Brennan notes with concern that "doctrines of disorganization, inarticulation, and circularity—all seen now as happy states, as heterotopias" have come to replace postcolonial studies' historical investment in an "ethos of progressive betterment, social reorganization, and education." Like Cooppan, Brennan wonders whether Hardt and Negri's *Empire* ultimately conflates the shimmering fractured newness of its authors' own method with that of the globalized world today, thus producing a deterritorialized critical language for a deterritorialized world.[25] Brennan insists on attending to the lingering and substantial effects of older kinds of imperial sovereignty and capitalist wealth extraction—phenomena that should not be mystified by the dazzling sign systems and image making of a new epoch and its sweeping dismissal of the politics of the past, whether hegemonic or oppositional.

Brennan's emphasis on the economics of culture points up the enormously demanding challenges faced by postcolonial studies today, which are compounded by the recognition that the brute force of military conquest constitutes far from the only (and, indeed, perhaps makes for the least efficient) form of neo-imperial power. Until the destruction of the World Trade Center changed US priorities, Western dominance over the global economy was affected largely through trade and technological imbalance, with international financial and banking systems, including the World Bank and the International Monetary Fund, adding to and enforcing structural disparities put into place during the long years of imperial rule. Neoliberal forms of globalization have of course been extensively debated—and challenged in more material and immediately political ways—for over a decade now.[26] Even as postcolonial studies is renewing itself by exploring the various forms of residually imperial power in the West, it is also moving beyond a monocular view of nation-based hegemony as the only force or form of neo-imperialism today. In other words, practitioners of postcolonial studies must and do recognize that there are newer as well as older forms of sovereignty and economic power subsisting side by side in the globalized world. Susie O'Brien and Imre Szeman argue that postcolonial studies has not yet managed to think its way beyond the conundrums of hybridity and authenticity in part because of its "commitment to a worldview that understands globalization as simply 'neoimperialism': something new, but not different in kind from earlier moments of global capitalist expansion and exploitation."[27] While this volume does represent (as we have emphasized so far) the insistence of many scholars in postcolonial studies on the interconnections between cur-

rent forms of globalization and older forms of capitalist expansion and exploitation, it also underscores the importance, for postcolonial studies as
an intellectual formation, to come to terms with what is *really* new about
globalization.

Indeed, postcolonial studies has the intellectual potential and tools for
subtly tracking both residual forms of national sovereignty within globalized institutions *and* emergent views of transnational power. For this effort,
it still draws vital conceptual resources from the decolonizing strategies
generated by struggles for national liberation, even while expanding the
frame of the nation so as to include different models of political mobilization and solidarity. The forced (and voluntary) movements of vast populations under colonialism and after has shaped one significant strand of postcolonial studies, generally gathered under the heading of diaspora studies,
and concerned with the struggles of minority or marginalized populations
(such as indigenous peoples) in various locations. Technological change in
the past five decades—and the acceleration of financial, media, and information flows in the past two—has demanded analytical attention to other kinds
of burgeoning transnational networks as well. Transnationalism, of course,
is not only the prerogative of multinational capital or of multilateral agencies like the International Monetary Fund, the World Trade Organization,
or the Asian Development Bank but also the source of many oppositional
sociocultural formations. The World Social Forum, an umbrella organization for antiglobalization activists and nongovernmental agencies, is one instance of the latter, even though critics worry that its radicalism, too, is compromised by the global nature of its funding.[28] Postcolonial analyses, which
have always paid systematic attention to the historical role of Western colonialism in managing and directing the global flow of persons, commodities,
and ideas, are now taking on the crucial vocation of highlighting various
forms of transnationalism from below as a collective counterweight to the
symbolic and material power of globalization from above.

Neoliberalism and the Postcolonial World

Two questions then face us: how to separate facile or tendentious visions of
a neoliberal "world without borders" from genuine or progressive forms of
transnationalism; and how to separate the abstract brand of freedom implied
by market liberalization across the globe from the internationalist vision of
freedom encapsulated in something like Fanon's rhetoric of liberation. We
recognize the great conceptual difficulties in separating the coercive constituent features of neoliberal globalization from forms of internationaliza-

tion that democratic and egalitarian thought supports. Some of the key terms in the debates surrounding these two questions—terms like *liberalization, liberalism, "free" markets, market rationalization, capitalism, democracy, modernization, development, consumer choice, empowerment*—codify histories and desires that not only mean different things to different policy planners and theorists but are also invoked to justify contradictory modes of national and international interaction. To take just one instance, parallel terms like *development* and *modernization* no longer stand for a transparent process of socioeconomic change, if only because postcolonial critics, among others, have shown how mainstream understandings of these processes—the move to greater privatization and capital-intensive agriculture and industry—are insensitive to local needs and, in many cases, ecologically unsustainable.

In her essay on "the end of history," Jean Comaroff takes up these questions, emphasizing the challenge to postcolonial work posed by the convergence of liberation, liberalism, and liberalization in moments of decolonization and their aftermath. Comaroff points out that in Africa, "agents of structural adjustment have labored to make democracy synonymous with privatization and minimal government, as well as with constitutionalism and an almost obsessional reliance on legal regulation." She notes that this problem, while truly global, is more obviously on display in postcolonies like South Africa, where the end of apartheid has provoked people to seize on history itself as a means to individual freedom and national redemption. Their efforts to anchor history to the ground of popular nation building unfold even as new forms of political economy threaten to erase it all together, as if the new South Africa had already appeared full-fledged, like a shrink-wrapped commodity.

The same challenge to postcolonial scholars—to separate (at the very least, conceptually) market liberalization from human liberation—recurs, in a somewhat different key, in Elizabeth Povinelli's essay "A Flight from Freedom." Through a dense linguistic-historical-philosophical genealogy, Povinelli reveals the very concept of freedom as one tightly, perhaps irretrievably, interwoven with a myth of individual autonomy that has only been intensified by neoliberalism and (neo)imperialism. Povinelli links her inquiry to the general question of postcolonial studies today by suggesting that colonized subjects have often been required to survive socially by performing their own distance from a metropolitan ideal of individual autonomy, that is, by claiming group identities based on ethnic or racialized forms of collectivity. She argues that the history of colonialism thus has left in its wake a legacy of worshipping freedom-as-individual-autonomy, and of defining freedom according to its distance from custom or tradition (rather than tracing freedom as a form of agency routed *through* custom and tradition). With reference to Australian Aboriginal land claims and queer US culture, Povinelli identifies a residual liberalism in critiques that hold onto dubiously narrow conceptions of freedom and political progress, proposing in their place a radical and relational model of agency.

But there are other paradoxes and pitfalls to confront once we take on board a more or less institutionalized critique of the related concepts of freedom, progress, modernization, and development in their classic Enlightenment (and colonial) forms. What happens, James Ferguson asks in this volume, when we dispense with the "evolutionist time lines and static essentialisms of older modernization paradigms" and sever the "automatic connection" between the West and modernity by advancing "a broader, pluralized notion of the modern, as constituting an 'alternative' modernity"? What happens when scholars focus too much on alternative modernity or, indeed, on cultural heterogeneity, and focus too little on the continuing wish of peoples to improve their conditions within what is left of modernity in the most basic of ways? Writing from the perspective of an Africanist, Ferguson notes that if modernity is no longer seen as a telos, then the hierarchies between different parts of the world are made more, rather than less, rigid:

> The developmentalist reassurance that history would, by its nature, transform status, that third world people needed only to wait, to have patience, for their turn to come, ceases to convince. . . . As understandings of the modern have shifted in this way, the vast majority of Africans today denied the status of modernity increasingly come to be seen, and may even (sometimes, and in complex ways) come to see themselves, not as less developed, but simply as less.

Ferguson suggests that although the modernization paradigm failed as a description of facts, its abandonment in the past two decades has left us prey to the hypostatization of global inequity under the culturalist alibi of alternative modernities. Ferguson's essay thus speaks to two of the many forms of double consciousness that postcolonial studies has to live with—first, it resonates with those essays in this volume that discuss the question of periodization and reminds us of the ways in which challenging the global and temporal divisions of the past is impossible without attention to the new divisions being created today. Second, it insists that our critique of the forms of modernity bequeathed to us as the aftermath of colonialism must be supple enough to insist that democratic values, egalitarian ideas, distributive justice, and secular forms of civil society are the right and the responsibility of all, both within and across nations.

Ferguson's skepticism about the practical effects of alternative-modernities theory represents a keynote in postcolonial studies today, which turns on the question of whether the field's investment in the myriad forms of genealogical critique ended up obscuring what was most salvageable from older metanarratives of social change. With that problem in mind, we can understand Kelwyn Sole's essay as an exemplary model of how to qualify metanarratives via scrupulous attention to local conditions, but without ceding the ground of larger historical destiny altogether to the neoliberal version of global progress. Sole shows to what extent and how appropriately postapartheid poetry in South Africa has been insisting on the importance of quotidian experience, as opposed to the more overt, more Manichaean politics of apartheid-antiapartheid that had become somewhat stultifying (both culturally and politically) during the struggle for liberation. As a reader of that poetry, Sole insists on the everyday as a category that questions rather than reflects the local pseudofreedoms bred and licensed by neoliberalism in the new South Africa. As he writes, "It is one thing to wish to downplay macro issues and political, economic, or theoretical determinism . . . so that the aspects of ordinary, everyday culture and experience can find greater definition; it is quite another to discount (to the point of invisibility) macro issues that structure and limit what is locally possible . . . in the first place."

Placing essays like Sole's and Comaroff's side by side, we can see the emergence (in this volume and in this moment of doubt, renewal, and expansion for postcolonial studies) of a new critical language for articulating the linkage between local, lived experience and the broadest structures of global economic and political power. These essays do not just call for this rearticulation of the theoretical relations among spatial scales and social registers under globalization but also attend to the specific practices and languages already in play. In Sole's work, for example, we have a close ear to the ground of South African poetry, proliferating as a dialogue between the minute, concrete sensuality of everyday life and the vast abstractness of its structural determinants.

Nivedita Menon reminds us that such political suppleness will involve unpacking the complex alliances and tensions that mark the relationship of globalization and nationalism, modernity and tradition. In many once-colonized parts of the world, she argues, resistance to globalization can be mounted in the name of both "tradition" and "nationalism." She observes that "the challenge for feminist politics in this context is the working out of a different space for a radical politics of culture, one differentiated from both right- and left-wing articulations of cultural and economic nationalism, as well as from the libertarian and celebratory responses to globalization from the consuming elites." Menon is wary of reestablishing the universalisms of older metanarratives, including the Marxist one. As she says in her disavowal of both Jürgen Habermas and Fredric Jameson:

I venture to suggest that the critique of the reification of cultural communities should take us in the opposite direction—toward a greater fracturing of universalism. Our politics and our democratic institutions must take on board the destabilizing implications of communities constituting themselves continuously around different axes, of which the cultural is only one. Other forms of community exist, building themselves around political ideals, but these are rarely recognized as such—communities built around sexual identity, displacement by development projects, language-based communities that undercut national boundaries, and so on.

Menon's essay argues that, from the perspective of feminist analysis, the dyad of tradition-modernity—and indeed even the general run of antineoliberal or antiglobalization discourse—offers too crude a reading of the effects of globalization in India, especially for Indian women. Her perspective constitutes a postcolonial beyond in that its optic of gender analysis points the way past a debate between globalization and traditional holdouts of ethnic/religious/national identity, calling for a way of seeing democratic politics that is neither one nor the other.

Beyond the Nation-State (and Back Again)

If Menon's work suggests the value of feminist analysis to postcolonial studies today, that is, the specific virtue of articulating a politics beholden neither to the nation-state nor to the globalized world in their respective official forms, it exemplifies a kind of postcolonial work that does not so much choose sides between national and transnational politics as reorganize the terrain altogether. Rob Nixon offers a similar expansion of vision in an essay that constitutes one of the first sustained considerations of what happens when postcolonial studies meets ecocriticism. As he began his work on this encounter, Nixon discovered that literary environmentalism had been

> developing, de facto, as an offshoot of American studies. The resulting national self-enclosure seemed peculiar: one might surely have expected environmentalism to be more, not less, transnational than other fields of literary inquiry. It was unfortunate that a writer like [Ken] Saro-Wiwa, who had long protested what he termed "ecological genocide," could find no place in the environmental canon. Was this because he was an African? Was it because his work revealed no special debt to Thoreau, to the wilderness tradition, or to Jeffersonian agrarianism? Instead, the fraught relations between ethnicity, pollution, and human rights animated Saro-Wiwa's writings. As did the equally fraught relations between local, national, and global politics.

Meanwhile, Nixon remarks, postcolonial studies has not engaged with environmental studies, "regarding them implicitly as, at best, irrelevant and elitist, at worst as sullied by 'green imperialism.'" Nixon's essay provides an eminently usable model for how disciplinary work in humanistic postcolonial studies can intersect with environmental knowledge, politics, and activism. Even more to the point, Nixon suggests (and shows) that the resources of postcolonial studies can prove useful, in their turn, to ecocriticism and other kinds of environmental humanities, not just because they help transnationalize a very US-oriented field but because they volatilize a category like "bioregional ethics," making it less likely to slide into a smug or xenophobic celebration of the pure, the local, the traditional.

Like many others in the pages that follow, Nixon points out that national traditions and national institutions cannot simply be dismissed in postcolonial/environmental analyses, even if the forces that structure ecologically hazardous enterprises (and the protest movements they inspire) are themselves quite thoroughly transnational. Indeed, many essays herein argue that reports of the death (or atrophy) of the nation-state as a vital organizing force in the contemporary world have been greatly exaggerated. Several contributors fear that such reports advance a facile or premature model of nationlessness that, however unwittingly, answers to the neoliberal fantasy of a borderless planet. To them, postcolonial studies appears especially well situated not just to resist that fantasy but to offer in its place a more detailed, more patient, more accurate representation of the reciprocal flow of power (economic, social, and cultural) between nation-states and globalized capitalism.

After all, despite the copious evidence that can be adduced to suggest the power of capital, media, or technology to circumvent national frontiers, even more powerful reminders exist that posit the nation as an extremely supple and enduring ideal.[29] Even as some states are forced to cede particular functions to multilateral agencies, other states—particularly the most powerful ones—confirm themselves in unilateral pursuit of their interests and of their vision for the rest of the world. The recent financial and economic crises in East Asia and Latin America, and the economic depression and human misery that has marked the "transition" between centralized state planning in the Soviet Union and the so-called market economies of the post-Soviet states, have all offered evidence that even as "hot money" flows opportunistically and destructively in and out of countries that do not have regulated capital markets, the forms of market regulation are often defined by regulators located not in these countries but in Washington agencies and New York banks. And of course, the boundaries of the powerful nation-states are far from porous: two recently proposed bills before the US Congress seek to

restrict the granting of US visas to foreign employees of American firms—
employees who will, it is feared, militate against the interest of American
workers. At the same time, some US firms have argued that call centers in the
third world (where employees are trained to speak with American accents
and pretend they are speaking from inside the United States) are depriving
American workers of jobs that are rightfully theirs. Postcolonial forms of
inquiry must not only adjudicate between national sovereignties and multinational treaty regimes but must also recognize that no necessary gap exists
between the one and the other and that, in fact, an enormously powerful
source of legitimacy for state actors is their participation in transnational
agencies.

What counts in these circumstances, and what the essays in this volume
try to exemplify, is how well one can grasp and describe the relations of national to transnational power—how one assesses the scale, ratio, and effect
of national forms of organization as against other micro and macro forms
of organization. If globalization scholars look beyond the nation, postcolonial studies scholars are trying to look afresh at the relation between national and transnational forms of government, economy, society, and culture.
As an instance of this, we might cite Laura Chrisman's essay, a close consideration of South African black intellectuals whose careers and writings
pose a challenge to received ideas in both postcolonial and Black Atlantic
studies. Specifically, Chrisman suggests that these hegemonic transnational
studies, with their consistent political antipathy to nationalism, tend to miss
the importance of certain complex and historically vital forms of national
affiliation. She uses her case studies of Sol Plaatje and Peter Abrahams to
show that the national and the transnational are not in practice structured
as antinomial terms, and thus need not be theorized as such. Moreover, the
case of Abrahams suggests that when national and transnational *are* posed
as antithetical, it is often because of an ideological commitment to romantic
individualism (as against collective or national politics).

The idea of the nation, of course, is available for appropriation by the
marginalized as well as by the elites—indeed, although some of the most
well-known anticolonial leaders of this century such as Fanon and M. K.
Gandhi were aware of the pitfalls of national consciousness, most anticolonial struggles have powerfully invoked alternative visions of a national community in order to challenge colonial hegemony. In an essay that asks postcolonial theory to engage more seriously than it has done with the history
of Latin America, Florencia Mallon reminds us that this continues to be
the case. As elite versions of the nation break down the world over, Mallon
asks,

Is there anything that might take their place? Tracing subaltern practices and alternative discourses across the past two centuries in Latin America would seem to suggest that there is, and contemporary indigenous movements have begun to demand it. Hybridity, difference, and decentralization, which for so long have been seen as impediments to national unification, turn out to be, in reality, key to national democratization. With all of its inevitable contradictions and limitations, might this notion still offer a potential pathway into a post-colonial nationhood?

Mallon does not propose that we "reinvent the wheel" and return to older certainties, but she does suggest that "today's enduring and ever more urgent need for a politics of solidarity . . . challenges us to take seriously, from a postcolonial perspective, the deep yearning that so many common folk across the world have had for the promises of national autonomy and development." Mallon sees in the future or beyond for both postcolonial Latin American studies and for Latin America itself the necessity to imagine fundamental ways of restructuring (not abandoning) the nation, especially given the resilience of its mechanisms for distributing power and of its capacity to organize its citizens' political hopes.

In thinking through the differences and connections between and within nations, especially as these have been constituted by the legacy of colonialism, Robert Stam and Ella Shohat urge postcolonial studies to engage more seriously with the politics of multiculturalism, which (like socialism earlier and postcolonialism today) has been "dismissed by the far Left as too soft and co-optive and denounced by the Right as too radical and incendiary." Examining the trinational trade in ideas among the United States, France, and Brazil, Stam and Shohat are interested in how debates about multiculturalism (which have permeated the public sphere far more widely than those about postcolonialism) travel across borders. On the one hand, their essay traces the ways in which racial and ethnic mingling and difference in each of these countries have been shaped by their interconnected colonial pasts (all three are touched by the Black Atlantic, for example). On the other, the authors warn us that in debates about multiculturalism and race relations, even oppositional intellectuals in these countries "too often operate within intellectual boundaries dictated by the nation-state." Mallon's case for comparative work that looks at a handful of related but not identical cases (Cuba, Chile, Mexico, and Bolivia) offers a glimpse of how future projects might be configured—not according to the pure exceptionalism of sui generis states, nations, or regions, but not according to the one-size-fits-all pattern of a blandly literal postcolonialism either. Likewise, Stam and Shohat's method of triangulation offers a promising new approach by tracing a specific set of linkages connected through related but different colonial histories—an approach in which neither the opaque soup of globality nor the isolated case predominates.

Bringing the local and international dimensions of nationalism into simultaneous play, Rebecca Stein's essay maps the connection between Israel's place in the new global order, its colonial maneuvers, and its attempts to define itself as a European entity. In the spring of 2002, as exchanges of violence intensified, the Israeli media became preoccupied with leisure, especially the café, which began "to stand in for the Jewish nation-state and its fragility." Mainstream newspapers represented Palestinian attacks on cafés as assaults on the cosmopolitan modernity of the nation-state (casting the situation as, in the words of one Israeli journalist, a "War for a chance of a Western society to survive in the Middle East"). Such a construction depended, Stein argues, on the obfuscation of "the historic and iconic status of the coffeehouse in the Arab world" and the construction of Israel as a Western society, "a nation-state that, given both its Palestinian and Mizrahi histories, had never been." Thus Stein shows how the colonial politics of Israeli settler-nationalism can be unpacked only by attending to its local operations. At the same time, she suggests, the "colonial comparativism" with which postcolonial theory engages can be effectively used to challenge "the terms of Israeli exceptionalism." Indeed, one canonical concept of postcolonial theory, ambivalence, plumbed most thoroughly by Homi Bhabha, illuminates the case of Israeli middle-class self-description, revealing layers of historical misdirection and colonial confession. What Stein's innovative and synthetic methodology highlights, from the point of view of academic knowledge production, is that postcolonial studies continues to reinvent and transform itself, generating new applications and ideas for specific cases in a transnational framework as it cross-fertilizes with an ever wider range of disciplines and subdisciplines in the contemporary academy.

Postcolonial Studies and the Disciplines in Transformation

It is hardly surprising that Israeli nationalism constructs itself as both a European and a modern entity under attack from people who live beyond the physical and temporal borders of civility. As several of our contributors show, in colonial rhetoric, time and space are inextricably connected; one of the most important directions for future work is a dynamic rethinking of the temporal and spatial reach of postcolonial studies, particularly the question of periodization. If postcolonial studies—as an intellectual field poised uncertainly among the disciplines—concerns itself with the full history of

European imperialism rather than simply its aftermath, just how far back should it go? There are, of course, obvious connections between the imperial present and colonial beginnings; Stam and Shohat point out in their essay for this volume that "George W. Bush's ultimatums against Iraq resonate with five hundred years of colonial ultimatums, going all the way back to the Spanish *requerimiento*, the document which the conquistadores read (in Spanish) to uncomprehending indigenous people and which told them, in sum, that they would have to give up their land, religion, and language, and that if they did not do so forthwith, the Spanish would burn their houses and rape their women, and that it would all be their own fault." But postcolonial scholarship has not systematically engaged with the long, intertwined histories of empire and race, even though over the past few decades, scholars in precolonial or early colonial periods have begun developing a critical but highly productive relationship with postcolonial studies.

There has been a long-established tendency to seal off premodern periods, as the home of the barbaric, from an enlightened early modern and modern Europe in much the same way as the geographic margins of colonial societies were differentiated from the metropolis. This rhetorical interplay between the "darkness" of medieval life and that of colonized spaces produces a plastic vocabulary often invoked to mark cultural and religious differences. But while postcolonial scholars question the colonial construction of African barbarism, or Islamic medievalism, they do not always examine the way "the Middle Ages" have been constructed as the barbaric other of "the Renaissance," and therefore of modernity. In his editor's introduction to *The Postcolonial Middle Ages*, Jeffrey Jerome Cohen writes that "postcolonial theory in practice has neglected the study of the 'distant' past, which tends to function as a field of undifferentiated alterity against which modern regimes of power have arisen. This exclusionary model of temporality denies the possibility that traumas, exclusions, violence enacted centuries ago might still linger in contemporary identity formations; it also closes off the possibility that this past could be multiple and valuable enough to contain (and be contained within) alternative presents and futures."[30] With this in mind, postcolonial scholars need to do more than insist on the alternate modernities of once-colonized worlds. Scholars of contemporary race and colonialism also need to question a traditional periodization that sanctions ignorance of earlier periods without which, as is becoming increasingly clear, we cannot understand contemporary ideologies of difference.

The idea that the roots of racial ideologies need only to be traced back to different *colonial* encounters has been challenged by recent medieval and early modern scholarship. Medievalists have both extended and revised the insights of postcolonial scholars and theorists by analyzing the Crusades as a form of early colonialism, characterized by a range of hostilities and hybridities every bit as complex as those of later times and crucial for understanding the latter. By illuminating the relationships between Muslims, Jews, and Christians at this time, medievalists have also traced the lineages of contemporary identity categories, making visible the foundational importance of religious difference in the development of racial ideologies. In this volume, Daniel Boyarin goes even further back in time, to late antiquity, and uses concepts developed in postcolonial theory in order to understand the separation of Christianity and Judaism in this period. Christian heresiologists, whom Boyarin calls a "religion-police," attempted to define and codify the difference between Jews and Christians; for them, Jews, so-called Judaizers, and Jewish Christians marked "a space of threatening hybridity" that had to be externalized in order to consolidate and identify Christianity as a religion. Inasmuch as "religion" as a singular idea can only be understood in terms of a posited difference between religions, Boyarin argues, this process of externalizing the hybrid, the not-pure, also marks the invention of religion itself. Judaism appropriates these heresiological moves, but then refuses "finally to become or be a religion"; it is only in this extended history that what Boyarin calls the ambivalence of Judaism about its own status as a religion can be located.

Today, it has become more necessary than ever for postcolonial scholars to engage seriously with such early histories. Etienne Balibar has argued that contemporary European neoracism draws freely on the earlier anti-Semitic rhetoric of the Reconquista.[31] The long history of Islamophobia has become increasingly visible after the destruction of the World Trade Center towers on September 11, 2001. Neo-imperial commentary has been quick to direct the rhetorical equation between barbaric pasts and uncivilized spaces toward first Afghanistan and then Iraq. Iraq, home to the oldest traces of civilization in the world, is seen to have progressed into the European Middle Ages and no further (or is it that it was bombed back into the Middle Ages after 1991?). The rhetoric of a clash of civilizations—and the fact of deep interdependence between cultures—can both be traced back to medieval and early modern European and Christian writings on Islam, as well as Judaism. At the same time, there exists a crucial difference between the power relations of the medieval world and those of contemporary times. In the medieval world, Islam did not simply constitute the Other of Christianity, nor was there an economic and military imbalance of the kind that exists today. Contemporary neo-imperialism revives key elements of the rhetoric of the Crusades not only because the vocabulary of religious confrontation plays to historical fears, including those compounded by modern-day racisms, but also because such fears make for a formidable accompaniment to the real business of empire, the perpetuation of global inequalities. We need to go to the past not just to understand the long roots of contemporary ideologies of difference but also to put these ideologies into perspective by historicizing them and glimpsing alternative ways of being, which the past also makes visible.

In the past few decades, some early modernists have moved to precisely this terrain, mapping the complexity and diversity of the relationships between European and non-European societies at that time. Many "Eastern" societies were far from being just the inferior Others of Renaissance Europe — in fact, Europeans desired to enter the powerful economic networks of the Mediterranean, the Levant, North Africa, India, and China; feared the military might of the Turks; and were dazzled by the wealth and sophistication of many Asian kingdoms. Indeed, as world-system theorists such as Andre Gunder Frank have argued, early modern Europe in fact constituted the junior partner in this "traffic," remaining on the periphery of a global economy whose center was located in the East. European domination of global commerce and colonial surplus does not begin till the eighteenth century.[32]

In the light of postcolonial theorists' demand that we learn to "provincialize Europe," such a perspective seems especially apropos.[33] At the same time, it seems equally important not to gloss over the fact that by the end of the seventeenth century, several European city-states and provinces had already begun trading in slaves, that plantations were well underway in several parts of the world, that native populations in the Americas had already been subjected to genocide, and, most important, that colonialist and racist ideologies and practices were fairly well developed in Europe. Thus a great many of the material practices and ideological features that came to define modern colonialism began to be shaped at this time, and a historical inventory of such details is important in helping us understand their power in the later periods.[34] Further, early histories of the coercive forms and ideologies of empire prove important because both the ideologues and adversaries of modern European colonialism debated them at length and understood them as leading up to their moment.

However, even as the dynamics of relationships between different religious, ethnic, and geographic groups in precolonial times can often be productively analyzed to reveal the roots of later colonialist ideologies, historical transformation cannot simply be understood as progression or decline. Earlier periods are more than simply precursors to later periods, and they must be understood in their own terms, a reminder that can often prove very productive for postcolonialists. In a recent essay, Bruce Holsinger has suggested that the work of the Subaltern School of Indian historians reveals a deep engagement with medievalist scholarship. He argues that many of the Subalternists' insights into the collective lives of the Indian peasantry under colonialism, and even after, are arrived at via a comparative consideration of medieval European modes of community and of the relationship to land of both peasants and proprietors. By tracing this "genealogy of critique," Holsinger thus suggests that these agrarian and communitarian practices, by virtue of their distance from those social forms made hegemonic by European colonial modernity, are useful in understanding non-European peasant communities under siege.[35] Thus he indicates an alternative way of conceptualizing the connections between the complexities of social formations in premodern periods and those of non-European spaces under colonialism.

Thus, at this juncture of history, we need to critically examine the grounds on which postcolonial studies has engaged with the past, and to think about the ways in which it needs to expand what Cooppan calls "the time and space of the postcolonial." By moving back into time beyond the usual boundary of 1492, and past those territories usually associated with European colonialism, we will be in a much better position to understand what Kenneth Pomeranz, a noted historian of modern China's place in the world-system, has recently styled the "great divergence" by which Europe came to dominate global political economy.[36]

Among the most challenging cases of expanded postcolonial consideration is indeed that of China, long seen by its specialist historians as exceptional in the history of modern imperialism and, more recently, subsumed into a model of semicolonialism. Tani Barlow's essay offers a brief review of the relevant positions in the debate over colonial modernity in China, concluding that the relevance of such a concept (and by implication, the potential applicability of the tools of postcolonial analysis) to an understanding of the modern traffic in ideas through the treaty ports is undeniable, despite its imperfect fit to the Chinese case. Specifically, Barlow suggests that it is difficult to grasp the full context for Chinese modernist thinking on the matter of eugenic feminism without placing it in the discursive networks that can be said to define colonial modernity itself. Like Nivedita Menon's essay, Barlow's suggests that feminist scholarship in the postcolonial arena offers alternative methods for reconciling the demands of local archives and conditions with broader paradigms of colonial and postcolonial history. Of course, even as Barlow's patient considerations exemplify the fruitful exchanges that emerge from the encounter between postcolonial studies and

East Asian history, her essay also registers the resistance of both historians in general and China specialists in particular to the perceived intellectual baggage carried by postcolonial scholarship.

Despite the supposedly porous boundaries of postcolonial studies, then, and despite the increasing interdisciplinarity of the humanities and social sciences, the genealogies of individual disciplines and area studies—and the evidentiary and explanatory protocols normalized within each—exert an enormous and often starkly differentiating influence on the ways in which various scholars approach colonialism and neocolonialism. Postcolonial critics and their critics, both those who work in Western universities and those in recently colonized countries, have also had to confront pressing questions of location germane both to the individual scholar and to the geographical or political unit under scrutiny. Of course, the question of the proper provenance of postcolonial studies only becomes more complicated—but also more interesting and timely—when its practitioners take stock of different concepts of the postcolonial established in different international academic settings. Especially outside of the Western academy, for example, there is a widespread perception that postcolonial studies' poststructuralist bias accounts for its popularity and institutionalization in the West, and also that this bias and location are inextricably connected with its political and philosophical weaknesses.[37] In the discipline of history, the work of the Subaltern School of Indian historians, which has been seen as the most substantial and controversial bridge between history and postcolonial criticism, is routinely critiqued on the grounds that depends (increasingly) on poststructuralist method, and therefore cannot theorize resistance in any meaningful way.[38] Branching disciplinary genealogies and discrepant institutional locations are indeed the two chief reasons for the wide divergence of views about the shape and relevance of postcolonial studies today. These debates partially explain why comparatively few scholars in places like India and South Africa (to take but two noteworthy examples) see themselves as postcolonialists.

At the same time, the conversations that resulted in this volume have suggested that there prevails a curiously consistent paradox across a number of disciplinary and institutions settings: many scholars reported their sense that postcolonial concerns and methods have been widely adapted, broadly influential, and even taken for granted as necessary in a number of scholarly domains. Yet those concerns and methods have been fairly shallowly integrated with some of the bedrock methodological and epistemological procedures that still define the traditional disciplines. For instance, even as various strands of postcolonial thought have proven crucial to the development of new forms of historiography, and even as the study of history has proven

[handwritten annotation: history not self-critical re: methodol. etc for post-colonial etc by]

crucial for the development of key texts of postcolonial studies, it is arguable that history (like political science) has only sporadically engaged with the crucial challenge of postcolonialism. This claim would certainly hold true by comparison to the impact of postcolonial questions on literary studies and anthropology, where each discipline was forced to confront its own origins and implication within the ideological and institutional apparatus of modern empires.[39] As a result, the work of many historians who do not call themselves postcolonialists, and also many critiques of postcolonial studies from historians all over the world, have contributed substantially to the conversations within the field and have enriched and extended debates about colonial and postcolonial dynamics.[40] In the case of anthropology, the fate of the discipline and the history of colonialism are so closely intertwined that much of the revisionary thinking in the discipline over the past three decades could be glossed under the heading of postcolonial studies. At the same time, and also unlike literary studies, not much overt theorization of the category of the postcolonial exists by practicing anthropologists.[41] Rather, one finds more of what we might understand as a convergence of concerns: the destabilization of received geopolitical categories, the critical focus on Western forms of power, the inquiry into global inequities and their local articulation, and the affirmative recuperation of subaltern voices. Meanwhile, in literary studies, the study of colonialism has been (along with several other intellectual developments since the 1980s) responsible for rethinking the social mission and institutional history of university literature departments. However, it is significant that despite the intellectual success of postcolonial methods (and their implied disciplinary critique), and despite the fact that postcolonial theorists have been most visibly and widely housed in departments of literature, the study of colonialism (and the teaching of non-Western literatures) still remains marginalized in the actual curricular and hiring practices of many literature departments, especially those most closely identified with the traditions of English studies.[42]

For these reasons, in part, postcolonial studies has been seen not just as invigorating to the disciplines but also as enormously irritating, perhaps even risky in some quarters. Very often this intellectual agon results in the characterization of postcolonial studies as an abstract, procrustean, and arcane set of theories that challenge the scrupulous, time-honored, and concrete practices of the traditional disciplines.[43] A widespread suspicion exists among historians, for example, that postcolonial studies functions as a carrier (and the metaphor was apt even before these virus-wary times) of other perspectives, such as poststructuralist thought, critical race theory, and next-wave feminism, that may destabilize the core of their discipline. Similarly, many anthropologists charge postcolonial studies with the decentering of ethnography—their discipline's distinctive form of knowledge production—which they trace quite directly back to Edward Said's *Orientalism* in particular. It is possible, in fact, to understand much anthropology written thereafter as a reaction to *Orientalism*. While not about the anthropological project per se, Said's argument regarding the discursive violence transported in representations of the Other could be readily transposed into all the practices of traditional anthropology. After Said, ethnographic knowledge could never be politically innocent (a position that a number of radical anthropologists had already articulated in the 1970s, but that only entered the anthropological mainstream in the 1980s).[44] Although it seems improbable from the point of view of the more empirical social sciences, various literary traditionalists, too, have lumped a Saidian/Foucauldian politics of representation into a general mélange of "bad" theories that they believe threaten the autonomy and specificity of the literary object per se, by allegorizing it or reducing it unfairly to a set of (generally baleful) political or ideological propositions.

Coming from different disciplines and backgrounds—and with diverse views about the future and provenance of postcolonial studies—many of our contributors nonetheless agree that postcolonial studies is now poised to move beyond some of the debates and methods that become ossified in the course of the 1990s. In anthropology, for instance, the mode of self-reflexive ethnography adapted in the wake of the postcolonial intervention and the "writing culture" moment has now lost some of its excitement. Once the case for self-reflexivity as such did not need to be argued any longer, the ritualized discussion of the ethnographer's position in the field began to seem forced, even gratuitous. In fact, the theoretical turn seemed to produce a newly formulaic ethnography that reiterated general lessons about cultural processes well established for a decade. In the past several years, this perceived impasse has led anthropologists to pursue a number of alternative modes of analysis; the five anthropologists represented in this volume each attempt to articulate a project for anthropology that reaches beyond, while being informed by, both the postcolonial and "writing culture" moments in the discipline.

. With this kind of capsule intellectual history in view, it is possible to understand why, in several disciplines, postcolonial studies has been (at times unfairly) hobbled by narrow association with a predictable and self-conscious kind of theoretical scholasticism that seems both politically attenuated with regard to the field's anticolonial origins and intellectually dull with regard to the complex ways in which creative scholars now try to represent the relation between culture and the state, between the imagination and the economy, between ideas and facts, evidence and interpretation. While it is possible to read many of the essays in this volume as retrieving a historical-materialist dimension of postcolonial studies (posed implicitly against its poststructuralist dimension), it is perhaps more apt to think of the work gathered here as moving beyond that particular binarized intellectual genealogy altogether.

While this may seem like a promising mandate for a reinvigorated postcolonial studies (embodied in the essays collected here), this volume also seriously entertains the views of those who believe that postcolonial studies has reached a dramatic point of crisis in its own intellectual and institutional trajectory. Indeed, one of the ironic juxtapositions on display here is that scholars like Rebecca Stein, Daniel Boyarin, and Tani Barlow—coming from intellectual precincts generally considered outside the purview of the postcolonial—are finding new ways to deploy classic postcolonial techniques of analysis, while scholars strongly associated with key statements within postcolonial studies—notably David Scott (in anthropology), Frederick Cooper (in history), and Neil Lazarus (in literary studies)—offer substantial critiques of the field designed to challenge its current methods and assumptions. Scott's essay, for example, issues something like an obituary for the field, while maintaining that it is crucial to continue to study (with fresh tools and new rubrics) the traces of colonial power in the history, culture, and economics of the present (the original raison d'être of postcolonial studies, of course). The endpoint of Scott's essay is to claim a new vocation for postcolonial studies or its successor, one that shakes off the intellectual cobwebs of "normal social science" and rededicates itself to the crises and problems of the contemporary world. That is, Scott wants postcolonialists to stop generating finer and finer models of the past operations of colonialism and to start orienting themselves to a full and insistent ideological differentiation of power based on its effects here and now. Taking us full circle to the opening question of the fate of postcolonial studies in the era of globalization, Scott identifies a potentially exhausted paradigm (the postcolonial) that seems to have answered the questions it posed originally; if not reformed, he suggests, postcolonial studies is thus doomed to continue formulating the same insights.

Even many of those not unsympathetic to the way in which the humanities and social sciences have been changed by the intervention of postcolonial studies, then, remain wary of the potential reification of its general insights about the relationship between colonizers and colonized. For instance, Frederick Cooper argues that postcolonial critiques have resulted in a flattening of Europe itself as a polity devoid of internal fragmentations and contestations, and suggests ways in which some of the excesses of postcolonial critique can be redressed by going back to certain key tenets of older historiography. Cooper offers a useful summary of one African historian's misgivings about the discursive-epistemic methods of postcolonial studies, including especially the danger that an emphasis on abstract knowledge-power patterns may interfere with our ability to recognize and recover the more determinate, more concrete, and ultimately more messy activities that advanced colonialism's economic and political interests, not to mention the manifold techniques for resisting them. Cooper's sharp criticism of certain excesses in the colonial-discourse approach modulates into a call for a more empirical, more wide-ranging, and more historically acute future for postcolonial studies—a future that several other contributors to the volume, sharing Cooper's concerns, are already helping to build.

Like Cooper, Neil Lazarus defines a strong vision for the beyond of postcolonial studies by articulating a stringent critique of certain prevailing interpretive protocols within the field. Lazarus's observations about the narrow structures of literary canonization—and the hermeneutical assumptions to which the metropolitan academy's postcolonial canon corresponds—crystallize an established critique of Eurocentric (and, not incidentally, Anglophone) postcolonial criticism. As Lazarus reminds us in his essay, only a handful of writers circulate in the postcolonial canon, and even these writers are interpreted only through a very narrow lens according to keywords such as "migrancy, liminality, hybridity, and multiculturality." Moreover, those keywords are themselves interpreted in restrictive ways—thus "migrancy" usually means the movement of once-colonized subjects to the West, an emphasis that leaves out (to take just one stark example) the displacement of millions of people during the partition of the Indian subcontinent. Lazarus here joins forces with a number of writers and critics working outside the Western academy to highlight this problem, urging postcolonial critics to expand their research into the immense and diverse body of contemporary non-Western literature that remains relatively unknown in US and UK classrooms. We might add that the canon of critical and theoretical work in postcolonial studies is itself more expansive than many trained within the narrow confines of a single discipline or scholarly language might suspect; indeed, in the coming decade, postcolonial scholars must continue to identify and translate the vital intellectual projects already produced in (but not always recognized outside) noncolonial, indigenous, and creolized languages from across the globe.

Conclusion

Postcolonial Studies and Beyond both calls for, and attempts to begin, a gathering of scholarly, critical political energies that is no longer detained by recycled debates and institutional jockeying, but instead is methodologically complex and eclectic, extroverted, experimental, and engaged in multiple sites of investigation and contest. One idea that this book clarifies, in its retrospect on postcolonial studies and its survey of the field's prospects, is that during the quarter century between 1978 and now, two simultaneous and overlapping, but not necessarily causally chained, events occurred: the disciplinary shift in postcolonial/global/third world studies from sociological and economic analysis to cultural and interpretive and theoretical/semiotic/discursive analysis; and the challenge to theorize models and metanarratives built on the dominant paradigms of modernization, development, and world-systems theory. This book in some ways tries to delink those legacies and reorganize them in two crucial ways. First, it imagines a study of culture that does not detach from the claims and conclusions of socioeconomic or structural analysis. Second, it revisits and revises broad models of global relations that insist on a systematic (yet critical) view of what is still the postcolonial world; that is, it argues that we need to keep alive particular metanarratives for critical purposes, while minimizing and accounting for their Eurocentric traces. This double disentanglement from the binaries of postcolonial studies in its formative period may now point the way to fresh insights and methods in the branching disciplinary and extra-disciplinary pathways that will define postcolonial studies in its current and future forms.

Our contributors here expand the project of postcolonial studies because they extend similar insights to new objects (geographically, methodologically), but particularly because their essays recapture the original importance of postcolonial analysis as a complement to other kinds of engaged intellectual and political work. Moreover, if there is something like a new empiricism on display in postcolonial ethnography, historiography, and criticism, it must be understood and appreciated not as a counter to the theoretical array characteristic of postcolonial studies but as a phenomenon that continues to emerge alongside and intertwined with it. Neither we nor the essayists represented here imagine that there is a choice to be made between empiricism or materialism, on the one hand, and theory, discourse, or culture, on the other. Instead, we are showcasing new methods for articulating the relation of material or socioeconomic facts with expressive art forms, new discursive histories, and abstract epistemological questions.

Taken together, the forceful critiques and inventive new applications of postcolonial methods on display in this volume suggest that the field has the resources and the momentum to reinvent itself and broaden its area of productive engagement. Indeed, stringent assessments of the limitations of the postcolonial paradigm prove essential to the work of assessing and creating its future directions. Our goal here has not been to defend the territory of postcolonialism, or the term, but to survey its usefulness in the past and meditate on its uses in the future, keeping a wary eye on narrow constructions of postcolonial studies too quick to paint it as passé, involuted, ethnocentric, or irrelevant. The many-handed and continual work of postcolonial studies—as an innovative, interdisciplinary, and self-proliferating set of practices—has always been self-renewing and should not be read as suddenly galvanized by an intellectual crisis in the field or by the new challenge of globalization. Faced with the diversity and ingenuity of work in postcolonial studies, it makes little sense now to restrict its range of interest to a small handful of theories, buzzwords, or classic texts. Only with a broad and ecumenical sense of the genealogy of the field (a tradition of anticolonial thought and sociocultural analysis stemming from a great many intellectual and historical developments) can current practitioners envision an urgent, wide-ranging, and productive future for postcolonial studies.

Notes

1. It is possible to think of postcolonial studies as having passed through an *auto-critical* phase (as evidenced by the essays collected in a 1992 special issue of *Social Text*—including oft-cited critiques by Anne McClintock, and Ella Shohat—and those collected in a 1994 special issue of *Oxford Literary Review* edited by Suvir Kaul and Ania Loomba). More recently, Kalpana Seshadri-Crooks has identified a kind of *melancholic* phase for postcolonial studies, a phase marked by the fact that the field's theoretical impasses can no longer go ignored at a time at which it has achieved relative security in academic institutions. See Seshadri-Crooks, "At the Margins of Postcolonial Studies," 3–4. While remarking the institutional critiques and theoretical limitations that have dominated self-reflexive postcolonial work in the last decade, *Postcolonial Studies and Beyond* rather emphasizes the array of vital and innovative new intellectual practices now enabled by engagement with issues of postcoloniality.

2. The work that we think of as postcolonial proceeds under many banners, including those listed by Robert Stam and Ella Shohat in their essay here: "revisionist 'bottom-up' history, diasporic indigenous studies, Afro-diasporic studies, critical race theory, transnational feminism, whiteness studies, antiracist pedagogy, media critique, postmodern geography, counter-Enlightenment philosophy, border theory, antiglobalization theory, and many other forms of adversarial knowledge." At several points in this introduction, we discuss questions of historical, temporal, and locational differences and how they alter conceptions of postcoloniality.

3. "Hip defeatism" is Martha Nussbaum's somewhat glib critique of Judith Butler. See Martha C. Nussbaum, "The Professor of Parody," *New Republic*, February 22, 1999, 37–45.

4. Sharpe, "Is the United States Postcolonial?" See also Frankenberg and Mani,

"CrossCurrents, Crosstalk"; Singh and Schmidt, *Postcolonial Theory and the United States*; and Hulme, "Including America."

5. See, for example, Schueller, "Articulations of African-Americanism in South Asian Postcolonial Theory."

6. Mignolo, *Local Histories/Global Designs*, 91–111. Similarly, Carlos Alonso and Alberto Moreiras have recently asserted the specificity of Latin American intellectual traditions within the archive of colonial modernity, citing documents that sometimes anticipate, sometimes reiterate, sometimes complicate, and sometimes challenge the key texts of postcolonial studies. For crucial or summary statements about the difference Latin America makes to the analysis of colonialism and globalization, see Alonso, *The Burden of Modernity*, 33–37, and Moreiras, *The Exhaustion of Difference*, 23.

7. Mignolo, *Local Histories/Global Designs*, 194.

8. See Moreiras, *Exhaustion of Difference*, 111–26; and Mignolo, *Local Histories/Global Designs*, 172–214. For a similarly rigorous rethinking of postcolonial hybridity through the specific historical and intellectual lens of Latin Americanism, see Moreiras, *Exhaustion of Difference*, 288–97.

9. See Miyoshi and Harootunian, *Learning Places*.

10. It is not possible to enumerate here the different ways in which postcolonialism has been theorized in relation to different places and histories, or even to provide a comprehensive reading list on the subject. However, in addition to books and essays already cited in this introduction, as well as by several contributors to this volume, a good starting point for thinking about the issue is the debate around the validity of subaltern studies beyond India and in relation to Africa and Latin America as conducted in the pages of *American Historical Review* 99, no. 5 (1994). Also useful are Young, *Postcolonialism*; Loomba, *Colonialism/Postcolonialism*; Prakash, *After Colonialism*; and Lewis and Mills, *Feminist Postcolonial Theory*.

11. Gikandi, "Globalization and the Claims of Postcoloniality," 13. Gikandi sees the field in a somewhat different way, viewing several recent figures in the field as postcolonial theorists *of* globalization (Appadurai and Bhabha), thus suggesting that postcolonial theory has in fact fed into (rather than resisted) the tendency of globalization discourse to privilege cultural products as against structural conditions.

12. O'Brien and Szeman, "The Globalization of Fiction," 606.

13. Arundhati Roy, "Instant-Mix Imperial Democracy," *Outlook*, May 26, 2003, 46–56.

14. David Cannadine's *Ornamentalism*, for instance, which describes itself as "characteristically entertaining and provocatively original" achieves both by scrupulously refusing to engage with the conclusions of economic historians, or indeed of any scholars whose writing on politics and culture have been central to the detailed revision of imperial certitudes and arrogance. In his book, *Empire*, Niall Ferguson goes one better by simply omitting the scholarly debates usually registered in footnotes.

15. Niall Ferguson, "The Empire Slinks Back," *New York Times*, Sunday magazine, April 27, 2003, 54.

16. Ibid., 57.

17. Paul Johnson, "Five Vital Lessons from Iraq," *Forbes*, March 17, 2003.

18. This failure to thrive is also understood in total isolation from the colonial

histories of these states, the deadweight of cold war allegiances, and, perhaps most important, the neocolonial power of banking, corporate, and military-industrial systems to intensify and perpetuate inequalities within once-colonized societies and across international borders.

19. Davis, *Late Victorian Holocausts*, 311.

20. Ibid., 312.

21. Ibid. In order to answer such questions, Davis focuses on a case study of the province of Berar, deriving his conclusions from the empirical and archival work of a host of economic historians, such as Laxman Satya (*Cotton and Famine in Berar*). For further sources on this topic, see also Guha, *Elementary Aspects of Peasant Insurgency in Colonial India*; and Sharma, *Famine, Philanthropy, and the Colonial State*.

22. Ferguson, *Empire*, 368; Amitav Ghosh, "The Anglophone Empire," *New Yorker*, April 7, 2003, 46.

23. See South Asia Citizens Wire, 13 June, 2003, available at sacw.insaf.net/pipermail/sacw_insaf.net/2003/001726.html.

24. Roy, "Instant-Mix Imperial Democracy."

25. See, in particular, Brennan, "The Empire's New Clothes"; Hardt and Negri offer a critical reply to Brennan in the same issue.

26. See, most recently, David Leonhardt, "Globalization Hits a Speed Bump," *New York Times*, June 1, 2003. Of the many full-blown critiques of the processes of coercive economic change described as globalization, Joseph E. Stiglitz's *Globalization and Its Discontents* has been particularly noteworthy not only because Stiglitz is a Nobel Laureate but because he has headed policy-planning bodies both in the US federal government and at the World Bank. At several moments in his scathing critique of "Washington Consensus" models, particularly of failed IMF policies, Stiglitz invokes colonialism as the appropriate referent for those policies: "All too often, the Fund's approach to developing countries has the feel of a colonial ruler" (40); developing countries dealing with the IMF have been forced to ask "a very disturbing question: Had things really changed since the 'official' ending of colonialism a half century ago?" (41). Stiglitz has no qualms about invoking a history that even so-called liberal commentators seem to have forgotten.

27. O'Brien and Szeman, "The Globalization of Fiction," 607.

28. See the *Economics and Politics of the World Social Forum* issue of *Aspects of India's Economy* 35 (September 2003), available online at www.rupe-india.org/35/contents.html.

29. For a brief recent summary of the ongoing power of "national hegemonies," see Bhabha, "Statement for the Critical Inquiry Board Symposium."

30. Cohen, *The Postcolonial Middle Ages*, 3.

31. Balibar, "Is There a Neo-racism?"

32. Frank, *Re-orient*.

33. The phrase comes from Chakrabarty, *Provincializing Europe*.

34. In an argument that is both expansive in its traversing of cultural frontiers and time periods and pointed in its recognition of enduring ideas about slavery and civil society, David Wallace has traced the relations of medieval European humanism and "a live discourse of slavery" that became "more or less active as economic conditions" dictated ("Humanism, Slavery, and the Republic of Letters," 78). Wallace suggests that "many of the features we associate with full-blown European colo-

nialism—as the slaving Mediterranean steadily evolves into the black Atlantic—are clearly forming during the earlier period" (67).

35. Holsinger, "Medieval Studies, Postcolonial Studies, and the Genealogies of Critique."

36. Pomeranz, *The Great Divergence.*

37. The most widely circulated statements of these positions are Ahmad, *In Theory*; Appiah, "Is the Post- in Postmodernism the Post- in Postcolonial?"; and Dirlik, "The Postcolonial Aura."

38. Prakash, "Subaltern Studies as Postcolonial Criticism"; O'Hanlon, "Recovering the Subject"; and Sarkar, "The Decline of the Subaltern in *Subaltern Studies.*" Other essays in Ludden, *Reading Subaltern Studies*, are also useful.

39. Of course, in *Provincializing Europe*, Dipesh Chakrabarty contends that the discipline of history, too, is deeply enmeshed in European and Eurocentric practices. Chakrabarty's claims parallel the work (for example) of Gauri Viswanathan in English literary studies and of Johannes Fabian in anthropology, so that all three of the disciplines in question have been reconceived in terms of their own origin stories, all of them variously but significantly interwoven with the history of colonial institutions in Europe. See Viswanathan, *Masks of Conquest*; and Fabian, *Time and the Other.*

40. Salient examples of influential historical work of this kind are Vaughan, *Curing Their Ills*; Sarkar, *Hindu Wife, Hindu Nation*; and Hofmeyr, "We Spend Our Years as a Tale That Is Told."

41. For exceptions, see David Scott, *Refashioning Futures: Criticism after Postcoloniality* (Princeton: Princeton University Press, 1999); and Gananath Obeyesekere, *The Apotheosis of Captain Cook: European Mythmaking in the Pacific* (Princeton: Princeton University Press, 1992).

42. See, for example, Hasseler and Krebs, "Losing Our Way after the Imperial Turn."

43. At the same time, others have argued that historians and anthropologists were in fact already aware of those methodological and critical insights that postcolonialists claim to have brought to the study of colonialism. For a relevant example of this discussion among historians, see the exchange between Vaughan, "Colonial Discourse Theory and African History," and Bunn "The Insistence on Theory."

44. Clifford and Marcus, *Writing Culture*, and Marcus and Fischer, *Anthropology as Cultural Critique*, were the two seminal publications of the 1980s that announced the arrival of a new anthropology—a discipline that would no longer claim political neutrality in the name of cultural relativism, but would instead see itself as a politically positioned field of knowledge production whose overarching goal was "cultural critique."

ONE ☉ Globalization and the Postcolonial Eclipse

Beyond the Straits: Postcolonial Allegories of the Globe

𝒪 𝒪 𝒪

PETER HULME

Mañana, mañana
Ojos sin brillo
Noche encalmada
Y no viene el día
No viene.
—RADIO TARIFA, "Mañana, mañana"

The conference on which this volume is based asked its speakers to reflect on the future directions that postcolonial studies might take. This essay begins by suggesting what new horizons might be glimpsed across the straits that have appeared in recent years to encircle postcolonial studies, defining it in narrow and restrictive ways. But it is also concerned to follow the implications of its title in ways literal, historical, and theoretical. The essay was written in the shadow of the reestablishment of one of the world's most influential frontiers, that between southwest Europe and northwest Africa: it revisits the shape of the earth verified by the European journeys from that portal, and it speculates on the survival of the allegories of globality that flowed from those journeys, allegories that might seem irredeemably tainted by the association with European imperial hegemony that they helped establish. On its own journey, the essay sails close to the contentious debates about globalization and cosmopolitanism that currently enrich postcolonial studies, but it takes too idiosyncratic and meditative a course to contribute anything of substance to them.

My personal commitment to the *idea* of postcolonial studies is probably as strong as it is because the appearance of that field in the late 1980s gave me a real sense of belonging: I recognized postcolonial studies as what I had been doing for fifteen years or so without realizing it. If there is one particular stance I take with respect to the current state of postcolonial studies, it is that we are still discovering, slowly, perhaps, and unmethodically, but—as far as I am concerned—with a continuing sense of excitement, the dimensions of the field. What I mean by this is both that the field is getting bigger as the characteristic language and thematic concerns of postcolonial studies spread across many disciplines and that at the same time we are unearthing a lot of earlier anticolonial work, often neglected at its time of writing, that is allowing us to piece together a fuller history of the development of postcolonial studies. So one of the fundamental "beyonds" suggested by my title is an encouragement to strip off the straitjacket of those accounts and definitions of postcolonial studies that simplify and narrow its range to the work of a handful of theorists and a handful of novelists. In the past, some of those who work within the field, or have a productive relationship to it, have even accepted that oversimplified picture of postcolonial studies. Fortunately, as this volume suggests, the picture is now beginning to broaden.

Perhaps the most obvious of my titular straits are the straits of Eurocentric thinking that postcolonial studies is dedicated to surpassing. As one might have predicted, the most resistant categories of Eurocentrism are those so deeply embedded that we have come to think of them simply as parts of a natural geohistorical landscape; and probably none of these categories has a deader hand than that of historical periodization. Until recently, postcolonial studies largely situated itself in the modern world, giving consistent attention to the notion of modernity, though that narrowness of historical range is beginning to broaden. However, even when postcolonial studies has looked back beyond the nineteenth century, it has tended to thump into the backstop of 1492, reinforcing the idea of the Middle Ages as some kind of dark hole out of which modernity seems magically to have emerged. Certainly by the eighteenth century, *medieval* had already become a colonial term in the sense of giving Western modernity a period into which to shunt at least some of the social formations it encountered.[1] Not accidentally, the term *medieval* has now made a reappearance as the period in which Islam, in at least certain of its forms, can be fundamentally situated: "the medieval savagery of the Taliban," for example—as if the Middle Ages could teach the modern world anything about savagery. Anyway, standing against these various simplifications and stereotypes there is now a growing body of work by self-defined postcolonial medievalists who tend to ask some of the most searching questions about the nature of nationalism and of colonialism.[2]

In geographical terms, to look back beyond the straits of 1492 would be to give more postcolonial attention to the Iberian Peninsula and to the empires developed there. One indication of what might be possible comes with the essay Gayatri Spivak contributed to a recent volume in honor of Edward Said, which takes the form of an extensive critical tribute to a book by a distinguished Native American historian, Jack Forbes, called *Africans and Native Americans: The Language of Race and the Evolution of Red-Black Peoples*. In this book, Forbes attempts to understand the shifting terminology of racial and color classifications by means of a detailed tracking of the fourteenth-century Arabic and Portuguese origins of words like *mulatto*, *pardo*, and *moro*—not to show what they *really* mean, but to demonstrate the vertiginous shifts in their meanings over the centuries, in fact to unmoor them from their conventional definitions. Spivak sees in this what she calls— in an unaccountably tender phrase—an "empirical intuition of affirmative deconstruction."[3]

Spivak relates Forbes to Said in a purely conventional way: Said is the groundbreaker, while "Forbes belongs to the group of social scientists who have been chipping away at the monolithic Eurocentrism of their disciplines . . . during the two decades after *Orientalism*" (which actually does Forbes less than justice since his first contribution to the rewriting of American history was published as early as 1960).[4] But by putting Forbes and Said in the same frame, Spivak both draws Forbes's work into the postcolonial field, where its intellectual and political allies are grouping, and extends and deepens that field by adding to it the complexity of Forbes's American concerns and the breadth of his lexicographical scholarship.

It is profoundly telling that it was a Native American historian, interested in why the mixing between Americans and Africans had remained so invisible to scholarship, who took the trouble to undertake this extraordinary work, which leads back to the equally invisible trafficking of Arabic terms into the developing European vernaculars—most traces of which would eventually be purged by the great European etymological dictionaries, those monuments to scholarship and amnesia. *Traffic*—a word now almost synonymous with modernity—may itself be of Arabic origin.[5] In any event, traffic—in this case human traffic across the straits—is where the main part of this essay will begin.

During September and October 2000, the Spanish photographer Javier Bauluz documented the illegal immigrants arriving on the southern coast of Spain near the towns of Tarifa and Zahara de los Atunes. An exhibition of his photographs has been shown in Spain under the title España: Frontera Sur (Spain: Southern Border). One particular photograph (figure 1) shows a young couple, presumably Spanish, almost certainly European, in swim-

FIGURE I. The beach at Zahara de los Atunes, Spain. Photograph by Javier Bauluz, White Star Photo Plus Text Agency

ming costumes, sitting on the beach at Zahara under a parasol. A few yards away lies a third figure, the body of a would-be refugee or migrant, drowned on the attempted crossing of the straits of Gibraltar and washed up onto the beach. The couple gaze with apparent indifference in the direction of the dead man, their own bodies betraying no evident discomfort or anxiety. If the corpse were removed from the picture, it would just look as if they were enjoying a pleasant day at the seaside. The photograph dramatizes contrasts in some evident ways: between the leisure and comfort of the young couple and the stillness in death of the single man; between their bronzed skin and his shabby clothes; between their togetherness and his isolation. In one sense, this essay meditates on the implications of that photograph, which casts its shadow back to the sixteenth century and beyond.

Zahara has more resonance as a place than might be immediately apparent. It owes its name to the Arab invasion of the Iberian Peninsula at the beginning of the eighth century which swept across these southern beaches, as did—in the other direction—the Jews and Muslims expelled in the fifteenth and sixteenth centuries so that Spain could define itself as white and Christian.[6] The final expulsion of the *moriscos* was ordered by Philip III in 1609, leading to the forced removal of 250,000 inhabitants of Spain over the following five years. One "representative" figure here—from the second part of *Don Quijote*, published in 1610—would be Sancho Panza's neighbor, the *morisco* Ricote, so acculturated that he even agrees with the king's decree, but so in love with the country of his birth that he returns to Spain in disguise after wandering through North Africa and much of Europe. "Wherever we are," he says, "we weep for Spain; for, in short, here we were born, and this is our native country."[7] Here we have an early representative of the hundreds of thousands of Europeans who have subsequently been seen as not *really* European.

Another image, this one dating from 1620, Simon van der Passe's engraving for the frontispiece of Francis Bacon's *Instauratio Magna* (figure 2), shows the ships of modernity sailing through the Pillars of Hercules into the Atlantic Ocean beyond. Bacon obviously intended this picture as a great visual monument to the alliance between European exploration and the development of scientific rationalism. The limits of traditional knowledge, symbolized by the Pillars of Hercules, were now being surpassed. As Bacon's epigraph to the engraving announces: "multi pertransibunt et augebitur scientia" (many shall go to and fro and knowledge shall be increased).[8] The northern pillar, pebbles and sand at its foot in the engraving, is traditionally located just a few miles from Zahara.

Europeans had in fact begun to sail out past that beach and through those straits early in the last millennium on voyages of exploration and colonization. The first major European colonization in the Western ocean was of the Canary Islands, the Fortunate Islands of classical mythology, which had been established by Claudius Ptolemy as the prime meridian for the calculation of longitude.[9] The Canarians were written about by Giovanni Boccaccio and by Petrarch, establishing within fourteenth-century European writing many of the tropes characteristic of the colonial accounts of indigeneity that would become more familiar after 1492 in respect to the newly discovered Americas.[10] In particular, Petrarch found in the Canarian the type of non-European man against which to define his ideal of secular individualism. The Canary Islands proved to be, ethnographically as well as geographically, the degree zero of European culture.

In a literal sense, beyond the straits lies the ever-receding horizon of the globe itself. The representation of the earth as a globe is indissolubly connected with the project of European colonialism, initially through Columbus's circumnavigatory plan, which finds its shape in the first surviving European globe, dating from 1492 (and therefore lacking the Americas). Eventually, in 1519, a truly pan-European voyage—Spanish in name but with German finance, a Portuguese captain, and an Italian chronicler—set off

FIGURE 2. Simon van der Passe, frontispiece to Francis Bacon, *Instauratio Magna* (London: Joannem Billium, 1620). Courtesy of the Beinecke Rare Book and Manuscript Library, Yale University, New Haven, CT

past the straits on a voyage that three years later returned to Seville having completed the first circumnavigation of the world, thereby engraving on European consciousness the sphericity of the earth, celebrated through the making of a series of terrestrial globes on which were plotted the courses of Magellan's ship and, eventually, those of his successors, such as Francis Drake and George Anson.[11]

There are many reasons to be suspicious of global thinking. On one level, globality—even in a restricted sense of the term—is clearly directed at the attainment of military and commercial power. The Spanish motive behind Magellan's voyage was to circumvent the papal division of the world enshrined in the Treaty of Tordesillas. Spain's global reach was never fully achieved, but it was that country's defeat in 1898, in the founding gesture of modern geopolitics, that gave the Unites States of America—through its acquisition of Cuba, the Philippines, and Guam, to go along with the recently acquired Hawai'i—an equatorial girdle, immediately reinforced by the building of the Panama Canal, itself one of those ruthlessly commercial projects presented by their backers as selfless attempts to unify the world: in Ferdinand de Lesseps's formulation, to "trace across this very globe the *sign of peace*."[12] Alfred Thayer Mahan, author of *The Interest of America in Sea Power* (and incidentally, or not, coiner of the term *the Middle East*) is rarely given his due as the great strategist behind this circumnavigatory policy that has underpinned US global power since the beginning of the twentieth century and whose sea channels are still crucial to waging war in places such as Afghanistan and Iraq.[13]

For the tradition of rationality that Francis Bacon represents, the global accomplishment foreshadowed by Columbus and achieved by Magellan's voyage across open seas and around the world offers an allegory of universal knowledge divorced from the local exploration of coastal waters. In the next section of the essay, I want at least to pose the question about the possible survival of versions of that global allegory in the face of postcolonial studies' fundamental commitment to ideas of the local and the marginal. The shape of the world always dictates return, so, having begun on the European coast, the essay will finally circle back to Europe—unlike Magellan himself, who only ever reached the Philippines.

The first word of Ella Shohat and Robert Stam's book title, *Unthinking Eurocentrism*, one of the early landmarks in postcolonial studies, needs to be taken in two ways.[14] The embedded categories of Eurocentrism give *unthinking* as adjective—the assumed, the naturalized. But the task the authors set about is verbal unthinking, the unraveling and remapping of what the West had once, from its own viewpoint, mapped so definitively in accordance with the universal coordinates it claimed to have discovered: the universalization of Western culture, as the Mexican historian Edmundo O'Gorman called it as long ago as 1958.[15] At a fundamental level—perhaps the deepest in the sense of the most embedded—that unthinking necessarily involves the dismantling and reassembling of the very literal terms in which areas of the world were divided and named and visualized within European maps. The conventional founding moment for postcolonial studies saw the unthinking of the geohistorical category of the Orient,[16] but the contribution of geohistorical unthinking to postcolonial studies has a much longer and broader tradition, initially in the work of figures such as Carl Sauer and O'Gorman himself, more recently in that of Arno Peters, Brian Harley, Enrique Dussell, Fernando Coronil, José Rabasa, Patricia Seed, Walter Mignolo, and J. M. Blaut.[17] The listing of those names—the enlisting of that work of what might be called cultural geography into postcolonial studies—is intended to make one of my points: the need to enrich postcolonial thinking by going beyond the usual suspects. As with Jack Forbes, let us pay some attention—and tribute—to where the work of unthinking Eurocentrism has actually been happening, for at least the past fifty years. And as those names suggest, much of that work has gone on in Latin America or at least in Latin American studies. To enlist Mignolo's work, in particular, means inevitably to raise the question he asks so persistently about the location of what he now prefers to call postoccidentalism.[18] For Mignolo, this work takes place "in the margins"— yet another spatial term, and one offering a location that seems more comfortably postcolonial than anything that global imagery might have to offer.[19] Beach, horizon: margins, globe: physical location, the rhetorical position of knowledge production. It is those dialectics to which I now turn.

Of the new European sciences developed in the early modern period, cartography probably has the most direct and unmediated relationship to colonial practice. Cartography helped European ships sail the oceans to their colonial destinations. The territory to be possessed or disciplined or taxed became subject to a regime of surveying and mapping. Cartography seems to be where Western rationality in one of its purest forms—geometry—serves an imperial practice, as what Arjun Appadurai calls "the prose of cadastral politics."[20] Following Brian Harley's pioneering work in this area, colonial historians such as Lesley Cormack, Barbara Mundy, and Matthew Edney have begun to detail the intimate relationships between cartography and imperialism.[21]

The founding text of Western cartography is Ptolemy's *Geography*, written in the second century AD, a text that also provides the classical demonstration of the sphericity of the earth, which ancient geographers understood long before Magellan's voyage demonstrated it. The shift associated with Ptolemy is one toward a deductive cartographic practice able to incorporate existing surveys into a synthetic whole constructed by means of the abstract numbered network we now call the lines of latitude and longitude, enabling the geographer to preserve the correct proportion of small areas to the whole earth.[22] It was the Latin translation of Ptolemy in the early fifteenth century that triggered early modern cartography, and his methodology guided European cartographers even when Ptolemy's own maps had obviously been superseded. Through the projections of sixteenth-century mapmakers, especially those of Gerardus Mercator, Europe produced an image of the world so powerful that we in the West still think that it is what the world actually looks like, with Europe at its center, Africa below, and America and Asia to each side: east is east and west is west, and north is on top.

All of this seems to run counter to the grain of postcolonial thinking. After all, the view from above is usually associated either with domination of a literal kind, as with the trope of the imperial eye, or with the claim to a scientific neutrality that merely constitutes the universalization of technological power, as exemplified, say, in spy satellites. So in light of this imbrication between cartography and imperialism, it is understandable why someone like Mignolo should reject the claim that Euclidean geometry might offer any "neutral ordering of the shape of the earth."[23] This seems an almost classically postcolonial point. Europe has taken the geometrical projections that allowed it to dominate the world and passed them off as neutral and unmarked. Postcolonial studies, one might assume, will remark that cartographic—even cosmographical—tradition as merely occidental, thus grounding, locating, and demystifying its global pretensions.[24] Indeed, in postcolonial discussions, mapmaking has frequently been offered as an emblem of the pretensions of rationality via reference to the now conventional topos of Jorge Luis Borges's tantalizing paragraph called "On Exactitude in Science," supposedly quoted from a seventeenth-century Spanish moralist who recalls an empire in which the art of cartography reached such perfection that a map of the empire was made "whose size was that of the Empire, and which coincided point for point with it"—and therefore proved entirely useless.[25]

However, in proposing a radically different set of projections of how the world looks, Arno Peters's "new cartography" from 1967 onward offered, in classically postcolonial fashion, to destabilize those earlier Western images of the world. The aim of Mercator's projections had been to allow navigators to plot straight-line courses. As a consequence, they represented European

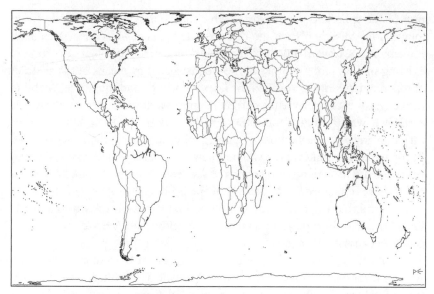

FIGURE 3. Arno Peters, *The Peters Projection.* Courtesy Akademische Verlagsanstalt and Oxford Cartographers Ltd. (for the English version)

landmasses as relatively larger than they are. Operating to a different imperative, Peters's postcolonial projections present landmass areas accurately in relation to each other, at the expense of distortion to shape (figure 3), thereby offering a salutary provincializing of Europe, and indeed of North America, especially with respect to Africa. But—and this is where I want to try to turn the tide of the cartographic argument—maps are not merely perspectival: size is a relative absolute, and landmass areas can therefore be represented accurately, or not, with respect to each other. That phrase "relatively larger than they are" belongs to Brian Harley himself,[26] who would have no truck with claims to the mere neutral truth of Western cartography, but who is prepared to make a truth claim that distances him from any suggestion that all maps merely offer a different perspective dependent on the position—ethnic, cultural, spatial, or whatever—of their maker. And the judgment about whether or not that accuracy has been achieved in any particular case can best be made from a position that might metaphorically be represented as global since, on a globe, landmass size and shape can *both* be represented accurately.[27]

Oddly, despite the current ubiquity of the discourse on globalization, and despite us nearly reaching the quincentenary of Magellan's voyage, the implications of the globe—in the cartographic sense of the term—have never fully infiltrated our critical language. As Spivak writes in an essay on Marshall McLuhan's notion of the "global village": "The 'globe' is counterintuitive. You walk from one end of the earth to the other and it remains flat."[28] The actual shape of the earth has had real difficulty in imposing itself on our ways of thinking and writing, leaving us with a language of "ends" and "margins," neither of which a sphere can actually possess. Such terminology, though rarely questioned, is deeply ideological: the biblical injunction "to the uttermost ends of the earth," based on the idea of a sacred center and heathen outskirts—and bolstered by the classical tag *ad termini orbis terrarum*— passed into common usage and has, even within the past two hundred years, underpinned two of the most savage of colonial genocides, in Tasmania and Patagonia, areas designated by Western imperial geographers as "the ends of the earth," and therefore apparently home to the lowest and most dispensable forms of humanity.[29] If that is what Eurocentric flat-earth imagery leads to, then allegories of the globe might possibly offer some improvement.

The globe seems almost to avoid scrutiny. It is a figure of perfection, completion, and universality. It has no truck with divisions or frontiers. The name of the object—the globe that sits in your study—is reassuringly the same as the name of what it represents: the earth, the planet, the globe. Scrutiny of global imagery has, however, recently arrived in two complementary studies, Denis Cosgrove's *Apollo's Eye* and Bruce Robbins's *Feeling Global*.[30] Cosgrove's book about the history of global imagery is deeply concerned with the genealogy of what Robbins calls "the ambiguity of the aerial perspective."[31] That perspective is not necessarily physically raised above the surface of the earth—indeed, it is only in the past one hundred years that such physical elevation has become possible. But rhetorically all maps occupy a position of overview or domination, with the globe itself even allowing its owner to imaginatively possess the whole world—that is why European monarchs commissioned so many globes in the sixteenth and seventeenth centuries. In Cosgrove's account, the Apollonian eye is synoptic and omniscient, intellectually detached from the earth, but never disconnected from it, which means that the knowledge invested in the Apollonian position is never separate from earthly power. The Apollonian vision is often an imperial gaze and is properly seen as the basis of a male-gendered Eurocentrism that rose to prominence during the early modern period, although Cosgrove rightly cautions that the issue is by no means simple: "The Apollonian perspective prompts ethical questions about individual and social life on the globe's surface that have disturbed as often as they have reassured a comfortable Western patriarchy."[32] Throughout the modern period in particular, representations of the globe have been connected "as closely to lust

for material possessions, power, and authority as to metaphysical speculation, religious aspiration, or poetic sentiment," Cosgrove writes, and he
is careful to pay attention to the development of a Eurocentric thinking
in which Europe's "totalizing globalism" transformed and destroyed non-
European worlds.[33] But at the same time, that potentially, or imaginatively,
global view has always also been associated with the detachment and disinterest of true knowledge. Apollo serves as Cosgrove's figure for that ambiguity—master of both the imperial and the poetic globes.

Robbins illustrates his book with photographs of Italian cities taken by his
father from the bomb compartment of his B-17 during and just after the Second World War, hauntingly beautiful photographs that illustrate that ambiguity of the aerial perspective in a fairly obvious way. Interestingly, Cosgrove
traces in some detail the twentieth-century fascination with the airman, who
took over from the circumnavigator in offering a figure whose vision could
be seen as disengaging from the limited perspective of earthbound mortals,[34]
a vision celebrated in the early 1940s in the writing of Archibald MacLeish
and in the mapmaking of Richard Edes Harrison, whose famous image of
a world map called *One World, One War* is sometimes invoked as preparing
the popular ground for US entry into the Second World War by placing the
viewer in an Apollonian position directly above the North Pole, from where
the globe's landmass appears shrunken and singular, nowhere very far from
anywhere else—apart from Australia and New Zealand.

If Peters's projections reverse the Eurocentrism of Mercator's without ever
escaping the misrepresentation intrinsic to the idea of projection itself, could
we imagine anything like a postcolonial globe? Cosgrove comes close to suggesting this possibility in the form of the photographs of the earth taken on
the Apollo space missions between 1968 and 1972—two of which have been
very widely reproduced (figure 4). There is obviously nothing neutral about
the origins of these photographs, but in their random angles and unplanned
coverings of cloud, they do further destabilize our remaining colonial certainties that north is at the top, that all writing runs a particular way, that
national borders are visible. The globe in the study turns on its own axis;
NASA's photographs give us a globe that is spinning in a larger universe.

Could any such global, Apollonian moment exist within postcolonial
studies, or at least in dialogue with postcolonial studies? Given the commitment of postcolonial studies to the work of the local, in the margins,
a commitment to allegorical globality could perhaps only survive counterintuitively—and, to be sure, against the grain of the term *Apollo*. But there
exists a contragranular tradition of this kind within postcolonial studies: I
am thinking—to keep within cartographic imagery—of something like Aimé

FIGURE 4. The whole earth. Courtesy NASA (photograph A S17-22727)

Césaire's attack on humanism in the name of "a true humanism . . . made to the measure of the world,"[35] a call that finds its echoes in Frantz Fanon and in Said and that encourages me to offer in shorthand three possible instances of such postcolonial globality.

It was Fernando Coronil who suggested the need to attend more care-fully to the actual textures of occidentalism itself the better to then formu-late postoccidental thinking.[36] But the term *postoccidental* itself has a much longer history, coined by the Cuban critic Roberto Fernández Retamar as early as 1961. Interestingly, for Retamar, the origin of postoccidental knowl-edge is to be found in the work of Karl Marx, the irony of history deter-mining that the occident would provide the material for its own unthinking underneath that suitably global dome of the British Museum reading room:[37] a theory of history thinking itself—and the metaphor seems unavoidable— *above* the circumstances and location of its production.

The second example is very different and comes from within cartographic studies itself. Shortly before he died, Brian Harley initiated, with David Woodward, a massive series of volumes called *The History of Cartography*, which is slowly offering a global account of the history of mapmaking. This is not an unpositioned history—it is mostly written by Western scholars and published by the University of Chicago Press—but it gives enormous weight to indigenous and non-Western traditions of mapmaking that not very long ago would not only have not been seen as important but would not even have been recognized as mapmaking at all. There is a universal claim at the heart of this project, but it is one spoken with due tentativeness: "There has probably always been a mapping impulse in human consciousness," Harley writes.[38] The determination to approach the history of "understand[ing] the world by depicting it in map form" in "a global way" is then finessed by imaginatively rising above the tradition of Western cartography, of which the whole project is obviously the inheritor, in order to recognize the unfamiliar, especially the indigenous, to engage it in conversation, and to allow it to change the terms describing the field of cartography.[39]

The question of indigeneity provides the third example. No other issue has pressed matters of locality so hard in places like Canada, Australia, Ecuador, and Mexico, where land constitutes a fundamental and burning issue. And yet the movement for indigenous rights has become a powerful force in the modern world at least partly because of its successful use of global opportunities, particularly in the forums of the United Nations where it is helping refashion the language of human rights, a language we often assume belongs to the Enlightenment, but that actually has its origins in the debate following contact with that indigenous Canarian population, victims of the first of Europe's genocides of native peoples.[40] So, perhaps, at moments, and with due caution, the development of postoccidental thinking might still operate some version of a global perspective without betraying its local commitments.

This ends the speculative circumnavigation, returning me to dry land, in Europe. I have referred both to the postcolonial tradition from the margins and to some more tentative global positioning, but I want to end in Europe for two reasons. First, to make the point that the attractions of global allegory do not involve divorce from the pressing circumstances of moment and location, which for those of us working in Britain currently involve grappling with the idea of Europe. And second, because it is important to remember that postcolonial studies has a purchase beyond the unthinking of Eurocentrism's view of non-European worlds: Britain itself, and Europe more generally, is deeply marked by its postcolonial condition, even as—and especially because—it has such difficulty recognizing that condition. The dimensions of the condition might be suggested by juxtaposing two very different "voyages in," to use Edward Said's term.[41] For most Europeans, though not all, the postcolonial condition might be grasped by coming to terms with the colonialism that preceded and enabled the establishment of the nation-states we inhabit. The eye has to turn inward and investigate that internal history, a history that Shakespeare witnesses and inscribes and to a degree enacts in plays like *King Lear* and *Macbeth*.[42] (Likewise in the United States, no taking of a postcolonial position should be able to ignore the genocidal violence that both preceded and followed the establishment of the nation-state and whose aftermath continues to disfigure American realities.) In other words, while postcolonial studies needs to move beyond various straits, it also needs to be recursive, testing the power of its analyses on the monuments of European culture: it must continue to unthink those cultural securities at home.

Inasmuch as British culture recognizes itself as postcolonial, that recognition is due to the presence in the UK of those who undertook the voyage in, during the 1950s and 1960s, largely from the Caribbean and the Indian subcontinent. Those inward voyages took many forms, but surely one of the most exemplary was that of the Barbadian novelist and critic George Lamming, whose book of essays, *The Pleasures of Exile*, was published in 1960 but only recognized nearly thirty years later as a landmark work in postcolonial studies, largely due to Rob Nixon's pioneering essay.[43]

One exemplary aspect of Lamming's work was his recognition of the centrality of what he called "the whole tabernacle" of English literature to the colonial system.[44] Lamming set out to shake the foundations of that tabernacle — by rereading *The Tempest*. On most grounds, that might seem a less radical move than hammering a nail into Prospero's head, which was what Caliban wanted to do in the course of that play. But Lamming was working in accordance with the first rule of guerrilla tactics: always take the enemy by surprise. Prospero will expect the nail in the head and take precautions, as the play itself shows; but he will not expect to be challenged as a literary commentator, a role Prospero and his descendants have long thought of as rightfully theirs.[45] Lamming's reading of *The Tempest* has changed our understanding of Shakespeare, opening the way for postcolonial scholarship of the kind that has now installed itself as the canonical reading of the play.[46]

The Tempest was probably the first literary beneficiary of circumnavigation. At that uttermost end of the earth that was Patagonia, Magellan encountered native people described by the Italian nobleman Antonio Pigafetta, the expedition's chronicler, as "Patagoni." Pigafetta tells of how Magellan captured two of these natives by a trick, imprisoning them in fetters. When they saw how they had been deceived, he wrote, they roared like bulls and cried out to their great devil Setebos to help them.[47]

The route from the Patagonian coast to Whitehall, where the word *Setebos* was spoken on the English stage, was by no means straightforward. The first published version of Pigafetta was an Italian translation of a French transla-

tion of the then lost Italian original. That Italian translation was itself translated into English in abbreviated form by Richard Eden in his *The Decades
of the New Worlde*, published in London in 1555, and then posthumously re-
printed in an augmented version in 1577 called *The History of Trauayle in
the West and East Indies*, which is where Shakespeare probably came across
it.[48] It is one of the oddities of the translation process that the non-European
word, precisely because it is unfamiliar to all parties in all European languages, once it finds its first European—in this case Italian—form as *Setebos*,
remains absolutely constant until it finally emerges in Caliban's description
of Prospero's power as such that "it would control my dam's god Setebos."[49]
That such a previously unknown word should reappear in absolutely identical form in *The Tempest* nearly a hundred years after its first recording off
the South American coast makes Pigafetta's text one of the very few certain
verbal sources for the play.[50]

The Tempest takes place in the dangerous waters between Naples and Tunis,
by implication between Christendom and Islam, and was first staged in 1611,
between Philip III's order and the final expulsion of the *moriscos* from the
Iberian Peninsula. For all of Fernand Braudel's emphasis on the deep currents
of Mediterranean history, the story he tells of the area in these years is in one
sense rather crude—an essential struggle between East and West, meaning
the Islamic world and Christian Europe. After centuries of the East's domination, by the sixteenth century the West "was far ahead of the East," a statement Braudel glosses as "more forceful and holding the Islamic world in its
dependence."[51] More interesting than the historical judgment itself is what
counts for Braudel as evidence of this Western domination—human migration. Not, however, as one might expect, human migration from East to West
or South to North, not the evidence of a superior civilization, richer and
more developed, that attracts the inhabitants of the less developed world like
bees to a honey pot—that is now the story we are told to explain migration
from South to North. Just the opposite, in fact: "Men flocked from Christendom to Islam, which tempted them with visions of adventure and profit—
and paid them to stay."[52] Braudel accumulates evidence for this. The grand
Turk paid handsomely for Europeans to work as artisans, weavers, ship-
builders; Spanish garrisons on the North African coast were decimated by
epidemics of desertion as soldiers embraced Islam; small boats left Sicily full
of candidates for apostasy, for "turning Turk," as the contemporary phrase
put it. This is a strange kind of dominance: Shakespeare's Alonso, pressured
into giving his daughter Claribel into a dynastic marriage in Tunis, would
certainly suggest a much more equal balance of forces at this moment. "Per-

haps unconsciously," Braudel says, "the Turks were opening doors just as Christendom was shutting them. Christian intolerance, the consequence of large numbers, did not welcome strangers, it repelled them."[53]

It is still repelling them. The second inward voyage to set alongside Lamming's is fictional: the disturbing and minatory novel by the French writer Jean Raspail, first published in 1973 and called *The Camp of the Saints*. The title is a biblical reference, from the book of Revelation (20:9), in which Satan is released from his one thousand–year imprisonment and unleashes the forces of Gog and Magog, which "compassed the camp of the saints about" until the fire from heaven came down to devour them. In the novel, a pilgrimage of a million starving Indians storm on board ships in Calcutta harbor and sail round Africa, through the Straits of Gibraltar, and into the Mediterranean, where they beach on the French coast. French army units, ordered to fire on the invading masses, desert in droves, and the novel ends with the establishment of a new world order dominated by the forces of the previously dispossessed. In the preface to the novel's second edition, Raspail explains that it was only "prudence" that had led him to displace the threat to Europe onto faraway India from where it actually lies—on the southern shores of the Mediterranean, ready to follow what he calls the "mighty vanguard already here . . . in the bosom of a people that once was French."[54]

In recent years, Raspail's novel has begun to look prophetic. In the summer of 1991, thousands of Albanians commandeered ships to take them to the Italian ports of Bari and Brindisi, where they were locked up in football stadiums before being forcibly repatriated. In February 1993, a small rusting freighter called the *Golden Venture* carried refugees from China to Kenya and then from Kenya to Rockaway, in the Queens district of New York City, where the boat ran aground, drowning several of the refugees.[55] Then, early in 2001, even more pointedly, the *East Sea*, a freighter flying a Cambodian flag, was beached by its crew near Nice with a cargo of nearly one thousand Iraqi and Turkish Kurds packed into the hold in conditions very close to those described by Raspail for his Indian ship (figure 5). Needless to say, this cargo of the dispossessed did not take over the government of the world.

Raspail's novel is a fascist cry of despair at the white race's supposed failure of will, or of "soul," as he calls it. Its four US editions in the past fifteen years have been embraced by white supremacist organizations such as Stormfront and American Renaissance as a warning to the white race that it must be prepared to defend itself against the threatening tide of the dispossessed who will soon attempt to overthrow its long and deserved hegemony—unless that white race rediscovers what Raspail unblinkingly calls "the inflexible courage to be rich."[56]

FIGURE 5. Migrants from the *East Sea* on a beach near Nice.
Photograph by Jacques Munch, Agence France Presse

On a small scale, it has become increasingly common, in many parts of the world, for the rich to need the protection of locked and patrolled housing estates to feel secure from the poor, just as, on a larger scale, the borders of the rich countries, and principally the long border between the United States and Mexico, need electronic surveillance, armed guards, wire fencing, and deep canals. Elsewhere, as with the Straits of Gibraltar, the natural frontier itself functions as a huge though often insufficient deterrent. Javier Bauluz's exhibition may carry the title Spain: Southern Border, but the man in his photograph has been cast ashore not just on the border between Spain and Morocco, but—since the accords that brought down most of the internal borders in Europe—on what has become the border between Africa and Europe itself (now practically synonymous with the European Union), and even the frontier between the first world and the third, the camp of the saints and the tents of the wretched, a frontier fortified and patrolled as never before, which is why so many people die trying to cross it.[57]

The most troubling aspect of Bauluz's Zahara photograph is the couple's unthinking, unseeing gaze, which must mark some sort of disavowal, some unconscious insistence that this stretch of sand is still a beach, rather than one of the contemporary globe's most significant fault lines. Cultural studies has taught us about the history of the beach.[58] For postcolonial studies, the beach has become, thanks to Greg Dening's work,[59] a prime contact zone of colonial history, an area that might become a theater for violence and killing, as well as for commerce and escape, that might be the crucible for new lives and new languages; but it was never meant to be the setting for indifference and denial.

The Tempest has a song for a drowned man—"Those are pearls that were his eyes"—but since the play is a comedy, Alonso, the man supposedly drowned in those waters and sung about by Ariel, turns out not to be dead at all. Radio Tarifa's words, the epigraph to this essay, sung by Faín Dueñas with that hoarse and keening edge that is a characteristic of the vocal traditions of both sides of the Strait, perhaps offer a better elegy for the drowned man on the beach at Zahara, for whom the day will never come.

Notes

1. On this "denial of coevalness," see Fabian, *Time and the Other*.

2. For examples, see the essays in Cohen, *The Postcolonial Middle Ages*; Linehan and Nelson, *The Medieval World*; and Ingham and Warren, *Postcolonial Moves*.

3. Spivak, "Race before Racism," 56; compare Forbes, *Africans and Native Americans*.

4. Spivak, "Race before Racism," 51. Forbes, *Apache, Navaho, and Spaniard*.

5. According to the *Oxford English Dictionary* (OED), *traffic* is probably a Romanic word with as putative a Latin origin as *transfacere* (to transact), about as neutral an origin as could be imagined, although even the OED recognises that there are "problems" with this derivation and even notes the possibility of a root in the Arabic word *taraffaqa*, meaning "to seek profit." Any amateur etymologist would also latch on to the recognized Arabic term *tariff*, with its various meanings such as "notification," "table," "list of customs duties," which are mostly associated with the commercial traffic that has, in different ways, always characterized the Mediterranean as a region. See the discussion in Menocal, *The Arabic Role in Medieval Literary History*, 1–26.

6. Resonating with Forbes's work, see Mariscal, "The Role of Spain in Contemporary Race Theory."

7. Cervantes, *Don Quixote*, 2:403. On some of the ways in which Cervantes and his writings deal with crossing the Straits, see Garcés, *Cervantes in Algiers*.

8. See Burnett, *The Engraved Title-Page*.

9. Ptolemy, *Ptolemy's Geography*, 134.

10. Boccaccio, "De Canaria et insulis reliquis"; and Petrarch, *The Life of Solitude*. See Hulme, "Tales of Distinction."

11. See Brotton, *Trading Territories*; and Randles, *Geography, Cartography, and Nautical Science*.

12. Quoted in Cosgrove, *Apollo's Eye*, 214 (emphasis Cosgrove's).

13. Mahan, *The Interest of America in Sea Power*. Recent recognition of Mahan's significance is given by Bové, "Can American Studies Be Area Studies?" 222. Compare Jacobson, *Barbarian Virtues*.

14. Shohat and Stam, *Unthinking Eurocentrism*.

15. O'Gorman, *La invención de América*; in English, O'Gorman, *The Invention of America*.

16. Said, *Orientalism*.

17. A very partial listing of this work would include: Sauer, *The Early Spanish Main*; Sauer, *Sixteenth-Century North America*; Peters, *The New Cartography*; Peters, *Compact Peters Atlas of the World*; Harley, *The New Nature of Maps*; Dussel, *The Invention of the Americas*; Dussel, "Eurocentrism and Modernity"; Coronil, "Beyond Occidentalism"; Coronil, "Listening to the Subaltern"; Coronil, "Toward a Critique of Globalcentrism"; Rabasa, *Inventing America*; Seed, *Ceremonies of Possession*; Mignolo, *The Darker Side*; Mignolo, *Local Histories / Global Designs*; and Blaut, *The Colonizer's Model of the World*.

18. Mignolo, *Local Histories/Global Designs*, 91.

19. Compare an earlier engagement with Mignolo's work in Hulme, "Voice from the Margins?"; and Mignolo's response, "I Am Where I Think," 235–45.

20. Appadurai, *Modernity at Large*, 121.

21. Cormack, *Charting an Empire*; Mundy, *The Mapping of New Spain*; and Edney, *Mapping an Empire*.

22. Woodward, "Maps and the Rationalization of Geographic Space," 84.

23. Mignolo, *The Darker Side*, 222.

24. Ironically, of course, historical study has begun to reveal how much of this so-called Western rationalism, including the geometrical and cartographical technology that underlies the very claim to a universal method of knowledge, was in fact learned in Europe from Jewish and Arabic scholars working in Spain and Portugal. See Seed, *Ceremonies of Possession*, 100–48. Such arguments undermine European exceptionalism, but also, ipso facto, take the ground from any simple assumption that universal rationalism is intrinsically or exclusively European.

25. Borges, *Collected Fictions*, 325.

26. Harley, "Maps, Knowledge, and Power," 290.

27. Claudius Ptolemy noted that "when the earth is delineated on a sphere, it has a shape like its own, nor is there any need of altering [it] at all." Quoted in Brown, *The Story of Maps*, 68.

28. Spivak, "Cultural Talks in the Hot Peace," 329.

29. See Gamble, "Archaeology, History, and the Uttermost Ends of the Earth."

30. Cosgrove, *Apollo's Eye*; and Robbins, *Feeling Global*. See also Brotton, "Terrestrial Globalism"; and compare Decker and van der Krogt, *Globes from the Western World*.

31. Robbins, *Feeling Global*, 2.

32. Cosgrove, *Apollo's Eye*, 3. See also Piper, *Cartographic Fictions*, 65–127.

33. Cosgrove, *Apollo's Eye*, 5, 80.

34. Ibid., 243.

35. Césaire, *Discourse on Colonialism*, 56.

36. Coronil, "Beyond Occidentalism."

37. Roberto Fernández Retamar, "Nuestra América y Occidente," 244.

38. Harley, "The Map and the Development of the History of Cartography," 1:1.

39. Woodward and Lewis, introduction, 1. See also Lewis, *Cartographic Encounters*; and Piper, *Cartographic Fictions*, 168–84.

40. See Muldoon, *Popes, Lawyers, and Infidels*.

41. Said, *Culture and Imperialism*, 295.

42. See Baker and Maley, *British Identities*.

43. Lamming, *Pleasures of Exile*; Nixon, "Caribbean and African Appropriations."

44. Lamming, *Pleasures of Exile*, 27.

45. For a development of this argument, see Hulme, "Reading from Elsewhere."

46. See Hulme, "Stormy Weather."

47. Pigafetta, *First Voyage around the World*, 17.

48. Eden, *History of Trauayle in the West and East Indies*.

49. Shakespeare, *The Tempest*, 1:2:372.

50. The word has never been identified within any of the indigenous Patagonian languages. Speaking of views from above, Setebos is now the official name of one of the moons of the planet Uranus, its nineteenth known satellite. According to the NASA Web site, "Setebos (S/1999 U1) is named after the character who enslaves Ariel in Shakespeare's play *The Tempest*. . . . Very little is known about Setebos." Available at solarsystem.nasa.gov/planets/profile.cfm?Object=Ura_Setebos. Very little indeed, since the character who enslaves Ariel is actually Sycorax.

51. Braudel, *The Mediterranean*, vol. 2, 799. I draw a couple of paragraphs here from two related essays of my own: "Dire Straits," and "Cast Away."

52. Braudel, *The Mediterranean*, 799.

53. Ibid., 800. See also Hess, "The Mediterranean and Shakespeare's Geopolitical Imagination."

54. Raspail, *Camp of the Saints*, xv.

55. A photograph of this incident provides the cover for the Social Contract Press edition of Raspail's novel.

56. Raspail, *Camp of the Saints*, xvi. See Matthew Connolly and Paul Kennedy, "Must It Be the Rest against the West?" *Atlantic Monthly*, December 1996, 61–68.

57. See Harding, *The Uninvited*. The huge number of illegal immigrants detained by the Spanish authorities on the southern coastal strip of Spain regularly include large numbers of Liberians, Somalis and South Africans, but also Filipinos, Chinese, and even eastern Europeans.

58. Lencek and Bosker, *The Beach*.

59. Dening, *Islands and Beaches*; and Dening, "Writing, Rewriting the Beach."

On Globalization, Again!

 ⊘ ⊘ ⊘

ALI BEHDAD

I have titled this essay "On Globalization, Again" to draw attention, first of all, to its belatedness in relation to the large body of research that already exists in the academy on the phenomenon of globalization.¹ My article relies on this literature to make its argument, and as such, it occasionally recapitulates what opponents, supporters, and "objective" theoreticians of the global flow have already stated in different ways. My essay does not claim to say anything new about globalization or the network of connectivity that characterizes it; instead, it tries to ask what is at stake, politically and intellectually, in contemporary theories of the global among cultural and postcolonial critics.² In other words, I am interested not so much in what globalization is as in the broader implications of how such an issue has garnered so much critical attention among these scholars. Does the issue of globalization offer a field of critical inquiry "beyond" postcolonialism? What are we to make of how the predicament of globalization has eclipsed, say, such crucial issues as imperialism and postcoloniality in our critical debates today? Does the focus on the global dissimulate neo-imperial relations of power?

Second, I have used the word *again* in my title polemically to suggest that the current academic research on globalization, especially in the field of cultural and postcolonial studies, itself constitutes a belated theoretical practice, describing a politico-economic phenomenon that precedes and goes beyond the discourse that theorizes its mechanism. This literature claims to state something utterly new, but it is itself belated, emerging after economists and political scientists have dominated the debate and borrowing extensively from earlier theoretical paradigms such as postcolonial theory, cultural studies, and postmodernism to support its claim about the novelty of our current sociocultural order. Consequently, it exhibits a critical anxiety about the political and cultural effectiveness of the critique it offers. Zygmunt Bauman's bemoaning observation that " 'globalization' is on every-body's lips; a fad word fast turning into a shibboleth, a magic incantation, a pass-key meant to unlock the gates to all present and future mysteries" speaks to both the predicament of belatedness and the critical anxiety of cultural and postcolonial critics who have jumped on the critical bandwagon of global theory.[3] I will return to the problematic relation of globalization and postcolonial theory below, but for the moment suffice it to say that the current crisis of postcolonialism can be partly attributed to how many of its theorists have acceded to the debate over globalization, instead of mapping the ways in which decolonization heralded the new global order or critically reflecting on the rise of corporate hegemony as a form of neocolonialism.

To unpack these rather general statements, I wish to discuss polemically three related predicaments in the academic literature on globalization. My first contention is that in spite of cultural and postcolonial critics' emphasis on the newness of today's global flow, the condition we call globalization is not new if viewed historically in the context of colonial relations of power and other earlier world-systems preceding European hegemony since 1492. The scale of economic, cultural, and technological connectivity is certainly larger, and the speed of the current global flow of capital, commodities, peoples, and ideas is certainly faster as the result of technological advances, but the flow and interconnection themselves are rather old, as is the discourse of novelty itself.[4] Postcolonial critics such as Enrique Dussel and Homi Bhabha locate the advent of global culture in 1492 with Columbus's so-called discovery of America.[5] Following Janet Abu-Lughod, Warren Cohen, and John Whitmore, I wish to argue for the need to remember that global flows and world-systems existed well before Spaniards began colonizing the New World, not only in the Americas but also throughout the Mediterranean, South Asia, and East Asia.[6] Postcolonial critics' fixation on the significance of 1492 as the beginning of modernity proves symptomatic of a North American form of historical interpolation. By this I mean that the United States always interpolates its citizens—including its citizens of color—with a triumphant history of discovery that always begins with Columbus.

Second, the current discourse of cultural globalization, I wish to suggest, is an academically mediated mode of representation, and as a result it borrows and imitates earlier theoretical interventions in the US academy, such as poststructuralism, postmodernism, and postcolonialism. Intellectually affiliated with these theories, this new discourse holds an intertextual relation with them as it often leans on their conceptual distinctions and regularly borrows from their theoretical vocabulary, while at the same time claiming itself as the newer form of theory with a whole new conceptual paradigm. This newer theory, by virtue of its novel vocabulary and conceptual framework, is supposedly capable of understanding the newer world system better. Consider, for example, how such key words as *postnation, disjuncture,* and *difference* in the writings of Arjun Appadurai and other denizens of *Public Culture* simultaneously depend on and differentiate themselves from earlier theoretical terms in poststructuralist, postcolonial, and postmodern theories. The academic literature on globalization, in short, contrary to its claims of novelty and originality, is a mimetic and intertextual discourse. Like earlier cultural and academic writings that attempted to articulate various politico-economic phenomena in theoretical terms, it, too, tries to describe, through critical language and conceptual frameworks borrowed from these earlier cultural discourses, a politico-economic condition incommensurable with the discourse's philosophical scope and discursive paradigm. It should come as no surprise that in many cases, the same theoreticians who tried to articulate postmodernity or postcoloniality are now describing our contemporary culture as globalization.[7]

The third problem in the academic literature of globalization, given the complexity and the great speed of current global flows, is that theoreticians of globalization are necessarily late arrivals to the critical and political scene dominated mostly by economists. The theories constructed by these academic intellectuals chase a phenomenon that incessantly changes in ways unpredictable, overdetermined, and rapid. The academic discourse on globalization constitutes a theoretical practice of interpretation, but it wishes to be a political practice that intervenes in and fashions the phenomenon it studies. Although this may be true of all theoretical works that define themselves as political, the fact that the circuitously complex geography of global flows imposes new limits on interventionary politics has resulted in cultural theories of globalization being unable to reconcile their discursive positions with their belated political critique. This split, on the one hand, results from the inevitable temporal delay between theory and its tortuously complex object; the gap renders theory's politics belated, and I mean here in the conventional sense of appearing past the proper time for it to prove politically effective. On the other hand, because the events of our current world-system have not yet run their course, they have not yet become "history" to be interpreted by cultural critics. And so like that of its precursors, the scope of the literature's interventionary possibilities remains extremely limited, in spite of the high hopes to the contrary of its belated practitioners. That figures such as the economist Joseph Stiglitz and the journalist Thomas Friedman, and not cultural critics like Fredric Jameson and Appadurai, have become the oft-cited experts on globalization speaks not only to the power of the popular language of the former in describing our current politico-economic condition but also to the discursive limits of cultural theories of globalization produced by the latter.[8]

In what follows, I want to elaborate on these three problems by considering particular examples from the cultural and postcolonial studies literature on globalization. My aim, however, is not to be merely critical but to suggest a more historically contextualized approach to studying our so-called cultures of globalization. Few accounts of cultural globalization have traced the historical roots of transnational cultural flows, contending with the fact that the extent of global reach today is historically unprecedented. But what do these critics mean by globalization as a new social order? Whence the resistance to offering an adequate conceptual purchase on the historical roots of globalization? What theoretical insights do they intend to offer about a putatively economic phenomenon marked by interdependencies of trade and monetary systems? And what are the political aims and implications of studying *cultures* of globalization ahistorically?

What Was Globalization?

In his essay, "Mexican Migration and the Social Space of Postmodernism," Roger Rouse remarks, "We live in a confusing world, a world of crisscrossed economies, intersecting systems of meaning, and fragmented identities. Suddenly, the comforting modern imagery of nation-states and national languages, of coherent communities and consistent subjectivities, of dominant centers and distant margins no longer seems adequate."[9] This is an early cultural studies description of the phenomenon that has been labeled globalization. The circuits of exchange, according to Rouse, have become complicated as a result of the border crossings of capital and people, commodities and identities. Echoing the argument of economists about the interconnectedness and interdependence of trade and monetary systems, Rouse describes globalization as a new social order marked by diasporic identities and fluid communities. As a result, the nation-state seems on the verge of disappearing, replaced now by a complex web of decentered and global economic and cultural relations. Like the recent boosters of globalization, Rouse equates, through a neoliberal economic logic, the emergence of a global market with the phenomenon of "denationalization," assuming that "nation-states have become unnatural, even impossible business units in a global economy," to use the words of one booster.[10]

Seminal as his essay seemed when it appeared in 1991 in the inaugural issue of *Diaspora: A Journal of Transnational Studies*, Rouse modestly acknowl-edged that he was only elaborating on the ideas of Jameson by extending the archive of "raw materials for a new cartography" to include "the cir-cumstances and experiences of those working-class groups whose members have been most severely affected by the changing character of capitalist ex-ploitation" in addition to the aesthetic forms analyzed by Jameson.[11] Rouse uses the case of the Aguilillan migrant farmworkers traveling between their native village in Michoacan and Redwood City in Northern California to make his argument about the new global order in which the category of nation-state has become obsolete. He borrows Jameson's theoretical model in "Postmodernism; or, The Cultural Logic of Late Capitalism"[12] to argue that "the gradual unfolding of the global shift from colonialism and classic forms of dependency to a new transnational capitalism has meant that, dur-ing the last 20 years, we have all moved irrevocably into a new kind of social space, one which our modern sensibilities leave us unable to comprehend."[13]

Striking in this rather typical description of the global flow by cultural and postcolonial critics is the emphasis on the novelty of the social ter-rain Jameson had earlier labeled "postmodern hyperspace." It is this new-ness that makes the theoretician suddenly "confused" and "unable" to com-prehend the new social space. All the changes seem to have occurred in the past twenty years or so, during which new technologies and economic changes have ushered in radical transformations in our everyday practices. And, given the radical differences of the new social order, both Rouse and Jameson feel the need for a new critical "cartography" to understand the broad politico-economic changes that characterize this new global order.

The tendency to describe globalization as an utterly novel phenomenon in need of a whole new vocabulary and conceptual framework is common in academic theories of the global flow. Jameson and Masao Miyoshi, to cite another example, begin their *Cultures of Globalization* by arguing that globalization is a "new kind of social phenomenon" that "falls outside the established academic disciplines" and as such remains an "unclassifiable topic" requiring a more "daring and speculative, unprotected" scholarly ap-proach.[14] The displacement of key words such as *culture, nation, state,* and *identity* in the works of Appadurai and other postcolonial critics by new notions of *diaspora, transnationalism, postnation,* and so on speaks to a similar desire to invent a *new* cartography of sorts to deal with a *new* cultural phe-nomenon that perpetually changes, a phenomenon whose transformations are both multifaceted and overdetermined. Such a desire, I should add, is symptomatic of the very difficulty of describing any multidimensional, com-plex, and rapidly evolving phenomenon. It is no accident that the issue of globalization has garnered such contradictory responses: while some have embraced it with outlandish hopes as a new epoch in human history marked by the erosion of the nation-state and the emergence of a novel form of cosmopolitanism, others have characterized it in dystopic terms as a race to the bottom in which a new phase of Western imperialism has intensified economic and social inequalities throughout the globe. I will discuss this particular predicament of representation below, but first I wish to take issue with the very assumption that globalization, as a worldly system of exchange, is as utterly new as academic intellectuals have claimed in their elaborate theories of contemporaneity.

One need not look solely at archeological discoveries of Polynesian artifacts in Africa or Chinese pottery fragments in the New World to claim that other world-systems existed well before Columbus's so-called discovery of America. There are now important historical studies that have shown the presence of world-systems existing before the one associated with European hegemony. Most recently, Warren Cohen in *East Asia and the Center* has insightfully demonstrated that contrary to the popular belief that Marco Polo opened up the "backward" Orient to the "civilized" Occident, East Asia has maintained four thousand years of economic and political relations with the rest of the world. Addressing a broad range of instances—for example, the extensive sea voyages of Chinese to the Middle East; the role of Ottoman and Egyptian military involvement in Indonesia against Western imperialism; and the influence of Indian cuisine on that of Chinese—Cohen's text offers a powerful corrective to the dominant misconception of the West as the originary source of global relations of power.[15] Similarly, Janet Abu-Lughod, in her seminal yet surprisingly marginalized text *Before European Hegemony*, offers compelling historical evidence for the existence of a complex and sophisticated world-system in the thirteenth century. Rejecting the Eurocentric views of Karl Marx, Immanuel Wallerstein, and even Fernand Braudel, all of whom have located the genesis of globalization in sixteenth-century Europe due to the rise of mercantilism and European colonialism, Abu-Lughod excavates a system of world trade in the thirteenth century to demonstrate the complex ways in which the globe was linked through a common commercial network of production and exchange. Her point is not to claim a new origin for today's globalization, for she agrees with Whitmore's claim that world-systems existed even much earlier, "with the zenith of the Roman Empire on the west, the Han Empire in the east, and the growth of commerce in India, the international trade route worked itself, via a series of links, through Southeast Asia toward China."[16] She even intellectually opposes the very idea of origin. Rather, her aim in focusing on the thirteenth century is to highlight a system of global flow three centuries before the Western hegemonic one, a system neither hierarchically structured according to modes of production nor one that entailed a capitalist/colonialist core hegemon. In the thirteenth-century world-system, according to Abu-Lughod, merchant mariners of Genoa and Venice did not just trade with the textile industrialists of Bruges and Ghent but also with the turquoise merchants of Persia and those in the crafts trades of Cairo and Baghdad. These Middle Eastern Sinbads themselves bartered with silk and pottery producers of China through the intermediaries of Indian merchants and sailors. The global circuits of capital that connected Europe (through the Mediterranean, the Red Sea, the Persian Gulf, and the Indian Ocean) with China and the Far East also brought a variety of people and ethnicities together, enabling a healthy and vibrant exchange of ideas among them. It is worth noting in passing that Thomas Aquinas's use of Aristotle's work on ethics was made possible by Arabic transmitters of these texts during this period, a fact that points to the intellectual and cultural interconnection that went hand in hand with commercial interdependency.

Moreover, Abu-Lughod demonstrates that "in spite of the tendency of western scholars dealing with the 'Rise of the West' to stress the *unique* characteristics of western capitalism, comparative examination of economic institutions reveal enormous similarities and parallels between Asian, Arab, *and* Western forms of capitalism," at least in the thirteenth century.[17] Among these, of course, were the invention of money and credit, elaborate techniques for pooling capital through partnerships, and various forms of merchant wealth independent of the state or imperial regulations. Like our global village today, the thirteenth-century world-system entailed a complex web of exchanging capital, commodities, people, and ideas, a system whose demise was historically necessary for the rise of European hegemony in the sixteenth century.

More recently, many social scientists have argued that neither today's increasing integration of the world economy nor the high rate of current immigration is by any means unprecedented. Paul Hirst and Grahame Thomoson, for example, have compared contemporary records of immigration with those of the nineteenth century to demonstrate that the greatest population movement occurred between 1815 and 1914.[18] Similarly, Martin Wolf has argued that judging by the flow of commodities and capital, and "despite the many economic changes that have occurred over the course of a century, neither the markets for goods and services nor those for factors of production appear much more integrated today than they were a century ago."[19] Other social scientists have maintained that "the historical high point of cultural globalization, in terms of its capacity to shape societies and identities, lies much earlier than the modern era in the form of world religions and imperial elite cultures."[20] In short, neither economic indicators nor cultural practices can be used to substantiate the claim that globalization constitutes a novel phenomenon.

A theoretical caveat is in order before we continue with the historical argument here. To compare the contemporary social and economic order with its counterpart in the thirteenth century or earlier is not to claim their exact sameness. Such a claim would constitute a historical misconception, one not very different from the ahistorical claims about the utter newness of globalization some academic scholars make today. Successive world-systems, as Abu-Lughod suggests, are always articulated differently because they always reorganize and restructure their precursors. And yet, the restructuring occurs in a "cumulative fashion" in which "the lines and connections laid down in prior epochs [tend] to persist even though their significance and roles in the new system may be altered."[21] The colonial model of center and periphery, for example, may not be at work today, but the geographical division of developed and underdeveloped worlds continues to persist. Every world-system rests on the ruins of the previous one, and because of this, world-systems are interrelated, albeit that the new system always expands and transforms the elements that it borrows from the previous one. In addition, technological advances in every epoch radically alter global relations of power. The invention of steam ships, the expansion of railroads throughout the colonial world, and advancements in the technologies of communication, for example, greatly accelerated and expanded the global flow of commodities and people in the mid-nineteenth century, just as today the democratization of airline transportation and the creation of the World Wide Web have radically sped the movement of people, objects, and ideas.

I draw attention to the predicament of novelty in the literature of globalization not to be solely critical but to suggest the need for an alternative set of historical inquiries in this emerging field of research. The academic literature on globalization privileges the phenomena of change and novelty over those of repetition and restructuring, undermining thus the mimetically mediated nature of paradigm shifts and the interconnectedness of social orders. While technological advances have dramatically altered the velocity of global flow, the general structures of economic and political power do not differ that radically from their colonial counterparts. As the economist Robert Gilpin observes, "Despite much talk of corporate globalization, FDI [foreign direct investment] is actually highly concentrated and distributed very unevenly around the globe. . . . When one speaks of corporate globalization, only a few countries [i.e., United States, Japan, and Western Europe] are actually involved."[22] On a cultural level, the convergence of the entertainment industry and of information technology have enabled a global media order dominated by a handful of corporations and owners—for example, Time Warner, Sony, Matsushita, and Rupert Murdoch—all of which are located in the so-called developed countries. In other words, as in the colonial model of center-periphery, political, cultural, and economic power is unevenly distributed and remains highly polarized between economic superpowers and the rest of the world.

We therefore ought to ask ourselves not "What is globalization?" but "What was globalization?" By this I mean that we need not to look for a new cartography to describe the elephant we call globalization, but should produce instead a genealogy of its historical formation. I say genealogy to underscore the critical and historical shifts that have occurred at each stage of its development and to avoid reducing globalization to a monolithic world-system precipitated by its precursors. The aim of genealogy is not to claim a linear development, but to locate the historically embedded nature of globalization's singularity. My goal, in other words, is to suggest the possibility of a differentiated grid of power relations to rectify the monolithic notion of globalization. Globalization, today, like earlier world-systems, encompasses a set of power relations articulated and mapped at different historical junctures in different, though perpetually unequal, ways. That Bretton Woods institutions differ from and function differently than the colonial trading companies of the nineteenth century, for example, should not blind us to the genealogical links between them that may illuminate how such managerial apparatuses enable and perhaps engender unequal development throughout the developing countries.

One direction, therefore, that this kind of genealogy can take is a mapping of the important connections that exist between our contemporary global flow and its colonial counterpart in the nineteenth century. In what ways, we may ask, for example, is the new transnational order new—that is, different—from its counterpart in the nineteenth century? How, for instance, is the paradigm of center-periphery of the nineteenth century restructured or displaced in our global village? Has the absolute spatial division between exploiters and exploited disappeared, as theorists of globalization claim? Or, is disparity still alive, as skeptical critics of globalization like Samir Amin and John Schmitt argue?[23] The quick academic shift from postcolonialism to globalization, I want to suggest, has ironically short-circuited the possibility of understanding the ways in which the geographical and cultural displacements of people and things by European colonialism informed the so-called cartography of globalization today. The tendency to invent a new vocabulary to make the contemporary global flow more transparent has ironically rendered its historical roots more opaque.

Postnational Forgetfulness

In his canonized essay, "Patriotism and Its Futures," Appadurai posits the concepts of the postnation and the postnational to describe the cultural and political condition we call globalization.[24] He uses these terms to elaborate three related implications of globalization. First, he employs these terms to mean "the [historical] process of moving to a global order in which the nation-state has become obsolete and other formations for allegiance and identity have taken its place." Second, he has in mind the "alternative forms for the organization of global traffic in resources, images, and ideas—forms that either contest the nation-state actively or constitute peaceful alternatives for large-scale political loyalties." And third, the notion of postnation implies what may be labeled diasporic nationalisms, which, encouraged by "the steady erosion of the capabilities of the nation-state to monopolize loyalty," are "largely divorced from territorial states."[25] The example Appadurai cites to drive these points home is interestingly the United States, an enormously wealthy nation that has been able to organize itself around "a modern political ideology in which pluralism is central to the conduct of democratic life"—a nation where various immigrant communities have been able to manufacture what he calls "delocalized transnations" that retain special ideological links to a putative place of origin but are otherwise thoroughly disasporic collectivities.[26] Insightful though Appadurai's argument is in locating the cultural implications of globalization, his claim about the disappearance of the nation-state appears problematic, especially since 9/11, a tragic event that not only rekindled a powerful form of patriotism in the United States but also helped fortify the power of state apparatuses such as the FBI, the CIA, and the INS, linked and centrally organized now under the rubric of the new Department of Homeland Security. Although the borders of nation-states have become increasingly porous with the emergence of global politics and the spread of free-trade zones, national governments continue to exercise a great deal of power in planning and shaping the ways in which their countries are globalized. Indeed, international organizations depend on individual state agencies to regulate trade and security, markets and systems of communication.

Not surprisingly, Appadurai's argument about the disappearance of the nation-state and the emergence of diaspora consciousness holds a mimetic relation with (post)colonial discourse on nation and nationalism. As one reads Appadurai's powerful argument about the disappearing of the nation-state, the specter of Fanon appears above and beneath every sentence— Fanon who first described the predicaments of national consciousness in *The Wretched of the Earth*.[27] Describing nationalism as an "empty shell," Fanon cogently observed that "the battle against colonialism [and oppression] does not run straight away along the lines of nationalism."[28] As a cosmopolitan intellectual, he considered internationalism the goal of the anticolonial movement, arguing that at the heart of the liberation movement, an "international consciousness lives and grows."[29] And yet, in the following chapter on national culture, Fanon claimed that "every culture is first and foremost national" and that the demand for nationhood, the desire for national culture, and the process of decolonization are intertwined.[30] The task of the colonial intellectual, then, was to help produce an "authentic national consciousness, freed from the psychological and ideological forces of colonialism"—a consciousness that involved a movement away from what he labeled "Western culture" toward a popular and democratic form of nationhood that empowered every social stratum.

What we encounter in the discourses of postnationalism and diaspora today is a similar ideological ambivalence toward what constitutes national consciousness and belonging. Whether we read Bhabha or Appadurai, we notice the paired critique of nationalism and the celebration of a more cosmopolitan, imagined community—for Bhabha, it is the "scattering of the people that in other times and other places, in the nations of others, becomes a time of gathering";[31] for Appadurai, it is the delocalized transnation that is celebrated against the white nation. What are we to make of these ambivalent articulations of the nation form? How are we to go beyond the problematic binary of good nationalism versus bad nationalism implied in this critical ambivalence?

A starting point to address these questions is to unpack the relation between state and nation and explore the roles of both in the global flow of people, capital, and commodities. What is striking about critiques of nation and nationalism by cultural and postcolonial theorists is the absence of any substantial discussion of the state, especially problematic because the nation and state are often linked—that is, the nation-state—if not fully equated. Often reduced to a repressive apparatus, the concept of the state is considered passé in today's academy, associated with an outdated Marxist paradigm that limited its function to maintaining class domination. But I want to suggest a return to this key term and question the extent to which the rhetoric of globalization has occulted the important role states and governments play in the process of globalization. We may ask, for example, what functions do states, as agencies of representation, perform in the broader system of international regulation? Do global agencies and transnational corporations undermine the sovereignty of national governments? Have states become the local agents of corporate interests? Or does the fact of their being answerable to their citizens make them the local shields against global capitalism? Can states recreate a sense of national identity in response to the political and economic constraints of globalization? Or, do state apparatuses mobilize the idea of the nation to enable the economic interests of transnational corporations?

Overlooking the roles of nation and state in recent theories of diaspora and postnationalism also seems problematic given the speed with which new nations and nationalisms are actually emerging today, and given the fortification of national borders in spite of the global flow of people across them, not to mention the forging of new partnerships between certain states and the global capital market. While national borders may no longer impede international trade and global economic transactions, they do nonetheless matter greatly when it comes to human subjects whose movements are carefully regulated. I have shown elsewhere that in the past twenty years, the principle of governmentality in the United States has actually solidified, as demonstrated, for example, by the expansion of the prison industry and the proliferation of technologies of border control at the US-Mexican border.[32] Similarly, the integration of Europe in the form of a union has also meant tougher restrictions on the movement of people from the Middle East, Africa, and most of Asia to Europe.

Moreover, in spite of the increase in global cultural contacts, nationalist sentiments persist throughout the world, and states continue to exert a great deal of power as to how a national community is globalized. On the one hand, as R. Radhakrishnan points out, "neither the deracinating multi- or inter-national spread of capitalism nor the Marxist theoretical assimilation of the national question within an internationalist Communism has been able to do away with the urgencies of the imagined communities of nationalism."[33] Nationalism and state apparatuses are everywhere, in Iran and the United States, in Serbia as well as France. On the other hand, even the social scientists who argue that "the contemporary globalization of politics is transforming the very foundations of world order by reconstituting traditional forms of sovereign statehood and reordering international political relations" have to acknowledge that the concept of state "sovereignty has by no means been rendered redundant" and that "political community continues to be shaped by the territorial reach of state sovereignty."[34] Neither the internationalization of politics nor the globalization of capital implies the disappearance of national form or state government. Quite to the contrary, globalization has actually reinforced their role as arbitrators in international processes. There remain indeed many questions yet to be answered about the problem of the nation-state and its ideological apparatuses. How, for example, is the nation-state reimagined in our globalized world? What roles do states play in the particular ways in which globalization is embraced and practiced in different locations? How are we to account for the rise of nationalist and ethnic fervor in a world that has become increasingly more transnational? What are the ways in which the formal universality of nationalism as a sociopolitical concept can be understood in the context of the irremediable particularity of nationalism's concrete manifestations? How can we simultaneously critique the regressive tendencies of nationalism in Bosnia and Rwanda while advocating, say, a Palestinian or Kurdish nation?

Saskia Sassen, in her illuminating essay "Spatialities and Temporalities of the Global: Elements for a Theorization," cogently suggests that globalization "persists as a partial condition," by which she means that significant overlap and interaction exists between the global and the national.[35] She writes, "Each sphere, global and national, describes a spatio-temporal order with considerable internal differentiation and growing mutual imbrications with the other."[36] One direction to take, she seems to suggest, is not to forget the nation in our postnational consciousness, but to study instead the "dynamics of interaction between the global and the national," a dynamic that sheds light on the "incipient and partial denationalization of domains once understood and/or constructed as national."[37] What more nuanced discussions of globalization such as Sassen's make evident is that the uneven flow between nationalism and globalization depends fundamentally on context and that while transnational circuits are appearing throughout the world, their formations are always sociohistorically contingent and culturally specific. Indeed, the strategic nature of economic globalization, as Sassen cogently argues, suggests that "most global processes materialize in national territories and do so to a considerable extent through national institutional arrangements, from legislative actions to corporate agenda."[38]

The second issue I wish to raise with regard to Appadurai's description of the global is the question of diaspora and its liberating potentials. According to Appadurai, diaspora is at once the cause and effect of postnational consciousness, and as such it occupies a central role in the way new identities are imagined in the global village. He views the presence of diasporic communities in the United States in salutary terms, considering them essential to fashioning a new "postnational politics" that would ultimately resolve "the tension between the centripetal pull of Americanness and the centrifugal pull of diasporic diversity in American life."[39] The emergence of delocalized transnations, he argues, forces American society to "confront the needs of pluralism *and* of immigration, to construct a society *around* diasporic diversity."[40] Contra Appadurai, I wish to argue that it is not evident that geographical displacement has necessarily led to any originality of political vision or the breaking of intellectual and cultural barriers in most cases, as global cultural theorists tend to suggest. Empirically, even the most superficial acquaintance with the ethnic politics of a city like Los Angeles reveals how stratified and conflicted third world–origin and minority communities can be. Not only do fundamental cultural and economic differences exist among various diaspora communities; these differences have also often sowed mutual hostilities across immigrant and minority communities, as the Los Angeles riots in 1992 painfully demonstrated. The supposedly postnational communities in Los Angeles are often more chauvinistic and nostalgic toward their countries of origin than the citizens of those nations, a fact empirically evident in the rise of ethnic enclaves throughout the city. In many cases, the sense of loss and disenfranchisement among many immigrant communities has led to a new form of tribalism characterized by antagonism and feelings of racial superiority toward other minorities. As James Clifford points out, "Indeed, some of the most violent articulations of purity and racial exclusivism come from diaspora populations."[41] In short, it is not clear that delocalized transnations remain free of the chauvinism of nationalism or the forces of state apparatuses, as Appadurai seems to suggest.

My aim in bringing up the issue of diasporic exclusivism is not to pose a simplistic binary relation between the symbolic and the real. Nor is it my aim to claim nationalist sentiment as an antidote to global disempowerment. Rather, my hope is to draw attention to the discrepancy between salutary explorations of diasporic consciousness by academics, writers, and artists and the complex and overdetermined itineraries of many immigrants caught in the tailspin of a globalization that has made them move to the West in hopes of upward economic mobility and political freedom. This discrepancy is symptomatic of the difference between what the political scientist John Armstrong calls "mobilized and proletarian diasporas."[42] Acknowledging the vagueness of the term *diaspora* to describe "any ethnic collectivity which lacks a territorial base within a given polity," Armstrong makes a useful distinction. Proletarian diasporas are "a disadvantaged product of modernized polities" (e.g., Mexican farm- and service workers in Southern California), while mobilized diasporas are "an ethnic group which does not have a general status advantage, yet which enjoys many material and cultural advantages compared to other groups in the multiethnic polity" (e.g., Iranians in Southern California or Indians in Northern California).[43] This kind of distinction proves useful because it helps us differentiate various trajectories of displacement and become attentive to the historical taintedness of metaphors of mobility fashionable among theoreticians of globalization. Part of the problem is the old Marxist predicament of a mobilized and privileged group of intellectuals representing proletarian diasporas.[44] To ignore the crucial economic and cultural differences among immigrant communities by labeling them all "postnational others" marginalized by the white nation-state, as Appadurai does in his essay, proves not only intellectually problematic but also politically dangerous.

Mahatma Gandhi once, when asked what he thought of Western civilization, responded, "It would be a good idea!" Gandhi's insightfully sarcastic response captures this essay's position with regard to the phenomenon of globalization. The popular rhetoric of globalization suggests that the world is becoming a better place to live through an intensification of economic interdependence, technological interconnectedness, and cultural linkage. The demise of state power, according to the boosters of globalization, has led to a positive diffusion of authority, while technological advances have enabled a more mobile and pluralistic sense of cultural and political identity. These would obviously constitute salutary developments were it not for the fact that they remain available only to a tiny and privileged minority. As Pico Iyer insightfully observes, "One of the most troubling features of the globalism we celebrate is that the so-called linking of the planet has, in fact, intensified the distance between people: the richest 358 people in the world, by UN calculations, have a financial worth as great as that of 2.3 billion others, and even in the United States, the prosperous home of egalitarianism, the most wired man in the land (Bill Gates) has a net worth larger than that of 40 percent of the country's households, or perhaps 100 million of his compatriots combined."[45] If I espouse the skeptical position in the globalization debate, it is not to undermine the advantages of cultural, economic, and political interconnectedness, but to draw attention to how its boosters have failed to address the contingent and uneven nature of global flow. What seems urgent now are not more paeans to the global ideal, but a willingness to confront the challenges that stand in the way of its realization. Counterintuitively perhaps, a global future demands a present engagement with the enduring issue of unequal and uneven development.

The word *beyond* in the title of this collection suggests a desire to look for new directions in postcolonial discourse by way of transcending the critical crisis this field of inquiry faces today. What I have been obliquely attempting throughout this essay has been a step in that direction by suggesting that postcolonialism can offer a historical corrective to the celebratory theories of globalization. Cultural theories of globalization have been blinkered by the misty notion of a "time/space compression," coined by David Harvey as a postmodern phenomenon to describe the ways in which new technologies of communication have shrunk geographical and temporal distance, enabling a condition of instantaneity in human interactions.[46] The speed and widening of global interconnectedness seem to have rendered history and geography obsolete as the global flows of people and commodities, ideas and images, capital and information are claimed to dismantle temporal and spatial barriers. This popular view of globalization not only dissimulates the spatial segregation that characterizes the current form of globalization but it also overlooks the (neo)colonial dimensions of its complex genealogy. A historically informed engagement with the unequal geography of globalization can offer a critical beyond for postcolonial theorists. Instead of going beyond what the postcolonial has already theorized about European forms of imperialism—which is the other connotation of the word *beyond* in the title—we may deploy the historical and political knowledge postcolonialism has already produced to explore the unequal geography of globalization and its historical links with European colonialism and the process of decolonization.

Economists have singled out two historical periods, 1870–1939 and 1950–73, as central to the rise of the global order: while in the first period "markets for key goods began to acquire a global dimension," during the second period, labeled the "golden age," "trade volumes grew at 5.8 per cent per annum, . . . [and] world output grew at an unprecedented rate of 3.9 per cent per annum."[47] What economists have overlooked, however, is the role of European colonialism and decolonization in the rise of the global order, and they neither acknowledge nor explore the fact that these periods coincided with the height of European colonialism and its dismantling, respectively. Postcolonial discourse is well positioned to map the colonial contexts of global flows to discern the unequal geography of globalization. In particular, postcolonial historiography can provide a critical genealogy to explicate the political shift from European colonialism to US imperialism. What are the conditions, we may ask, for example, that enabled the global spread of imperialism after the spectacular phenomenon of decolonization? What cultural attitudes, political practices, and economic strategies from the colonial period continue to persist today? Why have ex-colonized nations failed to reap the benefits of global trade? There are certainly no easy answers to these questions, but to grapple with the issues they raise may provide a spring-board, if not a framework, for a postcolonial genealogy of globalization.

Notes

1. To give an idea of the extensiveness of this body of literature: a cursory search in LexisNexis produced over seven hundred articles dealing with the issue of glob-alization in just the past two years.

2. I say "cultural critics" to draw attention to the fact that I will not be focusing on the works of economists and political scientists also engaged in a Manichaean de-bate in which globalization is viewed as either totally beneficial or utterly malignant. For a general work capturing these opposing views of globalization among social scientists, see Held et al., *Global Transformations*.

3. Bauman, *Globalization*, 1.

4. In a similar vein, some economists have also argued that little has changed about the global flow of capital and people since the late nineteenth century. Comparing trade and immigration indices from the turn of the century to those of the past de-cade, Martin Wolf, to cite an example, argues that neither global trade nor immigra-tion flows of today are higher than those at the turn of the century. See Wolf, "Will the Nation-State Survive Globalization?" 178.

5. Enrique Dussel, "Beyond Eurocentrism: The World-System and the Limits of Modernity," in Jameson and Miyoshi, *The Cultures of Globalization*, 3–31. Bhabha, *The Location of Culture*.

6. Abu-Lughod, *Before European Hegemony*; Cohen, *East Asia at the Center*; Whit-more, "The Opening of Southeast Asia."

7. An example of such a shift in the vocabulary of cultural critics occurs in Fredric Jameson's recent work, where he now describes the cultural logic of late capital-ism not as "postmodern" but as "globalization." See Fredric Jameson, "Notes on Globalization as a Philosophical Issue," in Jameson and Miyoshi, *The Cultures of Globalization*, 54–77.

8. Both Friedman's *The Lexus and the Olive Tree* and Stiglitz's *Globalization and Its Discontents* became national best sellers just as their authors were championed as experts on globalization by the media and various government agencies in need of advice.

9. Rouse, "Mexican Migration and the Social Space of Postmodernism," 8.

10. Ohmae, *The End of the Nation-State*, 5.

11. Rouse, "Mexican Migration and the Social Space of Postmodernism," 9.

12. Jameson, "Postmodernism."

13. Rouse, "Mexican Migration and the Social Space of Postmodernism," 8.

14. Jameson and Miyoshi, *The Cultures of Globalization*, xi.

15. Cohen, *East Asia at the Center*.

16. Abu-Lughod, *Before European Hegemony*, 141.

17. Ibid., 15.

18. Hirst and Thomoson, *Globalization in Question*.

19. Wolf, "Will the Nation-State Survive Globalization?" 179.

20. Held et al., *Global Transformations*, 328.

21. Abu-Lughod, *Before European Hegemony*, 368.

22. Gilpin, *The Challenge of Global Capitalism*, 24.

23. Amin, *Capitalism in the Age of Globalization*; Schmitt, "Inequality and Globalization."

24. Appadurai, "Patriotism and Its Futures."

25. Ibid., 169.

26. Ibid., 173.

27. Fanon, *The Wretched of the Earth*.

28. Ibid., 148.

29. Ibid., 248.

30. Ibid., 216.

31. Homi K. Bhabha, "DissemiNation: Time, Narrative, and the Margins of the Modern Nation," in Bhabha, *Nation and Narration*, 291.

32. Behdad, "INS and Outs."

33. Radhakrishnan, "Nationalism, Gender, and the Narrative of Identity," 83.

34. Held et al., *Global Transformations*, 85–86.

35. Sassen, "Spatialities and Temporalities of the Global," 215.

36. Ibid., 216.

37. Ibid.

38. Ibid., 228.

39. Appadurai, "Patriotism and Its Futures," 173.

40. Ibid.

41. Clifford, *Routes*, 251.

42. Armstrong, "Mobilized and Proletarian Diasporas."

43. Ibid., 393.

44. For an illuminating discussion of this issue, see Spivak, "Who Claims Alterity?"

45. Iyer, *The Global Soul*, 25–26.

46. Harvey, *The Condition of Postmodernity*.

47. Held et al., *Global Transformations*, 163–64.

The Ruins of Empire:

The National and Global Politics of

America's Return to Rome

🌀 🌀 🌀

VILASHINI COOPPAN

As any traveler of the contemporary academic scene will tell you, globalization is everywhere these days. Seized by many as an accurate descriptor
of contemporary politics, economics, and culture, and disparaged by a stal-
wart few as a kind of planetary white noise, global babble, or globaloney,
globalization (like money) nevertheless talks. And students and states, universities and corporations, publishers and politicians are all listening to its
stories of transnational migration, its parables of global citizenship, and its
omnipresent metaphors of flow. Even as the narratives of globalization command widespread attention on the strength of their claim to diagnose a profoundly new condition marked by the connection of persons, goods, ideas,
and capital across national borders, they strike a familiar, even uncanny, note
in certain corners of the academy long devoted to border crossing: anthropology, with its aspirations to a form of knowledge at once transcultural
and local, routed and rooted; comparative literature, with its founding vision
of a world literature produced by an international trade in letters and its
modern attention to increasingly more heterogenous forms of literary traffic across nations, periods, media, and disciplines; and, finally, postcolonial
studies.

Despite its relative newness, postcolonial studies has already seen its borders and boundaries interrogated and redrawn several times over, perhaps
nowhere more acutely than in speculation over the field's periodization and
the status of the nation within it—what we might call the time and space of
the postcolonial.[1] Like globalization, whose discourse it often mirrors, post-

colonialism emerges from historically deep processes of transborder contact, conflict, migration, and connection, as well as long traditions of oppositional thought. Just as postcolonial theory can be derived from the late-nineteenth-century nationalisms and mid-twentieth-century third-worldisms of intellectuals like José Martí in Cuba, W. E. B. Du Bois in the United States, Frantz Fanon in Martinique and Algeria, and Amilcar Cabral in Mozambique, so, too, can globalization theory be seen to emerge from the dependency theory and world-systems theory of Marxist thinkers like André Gunder Frank and Immanuel Wallerstein.[2] These prehistories of the postcolonial and the global, and their guiding concerns with national cultures and national economies in an international world, have been significantly elided in the present. Globalization theory's emphasis on its own newness and the newly mobile, transborder forms of nations and cultures that emerge in the wake of the twin territorial projects of imperialism and nationalism strikingly reproduces the version of postcolonial studies that purports to announce the end not just of empires but of nations too—and the ascendence of new hybrid forms of identity (of which it serves as privileged chronicler) over previous regimes of binarized difference. Even in this hegemonic form, however, the theory of the postcolonial never had anything near the name recognition and institutional power that globalization theory now wields.

It is this difference between postcolonial theory and globalization theory, as much as their similar structures of historical forgetting and premature postnationalism, that I wish to emphasize. My immediate purpose in identifying these points of contact and distinction is to begin to understand the substance of postcolonial theory's current Zeitgeist, its mournful sense not of its newness but its belatedness, not of its centrality but its displacement. Globalization now talks. But postcolonial criticism cannot seem to forget that in its day it also talked, albeit more softly and with a much smaller institutional stick. This essay marks an attempt to discern the whisper of the postcolonial in the contemporary clamor of globalization. If this exercise in double hearing describes a certain consonance between one version of postcolonial theory and a dominant strain of globalization theory, both of which announce the end of the nation, it equally envisions another version of postcolonial theory in which to speak the global is not necessarily to drown out the national. This second version of postcolonial theory is neither globalization theory's historical antecedent nor its institutionally repressed double but, rather, its interlocutor, its critic as much as its sharer. If we are to continue to practice postcolonial studies, if we are to participate in that continual reinvention that loyalty to an academic field demands, we must face up to globalization, articulating ourselves with it and against it.[3]

The Rise and Fall of Empires and Theories

Is it too soon even heuristically to diagnose the end of postcolonial studies? In what David Harvey has characterized as the profoundly accelerated space-time of postmodernity, are the two decades between the 1978 publication of Edward Said's *Orientalism* and the 2000 publication of Michael Hardt and Antonio Negri's *Empire* a long enough time for a field that once claimed a sizable chunk of the academic horizon to grow moribund? If *Orientalism* may be taken to mark the institutional rise of postcolonial studies in the North American academy, *Empire* may well mark its fall. For if *Orientalism* put the constitutive categories and concerns of postcolonial studies (colonialism, imperialism, nationalism) on the metropolitan academic map, Hardt and Negri's *Empire* might be taken to do something similar for globalization. However, Hardt and Negri situate their new "Empire" explicitly *after* the territorializing impulses of colonialism, imperialism, and nationalism: "The fundamental principle of Empire is that its power has no actual and localizable terrain or center."[4] Deterritorialized and decentered, endlessly mobile, and deeply networked, Empire works not within boundaries but across them. Empire is the very image of globalization and, not coincidentally, what disrupts and dissolves the operative paradigms of postcolonial theory. As what Hardt and Negri describe as "not a weak echo of modern imperialisms but a fundamentally new form of rule,"[5] Empire issues a claim to the present that pushes postcolonial theory into the past, effectively antiquating it. But I wonder if there is not still something to be gained from a postcolonial perspective on the ever more penetrating and powerful forms of contemporary imperialism.

My terms are deliberately chosen, their rubric of rise and fall, new and old, meant to echo a widespread return to Rome in contemporary critical and political discourse about the United States' role in the world. Jonathan Freedman, a journalist for the British *Guardian*, indexes the similarities between the two empires: overwhelming military, technological, and economic strength; an unparalleled global presence in garrisons or bases, Latin or English, gladiatorial games or Hollywood cinema; rule by remote control and the creation of client states; ethnically and culturally diverse societies; and a propensity to mythologize their origins and destinies.[6] Writing in the *New York Times* in 2002, Emily Eakin asserts: "Today, America is no mere superpower or hegemon but a full-blown empire in the Roman and British sense." Among conservative commentators making the case for the benign effects of American empire in a barbarian world, Eakin cites Charles Krauthammer, the ever quotable Robert Kaplan ("Times have changed less than we think," he observes in *Warrior Politics: Why Leadership Demands a Pagan Ethos*), and Max Boot, an editor of the *Wall Street Journal* who claims that "Afghanistan and other troubled lands today cry out for the sort of enlightened foreign administration once provided by self-confident Englishmen in jodphurs and pith helmets."[7] We have recently seen history repeating itself in yet another US war in Iraq under yet another President Bush. A full year before the US invasion of 2003, following the release of "Rebuilding America's Defenses," a 2000 report by the self-styled new imperialists of the Project for the New American Century (Bill Kristol, Donald Kagan, Dick Cheney, Donald Rumsfeld, Paul Wolfowitz, and others), Jay Bookman of the *Atlanta Journal-Constitution* characterized the tenor of the times. "This war, should it come, is intended to mark the official emergence of the United States as a full-fledged global empire, seizing sole responsibility and authority as planetary policeman. . . . Rome did not stoop to containment; it conquered. And so, the thinking goes, should we."[8] At the other end of the ideological spectrum from the interventionist architects of a new Pax Americana, we find Hardt and Negri's *Empire*, unmentioned in all the popular discussions of US empire, yet arguably offering the most extended illustration of our present moment's obsessive return to Rome.

At the core of Hardt and Negri's argument lies the notion that the United States is closer to ancient Rome—with its expansionist republicanism, networked power, and syncretic, englobing culture—than to the territorial sovereignty, linear ambitions, and differentialist logic of the modern imperial European nation-state: "Every time the expansiveness of the constitutional project ran up against its limits, the republic was tempted to engage in a European-style imperialism. There was always, however, another option: to return to the project of imperial sovereignty and articulate it in a way consistent with the original 'Roman' mission of the United States."[9] Reading Hardt and Negri's classical version of US history, we might well ask what it means to create a space-time in which imperialism is there (in Europe), not here (in the United States), then (in the nineteenth- and twentieth-century eras of the sovereign nation-state), not now (in the twenty-first century of globalization). Following the implications of Hardt and Negri's analogizing of the United States and Rome as mirror republican empires, it becomes impossible to name, analyze, and contest the simple fact of US imperialism here and now. And surely this is the urgent task of a postcolonial studies both in the present and in that disciplinary future we are calling the "beyond."

Both *Empire* and the wave of recent commentary on US empire argue for the unbroken return of a political form over a span of two thousand years. Such intimations of empire's immortality must be alarming to postcolonial critics, for whom empire is surely a phenomenon of local name and habitation. What strikes me in reading the contemporary apostles of US empire alongside Hardt and Negri is first and foremost a sense of loss. It is the loss that comes when they take your language from you. For isn't empire, or wasn't it, *our* term? How uncannily strange, then, to find it suddenly everywhere and so different from what we thought it meant: not a historically specific, territorially based, nationally directed, discursively managed system of domination that produced an oppositional practice of resistance, but rather a kind of vague, transhistorical, deterritorialized, postnational mode of contemporary existence tout court. There is no outside to Empire as Hardt and Negri conceive it. Where, then, is the space for postcolonial studies, given that the field conceived of itself in many ways as that outside, that place of critique? I will try to sketch a provisional answer to this question first through a survey of the distinct accounts of empire proposed by globalization theory and postcolonial theory, and then through an examination of several textual returns to Rome, culminating in Ridley Scott's *Gladiator* (2000), a film that is both *about* empire and *of* it—depicting Roman imperial rule while enacting US global cultural capitalism.

Mapping Postcolonialism onto the Borderless World of Globalization

An extensive debate exists on exactly when globalization happened and exactly what it did. Does it coincide, as David Harvey, Anthony Giddens, Fredric Jameson, and Arjun Appadurai would have it, with postmodern late capitalism? Can it be located earlier, in what Giovanni Arrighi calls "the long twentieth century," or earlier still, as Fernand Braudel and Immanuel Wallerstein claim, in the fifteenth-century origins of the capitalist world-system? Is globalization's process of cross-cultural flow traceable even back to the trade routes of the ancient world? We can see the resonance of this last genealogy in the various invocations of imperial Rome as the closest analogue to contemporary globalization. Shifting from globalization's periodization to its effects reveals a similar diversity of opinion. Does it create winners or losers, does it standardize or pluralize, does it represent the triumph of US sameness or the worldwide explosion of difference? In Mauro Guillen's words, "Is globalization civilizing, destructive, or feeble?"[10] No less than the imperial mission, globalization has been given and is being given a particular character, even a personality.

Globalization's split personality can be seen in the contrast between two opposing visions: first, globalization as a kind of ongoing decolonization characterized by the emergent claims of the local and the particular and reflective of the increasing heterogenization of the globe; and second, globalization as itself a new and potent form of colonialism in the shape of transnational capitalism's homogenizing imperium. Stuart Hall and Appadurai have been eloquent advocates of the first aspect, Masao Miyoshi and Jameson equally forceful voices for the second. According to Anthony D. King, at least two commonalities connect contemporary perspectives on globalization: "The rejection of the nationally-constituted society as the appropriate object of discourse, or unit of social and cultural analysis, and to varying degrees, a commitment to conceptualising 'the world as a whole.' "[11] Different theorists imagine distinct alternatives to the "nationally-constituted society as the appropriate object of discourse," for example, the world-system, the network, the global, the dyad of global and local, even what has been called the "glocal." The significant point is that for a large percentage of its critics, globalization's borderless world (to use Kenichi Ohmae's term) seems to imply the undermining, if not the much-vaunted end, of the nation-state.[12]

In an essay deeply suspicious of the seeming utopia of a borderless world, Miyoshi distinguishes old colonialism, which "operated in the names of nation, ethnicities, and races,"[13] from a new colonialism exercised through the transnational corporation and "tend[ing] toward nationlessness."[14] The new, nationless colonialism is "adrift and mobile," acting on behalf of its own interests and profits rather than those of a given state and for that reason is becoming harder to define or oppose than its predecessor. If capital occupies the unbounded space of postmodern global sovereignty in Miyoshi's argument, for Hardt and Negri that space belongs to Empire. Whereas old-style imperialism constituted its power through national territories, Empire unfolds along global networks, replacing the map with the route as the privileged emblem of power. Decentered and deterritorialized, articulated through the ideology of movement rather than place, independent of the construct of the nation-state, Empire enacts a form of global sovereignty that appears to do away with such outmoded categories as the national, the local, and the particular. "Nothing," Hardt and Negri insist, "can be outside the global flows of capital and Empire."[15]

Such a statement implicitly arrogates all theory making to itself. If the future belongs to Empire's peculiar form of nationless sovereignty, what does this mean for the future of postcolonial studies, a field concerned from its very beginning with the nation-state and a field that, at its best, has sought to name and understand *both* national and global forms of power and resistance?[16] This in no way means to argue for a single postcolonial studies that invests uniformly in the nation, nor does it attempt to dismiss the valuable work that has rendered that category less uniform within itself, more structured by contradiction and plurality, and more open to resignification and rearticulation at each historical turn. I mean simply that postcolonial studies cannot disavow the nation-state, or that it can do so only by disavowing an entire critical history to which the nation-state proved crucial: as the conceptual container of imperialist, anti-imperialist, and neocolonialist movements; as the terrain on which imperial and postimperial identities and identifications, no less than economies and politics, were worked out; and as the necessary complement, the silent second, that shadows any postcolonial naming of the global.

It is useful at this juncture to turn to Hardt and Negri's own genealogy of postcolonial criticism. Citing Jean Lyotard, Jean Baudrillard, and Jacques Derrida as their examples of postmodern theory and Homi Bhabha as their representative of postcolonial theory, Hardt and Negri argue that both postmodernism and postcolonialism advocate "a politics of difference, fluidity, and hybridity in order to challenge the binaries and essentialism of modern sovereignty."[17] The problem, as they see it, is that even as postmodernists and postcolonialists continue to recognize only one form of domination (the binary regime of modern sovereignty), a fundamentally new form of postmodern sovereignty has arisen (Empire), fully fluent in the very language so dear to postmodern and postcolonial critics. Thus combating an obsolete form of power, these critics "tumble unwittingly into the welcoming arms of the new power," a power that works not through dialectical or binary structures, but rather through the deterritorialized networks of difference itself.[18] Ultimately, Hardt and Negri conclude, postcolonial theory "may be a very productive tool for rereading [colonial sovereignty's] history but it is entirely insufficient for theorizing contemporary global power."[19]

Mired in the old-style politics of the nation-state, postcolonial theory for Hardt and Negri is fundamentally incapable of grasping, analyzing, or changing global power in its mobile, fluid, hybrid form. Such transformative work, they seem to suggest, is the sole province of critical theory that itself transgresses borders and valorizes flows: theory in the nationless shape of Empire. I want to suggest, by contrast, that it is precisely because of postcolonial theory's roots in the discourse of national sovereignty that it can understand the global. For the national and the global do not constitute antagonistic formations, the sites of an either-or choice, but rather are intercalated modalities of contemporary existence. And postcolonial studies has understood that for a long time, from such an originary stage of its own history as Fanon's observation in *The Wretched of the Earth* that "national consciousness, which is not nationalism, is the only thing that will give us an international dimension."[20]

The problem with Hardt and Negri's theory is that it enforces a choice between the national and the global, between the territorialized critical language of place they associate with postcolonialism and the deterritorialized critical language of placelessness, movement, and flow they make the hall-mark both of Empire and of their anatomy of it. By this logic, the path forward for postcolonial theory is nothing less than the path away from the nation. If, as Hardt and Negri appear to suggest, the critical future belongs to those who speak the language of deterritorialized flows, then postcolonial studies may perhaps be spared oblivion by virtue of its recent privileging of the category of diaspora. The critical lens of diaspora has undoubtedly altered the terms in which we think nations, forcing us to see them as more culturally heterogenous, more spatially unbounded, more fractured and fissured by the constant flows of the global into and out of the space of the state. But diaspora's rise does not necessarily signal nation's fall; the flows of diasporic movement and the border-crossing processes of diasporic identification have transformed the nation, not transcended it. A diaspora is both a flow and a space, both a process of deterritorialization and a mode of reterritorialization, in which diasporic subjects at once retain certain imaginative bonds with the nations they have left and forge others with the nations they have entered. Theories like those articulated in Hardt and Negri's *Empire*, which attempt to do away with the nation, lose a crucial capacity to name the most basic working of contemporary power, which for all its obvious globalization, nonetheless continues to function on the plane of the national. Just because we are globalized does not mean we are not also nationalized. In fact, it is very often through the processes of nationalization that the ideology of globalization takes place, and vice versa.

Let me summarize the train of the preceding argument: (1) the discourse of globalization or Empire seems in some sense to have superseded that of postcolonialism; (2) the nature of this apparent supersession turns on the axis of space rather than on that of time — what globalization appears to have that postcolonialism does not is nationlessness rather than newness; (3) as much as globalization or Empire lays claim to the deterritorialized ideology of nationlessness, the concepts are nonetheless undergirded by very specific forms of nationhood and nationalism; And (4) in light of this paradox, we could do worse than return to the toolbox of postcolonial studies, in which nation and globe are repeatedly joined, in order to interpret and analyze globalization.

Roman Returns

In Hardt and Negri's account of Empire, becoming global seems to preclude being national. Such a decisive separation is fantasy more than fact. And it may even be fantasy more than fiction, as a return to one text in particular suggests. Joseph Conrad's *Heart of Darkness* (1899) at once makes for an emblem of old-style territorial sovereignty with its maps and borders and for an account of the unsettling flows that lead out of, and back into, the space and time of imperial nations. Marlow's narration famously begins by turning the Thames, which "had known and served all the men of whom the nation is proud," into a prenational, un-English, peripheral blank space, the remote outpost of somebody else's empire and "one of the dark places of the earth":

> I was thinking of very old times, when the Romans first came here, nineteen hundred years ago—the other day. . . . darkness was here yesterday. Imagine the feelings of a commander of a fine—what d'ye call 'em?—trireme in the Mediterranean, ordered suddenly to the north. . . . Imagine him here—the very end of the world, a sea the colour of lead, a sky the colour of smoke, a kind of ship about as rigid as a concertina—and going up this river with stores, or orders, or what you like. Sand-banks, marshes, forests, savages,—precious little to eat fit for a civilized man, nothing but Thames water to drink. No Falernian wine here, no going ashore. Here and there a military camp lost in a wilderness, like a needle in a bundle of hay—cold, fog, tempests, disease, exile, and death— death skulking in the air, in the water, in the bush."[21]

Like the other upriver journey the novella will chronicle, Marlow's imagined voyage up a wild and distant Thames displaces the nation. The importation of Rome to the banks of the Thames inverts the novella's two predominant spaces, England and Africa, such that England becomes "the bush" and a place of "utter savagery," while Englishmen become "savages" and "wild men," the native foils to Rome's civilized men. The Romans, Marlow continues, were not colonists but conquerors, agents of an empire completely devoid of the famous idea that redeems British imperialism: "It was just robbery with violence, aggravated murder on a great scale, and men going at it blind. . . ."[22] Marlow sets up Rome in order to doubly differentiate it from England. Rome is both the empire to England's savagery and, by virtue of its conquering rather than colonizing mentality, the savagery to England's empire. It is Kurtz who at the novella's end will close the spatio-temporal gap between England and Rome. His degeneration from "an emissary of pity, and science, and progress,"[23] the *porte-parole*, the mouthpiece, of the civilizing mission, to ivory robber, murderer, primitive idol, and an advocate of the wholesale extermination of the native population marks not only the de-Englishification of the imperial project but also its return to an earlier, and less civilized, Roman form.

Heart of Darkness's multiple returns to Rome, by converting England from civilized imperial nation to raw subject territory to an imperial nation whose sovereignty is itself savage, occasion a narrative ebb and flow, a displacement and deterritorialization that far from simply replacing the idea of the nation (as Hardt and Negri would suggest), in fact enables the telling of a very national story of empire won and waning. That story is told as much through the properly national discourse of place as through the putatively nonnational mechanism of flow. It is certainly possible to argue that place crumbles before flow in the text, just as the shining power of the rainbow-colored imperial map that hangs in the Brussels offices of the Company dissolves in the face of the repeated narration of the futility and destruction of the project of national territorial sovereignty—from the French warship "firing into a continent" as "her ensign drooped limp like a rag,"[24] to the Belgian civil servant whose starched collars in the midst of the jungle are all that is left of imperial aspirations, to the tattered, unrecognizable flag that Marlow spots flying over an abandoned outpost, to Kurtz's final fall. The point is not that a narrative conceived from outside the space of the national destroys the placed idea of the nation, but rather that it is only through such a narrative that the idea of the nation, whether triumphant or tattered, can come into being. Nations cannot be thought without globes and globes cannot be thought without nations. This idea, so elegantly illustrated in the narrative structure of *Heart of Darkness*, remains altogether absent from Hardt and Negri's *Empire*.

I turn now to a cultural text that more directly mirrors Hardt and Negri. If England's late-nineteenth-century return to Rome can be condensed into *Heart of Darkness* and the particular anxieties of waning empire in an increasingly global world, America's late-twentieth-century return to Rome can be read in Ridley Scott's film *Gladiator*, released (like *Empire*) in 2000. The film's triumphal spread through the all-conquering vehicle of the Hollywood film, carrying the endorsements of several Oscars as well as a multitude of other domestic and international awards, constructs a very different image of national empire. Glamorously disguised as an historical epic of ancient Rome circa 180 AD, the film tells the quintessentially American story of, in the words of the trailer, "A soldier who became a general. A general who became a slave. A slave who defied an empire." Maximus (Russell Crowe) is the undefeated commander of the Roman legions in a long series of campaigns to annex ever more territory for the empire of Marcus Aurelius (Richard Harris). The emperor's unloved son Commodus (Joaquin Phoenix), enraged by his father's plan to name Maximus as his successor, kills his own father and orders the death of his rival and his family. Maximus escapes death, is enslaved, and subsequently sold to Proximus (Oliver Reed), a provincial gladiator trainer and contest organizer. Conquering all his opponents, Maximus becomes a legend who fights his way back from the empire's remote outposts to its center, where he defies and defeats the corrupt, antirepublican, pro-imperial rule of Commodus who cares for nothing but himself and his own reproduction through a properly corrupt, iconically decadent desire for his own sister (Connie Nielsen).

"*Ave!* Old knitter of black wool. *Morituri te salutant*," says Marlow, recalling his use of the ritual greeting of gladiators to spectators in bidding farewell to the two old women who guard the door of the Company's offices like classical fates or latter-day versions of Madame Defarges, silent witnesses to the scenes of death that await him in the Congo.[25] The difference between Marlow's gladiatorial journey and Maximus's is the difference between a deeply troubled account of imperial national sovereignty as a crumbling edifice, incapable of holding at bay the dark forces it has unleashed, and a relatively sanguine account of the project of empire.[26] In contrast to Francis Ford Coppola's Vietnam film epic *Apocalypse Now* (1978), which brilliantly mirrors Conrad's imperial anxieties, *Gladiator* ultimately dispels such ambivalence over US power. Maximus's final victory over Commodus in the gladiatorial arena implies the cleansing victory of the people over the crazed emperor and, in a familiar separation of powers, the restoration of the senate alongside Commodus's successor. It goes without saying that this vision of Roman rule directly echoes a prevailing vision of US democracy as a force for global good. When the noble senator Gracchus (Derek Jacobi of *I, Claudius* fame, in a Roman return of his own) joins the rowdy mob to watch one of the countless coliseum battles organized by Commodus to placate the population, he states: "I may not be a man of the people, but I do try to be for the people." Gracchus's line, voicing both the political and rhetorical form of representative democracy, reminds us that we can read—that we cannot *not* read—*Gladiator* as an account not just of Roman empire but of US empire too. Whereas *Heart of Darkness* positions Englishmen as Rome's slaves as a way of expressing the imperial mission's fragility, *Gladiator* positions Americans as simultaneously Rome's slaves *and* its saviors, the latter-day Maximuses who will redeem Rome's vision of democratic republicanism and make the world safe for a new empire.

The contrast between *Heart of Darkness* and *Gladiator* becomes even more clearly one of two imperial models when read through the lens of their respectively modern and postmodern textual strategies. With its formal oscillation between a sharply differentiated yet deeply imbricated Europe in Africa, *Heart of Darkness* emblematizes what Hardt and Negri characterize as the "striated space of modernity [which] constructed *places* that were continually engaged in and founded on a dialectical play with their outsides."[27] *Gladiator*, by contrast, can be seen, again in Hardt and Negri's terms, to "smooth" space such that its computer-generated ancient Rome seamlessly becomes America, speaking in its voice, expressing its ideology. "The space of imperial sovereignty," write Hardt and Negri, "might appear to be free of the binary divisions or striations of modern boundaries, but really it is crisscrossed by so many fault lines that it only appears as a continuous, uniform space. . . . In this smooth space of Empire, there is no *place* of power—it is both everywhere and nowhere. Empire is an *ou*-topia, or really a *non-place*."[28]

The analogy I am suggesting has its limits. For all its smoothing of space and time, *Gladiator* does not finally create the "non-place" of Empire. Instead, the film repeatedly conjures a distinctly placed, markedly national, unmistakably US, discourse of empire. For instance, in the North African section of the film, when the enslaved Maximus is shown rapidly conquering all his opponents in a provincial coliseum (custom-built on location in a Moroccan village), the town and its inhabitants are both Orientalized and Arabized. Viewers are treated to a shot of a dancing cobra on a gaming table, scenes of the bazaar, and an exotic, Armenian-influenced musical score. All of this despite the fact that there were no Arabs in the richly hybrid Berber-Roman culture of North Africa in this period.[29] The use of polymorphous Arab signs for African space offers yet another example of just how American the film is, imposing its own deadly iconography of difference onto a time and place in which it did not exist. Whether masterfully digitizing history (Rome) or lavishly reconstructing it (North Africa), *Gladiator* enlists Hollywood's technological and financial capital to produce an allegory of national reference and global reach. The film both trumpets and whispers "America," rendering it at once omnipresent and invisible.

The passage from the symbolic space of the Roman circus to that of the US cinema has long been mediated by the spectral presence of US politics. *Gladiator*'s American Rome, like that invoked in current discussions of US empire, is continuous with a broader tradition in which the nation returns to Rome in order to speak its own history: the founding, for example, with its republican language; or the cold war, with its global rhetoric of good and evil empires, its domestic concerns with new social movements of liberation, and its several filmic returns to Rome. Not only did the epic spectacles of the 1950s and 1960s represent Hollywood's effort to woo back an audience increasingly defecting to television as its preferred leisure activity, but they also served what Leslie Felperin calls "a more mass-psychological function," "working out anxieties about the west's imperial role in the new world order." Thus, she explains, *Gladiator*'s most direct predecessor, *The Fall of the Roman Empire* (1964), directed by Anthony Mann, depicts a civilization menaced by barbarians all around; William Wyler's *Ben-Hur* (1959) expresses fears about an increasingly diverse and secular nation; and Stanley Kubrick's *Spartacus* (1960) justifies the growing civil rights movement. Read in this trajectory, *Gladiator* reveals the newly muscular Americanism of a superpower in Roman guise. "Rome," writes Felperin, "here stands in for America: corrupt at its heart, based on enslavement, dedicated to sustaining pointless wars abroad while the mob happily forgoes a more civil society for bread and circuses."[30]

Gladiator and Hollywood's earlier sword-and-sandals spectacles share a signification of Roman empire that for all their historical anteriority and epic reach, are nonetheless deeply and referentially loyal to their respective US presents. *Spartacus*, for example, both echoes the cold war era's worst excesses of US nationalism and expresses its most powerful rhetoric. The popular 1951 novel that gave rise to the film was first conceived by the famous communist writer Howard Fast during a prison term for "un-American activities" and, thanks to a government-imposed publishing freeze on Fast's work, was subsequently published at its author's personal cost.[31] The film version of *Spartacus* illustrates the ways in which film form absorbs and deflects the particular contradictions of national history, nowhere more so than in the famous final scene. A group of fellow slaves who have fought and lost a gutsy battle against the Roman Empire are asked by their victors to identify their leader. Before Spartacus can step forward, another slave cries, "I am Spartacus," followed by another and another until all of them join in the general cry. The voice of the individual rises up as that of the many, denuding this ode to collective rebellion of any dangerous Internationale associations by virtue of an Americanized language of democratic individualism. Democracy (and America) has its victory even as the slaves are all crucified.

To read *Spartacus* or *Gladiator* as triumphs of the ideology of national place is to read against Hardt and Negri, who would likely see the films' refusal of firm boundaries between the contemporary United States and ancient Rome as an exemplary instance of the "smooth," "uncoded," "deterritorialized," placeless, and nationless space of Empire, as opposed to old-style imperialism's "machine of global striation, channeling, coding, territorializing flows of capital."[32] However, there are flows and flows: flows of the sort that Hardt and Negri describe through the language of deterritorialization, and others, like those mapped by world-systems analysis, critical geography, diaspora studies, and some strains of postcolonial theory and globalization theory, in which power does not diffuse itself across the flow but is seen to remain unequally divided between core and periphery, North and South, first world and third. If we think about *Gladiator* through some of these critical models, if we further contextualize the Hollywood form of the film, surely the "smooth" space of its American Rome will seem less smooth and more striated, marked by the differentiated boundaries of the world market itself. Read thus, *Gladiator* is not an expression of Empire, in the placeless sense that Hardt and Negri give it, but of imperialism—a specific kind of imperialism (cultural) emanating from a specific time and place (the late capitalist United States).

Imperial Flows

Social geographer Neil Smith calls Hardt and Negri's notion of a deterritorialized, decentralized Empire a "fantasy of financial capital, of entire periods in which financial capital dominates, a fantasy even of oppositions swirling too close to the necromancy of finance capital, that power no longer has any spatial definition." Such a reading of empire, Smith argues, altogether misses the profound spatiality of a system of domination that for all of its global rhetoric, remains territorialized, centralized, and national. What Smith calls "the nationalism of this globalism," starkly clear in the aggressive foreign policy of post–9/11 America, is a sober reminder of the particularly placed quality of contemporary empire.[33] To read the spatiality of empire it may be necessary, as Smith suggests elsewhere, to practice a "spatialized politics." To this end, he proposes a system of seven scales, each located within a particular space of identity (body, home, community, city, region, nation, globe). Although each scale is marked by a degree of internal coherence and internal difference, all the scales are constantly "jumping" the divides that separate one space of identity from another. This dynamic model, emphasizing "the active social connectedness of scales," as well as the simultaneous fixity and fluidity of borders, has as its ultimate aim "the recovery of space from annihilation and [the creation of] a language via which the redifferentiation of space can be pioneered."[34] The movement at the heart of Smith's scalar politics is not the same as the movement that preoccupies Hardt and Negri. Whereas the former specifies a process of spatial differentiation grounded in the inequitable division of global capital, the latter identifies a process of spatial homogenization, the creeping sameness of Empire everywhere. Read through the politics of scale, *Gladiator* becomes a film that though markedly national, is not *exclusively* so. A nationalism understood as expressed through globalism, to cite only one of Smith's other scales, has more relevance to our times and more utility for our critical practice than a nationalism dismissed as the obsolete residue of old-style territorial imaginaries.

Fredric Jameson provides another model for how to name the differentiating politics of global cultural flows in his description of a "fundamental dissymmetry between the United States and other cultures," a dissymmetry for which the Hollywood film and the broader "leveling power of American mass culture" bear serious responsibility.[35] If Jameson begins by noticing difference, he quickly concentrates his critical lens on the phenomena of sameness. Much like global English, that "lingua franca of money and power" dominating more local languages of culture and aesthetics, like the free-market "freedom" enabling worldwide penetration by US corporations, like the US culture system that, knowing no boundaries, "undertakes to incorporate exotic elements from abroad—samurai culture here, South African music there, John Woo films here, Thai food there, and so forth,"[36] Jameson sees the maw of Hollywood swallowing independent and nationalist cinemas and cultures. In this omnivorous aspect, the Hollywood film as described by Jameson closely resembles Empire as described by Hardt and Negri: a form of global domination that, like its Roman predecessor, "does not fortify its boundaries to push others away, but rather pulls them within its pacific order, like a powerful vortex."[37] But of course, for Jameson, the Hollywood film does not serve as the agent of Empire's placeless, nationless, decentered ideology of movement, but rather as the prize commodity of what he calls, eschewing the term *cultural imperialism*, "Americanization"—a profoundly placed, nationally centered, transnationally deployed regime of capitalist flow and consumerist desire whose ultimate aim is to remake the world in its own image.

Just when we are in danger of understanding the flows of global culture as purely unidirectional and wholly flattening, Jameson reminds us of globalization's dialectical nature. At once homogenizing and heterogenizing, it encompasses both the identity-based politics of certain nations with their transnational systems and the differentialist, multiplicitous politics of popular opposition to the national state and what lies outside it. "Paradoxically," Jameson observes, "it is often elements of that outside and transnational mass culture that are appropriated for such resistances: Hollywood films being sometimes the source of resistance to internal hegemony as well as the form external hegemony ultimately takes."[38] Even in this highly truncated, too abbreviated form, Jameson's signaling of a certain contradictory aspect to the phenomenon of global Hollywood opens a critically crucial, and for postcolonial critics, deeply familiar, ground. That power's force is multidirectional, that it effects various practices of domination and resistance, constitutes a central thesis of post-*Orientalism* postcolonial studies, as well as of Smith's scalar politics and, to some extent, of Jameson's anatomy of globalization. In a similar vein, Arjun Appadurai defines the new global cultural economy as "a complex, overlapping, disjunctive order that cannot any longer be understood in terms of existing center-periphery models,"[39] but must rather be comprehended through the more fluid model of "global cultural flow,"[40] in which "the United States is no longer the puppeteer of a world system of images but is only one node of a complex transnational construction of imaginary landscapes."[41] Naturally, a host of critical differences exist here. Appadurai's relativized America differs quite markedly from Jameson's cultural hegemon or Smith's global war machine, and the theorists themselves are quite differently positioned, probably in descending order of closeness, with regard to postcolonial studies. But taken together, these three models of global flows map for postcolonial scholars and others the possibility of a methodological alternative to Hardt and Negri's madness, a method in which to name (global) movement is by no means to forget (national) place.

Writing in the context of film studies and in critique of David Bordwell, Janet Staiger, and Kristen Thompson's account of global Hollywood, Miriam Hansen makes exactly this point in her definition of Hollywood classical cinema as "something like the first global vernacular." As her moniker *global* suggests, she understands Hollywood film as transnational and translatable—but only because it was first national and local, the particular expression of a specific historical experience of modernity:

> If classical Hollywood cinema succeeded as an international modernist idiom on a mass basis, it did so not because of its presumably universal narrative form but because it meant different things to different people and publics, both at home and abroad. . . . To write the international history of classical American cinema, therefore, is a matter of tracing not just its mechanisms of standardization and hegemony but also the diversity of ways in which this cinema was translated and reconfigured in both local and translocal contexts of reception.[42]

Hansen's model of vernacular modernism, essentially an effort to describe linguistically what others have described spatially, shows that to anatomize the workings of contemporary culture, we must be willing to name power's constitution within certain borders, as much as its spectacular flows across them. These flows themselves beg to be read not simply as the story of standardization (US cinema conquers the world) but also as the story of heterogenization (US cinema has been and is being received in a diversity of local ways).

An account of *Gladiator*'s international reception lies outside the bounds of this essay. I have tried merely to describe the film's simultaneous national meaning and global reach, and to suggest that it is in this simultaneity that the film reveals its deepest analogy with the now widespread rhetoric of US empire, a rhetoric that precisely veils nationalism with globalism. Despite a cast that includes British, Australian, Danish, and US actors; filming locations in Morocco, Italy, Malta, Britain, and the United States; a British director and an Australian star; and a joint US-British production unit (DreamWorks and Universal Pictures plus the increasingly European-oriented British Film Council), *Gladiator* remains a resolutely US film. As the authors of *Global Hollywood* observe, coproduction marks "a space where border-erasing free-trade economics meet border-defining cultural initiatives under the unstable sign of the nation." Coproduction, they continue, ultimately enables the triumph of a system both borderless (global) and bordered (national): "European audiovisual liberalisation largely fuels rather than challenges core aspects of the Hollywood NICL [New International Division of Cultural Labor]."[43] Though *Gladiator* was not produced by Hollywood alone or by one of Hollywood's emerging global partners such as the French-owned, pan-European pay-television giant Canal Plus, the film's extra- and transnational modes of coproduction, far from denationalizing it, render it even more representative of what I am suggesting is US nationalism's new shape. That shape—at once interdependent and hegemonic, worldly and national—finds clear expression in the production economics, no less than the cultural ideologies, of Hollywood.

As Hardt and Negri would have it, the most complete return to the model of Roman empire would be one that totally deterritorialized itself and became unbounded and networked—not simply postnational but unnational. Here is where a reading of *Gladiator* can provide a counterpoint to *Empire*, and possibly some schematic guidelines for postcolonial studies in an age of globalization. In *Gladiator* the United States is Rome and Rome is the United States. This spatio-temporal slippage demands something more than what Hardt and Negri give us, namely, a model that interprets the morphing of one space-time into another as evidence for the wholesale dissolution of borders, boundaries, territories, and, of course, nation-states. We might instead consider the morphing of Rome and the United States as an instance in which an emblematically national vehicle turns to Rome in order to both express and veil a resplendently national ideology. In other words, US empire is anteriorized and denationalized by a vehicle that if it puts the United States elsewhere, nonetheless returns us in its very form to America. The Hollywood film is something like the formal unconscious of US empire. And like the unconscious, the way it speaks us is often far more complex than the way we speak it.

Without a voicing of the national as an operative critical category, we are that much less able to name the workings of globalization, much less able to understand the insertion of a film like *Gladiator* into a specific network of US cultural and industrial capitalism worldwide and a particular tradition of Americanism at home (recall Hollywood's cold war Roman epics or *Bladerunner*, Scott's 1982 dystopic chronicle of US empire dethroned by Japanese capital). Whereas Hardt and Negri privilege the smooth space of Empire over the striated space of imperialism, I would stress the importance of continuing to look for the striations and, even more, for the dissymmetries—what Appadurai calls "the disjuncture and difference"—that shape our moment and remind us, time and again, that power in the contemporary world is not "no place," but rather is always placed, and often along national coordinates. Retaining the nation as a critical category does not mean giving up on the global. Rather, it simply means learning to move back and forth between them, learning to read each as the structuring condition of the other. This, I think, is the unfinished business of postcolonial studies, the work that returns us to our disciplinary history (where its models and methods partially lie), locates us in a globalized present, and enables us to construct a critical future.

Inherently corrupt, endlessly changing, and characterized by a fundamental "fluidity of form" that allows it to absorb all challenges, Hardt and Negri's Empire is a moving target.[44] Because Empire can be everything, there is no need to oppose or, more modestly, to critique it. But if Hardt and Negri's Empire contains its own critique, ours need not. Toward the end of their book, Hardt and Negri claim that "the coming Empire is not American and the United States is not its center. The fundamental principle of Empire . . . is that its power has no actual and localizable terrain or center."[45] Maybe the Empire to come is not American, but to an unavoidable degree, the present one is. And without an account of US imperialism in its various political, economic, military-industrial, and cultural guises, without a critical practice that puts power and national place, as much as resistance and global movement, at its heart, we cannot hope to move postcolonial studies into the space of the beyond.

Notes

This essay enjoyed the benefit of many people's contributions. I thank Suvir Kaul and Ania Loomba for the invitation to deliver the original talk, and the audience at the University of Illinois at Urbana-Champaign for their clarifying questions; James Tweedie, Jack Hitt, Jed Esty, and Neil Smith for conversation and references on the subject of US empire; and Jed Esty, Antoinette Burton, Dudley Andrew, and Michael Denning for incisive and generous readings of an earlier draft.

1. The time of the postcolonial has been elegantly parsed in McClintock, "The Angel of Progress"; Anne McClintock, "Postcolonialism and the Angel of Progress," in McClintock, *Imperial Leather*, 1–18; Shohat, "Notes on the Postcolonial"; and Hall, "When Was 'the Postcolonial'?"

2. I discuss the prehistory of the postcolonial in Cooppan, "W(h)ither Postcolonial Studies."

3. In a recent article, Simon Gikandi lays important groundwork for this project, particularly in his effort to describe a postcolonial theory of globalization focused less on the spatiality of the globe and its flows than on what he calls "the temporality of colonial and national modernity." Gikandi, "Globalization and the Claims of Postcoloniality," 636.

4. Michael Hardt and Antonio Negri, *Empire*, 384. *Empire*'s phenomenon has been extensively critiqued in a variety of disciplines. I have found the following particularly provocative: Gopal Balakrishnan, "Virgilian Visions"; Tim Watson, "An American Empire?"; Bashir Abu-Manneh, "The Illusions of Empire"; Arif Dirlik, "Empire?"; Timothy Brennan, "The Empire's New Clothes"; and Brennan, "The Magician's Wand." Hardt and Negri defend their book in an interview with Nicholas Brown and Imre Szeman, "The Global Coliseum"; and in Michael Hardt and Antonio Negri, "The Rod of the Forest Warden." Recently, two excellent collections of critical essays on *Empire* have appeared: Gopal Balakrishnan, *Debating Empire*; and Paul Passavant and Jodi Dean, *Empire's New Clothes*.

5. Hardt and Negri, *Empire*, 146.

6. Jonathan Freedman, "Rome, AD . . . Rome DC?," *Guardian* (London), September 18, 2002. A year later, as the arrival of the war turned history to farce, and with characteristic levity, Maureen Dowd asked her readers to imagine defense secretary Donald Rumsfeld "in a big metal breastplate, a skirt, and lace-up gladiator sandals. Rummius Maximus Pompeius." Maximus, of course, is the name of the hero of Ridley Scott's *Gladiator*. Maureen Dowd, "What Would Genghis Do?" *New York Times*, March 5, 2003. Some critics suggest that the US empire's Roman form does not signal its hegemony but its crisis and eventual end. See Johnson, *Blowback*; Kupchan, *The End of the American Era*; Nye, *The Paradox of American Power*; and Wallerstein, *The Decline of American Power*. For an overview, see Doug Saunders, "Imperial Decline," *Globe and Mail* (Toronto), October 5, 2002.

7. Emily Eakin, "All Roads Lead to D.C.," *New York Times*, March 31, 2002. A year earlier, Eakin had showcased Hardt and Negri's *Empire* in an article entitled "What Is the Next Big Idea? The Buzz Is Growing," *New York Times*, July 20, 2001. Robert Kaplan, *Warrior Politics*; Max Boot, "The Case for American Empire," *Weekly Standard*, October 15, 2001, 27.

8. Jay Bookman, "Bush's Real Goal in Iraq: Invasion Would Mark the Next Step toward an American Empire," *Atlanta Journal-Constitution*, September 29, 2002.

9. Hardt and Negri, *Empire*, 172. See the complete chapter 2.5 of *Empire*, "Network Power: U.S. Sovereignty and the New Empire," 160–82.

10. See Harvey, *The Condition of Postmodernity*; Giddens, *The Consequences of*

Modernity; Fredric Jameson, preface and "Notes on Globalization as a Philosophical Issue," in Jameson and Miyoshi, *The Cultures of Globalization*, xi–xvii, 54–77; Appadurai, *Modernity at Large*; Arrighi, *The Long Twentieth Century*; Braudel, *Civilization and Capitalism*; Wallerstein, *The Modern World-System*; and Guillen, "Is Globalization Civilizing, Destructive, or Feeble?"

11. King, *Culture, Globalization, and the World-System*, ix.

12. Ohmae, *The End of the Nation State*.

13. Miyoshi, "A Borderless World?" 740.

14. Ibid., 747.

15. Hardt and Negri, *Empire*, 43.

16. See the exemplary work of Said, *Culture and Imperialism*; Parry, "Problems in Current Theories of Colonial Discourse"; Parry, "The Postcolonial"; Brennan, *At Home in the World*; Lazarus, *Nationalism and Cultural Practice in the Postcolonial World*; Viswanathan, *Outside the Fold*; and Apter, *Continental Drift*.

17. Hardt and Negri, *Empire*, 138.

18. Ibid., 142.

19. Ibid., 146.

20. Fanon, *The Wretched of the Earth*, 247.

21. Conrad, *Heart of Darkness*, 8–10.

22. Ibid.

23. Ibid., 28.

24. Ibid., 17.

25. Ibid., 14.

26. In this regard I am in agreement with Linda Colley's suggestion that the "American empire has always mirrored British empire, while in the end exceeding it." Although Colley resists the analogy of the United States as Rome, preferring Britain as a closer and more consistent model, her argument nonetheless coincides with my own in its insistence on anteriorization as a crucial mechanism of imperial self-identification. Linda Colley, "What Britannia Taught Bush," *Guardian* (London), September 20, 2002.

27. Hardt and Negri, *Empire*, 190.

28. Ibid.

29. I am indebted to Mokhtar El Ghambou for discussion of this point.

30. Leslie Felperin, review of *Gladiator*, *Sight and Sound*, June 2000. For a contrasting point of view that resists allegorical interpretation of *Gladiator*'s Rome in favor of a strident critique of the film's flat characterization, wooden dialogue, repetitive violence, and pastiche aesthetic, see Andrew O'Hehir's review, "We Who Are About to Be Bored Salute You!" in the online magazine *Salon*, May 5, 2000, available at http://archive.salon.com/ent/movies/review/2000/05/05/gladiator.

31. Howard Fast provides a gripping personal account of these events in *Being Red*. I thank Katie Trumpener for alerting me to Fast's memoir.

32. Hardt and Negri, *Empire*, 332.

33. Smith, "Scales of Terror and the Resort to Geography," 636.

34. Smith, "Contours of a Spatialized Politics," 66.

35. Jameson, "Notes on Globalization as a Philosophical Issue," 59, 63. For an extended background to these arguments, see Jameson, *Postmodernism*.

36. Ibid., 59–60.

37. Hardt and Negri, *Empire*, 198.

38. Jameson, "Notes on Globalization as a Philosophical Issue," 75.

39. Arjun Appadurai, "Disjuncture and Difference in the Global Cultural Economy," in Appadurai, *Modernity at Large*, 32.

40. Ibid., 37.

41. Ibid., 31.

42. Hansen, "The Mass Production of the Senses," 68–69. See also Bordwell, Thompson, and Staiger, *The Classical Hollywood Cinema*.

43. Miller et al., *Global Hollywood*, 107. In Frederick Wasser's alternative reading, the rise of global film financing in Hollywood does not imply the international hegemony of the US film form but rather the transnationalization of the US film industry and, by implication, the "breakdown" of the very paradigm of national cinema created for national audiences. Wasser, "Is Hollywood America?" 424.

44. Hardt and Negri, *Empire*, 202.

45. Ibid., 384.

The Economic Image-Function of the Periphery

☉ ☉ ☉

TIMOTHY BRENNAN

The *idea* of the global periphery—not just the periphery's physical spaces where cheap manufacturing and resource extraction flourish—is itself an economic engine. A long discourse of dissent, of which postcolonial studies constitutes a particular phase, reminds us that the idea of the global periphery has often relied on inherited prejudices, cultural dissonances, or factual ignorance. In such an argument, the emphasis tends to rest on the offensiveness of the very concept, its epistemological violence (a periphery has inherently less value than a center, after all). But the moral emphasis deflects a more important aspect of the concept: its utility in the mundane, results-oriented process of profit making. Although not consciously perhaps, the periphery is an idea that is willed, and it governs perception under the quiet dictates of interest.

By *image-function*, I mean more than simply the ideological conditioning or the customs governing the dissonances of civilizational value. What should emerge from the term, rather, is a sense of the rules of perception—those demands made under capitalism in a phase when production has come prominently to include information as one of its commodities. The utility of perception does not in any way displace earlier commodity forms (machine tools, construction, clothing, luxury items, or other physical use-values), which, on the contrary, become heightened by the idea's agency. I am suggesting that the global periphery is a useable idea perceived as such, and that its existence is preserved by way of a fiercely defended set of regulations governing what can and cannot be said about it, at least if one wishes to maintain credibility in the United States and Europe. At the same time, critiques of Eurocentrism do not necessarily escape conformity to this highly policed need to preserve the idea of a periphery: for the idea may be weakened by exposing its underlying bigotry or civilizational slightings without losing any of its economic advantages.

For all these reasons, it seems puzzling that postcolonial critics have done so little to offer an original theory of the economy. Deriving many of its motifs and much of its language from the anticolonial independence movements of the 1950s and 1960s, postcolonial studies has always in one sense been about emancipation. This largely Marxist substratum should have led, one would think, to more creative attempts to explore development and profit. Not that these were its only goals, since postcolonial studies has also been about challenging the systems of cultural value, moving others to appreciate the cultural achievements of those outside the European sphere. There has always been a side to postcolonial studies that sought to expose those narrowly obsessed or tendentiously ignorant of many of the world's most consequential artistic and intellectual creations. Disagreements within the field have often occurred over the proper relationship between these twin motives of achieving emancipation and clarifying or expanding cultural value.

These conflicts arose out of a peculiar condition of emergence. Postcolonial studies entered the academy in the mid-1980s following several shifts of depressing and far-reaching dimensions, both within and outside the academy. A newly emboldened far right-wing political movement began to permeate government and the public sphere, pushing the previous social democratic common sense into the margins and making it appear a lunatic fringe. At just this time, literary theory entered the American academic scene. Although this is not the place to trace the complex process adequately, it should be appreciated that postcolonial studies was in a sense forced to occupy a preexisting landscape of literary theory, assuming the contours of an epistemological break rather than a deliberate attempt to link dissent with its historical past or create itself anew as a differently relevant anti-imperialist practice.[1]

From the start, in other words, postcolonial studies was caught in a double bind comprising incompatible intellectual traditions. Under the forces of the conservative public climate in which it came into existence, it found its authority in a veiled neomodernism hostile to its origins in the early anticolonial movements, and perhaps for that reason remained theoretically hostile to origins in any form. In some early practitioners, this departure was the aim; in others, it was a confusion about the past, but at all events, it was invested—given its theoretical lineage—in a mandate to reject and depart from the libratory language of national emancipation that had formed the intellectual basis for the political morality that later became postcolonial studies in the metropolis. The political and intellectual lineage of postcolonial studies, in other words, was radically suppressed by the development of the field in the 1980s under the conditions I have just described—that is, a far-right shift in American and British public politics and the reception of literary theory in the academy.

Three of the more pressing questions for anyone attempting to make sense of postcolonial studies today, then, are these:

(1)   Is postcolonial studies in its 1980s form (the one we still occupy today) a reaction against that rightward shift, one that, after all, was largely led in its early stages by former activists from the 1960s, who in a period of intense conservatism were forced to retreat into the academy in order to build the intellectual tools for fighting later, in practical ways, when more promising conditions arose?

(2)   Is it, by contrast, a radical alternative to materialist forms of activism first prompted in our thinking by literary and cultural theory's supposed turn to language?[2] In this case, it would still embody resistance to the Right's rise to power, but not in a period of preparation, yet rather as the fight itself in a higher, more sophisticated form—by way of "culture" and "language" through which all materialities (the argument goes) are ultimately mediated.

(3)   Or, to take perhaps the least considered option of all, is it the academic intellectual's version of that rightward shift itself as it seeped into the academy through the work of cold war high intellectuals of the French New Left, overwhelming its earlier liberationist drives and replacing the ethos of progressive betterment, social reorganization, and education with doctrines of disorganization, inarticulation, and circularity—all seen now as happy states, as heterotopias replacing the dangerous utopias of the past? I do not ask these questions coyly, or in order to imply that the third option wins out in the end. Postcolonial studies, I am saying, constitutes a genuine mixture, a schizophrenic combination of liberationist impulses and middle-class flight. The last of these options is neither more real than the others, nor *less* real.

It is easy to imagine, then, why an economic theory relevant to postcolonial studies has proven difficult to formulate. The economic as an intellectual category appears to offer postcolonial studies' transvaluation of values very little since the logic of the field is devoted to the obliteration of the business of being bourgeois. The economic emphasis in Marxist analysis does not appear radical enough, does not get deeply enough into the person, whereas the economics of the bottom line is positivistically bourgeois. Language and epistemology, by contrast, offer the critic a far more easily accessible reprieve from the world of instrumental calculation.

Such as they are, the economic discourses of postcolonial theory have devolved from a posteconomic poetics that sought to separate itself from any demotic or policy-oriented intervention, escaping both the world of business and the labor movement with equal force.[3] Despite apparent exceptions like Gayatri Chakravorty Spivak's provocative early essay, "Scattered Speculations on the Question of Value," for example, as well as elaborate treatments of material culture in critical anthropology circles (Fred R. Myers's *The Empire of Things*, for instance) and Fredric Jameson's suggestive writings on globalization, especially in *The Cultural Turn*, the overall picture remains.[4] Although not a literary critical or linguistic formation alone, postcolonial studies in history, anthropology, or the other social sciences has been recognizable—and therefore nameable—largely by way of a shift to what I am calling a poetics: in history departments, the discovery of memory over the archive, or seeing culture as a "ruin . . . linked to the incommensurable";[5] in political science, the rediscovery of anarchic states of noncooperation. Literary theoretical tropes are the ones that have stamped "theory" in the postcolonial corners of the social sciences, its poetics a sign of "metaphysical longing" according to Spivak, who made the observation almost twenty years ago.[6] Exceptions, at any rate, remain scarce. For the most part, they fail to draw on that merging of cultural criticism and the economic imagination found throughout theory's most prominent forerunners—Georg Simmel, Alfred Sohn-Rethel, Georges Bataille, Guy Debord, Jean Baudrillard, and Jameson himself among them.[7]

To approach the problem another way, through postcolonial studies' predecessors, notice how left cultural theory when confronting the colonial question turned to issues of agency and being (Jean-Paul Sartre) or the ethics of political violence and the psychology of otherness (Frantz Fanon), leaving the problem of economics to the increasingly specialized fields of policy studies, area studies, or development studies—all of them responding at some level to earlier Marxist or labor-liberal critiques of imperialism. The very different Marxism of the Frankfurt School (which has lately proven so influential on postcolonial theory) has witnessed a similar abdication. Following in the wake of the young Hegelians, especially Ludwig Feuerbach, the Frankfurt School enriched and elaborated dialectical thought as against the instrumentalist knowledge of the applied sciences and business efficiency. It set out to clean the house of thinking by sustaining the Hegelian distinctions between perception, intuition, knowledge, and self-consciousness against the pragmatist and crudely empiricist dominant of a reified knowledge. Lost in the extraordinarily productive years of contestation with the "cultural industry," however, was the recognition that Hegel's philosophy itself rested on an economic theory already implicit in *The Phenomenology of Mind* and elaborated in *The Philosophy of Right*.[8] Economics was inseparable from philosophy for Hegel.

And so, in spite of signs of investment in the trope of the economic in the ur-cultural theory of the young Hegelians and its offshoots in the nascent sociology of Simmel and Max Weber, not to mention the theorists of the Third International (particularly Antonio Gramsci and Georg Lukács), a theory-inflected postcolonial studies has seemed, at times, almost allergic to an application of even those economic theories that enliven its poststructuralist registers: namely, the Derridean supplement, Freudian libidinal economy, Bataille's expenditure, Baudrillard's political economy of the sign, or, more recently, the "new Italian" school's immaterial labor and the refusal of work.[9] A lot of classical cultural theory explicitly evokes the postcolonial problematic without being recognized as doing so: Simmel's thoughts on the city, for instance, with his notions of the blasé attitude and the culture of cold quantification emanating out from the hub of cities to rural districts in an act of territorial subordination; or Bataille's ecstatic writing on waste and excess as a deliberately self-destructive strategy of noncompliance with rational Western life; or Debord's psycho-geography, his attempt to upset the logic of the spectacle, with its creation of an isolated and paralyzed subject gawking at the world but unable to participate in it; and now Antonio Negri with his rehearsal of ideas taken from the council communists of the 1930s and 1940s about the inevitability of capitalist social relations and the opportunities that capitalism offers for greater forms of self-definition and biopolitical emergence.[10]

What we have to consider, then, is whether postcolonial studies has disqualified itself from taking part in a major conversation. Even in those moments when it did summon the economic, it failed to answer (or at least effectively ridicule) a question unfortunately still very much alive, the most important question for those interested in challenging Eurocentrism: why the West? Does Europe's triumph in recent centuries prove its intellectual and cultural superiority? Has it in fact triumphed, or is that the illusion to be dispelled? In a period when corporate CEOs are considered sages, when at least a third of all news reporting is dedicated to the stock market, and when the individual citizen hangs on the words of Alan Greenspan, the answer to this question must surely involve the economic, even if it cannot entirely rest on it. And the treatment of this question resides in an argument about value, although in a different sense from Spivak's, whose important reflections were designed to demonstrate the appropriateness of deconstruction to a reading of Marx (a demonstration she very much succeeds in making).[11]

None of this means to say that there exists no economic register in which the postcolonial critic speaks. The field's belief system takes the form of an atmospheric inheritance of a post-Fordist consensus established by the so-called New Times critics of 1980s Britain. The spin on cultural studies offered by Stuart Hall and his reliance, in turn, on the Althusserian and Foucauldian rereadings of Gramsci by Ernesto Laclau and Chantal Mouffe, both popularized a ready-made set of doctrines about the economy: namely, that production had given way to consumption as the site of political struggle; that the economy was primarily postindustrial; and that the welfare state constituted a "nanny state" that we should no longer place at the center of our demands.[12] It is important to note, though, that these findings in postcolonial studies were not arrived at after a process of painful reconsideration. They were rather a matter of inertia. They carried no sense of obligation to work through available scholarship on the world economy, patterns of investment, shifts in managerial strategies, or the actual relations of production. On the other hand, even if there was little work formulating a site-specific economic theory, there were patterns of research with economic consequences, including several valuable investigations of diasporic communities of labor, reflections on the key role played by women in local and transnational economies, and now extensive general commentaries on globalization itself, which is, however, often decoupled from capitalism as a systemic economic mode.[13]

Postcolonial theory needs now to explore an economics of culture in a way appropriate to its own field of play—to venture into the formal (that is, structuring) elements of thought recognized as economic and therefore to create a vocabulary that allows us to communicate a complex in terms of a serviceable abstraction, giving to the postcolonial endeavor tools comparable to those provided by Simmel's *blasé attitude* or Debord's *spectacle*. I am not saying that this is only possible today for the first time, or that such opportunities become evident only by way of a unique conjuncture. My argument concerns continuities rather than those ruptures that so dominate the vocabulary of globalization theory. Bataille's work on excess and death, after all, was based on a comparative analysis of Aztec sacrifice, Soviet planning, and Far Eastern religion in which expenditure stands in for accumulation and transgression substitutes for prohibition. This clearly provides a compelling lead for a postcolonial studies that tends to cast Marxism as the disenchanted horizon of capital, its pathetic reversal rather than its radical undoing (an undoing Bataille pretends to achieve through a reconceptualization of what the economy means). It is also clear that many critics are only now catching up to Marxists like Henri Lefebvre, whose inaugural writing on the consequences under capitalism of the decoupling of space and place played such a powerful role in globalization theory. In *The Production of Space*, he demonstrates how capital abstracts the spaces through which it flows so that it may engage in a continuous process of valorization, devalorization, and revalorization of spaces to allow for the continuous circulation of capital.

As the world map is being redrawn after 1989, postcolonial studies has done little to keep pace with the changing forms of imperialism as an actual set of strategies and developments. The great point of contact between economic history and postcolonial studies can be found in debates over the rise of modernity, although the rarefied nature of the discussion in our circles produces a deep uncertainty, even a deliberate ambiguity, about the status of value in the study of non-European or non-US parts of the world. The issue in the public sphere is very blunt: what is the third world worth? And debates over comparative civilizational value usually rest on a similarly brutal query about what Europe took from the colonies in the form of unpaid labor, material resources, or agricultural commodities. This provides a vital site of debate that postcolonial studies must enter (but has not), just as economists themselves need to learn what we know. That is, ours is a field that already casts the problem of the West in *relational* terms—a view overlooked in official economics circles. "Europe" is perceived by postcolonial studies to be the common ownership of the global cultures that created it. So, in any discussion of comparative value inflected by postcolonial studies, one would be forced to ask not only what Europe created, but what Europe was *forced to invent or adapt* in order to take advantage of its new holdings—the technological breakthroughs in shipping, navigation, astronomy; the impetus toward organizational precision for the purposes of better bookkeeping and unambiguous jurisdiction (moves that perhaps give us the form of the nation-state itself, and yet would be unimaginable without a system of colonies). What new styles of living became necessary for the production and sale of goods? The issue of colonies is one of absolute conditioning, not relative physical advantage.

Behind these questions lurk deeper structures of association. There is a nagging—some would call it unsentimental—concession that Europe is unique, and that that uniqueness has to do with science and pluralism and the life of the mind, that the rise of Europe has to do with its superior organization, its experimental sense, its free play of inquiry, and so on.[14] The ability of postcolonial studies to disrupt these views gives it a notorious centrality, even when it goes by other names. But it has to find a way to enter the discussion if it is going to play.

Development and Value: Key Positions

In historical circles, the paradigmatic statement of value as it relates to the postcolonial problematic is associated with D. K. Fieldhouse, whose original formulation of it in 1964 was deliberately pitched against the aspirations of the nonaligned movements and the first generation of postwar African and Asian intellectuals involved in newly independent states. In particular, their call for reparations and their search for an alternative to capitalist development constituted the targets of his career-defining arguments, which sought to stem the energies of both. It would be quite wrong to imagine that Fieldhouse represents a now obsolete, if not embarrassing, view in historical circles. On the contrary, his arguments continue to be honored and restated without modification.[15]

For Fieldhouse, the dominant myth about modern imperialism is "the belief that tropical empires were exploited to provide wealth for their masters."[16] Fieldhouse had maintained that colonies were not brought about to serve metropolitan interests. They developed haphazardly and anarchically, he claimed, and were only brought under the jurisdiction of the European crown after the fact, as a mere extension of the home country rather than a unique or separate space where a different kind of law, practice, or culture prevailed. Colonies did not develop according to economic theories or policies. Metropolitan prohibitions in the colonies, moreover, did not seriously prevent growth of manufactured goods, so one could not make the argument that differential wealth today resulted from earlier colonial restrictions. At any rate, not production was affected, but trade. However, even here, says Fieldhouse, the restriction on trade was simply an exaggeration of trade barriers that already existed within Europe. It is true, however, he concedes, that the colonies paid more for imports and earned less from exports than they would have if left freely to themselves.

There are many weaknesses in Fieldhouse's account, but let me limit myself here to the definitional ones. He defines profit from empire as the economic or fiscal advantages to the parent state that would not be available if its possessions were independent. Hence, he is forced to ignore any relationships other than those between European colonists and their rulers in the home country. Indigenous peoples do not factor. Slavery, similarly, although frequently mentioned in his study's pages, plays a minor role in accounting for the red and black columns on the imperial ledger. Never is there a systematic attempt to assess the profitability of unpaid labor, itself rather scandalously submerged beneath mercantilist verbiage. In the course of his argument, moreover, the emphasis shifts. What begins as a focus on profitability to empire changes to a focus on complementary (and therefore offsetting) advantages to the colony. At the same time, one is beckoned to forget that natural resources are a limit-text, not a comparative variable. That is, they dictate *all* profits in certain industries, and the entire course of future industries, not only relative gain within an indifferently structured system. Think only of the existence of natural rubber at the dawn of the automobile age, or the knowledge of foreign crude oil reserves. Focusing strictly on profits and gains in international exchange ratios obscures the reliance for profit making on the colony's goods (and on its remaining a colony in perpetuity). For even though neither commodity proved necessary to US factory owners so long as car manufacturing stayed at modest levels, mass production would never have been planned, nor would it have attracted investment, had there been no confidence that Malaysia and the Middle East could be controlled in due time.

The most vigorous riposte to the so-called critics of the imperial myth school has, of course, come from dependency theorists, who argue not so much for a rational or planned disparity of wealth growing out of colonialism (what Fieldhouse disparagingly called an "artificially constructed economic machine") as for a logic within capitalism that wishes to *block* development in specified areas of the world.[17] I am not arguing for dependency theory in this essay (as should become clear in a moment), although I am suggesting that many of its disparagers go too far.[18] For the dependency theorist, accumulation operates by division. One region, rather than another, is permanently subject to robbery, rapacious investment, and structurally unequal terms of trade. These regions, as a direct legacy of colonial administration, are ruled by a local lumpen bourgeoisie, a comprador class that makes its living in the interstices of multinational capital, cutting lucrative deals for its inner circles while ignoring development as such. Logically, dependency theory can no longer view capitalism as the extraction of relative surplus value from wage labor. Capitalism need have no other technical definition than the availability for exploitation; it exists for a region whenever that region has been integrated into the world market. The precise relation of exploitation (serf labor, petty commodity production, slave labor) proves secondary for dependency theory. Capitalism, in short, artificially preserves what appear as traditional or precapitalist forms in order to achieve superexploitation and a hidden transfer from peripheral to core countries.[19]

The more sophisticated critical rejection of dependency theory (for there are, of course, many who scoff at it without bothering actually to engage it) points out that it suffers from a central difficulty. The theory assumes not only that underdevelopment is produced by capitalism (which most bourgeois economists, not only Fieldhouse, would deny) but that underdevelopment is what capitalism actually sets out to do. In this sense, the theory confers an enormous strategic consciousness and control on a system that is in reality more brutal, shortsighted, and vulnerable. Second, it equates intense poverty with high rates of exploitation—a logical fallacy. In the end, one cannot get around the fact that if whole areas of the once-colonized world are still unavailable for capitalist production, there are long-term obstacles for capital expansion. Can one posit at once a cruel monolithic logic to capitalism while demonstrating such an illogical desire? Some have attempted to get around the contradiction by arguing that colonialism tried to adjust to conditions it could not dictate—primarily in Africa's case, where the active resistance of people to privatization, commodity production, industrial rhythms, and so on proved insurmountable. As Anne Phillips (a representative of this view) has argued, "If colonialism was indeed a product of capitalist forces—as most well-thinking radicals will be likely to presume— why were the interests of capital so ill-served?"[20]

Not all those who reject dependency theory belong, like Fieldhouse, to the Oxbridge-inspired narrative of imperial beneficence. Outside postcolonial studies, the debate over value has taken a more conventionally economic form. Paul Bairoch, Patrick O'Brien, and others have argued that although the European powers undoubtedly extracted large sums of material wealth from their colonies, and did so in a highly destructive fashion, the resulting benefits remained ambiguous.[21] The profits, we are told, accounted for a negligible percentage of overall European growth, and the real economic action took place back home in the form of increased labor productivity. (The relational point would, of course, be: how can one justify artificially separating increased domestic productivity from the global colonial system that must, at some level, be related to it?) While both admirers of empire (like Fieldhouse) and postcolonial theorists point to Marxist economists as the usual purveyors of the myth of the West's dependence on third world labor and resources, the truth is that there is a long tradition in Marxism that specifically derides this "myth." In the words of the Marxist economist William Tabb, "While much of the Left focuses on runaway shops to low wage venues, transnational capital avoids really low wage production sites, and indeed avoids investing in most developing countries. Nearly two-thirds of the world's population is basically written off as far as foreign investment is concerned."[22] The historian and economist Robert Brenner, similarly, has made an unassailable point about primitive accumulation: "Those Marxists who, like Wallerstein, stress the significance of an original amassing of wealth in either money or natural forms often tend to beg the fundamental questions. . . . They do not say why such a build-up of wealth 'from the outside'—from the periphery to the core—was necessary for further economic advance." Even more decisive, he continues, is answering "what allowed for, and ensured, that wealth brought into the core from the periphery would be used for productive rather than non-productive purposes."[23]

On their own terms, these responses are very difficult to counter, and perhaps cannot be refuted in the end. A speculative provocation, like my own, on the image-function of the periphery might at this point simply beg off, taking refuge in the position that even if my proposal has little statistical validity, it at least compels postcolonial studies to join the economic conversation. But the data seems to support the cultural theorists in this case, and there is no reason to make concessions since the economists' ripostes are based on an overly restricted line of sight.

With their taught reliance on a discourse of trade conditions, import percentages, financial instruments, and the creation of free labor (when, indeed, labor enters the equation at all, which is very seldom), Fieldhouse and Bairoch, I would argue, overlook entire areas of potential economic inquiry. Cultural theory's work on affect, desire, and ideology, although posed in terms of the wildly new, in fact works to return political economy to its classical self. Remember that the likes of David Hume or Adam Smith would have found it very strange to investigate the economy without supplying a theory of human nature. If psychological and emotional questions are not exactly banished from today's economic calculations (they play a large role in rational choice theory for instance), they are quickly forgotten in debates over the so-called imperial myth. What are these unexplored areas of economic inquiry? Among those things that need to be quantified—that must be assigned value—are unrecompensed, cost-saving services offered by the periphery; economically necessary conditions uniquely provided by the periphery; and, perhaps most crucial of all, the effect of the image-function of the periphery on the behavior of economic actors.

Zones of Invisibility

It is impossible to understand the image-function of the periphery without postulating a deliberate "making invisible" of profits via terminological narrowing. An elementary lesson in all critiques of the image is its subtractive function, even while it supposedly plays an illustrative or visualizing role.

The image of the periphery produces blindness to the recidivist elements of the new economy, suppression of first world material dependencies, and ignorance of the warehousing of labor. One can turn the tables on the critics of dependency theory. For, actually, if capital sought a world uniformly developed or developing, it would be illogical, for it would render a whole branch of profit making impossible. I am positing the necessity under capitalism of a zone of invisibility, and this is my bid for the "serviceable abstraction" I referred to above. Much of the living economy of contemporary capitalism has been rendered invisible by the terminological sluice gates of a Bairoch and a Fieldhouse.

Bairoch, for instance, feels he is merely explaining the confusion of his adversaries when, after a long section detailing why the colonial powers did not substantially benefit from colonial industries or trade, he concludes, "if the West did not gain much from colonialism, it does not mean that the Third World did not lose much."[24] He presents this indulgently in the form of a minor concession to what he considers now devastated interlocutors. But even if one were to agree that the removal from competition of an entire sector of the world economy did not necessarily advance the business of the center (which is by no means clear), Bairoch's point utterly ignores the piquant psychological effects on investment patterns, the limits placed on the demands of organized labor, or the calculus of desperation produced as a result in the peripheral territories. Each in turn is rubbed out of consideration as a noneconomic factor. His conclusion that "the economy is not a 'zero sum game,'" of course, means to rectify the outlooks of the naive who might think a lack of competition improved, rather than stunted, performance; on the other hand, seen as an environmental factor, the economy is indeed a zero-sum game. Put another way, the destruction of third world development subsidizes ecologically unsound businesses. The globe can only take so much, and therefore it can take more from some when others are not in the game. This is what I mean by a relational argument.

Responses to the critics of dependency theory have been eloquently staged by a variety of thinkers — James Blaut, most famously, but also David Harvey and Giovanni Arrighi.[25] But it is perhaps Robin Blackburn, in *The Making of New World Slavery*, who most effectively lays out the case for the intimate relations between Western capitalism's profitability and colonial theft, although a theft that extends far beyond a mere coerced surplus and, rather, entails a system of civilization value. I will not recount his argument here, which extensively documents the reliance of British industrialization on New World slavery by way of providing sources for investment and creating new plantation-related markets. I would only note that after laying the foundation for our enterprise in the American academy, postcolonial theory should now be ready to move beyond the ethical apprehension of othered subjectivity to a more sophisticated engagement with the public and professional discourses of an ongoing colonial system on which capitalism has feasted and continues to feast. It seems to me that Blackburn opens up a vast new field of research when he notes:

> Primitive accumulation . . . is not an episode or a moment, not a fateful biting of the apple located in an antediluvian past, but a continuing and relentless process whereby capitalist accumulation battens on pre-capitalist modes of exploitation, greatly extending their scope, until it has exhausted or transformed them. Capital's thirst for surplus-value and the necessarily uneven advance of mechanization has, indeed, repeatedly produced regimes of *extended primitive accumulation*, in which forced or sweated labour is driven to match the pace of machine industry, and expected to rely on "natural economy" or communal resources for their reproduction. New World slavery was the first and least-camouflaged expression of this capitalist logic.[26]

Here, at this kind of juncture, is where I would propose the sundered options of postcolonial theory (on the one hand, liberation; on the other, comparative cultural value) can be united and serve a common purpose.

A more mature economic theory would allow us to analyze that aspect of capitalism dedicated to rendering unpayment invisible. The hidden grounds of primitive accumulation are directly related to postcolonial work and lie at the heart of capitalist profit making (the introduction of a middle space of exchange, where confusion reigns in order to enact the trickery necessary for a legal appropriation of others' goods: like the "sign" of structural linguistics, capitalism might be seen as a materialist variant of that tripartite mediated space known, in literary studies, as "representation").[27] In globalization, the non-Western world—the former colonies that are still colonies—are assigned the role both as this metaphorical and actual space on a grand scale: an appropriately large middle space in which the unequal exchanges of globalization can be performed as legerdemain.

The colonial system is, following Blackburn, not "post" at all, but finds itself in the very heat of expansion, now wed unmistakably and in the clear light of day to all the most contemporary forms of postmodern image capitalism. Specific regions of the third world—our subdisciplinary object—perform their roles as sites of primitive accumulation. Even as op-ed columnists and pop economic journalists scoff at those who suggest the advanced countries have any use for the periphery at all, enormous (and utterly unacknowledged) profits are generated by its invisible middle spaces.

Companies, for instance, use these often politically defenseless zones for toxic dumping; its vast stretches of rain forest are relied on for the "scrubbing" of polluted air; consumers in poorer countries are routinely marked as subjects for trials involving potentially dangerous products, just as others are rendered experimental subjects for medical procedures. According to a publication of the Public Citizen Health Research Group (PCHRG), in April 1997, in a set of fifteen research studies involving HIV-positive pregnant women, only some of them were given AZT, "a drug that had been shown to reduce dramatically the transmission of HIV from mother to infant."[28] Instead, thousands of women were given placebos, with predictable consequences. Another scandal reported by the PCHRG involved a biotech startup company in Doylestown, Pennsylvania, called Discovery Laboratories that "in collaboration with Johnson & Johnson, manufactures an experimental drug called Surfaxin for the treatment of the often-fatal Respiratory Distress Syndrome (RDS) in premature infants. However, to sell it effectively in North America (where 40 percent of worldwide pharmaceutical sales occur), they need a placebo arm to their study to show that their product is better than nothing."[29] The company has therefore planned trials in Mexico, Bolivia, Peru, and Ecuador. Only a reflexive image of invisibility could erase such an acute advantage from the profit ledger in an argument over comparative value.

And then there is the business of war. Whole populations, often extending over regions or entire countries, by the magic of declaring them (as many US media sources did the Serbians in 1999) a "race of serial ethnic cleansers" are made to constitute a kind of field study on the effects of military weapons on the human body, mental functioning, and the fertility of land. Again, instead of an enemy to be conquered, the targets of US military action often play the valuable role of field experiments on the effectiveness of weaponry. A related source of profit once again lies precisely in the conditions created by neglect and social disarticulation for the weapons trade—one of international trade's most lucrative. Destroying infrastructures, massacring populations, achieving permanent instability is not conventionally thought to be profitable. "Capital hates instability" goes the ready maxim. This clearly no longer holds true. Half the planet lives on 2 billion dollars a day, a billion people on half of that sum. Poverty is profitable provided a low value on human life prevails. As Ted Fishman puts it,

> Countries that in the past counted on the garment and shoe industry now turn to producing for the low end of the arms market. In Mogadishu, there are one million assault rifles for 1.3 million people. Some six million have been killed

in armed conflicts around the world in the last decade, half of them with small arms. . . . There's profit in all that poverty, and it is most cheaply extracted in the form of war. Africa's battles are fought by a labor pool whose wages average 65 cents a day. An enterprising warlord can buy hundreds of willing combatants for the cost of a single American marine.[30]

Rather than being the passive outgrowth of desperate conditions of ambiguous origin, these conditions are implicitly tolerated and perpetuated as the investor feels him- or herself toward the exciting possibilities opened up by regions of chaos—undeveloped certainly, but not outside the market. The bountiful civil strife both feeds an industry and lays the groundwork for that peculiar product of colonialism—the state monopoly, which is not a monopoly because it is sold by the comprador warlord to a foreign state: diamonds and timber in Liberia, cocaine in Colombia, oil in Nigeria. And the old colonial powers have not emerged as the only beneficiaries either. In the new division of the world, Eastern Europe produces a majority of the 10 percent of worldwide illegal small-arms sales to Angola, Sudan, Ethiopia, Sri Lanka, and Congo-Brazzaville (feeding conflicts in which an estimated 10 million have died in the last decade).

Malaysia, Mexico, the Ukraine, and elsewhere have—again invisibly— become the necessary industrial sector of an economy that must officially proclaim itself postindustrial, that is to say, ethereal, beyond mere physical exertion, a product of intellect, skill, and insight as befits a truly futurological, "advanced" capitalism. Why is there no attempt to quantify the profits generated indirectly by the boost to morale or the unquestioning patriotism that grows out of believing the absurd proposition that we live in a postindustrial society? One will hear talk of business climates, but very little about the use-values of those ideological mechanisms that artificially produce climates, as here. These are image-functions inasmuch as they permit a discourse of postindustrialism that has the appearance of plausibility at home, thereby allowing a number of disabling conclusions to be drawn that disorient critiques of the overall crudeness of the operation.

Primitive accumulation, of course, is nowhere more pronounced than in the looting of vital plants used in medicine, or minerals crucial to military and aviation industries (bauxite, phosphorous, manganese), or geological formations or water resources necessary for generating energy or keeping population centers thriving in times of drought.[31] If not quite as profitable, these certainly compete with that old familiar, oil, the world's second most abundant liquid natural resource. Specific exotic plants, since they are not evenly distributed globally, are probably the most site-specific raw materials extracted in the current colonial era. Western doctors are learning from, borrowing, attempting to patent, or finding synthetic versions of nontraditional or culturally specific foreign remedies for diseases.[32] Senna pods from Egypt are used in Western commercial laxatives; Cichona bark from Congo, Zaire, and Uganda is used to treat cardiac arrhythmia; Adpergillus terreus (a fungus) from Pakistan lowers cholesterol; milk thistle from Argentina treats cirrhosis; and ipecac from Brazil, Bolivia, and Peru is a key ingredient in antidotes to poisons. Under the provocative title "Chairman Mao's Cure for Cancer," one article in the *New York Times* recently talked about how arsenic has been used to fight leukemia after its potential was discovered by "a folk healer in rural China" forty years ago.[33] A version of the treatment is now used at Memorial Sloan-Kettering.

According to Antonio Perez of the San Francisco–based NGO Global Exchange, official European and American groups, often set up under benign monikers, are involved in massive biopiracy. The Berlin-directed International Biodiversity Cooperation Group, which grew out of the 1992 UN-sponsored Rio Earth Summit and is funded by the US National Institute of Health, is, according to the Maya Quiche Indians who host them, a "for-profit scheme to put the Mayan herbarium on the global market."[34] Perez argues that 74 percent of all pharmaceutical discoveries are not made in the laboratory, but rather through identification by Indian doctors and healers.

In expanding the categories of utility to be considered in this ongoing debate over the values taken by the West from its periphery, it is important not to forget about the economic advantages of location, in which the peripheral countries provide not only land but the positioning required to host the intricate network of US military bases so vital for policing the financial and commercial dominance of globalization's main beneficiary, the United States. If a domestic real-estate market would naturally calculate the value of commercial property based on its location (proximity to traffic, state of existing infrastructure, etc.), why is this calculation abandoned in the periphery? Following World War II, the United States acquired the most extensive system of military bases that the world has ever seen. According to James Blaker, former senior advisor to the vice chairman of the joint chiefs of staff, "this overseas basing system at the end of the Second World War consisted of over thirty thousand installations located at two thousand base sites residing in around one hundred countries and areas, and stretching from the Arctic Circle to Antarctica."[35]

Among the most poignant image-functions provided by the periphery is simple political difference and variety. This proves a crucial function—one that globalization discourse obscures. For the nation-state system is a kind of smorgasbord of locally varied legal options: in one place offshore accounting; in another, relaxed environmental laws; in a third, a decent transit infrastructure; in another, the complete anonymity of the frontier—whatever can be made use of, in fact, in the juggling act of cornering markets, speculating on futures, outplanning competitors, or turning venture capital into a sure thing (prior to and separate from any interference). This system of "now-you-see-it-now-you-don't" could simply not exist without zones of invisibility. This utility of difference in the service of monopoly was graphically illustrated as the third world bulged with the collapse of the second. After 1989, the introduction of a new logic of property into the Eastern bloc brought with it widespread theft of industrial factories, raw materials, and nuclear material.

And then, of course, one would have to consider the cash boon of tourism, which relies on specific sites outside the territory of the richest countries because of available weather, scenery, anonymous sexual encounters, and cultural enrichment. These might be joined by a related, and alarming, development: the privatization of archaeological treasures, either to generate fees from those who would later study them or from eventual sales to private collectors and museums. None of these find their way into the economic calculations of the values generated for the metropolis by the peripheral countries of the former colonies.

However, I have so far drawn attention to the economic function of the periphery which, although concealed, is not always precisely an image-function except insofar as these material goods are disqualified from economic consideration by virtue of operating in a calculated zone of invisibility. But there is as well, I would argue, a great deal of work to be done on the material role played by immaterial images per se. The periphery, the third world, the regions of carnage and fly-ridden faces so shamefully and luridly depicted in the travel writings of Robert Kaplan, V. S. Naipaul, and Gustave Flaubert, for instance, is wielded as an image of the fearful potential of our own futures, thus serving to discipline labor and silence the middle-class critic. One is reminded of Wolfgang Fritz Haug's comments that "when trade unions made wage agreements during boom periods in the German Federal Republic it was always said that there was an invisible partner at the negotiating table, the Communists, out of fear of whom (or else with a clever eye to them) the ruling class made certain concessions or refused others."[36] Although negatively so, this scenario fairly resembles the role played by Mexico, Morocco, or Zimbabwe in incessant documentaries on television whose purpose is to remind the denizens of tenement halls that they are, for all that, members of the winning side.

The image-function is similarly (although contrarily) a repository of countermodernity—a refuge from capitalism's "libidos-for-sale" (the role it played, for instance, in early dada, the College of Sociology, in situationism, and other intellectual movements, including the left peasant ideology of John Berger). The more prevalent view in postcolonial theory—namely, that commodification has seeped into every pore of the world's most ostensibly premodern sites—is simply unsustainable. This view of a happily chaotic modernity generally considered to be ubiquitous—its penetration complete, and largely welcome—is false. The villages of rural India or of Latin America—with or without television—are hardly *in* modernity in any meaningful sense to metropolitan value. On the contrary (and this is one of the reasons for tourism), the periphery constitutes an important image that functions as a countersystem of value, a hope. Its attractions have to do with the art of conversation, the decrease of speed, the altruistic act of hospitality, and the decommercialization of artistic performance, all of them important psychological and emotional outlets for the negative energy overwhelming a metropolis characterized by anxiety, fear, and restlessness.

There is a vital call for many of us in postcolonial studies to turn our powers of decoding onto these image objects of everyday economic ideology, which remain the most powerful use-values in American imperial sovereignty. More attention to them, I think, would bring us into a fertile collaboration with the disciplines of social history and extramural forms of intellectual activism (from the *Harpers* of Lewis Lapham to speakers at the Porto Alegre summit). If the slavery reparations movement is the most visible example of resistance to an older legacy of primitive accumulation in Blackburn's sense, let me end with a not altogether serious proposal for a movement fitting capitalism's third world image-function.

The great postmodern myth about Las Vegas is that it is all fake. On the contrary, having just visited it, I would say just the opposite: the most striking thing about it is that it is all real. The mosaics are exact copies of those found in Bellagio and Venice, the result of hiring Italy's finest craftsmen. The frescoes are not photographic projections, but real frescoes painted by hand on wet plaster in the old manner. The rain forests in the lobby of the Mandalay Bay have been painstakingly transported from their original location, then planted and cared for to provide covering for its quaint Buddhist shrine. The pyramids of the Luxor are smaller, but built to scale. In the spirit of unpaid debts, and only half-jokingly, I propose that we demand that the owners of the theme casinos in Las Vegas pay royalties, as part of a counterpatent movement, to the governments of Egypt and Burma (let Italy and France fend for themselves) for the concepts in architecture, music, jewelry, and painting that they stole from abroad—concepts without which tourists would never have come. This human creativity—but more, their cultural associations—are what makes Las Vegas attractive, and its profits are to an unacknowledged extent based on them.

Capitalism cashes in on collectivist notions of common ownership in the others it destroys, using their self-sacrifice against them, and putting a for-sale sign on that common ownership while arrogating to itself the role of seller. The story could be told again and again in the electricity, aeronautics, plastics, and television industries, for example—all developed with public funds and later given to businesses—but this pattern could be extended also to the uses of cultural invention. Ideas are routinely stolen from other civilizations and sold to a docile public without even a thought to paying for the goods taken. In an entertainment economy like our own, where fatuous scriptwriters in Hollywood are paid large sums for options on some micro-twist to a clichéd story line (where, in other words, the *concept* is a very valuable commodity indeed), there is not even a hint that there might be a legal claim under the principle of intellectual property rights to folk healing or the copied designs of a theme hotel. If the demand for royalties might in this latter case seem absurd, let us by all means make it anyway to underline the absurdity of a system that sells patents on vitamins, on story lines, and in the future (why not?) on the air. To ask for payment is to expose the process of appropriation occurring asymmetrically on behalf of a country that seeks to extend its national property rights laws universally.

The force of the economic has arisen at punctuated moments in the history of cultural theory. Now, it appears, we are in a time when our work, so long as it turns outward to the social, is simply constrained to go beyond a few received truths cribbed from the New Times cultural studies luminaries of the age of Reaganism. We need to theorize the resilient fact of primitive accumulation and the system of image-functions that propels it.

Notes

1. I explore these arguments in more detail in my "From Development to Globalisation," 32.
2. I am not here opposing theory to some more practical, less elite or arcane practice, but criticizing the monopoly over theory by a collection of genealogical displacements, psychoanalytic treatments of the subject, analyses of discursive power, and ethical demands for decentering. A case both for the necessity of theory and against Theory's peremptory displacements of other theoretical traditions can be

found in Raymond Williams's "Language," in Williams, *Marxism and Literature*, 21–44, which, among other things, disputes that the so-called turn to language was novel.

3. Arjun Appadurai's valuable edited collection, *The Social Life of Things*, provides an interesting counterexample. Appearing in the discipline of cultural anthropology, and exhibiting some of the uneasiness of the social sciences generally, which, after theory, were forced to straddle two methodological imperatives (quantification and representation), the book's focus on commodities appears to be the logical result of the attempt to merge the two: the commodity as an exchangeable thing where exchangeability is a "socially relevant feature" (13). The book's findings are deeply relevant to postcolonial studies, which routinely cites Appadurai's *Modernity at Large*, but ignores this volume.

4. Gayatri Chakravorty Spivak, "Scattered Speculations on the Question of Value," in *In Other Worlds*, 154–78; Myers, *The Empire of Things*; and Jameson, *The Cultural Turn*.

5. Dirks, *In Near Ruins*, 8–9.

6. Spivak, "Scattered Speculations on the Question of Value," 154.

7. Although *For a Critique of the Political Economy of the Sign* remains both a brilliant and neglected book, my use of the term *image* is not taken from Baudrillard. Baudrillard posits a fusion in late capitalism of sign and commodity. The sign-commodity, for him, no longer submits to the dictates of a strictly capitalist logic. Leaving alone the argument's derivativeness (the image as commodity is worked through already in the Frankfurt School and in Debord), his view substitutes what it should supplement. In other words, he ignores the basic manufacturing on which the image is based.

8. Hegel, *The Phenomenology of Mind*, 514–58, esp. 523; G. W. F. Hegel, "Family Capital" and "The System of Needs," in Hegel, *The Philosophy of Right*, 116, 126–33.

9. Simmel, *Philosophy of Money*; Weber, *Protestant Ethic*; Derrida, "That Dangerous Supplement," in Derrida, *On Grammatology*, 141–64; Bataille, *The Accursed Share*, vol. 1; Baudrillard, *Political Economy of the Sign*; Hardt and Negri, *Labor of Dionysus*.

10. Simmel, "The Metropolis and Mental Life"; Bataille, *The Accursed Share*; Debord, *Society of the Spectacle*.

11. And yet this description does not wholly capture her intentions either. Like the present essay, Spivak's "Scattered Speculations on the Question of Value" directly sets out to question the "binary opposition between the economic and the cultural" (166), in order to defend deconstruction against the charge of idealism, and to reject the "metaphysical longing" of Deleuze and Guattari. Presciently, in 1985, she is busy turning our attention to the importance for postcolonial theory of "the globalization of markets" and the "international division of labor" (168).

12. I explore this process in detail in "Antonio Gramsci and Post-colonial Theory."

13. See, for instance, Enloe, *Banana, Beaches, and Bases*; Shiva, *Staying Alive*; Pattullo, *Last Resorts*; Schwarz, *A Master on the Periphery of Capitalism*; Huggan, *The Post-colonial Exotic*; Ginsburg and Rapp, *Conceiving the New World Order*; and Ong, "The Gender and Labor Politics of Postmodernity."

14. The classic work exposing both the structure and pervasiveness of this style of thinking is Blaut, *The Colonizer's Model of the World*.

15. See, for example, Burroughs and Stockwell, *Managing the Business of Empire*, which speaks of Fieldhouse's "shunning [of] monocausal explanation and interpretive strait-jackets," his "distinctive and complementary" approaches to complex issues, and his "illuminatingly traced and incisively analyzed" account of the economics of empire (11, 26).

16. Fieldhouse, *The Colonial Empires*, 84–99; 372–94.

17. Fieldhouse, *The Colonial Empires*, 87; Baran, *The Political Economy of Growth*; Frank, *Capitalism and Underdevelopment in Latin America*; and Amin, *Neocolonialism in West Africa*.

18. The concept that regions are actively underdeveloped is mercilessly ridiculed by the critics of dependency theory. They seem too peremptory in retrospect. One of the principal features of Nobel Prize–winning economist Joseph Stiglitz's recent criticisms of the IMF, for instance, has been his recognition that that institution did indeed cripple peripheral economies by coercing them to make economically harmful decisions. Even after Kenya was devastated by forced financial deregulation (wiping out small farmers), the IMF immediately sought the same remedy for Ethiopia. Eyal Press, "Rebel with a Cause: The Re-education of Joseph Stiglitz," *Nation*, June 10, 2002, 13.

19. A way around this difficulty, and one similar to my own intentions here, can be found in Hall, "Race, Articulation, and Societies Structured in Dominance." He points out that capitalism coexists with, or is "articulated" with precapitalist modes of production, but this coexistence is structured by the dominance of capitalism, which therefore benefits from it. My thanks to Ania Loomba for directing me to this reference.

20. Phillips, *The Enigma of Colonialism*, 156–63.

21. Although partially concurring with Fieldhouse's argument on the doubtful benefits of empire, Patrick K. O'Brien in "The Costs and Benefits of British Imperialism, 1846–1914," concentrates (unlike Fieldhouse) on labor. His conclusions are to that degree more socialized. He observes, for example, that whatever else one might say about it, the empire functioned as an "alternative to social reform and to structural changes within the domestic economy" (200). Precisely. A statement intended to stifle excessive claims of empire's worth to the center, in other words, actually enhances them.

22. Tabb, "Capitalism and Globalization," 317.

23. Brenner, "The Origins of Capitalist Development," 66.

24. Bairoch, *Economics and World History*, 88.

25. Blaut, *Eight Eurocentric Historians*; Arrighi, "Tracking Global Turbulence"; Harvey, *The New Imperialism*; for the attack on dependency theory from within Marxism, see Brenner, "The Origins of Capitalist Development."

26. Blackburn, *The Making of New World Slavery*, 554.

27. Its centrality to this phase of capitalism, as others, is not merely a matter of center-periphery relations, since it forms the cornerstone of domestic policy as well. This became clear, for example, in the Bureau of Land Management's recent collusions with private developers to trade away government lands at below-market values. Joel Brinkley, "A U.S. Agency Is Accused of Collusion in Land Deals," *New York Times*, October 12, 2002.

28. Public Citizens Health Research Group, *Health Letter* 17, no. 4 (2001): 1.

29. Ibid.

30. Ted C. Fishman, "Making a Killing: The Myth of Capital's Good Intentions," *Harpers*, August 2002, 34–35.

31. Bairoch at one point recites the major third world raw materials used in industry in order to show their insignificance to Western businesses (*Economics and World History*, 59–71). While conceding that there has been significant reliance on extraterritorial raw materials after 1950, especially in textiles and specialty metals, he stresses the period before 1950 (for the convenience to his argument, apparently, and without further comment). Before 1950, energy resources such as coal and oil were in sufficient supply in the West for its own uses. Leaving alone the fact that certain kinds of energy were critical to the development of certain industries (oil for the automobile, for instance), which would necessitate a long-term supply not found in Europe or the United States, Bairoch also inexplicably ignores luxury materials and monetary standards. Gold and silver, for example, receive no mention. Nor is there a word about diamonds, teak, or ivory, which played an appreciable role in the course of Western economic development regardless of their percentage of the gross domestic product (GDP). These absences can only suggest bad faith, and they are common throughout the literature.

32. Dawn Mackeen, "The Global Medicine Cabinet," *New York Times Magazine*, May 6, 2001.

33. Elizabeth Rosenthal, "Chairman Mao's Cure for Cancer," *New York Times Magazine*, May 6, 2001.

34. Quoted in John Ross, "Indian Doctors Battle the Devil to Save their Native Plants from Transnational Bio-Pirates," *Mexico Barbaro*, July 28, 2001, 1.

35. "U.S. Military Bases and Empire," *Monthly Review*, March 2002, 2.

36. Fritz Haug, "Some Theoretical Problems in the Discussion of Working-Class Culture," in Haug, *Communication and Class Struggle*, 95.

TWO ◉ Neoliberalism and the Postcolonial World

The End of History, Again?

Pursuing the Past in the Postcolony

❂   ❂   ❂

JEAN COMAROFF

> History as heritage, as an entitlement to rights others may not claim, is the latest
> ploy by those who still resent the fact that Britain changed the way it did when
> black and Asian Britons arrived and presumed to stay. We, the modernizers, the
> radicals and anti-racists, must watch out for the motives and the effects of this
> latest craze. We must be wary when Heritage History is flouted as the new
> gardening, or the new cookery.
> —YASMIN ALIBHAI-BROWN, "History Is Everywhere"

A strange thing happened in Johannesburg, South Africa, on May 24,
2000: five thousand students took to the streets of Braamfontein, near the
University of the Witwatersrand, looting market stalls and smashing car windows. The violence in itself was unexceptional; as one observer noted in a
personal communication, such things often occur at urban rallies organized
by the Congress of South African Students. What *was* surprising was the
stated object of the exercise: the organizers handed a petition to the head of
education for the province of Gauteng demanding that schooling be free of
charge and that history be made a compulsory subject in the upper grades.[1]

This event proved all the more remarkable because there is mounting evidence, in postapartheid South Africa, that young people have scant interest in actually studying history. Both in schools and universities, they show
strong preference for commercial subjects, subjects thought to give entrée
to the Promised Land of the Postcolony—its new entrepreneurial economy.
Not long ago, on August 31, 2001, academics and dignitaries met at the Old
Fort in Johannesburg—formerly a prison that "held freedom fighters in its
cells"—to show "support for the crisis facing history in schools around the
country."[2] The occasion marked the launch by the national education min-

ister, Kader Asmal, of the South African History Project, itself the fruit of
an investigation into the so-called deterioration of history. During the post-
apartheid period, the subject, tainted as a tool of Afrikaner indoctrination,
"virtually disappeared" from school curricula, having been blended into a
bland mélange of "social studies."[3] While the government encouraged public
rituals of remembrance, its critics accused it of fostering collective amnesia
in the classroom. The History Project, financed by the Carnegie Corporation
in the United States, undertook "the huge task of changing perceptions that
history [had become] a dead-end subject." In so doing, it caught the state in a
contradiction. For, having buried school history, the African National Congress (ANC) was now making an official commitment to what Asmal termed
"the relevance of the past . . . [to] the creation of a more liberated present."[4]
Was this perhaps the same contradiction as the one to be read in the riot of
students who both demanded that history be taught and yet seemed reluctant
to study it? One thing is clear, however: whatever its position on history-as-
learned, the ANC regime shows an active interest in history-as-lived, indeed,
in public memorialization. Note, again, that the History Project was inaugurated at the Old Fort, one of the most evocative sites on a new cartography
of popular struggle.

History-as-lived—or rather, history-beyond-the-classroom—is a preoccupation not only of the state in South Africa. For one thing, the liberation
of the media after the fall of apartheid has yielded a vibrant, argumentative
public sphere and a range of popular efforts to revise the colonial past in light
of the postcolonial present. One early instance was a TV series entitled *Saints
and Sinners*. A mix of fact and fantasy, it reevaluated South African history
through a sequence of criminal trials in which heroes and antiheroes alike
were called to answer for their actions—and then held to judgment. The first
episode was striking for its neoliberal denouement. It featured two of the
bitterest antagonists of the remembered past, the Zulu chief Dingane and
the white Voortrekker leader Piet Retief, meeting again in court; Retief is
commonly believed to have been killed on Dingane's orders in an encounter
that, even now, divides white from black historical consciousness. In the
final scene, the two men come to life again and are pictured standing on
the glorious coastline of KwaZulu-Natal. Here Retief makes a proposal to
Dingane: that they bury the historical hatchet, go into partnership, and develop a tourist resort on this sublime shore. This is truth and reconciliation
as farce: while it feigns to deliver a verdict on history, *Saints and Sinners*
is concerned, above all, to allow each protagonist his day in court, permit-
ting them both to tell their stories and to make a clean breast of their deeds.
Their redemption lies less in confronting their contested histories than in

transcending them by submersion into the market where, cleansed of strife, they can be profitably recycled as "heritage."

What sense are we to make of the simultaneous presence and absence of history here, of its assertion and its erasure, its curious new figurations? On the one hand, an ethnography of South African history making suggests that the postcolonial moment is exhilarating precisely for its freedom from the burden of the past, from the weight of historic responsibility: "We [are] tired of all that," says Oscar Warona, charismatic voice of *kwaito*, the hip musical-poetic genre born on Johannesburg's edgy streets after apartheid.[5] This mood has become ever more pronounced as liberation has given way to liberalization, to the mantra of a free-market unconstrained by society or history. Like most millennial visions, redemption through laissez-faire implies radical rebirth and the transcendence of a tainted past. In the postcolony, old sores and scores are settled by therapeutic or legal means, through confession, litigation, reparation; in other words, through processes that aim to reduce complexities of context and cause the better to "put history behind us." By their very nature, these processes discourage analytic evaluation—the sort that is the stock in trade of history as a scholarly discipline, for example. And that kind of history has felt the impact. As Alan Cobley notes, the intellectual debate that has raged for the past decade about the relevance of the discipline in postapartheid South Africa has taken on "an increasingly desperate tone."[6] Terence Ranger goes even further. "History is becoming today what Anthropology was in Africa in the 1950's," he declares, "the discipline that dare not speak its name."[7]

At yet there is copious evidence that the end of apartheid—which came amid seismic shifts in global geopolitics and momentous change in regular modes of communication and representation—has seen the birth of a host of creative new ways of engaging the past. Apart from all else, the project of nation building has called forth fresh forms of public recollection and monumentality: to wit, the government itself—most dramatically, through the Truth and Reconciliation Commission—has promoted the redemptive power of memory and personal testimony.[8] These are historically specific styles of self-narration, though, particular ways of framing what Achille Mbembe calls the "close relation of subjectivity and temporality."[9] They have captivated the popular imagination. Released from the "totally heroic" stance that Njabulo Ndebele has identified in most history making under apartheid,[10] ordinary South Africans have been avidly reclaiming their rights to the past, pressing it into the service of a host of identities, new and old, majestic and banal. On the face of it, this seems an ebullient instance of Simon Schama's "performative history," a genre whose unofficial pedigree in the West links Herodotus to Benjamin—and has vibrant, long-standing African counterparts. Schama notes that Benjamin was especially alive to the fact that those who seek to save history from cynical manipulation must capture memory where they can find it, not least in its fragmentary modern forms, "in the mesh of contemporary wiring" as it were.[11] In like spirit, Schama defends television history as "part of the democratization of knowledge," insisting that ours is not a time to "fetishize the meditative." We must respond to history in its diverse habitations, he goes on, acknowledging its special gifts of freedom, empathy, and community building.

A similar democratizing spirit has been fostered by a host of civic institutions in postapartheid South Africa: evangelical churches and NGOs, popular journalism and TV talk shows, have all endorsed the healing power of memory, life history, confessional narrative. Local traditions are reinvented, long-silent ancestors speak once more. Organic intellectuals offer so-called struggle tours, in which mundane urban scapes express vocal counterhistories—so much so that public life has been overtaken by a growing cacophony of testimonies, a Babel of ever more personal monologues. And so the question arises: amid all the speaking, is anyone listening? One is struck, once more, by the contrast between the parlous state of History, with a capital *H*, and its vitality as a "language of life."[12] But what sort of community can this kind of history be said to be building, given that *community* itself is invoked ever more vacuously, ever more as a beguiling linguistic fiction whose referent remains vague and elusive? Is History being privatized, dissolved into "his story" and "her story," disappearing under the weight of its own success? Does democracy in its neoliberal form, by encouraging novel genres of memory making, actually spell the end of modernist History as we know it?[13] Do all these personal stories add up to History or to its erasure?

In what follows, I can offer only a few rudimentary, anthropologically inflected thoughts on the paradox described. I approach the issue by viewing the pursuit of the past in the postcolony through another, metahistorical lens, one focused on the impact of current global conditions, conditions that have forced the coincidence of liberation and liberalization. This conjuncture is unique neither to Africa nor to the postcolony; much of what I have said about the fate of history is identifiable elsewhere, if in less condensed, dramatic form. The vivid South African case, then, invites broader generalization, of which more in a moment. The urgent debate surrounding the state of South African history, at least for the past decade, has had two major foci: the loss of a sense of paradigm and purpose with the collapse of the coordinates of the late colonial world; and the impact of new theoretical perspectives—poststructuralist, postcolonial—that raise questions about the nature of texts and about the authority, veracity, and transparency they presume.[14] Yet energetic as it has been, this debate has failed, by and large, to connect these two foci—the loss of paradigm and the impact of new theoretical perspectives—or to treat them as integral to the Weltbild of the post–cold war world.[15] In what ways, one might ask, have recent changes in the nature of economy, technology, and the nation-state affected the very experience of social being in time and place? And what are the implications of such shifts for the ways in which we comprehend history, in the here and now, both as a scholarly and as a popular practice?

Reflections on the Postcolony

Let me approach this global moment from an African vantage.[16] It was widely noted in the 1990s that *postcoloniality*, one of many contemporary terms marked by a prefixation on what they are not, is only inadequately translated as "after colonialism." But in the lively debate over what it actually *does* mean, there has been a marked tendency to leave unaddressed the political sociology of actually existing postcolonies. As a result, the postcolonial nation-state has become something of a theoretical stereotype, on whose ground arguments about history, subjectivity, agency, and a lot more besides might proceed unencumbered by facts about particular pasts, particular economies, or particular societies. In fact, *the* postcolonial state refers to a class of polities in motion that is quite diverse, a class to which South Africa is the newest, most celebrated recruit. Yet as I have already implied, this case reveals much about the condition of postcoloniality tout court, making plain the contradictions involved in belated efforts to create modernist polities in postmodern, neoliberal times. In the newly liberated South Africa, history, where it is still offered, is taught for the most part from apartheid-era texts. And the new national History Project is financed not by the state, but by a private American foundation.

Postcolonial state making reaches into diverse realms of collective being-in-the-world: into the struggle to construct a meaningful sense of belonging—and, hence, of moral and material community—in circumstances that privilege difference; into the endeavor to regulate sovereign borders under global conditions that make the transnational movement of labor and capital, money and goods, a necessary condition of the wealth of nations; into the often bitter controversies that rage as people assert various kinds of identity-based claims on the past to secure entitlements in the present; into troubled public debates about the proper reach of twenty-first-century constitutions and, especially, their protection of collective rights; into the complicated processes by which governments, and nongovernmental organizations, seek to carve out a division of political and social labor; into angst about the decay of public order, about crime, corruption, and their policing.

These conditions clearly have broad implications for the ways in which history is defined and deployed. For present purposes, I confine myself to just two of them: the changing basis of belonging and the shifting nature of politics.

First, belonging. If the modernist polity, to recall Benedict Anderson, was erected on a fantasy of cultural homogeneity, on an imagined (if never fully realized) sense of "horizontal fraternity," then most postcolonial nation-states must make themselves out of difference. Born of long histories of colonization, these polities entered the new world order with their own legacies of ethnic division and political incoherence, owing largely to the fact that colonial states, intent on the management of racial capitalism, nowhere constituted nations in the Euro-modernist sense of the term. To this have been added neoliberal conditions that, especially since 1989, have not merely transformed the moral and material sovereignty of nation-states everywhere but have compounded their social heterogeneity: the transnational mass mediation of signs and styles, information and ideologies, therapies and theologies; the rise of an electronic commons; the migration of ever more people in search of work and opportunity; the growing hegemony of the market and, with it, the notion that personhood is constructed through consumption, that culture and history are intellectual property to be possessed, patented, and exchanged for profit. In this world, goes the truism, freedom represents itself as choice: most of all, as choice not merely of identities but of modes of producing them. In light of this, it is one of the great existential ironies of our age that identity appears to have become, simultaneously, a function of voluntary self-production *and* a matter of ineluctable essence, even genetic inscription.

As this suggests, postcolonies do not differ in kind from the modernist nation-states on which they have little option but to model themselves. They are speeded-up, hyperextended transformations of those nation-states; sedimentations, if you will, of the history of Euro-politics running slightly ahead of itself. Hence the familiarity—and analytical relevance—of many of the issues identified here.

Salient among these issues is the changing shape of citizenship. The *im*plosion of identity politics since 1989—which has occurred in rough proportion to the erosion of local communities of labor and political participation—has expressed itself in the marked proliferation of claims to rights and resources made in the name of gender, generation, race, religion, sexuality,

style, culture, and various displacements of class. Also, and more complicated still, in conglomerates of these identity markers, some of which transcend national boundaries, mandating ever more strident demands within
them against the commonweal. As a result, while most postcolonials continue to live as citizens *within* nation-states, they tend only to be condition-
ally citizens *of* nation-states. And the state itself—increasingly assuming the
role of a metamanagement enterprise that attracts investment, subcontracts
its functions, and regulates business—is compelled to treat its subjects as
stakeholders who, while entitled to shares in the polity as corporation, are
also free to indulge their own affiliations, to pursue their distinct interests in
an increasingly planetary field. Herein, then, lies the complexity. The condi-
tionality of citizenship—the fact that it is overlaid and undercut by a fractal
politics of difference—does not necessarily involve the simple negation of
the national identity and national narratives of belonging, but merely their
uneasy coexistence with other priorities.

Of those priorities, cultural identity, congealed in ethnic consciousness
and the imperatives of autochthony, is often taken to be the most elemen-
tal. Such attachment is an historical construction, to be sure. But its aura
as the ineluctable basis of existence rests precisely on the assumption that it
transcends history. As such, as I have already implied, ethnicity partakes of a
doubling: it represents itself as grounded both in a commonality of interest
and entitlement *and* in primordial connectedness; in myth *and* in materialities like soil, bodies, bones, and blood. This doubling, in turn, promotes a
process of reduction: first from history to culture, then from culture to intellectual property as a naturally copyrighted, legally protected collective possession. We are, to put not too fine a point on it, witnessing the dawn of the
Age of Ethnicity, Inc., of Heritage PLC.[17] Indeed, it comes as no surprise that
some ethnic groups struggle to brand distinctive shares in the past, some even
incorporating themselves nowadays as corporations. All of which is why history and identity, in the age of conditional citizenship, are increasingly defined by the capacity to possess and to consume, why social wrongs are translated into the language of rights, why politics, in so many places, threatens
to dissolve into Tom Vanderbilt's specter of "a host of special-interest groups
clamoring in the trading pits of pluralist relativism."[18]

Regarded thus, heterogeneous postcolonies, often benignly characterized
as "multicultural" or "rainbow" polities, take on a more troubling aspect.
As we have argued elsewhere,[19] nation-states in which ethnicity plays simultaneously on primordial connectedness, natural right, and corporate interest
are less multicultural than they are *poli*cultural. The prefix marks two things:
plurality and its politicization. Policulturalism is not a bland agreement to

respect the customs, costumes, and cuisine of minority populations. It is a mode of argument, grounded in a cultural ontology, about the very nature of the pluri-nation, about its constitution, its history, and membership within it, about the spirit of its laws and the terms of its governance. In rural South Africa at present, it takes the form of an ongoing argument between, on the one hand, Euro-modern liberalism and its axioms of politics and history, and, on the other, variously formulated notions of political, legal, and moral difference.

This brings me to the other dimension of the postcolonial present with which I am concerned here: the implication of current conditions for the nature of politics itself, and for the political deployment of the past. As I have intimated, current global conditions have had a marked impact on the terms of liberal-modernist politics, especially in Africa. To many, this has seemed tantamount to a depoliticization of politics itself. The argument goes like this: neoliberal capitalism, in its triumphal phase, offers no ideological alternatives to laissez-faire; nothing else—no other political-economic system— seems even plausible, save as an embodiment of primitive or "fundamentalist" unreason. The primary question left to public policy is how to succeed in the new world order. Why? Because this new order hides its ideological scaffolding in the dictates of economic efficiency and capital growth, in the fetishism of the free market, in the exigencies of science and technology. For those who believe in the fetish, who worship at the altar of the market, its triumph is a matter of manifest destiny, the final victory of rational choice over the axes of evil and error. Under its hegemony, there really exists no such thing as society; the social is dissolved into the natural, the biological, the transactional, or the mythic chimera of community. In this world, there is a strong tendency for politics to be reduced to struggles over so-called special interests and issues: the environment, abortion, health care, child welfare, domestic abuse, human rights, crime, capital punishment. Urgent questions of the moment, often addressed with reference to technical imperatives, become the stuff of collective action, cutting across older lines of ideological and social commitment. Each takes the limelight as it flares into public awareness and then burns down, its embers consigned to the recesses of collective consciousness—only to flame up again if kindled by contingent conditions or vocal coalitions. Or both.

Not that the institutional forms of liberal democracy—the politics of parties and unions, of election and representation—have disappeared. But here, as elsewhere, their significance is shifting in relation to other, ever more compelling modes of understanding and negotiating the operation of power. In Africa, for instance, agents of structural adjustment have labored to make democracy synonymous with privatization and minimal government, as well as with constitutionalism and an almost obsessional reliance on legal regulation. The modernist state, as Leviathan, has always rested on jural foundations, of course. Its citizen has always been a right-bearing subject, all the more so under the impact of neoliberalism, which depends heavily on the ways and means of the law. This reaches its acme in those postcolonies that seek to reinvent themselves as liberal democracies. In such conditions, legal instruments — constitutions and contracts, statutory enactments and judicial procedures — are attributed an almost magical capacity to accomplish order, civility, and justice. Note, in this regard, how many new national constitutions have been promulgated since 1989. In South Africa, the language of legality has become so ubiquitous, the constitution so biblical, that almost every organization feels the need for one.

Why this fetishism of the law? In policultural nation-states, the language of the law offers what is putatively an impartial medium for communicating across lines of difference, thus making it possible to equate unlike values and adjudicate competing claims. In so doing, it creates consonance amid contrast, providing a currency that permits trade in what are otherwise incommensurable interests, across otherwise intransitive borders. Hence the law's capacity, under conditions of social and ethical incoherence, to forge a single discourse, to transmute difference into the appearance of likeness. Hence, too, its hegemony, despite the fact that in the absence of a politics of redistribution, it hardly functions as a guarantor of equality.

The legalism of the postcolony has had a direct impact on the shape and uses of history. The South African Truth and Reconciliation Commission provides a telling instance; its widespread popularity as a model of appeasement in the post–cold war world is evidence of how appealing the legal idiom has become in arbitrating the meaning of the past, even beyond the purview of the courts. The law is given the authority to reduce complex historical processes to narratives of intent and culpability, suffering and victimhood, and hence, to arbitration. The judicial process promises to deliver a verdict, to exact restitution, to settle past inequities, and this on an ever more international scale. In practice, as illustrated by several European precedents,[20] it has proved easier to exact damages for physical atrocities or to demand expropriations of private wealth than to press subaltern claims of historical injustice and dispossession; that much is evident from the furore surrounding recent arguments about reparations in South Africa and the United States. But this, too, is changing. Recently, Kenyans injured by British Army munitions left behind after independence have been awarded significant damages; the London law firm that assisted them is now preparing another case against the British government, this time on behalf of Mau Mau veterans tortured in detention camps in the 1950s.[21] As one reporter noted, success in such a suit might "inspire . . . others . . . from former British colonies."[22] Clearly there are efforts afoot to redefine colonialism as a culpable offense—again reducing history to a charge sheet of individual intentions and personal injuries, to perpetrators and victims.

This effort to put history on trial resonates, I have suggested, with a more general neoliberal ethos, one evident especially in civil courts, where private corporations, like the Swiss banks recently forced to pay $1.25 billion to Holocaust survivors, have proven more indictable than state governments. The Swiss precedent has been cited in a current suit, filed in the US district court in Manhattan by a "group of apartheid's victims,"[23] who seek damages of $50 billion against three banks for breaching international sanctions and, hence, for collaborating in forced labor, murder, and torture.[24] Among the plaintiffs is Lulu Peterson, whose twelve-year-old brother Hector died in the 1976 Soweto uprising and was immortalized by one of the most famous photographs of the struggle years. The two siblings have become iconic of antiapartheid resistance. "We want reparations from those international companies . . . that profited from the blood and misery of our fathers and mothers, brothers and sisters," Lulu Peterson declared, echoing the rationale for a similar movement among descendants of slaves in the United States.[25] As in the American case, the South African action has proved controversial; critics fear that attempts to criminalize liability will undermine efforts to frame a more embracing political settlement authorized in terms of the new constitution. Some in high places even argue that it will discourage foreign investment!

In the legal pursuit of victims' rights, as in the politics of special interest, history is in danger of being made into a commodity, into evidence of entitlement, a charter for stakeholders. These uses of the past brook no indeterminacy; nothing of what Schama identifies as "history's subversion," its attachment to the "bud of awkward alternative outcomes."[26] Litigation also encourages other tendencies associated with the privatization of the past: the assertion of ever less tolerant sectarian differences, of an incorrigible plurality irreducible to common social denominators or collective narratives; indeed, irreducible even to a common argument, save through such universalizing media as money or the law. Hence also the fetishism of the life story and of therapeutic disclosure: these all constitute ineluctably individual atoms of narrated existence that, however they are put together, cannot—with apologies to Adam Smith—add up to the Health of Nations, let alone to a History of the Body Politic or the Body Social.

These conditions pose conundrums for historians everywhere, above all for those who have long argued that decolonization requires a popular rec-lamation of the past (by the 1980s, for instance, the South African His-tory Workshop was sponsoring titles like *Write Your Own History*).[27] On the one hand, they have witnessed a fulsome repossession of this past in places like South Africa. Who would not be deeply moved, as was Shula Marks, by efforts to retrieve the bones of ancestors abducted by former colo-nial rulers or scientific researchers, and this in a context where the restora-tion of the blighted black body has become a powerful ritual for recovering national dignity?[28] Yet, as Marks implies, the poignant pursuit of relics in postapartheid South Africa raises new challenges for critical scholars. Many of us are made uneasy by the fact that, here as elsewhere, the repatriation of remains ironically reproduces the efforts of former oppressors to reduce their subjects to physical ciphers. We are made uneasy, too, by the way in which it reinforces a politics of identity that reduces things historical to car-nal essence. Even more than this, we are unnerved by the spin given to lib-eral terms under neoliberal conditions: how *democratization* comes to de-scribe the pursuit of sectarian interests, how managers and NGOs govern in the name of popular *empowerment*,[29] how arguments for historical justice give way to myths of entitlement that silence the flux and indeterminacy of the past.

This predicament is all too familiar to anthropologists who, having cham-pioned the salience of culture, now see it invoked on all sides, returning to haunt them in a host of embarrassing guises: as race, as entitlement, as prop-erty, as ethnic essence. In arguing that history and culture should continue to inform critical perspectives, then, scholars are often pitted uncomfortably against those who lay exclusive claim to collective patrimony as one of the few resources at their disposal to press their rights and produce a livelihood. One is reminded of Benjamin's assertion that "there is no document of civili-zation which is not at the same time a document of barbarism."[30] Yet as all this suggests, it is increasingly impossible to presume a priori whence, and in what form, comes meaningful social insight. The media and the market democratize the ivory tower in ever more radical ways, both liberating and banalizing our forms of knowledge. It is a matter of record that the popu-lar historical imagination has been fired by a multitude of new opportuni-ties, not all of them demeaning. As critical scholars, we must be prepared to judge when these new means enhance history's enabling possibilities, and when they form part of a mercenary impetus toward ever more profitable, privatizing, and alienating visions—visions dispossessing the past.

Pursuing the Paradox: History in the North West Province

This conundrum, and its implications for the supposedly new South Africa, were palpable during my recent stay in the North West Province, which may serve, here, as a microcosm of the wider field of postcolonial history making. Mafikeng-Mmabatho, the provincial capital, offers a palimpsest of competing pasts. It is the site of the famous Boer War siege, the historic center of the Tshidi-Rolong people, the former administrative headquarters of the ethnic "homeland" of Boputhatswana, and the location of a historically disadvantaged (aka black) university, born in the apartheid era—where I have taught as a volunteer in the Department of History. Soon to be merged with the once exclusively white, ultraconservative University of Potchefstroom, this institution has seen its history enrollments plummet in recent years.[31]

Beyond the academy, however, there exists a heady array of activities that seek to take hold of the past: again, the difference between history-as-learned and history-as-lived. The Tshidi-Rolong boast famous lay historians like Dr. Modiri Molema and Solomon T. Plaatje,[32] and their legacy lives on. "I [cannot] claim to be some . . . expert," wrote Tswagare Namane in "Searching for Tswana Heritage" on the op-ed page of the (Mafikeng) *Mail* a few years back, "and yet . . . I feel deserving to be heard." The future of the North West region, like the rest of postcolonial Africa, he noted, was likely to become ever more reliant on tourism. This would require more than hotels or game parks. It would necessitate uncovering "what is authentically Tswana." But commercial motives do not necessarily cheapen the quest for identity. Added Namane: "I have walked around in search of anything genuinely mine; something I could hold on to [in] my heart and cherish as a true achievement of my forebears, something to affirm my humanity and assert my equality to all."[33]

This restless urge, he suggests, might well be particularly urgent among those deliberately dispossessed of their past. "What I am reclaiming is my ethnicity, my heritage, not my 'ethnicism,' a propagation of apartheid." Heritage, I have stressed, is history and culture as legacy, a quality to be alienated in the market, thereby reproducing identity in its postcolonial form. This alienation of cultural essence in the current age seems, in fact, to have replaced the sale of labor power that underpinned subaltern existence in the colonial industrial economy, during an age when identities were a matter of race and class, rather than location in an ethnically coded marketplace.

In short, difference has come to be a source of opportunity and entitlement rather than the invidious discriminations of capitalism, colonial-style—although the latter, alas, are by no means extinct. Namane's effort to draw a nice distinction between ethnicity and ethnicism underlies an enduring ambivalence about the status of culture as political force in South Africa, one which separates supporters of the modernist ANC regime from proponents of ethno-nationalism. For the modernists, history exemplifies the triumph of secular civility over parochial distinctions, a view that makes culture a matter merely of the ceremonial; it might give local color to citizenship, but it cannot provide its substantive basis. In contrast, ethno-nationalists of all hues invoke what they term tradition to challenge, ever more vociferously, the very crux of identity and the sovereignty of the constitution. Hence *poli*culturalism. This tension cuts to the heart of everyday life in the countryside, where the ruling regime has been drawn into increasingly strident, often litigious debate with customary authorities. The funeral in Mafikeng of chief Setumo Montshiwa of the Tshidi-Rolong, himself both an ANC sympathizer and an active member of the national House of Chiefs, proved a ready site for pursuing this conflict on a cold gray morning in July 2000. Much of the proceedings, which attracted five thousand mourners, several representatives of the national government, and TV crews from across the nation, was given over to competing orations of history. State functionaries commended Setumo's loyalty to the liberation movement and his participation, as a voice for enlightened custom, in the South African rainbow coalition. By contrast, Tshidi royals intoned a history of local political independence, recounting a long struggle by their rulers to remain free of overlords of all stripes.

But the story did not end there. For the neoliberalization of history's means and motives has also affected vernacular ways of contesting the past, among them the genealogical arguments that frame the bitter succession disputes that often mark chiefly deaths here—as elsewhere where blood and inheritance determine the distribution of spoils, a principle revitalized in many parts of the world in the age of Ethnicity Inc. The case of Setumo Montshiwa proved no exception, the value of his office now enhanced by a regular salary and benefits. Accordingly, late one afternoon in March 2000, we received a harried phone call from the anthropologist at the provincial Department of Traditional Affairs. He needed to consult us urgently on the matter of the Tshidi-Rolong royal family tree, soon to be debated in an action brought to the high court by rival factions contesting the chiefship. The conflict had more than once brought the Public Order Police to the tribal office, where disputants came to blows over rival accounts of history, waving genealogical charts with dramatic flourish. At issue was the status of polygynous houses and the seniority of descent lines dating back more than a century. One party commissioned a video chronicle of the dispute, gathering testimony from various authoritative elders and selections from the copious coverage of the conflict on local TV. The well-established art of arguing over succession has now become a media spectacle, drawing on the services of legal and cultural consultants—and abetted by the ever more lucrative rewards of laying claim to tradition.

The neoliberalization of history has fueled the reclamation of other historical figures as well, some of them predictable, others quite bizarre. There exists a new sense of license among many South Africans to explore the subjectivities of those who, until recently, were the very embodiment of otherness past. A form of *jouissance*—to use Lacan's term for the mix of enjoyment and outrage at play in this sort of impersonation—has become visible in a range of locations: in novels like Achmat Dangor's celebrated *Kafka's Curse*, notable for the virtuosity with which the protagonist assumes an array of ethnically diverse identities, of selves both old and new.[34] Or in the less conventional register of the supernatural, postapartheid citizens of all stripes appear very susceptible, at present, to possession by restless ghosts who haunt public battlegrounds and private consciences, and whose appeasement is the work of a wide array of exorcists, evangelical healers, or diviner detectives.[35] But there are also more quotidian cases: like the Christmas play in a Mafikeng junior school in 1999, where a group of Tswana girls enthusiastically donned the headdress and skirts of nineteenth-century Afrikaner Voortrekkers to perform a spirited version of "Sarie Marais," a well-known Boer folk song, while their white male counterparts endeavored, not quite so successfully, to execute a Zulu war dance in blackface.

In the case of some especially charismatic historical figures, spirited struggles have taken place to claim possession of their aura. This has been evident with respect to Solomon T. Plaatje, acclaimed writer, articulate black nationalist, and diarist of the siege of Mafikeng, about whom there have been numerous radio and TV documentaries at home and abroad. Reinstated as a leading black intellectual of the early twentieth century, Plaatje's house in Kimberley (where he lived between 1894 and 1898) has become a national museum, and his works are now read in schools across the nation. Raised on a mission station at Pniel, he married into the royal family of the Tshidi-Rolong and lived in Mafikeng for some years, first as court interpreter during the siege, then as editor of one of the first African language newspapers, *Tsala ea Batho* (*Friend of the People*). Since the transition, civic leaders in Mafikeng have been eager to patent his image, expressing irritation at having to share his luster with their counterparts in Kimberley. A school and a street now bear his name, and his visage—under the legend "Bard of the Batswana" and "indefatigable fighter for human rights"—graces local postcards and tourist posters. Meanwhile, faculty at the University of the North West, while expressing distaste for such commercialization, have themselves established the annual Plaatje Lecture. Those who claim to be direct descendants, not to be outdone, have produced a range of personalized heirlooms and anecdotes, his great nephew having striven to have his own Victorian home, in which Plaatje lived during the siege, declared a private museum—all this in the fervent hope of attracting sightseers. As Gary Minkley and his colleagues observe of the country as a whole, the competition to "[bring] home the tourists" has become an integral part of the rhetoric of establishing and developing a postapartheid "community"—that elusive word again.[36] If history is to be the source of commonwealth here, clearly it will be as commodity. But the Plaatje legacy also proves a bankable political asset. At least one descendant, prominent in the new provincial administration, has taken "Plaatje" as a second surname.

Refiguring historical subjectivities has sometimes entailed a rereading of epic events and relations. A prime instance of this was occasioned by the centenary of the Anglo-Boer War, which provided funding to local communities to develop sites on a commemorative route that enabled visitors to trace the progress of the conflict across the country. We were startled, on our return to the Tshidi-Rolong royal court in 1999, to find a prominent bronze bust of Besele I, who was chief during the siege of Mafikeng. Thirty years before, when apartheid reigned supreme, Besele was all but forgotten, his drunken and ineffectual governance taken as emblematic, by both blacks and whites, of the decline of a once historically significant people. During those years, this ignominious past was illuminated by one proud memory: the alliance between the Tswana residents of Mafikeng and their British allies during the famous investment of 1899–1900. But those were different times, when the past truly *was* another country. We were soon to learn that, with the end of apartheid, colonial history was being rewritten, sometimes in surprising ways.

It had, indeed, become obvious that in the rapidly desegregating towns of the North West Province, Africans and Afrikaners had reached a new accommodation. It has now become chic for Tswana speakers to punctuate their conversation with Afrikaans, that once reviled language; just as the acting vice chancellor of the University of the North West, whose own research focused on a thoroughly postcolonial concern with Afrikaner supernaturalism, could comfortably perform a Tswana praise poem of his own composition at a gala dinner in 1999. The two populations might not yet be on intimate terms, but they are increasingly drawn together in commerce and on the sports field. And they are wooed, side by side, into the rousing new-age churches whose healing rites and prosperity gospels mark out a vital, enchanted public sphere that speaks to a shared sense of thwarted desire, of development deferred, in the arid countryside. Above all, current conditions have occasioned a palpable revaluing of *past* alignments: as a venerable Tshidi elder, himself a former teacher of history, informed us at a meeting in 2000, his brethren had come to see that it was in fact the British who had been their most insidious historical enemy. The Boer War, he declared, constituted an archinstance of imperial plunder. Far from being allies of the British, the Tswana had been betrayed by a perfidious liberalism (he intoned the phrase in English). Despite copious promises of reward, their coopera-tion had not prevented them being sold into colonial bondage like all the rest. Blacks and Boers had in fact shared a similar fate at the hands of such imperialism—a claim increasingly echoed in the popular and political cul-ture of those who now like to style themselves as "white Africans."[37] For their part, local Tshidi elites tell a revised story of the (renamed) South Afri-can War. An independent, ethnically indexed account, it is one in which their own heroes and rulers—among them, the hapless Besele—are named and re-instated. And one in which the British are said to have reneged on a loyalty-for-land deal. In the age of policulturalism, there is a strong impetus to pri-vatize great historical events and, simultaneously, to root chronicles of local difference and material entitlement on the terrain of grand history—thereby restoring a sense of distinction and a brand of marketable difference. For, as I have stressed, the two have increasingly become conditions of each others' possibility.

But the circumstances that have abetted all this organic history making have also undermined the status of history as academic discipline. I return, here, to my opening paradox. At the University of the North West, the multi-racial faculty responsible for the subject have been marginalized both by stu-dent disinterest and by their distance from the remaining strongholds of re-search scholarship in South Africa. Yet they have also sought to make virtue of necessity, joining the national debate about how the discipline might be revived. As former history lecturer Neil Roos wrote to the director of the South African History Project:

> My teaching experience at UNW, where most of the students are from rural areas and country towns, has alerted me to the pitfalls of "national" history, and suggests a need to move beyond the iconographic level, with its predict-able focus on "big" national events and figures. . . . I teach a course in heritage studies, and my students have frequently expressed frustration at the tenuous connections between their own lives and the way in which the emerging na-tional narrative (e.g. the Sharpeville massacre, the symbolism of Robben Island; Mandela-ism) is commemorated. . . . I have tried . . . to [encourage them] to re-call their own family and local stories of poverty, oppression and resistance . . . experienced mainly in the Bophuthatswana homeland.[38]

Incorporating stories from the margins, he went on, would lend credibility to history as a scholarly discipline, especially on the rural periphery. His views echo the appeals of others, like Colin Bundy, then vice chancellor of the University of the Witwatersrand, who has called for a school curriculum that stresses the complexity of the past, rather than offering a "bland, sanitized" narrative of nation building.[39] Some also reinforce Roos's methodological concerns: Haroon Mahomed, of the Gauteng Institute of Curriculum Development, fears that "the history revivalists are reverting to a pedagogy that focuses on the old fashioned pursuit of objective historical truth through texts, instead of looking into oral traditions, culture, and other forms of knowledge."[40]

But, in the North West Province, those who advocate studying local traditions tend to talk past those who live them, and vice versa. To underscore the ironies that flow from this, local Tshidi-Rolong elders have been assembling oral and documentary evidence stretching back to the late nineteenth century in order to press a claim that the University of the North West, and its history department, are built on their ancestral cattle posts, that, by rights, this house of learning belongs to them.

Conclusion

I began this reflection by noting the signal irony that, in South Africa, history seems to have been disappearing in the academy in direct proportion to the degree to which it is being made elsewhere—as popular revolution, as media spectacle, as national pageant, as intellectual property, as recovered memory, as therapy. True, the present might be a moment of hiatus between a discredited past and a time when new narratives take shape that are more suited to the postcolonial present, narratives that might inform a long-awaited new school curriculum and the rewriting of text books. To be sure, the emergence of a grand narrative—whether as the triumphal tale of "new nationalist masters"[41] or a more multivocal, rainbow chronicle—has thus far been deferred, not merely because of a necessary debate about the form and content of a new history, about the balance of Western and Afro-centered perspectives, of texts and oral traditions of fact and theory—although, patently, there *is* plenty of debate.

At work, also, I have suggested, is something else. A history of history, so to speak, itself the product of forces reshaping the postcolony along with the rest of the neoliberal world; forces ushering in an age of policulturalism and a pluralization of the past; forces that have radically privatized memory, multiplying the means of communication and the bases of belonging.

Under such conditions, history is endangered less by its appropriation by the powerful than by its unrestrained indulgence, its diffusion to everywhere and hence to nowhere in particular. There may be situations in which there is just too much history, as Terence Ranger recently remarked.[42] An infinite regress of assertive voices threatens to postpone, indefinitely, the process of shared *re*collection, the subsuming of difference into an overarching totality—even if only as a field of dispute—against which claims can be relativized and difference measured. Let us hope that in contexts like the new South Africa, where so much hangs in the balance, a moment of recollection will soon be reached; that history will emerge not as a trading pit of alterities, nor as a "triumphal procession in which the present rulers step over those who are lying prostrate," but as an argument joined about various, reciprocally entailed histories in a *field* of interrelated narratives.[43]

In contemporary Britain, where the old monologue of empire finds itself disrupted ever more audibly by the assertive presence of postcolonial populations and where heritage has become a public passion, there is also—at least, according to Yasmin Alibhai-Brown—a troubling lack of "interactive debate" across lines of historical difference.[44] Yet the very possibility of a new history rides on promoting such argument, she insists, argument that requires recognition of the interdependence of what were once colonizer and colonized. At issue is a willingness to see one another as "joint [if not yet equivalently endowed] custodians of the past and the future." It is only by accepting the analytic and political challenges of a shared fate that it will be possible to arrive at a critical history of the postcolony itself and, because it is inseparably part of this process, of the postcolonial metropole. Only thus will we be capable of reconsidering the role of history, both learned and lived, in an ever more unequal, interdependent world.

Notes

1. "Stalls Looted, Car Windows Smashed as Students March," *Pretoria News*, May 25, 2002.
2. Nawaal Deane, "New Lease for History," *Weekly Mail and Guardian* (Johannesburg) August 31, 2002.
3. Sasha Polakow-Suransky, "Reviving South African History: Academics Debate How to Represent and Teach the Nation's Past," *Chronicle of Higher Education*, June 14, 2002, available at chronicle.com/prm/weekly/v48/i40.40a03601.htm.
4. Deane, "New Lease for History."
5. Quoted in Douglas Rogers, "Straight Outta Jo'burg," *Guardian*, July 20, 2002.
6. Cobley, "Does Social History Have a Future?" 624.
7. Terence Ranger, "History Matters," valedictory lecture, University of Zimbabwe, May 31, 2001, 4. Ranger argues that history has remained more vital in Zim-

babwe than South Africa—this for various reasons, mainly the greater dependence
of the Zimbabwean regime on historical validation. In fact, the protracted political
crisis in that country probably mediates many of the influences considered here. At
the same time, Ranger does provide evidence that both in schools and university,
Zimbabwean history might well be "dying a natural death" (8).

8. Cobley, "Does Social History Have a Future?" 618.

9. Mbembe, *On the Postcolony*, 15.

10. Ndebele, *Rediscovery of the Ordinary*, 47.

11. Simon Schama, "Television and the Trouble with History," *Guardian*, June 18,
2002.

12. Mbembe, *On the Postcolony*, 15.

13. See Joyce, "The End of Social History?"

14. See Bunn, "The Insistence on Theory"; Nuttall and Wright, "Exploring History with a Capital 'H,' " 38; Gary Minkley, Ciraj Rassool, and Leslie Witz, "Thresholds, Gateways, and Spectacles: Journeying through South African Hidden Pasts
and Histories in the Last Decade of the Twentieth Century" (unpublished paper);
McGrath et al., *Rethinking South African History*; and Cobley, "Does Social History
Have a Future?"

15. See Rich, "Is South African Radical History Becoming Irrelevant?"

16. This section draws on several previously published accounts of the making of
the postcolony: Comaroff and Comaroff, "Alien-Nation"; Comaroff and Comaroff,
"Naturing the Nation"; Comaroff and Comaroff, "Millennial Capitalism."

17. John Comaroff and Jean Comaroff, "Ethnicity Inc.: On the Commodification,
Consumption, and Incorporation of Cultural Identity." Deutsche Bank AG guest lecture, Johann Wolfgang Goethe Universität, Frankfurt/Main, November 18, 2002.

18. Vanderbilt, "The Advertised Life."

19. Comaroff and Comaroff, "Ethnicity Inc."

20. The compensation paid to victims of Nazi dispossession, for instance, or to
survivors of Japanese detention during World War II.

21. Gakuu Mathenge, "British Lawyer Prepares for Mau Mau Suit," *Daily Nation
on the Web*, November 25, 2002, available at www.nationmedia.com/dailynation/
olderarchives.asp?archive=true; Mike Thompson, "Mau Mau Rebels Threaten
Court Action," BBC News–World, Africa, available at news.bbc.co.uk/1/hi/world/
africa/2429227.stm.

22. Mathenge, "British Lawyer Prepares for Mau Mau Suit."

23. There is a growing tendency for non-Americans to turn to US tort law in efforts
to press claims for social justice against international bodies (both corporate or political), whether or not the latter in any key sense constitute US operations. This
underlines the extending hegemony of American legal culture across the globe.

24. McGreal, "Banks Sued for $50bn in SA Class Action," *Guardian*, June 18,
2002.

25. In the South African case, however, it is agents of international capital who
are the object.

26. Schama, "Television and the Trouble with History."

27. Witz, *Write Your Own History*; see also Minkley, Rasool, and Witz, "Thresholds, Gateways, and Spectacles."

28. Marks, "Rewriting South African History." Marks is most directly concerned
with the search, in the Scottish highlands, for the head of Hintsa, the Xhosa king

killed and dismembered in 1835 in a military effort to prevent the colonial expansion of the British in the Eastern Cape. Other South African instances include the successful campaign of the Khoi people for the return of the remains of Saartje Baartman, the so-called Hottentot Venus abducted to Europe in the early nineteenth century and whose genitalia were, until recently, on show in the Musée de l'Homme in Paris; and the bones of Griqua leader Cornelius Kok II, recently returned to his descendants by Dr. Phillip Tobias of the University of the Witwatersrand Medical School. See Adam Cooke, "Griqua Chief Fumes as Tobias Hands over Bones," *Star*, August 21, 1996; and David Hearst, "African Woman Going Home after Two Hundred Years," *Guardian*, April 30, 2002. A further case, as yet unresolved, involves the missing skeleton of the man held to have been the first king of the rapidly "retraditionalizing" Mamone Bapedi of Sekhukhune, who was hanged by the Boers a century ago. See Oomen, "Chiefs, Law, Power, and Culture," 164–65.

29. See Gabriel Cwele on the changing politics of student government in contemporary South Africa. Cwele, "Student Politics in Postapartheid South Africa," paper presented at the Social Science Research Council workshop on youth and globalization, Dakar, June 7–10, 2002.

30. Benjamin, *Illuminations*, 256.

31. For details of this reorganization, see B. Mbenga, "Re: Staff Profiles at South African Universities #5," March 16, 2000, posted on H-SAfrica@H-Net.MSU.EDU; see also Cobley, "Does Social History Have a Future?" 624.

32. See Molema, *The Bantu, Past and Present*; Molema, *Chief Moroka*; and Molema *Montshiwa*; Plaatje, *Native Life in South Africa*; Plaatje, *The Diary of Sol T. Plaatje*; Plaatje, *Selected Writings*; and Willan, *Sol Plaatje*.

33. Tswagare Namane, "Searching for Tswana Heritage," *Mail*, March 4, 1994.

34. Dangor, *Kafka's Curse*.

35. The latter range from "traditional" practitioners to members of the Occult Related Crimes Unit of the South African Police Services. See Comaroff and Comaroff, "Millennial Capitalism."

36. Minkley, Rasool, and Witz, "Thresholds, Gateways, and Spectacles," 25.

37. Witness the South African movie, *Final Solution* (2001; directed by Cristobal Krusen), whose Afrikaner hero, a champion of reconciliation, is described as a member of "Africa's white tribe" and as the son of a famous "freedom fighter" executed by the British during the Boer War. The theme appears again in the political rhetoric of the leader of the New National Party, Marthinus van Schalkwyk, who seeks to link Afrikaner and African identities by citing their common history of British oppression.

38. Dr. Neil Roos, letter to Dr. June Bam, December 10, 2001, Mafikeng.

39. Polakow-Suransky, "Reviving South African History."

40. Ibid.

41. Charles can Onselen, as quoted in ibid.

42. Ranger, "History Matters," 12. Ranger was in fact speaking, in a slightly different sense, of apartheid South Africa, but I find his phrase even better suited to the present.

43. Benjamin, *Illuminations*, 256.

44. Yasmin Alibhai-Brown, "History Is Everywhere—But Whose History Is It?" *Independent*, July 22, 2002.

A Flight from Freedom

⊘ ⊘ ⊘

ELIZABETH A. POVINELLI

> Why is it that the very name which allows modern philosophy to think and designate
> the originary freedom of the human being—the name of "subject"—is precisely the
> name which historically meant suppression of freedom, or at least an intrinsic
> limitation of freedom; i.e. subjection?
> —ETIENNE BALIBAR, *Supposing the Subject*

Freedom: not God, and yet as difficult to approach and as surely the
banner under which we have witnessed centuries of both extraordinary social good and social terror. Even as I write, states are inching toward and
resisting a potential global upheaval in its name. Such indeed is the nature
of freedom that it can seem more godlike than God. Any evil perpetuated in
freedom's name is exiled from its truth. We hear: Well, that was not really
about freedom but about the interests of oil companies; or, worse, about the
interests of particular CEOs and statespeople who use business corporations
and political positions to swell their private bank accounts. In secular states
we are free to worship any god we choose. But can we choose not to worship
freedom? In this way, freedom is the Law of law; it distributes the values of
truth and falsity, good and evil, without being subject to them. How can one
think critically in its vicinity, even in such explicitly secular spaces as the
academy, especially during these decisive times? More important, how can
one refuse freedom without embracing its twin, unfreedom; or, I should say,
without embracing the various names given to the condition of unfreedom
by a discourse of freedom: bondage, oppression, subjection, enthrallment.
Social subjection—note, not self-subjection—seems to exist merely as freedom's negation.[1]

I want to speak here against freedom, notwithstanding the reverence I
hold for social critique and the benefits I have derived from it. After all, the

first critical response to this essay could well be that it is a social orientation to freedom that allows me to speak against freedom in the first place—that social critique is only authorized in, and by, freedom. An equally cogent critique might point out that, no matter the ultimate reality of freedom as a state of being, its authority has been constitutive of a variety of social goods for a variety of subjugated social groups. Homosexuals, colonial subjects, women, and indigenous worlds: all have seemed to benefit from their struggle for freedom. So let me be careful at the start to say more precisely what I want to speak against, and for.

By assuming a stance against freedom, I am not assuming a stance against the aspiration to be rid of any specific form of social life, to be done with the social relations that enchant power today. I am instead contesting a normative orientation to, and aspiration for, a state of social nondetermination, something generally understood as self-governance, whether that self be at the scale of an individual, a couple, a culture, or a state. The notion of freedom as a freedom from social hindrance—the notion that we can, or should, be moving toward not only a world of less social hindrance but an ideal world of no social obstruction at all—is typically conceived in the political science literature as a form of negative freedom. But it will be clear that I am strongly distancing myself from positive formulations of freedom as well. Indeed, the premise of this essay is that freedom is not a good orienting device for subaltern social struggles, not merely because it is "wrong" in a descriptive sense, though this, too, is true—life does not, and cannot, operate in a state of radical freedom. Instead, an orientation to freedom as a state of social nondetermination (1) sets into place a specific vector of responsibility and accountability for the harms of given social life away from those who profit toward those who suffer; (2) aligns itself to the worst excesses of capitalism; and (3) reduces possibilities for social elaboration and social critique. I want to explore, in contradistinction to this imaginary of freedom, an alternative ground for social struggle—an orientation to the irreducible, and necessary, embeddedness of life. I will be arguing that the form of a given embeddedness is the sedimented result of a history of social composability in the context of institutions of social intelligibility and livability. This essay elaborates what I mean by these notions of *embeddedness, social composability, social intelligibility,* and *livability.* I hope the notion of embeddedness and the histories of its composability contribute to a positive detour around the dialectic of freedom and dependency.

In spirit, this essay constitutes an extended meditation on a long passage in Frantz Fanon's "Concerning Violence" and the trouble Fanon's work poses to approaching the problem of freedom critically. Less than a third of the way into his difficult essay, Fanon posits what a "genuine eradication" of the colonial order would consist of after a "real struggle for freedom" had taken place. "Individualism is the first to disappear," Fanon argues, carefully describing what he means by individualism—"the idea of a society of individuals where each person shuts himself up in his own subjectivity."[2] This disappearance responds to a social and a philosophical field—to the Algerian struggle, as well as the existential struggle so well put by Fanon's French colleague Simone de Beauvoir: "If man is once enclosed within himself, how can he get out?"[3] Fanon's answer on both fronts is equally, if deceivingly, clear: "The very form of organization of the struggle will suggest [to the native intellectual] a different vocabulary. Brother, sister, friend—."[4] These forms remind the native intellectual of the positivities of social embeddedness. Lest he be mistaken as an anthropologist of naive communalism, Fanon insists that "self-criticism" and "analysis" are immanent in and to the relational terms he evokes.[5] If we do not rush to understand this "group-criticism" as just another Stalinist form of social subjection, how might an orientation to a critical social embeddedness solve the problem of the individual's self-encasement without triggering the specter of his or her oppression? Put another way, why doesn't a real struggle for freedom oppose social reabsorption? If I am irreducibly in, of, and through *my sister*, what of *my* freedom?

To answer these questions, this essay engages the enthrallment of freedom by first reengaging the persistence of the sovereign subject as a social aspiration and an institutional condition of postcolonial value. This engagement has a specific end: to understand how international social struggles are continually deflected by, if not into, a hierarchy of values produced and institutionalized by the subject of freedom. Concretely, I want to address why some techniques of the self or the social—worlds of religious piety, of kinship, of sexual carnality—are liable to, and disabled by, a characterization of them as unfree? I think part of the answer depends on developing a symptomatic reading of contemporary metadiscursive approaches to subjectivity in language.[6] My wager is that in grappling with the social nature of linguistic subjectivity, metadiscursive approaches have generated a privileged, if symptomatic, insight on one aspect of the form of power that is freedom. This symptomatic reading—inspired equally by V. N. Volosinov's *Marxism and the Philosophy of Language* and Louis Althusser's *Reading Marx*—is not a critique of contemporary metadiscursive approaches, but an acknowledgment of the clarity they provide to a reading of liberal ideological foundations of freedom.

No matter how closely this essay examines the metadiscursive form of subjectivity, it refuses the claim that the formation of social subjectivity can be reduced to abstracted linguistic forces and functions. I hope to show how institutions of intelligibility and livability overdetermine the grammatical surface of language and, thus, the function of language as an intuitive resource, and brace, of the subject. The linguistic resources of subjectivity are embedded in these institutions. These in turn disturb the global terrain of social struggle, differentially distributing discursive and material values. It is the disturbance these institutions create on the surface and in the depths of social struggles that this essay seeks. Thus if this essay begins with the semiotic conditions of freedom, it ends with discussing how they establish and maintain an international division of civilizational authority and material distribution such that Western and non-Western worlds are projected out into global social space, and projected out of a specific hierarchy of value. The worth of the sympto-analytic reading this essay produces depends, for me, absolutely on the insight it provides us on the uneven terrain of global social struggles, their rhetorics of responsibility and accountability, and their production of life, death, and rotting worlds.

Surely, the sovereign subject can now be left for dead? After all, first desire then discourse long ago loosened man's (reasoned) authority over himself. What is the sovereignty of reason since Freud but the anxious agency of discourse halfway between the speaking subject and the social norms she or he depends on to speak? From Freud to Michel Foucault we have witnessed the inauguration of new questions. We ask no longer who speaks but from where this discourse comes and what objects it produces. So let us ask these questions, paying close attention to the semiotic features of the sovereign subject: What are the conditions of intelligibility and livability in which this subject—who remains, if wounded, an ideal even after desire, even after discourse—is embedded? What work do these conditions of intelligibility and livability do in organizing the global distribution of social values?

A critical aspect of these conditions of intelligibility and livability is the characterization of the reflexive enclosure of the subject as freedom and the subject projected out of this enclosure as free. The self-made man, who emerged with a historical force during the age of revolution, is possible only under very specific metadiscursive social conditions. Etienne Balibar suggested as much in his discussion of the subject in the early modern Western canon. In "Subjection and Subjectivation," Balibar argued that even those Europeans who saw the sovereign subject as not only possible but vital, understood this subject's relation to freedom as inaugurating a new form of subjection. In Augustine's discussion of how a man "subjects himself to himself," Europeans glimpsed for the first time a form of obedience, self-obedience, that was not "an inferior degree of humanity, but on the contrary a superior destination, whether terrestrial or celestial, real or fictitious."[7]

And yet, this subject was anything but free, in the sense of undetermined, in two ways. First, in projecting himself as his own authentic ground, the Augustinian subject could be said to become sovereign. But at this moment, self-discipline emerged not only as a viable but also as a necessary practice of human freedom—the telic and ontic truth of man would not be in his *essence* but in his obedience to a specific *semiotic practice*. As Foucault long ago observed, the price Europeans paid to free themselves from the external social constraints of familial, aristocratic, and religious power was that they assumed their own self-management. This self-management would later, especially under the pressure of the psychoanalytic mandate, become rethematized as the anxiety that the subject paid for the price of becoming a subject as such. But by that time, the contract between power and self-authorization would have insinuated itself into the very tissues and membranes of practices of care, as Foucault's student, Jacques Donzelot, would show in his study of the emergence of the bourgeois family and social welfare in France, and as Ann Stoler would demonstrate in practices of colonial childcare.[8] That is, the self-made subject is not determined merely because it is self-determined but because it is a social mandate—a social determination.

How self-obedience came to be understood as self-autonomy and freedom is, of course, the subject of no little controversy. Marxist historians like E. P. Thompson and Eric Hobsbawm have located the origin of self-subjectification as a liberatory project not in the canonical texts of traditional philosophy but in the historical struggles of specific groups. Contests over the meaning and direction of social revolutions in the seventeenth and eighteenth centuries spawned a new form of human being from the ashes of aristocratic society—the parvenu, that is, the self-made man.[9] History was inverted: man would be measured by his end rather than by his beginning. One of the projects of the academic Left has been to understand how struggles for freedom from specific forms of social oppression were transformed into institutions of individual "liberty," that is, the movement from an action-oriented socially embedded politics to a state-oriented politics and the transformation of radical social projects into liberal individual contracts.

A different set of European historians have challenged the claim that the individual was first freed from the chains of familial and feudal ties in the seventeenth century. Let me mention briefly two such arguments. The twelfth-century Gregorian reforms of the consolidating Catholic Church have been seen to pose interesting challenges to Enlightenment exceptionalism. The Gregorian reforms are usually described as a reaction by conservative Catholic theologians to the excess of the Carolingian period, especially the increasing penetration of the church by secular society as the aristocracy, the church, and commoners maneuvered to gain, or keep, control of land and wealth. One of the tactics deployed by the church to outmaneuver the aristocracy was its insistence that individuals rather than households be the locus of the felicity and fidelity of the marriage contract. Arranged marriages continued to be valid, but their validity increasingly depended on the consent of the two individuals concerned, rather than the marriage ceremony itself.[10] What "consent" referred to was itself a form of great contestation, but was increasingly narrowed to one discursive form. The betrothal became a proto-contract, a public first-person present tense announcement—and note, this protocontract predated the Hobbesian contract by four hundred years (the *Leviathan* was published in 1651).[11]

And yet, at the same time that the Gregorian reforms placed individual consent at the center of the marriage ritual, they vastly expanded the sphere of kinship in which individuals had to maneuver. The church doubled overnight the number of kin prohibited from marriage by substituting Roman law for German law as the basis for reckoning kinship degrees and by instituting new, sexually restricted kinship categories like godparent, widow, and spiritual parent. British social anthropologist Jack Goody has argued that the Gregorian reforms were not merely aimed at the aristocratic control of social life but at the control of property by collateral kin at all levels of society.[12] Even if we remain agnostic about whether these reforms stood primarily in the service of property accumulation or doctrinal purity, there seems little disagreement that the tension between the contractual couple and the expansion of the genealogical grid instigated an enormous struggle across all orders of society over these new disciplines of sexuality and kinship. The genealogical grid became a pervasive constraint at the very moment the individual was freed from its dictates. The church increasingly monopolized the role of arbiter, verifying licit unions and dissolving or dispensing absolution for illicit marriages where it saw them as appropriate (or lucrative). But everyone was in real or potential danger of a dangerous liaison. It was not until the Protestant Reformation that the genealogical grid contracted around the contractual couple and their immediate filial relations.

Alan Macfarlane's work is perhaps best known in challenging the claim that the individual first emerged in the seventeenth century.[13] Focusing on English exceptionalism rather than Gregorian reforms, he argues in *Origin of English Individualism* that with regard to marriage and property, an English person's freedom from the family existed long before the age of revolution.[14] In this sense, England was "diametrically opposed" to the rest of the continent. In England, the great constitutional compromise of the Glorious Revolution of 1689 foregrounded the liberty and freedom of the subject from the tyranny of the crown in ways quite distinct from the rest of Europe. The individual was "not merely an eighteenth-century difference, but can be traced back to the fifteenth-century, before the supposed dramatic changes caused by Protestantism and the rise of a new capitalist economy."[15] Macfarlane is not alone in considering England the oddball of Europe and arguing that the spirit of liberty predated the Protestant Reformation. Alexis de Tocqueville noted the intractability of English individualism. And Montesquieu famously quipped that the English were too busy amassing wealth to develop a taste for social refinements. According to Macfarlane, from the perspective of law and custom, the household seemed relatively unimportant to matters of property, residence, or marriage; by and large, children made their own choices about marriage, employment, and household location, and the relations between the sexes and the classes appeared fairly relaxed. Indeed, to the modern ear, some accounts of English parental attitudes toward their children might sound like a form of child neglect. Little wonder that capitalism took root so quickly and extensively there. And little wonder that when it did, many English workers experienced its demands as a violation of their status as self-motivated persons.[16]

While a fascinating historical correction, the discovery that English men and women had great flexibility in their choice of marriage, work, and residence does not discount the revolutionary form of social detachment that emerged alongside the notion of self-authorization in the seventeenth and eighteenth centuries. The early American historian Gordon S. Wood would speak to this point in his discussion of the utter Englishness of prerevolutionary colonial Americans.[17] Reviewing in detail the record on English exceptionalism, Wood concludes that no matter the great national chauvinism regarding liberty, inequality was presupposed, and it was based on a monarchical necessity: "In the eighteenth century, as in the time of John Winthrop, it was nearly impossible to imagine a civilized society being anything but a hierarchy of some kind" based on "a long train of dependence . . . that linked everyone from the king at the top down to the bonded laborers and black slaves at the bottom."[18] People like Edmund Burke, after all, valued the great compromise as much as radical compatriots. But he saw the unique British liberty it entailed as thoroughly dependent on the coordination of the social field under the monarchical necessity.

What social theorists such as Fanon and Balibar are tracking is this seemingly subtle but socially significant normative shift that begins with struggles aimed at freeing persons from some specifiable form of social organization or social injustice within a field of tactical power and ends with a devotion to freedom as a radical and ultimate break from all social conditions/horizons.[19] Aristocratic trappings might have remained in the self-stylizations of titles and manners that the emergent bourgeois society adopted. And the actual personages of king and court resurfaced during the Restoration (1789–1848), as did radically delicious crackpots such as Charles Fourier and the Icarians and less dreamy social reform movements like the Anti-corn League. And yet underneath these restoration costumes and utopian visions emerged a decisive new presupposition, an expectation that the course of a man's life should be determined by *his* life, the life *he* made—and made with another deracinated subject—rather than from his placement before his birth in a genealogical, or any other socially defined, grid. The modern form of human freedom was not inaugurated until the notional realm of freedom and radical self-detachment were coordinated, and the narrowing of the sources of the self was thematized as the unfurling of freedom. Authentic self-naming (auto-nym) came to be opposed to all forms of critical social attachment. The "experiments with the subjectivity discovered in the close relations of the conjugal family" rife in the eighteenth century were revolutionary exactly in so far as they considered other sources of self-opinion and thought as constraining the freedom of the individual.[20] Do we orient our opinions and actions based on our relationship to our spouse, our kin, and our social group? Is kin-based self-heteronomy opposed to self-autonomy? What about other social forms such as the demands of religion or custom? Are these religious or custom-based forms of self-heteronomy opposed to self-autonomy?

In other words, the aspect of the parvenu that these theorists seek is not so much the individual in some general sense, nor the individual as an essential category, but rather the semiotic form this subject took, as well as its social effects. This semiotic form absolutely distinguishes these older English and medieval forms from modern forms, and, as a global discourse, initiates a decisive cut—or bar, or barricade—between whatever is figured as a normative Western claim on freedom and all other such claims. To understand why, let us pursue our two questions more delicately. If not an essentialist discourse, what are the semiotic specificities of this practice of self-subjection from the perspective of language theory? And why do we name this form of semiotically meditated social relation—man to himself—"freedom," as opposed to naming it something else or as opposed to calling some other form of social composition "freedom"? If self-subjection is thoroughly social in its origins and effects, its brace and brakes, why is it more free than any other form of self-subjection?

Figuring the self-enclosure of the parvenu as freedom par excellence depends on a specific linguistic ideology centered on (pro)nominal categories and their relationship to social context and social practice. This ideology proves metapragmatic insofar as it constitutes a social practice (or discourse) whose object is a linguistic form. There is no better way of seeing this than beginning with Emile Benveniste's discussion of subjectivity in language in *Problems in General Linguistics*. What interests Benveniste, and others, about the first person singular is that, viewed from a semantic perspective, *I* stands radically alone, naked and momentary. The "meaning" of *I* is radically dependent on social context; it is pragmatic (or performative) in this sense: in saying "I" or assuming the position of *I* in language, the subject is not so much projected into social space as social space is established as a set of values emanating from the null-space of the subject. As opposed to what are generally considered to be other true pronouns (other person pronouns, demonstratives, reflexive pronouns, etc.) and lexical nouns (common or proper), the first person singular pronoun (*I, ipse, ego*) refers to, and creates, an axis of enunciation without adding any further semantic details about that axis or the subject marked as the null-space at the center of that axis. In other words, *I* sets, but does not describe, the time, aspect, place, or social status of the speaker. It does not tell us the gender, race, time, or social status of the speaker. In noticing the function of *I* in establishing discursive space, the students of Benveniste noticed something else about the semiotic effect of *I*: it set into place an asymmetrical system of values. If *I* constitutes the zero-coordinate of social space, all other social forms and temporal-spatial locations are marked by various values such as gender, number, distance, and tense.

A further order of semiotic complexity is introduced when *I* is used as a source of a speaker's own authorization. Positing oneself as addresser and addressee creates a new I, a type of first-person you. This I is not the subject who asks the question "What do I think?" but the I entailed as the object (you) of the question and placed in the role of the potential subject of response. Object and subject of enunciation appear to collapse into each other, "Hey, You, yes, You-who-are-I/Me, tell me. . . ." This discursive form creates neither the Freudian split subject nor the Deleuzian subject of surplus; it creates them both. The more I ask myself to speak my own truth, the richer and more multidimensional the interior terrain of *I* becomes, literally the more of myself there is. But, at the same time, the more I query (produce) myself—

thematizing the different aspects of myself that I am interested in (thinking me, inner me, wounded me, spiritual me, gay me)—the more I build my own removal from myself. Self-elaboration and self-alienation are born at the exact same moment because they constitute the dialectical consequences of this type of self-referentiality. As a result, the parvenu that emerged in the long seventeenth century emerged as a split and a surplus, and within an asymmetrical structure of value. We might say it was born with an agitated detachment from any and all other forms of social attachment.

I will come back to this agitated detachment. But first it would be wise to ask what the relationship is of this I to other actual or possible, even as yet to be conceived, nominalizable social forms and relations. If we examine *I* from the vantage point of other social forms, we immediately notice its radical promiscuity—and this exact promiscuity is what makes it so suitable to a liberal discourse of social disinterest and detachment. *I* can refer to any nominal form that is culturally construable as able to speak in one or another of possible worlds. A woman, man, cat, god, breeze, freedom, or golem could be *I* from the perspective of one or another of possible worlds. Moreover, a woman could speak from the perspective of I but be seen as channeling a demon, as in the movie classic *Rosemary's Baby* (1968; directed by Roman Polanski)—that is, following Erving Goffman's classic distinctions, she could be the animator of another author's words.[21] Indeed, the I may have spoken two thousand years ago by a donkey carrying Don Quixote. The point is that knowing who is "speaking" depends on elaborate, and elaborating, metadiscursive frames—discourses about the intelligibility of the place, time, and value of various discourses. Explicit political struggles, no less than implicit attempts to gain the upper hand in a romance, are exactly about these contestable conditions of intelligibility—the whether, where, and when so-and-so kinds of persons constitute intelligible, or viable, lifeworlds.

But intelligibility is not the only value in play. Corporeal viability—livability—is equally at stake in confrontations with the social institutions of risk and pleasure that make up human life. For example, speaking as a golem is intelligible in a Western European or US court of law, but intelligible under a regime of madness and so a regime of real risk to the subject of enunciation, unless some new metadiscursive composition is made. The radical psychiatry of Saint Alban's, associated with François Tosquelles and Felix Guattari, was just such a space of metadiscursive play—a space of discursive play in the physical sense of a scope for motion or action within a certain material environment. Within these discursively saturated material environments the viability and intelligibility of social identities are contested, new identities composed; the social formed, deformed, and reformed.

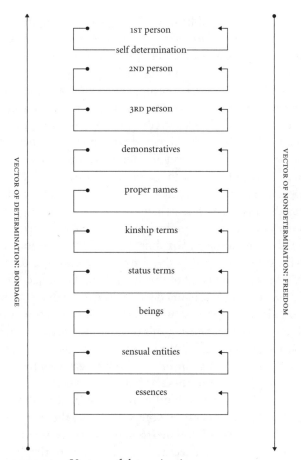

FIGURE I. Vectors of determination

I has a second relation to other nominal categories fundamental to understanding the play of social struggle in the postcolonial condition. As Michael Silverstein has shown, an elaborate nominal hierarchy can be projected out of Benveniste's project of grounding language form and function in these conditions of socially situated speech.[22] From this point of view, noun phrases extend outward from *I* on the basis of degrees of distance from the coordinates of speech events. This, too, might be better visualized with the aid of figure I. Hopefully there one can see how, say, *uncle* depends on, refers to, and describes a type of social role relative to the position of *I* (ego) in discourse. Indeed, social anthropologists are infamous for calibrating kinship degrees based on the horizontal and lateral distances from ego and for distinguishing between ego- and alter-centric kinship systems. (In alter-oriented systems, a person would address a person from the addressee's perspective of the kinship order.) *Custom* refers to, encompasses, and quantifies the totality of social beliefs and relations. Like *culture*, the terms *ideology*, *tradition*, and *custom* presuppose and stand in for a whole/part relationship to social roles. For example, *custom* presupposes *kinship* and other social forms; it is the whole of which these social forms are parts. All the ascending terms presuppose the prior term and describe a degree of divergence from actual situated social reality, from the here and now of an utterance, of phenomenological being, of argument, struggle, and its institutional effects. *Freedom* is, therefore, a term of quality that lies at the furthest degree of removal from the social context. And, unlike *belief*, which sits alongside it, *freedom* characterizes this distance as detachment.

The two ends of the above nominal hierarchy meet in their mutual revulsion of social determination and qualification, suturing the impartial and impersonal to the subject of speech, the abstract and universal to the particular and local. We have, on one end of this hierarchy, the subject that initializes social space but remains unqualified by any social qualia; and on the opposite end of this hierarchy, we have nouns maximally distal from the context of speech and self-reflexively figuring this distance as a break from all contexts of speech. What grammatical first-person singular and abstract nouns such as *freedom* seem to share is an insularity from inscription by social context. It is not surprising, then, that these are the "representations" that Timothy Mitchell has noted were left behind in the colonial world to act as virtual agents of the colonizing process.[23] Note as well that these "representations" are also the calling cards of colonizing capital—to be free to move across social space without being subject to the constraints of that social space.

The problem with this theoretical approach to subjectivity in language —and its revolutionary insight—is that it itself depends on, as it makes visible, a set of metadiscursive, socially embedded protocols shaping language's grammatical surface and the function of language as the intuitive backdrop of the subject. Every significant level of linguistic grammaticality and pragmatics bears the social history of this ideological struggle. Let me note two ideological protocols that have shaped grammaticality and our understanding of it, and are significant to the international division of civilizational authority and material distributions.

The first protocol is the claim that *I* sets the zero- (or null-) point for enunciation without signaling anything further about the social qualities of the subject. This characterization is problematic for two reasons. First, it reads grammatical function off ideological form, rather than the other way around. In many languages, such as Thai, Japanese, and Javanese, gender or social status is signaled in first-person and second-person pronouns. Speakers must select among a set of first-person singular forms, each of which assumes, and entails, a social relation between speaker and spoken to. The transformation of these grammatical categories is a social transformation with a social history. The English you/thou and the French *tu-vous* distinctions are good examples of how such social signals are carried by the second person—and how the social is entailed by the second person, a point of which Frantz Fanon was well aware.[24] But the historical emergence of Indonesian as a national language provides another, different kind of example.[25] In other words, when Benveniste describes the first person as setting up a null-point in the speech event, this is true only in so far as all additional social information has been stripped from the grammatical first and second person *and* in so far as this stripped form has been characterized as its true grammatical form and function. This characterization proves problematic for a second reason. It reads universal forms—what grammatical forms and functions can be abstracted from actual speech—through the privilege of liberal discourse of social disinterest and detachment. In both cases, *I* reemerges not as the null-point of the social, but as a value irreducibly embedded in socially saturated and coordinated value systems.

A second ideological protocol details how the nominal hierarchy discussed above is read in relation to "freedom." For simplicity's sake, we can describe this mandate of reading the protocol of freedom. The protocol of freedom has the crucial characteristics of "fractal recursivity," what Susan Gal and Judith Irvine describe as a linguistic operation in which a set of ideological oppositions are projected from one level to another.[26] The various suboperations of freedom within this ideology of fractal recursivity are simple enough, as figure 2 suggests. We can summarize them as: (1) all self-reflexive forms are describable as "free"—the following forms are construable as "free": I determining I, Kinship determining Kinship, Social determining Social, Culture determining Culture; (2) (pro)nominal forms can determine any form to the "right" of it without violating freedom—I can determine Kinship, Society, and Culture and remain free. But no (pro)nominal form can determine any form to the "left" of it without violating the protocols of freedom. The protocols of freedom are not grammatical in the sense of issuing from a universal grammatical law. *Freedom* is the name that specific people, within immanent institutions of the subject and social, gave this specific linguistic hierarchy.

The protocol of freedom links the very organization of language—the form and function of the (pro)nominal hierarchy discussed above—to empire. On the one hand, not only was the normative source of opinion and

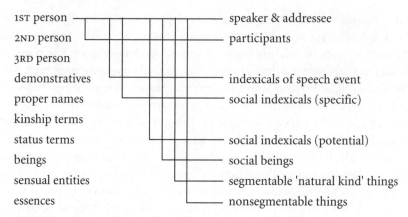

FIGURE 2. Metapragmatic freedom. Adapted from Michael Silverstein, "Case Marking and the Nature of Language," 1981

value narrowed to the self but all other sources were characterized as limiting rather than expanding the self, as primitive rather than modern forms of the subject. Social relations went from being the presupposed source of the self to its Waterloo: You should do it yourself; you can do it yourself; if you cannot do it yourself, something is wrong with you. On the other hand, a new type of hindrance emerged from which the subject had to struggle to detach itself—the abstract notion of a society as a collectivity with a custom. Does a man wish to free himself into the authority of his own reason, his own feelings, his own destiny? Well, the first place he might begin working is on what David Hume referred to as the customary nature of causal connections. Many names have been given to this domain of habituated unfreedom before and after *A Treatise of Human Nature*. The American semiotician Charles Sanders Peirce would call it "extreme abduction."[27] And social scientists would provide a host of other names: the real, doxa, hegemony, culture, ideology.

Whatever this source of semiotic determination is called, there can be no history of the emergence of a society of nations and customs that does not place its smelting in the furnace of the imperial and colonial world.[28] Since Bartolome de las Casas challenged the legal and moral basis of Spanish rule in the Americas, the emergence of freedom's struggle with custom constituted the continuation of struggles between peoples about the meaning of custom and its relation to the subject. Mary Wollstonecraft, eighteenth-century champion of men and women's freedom, could and did compare the world she envisioned to "Mahometanism," the eighteenth-century term referring to Islamic societies.[29] She was by no means alone. Colonial societies and their customs rolled off the tips of many tongues. As Uday Mehta has noted, though few explicit reflections exist on the link between emergent social theory and social practices in empire, this link formed new categories of thought (customs), brought new comparisons to mind, and further removed freedom from everyday life.[30] What changed in the long *durée* of revolution and colonization was not so much the orientation of the self to itself, but the beginning of a robust discourse that produced "society" and "custom" as natural entities—things, forces, agents—that organized, qualified, and mystified more particular social relations and beliefs; and the beginning of a robust discourse of freedom that expanded to encompass this new level of social abstraction and quantification. In other words, empire built the middle range of the nominal hierarchy—kinship, society, custom—and its place in a scale of human value.

For all this attention to the semiotic details of the parvenu, the modern, self-authorizing I and its coordination to desubstantialized nominal categories like freedom are not the consequence of linguistic form and function. In other words, we would be greatly mistaken if we viewed the above diagrams as universal facts of linguistic grammaticality, or even speech events as abstractable forms. These diagrams explicate the historical sedimentation of language as a social event, as socially composed and composable materials in the midst of specific language-saturated social risks and pleasures. The revolution in thought that the metapragmatic perspective on language inaugurated, and its usefulness for analyzing radical social struggles, is its placement of immanent social practice—the asymmetrical nature of here-and-now social life—at the center of any explanation of language form and function. In this sense, the above metapragmatic approach opposes absolutely the essentializing tendencies of semantics and foregrounds instead the social dependency of these new forms themselves on spaces of experimentation, expression, and elaboration.

To understand how this pyramid scheme of freedom is projected into postcolonial worlds and settler-colonies, we must begin again, but this time we have to examine how the subject of freedom intersects with the authentic subject of international recognition. When these two subjects meet, something quite odd occurs. Suddenly, the nominal hierarchies of self-subjectification and freedom not only serve as descriptions of levels of human freedom but also as assertions about the differential truth of global "civilizations." These sources of self-determination characterize the truth of so-called civilizational types and calculate their degrees of divergence from human destiny. It is at this point that the politics of freedom becomes an exceedingly complicated discourse for those outside of Western Europe and its settler-colonies. In some cases, the price of maintaining actual life is the command performance of unfreedom.

In Australia, where I have done most of my work, for indigenous persons to be recognized as the owners of their land by the state, they must demonstrate that they are members of what is legally and anthropologically known as a local descent group. Foucault would probably have described the local descent group as an example of a deployment of alliance—a family tree organized on the basis of some rule of kinship, marriage, and descent, rules that situate persons before they are born in a generational flow of people, affects, and goods; place them under certain fixed obligation and duties; and provide them with certain rights and responsibilities with regard to that flow. For us it is important to remember that the deployment of alliance as the grounds for self-action is not merely, or even necessarily, a function of indigenous social life, but a mandate of state law. No matter what an indigenous person in Australia says motivates her or his beliefs, actions, and opinions, in the context of the two major pieces of legislation pertaining to land rights, only her or his determination by "custom," "culture," or "Aboriginal law" proves felicitous in court. Courts hold that kinship, marriage, and descent rules constitute the Aboriginal society as truly distinct and authentic to itself and for the nation, not any other form of self or social authorization—not love, not friendship, certainly not self-autonomy. Aboriginal activists since the 1950s, and certainly during the crucial years of the early 1970s when federal land rights legislation was written, argued that a variety of social forms should be considered as valid means of land and social attachment. But these were put aside. To put it bluntly, if human freedom depends on some form of self-autonomy, Aboriginal persons are called on to dehumanize themselves as the price of material reparation and public recognition.

The demand on Aboriginal subjects to produce what would appear to be unfree forms of determination has only intensified over the last twenty years. In the first ten years of land claim hearings in the north of Australia, juridical procedures focused on the epistemological aspects of statements about local beliefs and practices; that is, on what people said was the content of their cultural beliefs about land, kinship, and social behavior. As urban Aboriginal men and women entered into the land-claim process, suspicion increased about the truth of such statements. Were some Aboriginal persons just talking the talk? Increasingly, land, native title, and heritage claims focused on the degree to which statements correspond to a form of social heteronomy, and on the degree to which these forms of social heteronomy determine the interior disposition of a subject. In other words, some evidence is sought of an even deeper form of compulsion of the self by its custom—not only a statement about the social sources of the self, but some evidence that the actual person making these statements is deeply and irrevocably compelled by these social sources. In short, land claims demand ever-increasing orders of externally derived compulsion as the condition of material reparation and a politics of cultural dignity.

Tolerance, it seems, has a trapdoor that drops subaltern people back into the dehumanizing gesture of humanist freedom. Gayatri Spivak long ago noted this trap of *"speaking as."*[31] The postcolonial subject is continually called on to speak from the position of her or his social location, a location with a specific value within the general system of humanistic freedom. The entire legal and public apparatus of recognition—the legislation that describes the grounds of legitimate self-authorization, the celebratory and critical public discourse that circulates around this form of "traditional" authorization, the mode of social welfare organized on the basis of the recognition of this mode of authorization—forms part of a network of institutions of risk and pleasure that restrict and direct the values and meanings of indigenous and nonindigenous forms of social experimentation without necessarily referring to them. They might be something like a front-page story in the *Los Angeles Times*, reporting on the "honor killing" of Fadime Sahindal, the immigrant daughter of a Kurdish man, for refusing an arranged marriage: "Even after 20 years in Sweden, Sahindal's father, Rahmi, was guided more by pressure from his Kurdish clansmen than by the rule of law or love for his daughter."[32] We must ask why this story is newsworthy? A front-page story? The *Los Angeles Times* gives as a reason the importance of such incidents to public debate about the form that Western European democracies will take in the context of cultural diasporas. It reports that the case has caused Swedes to pay attention to "religious and cultural clashes." But this metadiscursive frame is needed not simply to justify its place in a circulatory system of news but to separate Europeans from Kurds (and metonymically all other non-Europeans) based on their differential allegiance to freedom and social attachment.

It is within the context of these globally circulating discourses of freedom and subordination that persons contend when they take seriously alternative forms of self-determination such as the "narratives of community" Partha Chatterjee has explored.[33] Saba Mahmood's work on Islamic women's piety movements in Egypt captures some of the stakes of this position. In a recent essay, Mahmood begins by asking why social categories such as sexual, racial, class, and national difference have become topics of debate about the cultural and historical specificity of the feminist project, while religious difference has not.[34] Her intuition is that the difference has something to do with the latter's relation to secular-liberal notions of freedom. She then carefully demonstrates the problematic relationship that the specific form of self-obedience to (or through such notional categories as) God has to the dominant understanding of agency. Mahmood asks again and again why it is so difficult to conceptualize agency "not as a synonym for resistance to relations of domination, but as a capacity for action that historically specific relations of subordination enable and create."[35] As she notes, paying attention to this level of agency does not stifle critique, nor does it disable a potentially negative critique of the specific methods or goals of these women. What it does do is query the assumption of certain scholars that custom constitutes freedom's limit, and that freedom is the necessary orientation of positive social action.

In sum, what emerged in the long humanist revolution was not only the normative ideal that the most legitimate source of authorization for a person's opinions, actions, and beliefs was his or her self; and not only the normative sense that this form of self-authorization best expressed the quality of freedom. What emerged were new institutions of risk and pleasure that make freedom from social relations seem natural and desirable: for instance, voting, wage labor, and love; subjective acts and orientations that crisscross the state, civil society, and the person. The spatial and temporal nature of democratic voting is perhaps the form par excellence of this radical fantasy of detachment. Face to the mirror of one's own ballot, back to the social world, and "influence" legally distanced, persons are incited to strip away their world.

These institutions short-circuit alternative sources and descriptions of the self, sources that might derive from social relations or particular godly traditions. They continually orient agitated detachment back to itself as the source of the authority of all opinions, actions, and beliefs. While linguistic facts such as the above nominal hierarchies do not create the social, they make for the intuitive resources of arguments concerning how the social should be organized. The semiotic features of language, metadiscursively organized, become an essential unconscious element of a variety of historical arguments about the legitimate sources of the self—from what perspective it can legitimately speak, in what context. But because these arguments are metadiscursive in nature, institutions that make certain sources of the self more or less risky, more or less pleasurable, exert a certain force on social life. And—this force is exerted on subjects who themselves constitute the effects of a world in which freedom is already the presupposed horizon of all actual and possible good worlds. Foucault was certainly right when he noted, "The contemporary world is teeming with ideas that spring up, stir around, disappear or reappear, and shake up people and things."[36] Can women subject themselves to piety? Can indigenous people be kin? Can subaltern woman speak as her social form? If these social experiments have a hard time flourishing, it is not because language does not provide the resources, but because the particular metapragmatic coordination of linguistic categories is now embedded in institutions that make these flourishings dangerous, difficult, without any context. Freedom does not authorize us to speak, to critique, to find new modes of association. We authorize each other, within the necessarily constraining (dependizing) nature of linguistic intuitions and social institutions.

What then of social composability and the "real freedom" of Fanon? What if we were trained to seek, and inspect, practices of social coordination rather than practices of detachment? Wouldn't we open up a space for a very different form of politics if we asked what types of attachments we should have in different contexts? Would we not first and foremost ask what our commitments are to one another, rather than to an abstraction? What practices of care for others need to be established, elaborated, closed down? Can these questions be asked underneath the domineering light of freedom? The domination of social life by freedom, such that having freedom is worth personal and social amelioration, is suggested in a conversation generated by a *New York Times* reporter in a small town in Russia. Asked about the difference between the world of her parents and her own, a tenth-grader replied, "Sure things were fine and good in the past when everyone had work and could afford to live well, but now we have freedom."[37]

Give me freedom or give me death. Surely there is another option: an ongoing, critically oriented search for a better social life.

Notes

I would like to thank Susan Gal for her critical reading of this essay, as well as audiences for their comments at the City University of New York (CUNY) Graduate Center, the Department of Anthropology of the University of Pennsylvania, and the University of Illinois, Urbana-Champaign, where I presented versions of this essay.

1. Kirstie McClure has made a related point in her discussion of tolerance, in which she argues that "a focus on the logical opposition alone" between tolerance and intolerance "serves only to obscure the discursive construction of the binary itself." McClure, "Difference, Diversity, and the Limits of Tolerance," 265.

2. Fanon, *The Wretched of the Earth*, 47.

3. De Beauvoir, *The Ethics of Ambiguity*, 16.

4. Fanon, *The Wretched of the Earth*, 47.

5. Ibid., 47, 49.

6. Four edited volumes provide an overview of this field: Lucy, *Reflexive Language*;

Silverstein and Urban, *Natural Histories of Discourse*; Schieffelin, Woolard, and Kroskrity, *Language Ideologies*; and Gal, *Languages and Publics*.

7. Balibar, "Subjection and Subjectivation."

8. Donzelot, *The Policing of Families*; Stoler, "Carnal Knowledge and Imperial
Power."

9. Hobsbawm, *The Age of Revolution*, 183.

10. Duby, *The Knight, the Lady, and the Priest*.

11. Other discursive forms like the first-person future (e.g., "I will marry thee . . .")
were, for a long time in many places, seen as performative at the moment of sexual
consummation.

12. Goody, *The Development of the Family*.

13. Macfarlane, *The Origins of English Individualism*. See also, Wilson, "The Enlightenment Came First to England"; Brewer, *Party Ideology and Politics*; Stone, *Uncertain Unions*; and Houlbrooke, *The English Family*.

14. Macfarlane, *The Origins of English Individualism*.

15. Ibid., 166.

16. E. P. Thompson provides a useful example in his discussion of the struggle between wool weavers and hand-loom factories. Thompson, *The Making of the English
Working Class*, 269–313.

17. Wood, *The Radicalism of the American Revolution*.

18. Ibid., 19.

19. Thompson's *The Making of the English Working Class* is of course a classic archive for the historical unevenness and incompleteness of this movement.

20. Habermas, *The Structural Transformation of the Public Sphere*, 49. A number of
scholars have examined how these experiments with subjectivity were themselves refracted across new forms of text and textual circulation. See, for instance, Lee, "Textuality, Mediation, and Public Discourse"; and Warner, *Publics and Counterpublics*,
65–124.

21. Goffman, "Footing." Several linguistic anthropologists working in the legacy
of Emile Benveniste and Erving Goffman have demonstrated the potential complexity
of the matrix located at this axis. See, for instance Urban, "The 'I' of Discourse in
Shokleng."

22. Silverstein, "Hierarchy of Features and Ergativity"; and Silverstein, "Case
Marking and the Nature of Language."

23. Mitchell, *Colonising Egypt*.

24. For example, see the debate among Roger Brown, Albert Gilman, and Kath-
leen Wales. Brown and Gilman, "The Pronouns of Power and Solidarity"; Wales,
"*Thou* and *You* in Early Modern English"; and Brown and Gilman, "Politeness
Theory and Shakespeare's Four Major Tragedies."

25. See, for instance, Siegel, *Solo in the New Order*; Keane, "Public Speaking"; and
Errington, *Shifting Languages*.

26. Irvine and Gal, "Language Ideology and Linguistic Differentiation."

27. Hume, *A Treatise of Human Nature*; Peirce, "Pragmaticism."

28. See, for instance, Porter, *Critics of Empire*; Said, *Orientalism*; Chatterjee,
Nationalist Thought and the Colonial World; Mehta, *Liberalism and Empire*; and
Young, *Postcolonialism*.

29. Wollstonecraft, "The Vindication of the Rights of Woman."

30. Mehta, *Liberalism and Empire*.

31. Gayatri Chakravorty Spivak with Sneja Gunew, "Questions of Multi-culturalism," in Spivak, *The Post-colonial Critic*, 59–66.

32. Carol J. Williams, "Price of Freedom, in Blood," *Los Angeles Times*, March 7, 2002.

33. Chatterjee, *The Nation and Its Fragments*.

34. Mahmood, "Feminist Theory, Embodiment, and the Docile Agent."

35. Ibid., 203.

36. Quoted in Eribon, *Michel Foucault*, 282.

37. Patrick E. Tyler, "In Stalin's Town, A School Divided." *New York Times*, March 3, 2002.

Decomposing Modernity: History and

Hierarchy after Development

☉ ☉ ☉

JAMES FERGUSON

Africa always seems to come to the question of modernity from with-out. Generations of Western scholars have considered Africa as either be-yond the pale of the modern (the savage heart of darkness that lurks beyond the edges of the civilized world) or before it (the "primitive," "traditional" place always not yet in the time of the up-to-date present). Today, scholars critical of the evolutionist time lines and static essentialisms of older modern-ization paradigms struggle to redescribe Africa as within the modern. Seek-ing to deprovincialize the notion of the modern, and to sever its automatic connection with the West, they prefer to locate contemporary African social realities within a broader, pluralized notion of the modern, as constituting an "alternative" modernity.[1]

What are the implications of the different sorts of answers given to the question of Africa's relation to modernity? Is the idea of alternative or mul-tiple modernities a useful one? What is at stake in the assertion that African societies are "less modern" than North American and European ones, and what is accomplished by the contrary claim that they are instead only differ-ently modern, alternatively modern?

I raise this issue not in an attempt to prescribe ways of thinking about modernity, but rather to foreground an important dimension of the discus-sion that I think has not yet received enough attention. In the course of fore-grounding this dimension, I will deliberately ignore or move into the back-ground other significant dimensions of the debates about modernity. If the picture sketched here seems exaggerated and one-dimensional, it is by de-sign. It should also be noted that I treat *modernity* here not as an analytic term to be defined and applied, but as what anthropologists call a "folk category," in this case, a folk category shared by an enormously heterogeneous population of natives. Vague and confused as the term undoubtedly is when considered as an analytical tool, it remains the center of a powerful "discourse of identity" (as Mary Louise Pratt has termed it),[2] and a keyword that anchors a host of transnational discussions in and out of the academy about an emerging global social order.[3]

The Time of Modernization

It is perhaps appropriate to begin by going back to the days when people thought they knew what they meant by modernity: the years following World War II, the days of decolonization and so-called emerging nations, modernization theory and nation building. At the end of empire, a story about the emergence of "new nations" via processes of "modernization" or "development" provided a new grid for interpreting and explaining the world's inequalities. As the "backward nations" advanced, in this optic, a "modern" form of life encompassing a whole package of elements — including such things as industrial economies, scientific technologies, liberal-democratic politics, nuclear families, and secular worldviews — would become universalized. In the process, poor countries would overcome their poverty, share in the prosperity of the "developed" world, and take their place as equals in a worldwide family of nations.

This vision, so crudely sketched here, amounted to a powerful political and economic charter. With the world understood as a collection of national societies, global inequalities could be read as the result of the fact that some nations were further along than others on the ladder to a unitary modernity. In this way, the narrative of development mapped history against hierarchy, developmental time against political economic status. The progressive nature of historical time so taken for granted, nations could anticipate their inevitable, if gradual, rise in the global order through a natural process of development. The diagram in figure 1 is painfully simple, but its virtue is to allow us — even to force us — to apprehend this sense of time *analytically* as composed of two dimensions (the two axes, labeled "time" and "status").[4] If so-called backward nations were not modern, in this picture, it was because they were not *yet* modern. Modernity figured as a universal telos, even for the most traditional of societies. And the extent to which societies differed from the modern (and, implicitly or explicitly, Western) ideal neatly indexed their supposed level of development toward that ideal.

This powerful narrative effectively transformed a *spatialized* global hierarchy into a *temporalized* (putative) historical sequence. Poor countries (and

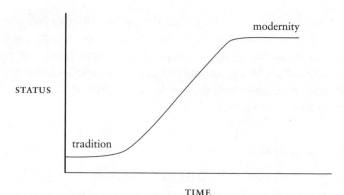

FIGURE 1. The time of modernization

by implication, the poor people who lived there) were not simply at the *bottom*, they were at the *beginning*. And the clear implication was that history—the passage of developmental time—would in the nature of things raise the poor countries up to the level of the rich ones. For those at the bottom of the global hierarchy, the message was clear: wait, have patience, your turn will come.

This picture is so familiar as to appear banal. But before my argument can proceed, it is necessary to take this only too familiar story line and make it strange. To do this, it will help to look briefly into the past, to a time when such a progressive temporalization of human and societal difference did not at all appear commonsensical.

Nineteenth-century schemes of social evolution, as anthropologists know well, relied on a temporalization of spatial and societal difference very close to that found in mid-twentieth-century modernization theory. This was the key device that marked the social evolutionism of our discipline's so-called founding fathers, conventionally recognized as Lewis Henry Morgan in the United States and Edward B. Tylor in Britain. In their speculative schemas of human history, societies deemed primitive revealed the earliest history of the human species, while more "advanced" societies showed intermediate stages in a universal human journey from (to use Morgan's categories) the various "statuses" of "savagery" through "barbarism" and finally to "civilization."[5]

However familiar such conceptions may have become, it is worth recalling that in the nineteenth century, they were radically new. As students of the history of anthropology have long observed, the idea of social evolution entailed a radical break, as well as a certain continuity, with older, theological conceptions of the Great Chain of Being. The idea that the various creatures of the world formed a great and continuous chain, ranked from highest to lowest, is an idea the intellectual historian A. O. Lovejoy famously traced from ancient Greek philosophy all the way up to the eighteenth-century European philosophers.[6] According to the principle Lovejoy termed "plenitude," a perfectly created world would necessarily contain all possible types of existence within it. And these various types of existence could be ranked according to their degree of "perfection," as Aristotle would have it, or according to their distance from God, as later Christian theologians would prefer. Man, having been created in God's image, was clearly "higher" in this sense than the "lesser" creatures. But nonhuman creatures themselves were ranked according to the same principle; thus the dog or the horse held a higher position than the rat, which in turn was located higher up on the chain than the frog or the worm, and so on. And, of course, for medieval thought, Man was not the only sort of being close to God: a variety of types of angels (themselves arranged in a "celestial hierarchy") continued the chain of existence upward, providing a continuous series linking the lowest forms of creation to Man, and ultimately to God.

In keeping with such thinking, the various types and conditions of human being also found their place in a natural hierarchy of existence. The religious hierarchy itself, of course, took this form, with church offices ranked (like the angels) from high to low. So did relations among different religions, since Christians were understood to be closer to God than adherents of other religions, while "savage" pagans were clearly understood to inhabit the lowest of human conditions. The different social estates, too, were understood as distinct cosmological conditions that could be ranked by their distance from God. Thus the serf's obligations to his master, like the wife's submission to her husband or a child's to its father, constituted but another form of the legitimate hierarchy that linked Man and God.

As racial thinking emerged in its modern form in eighteenth- and nineteenth-century Europe, the supposed racial "types" of Homo sapiens were fitted into a similar scheme. The doctrine of polygenism held that the different "races" were created separately by God and that they held—by nature and by divine plan—different ranks in the overall scheme of things. Opponents of such views often protested that "inferior" races did not constitute an original creation, but rather the result of a fall from grace, sometimes understood through the biblical story of Noah's curse on his dark son, Ham. In this alternative view, racial difference resulted from history, but it was a history understood as a fall from an original state of grace. Later variations on this theme notoriously introduced the idea of racial degeneration, a kind of biologicized version of the Fall.[7]

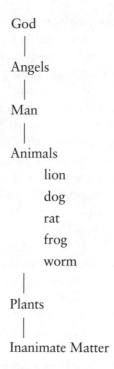

God

|

Angels

|

Man

|

Animals

    lion

    dog

    rat

    frog

    worm

|

Plants

|

Inanimate Matter

FIGURE 2. The Great Chain of Being.
Adapted from A. O. Lovejoy, *The Great Chain of Being*, 1936

What is worth underlining in all of this is that such hierarchical rankings of different forms of human and nonhuman being were *not* understood as forming a historical or evolutionary progression. It is all too easy for modern eyes to look at figure 2 and see in it a primitive evolutionary schema. But the conception was actually a very different one. As Lovejoy insists, if God's creation was perfect and complete (and how could it have been otherwise?), then it was also timeless and immutable. The principle of plenitude, he noted was "inconsistent with any belief in progress, or, indeed, in any sort of significant change in the universe as a whole. The Chain of Being, in so far as its continuity and completeness were affirmed on the customary grounds, was a perfect example of an absolutely rigid and static scheme of things."[8] If some form of temporality did enter into a specifically human history, it was decidedly a nonprogressive one. Whether in the form of the fateful expulsion of Adam and Eve from the Garden of Eden, or the degeneration of pagan races, the dynamic was that of the original Fall. It is for this reason that the transformation of the Great Chain of Being from a timeless ranking to a progressive temporal sequence (a transformation Lovejoy traces to the eighteenth century) proved a true intellectual revolution. Not only did such a shift make possible the Darwinian idea that new species might emerge, via chance variation and natural selection, from older ones; it also licensed the key social evolutionist idea that so-called primitive peoples might represent earlier stages of a universal human history and that historical time was—in the very nature of things—progressive.

Development and Its Aftermaths

If the move from a Great Chain of Being to a temporalized evolutionary progression made for a sort of epistemic break, the shift from nineteenth-century evolutionism to mid-twentieth-century modernization schemes constituted a break of a quite different kind. For it entailed not a revolutionary new notion of time, but instead an insertion of an only-too-familiar evolutionist temporalization of difference into a quite specific political and historical moment. In the context of decolonization and movements for national independence, the development story constituted no abstract scientific theory. On the contrary, it provided a vital, necessary narrative that could serve both as a charter legitimating and justifying the abrupt withdrawal of the colonial powers and as a blueprint for the nation-building and economic development programs of the new, postindependence elites.[9] I will return to this point shortly.

It has been widely observed that developmentalist models have in some measure lost credibility in recent years. Some scholars have interpreted this conjuncture as the advent of a new, hopeful "postdevelopment" era.[10] Such formulations should give us pause, not least because such era-thinking is itself closely tied to a developmentalist conception of history. But the more fundamental problem with such claims is that they are not quite true, at least not everywhere. The claim that development is over would surely sound strange to many people in, say, South Korea or China, who seem to take both development and its promises very seriously indeed (and not without reason). A more precise way of posing the problem might be to say that while developmental narratives have hardly disappeared, they have undoubtedly lost much of their credibility for certain people in certain places. This way of putting it underlines a fact that seems quite crucial to grasping the specificity of the present: that is that the loss of credulity toward narratives of social and economic development has occurred not universally, but in specific ways and in specific places (i.e., there is a *regional* specificity to this loss of credibility).

Critical social scientists are familiar enough with the intellectual and explanatory failings of developmentalist evolutionary narratives. Modernization theory suggested that the different elements of modern society formed a necessary and integrated package, implying that things like industrial economies and modern transportation and communications systems necessarily "came with" political democracy. As did a transition from extended to nuclear families and from communal to individual identities; the rise of bounded, monadic individuals; the secularization of worldviews; the rise of scientific rationalism and critical reflexivity; and so on. Critical ethnographic studies have shown the need to take apart that package. It is now well established that so-called traditional elements can fit together with the various elements of an archetypal modern industrial society without any necessary contradiction. Thus we have become accustomed to accounts of industrial workers with so-called extended family structures, of transnational business executives who fear witches, and of white-collar workers who fly in jet airplanes to visit their matrilineal clan elders. Anthropologists of Africa no longer regard such juxtapositions as entailing any contradiction or lag; modern Africa is today understood as a place of bricolage and creative invention, where bits and pieces of what used to be called Western modernity are picked up, combined with local (and not-so-local) resources, and put back together.[11]

But the developmental narrative is increasingly visible as a failure not only in the domain of academic theory but in practical economic terms as well. The basic premise of postwar developmentalism, of course, was socioeconomic convergence. Yet few talk about African economic convergence with the first world these days. On the contrary, the economic gulf between the richest and the poorest countries—as indexed by such standard measures as gross domestic product (GDP) per capita—is in fact growing rapidly, and most African countries are much further from economic parity with the first world today than they were twenty or thirty years ago (indeed, many are worse off even in absolute terms).[12] This may not be "the end of development," as some have perhaps overreached in claiming. But the absence of economic convergence in Africa and some other parts of the world is indisputable, even as living standards have indeed risen sharply in some parts of the former third world, thereby sustaining continuing dreams of an ascent to first world levels of wealth and security. If development is over, it is apparently over in some places, but not in others.

The logical consequence of this, and a crucial one, is a splitting of the world into places offered a role in the convergence narrative (e.g., Poland, Turkey, or the handful of neoliberal success stories of East and Southeast Asia, where people still speak unselfconsciously of "transition" and readily imagine an ultimate convergence with the economic standards of the first world), and others tracked into that vast, nonconvergent holding tank Manuel Castells has called the "fourth world."[13] (Many ex-Soviet areas seem now to be in the position of anxiously awaiting the news about which tracking they will receive.) Most of Africa finds itself at the far extreme of the nonconvergent, where developmentalist narratives have the least plausibility.

For this reason, the deployment of the idea of alternative modernities in Africa has a rather different significance than it has had in Asia. East and Southeast Asian versions of alternative modernity have mostly argued for the possibility of a parallel track, economically analogous to the West but culturally distinctive. Broadly, the idea has meant the possibility of achieving a first world standard of living, while retaining so-called Asian values, or maintaining a more restricted notion of individual rights, or avoiding the West's perceived moral vices.[14] But in Africa, where the idea of economic convergence has lately lost so much plausibility, pluralizing the concept of modernity has proven attractive for very different reasons. Academic and nonacademic understandings of African societies and cultures have long misunderstood Africa's difference from the West as anachronistic relic, as somehow not really of the present, as a symptom of backwardness and incomplete development: in short, as "tradition."[15] In the face of this, there is certainly something very appealing, and undoubtedly correct, about emphasizing the modernity of African society, its status as coeval with the West and part and parcel of the modern. In this spirit, it has been very useful for, for example, Peter Geschiere to insist on "the modernity of witchcraft," much as it was helpful for Paul Gilroy to identify slavery and its aftermath as unfolding within, rather than outside of, the modern.[16]

And yet, I want to argue that the alternative modernity formulation misses what may be most important about the current mutation in the meaning of *modernity* for Africans. To understand why this might be, it may be illuminating to return to the old modernization narrative and ask what is at stake in the current collapse of that narrative.

Modernity: From Telos to Status

The modernization narrative was a story, not just about cultural difference but also about global hierarchy and historical time. It combined these three elements in a unique and powerful (if ultimately mistaken) way. Figure 1 shows us the time line of development and its two dimensions. As time moves forward, status in a global system rises. History and hierarchy are indissolubly bound to each other, and a movement forward in time is also—necessarily, so long as the developmental time line holds—a movement upward on the scales of development and modernity. This story about history and hierarchy encoded a set of factual claims (about the relation between social, cultural, and economic change) that turn out to be mostly wrong. But it also encoded a set of political promises (in the context of decolonization and national independence) that remains quite important.

Anthropologists today, working to combat old stereotypes, are eager to say how modern Africa is. Many ordinary Africans might scratch their heads at such a claim. As they examine the decaying infrastructures, nonfunctioning institutions, and horrific poverty that surround them, they may be more likely to find their situation deplorably nonmodern and to say (as Zambian mine workers used to sigh to me, ruefully shaking their heads): "This place is not up to date!" Of course, the two claims have different referents. The anthropologists refer to cultural practices and their previously unappreciated historicity; hence Africa is modern, not traditional. But Africans who lament that their life circumstances are not modern enough are not talking about cultural practices; they speak instead of what they view as shamefully inadequate socioeconomic conditions and their low global rank in relation to other places. The developmental time line narratives squarely addressed these questions of status and standard of living, if only in the form of a promise: "If you are dissatisfied with your conditions, just wait; your society is moving forward and moving upward." Today, they are more often evaded—by culturally minded anthropology and neoliberal economics alike.

Under the circumstances, it appears unsurprising that some contemporary Africans seem to feel a sort of nostalgia for the modern. In my own research in Zambia, for instance, mine workers did not say, "We are modern, but in our own, alternative, way!" or even, "We have never been modern" (as Bruno Latour would have it);[17] they said, in effect, "We used to be modern—or at least well on our way—but now we've been denied that opportunity." Modernity, for them, was not an anticipated future, but a dream to be remembered from the not-very-distant past. The real future was almost universally understood as bleak, even apocalyptic.[18]

Once modernity ceases to be understood as a telos, the question of rank becomes dedevelopmentalized and the stark status differentiations of the global social system sit raw and naked, no longer softened by the promises of the not yet. The developmentalist reassurance that history would, by its nature, transform status, that third world people needed only to wait, to have patience, for their turn to come, ceases to convince.

I thought of this old call to patience recently, when the Swedish anthropologist, Mats Utas, showed me a photograph from his fieldwork with young men in the Liberian civil war. The photograph showed a young man, standing at a roadblock, waving an assault rifle in the face of a driver he had stopped. The young man with the rifle wore a T-shirt with the following English words on the back: "Patience my ass!"

In a world where developmentalist patience has little to recommend it, the promise of modernization increasingly appears as a broken one, and the mapped-out pathways leading from the third world to the first turn out to have been bricked up. The status categories of the contemporary global order, when detemporalized in this fashion, may even come to resemble the fixed status categories of the preindependence era, when the color bar segmented the social world into a rich, white, first-class sector and the poor, black, second-class world of the "natives."

To be sure, there are those who manage to live a "first-class" life even in the poorest countries, enjoying fully modern standards of living in the midst of general deprivation. In contrast to colonial times, these lucky few today include not only white expatriates but also the considerable numbers of local elites who have found great wealth in the wide open spaces of neoliberal Africa. Yet the fact remains that the new rich of today do not, for the most part, seem to be understood as early examples of a soon-to-be generalized societal destination (as the new elites of the 1960s often were). On the contrary, today's success stories are more likely to be seen as proving the power not of education and developmental uplift, but of luck, ruthlessness, or even criminality. If the new elites enjoy, as few of their compatriots can, a modern way of life, it is not because they are further along, but because they are on top.

Modernity, in this historically specific conjuncture, appears not (as it does to many contemporary anthropologists) as a set of wonderfully diverse and creative cultural practices, but as a global status and a political-economic condition: the condition of being first class. Some people and places have it, others don't; the key issues concern membership and rank. Such a conception directly opposes the anthropological urge to construct a plurality of cultural alternatives while refusing to rank them. Hence two questions: How does one term yield two such different discussions? And why are the anthropologists so out of step with the locals on the meaning of modernity?

To answer this question, it may prove useful to think a bit more about what sorts of thinking are possible and necessary in the aftermath of the modernization story.

Decomposing Modernity

Let us return to figure 1, the time of modernization, and take seriously the idea that this picture is, in some sense, falling apart. What does it fall apart *into*? If it falls apart, what are its *parts*? We might think of this falling apart as analogous to the chemical process of decomposition. The word, *decomposition*, suggests death and decay, but it is, in fact, a more basic sort of operation. In a laboratory, for instance, a chemist might perform a decomposition of a compound by cracking it (normally, through the application of heat), thereby decomposing it into its constituent elements. A similar conceptual operation is called for if we are to understand the decomposition of the developmentalist time line of modernization. As the mythical coupling of historical time to societal location in a spatialized global hierarchy breaks down, it becomes necessary to take the two axes of figure 1 and peel them apart, cracking the compound and releasing the elements that the developmentalist time line for so long fused into a single figure. Such a decomposition yields two elements, deriving from the two axes of figure 1.

The first element comes from the horizontal axis of the diagram, which may now be understood simply as history. With the time axis now unhinged from questions of status, history now does not constitute a teleological unfolding or a gradual rise through a hierarchical progression, but simply a movement through time (no longer a passage through various "stages of development"). Such a dedevelopmentalized notion of history no longer has modernity as its telos; insofar as different societies share the modern world, in the new conception, they negotiate modernity in different ways, through a variety of coeval paths. Hence we come to speak not of sequential stages of modernization, but of a variety of alternative modernities. With social and cultural difference no longer serialized, modernity is plural, history contingent. The telos is gone. Plurality, fragmentation, and contingency here emerge as key themes.

But there is also, less remarked, the second axis of the diagram, the axis of hierarchy. Now, with the idea of temporal sequence removed, location in the hierarchy no longer indexes a stage of advancement, but simply a rank in a global political economic order. Insofar as such ranks have lost any necessary relation to developmental time, they become not stages to be passed through, but nonserialized statuses, separated from each other by exclusionary walls, rather than developmental stairways. Modernity in this sense comes to appear as a standard of living, a *status*, not a telos. The global hierarchy is thereby dedevelopmentalized and appears as static, without the promise of serialization. Key questions here concern not development and sequence, but edges, walls, and borders.

The first axis (dedevelopmentalized time) yields a nonserialized, coeval cultural difference. This is the element of the decomposition that so many anthropologists have lately seized on with such enthusiasm, the terrain of alternative modernities. The anthropological excitement is not misplaced; the insistence on viewing cultural differences as nonserial and contemporary, as coeval in Johannes Fabian's sense,[19] and the determination to dedevelopmentalize our understanding of a global modernity has undoubtedly proven very revealing. It has opened up for analysis a vast terrain of hybrids and bricolage, of creative invention and emergent new possibilities. It is undoubtedly an area where a great deal of valuable work has recently been done.

But what about the second axis? Here, the decomposition procedure yields a second, less benign residue: nonserialized, coeval, but ranked political-economic statuses. If the first axis (once unhinged) shows us a modernity newly understood as plural, the second one shows us a different understanding of modernity in which, no longer promised as a telos, it has come to be simply a status—a standard of living to which some have rights by birth and from which others remain simply, but unequivocally, excluded.

As understandings of the modern have shifted in this way, the vast majority of Africans today who are denied the status of modernity increasingly come to be seen, and may even (sometimes, and in complex ways) come to see themselves, not as less developed, but simply as less. As people lose faith in developmental time, the global status hierarchy comes to be understood in new and disturbing ways.

Among the emergent possibilities coming into view, perhaps the most obvious one is an understanding of global statuses as detemporalized. Rather than poor countries being understood as *behind* the West—playing catch-up, developing, or emerging—they are increasingly understood as naturally, perhaps even racially, *beneath* it. This is visible both in popular ideology and some journalistic treatments in the West, which seem increasingly content these days to treat the economic and humanitarian crises in Africa as just more evidence of the way "those places over there" *are*. But it has also become evident in some African self-conceptions, where the optimistic mood of a developmentalist era has, at least in some specific social locations, given way to a much bleaker view that identifies "Africa" with an unchanging future of hardship and suffering.[20]

What is new here is not the existence of negative and even stereotypical images of Africa, for those go back a very long way, but rather the fact that such pictures today seem less dependent on a temporal frame that would fit "African troubles" into a progressive developmental trajectory. In such detemporalized visions of Africa as a continent by nature given to poverty, turmoil, and low global status, the Great Chain of Being threatens to reappear, with the different conditions of different statuses of people appearing simply as a naturally or divinely ordained, unchanging order. If the postcolonial condition is, as some have suggested, most fundamentally characterized by a perceived temporal disjuncture (with postcolonial nations and societies imagined as "behind" or "belated" in developmental time),[21] then the dedevelopmentalization of historical time promises to leave postcoloniality itself ironically out of date, not by ending or overcoming colonial inequality, but by rendering obsolete that very hope and dream.

Yet the detemporalization of global statuses is not the only alternative to the developmentalist vision of progressive stages. Another possibility (though perhaps no less problematic) exists in the form of nonprogressive temporalizations. That is, statuses and conditions of peoples and nations may be understood to change over time, but not in a progressive way. One version of such a nonprogressive temporalization, of course, is found in the idea of degeneration, where the temporal dynamic is one not of progress, but of decline, decay, and disintegration (again, a world picture with a long and disturbing pedigree). This may be readily observed in accounts of Africa in the genre we might term journalistic Malthusianism. Robert Kaplan's *The Coming Anarchy* stands as perhaps the best known (though hardly the only) example.[22] Kaplan paints a vivid picture of an Africa at the leading edge of a downward spiral into chaos, poverty, and war that might eventually sweep up the entire planet. This picture is not detemporalized or static, but neither is it a progress story. The worst off, in such a view, are not the "least developed," those still at the beginning of their long journey of uplift and improvement. Rather, the worst off are those furthest along on a very different journey: a downward slide into degeneration, chaos, and violence.[23]

Yet another sort of nonprogressive temporalization of economic distress may be detected in what we might call "apocalyptic temporalizations." At a time when more and more people (both in Africa and in much of the rest of the world) reckon world-historical time by referring not to the calendar or the five-year plan, but rather to the Book of Revelations, the question of development threatens to be displaced by the question of the end times. Many examples of this might be cited. The one that most recently struck me was the televised comment of a refugee from the recent volcanic eruptions in Goma, in the Congo. Having lived though genocide, civil war, starvation, cholera, and years of life in a refugee camp, the man betrayed little fear in the face of the terrifying volcano. After all, he reasoned, "we have read about these things in the Bible. The Lord will be coming for us soon." One should be wary of forcing overly simple interpretations on this kind of material, but it is perhaps worth suggesting that there may be some relation between the fading credibility of developmental time, on the one hand, and the rise of new spiritualities, and their associated temporalities, on the other.[24]

Such new understandings of the temporal dynamics of social and economic well-being (of the relation, that is, between history and hierarchy) may bring with them new strategies through which people seek to secure their own futures. One thing that seems to come up all over the continent in recent years is a shift from a focus on temporal dynamics of societal progress toward a new reliance on individual and familial strategies of spatial mobility. How is one to escape the status of being a poor African? Not by patience and the progress of national or societal development, but by leaving, going elsewhere, even in face of terrible danger.[25] Today, anthropologists in Africa tend to be asked not, "What can you do for us" (that time-honored question), but rather, "How can I get out of this place?" Not progress, then, but egress. If escape, too, is blocked, other avenues may involve violently crashing the gates of the first class, smashing the bricked-up walls and breaking through, if only temporarily, to the other side of privilege and plenty. As Achille Mbembe has observed, the contemporary African experience is not simply one of economic deprivation; rather, it involves "an economy of desired goods that are known, that may sometimes be seen, that one wants to enjoy, but to which one will never have material access"; the appropriation of goods "through pillage and violent seizure" here finds its logical place alongside a range of "shadow interventions in the phantasmatic realm."[26] In this way, the developmental life course is displaced by a life course "assimilated to a game of chance, a lottery, in which the existential temporal horizon is colonized by the immediate present and by prosaic short-term calculations."[27] Patience my ass.

To the extent that the global status system is detemporalized, or retemporalized in nonprogressive ways, the nature of the relation between the global rich and the global poor is transformed. For in a world of nonserialized political economic statuses, the key questions are no longer temporal ones of societal becoming (development, modernization), but spatialized ones of policing the edges of a status group. Hence the new prominence of walls, borders, and high technologies of social exclusion in an era that likes to imagine itself as characterized by ever-expanding connection and communication.[28]

My thesis has been that anthropologists have lately tended to focus on the first axis of the developmental diagram, the first product of modernity's decomposition—a happy story about plurality and nonranked cultural difference—to the neglect of the second, which yields relatively fixed global statuses and a detemporalized world socioeconomic hierarchy. In this way, the application of a language of alternative modernities to the most impoverished regions of the globe has become a way of *not* talking about the non-serialized, detemporalized political economic statuses of our time—indeed, a way of turning away from the question of a radically worsening global inequality and its consequences. Forcing the question of Africa's political-economic crisis to the center of contemporary discussions of modernity is a way of insisting on the second product of modernity's decomposition: the enduring axis of hierarchy, exclusion, and abjection, and the pressing political struggle for recognition and membership in the emerging social reality we call the global.

Notes

1. For recent general discussions on alternative or multiple modernities, see Appadurai, *Modernity at Large*; Gaonkar, *Alternative Modernities*; and "Multiple modernities," a special issue of *Daedalus*. For the discussion on African modernity, see Comaroff and Comaroff, *Modernity and Its Malcontents*; Piot, *Remotely Global*; Englund, "Witchcraft, Modernity, and the Person"; Diouf, "The Senegalese Murid Trade Diaspora"; Geschiere and Rowlands, "The Domestication of Modernity"; Geschiere, *The Modernity of Witchcraft*; and Hodgson, *Gendered Modernities*.

2. Pratt, "Modernity and Periphery," 183.

3. Ethnographic accounts by anthropologists often contain key terms or concepts that are important to the people being studied but that are distinct from the ethnographer's own terms of analysis. Sometimes this distinction is insisted on for epistemological reasons (as when an ethnographer of religion analyzes named mystical forces or beings while retaining a skepticism about their literal existence); in other cases, the inclusion of special terms is a linguistic necessity (as when the category in question does not correspond even approximately with any term in the ethnographer's own language). Such "folk categories" or "native categories," normally appearing as untranslated vernacular terms in the ethnographic text, have long been central to anthropological accounts of cultural "others." While anthropology has traditionally tried to keep "folk" and "analytic" terms distinct, the case of modernity illustrates the important tendency of apparently analytic terms to "go native" and take on a life of their own.

4. I label the vertical axis "status" as a way of insisting on the way that narratives of modernization encoded claims to a rising standing in the world that involved more than simply questions of income or gross national product. I wish thereby to foreground the idea of the tradition-modernity system as what anthropologists call a "prestige system," a matter not simply of ahead and behind but also of what is known —again, in the language of political anthropology—as "rank." As my later discussion will show, I also seek to make connections with what the nineteenth-century social evolutionist Lewis Henry Morgan termed the "statuses" of "savagery," "barbarism," and "civilization," and with the idea of a status as a durable, and even static, condition.

5. Morgan, *Ancient Society*.

6. Lovejoy, *The Great Chain of Being*.

7. See Gould, *The Mismeasure of Man*; and Mosse, *Toward the Final Solution*.

8. Lovejoy, *The Great Chain of Being*, 242.

9. See Cooper, *Decolonization and African Society*; Cooper, "Modernizing Bureaucrats, Backward Africans, and the Development Concept"; and Chatterjee, *Nationalist Thought and the Colonial World*.

10. Sachs, *The Development Dictionary*; Escobar, *Encountering Development*; and Rahnema with Bawtree, *The Post-development Reader*.

11. See Meyer and Geschiere, *Globalization and Identity*; Comaroff and Comaroff, *Modernity and Its Malcontents*; Donham, *Marxist Modern*; Werbner and Ranger, *Postcolonial Identities in Africa*; Piot, *Remotely Global*; and Hansen, *Salaula*.

12. Easterly, *The Elusive Quest for Growth*.

13. Castells, *End of Millennium*.

14. See, for instance, Ong, *Flexible Citizenship*.

15. See Fabian, *Time and the Other*.

16. Geschiere, *The Modernity of Witchcraft*; and Gilroy, *The Black Atlantic*.

17. Latour, *We Have Never Been Modern*.

18. Ferguson, "The Country and the City on the Copperbelt"; and Ferguson, *Expectations of Modernity*.

19. Fabian, *Time and the Other*.

20. Ferguson, *Expectations of Modernity*.

21. See, for instance, Gupta, *Postcolonial Developments*.

22. Kaplan, *The Coming Anarchy*.

23. On visions of degeneration in journalistic depictions of Africa, see Liisa Malkki, "Figures of the Future: Violence, Dystopia, and the Imagination of Africa," unpublished manuscript.

24. On new forms of Christianity in Africa, see Englund, "The Dead Hand of Human Rights"; van Dijk, "Pentecostalism, Cultural Memory, and the State"; Bornstein, *The Spirit of Development*; Meyer, *Translating the Devil*; and Meyer and Geschiere, *Globalization and Identity*.

25. See Ferguson, "Of Mimicry and Membership."

26. Mbembe, "African Modes of Self-Writing," 271.

27. Ibid.

28. Ferguson, *Expectations of Modernity*, 234–54; and Ferguson, "Of Mimicry and Membership."

"The Deep Thoughts the One in Need Falls Into":

Quotidian Experience and the Perspectives of Poetry in

Postliberation South Africa

☉ ☉ ☉

KELWYN SOLE

From 1984 onward, South African academic Njabulo Ndebele launched a wide-ranging critique of creative literature within the country. Overwhelmed by apartheid oppression, all expression—even of those who saw themselves in opposition—was trapped, he suggested, in apartheid's bogus "normality" of polar opposites. Moreover, a culture of the spectacular —the flaunting of material excess cheek by jowl with social poverty, the brutal displays of power and victimhood—had come to delimit even the worldview of apartheid's literary opponents. Writers downplayed all facets of social life among black people other than those of direct political relevance, Ndebele claimed. This allowed readers only an aesthetics of recognition, indictment, and ideological confirmation. Impatient with these categories and assumptions, Ndebele argued for a new phase of literary expression, suggesting that if the entire society has to be recreated, then writers, especially black writers, needed to realize that no aspect of society could be deemed irrelevant to the progress of liberation. Therefore they should widen their focus considerably to include the complex details of black people's ordinary experiences. The day-to-day lives of people constituted the content of the antiapartheid struggle. This should be a direct focus of interest: the new society being struggled for in South Africa should be based on a concern with the way people actually lived.[1]

In distinction to the predictability of political literature, Ndebele acclaimed popular songs, music, and the anonymous stories exchanged on buses and trains as examples of the types of utterance that showed Africans to be "makers of culture in their own right . . . asking ultimate questions about life, moral values and social being." Black culture and a revitalized cultural creativity were, it can be noticed, the principal wellspring feeding Ndebele's vision of a "post-protest" society and literature. In a 1986 discussion of contemporary black short fiction, for example, he highlighted the manner in which one particular short story demonstrated "African folk culture ['s] . . . independent life . . . right bang in the middle . . . of western 'rationality.' " Referring to other stories, he praised the way in which they validated the rationality, philosophical insights and self-knowledge of ordinary black people.[2] Although the inconsistencies and ambiguities of popular quotidian behavior and attitudes might exasperate politically motivated intellectuals, focusing on the ordinary would, Ndebele believed, open up a number of questions and lessons in literature that related to ethical issues, social processes and relationships, and the interiority of individuals. In a country where white rule had never nurtured "a civilisation based on the perfection of the individual in order to perfect maximum social creativity," the investigation of ordinary black livelihood constituted a keystone of the postapartheid future, part of Ndebele's agenda "to free the entire social imagination of the oppressed from the laws of perception that have characterised apartheid society," so that "the social imagination of the oppressed can be extended considerably in concrete terms and made ready to deal with the demands of a complex future."[3]

The Ordinary in South African Literary Studies

Many of these points have since become commonplaces of South African literary criticism. Generally speaking, at worst (and contrary to his intentions), some critics have directed Ndebele's suggestions into new forms of binary opposition rather than allowing them to invigorate more complex questions. Here, his call for attention to interiority is used to motivate postapartheid writers to focus exclusively on "introspection and the inner life," while his concept of the ordinary is employed to discredit any form of political expression—literature should simply affirm "the capacity for survival in the day-to-day ingenuity of townships dwellers," rather than become bogged down in the "baggage of politics."[4]

However, it is among critics who situate themselves within the terrain of postcolonial studies and poststructuralist theory that more intricate programs based on the foundation of Ndebele's views have been developed. Graham Pechey, one of his most loquacious supporters, provides an instructive example with regard to the stakes in such critics' commitment to the quotidian. For Pechey a "post-heroic culture of irony, the local, the ordinary" allows writers to explore textures of life that have eluded the Manichaean battles between state and "people" common to antiapartheid literature. Interrogating the contradictory details of the local and the quotidian, writers might learn to display social difference in nonhierarchical terms while approaching a more encompassing view of social reality. For Pechey, this commitment to local realities would in turn engender a whole range of "hybrid articulacies" resistant to the reification of totalizing theory and history, independent of metropolitan models, and no more answerable "to those good intentions of the [postliberation] state than . . . to the bad ones of . . . apartheid." Focusing on cultural aspects encompassing both "pre-colonial residues and transcultural strategies that have survived colonial acculturations" would, furthermore, bring to light African perceptions and experiences that had eluded discourses of modernization brought to the country by colonial modernity—discourses that (whether pro- or antiapartheid) Pechey believes disabled black subjectivity.[5]

Thus according to the poststructuralists, writers and critics explicating the concept of the ordinary are seen as having the potential to incapacitate the hegemonic ballast of the old apartheid state, as well as any hasty realignments seeking to ensure that the new social order resembles the old. Subverting master narratives and transforming victory over apartheid into "a gain for postmodern knowledge," this emphasis on the quotidian—on the heterogeneity of local institutions, representations, and their experienced histories—is meant to ipso facto act as a powerful counterforce to totalizing proclivities and homogenizing fabrications.[6]

Inflections of the Everyday

Studies of ordinary behavior outside of South Africa have been most fruitfully conducted through the term *the everyday*, a term that, for the purposes of this essay, sufficiently resembles *the ordinary* to allow for a comparison. Studies of the everyday reveal both the term's referential instability and the degree to which it both tends to elude theoretical or descriptive precision and to become weighted down with diverse, even contradictory, associations.[7] Its most significant area of operation appears in the rift between institutional codes and systems and private, individual perceptions, thus calling for a study of what Henri Lefebvre, possibly the preeminent formulator of studies of the everyday, perceives to be an *organized* passivity, whereby its routines and familiar settings are kept in place by their own (often unacknowledged) ethics and aesthetics, those widespread aspects of experience taken for granted such as domesticity, family and private life, leisure, and habitual repetitive behavior.[8]

For Lefebvre, the apparent diversity of quotidian experiences of modernity occludes the manner in which people's lives have been incrementally subordinated to a totalizing system constructed around what he designates "things" and a "bureaucratic society of controlled consumerism."[9] The apparent betterment of life under capitalism has paradoxically engendered a devaluation and regimentation of experience, felt temporally both linearly (as accelerated change) and cyclically (as monotony and stagnation). Everyday life is a product of the interlinked wealth and misery generated by capitalism, combining programmed abundance and planned obsolescence for some (especially in the so-called first world) with destructiveness—the devastation and impoverishment caused by a worldwide colonialism that goes hand in hand with a destruction of nature.

Despite being saturated with what is "numbered and calculated," however, the quotidian contains a residuum where "conquest and creation" can take place. In a world dominated not only by capitalist penetration but also by the postmodern proliferation of "aimless signifiers and disconnected signifieds," signs that "ratify the commentaries that determine their meanings," there is still a choice available for the individual: to become either a "passive victim" or an "active interpreter of signs."[10] Amid banality and repetition in those spaces where constraints and boredom are produced, in a global arena where abundance and lack occur side by side, dissatisfaction and unfulfilled desires emerge as natural consequences. This observation proves, in my opinion, pertinent for any understanding of contemporary South African experiences of the ordinary. In a scenario where the nation, and especially its poorest citizens, bear the brunt of the uneven development characterizing the postcolonial world, basic needs such as clean water, sanitation, electricity, transport, and housing serve as a point of negative comparison for many South Africans vis-à-vis others both in their own country and in the developed world.

Lefebvre's degree of optimism is fueled by a belief that it is within the commonplace of everyday life, "where the dominant relations of production are tirelessly and relentlessly reproduced," that utopian and political aspirations may crystallize.[11] Even at its most degraded, the quotidian offers the possibility of its own transformation, as the political lurks in the everyday. It is within everyday actions and attitudes that resistance may be perceived.[12]

Furthermore, in Lefebvre's view, any study of the everyday brings certain other questions to the forefront. In studying the everyday, one starts to ask: "Why should the study of the banal itself be banal? Are not the surreal, the extraordinary, the surprising, even the magical, also part of the real? Why wouldn't the concept of everydayness reveal the extraordinary in the ordinary?"[13] Cryptic as this quote may appear, it implies that transformative possibilities include, but are not exhausted by, political action in the conventional sense; and it implicitly points to something close to an understanding (an epiphany, if understood in literary terms) available to those who learn to "read" the untapped human potential still adhering in everyday life. It is immediately noticeable that contemporary South African cultural and literary critics who similarly recognize the "extraordinary" nearly always avoid, or refuse clear distinction to, the political ramifications of the quotidian, at the same time as they stress the more "magical," individualized connotations of the extraordinary residing in everyday life.[14]

Furthermore, many South African critics during the 1990s employed poststructuralism's critiques of "liberal humanism" (the dominant discourse in oppositional literary studies under apartheid) to construct, paradoxically, a new humanism: one they hope will bypass both the legacy of apartheid's antihumanism, as well as antihumanist strains in the poststructuralist theory they have up to this point invoked.[15] According to the poststructuralist John Noyes, for instance,

> To engage in intellectual work in South Africa means, perhaps at this present moment more so than in many other countries, to engage in the reluctant articulation of utopia and the form in which it announces itself in everyday life, the idea of the human. I permit myself this leap from the idea of utopia to that of the human via practices of everyday life, because one of the first moves in reconstituting our damaged civil society will have to be countering [a] particular idea of the human—the one that held sway over the ideology of apartheid.[16]

For Pechey, a reconceptualization of South Africa may optimally result in a scenario in which

> the peculiarity of [South African] history would no longer be a matter of territory and the economy . . . it would instead be a way of understanding the distinct . . . yet coinciding temporalities lived by South African communities as they have journeyed together . . . towards modernity. We need to see that what coincides in South Africa are not two "superstructural" spheres on one "infrastructure" but rather so many "nows" lived alongside each other . . . a redescription of "South Africa" that bypasses the grand categories of the geopolitical and the world-historical in a new emphasis upon the *dialogue* that underlies all antagonism.[17]

Such formulations of postliberation intellectual priorities seem attenuated. Crucially, discussions of the everyday outside of South Africa have tended to concur that the term cannot be conceptually seen as equivalent to *culture*.[18] Yet South African commentators appear to infer precisely this association. Even if a degree of imbrication of the everyday/ordinary with cultural identifications is granted, as of course it must be, the everyday aligns more specifically with the "cultural activity of the non-producers of culture"—to "whatever remains after one has eliminated all specialized activities."[19] In other words, the term should not be approached as a label for a generalized cultural studies.

Nevertheless, in South Africa, culturalist and humanist discourses of the quotidian are at present usually deemed sufficient in themselves and feed into utopian, pluralist conceptions of benign multiculturalism—of "dialogue" and negotiation between racial and cultural groups. At the same time, academic and media commentators hint that literature or criticism referring to political and economic imperatives or to unbreachable social differences appear merely redundant. Intent on avoiding any suggestion of politico-economic determinism in his or her own work, critic after critic falls prey to cultural reductionism instead.[20] Indeed, the dogged refusal of some critics to engage with structural (over)determination presents, eventually, a curiously one-sided picture of the experiences accompanying globalization. The ludic, multicultural potentialities of a burgeoning "hybridity" are stressed until one begins to lose sight of another important aspect of uneven global development: the fact that its processes simultaneously create a far more toxic reality for many people who, "bound to the global circulation of capital by only the thinnest of threads," are reduced to "being monetary subjects without money."[21] In light of this, a continued preoccupation with experiences of material poverty by many South African poets—including some of those quoted below—appears less idiosyncratic.

It should be pointed out that such gestures toward the ordinary are themselves susceptible to managed and top-down agendas every bit as teleological as any master narrative they strive to replace. In the long run, they serve ideological ends, bolstering those particular notions of human social identity, negotiated pluralism, and overarching unity-in-difference that their proponents believe are appropriate for a new society. Whatever passing genuflections are made to the pressures of globalization, commodification, and consumerism on both culture and the everyday (or the possibility that the country might be entering "the latest of its neocolonial phases"), they stay almost without exception on the level of asides.[22] Little evidence exists of a desire to follow through their implications by carefully scrutinizing how such factors impinge on, or help form, South African experience.

It is one thing to wish to downplay macro issues and political, economic, or theoretical determinism and mechanical articulations of "base/ superstructure" so that aspects of ordinary, everyday culture and experience can find greater definition; it is quite another to discount, to the point of invisibility, macro issues that structure and limit what is locally possible experientially in the first place. Yet this is precisely what has happened. The utopian nature of the studies I have described might open up interesting possibilities for more democratic, generous, and inclusive ways to view everyday South African reality. Yet in the absence of painstaking studies of the multiple levels of delimitation and effect at work — such as the effects of the economic and the political on culture and experience, or the ramifications of the complex dialectical interactions between the local and the global — what emerge in general are, it can be argued, curiously haphazard, idealist, and idealistic notions concerning the constitution of ordinary experience (or even the terrain of "culture") within South Africa.

If, as poet Peter Horn suggests, the destruction and devaluation of human space and experience under apartheid was total, then it is difficult to see precisely where one will find spiritualities and cultures falling sufficiently outside of the universalizing project of Western modernity; or why such phenomena should serve to downplay the relevance of macro issues.[23] The fact that there exist areas of communal and local micro politics that are nonreducible to macropolitical consumption should not result in amnesia about the manner in which macro issues impinge on the configurations of everyday life. Nevertheless, by 2001, in a climate of escalating retrenchments, joblessness, and inadequate social services, veteran poet and antiglobalization activist Dennis Brutus has seen the need to reemphasize this connection, bewailing the failure in local protests "to connect poverty in this country to the government's economic policies."[24]

Poets, GEAR, and Civil Society

When intellectuals and critics cast the everyday into the terms discussed above, one can argue that the only obvious beneficiaries are the country's powerful new and old political and economic elites. In distinction to this viewpoint, a significant number of contemporary South African English-language poets do not seem to subscribe to the view that their role and work lie outside of the province of capitalist reproduction or political conflict. Proposing that after liberation it was time to search "beyond the monolithic political categories . . . frozen into their [the poets'] minds by traumatising social engineering," Grahamstown poet Robert Berold expressed a hope (echoed by many poets from differing social and political positions) that a more multireferential and multidimensional art might start to emerge.[25] Yet while some white liberal poets used the opportunity to stress the priority of the free-floating individual, poets who had been closer to the antiapartheid struggle tended to suggest that postliberation livelihood remained "a struggle" for many. In 1990, the trade union–based Cultural and Working Life Project in Durban noted that "we see struggle as *part* of us, part of our everything—you wake up in the morning and it starts *coming* to you . . . it's about surviving, being resilient."[26] Eight years later, the Gauteng-based poetry collective the Botsotso Jesters remarked that while its members perceived an expanded horizon of subject matter and focus for themselves, they would continue to address a politics related to the "everyday life struggle of the individual" and to use poetic metaphors and images "taken from daily life, but . . . connected to broader political concepts."[27] Others, such as Cape Town poets Tatamkhulu Afrika and Karen Press, pointed to enduring issues—psychological, socioeconomic, and political—that would not disappear readily: Press noted that while "some people are starving, some people have three houses and five cars, and there are connections between them. Writing poetry doesn't excuse you from having to understand how power really works in the world you live in," while Afrika maintained that protest "against dominance of wealth, of privilege" was still necessary.[28] These statements indicate that in the first decade of liberation, (at least some) poets recognized the structurally overdetermined nature of ordinary life.

Despite the huge expectations of rapid social transformation that emerged after the demise of apartheid, from the first the new African National Congress (ANC) government found its power constrained by structural difficulties. Working within a situation in which, in the words of one member of parliament (MP), the party's continuing popularity depended on the degree to which it could win hearts and minds through delivering those benefits it promised before the election, it battled to gain adequate control of key economic and ideological institutions.[29] This problem has been made more acute by the continued presence of key old regime bureaucrats hindering implementation of new policies.

By the mid-1990s, it had become clear that the government was deviating from its previous position of "national democracy plus economic egalitarianism" in order to create a local climate that might gain access to and compete on world markets. The ANC's Reconstruction and Development Programme (RDP), formulated before the first election as the hub of its equity and development strategy, was replaced (despite disagreement from the party's traditional trade union and Communist Party alliance partners) with the 1996 Growth, Employment, and Redistribution Policy (GEAR), which formulated national economic policy in terms of neoliberal principles compliant to the dictates of the global market. The GEAR policy emphasized growth of exports and foreign investment as the principal machinery for stimulating economic growth. Development goals, and the eradication of the country's huge apartheid-given legacy of social inequities, were seen as realizable through a so-called trickle-down effect that would result from macroeconomic gains.[30] Both the IMF and the World Bank became significant players in steering the country in this direction through advice and expertise, with policies encouraging privatization, tight fiscal discipline, downsizing, and retrenchments. Such structural adjustment policies limited autonomous policy choice on a national level.

The bureaucratic, centralized, and top-down style of government that has more recently characterized Thabo Mbeki's presidency has not helped matters. While Mbeki and his circle see themselves as part of a global faction aiming to reform the global system to obtain greater de facto market equality for developing countries, they appear to question the structure of the world market only insofar as it prevents equal competition by the elites of the South who, it is implied, will use accruing wealth to ensure national development for all their citizens. This vision is put forward as a racial-cum-continental "revolution." Tight party discipline is seen as essential to achieve this goal, and the latter's opponents have heard themselves labeled "Afro-pessimists." The ANC excoriates members of the new bourgeoisie only if they do not use their wealth "patriotically." The government thus simultaneously displays itself on the world stage as a champion of the poor and puts in effect policies that are little more than a "negotiated path to austerity."[31]

This austerity has impacted most heavily on the poor and least-organized groups in society, particularly on the youth and women. Public services, such as water, have been commodified with devastating, and sometimes deadly, results for those unable to pay for them. Donor requirements to make the country more efficient and competitive have become linked (especially in the eyes of the poor) with a further degeneration, rather than regeneration, of living standards. Moreover, instead of growth and investor confidence, the South African economy has suffered many downturns since 1995 and has fared badly due to continuing North-South inequities. By the mid-1990s, the country had clearly fallen victim to outside financial speculation and an emerging markets' crisis, especially noticeable in 1996 and again in 1998 with the collapse of the so-called Asian Miracle—those "miracle" markets in the East that poet and inner-circle presidential adviser Vusi Mavimbela had previously put forward as a model for South Africa.[32]

Many ordinary people continue to feel the effects of economic and social devastation. The 1998 Speak Out on Poverty campaign calculated that 6 percent of the country's population earned more than 40 percent of the income. Sixty-three percent of the income went to the richest 20 percent of the population, who were still (due to the legacy of apartheid) predominantly white. Fifty-three percent of the population was estimated as living below the poverty datum line, and nearly 9 million people lived in informal settlements and shack communities. Africans in rural areas constituted 70 percent of the country's poor. While segments of the poor have received better basic services since 1994, the targets reached fell far short of inflated election promises and expectations on the ground. By the millennium, the situation had further deteriorated. Some surveys now contend that it may be worse than official figures suggest, with wage differentials both within and between race groups increasing, unemployment rates of up to 45 percent— with women, people in nonurban areas, and Africans bearing the brunt— and almost half the population living in poverty. A crisis of overcrowding, poor living conditions, and lack of basic services extends, in a differentiated fashion, into every aspect of the lives of the poor.[33]

Although the institutions of civil society can by no means be conflated with the terrain of the everyday, the relative health of such institutions gives some indication of the manner in which social life is experienced in domains not immediately connected to the state.[34] In apartheid South Africa civil society was highly developed, though exceedingly disproportionately so, usually along racial lines. Despite the fact that the apartheid state made every attempt to root out of civil society all actual or potential pockets of resistance to its workings, by the 1980s, a grassroots civil society had come into being in many black townships, comprising women's and youth groups, civic associations, street committees, NGOs, and other groupings. Many commentators expressed a hope that despite a daunting residue of apartheid's "constructions and representations" after liberation, a "new civic language . . . [and] forms" (the words belong to poet Ingrid de Kok) might act as catalysts for a widely participatory new society in ways that went beyond formal democracy.[35]

However, the confines in which organs of civil society have been able to operate during the 1990s have been reduced, and their relative freedom from immediate state influence have seen fierce contestation.[36] Despite the formation of a national civil society and NGO organizations in 1992 and 1996, respectively, a devastating decline in civil society occurred after the 1994 elections. Many pro-ANC, independent antiapartheid civic associations were seen as competition to, and therefore dissolved into, newly formed ANC branches. Government saw its own role in directing development as para-

mount, absorbing many experienced grassroots activists into new state structures. Many NGOs experienced a drastic reduction in overseas funding, while
a national funding body set up by the government hastened the demise of
more interstitial projects and itself proved a far-from-efficient distributor of
funds. Factionalism, corruption, and an ongoing dispute over the relationship of civil society to the state continue.[37] Even though the NGO and civic
sectors seemed to stage a partial recovery in the final years of the decade, by
the late 1990s, a serious question mark hovered over the ability of organizations of civil society to maintain a critical space between the government
and themselves. This has resulted in considerable distress, resentment, and
opposition, to the point that in 2000, some previously government-aligned
civic associations in the Eastern Cape chose to oppose the ANC in local elections.[38]

In such a milieu, Cape Town poet and community activist Donald Parenzee contrasts the idealism and comradeship of civic organizations during the
1980s with the atmosphere of the present, observing: "Now that apartheid
has been removed, there's a popular tendency to believe we're living in a free
society, which we're not. Society is driven, basically, by the same economic
structures as before. People have become much more aware of just how repressed their psyches have been, and it's been quite a shock. But there is
hardly any redress for this through political structures."[39]

Postliberation Poetry and the Everyday

It is evident that both utopian expectation and grim reality continue to coexist in people's experience of daily life, and that there exists a body of
poetry that attempts to explore the interstices at which these extremes are
felt and acted on. For example, commenting on Johannesburg poet Kgafela
oa Magogodi's depictions of inner-city Hillbrow, Phaswane Mpe acknowl-
edges that this poet's examination of the dire aspects of urban inner-city life
is offset by examples of positive human agency.[40]

In the postliberation milieu, there has been some disagreement as to the
future role of poetry. At one extreme, a number of short "What makes you
black?" poetry video inserts have recently been made for television featuring Pretoria poet Tumi Molekani in order (according to Metro FM manager
Lesley Ntloko) to create associations "with sophistication and upwards mobility among blacks . . . (and) an emotional bond between the brand [ad-
vertised in accompanying commercials] and its listeners."[41] In ruling party
circles, some poets such as diplomat Lindiwe Mabuza seem to see their role
as simply praising the new dispensation or its office bearers. Others close to

government stress the positive requirements of nation building and a widening of opportunities for democratic public discourse. For example, ANC MP
Jeremy Cronin argues the need for poetry to "emerge from public conversation and return to it. . . . it should not have to choose always between either
the street or the study."[42]

Poets at a distance from government, however, tend to be less forgiving of
its failings and more prepared to take on a dissident, acerbic role castigating
those in power. Says Gauteng poet Lesego Rampolokeng in "The Rampster
Comes Straight":

> it's another struggle stage
> bungle next age same page
>
> . . .
>
> no government under any firmament worth fundament
> i'm poet not ornament in cabinet / house of parliament
> get it   sillybitcharsellout?

As far as representations of quotidian experience are concerned, while it
is clear that some recent poems do not, in the words of Magogodi, concern themselves with anything more than "waking up in the morning . . .
[and] romantic relationships," a sizeable number of poets "in a fairly tough
[era] . . . really want to see questions that were posed or promises that were
put up in '94 being responded to."[43] Any sustained reading of contemporary South African poetry throws to light a frequent implicit, and sometimes
explicit, recognition of the quotidian as a politicized domain. For example,
Eastern Cape poet Mzi Mahola's elliptical "Strange things," quoted here
in full, directs the reader toward scrutinizing his or her own point of view,
habits of understanding, and stereotypes and prejudices through a series of
descriptive statements and conflicting inferences about a possibly banal, possibly highly charged series of everyday interactions involving three people
(one obviously of different social status and racial group to the others):

> A man followed a madam
> Into a house . . .
>
> When he went home
> She was at the window
> Listening to his footsteps
> Gazing at the township.
>
> When her husband returned
> He helped her into a chair.

In Press's collection *Home*, she interweaves questions relating to the quotidian and the political, the public and the personal, the global and the local, ancestry and identity, home and exile, within the fraught context of post-1990 reality. The local is suffused with "seeds . . . from all parts of the known world" ("I who Live Here, It is I") while, after liberation, reclaiming the land (in a poem of the same name) seems like an arduous, perhaps impossible, task, for "Every map is out of date. / . . . Put up a mirror where you are / and make yourself at home in your familiar eyes. / Outside the wind blew it all away."

Other poets are more forthright in their association of daily life with political and economic issues. Some of the poems of Vonani Bila, an NGO worker and cultural activist living in Limpopo province, deal forcefully with politically charged experiences of the everyday in one of the poorest areas of the country. Questions of gender and the degradation of women permeate his work, for instance in the lengthy "Dahl Street, Pietersburg," which links prostitution directly with the economic and cultural destruction of social networks and the policies of what he calls "a cocacola regime": "Sex workers are burgers / we chew the fresh ones / . . . Leaders smoke Cuban cigars / . . . In Holiday Inn they buy beers with credit cards / Next plane to US / . . . Trapped in crony capitalism." For him, issues of social placement and identity, and personal and communal experience, are immediately bound up with wider issues of national economic policy and direction. Cape Town poet Mark Espin's delineation of the Company Gardens, a tourist destination in the center of the city, makes a similar point using understatement. Benign as it may seem, the everyday constitutes a surface below which strong undercurrents moil in "The Company Gardens":

All trees are labelled according to their origins.

The strawberries have the taste of the earth.

The image of Madiba has been discounted
With the sale of keyrings and postcards.

Street beggars provide the necessary entertainment.
Show their bruised faces as an illusion.

. . . Sunlight remains a charade amidst the lush leaves.

The foreign accents irritate the tame doves.

The currency of pretension is suitably exchanged.

The Elaboration and Questioning of
Traditional Spheres in Women's Poetry

Rita Felski observes that feminism has usually conceived of itself as a politics of everyday life, due in part to the traditional linking of women with the domestic sphere and other sites of reproduction. Feminists have generally perceived this ambivalently, deploying "a hermeneutics of suspicion vis-à-vis the everyday, showing how the most mundane, taken-for-granted activities . . . serve to reinforce patriarchal norms," while simultaneously honoring everyday life as a "distinctively female sphere and . . . source of value."[44] While Ndebele's work generally remains silent about gender and feminism, Anthony O'Brien suggests that the attention to the ordinary it has generated opens up a wider range of possibility for such concerns, displacing questions of power toward the private sphere, traditionally coded female.[45]

While O'Brien's statement is hypothetical, in practice it has become apparent that since 1990, a number of women poets in South Africa have challenged, refined, or shown the complexities of notions of a female sphere in ways extending the term. At the onset of the postapartheid era, women active in the antiapartheid struggle such as Durban poets Nise Malange and Boitumelo Mofokeng were already writing a poetry commenting on the problems of the double—for some, triple—oppressions of race, class, and gender suffered by some women, or about workaday burdens relating to mothering and the double shift. "Help me to remove my baby from my back," Mofokeng ironically comments, "because it is time to make love: / the only chore I do without / my baby on my back" ("With My Baby on My Back").[46] Similarly Joan Metelerkamp, citing Adrienne Rich, speaks of her desire to move "out of the realm of men . . . [but] also to move into the realm of the brilliance of men, but in my own terms," defining her writing as from "the white suburbs. . . . I accept it. Mothering in the white suburbs." She therewith highlights the attention to detail and domesticity, but also to intellectual and creative work (spheres traditionally designated male) associated with her poetics.[47] From a very different social position but contemporaneously, Malange notes, "I don't think South Africa will be different from any other country. As black women, we are still going to fight for our recognition and acceptance in political structures as well as culture."[48]

Any careful examination of contemporary women's poetry requires an exploration of not only unifying but also differing experiences of race, class, locality, and citizenship between and within the sexes. Such an exploration would take us into the realm of the everyday and would scrutinize and query the stereotypes and generalizations that condemn South African women to their supposed "traditional" spaces of importance.[49] This is not to underplay the fact that more than two-thirds of South African households are (according to minister of housing and poet Sankie Mthembi-Mahanyele) headed by women, and that the strength and power of these households depend on women.[50]

However, despite a number of parliamentary and civil organizations set up since 1990 to address the plight of women, and despite the promulgation of new, favorable legislation, "betrayal, and sexploitation are the order of the day."[51] Empowerment strategies appear to have resulted mainly in advantages for middle-class and/or white women.[52] While changes in the economy and legislation have altered (and sometimes assisted) women's structural position in households, various forms of abuse and violence have also spiraled out of control.[53] The existence of legal frameworks to enable an end to gender discrimination remains at odds with experiences of many people on the ground. Notwithstanding government attempts at resourcing, the ex-homelands and rural areas continue to be epicenters of poverty and lack—for women as for men. Estimates say that just less than half of the country's population is rural, with women making up just over half of this figure. Structurally crucial to the rural economy, women nevertheless remain the most impoverished group.[54]

Of course, we cannot assume that the experiences women undergo within race and class enclaves remain static, or are lacking in diversity. In a long poem, Cape Town poet Gertrude Fester, on an "official visit" to a poor rural area, muses on the social differences that render South African women "Sisters of sorts." Elsewhere, Eastern Cape poet Nosipho Kota claims her poem "Township woman" (which looks at a number of township women with widely differing social placements and personal histories in order to focus on the stereotypical labels they have received from the local community) became possible for her to write because her own life history was marked with rapidly changing social positions, expectations, and fortunes.[55]

Two individual poets have explored the intersections of social life with quotidian experience and local geography at book length. Joan Metelerkamp's *Into the day breaking* traces her determination to map out her life, role, and relationships with her family and wider social and natural surroundings in a small sawmill town inland from Knysna. The poems, written in her characteristic meditative style, deal with the straitened circumstances she finds herself having to confront on a daily basis. Karen Press evinces a similar urge (despite differences in style and focalization) in *Echo Location*, with poems centered around the spatial, imaginative, and social geography of the high-rise suburb of Sea Point in Cape Town.

An examination of poetry reveals that women—and black women in particular—restrained by habits of privacy and social decorum, often use creative writing to facilitate a more direct expression of taxing issues and emotions than they feel comfortable with face to face.[56] This is sometimes conjoined with a determination to maintain a profile of social responsibility, or remain optimistic to the possibilities of communal and individual self-betterment despite adversity. "Victimised But Never a Victim," by Brigitte Nxele (a pseudonym), demonstrates this: writing of a childhood of familial displacement, verbal and sexual abuse, and psychological trauma, she speaks of eventually obtaining a university degree and her "new dream / . . . to free and help homeless people / Because I know what it is like to live / Without a future ahead of you. . . ."

Structural Underdevelopment and the Everyday

Many contemporary poems implicitly or explicitly acknowledge that personal experience and the quotidian are shot through with enduring macro issues of a sociopolitical, cultural, or economic nature, while others demonstrate a psychological and personal precariousness that one can say relate in part to the country's fragile social coherence and tenuous global economic standing. Mahola, for one, remarks that "Rulers are shifting the ground / Under our very feet / This night of our freedom / . . . the wind / Has blown the country down" ("They've grown to love killing"). Thus we can read observations like Press's that "no one is nailed down properly here" in "Can't Stand, Can't Dance" on several levels.

Cape Town poet Weaam Williams has observed in "Derailed" that South Africa has emerged from racial oppression into a global milieu exhibiting the "contradictory reality of liberation and abuse / With anorexic millionaire models / And starving populations." For the poor, lack is always experienced through the prism of the excesses of wealth and indulgence of a consumerist society. In a society where the burgeoning of poverty next to enclaves of privilege and technological sophistication endures, retrenchments, housing shortages, and other reminders of social inequity become common poetic themes. Thus, in "Under the bridge," Johannesburg poet Thomas Hartleb describes a scene of homeless people living under billboards "Between the Kodak moments / And the Colgate smile," while the homeless narrator in Gauteng poet Johannes Buti Makama's "To sit in there" sees "a sit-in food outlet / Fifty steps from where I sit / This is the distance I have to keep / They claim I'll be bad for business / If I go any nearer." A powerful trope in a number of poems revolves around the poor's reliance on waste: Durban poet and cultural activist Ari Sitas's "RDP—Film Documentary" focuses on people's attempts to gain access to a rubbish tip; "They Claim," by Limpopo province–based Mashudu Mashige describes the scramble for food that takes place around a truck overturned in a traffic accident; and Vigilance Ndama from the Eastern Cape, at one time homeless himself, praises, in "Dust Bin, a Sustainer," a rubbish bin as "sustainer / in times of starvation."

In a climate where the gap between rich and poor is widening at the same time as the political and business elites put themselves forward as the agents of growth and development, a number of poets such as Seitlhamo Motsapi, based in Gauteng, denounce these elites and the forms of corruption and parasitism they engender in this way: "the sun recedes / into the quaking pinstripe / of my warriors / grinning & vulgar in their muddied dreams / of power" ("sol/o"). Those "mimics," in Mahola's words, "of their former masters" who "with elastic hands / . . . pluck / Fruits of other's sweat / Like a flight of birds" ("Sweat of their Brows"). This goes hand in hand with a degree of cynical incredulity at those who, in the words of Soweto poet Mbongeni Khumalo, sit at conferences "talking rubbish / beautified with English" ("My dream has died"). Moreover, while younger poets increasingly use electronic media (in forms such as beat boxes and homemade videos), the manner in which commerce and the media manipulate and dull human consciousness to benefit the rich locally and globally emerges as a pervasive theme for those living, as Magogodi's "rhymes of the times" has it:

in a storm
of stereoform
of
censorship
in radioform
of
dictatorship
in djform
of
an afrika
made in america

Such poems bear witness to exacerbated class friction, new forms of social fissuring, and widely divergent life experiences: noting that GEAR should rather stand for "Government Entrenches Avoidance of Reality" in "The People Have Spoken," Johannesburg poet Righteous the Common Man, addressing the well-off in "My Reality," finds it "amusing / the way you have a tendency of assuming / whenever you speak of solutions and resolutions / concluding that we all share the same reality."

Recent work by Bila and Sitas marry the quotidian to enduring social and economic issues within poorer communities especially powerfully. In a concatenation of short poems, "Living rites," for example, Sitas measures the beauty of the rural Kwazulu-Natal landscape against the rigors of livelihood in a social environment beset by AIDS, cholera, and other health and social issues:

> The foothills
> and the meadows
>
> . . .
>
> the beautiful Dhlomo Paton-ted landscape
> of the river that kills
>
> . . .
>
> The inhale exhale of the
> intimacy of man, woman, beast
> The thousands in their lines
> sharing a drip.

Bila, in turn, utilizes the antiapartheid slogan *Amandla ngawethu!* (power to the people) as a point of comparison when he asks in "In the name of Amandla":

> In the name of Amandla
> Tell me what has changed in this village
> There's no food in the kitchen
>
> . . .
>
> It's winter, the school has no desks, textbooks & windows,
> Our leaders send their children to private schools
> Ask them
>
> . . .
>
> We are in trouble
> The electricity is weak
> Switch off everything else when you use a stove
>
> . . .
>
> Come winter—the municipality will cut it off
>
> . . .
>
> Our RDP house leaks when it rains
> We can't fit, it's a toilet
>
> . . .
>
> Verwoerd, my enemy, built much bigger houses
> Trevor Manuel can't stop buying submarines, corvettes and jet fighters.[57]

In poems such as these, the anger is direct and the political targets clear. They insist on the awareness that ordinary life is inextricably intertwined with macro issues. Therefore many contemporary poets palpably attempt to lay bare a "geopolitical reality" of structural cause and effect in ways which "used to be called self-consciousness about social totality."[58]

Conclusion

The politically charged nature of the term *the everyday* makes it potentially the bearer of different associations and versions. This essay has tried to examine, via poetry, what is singular and typical about South Africans' experience of the quotidian, especially in terms of the country's position as a so-called developing country; at the same time, it implicitly suggests that intellectuals cannot simply presume that their delineations of, or wishes for, quotidian life are always accurate or generally felt. Yet it is clear that the spaces in which boredom, routine, and stereotyped roles are manufactured also function as a springboard for the possible, as they implicitly demonstrate the need for a far different state of affairs and at times contain powerful significations of human resistance. Currently, a group of poets is writing in South Africa that positions itself at a greater distance from the promises of the present government than some of its peers, and their work bears this out. This group comprises both politically aware middle-class poets and many who have themselves brutally and firsthand experienced the suffering brought about by globalization and neoliberal policies.

Ndebele's intervention in the arena of the ordinary certainly does not constitute a plea for the status quo: it bears an activist desire for a space where the resilience of "African" cultural experience can begin to reach beyond itself to form and transform a new civil society and lived experience of nationhood. This is to the point. Achille Mbembe argues trenchantly that extrapolations of the notion of civil society and the everyday into Africa have tended to ignore the traces of distinctly African forms of categorization, organization, and experience.[59] It should be noted that Lefebvre's work tends to situate the everyday in developed or affluent societies (at least officially affluent), so there is a need to both extend and reformulate his concepts when considering developing and postcolonial societies. In recent studies, I would contend, discussion of the lineaments of everyday experience has tended to presuppose too readily that the ambience of contemporary quotidian social experience in the West constitutes the norm. Critics like Rita Felski misrecognize the possibility that everyday experience and behavior can in fact be interwoven with a routine experiential dissonance. An erasure between "extremity and the everyday, the terrible and the ordinary . . . a topsy-turvy world [where] the unthinkable becomes mundane, even expected" does not emerge only in "abnormal societies where terror and torture are systematized," as she maintains.[60] Such an erasure is also—to a less extreme degree—a factor of experience of the poor, the homeless, refugees, and other marginalized groups in countries lower down the global food chain such as South Africa, even as individuals in these groups strive toward a life of greater affluence and normality. It is moreover not beyond possibility that a partial erasure still exists of Felski's own milieu.

However, Ndebele's emphasis on race and culture in his version of the ordinary bears crucial aporias. Similarly, poststructuralist theorists who use Ndebele as a starting point too often ignore aspects of South African experience that lie athwart their particular emphasis on the politics of culture and discourse. In a country presently awash with the banalities and selective interpretations of politicians and businesspeople and the myopic felicities of feel-good journalism, the incisive testimonies borne by poetry give some indication that this medium (rather than being rendered obsolete by new technologies) continues to have a relevance indispensable to human livelihood and expression. As the poet Dineo Veronica Mosiane has noted, "the deep thoughts the one 'in need' falls into are much deeper than of those who have all they want."[61] The utterances quoted here, some by poets not individually celebrated or recognized by the academy, attest to the experience of quotidian tedium and lack and give notice of the ways in which individuals perceive, and resist, the impositions of the powerful. As Port Elizabeth poet Mxolisi Nyezwa implies in his collection *song trials*, realizations of scarcity and sorrow necessarily exist alongside, and bring into being, expectation, longing, and a determination for change. In "i won't forget" he writes

> i won't forget those men who tug at night
> and who sleep in the bay
> with hope of seeing light,
> the blue light of the next day.
> . . .
> i won't forget that we are men on this earth
> with numbed emotions,
> nabbing at shadows
> hidden from sight.

Notes

1. See the discussion in Ndebele, *South African Literature and Culture*, 30–34, 48, 56–57, 70.
2. See the discussion in ibid., 37–38, 51–56.

3. Ibid., 50, 67, 73, respectively.

4. Quotes are from Mbulelo Mzamane, "From Resistance to Reconstruction," 18; and Andries Oliphant, "SA Needs to Escape Baggage of Politics," *Sunday Times* (Johannesburg), May 22, 1994.

5. See Pechey, "Post-apartheid Narratives," 155–56; Pechey, "Introduction," 6; and Pechey, "The Post-apartheid Sublime," 57, 64.

6. Pechey, "Post-apartheid Narratives," 153. See also Pechey, "The Post-apartheid Sublime," 58; O'Brien, *Against Normalization*, 101; and de Kock, "The Pursuit of Smaller Stories," 86.

7. See the discussion in Langbauer, "Cultural Studies and the Politics of the Everyday," 48–50; and Felski, "The Invention of Everyday Life," 30.

8. Kaplan and Ross, introduction, 3–4; Lefebvre, "The Everyday and Everydayness," 10; and Lefebvre, *Everyday Life in the Modern World*, 24.

9. See Lefebvre, "The Everyday and Everydayness," 8–9.

10. Lefebvre, *Everyday Life*, 21, 25.

11. These are Lefebvre's terms; see Kaplan and Ross, introduction, 3.

12. For discussion of the political emphasis in Lefebvre, see Langbauer, "Cultural Studies and the Politics of the Everyday," 50–52.

13. Lefebvre, "The Everyday and Everydayness," 9. Similarly, new South African writing should, Pechey suggests, not only "rediscover the ordinary" but also "point to its equal and opposite generation of the extraordinary." Pechey, "The Post-apartheid Sublime," 64.

14. Reviewer Dirk Klopper, for instance, reads the work of perhaps the most exemplary delver into the ordinary—poet Tatamkhulu Afrika—in a way that blurs completely the cramping political-cum-economic into the emancipating spiritual-cum-human. He notes that Afrika's poetry deals with the "dissipation and imminent violence" of the "other Cape Town not referred to in travel brochures . . . which appears to be divorced from the sobriety of civil society but is in fact intimately related to it," as well as with chance meetings "pointing to an unknown beyond themselves of which they may be said to be the astonished trace . . . transforming everyday eventualities into encounters with the numinous other," but he does not discuss the different connotations of these two aspects. Dirk Klopper, "Tatamkulu [*sic*] Afrika: *Dark Rider*," *New Coin* 29, no. 1 (1993): 59; and Dirk Klopper, "Tatamkhulu Afrika: *The Lemon Tree* and Other Poems," *New Coin* 31, no. 2 (1995): 76–77.

15. All of these critics have (rather unhappily) appropriated Spivak's "strategic essentialism" in order to enable "the oppressed" viable, continuing self-determination and self-expression in a transitional South Africa. For a longer discussion of this aspect in David Attwell, David Bunn, Annemare Carusi, de Kock, and others, see Sole, "South Africa Passes the Posts," 120–25. Spivak, *In Other Worlds*, 205.

16. Noyes, "The Place of the Human," 53.

17. Pechey, "Post-apartheid Narratives," 155; emphasis original.

18. Lefebvre, *Everyday Life in the Modern World*, 30–37.

19. Quotes are from de Certeau, *The Practice of Everyday Life*, xvii, and Kaplan and Ross, introduction, 2.

20. Albeit focused on a different historical context, James Holstun's comment is germane: "Contemporary practitioners of cultural studies seldom take the time to specify what is *other than* culture, so by definition . . . they never define culture itself.

They post clear warning signs on the road to reductive economism, but leave unmarked the equally reductive road to culturalism." Holstun, *Ehud's Dagger*, 93.

21. See the discussion (especially of the work of the economist Robert Kurz) in Larsen, *Determinations*, 48–57.

22. The quote comes from Pechey, "The Post-apartheid Sublime," 59.

23. Horn, "A Radical Rethinking," 100.

24. Glenda Daniels, "Veteran Activist to Speak at Race Talks," *Mail and Guardian* (Johannesburg), August 24, 2001.

25. Robert Berold, "Interview: Karen Press," *New Coin* 29, no. 1 (1993): 28.

26. Malange et al., "Albie Sachs Must Not Worry," 99.

27. See the statements by poets Ike Mboneni Muila, Allan Kolski Horwitz, and Anna Varney in Robert Berold, "Interview: Botsotso Jesters," *New Coin* 34, no. 1 (1998): 24.

28. Berold, "Interview: Karen Press," 27; and Berold, "Interview: Tatamkulu [*sic*] Afrika," 39.

29. Ben Turok, "ANC: Torn between Two Roles," *Mail and Guardian* (Johannesburg), August 10, 2001.

30. For further discussion, see Adelzadeh, "From the RDP to GEAR"; Habib et al., "South Africa and the Global Order"; and Bond, *Elite Transition*.

31. Alan Zuege, quoted in Bond, *Against Global Apartheid*, 118. For an extended critique of Mbekism, see ibid., 116–51. See also Ferial Haffajee, "ANC National General Council: Rationality Gains Ground on Rhetoric," *Financial Mail* (Johannesburg), July 20, 2000.

32. Bond, *Against Global Apartheid*, esp. 3–53; Vusi Mavimbela, "How to Build an African Renaissance," *Sunday Times* (Johannesburg), June 8, 1997.

33. See Marais, *South Africa: Limits to Change*, 107–8; André Koopman, "Break the Silence on Poverty, Destitution," *Mail and Guardian* (Johannesburg), March 5, 1998; Glenda Daniels, "New Survey Puts SA Jobless Rate at 45 percent," *Mail and Guardian* (Johannesburg), March 1, 2002.

34. For the purpose of this essay, civil society will be defined as a spatial metaphor for "those organizations that operate between the level of the state and the level of the individual and household." Mayekiso, *Township Politics*, 145.

35. De Kok, "Cracked Heirlooms," 70. Pechey notes that civil society can act as a "powerful counterweight" to neocolonial solutions (Pechey, "The Post-apartheid Sublime," 59). Ndebele, as well as poet Mongane Serote, had similar views concerning civil society's contemporary importance in South Africa. See Ndebele, *South African Literature and Culture*, 108–10; and Serote, *Hyenas*, 187.

36. For further elucidation, see Daniel Nina, "Beyond the Frontier: Civil Society Revisited," *Transformation*, no. 17 (1992): 61–73; and Mayekiso, *Township Politics*, 145.

37. Newspaper reportage on these issues is too voluminous to be cited fully. See, for example, David Macfarlane, "NGO Sector Rocked by Divisions," *Mail and Guardian* (Johannesburg), July 6, 2001; Evidence wa ka Ngobeni, "ANC, Sanco Fight for 'God's Paradise,'" *Mail and Guardian* (Johannesburg), July 20, 2001; David Macfarlane, "NDA Mired in Controversy," *Mail and Guardian* (Johannesburg), August 24, 2001; and Marianne Merten, "Sanco Torn by Byzantine Wrangle," *Mail and Guardian* (Johannesburg), July 26, 2002.

38. Abbey Makoe, "Local Poll Renegades Tackle ANC Head-On," *Sunday Independent* (Johannesburg), November 26, 2000.

39. Robert Berold, "Interview: Donald Parenzee," *New Coin* 36, no. 1 (2000): 48–49.

40. Mpe, "Introduction," vii.

41. Thebe Mabanga, "Hearing the Beat on the Box," *Mail and Guardian* (Johannesburg), February 1, 2002.

42. Robert Berold, "Interview: Jeremy Cronin," *New Coin* 34, no. 2 (1998): 35, 37.

43. Matthew Krouse, "Talkin' Loud," *Mail and Guardian* (Johannesburg), June 14, 2002.

44. Felski, "The Invention of Everyday Life," 30.

45. O'Brien, *Against Normalization*, esp. 50–56.

46. DeShazer, *A Poetics of Resistance*, 226. DeShazer quotes Mofokeng's "With My Baby on My Back."

47. Colleen Crawford Cousins, "Interview: Joan Metelerkamp," *New Coin* 28, no. 2 (1992): 24, 28.

48. "Nise Malange," 45.

49. Massey, *Space, Place, and Gender*. Massey is at pains to emphasize the changing roles and positions working women occupy in different temporal and spatial contexts. For an incisive discussion of the problems associated with prior South African studies of motherhood, see Walker, "Conceptualising Motherhood."

50. Mark Gevisser, "The Poet with a Politician's Instincts," *Mail and Guardian* (Johannesburg), January 26, 1995.

51. Mzamane, "From Resistance to Reconstruction," 16.

52. Shamim Meer, "Which Workers, Which Women, Which Interests? Race, Class, and Gender in Post-apartheid South Africa," paper presented at the Centre for African Studies, University of Cape Town, August 16, 2000, 1.

53. For an example of structural repositioning, see the study of Duncan Village near East London in Bank, "The Social Life of Paraffin." For the burgeoning of abuse, see Jane Bennett, "Enough Lip-Service! Hearing Post-colonial Experience of Gender-Based Violence," *Agenda*, no. 50 (2001): 88–96.

54. For further discussion see inter alia Daymond, *South African Feminisms*, xvii–xxiv; and Tara Turkington, " 'We Are in the Dark,' " *Mail and Guardian* (Johannesburg), October 19, 2001.

55. "I think it was God's purpose for me to experience those places, so that I am in a position where I can say, I know what it is to live in a one-room, as well as living in a backyard shack." Kota, "Introduction: A Frank Poet," 35–36.

56. See the remarks in Mofokeng, "Workshop on Black Women's Writing and Reading," 87.

57. Trevor Manuel is the present national minister of finance.

58. Jameson, *The Geopolitical Aesthetic*, 2.

59. See Mbembe, *On the Postcolony*, esp. 36–39, and "African Modes of Self-Writing," 258.

60. Felski, "Introduction," 617. As regards Africa, Ato Quayson remarks, "Much of the continent is pervaded by what might be called *cultures of impunity*. A minor traffic infringement might cause a person instant and violent retribution from bystanders. To fall in love with the wrong partner may invite physical mishaps of un-

imaginable sorts. . . . The worrisome thing is that this culture of impunity often marks *all* levels of civic society and polity" ("Obverse Denominations: Africa?").

61. Quoted in Hemsley and Blumenthal, *Of Money, Mandarins, and Peasants*, 89.

Bibliography of Poetry

Bila, Vonani, ed. *Timbila 2001: A Journal of Onion Skin Poetry*. Elim: Timbila Poetry Project, 2001.

Ferguson, Bus, and Ingrid de Kok, eds. *City in Words*. Cape Town: David Philip/New Africa Books, 2001.

Finlay, Alan, and Siphiweka Ngwenya, eds. *Insight: Nosipho Kota, Alex Mohlabeng, Myesha Jenkins, Ayanda Billie, Themba ka Mathe, Righteous the Common Man*. Elim: Timbila Poetry Project/Bila, 2003.

Gardiner, Michael, ed. *Throbbing Ink: Six South African Poets: Linda ba Ndlovu, Wisani Nghalaluma, Vonani wa ka Bila, Mbongeni Khumalo, Phomelelo Machika, Allan Kolski Horwitz*. Johannesburg: Botsotso Publishers, 2003.

Helmsley, Joanna, and Roy Blumenthal, eds. *Of Money, Mandarins, and Peasants: A Collection of South African Poems about Poverty*. Johannesburg; SANGOCO/Homeless Talk, 2000.

Howe, Hannah, ed. *Pulse—The Peripherals: Street Poetry by Homeless Writers*. Johannesburg: Peripheral Vision, 1997.

Magogodi, Kgafela ba. *The Condom Come*. Amsterdam: New Leaf, 2000.

Mahola, Mzi. *Strange Things*. Cape Town: Snailpress, 1994.

———. *When rains come*. Cape Town: Carapace, 2000.

Metelerkamp, Joan. *Into the day breaking*. Pietermaritzburg: Gecko/University of Natal Press, 2000.

Motsapi, Seitlhamo. *earthstepper/the ocean is very shallow*. Grahamstown: Deep South, 1995.

Ndlovu, Malika, Shelley Barry, and Deela Khan, eds. WEAVE's *ink@boilingpoint: A Selection of 21st Century Black Women's Writing from the Tip of Africa*. Cape Town: WEAVE Collective, 2000.

New Coin 37, no. 1 (2001).

New Coin 37, no. 2 (2001).

Nyezwa, Mxolisi. *song trials*. Pietermaritzburg: Gecko/University of Natal Press, 2000.

Press, Karen. *Echo Location: A Guide to Sea Point for Residents and Visitors*. Durban: Gecko, 1998.

———. *Home*. Manchester: Carcanet, 2000.

Rampolokeng, Lesego. *The Bavino Sermons*. Durban: Gecko, 1999.

Between the Burqa and the Beauty Parlor? Globalization, Cultural Nationalism, and Feminist Politics

☉ ☉ ☉

NIVEDITA MENON

Debates on globalization in India tend to harden into polarized rhetorical stances — either an uncritical celebration of globalization by the dominant consuming elites or a condemnation, equally lacking in nuances, by so-called antiglobalization forces, which range across the political spectrum, from right to left. This essay speaks to some of the issues circulating around these debates and explores significant disjunctures and contradictions on both sides.

To begin with, the boundary between the sides is more blurred than might appear from the rhetoric. Some sections of the pro-globalization consuming elites referred to above also form part of the support base of the supposedly antiglobalization Right. However, left-wing antiglobalization critiques seldom unpack these tensions, and tend to conflate the antidemocratic majoritarian politics of the Hindu Right with corporate globalization. Growing communalism is thus assumed to be tied to and drawing from the globalizing forces; further, India's nuclear bomb is also given a specifically Hindu Right color. As a result of this conflation, counterhegemonic political practice, specifically feminist politics, fails to recognize the full complexity of the forces we are dealing with — we miss out both on the real dangers and on potential opportunities. Although I address material generated largely in debates in India, it is not far-fetched to assume that strong resonances exist with similar debates in other postcolonial societies, marked as they are by a shared uniqueness best characterized, following Partha Chatterjee, as "our" moment of modernity, a term I explain below.

Indeed, there are three terms that I need to clarify before I continue — *postcolonial*, *modernity*, and *our modernity*. At least two of these terms have been rather overdebated, and here I intend simply to point to where I stand, assuming the prior existence of those debates. I use *post-colonialism* not simply as *after* colonialism but in another well-known sense, as the discourse of oppositionality that the encounter with colonialism brings into being—postcoloniality thus begins from the very first moment of colonial contact.[1] Second, with reference to *modernity*, I find useful Sudipta Kaviraj's outlining of "the historical constellation of modernity" as generally understood to consist of three primary processes: (1) capitalist industrial production; (2) political institutions of liberal democracy and the evolution of a society based on the process of individuation; and (3) a gradual decline of communal forms of belonging yielding place to the modern form of interest-based voluntary associations.[2] Third, when this modernity is encountered through colonialism, it assumes a particular form that Partha Chatterjee calls "our" modernity.[3] While modernity proved equally disruptive in Europe, the way these other societies entered into modernity involved a double violence—that of an alien structure of power embodying, in addition to the disruption of modernity itself, the violence of imperialism. The relationship with modernity in such societies has therefore had a specific character: local elites on the one hand, and subaltern groups on the other, entering into differentiated negotiations at two interrelated levels, with colonial authority and with modernity, each group developing different degrees of investment in the twin, related projects.

When we look at the articulation of resistances to globalization in those parts of the globe that have been colonized, we find that some antiglobalization arguments position themselves as identical to "tradition"; others, to "nationalism"; and with many, the two are linked, that is, the Nation *is* Tradition. The challenge for feminist politics as a radical critique of capitalism and dominant culture is to disaggregate the strands of these assertions and to carve out a different space of resistance. This task is complicated by the fact that, as I have already suggested, the kinds of positions outlined above do not simply fall into the Right/Left opposition, particularly when it comes to nationalism, a value asserted by both sides equally vociferously.

A useful entry point into the questions I have gestured toward is the recent drive by some militant groups in Kashmir to enforce the veil for Muslim women in the state. This drive is several years old now and began with an ultimatum issued by a little-known militant group in Kashmir, the Lashkar-e-Jabbar. In September 2001 the group announced that all Muslim women in the valley of Kashmir would have to wear the burqa (a form of hijab) and that those who did not would be "punished." There followed attacks with acid on the faces of unveiled women and threats to shoot after the deadline passed. Apart from one major women's organization, Dukhtaraan-e-Millat, which supported the call, all other militant groups denounced this ultima-tum and raised doubts as to the existence of the group calling itself Lashkar-e-Jabbar, suggesting it could be part of the Indian state's strategy to discredit militancy in Kashmir. However, the threat proved real, and many women have taken to the burqa who did not wear one till now. After what seemed like a lull, once again the drive intensified in 2002, this time in the name of another organization. In this phase, the threat was even more potent—three young women were killed for going unveiled.

Mehbooba Mufti, the leader of what was then the opposition party in Kashmir (now, after the recent elections, in power), who herself adopted the head scarf after she joined politics, came out with a strong statement against forcing such dress on women. She said, "When women come out to demonstrate, their headgear is always missing, they even have torn clothes, there is no purdah at all. Then nobody has a problem. But when one of these women is on her way to school or office, she has acid thrown on her in the name of vulgarity. It is nothing but hypocrisy."[4] This is a woman from a po-litically powerful family, emphasizing the way militant groups use the sub-versive agency of women in "extraordinary" moments as a counterpoint to the expectation that in "ordinary" moments, these very women will com-ply with tradition. But this is also a woman who, when she entered public life, decided to conform to what so-called tradition demanded of women by wearing the head scarf.

For those struggling to protect democratic rights in India, this situation constitutes yet another attempt in several over the past few years to control women's dress and behavior in the name of cultural purity. With the increas-ingly free circulation of images from Western consumerist culture through television channels as a result of lifting of restrictions in the so-called era of liberalization, various groups have expressed concern about the threat to "Indian" culture. Organizations of the Hindu Right such as the Bajrang Dal and the Akhil Bharatiya Vidyarthi Parishad (both with close links to the Bharatiya Janta Party [BJP], leading the alliance currently in government) have been trying to enforce dress codes for women in universities, claiming that sexual harassment would decrease if women dressed "respectably" and according to "Indian tradition." Interestingly, the Lashkar-e-Jabbar in Kash-mir also "appealed" to unveiled "Hindu and Sikh sisters" to wear a *bindi* (a dot on the forehead) in order to be spared from attack.[5] Clearly, when it comes to the marking of female bodies with cultural signs, the Right is united across ideological lines. Additionally, one witnesses the characteristic homogenization of the Other (in this case, the non-Muslim), for Sikh women do not wear the *bindi*.

It is by now a phenomenon well recorded by feminist scholarship and politics that communities vest their honor in "their" women, and that cultural policing begins with first marking and then drawing women "inside" the community.⁶ Particularly when a community feels its identity or existence under threat, its proud assertion of identity always appears marked on the bodies of "its" women first. For instance, the increasing numbers of Muslim women wearing the burqa in the state of Kerala, where this practice was rare, is often dated from the demolition of the Babri Masjid, a four-hundred-year-old mosque, in 1992 by the Hindu Right, an act widely perceived to have decisively reshaped the contours of India's secular and democratic polity.⁷ This phenomenon does not remain restricted to minority communities alone; majority communities, too, respond to the threat of "Western" culture in this way, as is evident from the violent reactions to the holding of the Miss World contest in India from the Hindu Right and in Nigeria from the Muslim Right. But feminists have written and talked about such things for a long time now. What I am interested in here is another aspect of the phenomenon. Let me take up a statement made by a young Muslim woman in Kashmir who took to the veil after the threats. In an interview with a journalist critical of the diktat, she said that she had never worn a burqa before, that it made her terribly unhappy, and that she felt restricted and bound. "I used to go the beauty parlour regularly," she said plaintively, "but now I don't have to bother about my face." This statement also runs in a bold blurb across the article, so that it is what first strikes the reader—the poignancy of a young girl declaring sadly that she no longer has to bother about her face because she has been imprisoned inside a burqa. However, at another point in the interview, she conceded that she felt safer in public because men were more respectful. "It can be liberatory," she said, "you can go wherever you want to go."⁸

So there you have it—the burqa offering a refuge from sexual harassment and some of the restrictions in mobility faced by young girls, and the beauty parlor standing in for the realm of self-expression, for emancipation from enforced veiling. A painful seesaw for a feminist to be trapped on! Is cultural policing any less effective when not backed by a gun but by societal consensus? Or any less restrictive on the "beauty parlor" side of the equation? When Brazilian women die on plastic surgeons' tables, or when American teenagers risk death and eat less and less in order to stay beautifully thin, is that cultural policing too, or an expression of "free will"? If that young Kashmiri girl could have continued to go to beauty parlors, would she have been much freer to express herself? I must emphasize that this by no means constitutes a simple rhetorical question, but a significant dilemma. Consider the increasing numbers of middle-class Indian women, who would have been housewives with no income of their own, now setting up beauty parlors in their homes. In doing so, they become small entrepreneurs (government documents recording loans given for this purpose list it as a "nontraditional" method of income generation, along with enterprises like desktop publishing and managing public phone booths). Presumably, these women then acquire a slightly greater degree of control over resources than they had as housewives. However, the mushrooming of such beauty parlors also reflects the new overwhelming pressure on even women from traditional backgrounds to "look good" in the new way, and to spend time and money doing so.[9]

There is a peculiarity to this moment in history, particularly when one is located in a postcolonial democracy like India. In the face of a renewed and relentless moral rhetoric throughout the 1990s from the Right, which targets women as the repositories of cultural purity, one kind of critical response has come from the globalized elite, celebrating "choice," "individual freedom," and "women's right to their bodies." For instance, a story in the *Wall Street Journal* about beauty contests in Pakistan was titled "Lifting the Veil from Pak Ramps."[10] Thus when the Right has attacked beauty contests and celebrations of Valentine's Day as "Western" and "morally corrupting," the Westernized Indian elites have reasserted pride in our "modernity" and "our women's" confidence on the international stage (several Indian women have been Miss Universe and Miss World in the past few years). In this debate, the Left seems to have fallen into the trap of equating *antiglobalist/antiimperialist* with *nationalist*. In the process, it has taken positions similar to those of the Right. For instance, the two state governments that banned beauty contests in 2001 were the BJP-ruled Uttar Pradesh and the Left Front–ruled West Bengal. Neither party made the move from the perspective of a critique of the commodification of women's bodies; rather, the justification came in terms of "cultural purity" in both cases.

The challenge for feminist politics in this context is the working out of a different space for a radical politics of culture, one differentiated from both right- and left-wing articulations of cultural and economic nationalism, as well as from the libertarian and celebratory responses to globalization from the consuming elites. Do we need to recover an older feminist and Marxist critique of commodification that will address both kinds of cultural policing—the coercion of the Right, as well as the hegemony of the so-called free Western world? Or will that older critique need substantial refashioning?

The all-too-familiar binary opposition of tradition and modernity has faced substantial and by now well-known lines of critique. Nevertheless, there continues to exist a way in which critiques of modernity are perceived as set up only from within the site of tradition, and critiques of tradition only from within modernity. The political task is precisely to deconstruct this binary in order to demarcate (and recognize) a third, or at least, other, site from where we can scan our landscape. From this site it becomes possible, first, to remind ourselves that modernity and tradition do not always constitute two clearly distinguishable moments. What is called tradition, especially in postcolonial societies, is unavoidably located within modernity, irretrievably constituted by modernist discourses. Neither pole of the opposition remains hermetically sealed from the other. There is a vast body of scholarship demonstrating that "custom," "religious practice," and so on have been decisively fashioned by colonial administrative fiat and continue to be reinvented apace.[11] Yet these categories still circulate, both intellectually and in political practice, as if they were primordial.

Second, we recognize, from our vantage point on the "other site," that critiques of each do not only come from the other. That is, modernity comes under attack not only from tradition but also from opposing tendencies within itself, while, similarly, tradition is challenged not only by the language of rights and modernity but is internally contested in its own terms. A politics of radical democratization would have to recognize the specific oppressiveness of both modernity and tradition. For feminists especially this appears a crucial step to take because in postcolonial societies, tradition seems to offer a refuge from the alienation and commodification set in motion by modernity. One kind of critique of the new ways in which forces of modernization oppress women can be and very often is cast in terms that valorize a reconstituted tradition. Take, for example, what is called the Islamic feminist defense of the veil as a mode of challenging the commodifying Western (and male) gaze. Fadwa El Guindi puts it this way in the context of Egypt: "It [Islamic feminism] is feminist because it seeks to liberate womanhood; it is Islamic because its premises are embedded in Islamic principles and values. Yet in some senses, the liberal Western-influenced feminism of the aristocracy and the Islamic one are not far apart. Both are about the emancipation of women. The early feminist lifting of the face-veil was about emancipation from exclusion; the voluntary wearing of the hijab since the mid-seventies is about liberation from imposed, imported identities, consumerist behaviours, and an increasingly materialist culture."[12] El Guindi also explicitly locates the mid-seventies as the period from which Western imperialist demonization of Islam goes on the ascendant.[13]

But of course, at the same time feminist critique has to be aware of the oppression institutionalized by tradition, and against which the values and institutions of modernity have seemed to offer the handiest weapons of critique. Thus despite decades of feminist scholarship and politics, we continue, in many senses, to be trapped inside the swing of this particular pendulum, unable to make a critique of modernity and tradition simultaneously. Consider another instance, one cited by South African scholar Thandabantlu Nhlapo at a conference in order to illustrate his attack on the pretensions to universality of the modernist discourse of rights. He referred to the case of a beauty queen debarred from SPCA (Society for the Prevention of Cruelty to Animals) events because she declared at a press conference that she would celebrate her victory in the traditional way, by slaughtering an animal. Nhlapo used this incident to outline a defense of the rights of communities to their traditional ways of life against the overwhelming and homogenizing drive of modernity.[14] As I see it, however, this offers a good example of what we may call the prison of the pendulum between tradition and modernity. What is at stake in this episode, but rendered invisible in Nhlapo's telling of it, is modernity—not only as the force eroding the traditional rights of communities to their ways of life but as the force objectifying the female body. Nhlapo remains unaware of the paradox involved in defending the "traditional" forms of celebration of the community in this specific context—what the woman in question is celebrating, of course, her beauty contest crown, exemplifies the commodification and alienation of the self, particularly of the female body, which is typical of modernity.

The point I wish to make is that modernity can be shown to be running counter to an emancipatory ethic in several ways, and that tradition is only one of the lenses through which this may be made visible. In fact, modernity itself offers the values that can form one basis of attacking it—autonomy, equality, and freedom are archetypically modern values, all of which Nhlapo invoked in the instance above. Our political practice needs urgently to work on the delineation of the "third space" from which a critique of the oppression of both tradition and modernity can be made.

A passing reference here would not be out of place to the fascinating ways in which beauty contests, sponsored by giant multinational companies in so-called third world countries, occupy contradictory and shifting positions on the grid of tradition/modernity. A considerable amount of feminist scholarship exists along these lines, on beauty contests in Southeast Asia and Latin America.[15] In India, we see the phenomenon of women from traditional, middle- to lower middle-class families, who would have been "married off," aspiring to beauty crowns and modeling as a career. If they succeed, they then totally escape the patriarchal controls of the family and live in the style of "liberated," wealthy women: their love affairs in the public eye, they are the darlings of the media and remain unconcerned about middle-class public opinion. They are confident, have control over their earnings, and many of them invest for a soon-to-come future in which they will no longer be models and move into business ventures of different kinds. On the other hand, the ideal they explicitly stand for, especially in the winning round of the beauty contests, is that of "womanhood," especially "Indian womanhood," represented as a perfect mix of tradition and modernity. The answers they give to the question of what they aspire to has to be in terms of acceptable womanly virtues—some kind of nurturing, caring answer is expected of them. An interesting incident from the history of Indian participation in international beauty contests comes with the story of Madhu Sapre, today a top model. In the period before a spate of Indian women began to win Miss World contests, Sapre missed the crown by a whisker, becoming merely first runner-up. The innumerable analyses in the English media of her failure to win the Miss World crown focused again and again on the "wrong" answer she gave to the question in the final round, "What would you do if you were the leader of your country?" Sapre, a champion of her state (Maharashtra) in badminton, replied that she would build the best sports facilities so that India could excel in the international arena. This was unanimously and endlessly identified as a "selfish" answer to have given, which cost her the crown. Every single finalist since then has given an answer that involves children, old people, the poor, or all three.

It is also no coincidence that Indian women started winning international titles seemingly all of a sudden in the 1990s. A much-analyzed phenomenon, it has been pointed out by journalists and feminist scholars that the great Indian consumer middle class was created during that decade, with the new structural adjustment policies putting into place greater purchasing power for a relatively small class, which in absolute terms, given India's population size, proved quite large. India opened up as a consumer market for multinational companies, with cosmetics in particular being especially targeted at Indian coloring and requirements. International beauty contests became a way of wooing hitherto untapped markets in Asia and Africa.[16] A second, less commented-on factor is the conscious strategy adopted by Satya Saran, the editor of *Femina* (the magazine that sponsors the Indian contest, and the winners of that to the international one). Writing after the spectacular string of successes began, she explained how the magazine started to select the so-called international look, which was very far from the Indian idea of beauty—taller, thinner, with the color of skin not really mattering; indeed, "dark" might even prove an advantage on the international stage. Another change made seems significant. Earlier, the Miss India contest featured the winners of preliminary contests in the states. However, as Saran pointed out, the winner from a small town was likely to be much less sophisticated than even the top ten contestants from a cosmopolitan city like Mumbai. After the restructuring, regional representation no longer received any weightage, and if all the top contestants came from three big cities, it did not matter. This meant that a particular type of look was expected, and the large variations that one could expect to see in a contest featuring women from different parts of the subcontinent was deliberately ended. One more instance of the homogenization we have come to associate with globalization.[17]

However, as the above discussion illustrates, homogenization is not the only result of globalization, which unleashes complex, often contradictory forces. In the next section I will examine how one can flatten globalization by understanding it as either simply empowering or simply oppressive.

The complexity of the negotiations between tradition and modernity is particularly evident in the phenomenon of migration from the global South to the North, as well as the transformations within these relocated communities. Naila Kabeer's book on Bangladeshi women workers addresses the apparent paradox that while women garment workers in Dhaka have entered garment factories and work unveiled, Bangladeshi women in the garment industry in London are almost entirely confined to home working. One of Kabeer's main explanations for this is that women in Dhaka come from diverse geographical backgrounds into a relatively anonymous urban setting, while the women in London came mostly from one province, Sylhet, with an extremely conservative society, even by Bangladeshi standards. In London, they tend to settle in one part of East London because of community networks drawing new migrants into that area where Bangladeshis have become concentrated. This concentration and regrouping of the community is, of course, set within a context of growing racist hostility, leading to the familiar phenomenon of drawing "our" women "inside." Men, then, work in the factories and women at home—with the additional labeling of women's labor as unskilled and men's as skilled. Kabeer argues that the processes of globalization by which garment factory sweatshops get located in countries like Bangladesh empower women who, despite exploitative conditions of work, find their options increased. She suggests that the "agency" of women is enhanced by the effects of globalization in the South.[18]

However, Kabeer's significant argument, which seems to run counter to feminist wisdom on globalization, misses a critical component. It therefore stops the pendulum too easily at the beauty parlor, as it were. In the scenario she outlines, there are, it seems to me, two axes at work that map onto each other, not only in London but also in Dhaka—tradition/modernity and home/not at home—but that produce contradictory results: anonymity and dispersal of community in Dhaka, regrouping and reassertion of community in London. Is it possible, then, to suggest that the critical distinguishing element here is not the *economic* operation of globalization—which, after all, takes the Bangladeshi immigrants to London as much as they bring women to factories in Dhaka—but the *cultural* hegemony produced by globalization, more violently experienced in the West than in a poor country like Bangladesh. In India, with a much more numerically significant middle class targeted by multinational companies and where this cultural hegemony is experienced right "at home," the phenomenon of cultural nationalism is more evident. Indeed, even within Bangladesh, the reassertions of community would take place at the points where cultural hegemony is experienced as a threat, regardless of the anonymity produced by factory production. In other words, the factory women in Dhaka are not forever immune from retraditionalizing moves—as and when "Western" or "Indian/Hindu" culture gets perceived as a threat in Bangladesh, either through television or the growing presence of middle-class consumers. At that point, the familiar moves to mark out "our" women as different will come into play.

I move now to an argument that presents globalization in another unidimensional mode, but from the opposite direction. That is, the mode that presents globalization as uniformly oppressive, especially because of what is presented as its seamless compatibility with the politics of the Hindu Right in India. Kumkum Sangari, in a paper titled "New Patriotisms: The Beauty Queen and the Bomb" correctly points out that both the defense of the beauty contest by the new Indian middle class as well the opposition to the event from the Hindu Right "hinge on nationalism and carry an overt anti-feminism."[19] However, she attempts to understand this contradictory response exclusively within the frame of political economy. She delineates the two responses as corresponding to "two distinct historical moments": (1) the Hindu Right representing "the era of merchant capital, which favoured extraction through maintaining precapitalist relations in colonized formations," during which " 'backward' enclaves cordoned from the market and 'the west' became synonymous with authentic indigenous culture"; and (2) the new middle classes representing the " 'modernized' enclaves" that in the current period are becoming the "epicentre of authentic culture."[20] Thus Sangari separates the two responses as corresponding to temporally different moments of capitalism. However, as the argument proceeds, the distinction becomes impossible to maintain, for too many contradictions surface. After all, the new middle class also forms part of the Hindu Right's support base, and this is partly the reason why the prime minister leading the right-wing coalition applauded the successes of Indian women in beauty contests. Sangari dismisses this fact too easily as a "division of labour in the Hindu right between 'moderate' parliamentarians and street-smart vandals," with the former supporting structural adjustment and liberalization policies, while the latter maintain the myth of Hindu right-wing nationalist claims through overt opposition to "some of its epiphenomenal forms." The latter (whom she exemplifies by the Vishwa Hindu Parishad and the Bajrang Dal), she holds, "no longer even mention the economy."[21]

This is not in fact the case. There is certainly a division of labor in the Hindu Right, but it works differently. The Vishwa Hindu Parishad and the Bajrang Dal generally focus on "culture," while it is the Swadeshi Jagran Manch that deals with the "economy." The latter is specifically devoted to raising the emotive slogan of *swadeshi*—a term from the era of the struggle for independence which refers to a nationalist economy. This organization, as well as other wings of what is called the Sangh Combine—the loose conglomeration of different Hindu right-wing formations—continuously puts pressure on the government to roll back liberalization policies on the World Bank prescription.[22] Indeed, Hindu right-wing organizations have teamed up with left organizations on more than one occasion in Delhi and Mumbai to stage massive demonstrations against globalization.[23]

On the other hand, the Left Front government in West Bengal led by the Communist Party of India (Marxist), CPI(M), has been proactive in inviting foreign capital and has shown considerable alacrity in implementing all the structural adjustment policies required for this program's success. For instance, Harkishan Singh Surjeet, the general secretary of the CPI(M) has clarified on several occasions that the party does not oppose multinational companies such as Coca-Cola coming into the country with investments.[24] The CPI(M) chief minister of West Bengal, Buddhadev Bhattacharya, said in a recent interview, "The world needs new understanding . . . we have to understand capital and its requirements. Capital is very important." In the same interview, he said that jobs would have to be created "not in the old sense," but through encouraging entrepreneurial energies.[25] His government has endorsed a contract system for workers and is committed to selling off the state's sick industries.[26] The complexities and contradictions in the attitude of the Left toward globalization Sangari does not touch on at all. The silence in her paper implicitly suggests that the Left is "really" anti-globalization, as opposed to the hypocritical stance of the Right. However, if the "schizophrenia" on this issue that she attributes to the Hindu Right is equally evident on the Left, then surely we have to give up trying to understand these contradictory responses in terms of a pathology, that is, as the "abnormal" condition of schizophrenia.[27]

A quick detour to consider a more striking illustration of left-wing nationalism as a response to globalization might illustrate this point better. Consider left responses to the position taken by the governments of the third world/developing countries on the "social clause" of GATT (which includes universal standards on labor, as well as environment and human rights standards). These governments generally oppose the social clause because it will reduce the trade advantage, that is, "cheap labor," enjoyed by third world countries. In a provocative paper, Aditya Nigam outlines the very strange scenario that unfolded on this front. In 1995, the Delhi Declaration was adopted by the Fifth Conference of Labour Ministers of Non-aligned and Other Developing Countries, which expressed "deep concern about the serious post-Marrakesh efforts at seeking to establish linkage between international trade and enforcement of labour standards through the imposition of the social clause."[28] The social clause attempts to impose labor standards (such as ending child labor, enforcing minimum wages, and providing the right to organize) as a precondition to trade.[29] The Indian government's position, denouncing the linking of labor standards to trade as an attempt to neutralize the third world's trade advantage of cheap labor, had the backing of all the major Indian trade unions (including both left- and right-wing trade unions) attending the thirty-second session of the Standing Labour Committee held a few months earlier. Reporting on the trade union conference, the official organ of the Communist Party of India (Marxist) said that "the social clause is a singular issue on which there is unanimity not only among trade unions and employers, but also on support to the government on wanting to reject the US move."[30] The central trade unions went to the extent of appealing to the conference to resolutely oppose the linking of labor standards to trade as a nontariff protectionist measure.[31] Thus, as Nigam points out, the position taken by the trade unions was not at the level of a strategic agreement among themselves, but amounted to an unconditional declaration of support to the government: "It did not matter that precious little had been done by the government on this front for close to five decades. . . . What mattered was the 'fact' that imperialism was blackmailing the 'nation' and 'the working class' was historically destined to play its 'anti-imperialist role.'"[32] Nigam further points out that the response of Indian trade unions also proves illustrative of the higher degree of hegemony of the organized, public-sector workers (enjoying relatively better working and living conditions) over the trade union movement in India. In several other third world countries such as Malaysia, Peru, and many African countries, the situation is such that even mainstream trade unions find it difficult to take a straight-forwardly nationalist position on the social clause, which in effect would mean defending "our" bourgeoisie's right to cheap labor.[33]

So we are left with a picture in which left- and right-wing governments at some points succumb to structural adjustment, while at others, left- and right-wing nationalist protests come together against the social clause and the Western culture represented by beauty contests. At other points still, the Left and the Right come together in nationalist pride over the bomb—one of the first reactions to India's nuclear explosion came from the CPI(M), applauding Indian scientists for their "achievement." The Left emerged in open opposition to the bomb only after Pakistan's reciprocal nuclear explosions a little later.[34] In a fascinating discussion, Sangari argues that while the bomb revolves on an "axis of masculinity," and the beauty contest on an "axis of femininity," "both are rooted in feelings of relative deprivation": "National accumulations of beauty and the capacity for violence can redress all economic and social problems."[35] The narrative here proves persuasive and insightful, but the problem is that Sangari follows the general trend in India of left opposition to the bomb in characterizing it as "embedded in a Hindutva vocabulary," conflating the "Hindu Right" with "support for globalization/beauty contests and the Bomb."[36] However, although the Hindu Right–led coalition government exploded the actual bomb, India's nuclear policy was not originated by the Hindu Right, which has merely inherited a longstanding nationalist project of "putting India on the world stage," a project to which both Right and Left have contributed.[37]

Thus it does not prove very useful to try to understand the effects of globalization (or right-wing politics in India) as a function of the political economy alone, nor to assume that there exists a pure antiglobalization position on the Left and a necessarily compromised one on the Right. As we have seen, the responses vary from government to party to trade union fronts of the Left and Right, and to collapse the several distinct strands into two homogenized positions is to lose a sense of the textured nature of both globalization and responses to it.

In this context, I find insightful Fredric Jameson's identification of "five levels of globalization"—"the technological, the political, the cultural, the economic, the social." This exercise helps in "taking an inventory of their ambiguities," as he puts it.[38] In the Indian context, Kancha Iliah offers a parallel argument in which he suggests that while globalization in the *economic* sphere "has offered an expanded and varied life for the rich and made the poor poorer," in the *cultural* realm, it has "opened up a new channel of hope for the historically suppressed masses," that is, the lower castes that he calls "Dalit-Bahujan." He characterizes the access of these castes to English as a means of coming into contact with "the world's egalitarian knowledge systems." While Western culture threatens the Brahmin, it liberates the Dalit-Bahujan: "Cultural globalization negates the Brahminic myth of purity and pollution."[39] Both Jameson and Iliah offer the potential of complicating our understanding of globalization and its effects.

However, Jameson's project, after identifying the different levels of globalization, becomes that of demonstrating their "ultimate cohesion," and in the process of doing so, he tends to iron out their ambiguities.[40] As we will see in the next section, this move takes us more or less back to the moves that conflate anti-imperialism with nationalism. I will argue later in this essay that nationalism is only one of the platforms from which to counter the imperialism of corporate globalization, and from the point of view of attempting a radical critique of capitalism, it is certainly not the most just or productive.

In conclusion, let us return to the question of framing a space for a radical critique of capitalism and dominant, patriarchal culture. In the light of the discussion above, I suggest that such a project would have to take into account three dimensions:

As a first dimension, the complex nature of political subjectivities as they are constituted at this moment. Let me suggest just two instances as an illustration of these complexities. First, consider a contradiction that we have not adequately confronted in our politics, the contradiction between our belief in the need to assert and protect the autonomy of the individual citizen and our simultaneous belief in the operation of the hegemony of dominant, power-laden values that makes the "freedom to choose" so problematic. That is, the values that *we* consider desirable are not hegemonic in society, so that the freedom to choose most often simply reasserts dominant values. Consequently, democracy, with its assumption of the rights-bearing citizen endowed with free will, poses a problem for us until the values *we* hold to be crucial become hegemonic in society. When, for instance, a woman chooses to abort a fetus because of its female sex, or to acquiesce to a marriage in which her natal family will be made bankrupt by dowry requirements, or to participate in a beauty contest, what operates is not free will in the feminist/modernist sense, but at the same time, the situation is so complicated that it cannot simply be characterized by a *lack* of free will either.

Second, an unqualified defense of the notion of universal human rights has become increasingly problematic. In the current world scenario, such a defense has all too often become linked to the United States of America as

the global champion of universal human rights. The universalism espoused
by philosophers like Martha Nussbaum, for instance, includes the idea that
nations that have adopted the norm of "universal human capabilities" should
"commend this norm strongly to other nations," using whenever necessary
"economic and other strategies to secure compliance."[41] The fact that the
only nation in a position to "secure compliance" today is the United States,
with its selective regime of sanctions and human rights conditionalities pro-
tecting the interests of American and multinational corporations all over the
world, remains unremarked on.[42] Thomas Friedman puts it succinctly when
he says that "the hidden hand of the market will never work without a hidden fist . . . and the hidden fist that keeps the world safe for Silicon Valley's technologies to flourish is called the US Army, Air Force, Navy and
Marine Corps."[43]

In the new unipolar world, the question of universal rights appears in
the form of an unavoidable choice—barbarity or civilization. In public discourse, the debate is all too often seen in terms of three positions: pro-
human rights, pro-intervention by the United States; anti–human rights,
pro–religious fundamentalists/dictators; and those who don't care either
way—"It's not our business, let Milosevic/the Taliban do what they want."
But there are voices that raise another, more disturbing issue, namely, that
US action usually ends up strengthening the Milosevics and the Taliban-like
forces and swamping democratic opposition *within* those countries on a tide
of resurgent nationalism. For instance, leading peace activist in Serbia, Veran
Matic, editor in chief of Belgrade's Radio B92 banned by Milosevic, wrote
in the *Guardian*, "I sat in a Belgrade prison on the first day of the NATO attack on my country. . . . NATO's bombs have blasted the germinating seeds
of democracy out of the soil of Kosovo, Serbia and Montenegro and ensured
that they will not sprout again for a very long time. . . . The free media in
Serbia has for years opposed nationalism, hatred and war. As a representative of those media and as a man who has more than faced the consequences
of my political beliefs, I call on President Clinton to put a stop to NATO's
attack on my country."[44]

Similarly, can we remain indifferent to the specific moment at which the
Revolutionary Association of Women of Afghanistan (RAWA) was recognized by the United States as an organization of heroines? For decades these
women had struggled against the Taliban with no support or recognition
from anywhere. Suddenly, when the United States launched its so-called war
on terror, RAWA became the staple of CNN broadcasts. At the time, representatives of RAWA emphasized that they opposed the American bombing of
Afghanistan, as it formed part of the strategic agenda of the US government
and not of the struggle that RAWA had long conducted. They also pointed

out that the Northern Alliance, whom the United States backed, was no less oppressive and patriarchal than the Taliban. Nevertheless they found themselves appropriated into the battle as allies of the United States in the war on terror and used to legitimize US state policy.

What these two instances suggest in the context of negotiating the contradictions generated by globalization on the one hand and cultural nationalism on the other is the need for feminist politics simultaneously to deconstruct both the "freedom of choice" presented by the beauty parlor and the "nationalist" resistance to globalization offered by the burqa. In the process, we might well end up using the idea of the autonomy of the individual to challenge cultural nationalism and, conversely, employing the idea of historical, temporal, and spatial specificities to challenge the homogenizing drive of globalization. In each case, the danger exists of falling back into the capitalist myth of the freely choosing individual or, conversely, into the opposite tale of internally consistent cultures. The crucial recognition, however, is that no subject position is closed, that no hegemony is complete. This recognition has to inform and transform our political practice.

As a second dimension I would like to name the need for an uncompromising critique of the nation-state. Jameson states baldly, despite several caveats later in the same article, that "the nation-state today remains the only concrete terrain and framework for political struggle."[45] He holds onto this idea despite his recognition of the United States co-opting the language of nationalism and using the language of universalism to defend its specific national self-interest. He further recognizes that the universal and the particular are embedded as contradictions within the existing historical situation of nation-states inside a global system. This latter recognition is perhaps the deeper philosophical reason, Jameson concedes, why the struggle against globalization can only partially be fought on national terrain. Nevertheless, Jameson tries to rescue nationalism by engaging in an exercise familiar to those who follow Indian historiography—by distinguishing between "'good' nationalism," which is "the great collective project" of attempting to construct a nation, and "'bad' nationalism," which is the attempt to win state power with the aim of national bourgeois hegemony: "Nationalisms that have come to power have therefore mainly been the bad ones," Jameson concludes. In addition, he believes "it is misleading to confound nationalism with phenomena like communalism, which strikes me rather, as a kind of (for example) Hindu identity politics, albeit on a vast and indeed, national scale."[46]

On the contrary, I would argue that nationalism is itself one of the earliest forms of identity politics. It is not self-evident that identity politics can only refer to "smaller" identities within the nation, although this assumption is a familiar one in Indian historiography. For example, one set of Indian historians argues that the rise of religious, regional, and other particularistic identities has resulted from "the degradation of nationalism to an ideological ploy for the reinforcement of the interests of the ruling elites."[47] The assumption here is of a genuine nationalism that would be democratic and secular, an assumption that marks even analyses such as that of Purushottam Agarwal, who recognizes that what is called communalism is not so much a particularism vis-à-vis the nation, but simply another modern project of nation-building.[48] For Agarwal then goes on to distinguish the communal project of nation building from the secular one on the basis of the (assumed, not demonstrated) democratic orientation of the latter, as opposed to the authoritarian orientation of the former.

However, I would emphasize that no project of community formation can be assumed to be inherently or a priori democratic. On the contrary, the nation can only represent dominant, majoritarian values—minorities reasserting "their" culture can never claim the legitimacy of representing the nation, whether it is Muslims in India or Indians in the United States. Further, historically the secular nation, too, has constituted the citizen through equally antidemocratic measures. In the classic case of France, Eugen Weber writes of the "acculturation" process in the nineteenth century by which the inhabitants of the area that became France were made "French," that is, "the civilization of the French by urban France, the disintegration of local cultures by modernity and their absorption into the dominant civilization of Paris. . . . Left largely to their own devices until their promotion to citizenship, the unassimilated rural masses had to be integrated into the dominant culture as they had been integrated into an administrative entity. What happened was akin to colonialism."[49]

In the Indian context, secularist discourse has been intimately tied to a notion of development predicated on the large-scale sacrifice of sectional interests in the greater interest of the "Indian citizen." Hence the massive displacements of populations in irrigation, power, and defense projects. As had already been extensively documented by the 1980s, this "development" has benefited specific sections of society and particular regions of the country.[50] The highly centralized, capital-intensive, and high-technology–based development model adopted by the Indian elites requires the homogeneous subject constructed by the discourse of citizenship. In response, the struggles against marginalization have involved posing specific identities and particularity against the universalizing thrust of development discourse.

In such a context, the assumption of an easy link between anti-imperialism and nationalism appears deeply problematic from the point of view of a democratic project. We who would practice democratic politics cannot afford to be unreflexive of the founding moment of discursive violence that both presupposed and produced the nation, nor of the repressions and marginalizations on which hegemonic nationalist discourse is predicated, at any point in history and on any part of the globe—even in Cuba and China, offered by Jameson as "the richest counter-examples of the way in which a concrete nationalism could be completed by a socialist project."[51] No project of nationalism is ever "completed"—it is frozen at some point or the other through a coercive apparatus backed by the sanction of violence that prevents the further articulation of other voices and identities with similar aspirations.

As we have come to recognize, the "demise of the nation-state" in the era of globalization is a myth. Simultaneously with its retreat from development and welfare responsibilities, the nation-state is being reconstituted in all its oppressive aspects. Whether in the United States, in India, Bosnia, or Rwanda, the discourse of xenophobic and jingoistic nationalism is audible in full volume, and the nation-state's repressive face is very much in evidence toward the dissident and/or marginalized voices within it. The so-called retreat of the state is only visible in sectors in which it previously had some responsibility for health, education, and so on. This retreat in fact constitutes a proactive step making it easier for global capital to penetrate: restrictive measures to control labor mobility and trade unions are very much in force, and new measures are being enacted that empower the state in all sorts of ways to ensure a healthy climate for investment. Indeed, the delegitimation of the state's authority only pertains to whatever positive effects (from a democratic point of view) were generated in anti-imperialist struggles. As a result of this complex process, what can be called a democratic response is itself very much more complex than our experience so far has prepared us for.

This is why both kinds of reactions—of turning to the nation-state to reassert the old authority *and* assuming its demise and celebrating globalization—are entirely misplaced. I should therefore clarify that the argument made above, rejecting the nation-state as a position from which to critique imperialism, is the very obverse of corporate globalization's postnationalism "from above," in which the sovereignty of the nation is sought to be bypassed in the interests of global capital. Rather, the kind of postnationalism I refer to is better described as being "from below," that is, the cross-border solidarities of women's movements, movements for the rights of minorities, and pro-democracy and peace movements.

The third dimension required for a new kind of radical politics is a critique of multiculturalism, which currently involves a reification of religious and cultural communities. The debates on multiculturalism tend to capture communities as constituted by cultural boundaries that are more or less fixed. A typical instance is the following statement by Amy Gutmann, who sets out the problem as one of how public institutions should recognize the identities of "cultural" and "disadvantaged" minorities she says "are often based on ethnicity, race, gender and religion."[52] Gender is simply listed as one of the identities here, with no understanding of how gender can in fact complicate the other three identities. Take, for example, this statement a little later in the same essay: "Recognizing and treating members of some groups as equal now seems to require public institutions to acknowledge rather than ignore cultural particularities, at least for those people whose self-understanding depends on the vitality of their culture."[53] Here "cultural particularities" cannot possibly refer to gender, for, much as we may wish it, women have no recognized "culture" specific to them, nor do they form a community in the sense in which Gutmann uses the term. On the contrary, gender is often one of the axes on which the assumed "vitality" of cultures is internally challenged, for this vitality too often depends on demarcating an oppressive space for "their" women. It seems to me inadequate, therefore, to identify the problem for liberal democracies as Gutmann does, as one of whether they should "respect those cultures whose attitudes of ethnic or racial superiority, for example, are antagonistic to other cultures."[54] This problem involves only the *external* relationship of different communities to other communities, while the problem of gender (or, say, caste in India) is *internal* to the very constitution of the community itself.

That is, the real dilemma is that the very vitality and identity of the community so often depends on denying autonomy to sections within itself. Within the boundaries of a multicultural politics, recognition involves only external recognition by the state of different communities and by communities of one another. Thus French feminists would understandably hesitate to support the French government's prohibition on wearing the head scarf in schools, fearing that such a prohibition would feed into processes marginalizing and demonizing the Muslim community in France. But there are also voices internal to the community that are critical of the marking of "their" women by the community in specific, coercive ways. These voices may be delegitimized within the community, not strengthened, by open support for the French government's policy from the mainstream feminist movement.

In short, feminist response to this mode of constituting the community (of drawing "their" women in and marking out women's bodies in specific ways) has to be mediated by a recognition of the complex dynamics involved —

both of the threat to minority identity in a multicultural society with a substantial majority community, as well as of the internal coercion involved in the very constitution of this minority identity. This recognition problematizes both the straightforward "feminist" response that could simply feed into racist (in the West) or Hindu (in India) stereotyping of minorities as reactionary and backward and the "multicultural" response of "respecting differences."

Thus the recognition of the complexity of cultural identity in a globalized world requires us to challenge both the reification of cultural boundaries by the advocates of multiculturalism and the unproblematic assertion of "universal" rights by its opponents. Jürgen Habermas, for example, speaking from the second side, terms constitutional protection of group rights as "questionable from a normative point of view." He argues that such protection is supposed to serve the recognition of their individual members, and that it should not become the "preservation of the species by administrative fiat."[55] He, or Jameson, would assert the need for a greater universalism—Habermas of *demos* and Jameson of class, as opposed to *ethnos*. I venture to suggest that the critique of the reification of cultural communities should take us in the opposite direction—toward a greater fracturing of universalism. Our politics and our democratic institutions must take on board the destabilizing implications of communities constituting themselves continuously around different axes, of which the cultural is only one. Other forms of community exist, building themselves around political ideals, but these are rarely recognized as such—communities built around sexual identity, displacement by development projects, language-based communities that undercut national boundaries, and so on.

If Jameson's "five levels" of globalization are to be taken seriously, we need to move in the direction of characterizing globalization as a complex articulation of differentiated, sometimes mutually contradictory processes. The intersection of these processes can produce spatially and temporally differentiated moments that generate constraint as well as freedom—whether any given moment will produce constraint or freedom cannot be predicted in advance. A radical transformative politics cannot afford not to recognize the full significance and potential offered by this unpredictability.

Let me present a series of instances to illustrate the complex nature of the field that a radical politics has to confront. Forces of globalization can work against those of the religious Right. Why, for instance, has corporate India come out so strongly and publicly against the ethnic cleansing attempted by the Hindu right-wing government in Gujarat a year ago? Because an India torn by violence is not an India in which investments are secure. Or to take another instance, let us consider the national daily newspaper the *Indian Express*, which has conducted one of the most hard-hitting and thorough campaigns against the Gujarat carnage and which has taken a strongly secular position both editorially and in all its stories. This newspaper, however, has also emerged as one of the strongest voices in favor of globalization and consistently approves of anti-poor measures such as "cleaning up" Delhi by removing hawkers and vendors, banning begging, and so on. The two sentiments—pro-globalization and antireligious fundamentalism—are perfectly compatible with each other. Why, for instance, has the increasingly popular Valentine's Day become a target of violent attack by the Hindu Right in India? For feminists who have been critical of both the notion of romance and of the consumerism underlying Valentine's Day, the Hindu Right's opposition brings into relief another aspect—the potentially subversive power of two *individuals* in love—oblivious (perhaps) of caste, class, and religious identities. This potentially subversive character of romance certainly constitutes a threat that the Hindu Right takes very seriously.[56]

Some other messy alignments: How are we to understand the active presence of the Hindu Right in some of the movements against big dams, for example, in the Tehri region? Their rhetoric draws on "Hindu" imagery, but does so in order to defend traditional ways of life against destructive modern development, as Mukul Sharma's work shows.[57] Sharma himself attributes a "communal" motive to the Hindu Right's involvement with such movements. Even if that were the "real" motive, surely the active participation of the Hindu Right in an ecology movement generates both possibilities equally: if there is a possibility of its succeeding in communalizing the movement, there should be an equally strong possibility of the ecology movement restricting/transforming the Hindu Right's communalism. We cannot assume either eventuality in advance. Conversely, a pro-Dalit/lower caste voice exists that strongly favors globalization and big dams because for lower castes, "tradition" and the coerciveness of traditional occupations can only always prove oppressive.[58]

In the face of such complex intersections of the reactionary and the progressive, there are no clear-cut strategies to offer—indeed, the specificity of "our" modernity is precisely that no overarching, ever-valid strategy remains available to us. The clearest conclusion we can arrive at is that the other space that feminism seeks to define will have to be marked by the continual refusal of choice—between tradition and modernity, between universal rights and cultural specificities, between individual uniqueness and community identity, between capitalist consumerism and the demonization of desire. As the different levels of globalization intersect at different spatial and temporal moments, different and unpredictable energies will be generated that cannot be known in advance. Our politics has to remain flexible enough to seize the moment, whenever and however that moment may occur.

Notes

I would like to thank the following people for their challenging comments—Antoinette Burton, Ania Loomba, Priyamvada Gopal, and Aditya Nigam. I also thank Faranak Miraftab for her interest in my argument and for taking the trouble to help me get hold of a crucial reference.

1. Ashcroft, Griffiths, and Tiffin, *The Post-colonial Studies Reader*, 117.

2. Kaviraj, "Democracy and Development in India," 98.

3. Chatterjee, *A Possible India*, 263.

4. Mehbooba Mufti, "Kashmiri Women Don't Need Morality Lessons," interview by Muzamil Jaleel, *Indian Express*, September 7, 2001.

5. News report, *Indian Express*, September 5, 2001.

6. Sarkar and Butalia, *Women and the Hindu Right*; Mernissi, *The Veil and the Male Elite*.

7. M. P. Basheer, "Behind the Veil," *Communalism Combat*, January 1992, 8.

8. Muzamil Jaleel, "Look at Me, Don't Look at Me," *Indian Express*, September 9, 2001.

9. The beauty parlor as an ambiguous space of empowerment and objectification has been studied extensively by feminist scholars. See, for example, Black, " 'Ordinary People Come through Here' "; and Black and Sharma "Men Are Real, Women Are Made Up." In "Men at Work: An Inquiry into the Survival Aspects of Men in Beauty Work," S. M. Faizan Ahmed, through a study of men who do "beauty work" in two cities of India, has suggested that the care of the body in many ways constitutes a form of unalienated labor that links work and worker through an ethic of care, offering the potential of subverting dominant constructions of masculinity.

10. Mei Fong, "Lifting the Veil from Pak Ramps," *Indian Express*, March 31, 2002. The article was originally published in the *Wall Street Journal*, March 26, 2002.

11. See, for instance, Mani, "Contentious Traditions"; Kumar, *The History of Doing*, ch. 2; Kaviraj, "The Imaginary Institution of India"; and Chakrabarty, "Modernity and Ethnicity in India."

12. El Guindi, *Veil*, 184.

13. Ibid., 131–32.

14. Thandabantlu Nhlapo, "The African Customary Law of Marriage and the Rights Conundrum."

15. See, for instance, the essays in Cohen, Wilk, and Stoeltje, *Beauty Queens on the Global Stage*.

16. Sangari, "New Patriotisms," 154–55.

17. Local beauty contests have proliferated since the run of successes began, but only the winners of the *Femina*-sponsored contests go to the international one.

18. Kabeer, *Bangladeshi Women Workers*.

19. Sangari, "New Patriotisms," 156.

20. Ibid.

21. Ibid., 158.

22. "Swadeshi Hawks Attack PM's Reforms," *Indian Express*, December 12, 1998; "Rashtravirodhi aarthik neetiyon ko chalne nahin dega Sangh" [The Sangh Will Not Allow Antinational Policies to Be Implemented], *Jansatta*, March 13, 2000.

23. For instance in Mumbai on April 25, 2001, and in Delhi on February 27, 2003. See Smruti Koppikar "United Colours of Politics," *Indian Express*, April 27, 2001.

24. "Surjeet Rules Out Probe into Cola Row," *Hindu*, February 8, 2003.

25. "Regarding Industrial Policy There Is Some Friction between Government and the Unions," *Indian Express*, June 10, 2001.

26. Ibid.

27. Sangari, "New Patriotisms."

28. Nigam, "Radical Politics," 160. All documents cited by Nigam in this section come from a dossier prepared by the Centre for Education and Communication, New Delhi, "Social Clause in Multilateral Trade Agreements (A Dossier on Social Clause)" (1995).

29. The pressure on advanced capitalist countries to impose labor standards on the poorer states has a complex origin, for it reflects both the anxiety of organized labor in the former at the flight of capital to poorer regions of the world and the re-sulting fall in employment, as well as the need of corporate capital to neutralize the trade advantage of the third world bourgeoisie.

30. Nigam, "Radical Politics," 162.

31. Mahendra, "A Protectionist Measure," 47, quoted in Nigam, "Radical Politics," 162.

32. Nigam, "Radical Politics," 162.

33. Ibid., 164. Nigam underlines the complexity of the responses to globalization when he argues that at least five different positions on globalization can be discerned: (1) The pro-globalization, pro–social clause position of the Western powers; (2) the antiglobalization, anti–social clause position of the Indian trade unions and left-wing parties; (3) the pro-globalization, anti–social clause position of the Indian elites, the Indian government, and the World Bank; (4) the antiglobalization, pro–social clause position of some representatives of the nonorganized sector in India, as well as trade union voices in other third world countries like Malaysia, Peru, and so on; and (5) the ambiguous stand on globalization combined with a pro–social clause position of some major NGOs working on child labor. Ibid., 168.

34. In a book that follows a similar line of argument to Sangari's in linking the bomb to the agenda of the Hindu Right, Praful Bidwai and Achin Vanaik put it this way: "Only the left came out *(after initial hesitation and confusion)* against the tests." Bidwai and Vanaik, *South Asia on a Short Fuse*, 107; emphasis mine. What the hesi-tation and confusion was about is not explained.

35. Sangari, "New Patriotisms."

36. Ibid., 168.

37. India's "ambiguity" about the bomb after its first nuclear explosion in 1974 left open the possibility of any subsequent government deciding on the nuclear option. The United Front coalition in power immediately before the BJP-led government that exploded the bomb, and which had included the Communist Party of India and the CPI(M), also claimed some of the "credit" after the 1998 explosion by saying that it

had already made the first preparations for the bomb. See Bidwai and Vanaik, *South Asia on a Short Fuse*, 107.

38. Jameson, "Globalization and Political Strategy," 49.

39. Kancha Iliah, "Cultural Globalisation," *Hindu*, February 22, 2003.

40. Jameson, "Globalization and Political Strategy," 49.

41. Nussbaum, *Women and Human Development*, 104.

42. For a fuller critique of Martha Nussbaum, see my review essay of *Women and Human Development*, Menon, "Universalism without Foundations?"

43. Friedman, *The Lexus and the Olive Tree*, 64. quoted in C. T. Kurien "Globalisation—An American Perspective," *Hindu*, April 5, 2001.

44. Quoted in Nivedita Menon and Aditya Nigam, "The 'War' in Europe," *Economic and Political Weekly*, May 1, 1999, 1021.

45. Jameson, "Globalization and Political Strategy," 56.

46. Ibid., 64.

47. Bhagwan Josh, Dilip Simeon, and Purushottam Agarwal, "Rethinking Secularism," *Mainstream*, December 30, 1990, 7–10.

48. Agarwal, "Surat, Savarkar, and Draupadi," 32.

49. Weber, *Peasants into Frenchmen*, 486.

50. See Bardhan, *The Political Economy of Development in India*; the collection of essays in "Development and Displacement," special issue of *Economic and Political Weekly*, June 15, 1996; and the *Lokayan Bulletin*, March–April 1995.

51. Jameson, "Globalization and Political Strategy," 65.

52. Gutmann, *Multiculturalism*, 3.

53. Ibid., 5.

54. Ibid.

55. Habermas, "Struggles for Recognition," 130.

56. Nazila Fathi, "A Little Leg, a Little Booze, but Hardly Gomorrah," *New York Times*, April 15, 2002. Similarly, in Iran, the island of Kish became a free-trade zone in 1989, since when the strict rules regarding clothing and intermingling of the sexes have been relaxed for both foreign and domestic tourists. Occasionally, the authorities have to "tighten up" to avoid interference from the hard-liners, but by and large, Kish is "known as an oasis of luxury and laxity." Conversely, of course, corporate globalization can appropriate feminist slogans into traditional images of women—for instance, many consumer goods advertisements on March 8 this year celebrated the "Day of the Wife."

57. Mukul Sharma, "Nature and Nationalism," *Frontline*, February 16, 2001, 94–96.

58. Gail Omvedt, "Marx and Globalization," *Hindu*, March 1 and 2, 2001; and Chandra Bhan Prasad, "New Life Movement versus Narmada Bachao Andolan," *Pioneer* (New Delhi), October 22, 2000.

THREE · Beyond the Nation-State
(and Back Again)

Environmentalism and Postcolonialism

ROB NIXON

What would it mean to bring environmentalism into dialogue with postcolonialism? These are currently two of the most dynamic areas in literary studies, yet their relationship continues to be one of reciprocal indifference or mistrust. A broad silence characterizes most environmentalists' stance toward postcolonial literature and theory, while postcolonial critics typically remain no less silent on the subject of environmental literature. What circumstances have shaped this mutual reluctance? And what kinds of intellectual initiatives might best advance an overdue dialogue?

Let me begin with the events that set my thinking on these issues in motion. In October 1995, the *New York Times* Sunday magazine featured an essay by Jay Parini entitled "The Greening of the Humanities."[1] Parini described the rise to prominence of environmentalism in the humanities, especially in literature departments. At the end of the essay, he named twenty-five writers and critics whose work was central to this environmental studies boom. Something struck me as odd about the list, something that passed unmentioned in the article: all twenty-five writers and critics were American.

This unselfconscious parochialism was disturbing, not least because at that time I was active in the campaign to release Ken Saro-Wiwa, the Ogoni author held prisoner without trial for his environmental and human rights activism in Nigeria.[2] Two weeks after Parini's article appeared, the Abacha regime executed Saro-Wiwa, making him Africa's most visible environmental martyr. Here was a writer—a novelist, poet, memoirist, and essayist— who had died fighting the ruination of his Ogoni people's farmland and fishing waters by European and American oil conglomerates in cahoots with a despotic African regime. Yet, clearly, Saro-Wiwa's writings were unlikely to find a home in the kind of environmental literary lineage outlined by Parini.

The more ecocriticism I read, the more this impression was confirmed. I encountered some illuminating books by Lawrence Buell, Cheryll Glotfelty, Harold Fromm, Daniel Payne, Scott Slovic, and many others.[3] Yet these authors tended to canonize the same self-selecting genealogy of American writers: Ralph Waldo Emerson, Henry David Thoreau, John Muir, Aldo Leopold, Edward Abbey, Annie Dillard, Terry Tempest Williams, Wendell Berry, and Gary Snyder.[4] All are writers of influence and accomplishment, yet all are drawn from within the boundaries of a single nation. Environmental literary anthologies, college course Web sites, and special journal issues on ecocriticism revealed similar patterns of predominance. Accumulatively, I realized that literary environmentalism was developing de facto as an offshoot of American studies.

The resulting national self-enclosure seemed peculiar: one might surely have expected environmentalism to be more, not less, transnational than other fields of literary inquiry. It was unfortunate that a writer like Saro-Wiwa, who had long protested what he termed "ecological genocide," could find no place in the environmental canon.[5] Was this because he was an African? Was it because his work revealed no special debt to Thoreau, to the wilderness tradition, or to Jeffersonian agrarianism? Instead, the fraught relations between ethnicity, pollution, and human rights animated Saro-Wiwa's writings. As did the equally fraught relations between local, national, and global politics. It was futile, he recognized, to try to understand or protest the despoiling of his people's water, land, and health within a purely national framework. For Ogoniland's environmental ruin resulted from collaborative plunder by those he dubbed Nigeria's "internal colonialists" and by the unanswerable, transnational power of Shell and Chevron.[6]

Saro-Wiwa's canonical invisibility in the United States seemed all the more telling given the role that America played in his emergence as an environmental writer. The United States buys half of Nigeria's oil and Chevron has emerged as a significant Ogoniland polluter.[7] More affirmatively, it was on a trip to Colorado that Saro-Wiwa witnessed a successful environmental campaign to stop corporate logging.[8] This experience contributed to his decision to mobilize international opinion by voicing his people's claims not just in the language of human rights but in environmental terms as well. Yet it was clear from the prevailing ecocritical perspective in literary studies that someone like Saro-Wiwa—whose environmentalism was at once profoundly local and profoundly international—would be bracketed as an African, the kind of writer best left to the postcolonialists.

I became aware, however, of a second irony: that postcolonial literary critics have, in turn, shown scant interest in environmental concerns, regarding them implicitly as, at best, irrelevant and elitist, at worst as sullied by "green imperialism."[9] Saro-Wiwa's distinctive attempt to fuse environmental and minority rights was unlikely to achieve much of a hearing in either camp.

These, then, were the circumstances that got me thinking about the mutually constitutive silences that have developed between environmental and postcolonial literary studies. Broadly speaking, there are four main schisms between the dominant concerns of postcolonialists and ecocritics. First, postcolonialists have tended to foreground hybridity and cross-culturation. Ecocritics, on the other hand, have historically been drawn more to discourses of purity: virgin wilderness and the preservation of "uncorrupted" last great places.[10] Second, postcolonial writing and criticism largely concern themselves with displacement, while environmental literary studies has tended to give priority to the literature of place. Third, and relatedly, postcolonial studies has tended to favor the cosmopolitan and the transnational. Postcolonialists are typically critical of nationalism, whereas the canons of environmental literature and criticism have developed within a national (and often nationalistic) American framework. Fourth, postcolonialism has devoted considerable attention to excavating or reimagining the marginalized past: history from below and border histories, often along transnational axes of migrant memory. By contrast, within much environmental literature and criticism, something different happens to history. It is often repressed or subordinated to the pursuit of timeless, solitary moments of communion with nature. There is a durable tradition within American natural history writing of erasing the history of colonized peoples through the myth of the empty lands. Postcolonialist critics are wary of the role that this strain of environmental writing (especially wilderness writing) has played in burying the very histories that they themselves have sought to unearth.

Postcolonial critics understandably feel discomfort with preservationist discourses of purity, given the role such discourses have played historically in the racially unequal distribution of post-Enlightenment human rights. In the context of a romantic primordialism, the colonized, especially women, have been repeatedly naturalized as objects of heritage to be owned, preserved, or patronized rather than as the subjects of their own land and legacies. Once cultures have been discursively assimilated to nature (not least through the settler tradition of viewing the United States as "nature's nation"), they have been left more vulnerable to dispossession—whether in the name of virgin wilderness preservation or the creation of nuclear test zones.[11]

Autobiographical divergences have doubtlessly sharpened intellectual differences between postcolonial writers and ecocritics over the politics of purity, place, nation, and history. The preeminent critics associated with postcolonialism—Kwame Anthony Appiah, Homi K. Bhabha, Edward Said, Sara Suleri, Gayatri Chakravorty Spivak, and Gauri Viswanathan, among others—have lived across national boundaries in ways that have given a personal edge to their intellectual investment in questions of dislocation, cultural syncretism, and transnationalism. Conversely, the most prominent environmental writers and critics are mono-nationals with a deep-rooted experiential and imaginative commitment to a particular American locale: Vermont for John Elder, the Sierra Nevada for Gary Snyder, Appalachian Kentucky for Wendell Berry, Utah in Terry Tempest Williams's case.

This tension between a postcolonial preoccupation with displacement and an ecocritical preoccupation with an ethics of place needs to be further situated in terms of cosmopolitanism, on the one hand, and bioregionalism, on the other.[12] Bioregionalism, in Parini's words, entails a responsiveness to "one's local part of the earth whose boundaries are determined by a location's natural characteristics rather than arbitrary administrative boundaries."[13] Gary Snyder and ecocritics like John Elder and David Orr are all vocal advocates of a bioregional ethic. Orr connects ecological destruction to the way people can graduate from college "with obligations to no place in particular. Their knowledge is mostly abstract, equally applicable in New York or San Francisco."[14] Similarly, Elder argues that "the traditional model in education has been cosmopolitanism. I've come to prefer a concentric and bioregional approach to learning. . . . It makes sense—educationally—to begin with local writing; then you expand, adding layers of knowledge."[15]

There is much to be said for this approach: it can help instill in us an awareness of our impact on our immediate environment, help ground our sense of environmental responsibility. However, from a postcolonial perspective, a bioregional ethic poses certain problems. For the concentric rings of the bioregionalists more often open out into transcendentalism than into transnationalism. All too frequently, we are left with an environmental vision that remains inside a spiritualized and naturalized national frame.

Much of the American imaginative and critical literature associated with bioregionalism tends toward a style of spiritual geography premised on what I call spatial amnesia. Within a bioregional center-periphery model, the specificity and moral imperative of the local typically opens out not into the specificities of the international but into transcendental abstraction. In this way, a prodigious amount of American environmental writing and criticism makes expansive gestures while remaining amnesiac toward non-American geographies that vanish over the intellectual skyline.

The environmentalist advocacy of an ethics of place has, all too often, morphed into hostility toward displaced people. Edward Abbey's rants against Mexican immigrants, Mary Austin's anti-Semitism, and the Sierra Club's disastrous referendum on zero immigration all evidence a xenophobic strain running through ethics-of-place environmentalism.[16] With the Sierra Club in mind, Richard Rodriguez has noted how the weeping Amerindian in the public service commercial first became an environmental talisman and then, in a grim historical irony, was invoked against the immigrant descendants of indigenous populations heading north from Mexico and Central America.[17]

An exclusionary ethics of place can easily lapse into jingoistic transcendentalism, as in an essay that the Montana author, Rick Bass, wrote in defense of southern Utah's Red Rock country. "The unprotected wilderness of the West," Bass declared

> is one of our greatest strengths as a country. Another is our imagination, our tendency to think rather than to accept—to challenge, to ask why and what if, to create rather than to destroy. This questioning is a kind of wildness, a kind of strength, that many have said is peculiarly American. Why place that strength in jeopardy? To lose Utah's wilderness would be to strip westerners and all Americans of a raw and vital piece of our soul, our identity, and our ability to imagine. . . . The print of a deer or lion in the sand, in untouched country, as you sleep—it is these things that allow you, allow us, to continue being American, rather than something else, anything else, everything else.[18]

In trying to rally Americans to a worthy preservationist cause, Bass may be resorting here to what Spivak calls "strategic essentialism."[19] After all, it is the American people's representatives who will determine the fate of Red Rock country. But such essentialism, strategic or otherwise, comes at a cost, for Bass aggrandizes and naturalizes the American national character in ways politically perturbing. How do we square his intimation that creative questioning is "peculiarly American" with Americans' widespread, unquestioning ignorance of the disastrous consequences (not least environmental consequences) of US foreign policy? Bass's position is predicated on, among other things, a failure of geographical imagination—a kind of superpower parochialism.

If your frame is Red Rock country, the United States may seem quintessentially a nation of questioners who seek to "to create rather than to destroy." But from the vantage point of the 1 million Vietnamese still suffering the health consequences of Agent Orange, or from the perspective of vulnerable microminorities in Nigeria, Ecuador, or West Papua, places where American extraction industry giants like Chevron, Texaco, and Freeport McMoran run rampant, a reluctance to destroy may not seem as definitive an American value. We should temper Bass's blinkered econationalism with Aldo Leopold's sobering reminder of what else it means, in environmental terms, to be an American: "When I go birding in my Ford, I am devastating an oil field, and re-electing an imperialist to get me rubber."[20]

Bass's exaltation of the American soul as pure imagination—a higher soul in search of "untouched country"—has, moreover, a dubious settler lineage. It is precisely such thinking that has impeded the American environmental movement's efforts to diversify its support base. From the perspective of North America's First Peoples, the white soul dream of "untouched country" has meant cultural erasure and dispossession. It contributed, classically, to the Ahwahneechee's eviction from Yosemite as part of Yosemite's reinvention as pure wilderness.[21]

For people relegated to the unnatural margins of nature's nation—like gay minority writers Rodriguez and Melvin Dixon—the wilderness experience can look ominously purified (as opposed to pure). In his ironically titled essay "True West," Rodriguez describes how, setting off on a hike, he hears, three minutes beyond the trailhead, rustling in the bushes. Instead of experiencing transcendental uplift, he fears ambush by "Snow White and the seven militias."[22] And in *Ride Out the Wilderness*, poet-critic Dixon has chronicled how African Americans have associated wilderness with the travail of exile: it is more a place of eviction and historical hauntings than of redemptive silences.[23]

Our intellectual challenge, then, is how to draw on the strengths of bioregionalism without succumbing to ecoparochialism. Here one might heed the call by the British natural historian Richard Mabey for a less brittle, less exclusionary environmental ethics. As Mabey writes, "the challenge, in a world where the differences between native and stranger are fading, is to discover veins of local character which are distinctive without being insular and withdrawn."[24] Yet in response to the blurring of the distinction between native and stranger we have frequently witnessed a defensive tendency to naturalize rootedness and stigmatize as alien people who look or talk differently. Precisely this kind of defensiveness prompted, in a British context, Paul Gilroy to question the racial implications of Raymond Williams's ethics of place.

Williams (whose *The Country and the City* stands as a compendious precursor to ecocriticism) championed what he called "rooted settlements" or "natural communities." These were communities in which "lived, worked and placeable social identities" provided anchorage against the dislocating effects of global capitalism and the abstractions of national identity.[25] However, Williams's advocacy of "natural communities" was accompanied, on occasion, by a suspicion not just of capitalism's dislocating effects but of dislocated people themselves, as when Williams expressed sympathy for local resistance, in rural British communities, to "the most recent immigrations of more visibly different peoples."[26] It proved insufficient, Williams argued, to say that these newcomers "are as British as you are." Because that was to invoke "a merely legal definition of what it is to be British. . . . Any effective awareness of social identity depends on actual and sustained social relationships. To reduce social identity to formal definitions . . . is to collude with the alienated superficialities of 'the nation.' "[27] Writing from a more cosmopolitan, postcolonial perspective, Gilroy voiced alarm at such sentiments. He pointed out that Williams's vision of natural community meant that minority immigrants and their British-born descendants would find themselves typecast as innately foreign and treated as second-class citizens.[28] How many generations, one might ask, does it take to get upgraded to "natural"?

The terms of this exchange are directly pertinent to the project, still in its infancy, of giving environmental literary studies an international dimension.[29] Gilroy's unease with the implications of Williams's remarks dramatizes the need for us to recuperate, imaginatively and politically, experiences of hybridity, displacement, and transnational memory for any viable spatial ethic. Postcolonialism can help diversify our thinking beyond the dominant paradigms of wilderness and Jeffersonian agrarianism in ways that render ecocriticism more accommodating of what I call a transnational ethics of place.

Such an ethics can help us, for example, rethink the pastoral in terms of colonial and postcolonial transnationalism. As an imaginative tradition, English pastoral has long been both nationally definitive and fraught with anxiety. At the heart of English pastoral lies the idea of the nation as garden idyll into which neither labor nor violence intrudes.[30] To stand as a self-contained national heritage landscape, English pastoral has depended on the screening out of colonial spaces and histories, much as the American wilderness ideal has entailed an amnesiac relationship toward the Amerindian wars of dispossession.[31]

But what happens when memories of colonial space intrude on pastoralism, disturbing its pretensions to national self-definition and self-containment? The result is a kind of writing that I call postcolonial pastoral, writing that refracts an idealized nature through memories of environmental and cultural degradation in the colonies. Postcolonial pastoral can be loosely viewed as a kind of environmental double consciousness.

We can see this double consciousness at work in V. S. Naipaul's autobiographical novel *The Enigma of Arrival*, which draws on his life on a manorial estate in Wiltshire—Thomas Hardy country, the heartland of English pastoral.[32] Naipaul self-consciously appends himself, in this novel, to the imaginative lineage of English pastoral by invoking William Constable, John Ruskin, Oliver Goldsmith, Thomas Gray, William Wordsworth, William Cobbett, Richard Jeffries, and Hardy. In the process, Naipaul engages the centuries-long English tradition of *hortus conclusus*, the enclosed garden.

However, Naipaul's perspective is that of an uprooted immigrant whose vision of England can never be nationally self-enclosed. In other words, his experience of pastoral cannot be contained by the historical and spatial amnesias demanded by an all-English frame. Instead, through the double consciousness of postcolonial pastoral, Naipaul experiences the *hortus conclusus* as indissociable from transnational, colonial environments and memories. The counterpoint to the Wiltshire manor garden that he inhabits is the Trinidadian sugar plantation to which his grandparents were indentured from India. Thus Naipaul views his environment through the double prism of postcolonial pastoral: behind the wealth and tranquility of an English idyll, he remembers the painful, dystopian shadow garden of the transatlantic plantation that helped make that idyll possible.

The most exhilarating recent exploration of transnational shadow gardens has come from the Caribbean historian Richard Drayton. In *Nature's Government* — on the surface, a history of the Royal Botanical Gardens at Kew — Drayton examines, in his words, "how the natural sciences became included in an ideology of 'Improvement' which ordered enclosure at home and expansion abroad."[33] Kew, for Drayton, constitutes not a self-enclosed English space, but part of an extraordinary web of imperial gardens stretching from St. Vincent to South Africa, Ceylon, Australia, and beyond, gardens that became implicated in global developments not just in botanical knowledge but also in economic power, political policy, and imperial administration. Drayton's book provides some answers to a question that Jamaica Kincaid has posed repeatedly in literary form. Kincaid, the *New Yorker*'s former gardening columnist (and the only anticolonial gardening columnist the magazine will likely ever have), is equally impassioned about lupines and colonial history. At the heart of much of her nonfiction stands this blunt question: "What is the relationship between gardening and conquest?"[34]

Kincaid herself exemplifies that relationship. The British transported her violated ancestors to Antigua. But colonial ships also carried to Antigua the alien plants and animals that have since spread across the island. Kincaid's interest in Antigua's environmental viability thus becomes inseparable from her obsession with her ancestral memories of displacement. From where she stands, the separation of botany from the history of slavery seems profoundly unnatural. That much becomes apparent in "The Flowers of Empire," an essay in which Kincaid recounts how, in a moment of botanical rapture, colonial history ambushed her:

> One day I was walking through the glasshouse area of Kew Gardens in London when I came upon the most beautiful hollyhock I had ever seen. Hollyhocks are among my favorite flowers, but I had never seen one quite like this. It had the characteristic large, flared petal, and it was a most beautiful yellow, a clear yellow, as if it—the color yellow—were just born, delicate, just at the beginning of its history as "yellow." It was on looking at the label on which was written its identification that my whole being was sent awhirl. It was not a hollyhock at all but gossypium, the common cotton. Cotton all by itself exists in perfection, with malice toward none. But it played a tormented, malevolent role in the bondage of my ancestors.[35]

Here, as in Naipaul's *Enigma of Arrival*, Kincaid's passion for nature is complicated by her postcolonial double consciousness.

One can read Kincaid's writings against John Elder's insistence that bioregionalism constitutes a more responsible pedagogical model than cosmopolitanism. For Kincaid confounds such oppositions. *A Small Place*, her nonfictional book about Antigua and tourism, could be read as bioregional in approach: it takes, as its starting point, the natural boundaries of this tiny island. Yet the small place where Kincaid stands, the place where knowledge must begin, is inextricably local *and* transnational.[36] Place is displacement, for British colonists killed off the indigenous inhabitants and replaced them with transported slaves. In the process, the colonists turned what was a well-wooded island into a desert, clearing the forests to grow slave crops—sugar and cotton.[37] As a result of this slave-era environmental degradation, the island has lost its ability to retain water and, to this day, is forced to import it.

This colonial-induced drought has deepened Antigua's economic reliance on tourism. So, ironically, a place scarred by a long history of coercive labor and violence has been reinvented as an Edenic retreat where Europeans and North Americans can experience nature as pure—a paradise beyond reach of work and time. We can thus read *A Small Place* as Kincaid's effort to return this Eden to a transnational ethics of place. In this way, Kincaid allows us to see Antigua, like Naipaul's Trinidad, as a shadow island, a corrective to the spatial amnesia of a self-contained, regenerative English pastoral of the kind evident in, for example, the conclusion to E. M. Forster's *Howard's End*.[38]

"Alien Soil," Kincaid's essay on English and colonial nature, captures the paradox of her position. In England, she is on alien soil; in Antigua, an island where none of the people and few of the plants are native, the soil constitutes the historic ground of her alienation. In Kincaid's words: "I come from a people with a wretched historical relationship to growing things."[39] However, despite that relationship, Kincaid retains a huge passion for botany and gardening—a passion that she recognizes as part of her English inheritance through conquest. Yet she turns that inheritance against itself by insisting that her botanical enthusiasms be refracted through the prism of colonial history.

This is well-illustrated by her response to an entry in the *Oxford Companion of Gardens* on George Clifford, the eighteenth-century Anglo-Dutch banker who built a gargantuan glasshouse filled with plants collected from around the world. That glasshouse proved indispensable to Linnaeus when "Adam-like [he] invented modern plant nomenclature."[40] Kincaid observes how

> the plants in [Clifford's] glasshouse could only have come to him through—and I quote from *Oxford Companion to Gardens*—"the influence of the world trade being developed by maritime powers such as the Netherlands and Great Britain." This being way of expressing an extraordinary history event—"trade being developed," leaving out the nature of the trade being developed: trade in people and the things that they possessed, plants, animals, and so on—never ceases to amaze me.
>
> I do not mind the glasshouse; I do not mind the botanical garden. This is not so grand a gesture on my part. It is mostly an admission of defeat—to mind would be completely futile; I cannot do anything about it anyway. I only mind the absence of this acknowledgment: that perhaps every good thing that stands before us comes at a great cost to someone else.[41]

Kincaid's pained reflections here echo Walter Benjamin's insistence that "there is no document of civilization which is not at the same time a document of barbarism."[42]

Ecological literary critics have been slow to absorb the kinds of provocative transnational thinking that has gathered strength in other disciplines central to the greening of the humanities, disciplines like history, geography, and anthropology.[43] Postcolonial literary critics, by contrast, have tended to shy away from environmental issues as if they were soft, Western, bourgeois concerns. But the notion that environmental politics are a luxury politics for the world's wealthy is clearly untenable. As Gayatri Spivak, one of the few postcolonial literary scholars to even allude to environmental issues, has argued, "the local in the South directly engages global greed."[44]

Any postcolonialist dismissal of environmentalism as marginal to "real" politics is belied by the current proliferation of indigenous environmental movements across the global South. Saro-Wiwa was not some isolated epic hero: his actions were indicative of a myriad non-Western environmental campaigns locally motivated, locally led, and internationally inflected. We are witnessing, on the environmental front, something similar to the mutation of feminism, which was often dismissed, twenty or thirty years ago, as white, privileged, and irrelevant to the needs of third world women. We have seen what counts as feminism radically changed by the rise of local social movements that have decentered and diversified the agenda of women's rights in ethnic, geographic, religious, sexuality, and class terms. In recent years, we have witnessed a similar decentering in environmentalism, one that has begun to shift the terms of the decisive debates away from issues like purity preservation and Jeffersonian-style agrarianism.

As William Beinart and Peter Coates have argued, "all human activity alters the composition of the natural world which in itself is never static. A critique which regards all change as decay begs the very legitimacy of human survival."[45] Non-Western environmental movements are typically alert to the interdependence of human survival and environmental change in situations where the illusion of a static purity cannot be sustained, far less exalted as an ideal. Such movements are also typically aware of how easily foreign forces—transnational corporations, the World Bank, or NGOs, often in cahoots with authoritarian regimes—can destroy the delicate, always mutable, mesh between cultural traditions, social justice, and ecosystems.

In Ecuador, one such locally led campaign, Acción Ecológica, mobilized the nation's Confederation of Indigenous Nationalities against Texaco, whose ransacking of the environment echoed the plunder, ten thousand miles away, that generated Nigeria's Movement of the Survival of the Ogoni People.[46] In India, the corporatizing of biodiversity has proved a major rallying point: 200,000 Indian farmers descended on Delhi in the so-called Seed Satyagraha to protest transnational efforts to wrest control over the reproduction and distribution of seeds from traditional farmers.

Wangari Maathai, Kenya's first woman professor, has been imprisoned and tortured for helping instigate mass tree plantings to protest rampant deforestation. In 1998, when Kenya's kleptocractic government began expropriating and selling off the publicly held Karura Forest to developers of luxury housing, students at the University of Nairobi and Kenyatta University launched another dissident tree planting. The government's brutal response produced campus riots that closed down both universities in defense of what student leader Wycliffe Mwebi called the "moral right to defend the environment against a corrupt land grab."[47]

If it is no longer viable to view environmentalism as a Western luxury, how are we best to integrate environmental issues into our approach to postcolonial literature and vice versa? Among many possible productive starting places, one could turn to the current wave of interest in Black Atlantic studies and seek to give it an environmental dimension. Black Atlanticism stands as one of the most energizing paradigms to have emerged in literary and cultural studies during the past decade. Yet the questions it raises—about transnational identities, the triangular trade in people and commodities, the multiple passages of modernity—remain cordoned off from environmental considerations. The literary possibilities are alluring: not just in Kincaid's oeuvre but also in the work of writers like Derek Walcott (starting with his assertion, "the sea is history"), Aimé Césaire, Wilson Harris, Michelle Cliff, and Patrick Chamoiseau, among others.[48]

By integrating approaches from environmental and Black Atlantic studies, we might help bridge the divide between the ecocritical study of America's minority literatures (a recent growth area) and the ecocritical study of post-colonial literatures, which remains extremely rudimentary. The recent influential anthology, *Literature and the Environment* evidences the problems with this divide.[49] In one important regard, this makes for an encouraging volume: it is the first environmental anthology to include a significant spread of minority writers, many of them foregrounding issues that the environmental justice movement has prioritized. By acknowledging what Langston Hughes, bell hooks, Louis Owens, Clarissa Pinkola Estes, and Marilou Awiakta (among others) add to environmental debate and testimony, the anthology marks a shift away from the American ecocritical obsession with wilderness writing and the literature of Jeffersonian agrarianism. Several of the essays address indigenous land rights, community displacement, and toxicity, often in the context of urban or poor rural experience. Encouragingly, these are some of the American concerns that most readily connect with the environmental priorities that predominate in postcolonial writing. It is here that one recognizes the richest possibilities for a more transnational rapprochement.

However, in helping redefine the field, *Literature and the Environment* (despite its expansive title) restricts itself to an almost all-American cast. Of the 104 contributions, only one is non-American: a maverick Wordsworth poem. So while applauding this diversification of environmental literature, we should be careful not to confuse American multiculturalism with international diversity, or assume that the latter flows automatically from the former. The urgent need for a more global inclusiveness remains unaddressed.

The geographical distribution of interest in Lawrence Buell's otherwise brilliant recent study, *Writing for an Endangered World: Literature, Cul-*

ture, and Environment in the U.S. and Beyond, raises some similar issues.[50] Buell's earlier, and justly influential, study *The Environmental Imagination* centered on American nature writing and was composed in the shadow of Thoreau. Buell's sequel, however, takes a more generous, creative view of what counts as environmental literature, opening up questions of toxicity, biodegradation, urban experience, and "engineered environments."[51] This enables Buell to engage, through detailed readings, a series of American minority writers: Gwendolyn Brooks, John Edgar Wideman, Richard Wright, and Linda Hogan, among them.[52]

However, the expanded American diversity of Buell's later work is not matched by an attentiveness to diversity elsewhere. The limitations of trying to generate a global vision from an American-centered account of environmental writing becomes evident in Buell's solitary reading of a postcolonial text, Mahasweta Devi's "Pterodactyl, Puran Sahay, and Pirtha," a Bengali short story translated into English by Gayatri Spivak.[53]

After praising "Pterodactyl" as a trenchant fiction of environmental justice, Buell remarks that the novella's "sometimes esoteric cultural particularism . . . may seem to make it an odd detour from the U.S.-focused texts I have mainly been discussing."[54] The image of a "detour" and the reference to Devi's "esoteric cultural particularism" foreground the intellectual challenge for ecocritics of moving beyond a center-periphery model. The unsettling implication is that somehow American texts transcend "cultural particularism," are always already universalized in ways that postcolonial ones are not.

In terms of bridging possibilities, Buell's work on toxic discourse represents the most promising recent theoretical initiative.[55] The prospects it opens up for comparative international readings are almost inexhaustible. Rebecca Solnit, for instance, has brilliantly evoked the resistance to nuclear testing in Nevada by Western Shoshone battling for their land rights in collaboration with environmental protestors. Yet instead of placing Solnit's *Savage Dreams* within the standard Americanist ecocanon, it could be repositioned in an international context that would engage, comparatively, the land claims and toxic history of Australia's Aboriginal downwinders, as recounted in *Yami: The Autobiography of Yami Lester*.[56] Solnit and Lester, in turn, could be read productively alongside Arundhati Roy's *The Cost of Living*, Marilynne Robinson's *Mother Country*, and Scott Malcomson's *Tuturani*, which explore, respectively, the lethal repercussions of nuclear testing and nuclear pollution in South Asia, Britain, and the Marshall Islands and Bikini Atoll.[57]

Much of the new work to be done is comparative: the Australian Aboriginal environmentalist Fabienne Bayet's reflections on indigenous traditions of nonproprietary land possession bear fruitful comparison, for example, with Leslie Marmon Silko's account of Pueblo land values.[58] However, for the work ahead, we cannot rely only on American terms of comparison. How, for example, would our assumptions about what constitutes environmental literature have to change if we generated eco-inflected rereadings of classic African novels like Bessie Head's *Where Rain Clouds Gather*, Chinua Achebe's *Things Fall Apart*, Cheikh H. Kane's *Ambiguous Adventure*, J. M. Coetzee's *Life and Times of Michael K*, and Ngugi wa Thiong'o's *A Grain of Wheat*?[59]

International oil literature offers us, pedagogically, an unusually rich resource. We can draw on it both to diversify the environmental literary canon and dramatize for students the connections between questions of transnational environmental justice and their local consumer choices.[60] Oil literature allows us to connect writers as various as Upton Sinclair (on the California oil boom), the Nigerians Saro-Wiwa, J. P. Clark, and Tayo Olafioye, the great Jordanian-born novelist Abdelrahman Munif, and Joe Kane (on Texaco in Ecuador).[61]

But we need to go beyond simply diversifying the canon; we need to reimagine the prevailing paradigms. That much is evident from the enormous difficulty Saro-Wiwa had in gaining an audience in the United States and Europe. When he first appealed to Greenpeace representatives, they said they did not work in Africa—it was off their environmental map.[62] Wherever he went, Saro-Wiwa was treated as an unfathomable anomoly—an African writer claiming to be an environmentalist? And claiming, moreover, that his people's human rights were being violated by environmental ethnocide? Part of Saro-Wiwa's problem in gaining a hearing for the Ogoni was not just economic and political—it was imaginative as well.

Saro-Wiwa campaigned for environmental justice. But he also campaigned, in effect, against a center-periphery paradigm. He had to contend not just with environmental racism but with prejudicial failures of geographical imagining. In American intellectual and media terms, a region like Ogoniland is almost completely unimaginable.[63] Yet the writings of Saro-Wiwa, like those of Arundhati Roy, allow us to engage (in ways that the self-perpetuating national lineage of Thoreau, Muir, Abbey, Snyder, and the others does not) environmental politics through conflicts between subnational microminorities, autocratic nation-states, and transnational macroeconomic powers.[64]

In trying to diversify our thinking, we need to ensure that we do not end up asking an environmental variant of Saul Bellow's dismissive question:

"Where is the Zulu Tolstoy?" If we go scouting the equatorial forests for the Timorese Thoreau (or his Cameroonian cousin), we will return alone. Nor can we content ourselves with the current move toward nominal international variety—an Ishimure Michiko or Wordsworth text decorating the American ecocanon much as Virginia Woolf or Jane Austen once graced otherwise all-male courses and, later, a nominal Toni Morrison or Alice Walker was used to "diversify" white courses on women's writing.[65]

To reject an add-on solution to the challenges of diversity is to refuse a vision of environmentalism as invented at the center and exported to (or imposed on) the periphery.[66] Such center-periphery thinking constitutes both a source of postcolonialists' pervasive indifference to environmentalism and, conversely, a source of the debilitating strain of superpower parochialism that lingers among many American ecocritics and writers. Just as subaltern studies embarked on a project of provincializing the West, so, too, we need to provincialize American environmentalism if we are to regenerate and diversify the field.

Ours is an age in which the combined wealth of the world's 550 billionaires exceeds that of the 3 billion humans who constitute the planet's poorest 50 percent. Five hundred corporations command 70 percent of world trade. In an era of giga-mergers and nanosecond transnationalisms, we cannot persist with the kind of isolationist thinking that has, in different ways, impeded both postcolonial and ecocritical responses to globalization.[67] The isolation of postcolonial literary studies from environmental concerns has limited the field's intellectual reach. Likewise, ecocriticism's predominantly American studies frame has proven inadequate, not least because we cannot afford to stop seeing the broader connections. Invisibility has its costs, as Arundhati Roy reminds us: globalization, she observes, is "like a light which shines brighter and brighter on a few people and the rest are in darkness, wiped out. They simply can't be seen. Once you get used to not seeing something, then, slowly, it's no longer possible to see it."[68] In the classroom, in our writing, and in the media, we need to widen that beam.

The dialogue I have sought to outline can help us rethink oppositions between bioregionalism and cosmopolitanism, between transcendentalism and transnationalism, between an ethics of place and the experience of displacement. Through such a rapprochement, we can begin to think, simultaneously, for example, about nature-induced states of transport and the vast, brutal history of humans forcibly transported. In the process, we can aspire to a more historically answerable and geographically expansive sense of what constitutes our environment and which literary works we entrust to voice its parameters. This is an ambitious but crucial task, not least because, for the foreseeable future, literature departments are likely to remain influential players in the greening of the humanities.

Notes

1. Jay Parini, "The Greening of the Humanities," *New York Times* Sunday magazine, October 23, 1995, 52–53.
2. Rob Nixon, "The Oil Weapon," *New York Times*, November 17, 1995. For a fuller discussion of the issues at stake, see Nixon, "Pipedreams."
3. Buell, *The Environmental Imagination*; Glotfelty and Fromm, *The Ecocritical Reader*; Payne, *Voices in the Wilderness*; and Slovic, *Seeking Awareness in American Nature Writing*. Buell does stress the need to give international dimension to environmental literary studies, but in design and emphasis, *The Environmental Imagination* remains within an Americanist paradigm.
4. For a classic instance of these limitations, see Oelschlaeger's *The Idea of Wilderness*.
5. Saro-Wiwa, *Nigeria*, 71.
6. Saro-Wiwa, *A Month and A Day*, 7.
7. Ibid., 80.
8. Ibid., 79.
9. For an influential postcolonial challenge to the American wilderness obsession, see Guha, "Radical American Environmentalism and Wilderness Preservation."
10. For an invaluable critique of the wilderness tradition of "purity," see Cronon, "The Trouble with Wilderness."
11. See J. M. Coetzee's terse assessment that "it is certainly true that the politics of expansion has uses for the rhetoric of the sublime." Coetzee, *White Writing*, 62.
12. For an excellent discussion of the dangers of an excessive preoccupation with displacement, see Kumar, *Passport Photos*, 13–14. See also, Ian Buruma, "The Romance of Exile," *New Republic*, February 12, 2001, 23–30.
13. Parini, "The Greening of the Humanities," 53.
14. Quoted in ibid., 53
15. Quoted in ibid., 53.
16. On Abbey's anti-immigrant environmentalism, which became more prominent in his later years, see Scarce, *Eco-warriors*, 92. For Austin's anti-Semitism, see Athanasiou, *Divided Planet*, 297.
17. Rodriguez, *Days of Obligation*, 5.
18. Rick Bass, "A Landscape of Possibility," *Outside*, December 1995, 100–01.
19. Spivak, *The Post-colonial Critic*, 72.
20. Aldo Leopold, "Game and Wildlife Conservation," in Leopold, *Game Management*, 23.
21. For a brilliant account of this process, see Solnit, *Savage Dreams*, 215–385.
22. Rodriguez, "True West," 331.
23. Dixon, *Ride Out the Wilderness*.
24. Mabey, *Landlocked*, 71.
25. Williams, *Towards 2000*, 195. For a related perspective on community and

place, see Williams, "Homespun Philosophy," *New Statesman and Society*, June 19, 1992, 8–9. See also his *The Country and the City*.

26. Williams, *Towards 2000*, 195.

27. Ibid., 195.

28. Gilroy, *"There Ain't No Black in the Union Jack,"* 49–50. Stuart Hall questions Williams's prioritizing of rooted settlements in similar terms. See Hall, "Our Mongrel Selves," *New Statesman and Society*, June 19, 1992, 6–7.

29. To date, the most useful resource on environmental writing beyond the United States is Murphy's *Literature of Nature*. Scott Slovic has sought to counter the complaint "that environmental literature is an exclusively Americanist preserve" by pointing to, among other things, the rise in international submissions to the premier journal in the field, *ISLE: Interdisciplinary Studies in Literature and Environment*. Yet the subjects and authors of environmental literary criticism remain overwhelmingly American. The internationalizing of ecocriticism, moreover, should not simply involve additive diversification in a center-periphery fashion. As I have argued above, we need to address the way ecocriticism's dominant models and intellectual priorities remain skewed by their American genesis, not least, by their failure to engage the rich traditions of postcolonial literature and thought. See Slovic, "Forum on Literatures of the Environment," 1102.

30. Williams's *The Country and the City* remains the most wide-ranging account of the English pastoral tradition.

31. For the most eloquent and economical account of the relationship between wilderness thinking and Amerindian dispossession in the United States, see Cronon, "The Trouble with Wilderness," 95–96. Solnit's *Savage Dreams* is also quite brilliant in this regard.

32. Naipaul, *The Enigma of Arrival*.

33. Drayton, *Nature's Government*, xvi.

34. Kincaid, *My Garden*, 132.

35. Ibid., 139.

36. Kincaid, *A Small Place*.

37. Ibid., 16.

38. Forster, *Howard's End*.

39. Kincaid, "Alien Soil," in Kidder, ed., *The Best American Essays*, 211.

40. Kincaid, *My Garden*, 143.

41. Ibid., 137.

42. Walter Benjamin, "Theses on the Philosophy of History," in Benjamin, *Illuminations*, 256.

43. One thinks here of innovative works like Grove, *Green Imperialism*; Griffiths and Robin, *Ecology and Empire*; Arnold and Guha, *Nature, Culture, Imperialism*; and Beinart and Coates, *Environment and History*.

44. Spivak, "Attention: Postcolonialism!" 166.

45. Beinart and Coates, *Environment and History*, 3. This book offers a fine comparative history of national parks in the United States and South Africa.

46. See Kane, *Savages*; Sawyer, "The Politics of Petroleum"; and Selverston, *The 1990 Indigenous Uprising in Ecuador*.

47. Quoted in ibid., 18.

48. For the rich possibilities to be found in this kind of intellectual rapprochement, see the Canadian critic Casteel's, "New World Pastoral."

49. Anderson, Slovic, and O'Grady, *Literature and the Environment*. Of the 104 essays and poems included by the editors, 26 are by African American, Amerindian, Latina/o, or Asian American writers. This marks a significant advance over the more typical spectrum of Glotfelty and Fromm's influential *Ecocriticism Reader*, which found room for only two "minority" essays out of twenty-six.

50. Buell, *Writing for an Endangered World*.

51. Ibid., 24.

52. The broader scheme of the second book also encourages Buell to discuss some urban European writers, notably Charles Dickens, Virginia Woolf, and James Joyce.

53. Mahasweta Devi, "Pterodactyl, Puran Sahay, and Pirtha," in Devi, *Imaginary Maps*, 95–96.

54. Buell, *Writing for an Endangered World*, 230.

55. Ibid., 30–54.

56. Lester, *Yami*.

57. Roy, *The Cost of Living*; Robinson, *Mother Country*; and Malcomson, *Tuturani*.

58. See Bayet, "Overturning the Doctrine"; and Silko, *"Yellow Woman" and "A Beauty of the Spirit."*

59. Head, *Where Rain Clouds Gather*; Achebe, *Things Fall Apart*; Kane, *Ambiguous Adventure*; Coetzee, *Life and Times of Michael K.*; and Thiong'o, *Grain of Wheat*. Are there ways, for example, to link Ngugi's account of a resistant Gikuyu culture of the forest during the anticolonial struggle with student efforts, in the 1990s, to safeguard Kenyan forests from neocolonial rapacity? For a preliminary foray into connections of this sort, see Slaymaker, "Echoing the Other(s)."

60. Rob Nixon, "The Hidden Lives of Oil," *Chronicle of Higher Education*, April 5, 2002, B7–B9.

61. Sinclair, *Oil!*; Clark, *All for Oil*; and Olafioye, *A Carnival of Looters*; Kane, *Savages*. The finest, and certainly the most teachable, of Munif's novels is *Cities of Salt*.

62. See Saro-Wiwa, *A Month and a Day*, 88.

63. Ogoniland belongs to the tropical belt that runs through the Amazon, West and Central Africa, Indonesia, and Papua and New Guinea, a zone that possesses the world's most diverse, ethnically fractured populations (four hundred ethnicities in Nigeria, several thousand in New Guinea), as well as unusually rich natural resources—oil, precious minerals, and timber. It is in this strip that American, European, and Japanese extraction-industry multinationals operate (frequently supported by dictatorial regimes) with maximum violence and impunity.

64. Pedagogically, an excellent place to start would be to read Saro-Wiwa's prison diary, *A Month and a Day* alongside both Wole Soyinka's prefigurative early play *The Swamp Dwellers* and recent work by Nigerian environmental philosopher Kolawole Owolabi, for instance, *Because of Our Future*. For a resonant comparison, one could turn to Joe Kane's account in *Savages* of another contest between an equatorial microminority (Ecuador's Huarorani Indians) and a petroleum multinational (Texaco).

65. The two contemporary ecocritics who seem most alive to the need to inter-

nationalize the field are Jonathan Bate and Patrick D. Murphy. Bate's *The Song of the Earth* places English romantic poetry center stage, but includes ecocritical readings of several contemporary British and American poets, as well as the West Indian poet Edward Kamau Brathwaite and the Australian writer Les Murray. Murphy's analyses, while predominantly American, are more geographically expansive than most. He includes a fine chapter on Ishimure Michiko and another entitled "Worldly Diversity." Murphy's title, *Further Afield in the Study of Nature-Oriented Literature*, however, suggests (like Buell's "detour") the tenacity of ecocriticism's center-periphery model.

66. For an excellent theoretical account of the conceptual limitations that result from a center-periphery model, see Timothy Mitchell, "The Stage of Modernity," in Mitchell, *Questions of Modernity*, 1–34. Mitchell's critique focuses on Western-centered genealogies of modernity, but many of his insights can be applied adaptively to ecocriticism.

67. Clearly, a narrowing of the divides between these two powerful intellectual currents only marks a beginning. In search of a truly international, interdisciplinary response, we would need to move beyond postcolonialism's Anglo- and Francophone emphases toward more fully global imaginings. But a postcolonial-environmental rapprochement would represent an invaluable start.

68. Roy quoted in Madeleine Bunting, "Dam Buster," *Guardian* (London), July 28, 2001.

Beyond Black Atlantic and Postcolonial Studies:

The South African Differences of Sol Plaatje

and Peter Abrahams

☉ ☉ ☉

LAURA CHRISMAN

In 1915, the British imperial administrator Sir Harry Johnston refused to preface a manuscript titled *Native Life in South Africa*. In the process, he gave its black South African author, Sol Plaatje, some badly misjudged transnationalist advice: "You must call it something like 'The Negro Question in South Africa.' Do not abuse the term 'native,' for it applies nowadays to 2 millions of white and yellow people born in and native to South Africa. Never be ashamed of the term Negro, for the Negro race has many great qualities and will yet play a potent part in the affairs of the world of the future as it did in the world of 100,000 years ago."[1] These Black Atlantic injunctions did not sway Plaatje, and in 1916, *Native Life* came into print.[2] Sir Harry, whose previous book publications included *The Negro in the New World* (1910), went on to publish a book titled *The Backward Peoples and Our Relations with Them* (1920). Plaatje spelled out his own reasons for preferring the terminology of *native* to *Negro* in his 1921 Pan-African Congress speech. In it, he argued that "everybody knows that the negro races throughout the world occupy an inferior position to that of other sections of the human race; but it is not so generally known that the Natives of British South Africa are assigned to a far lower level than that occupied by negro races in the rest of the civilized world."[3] Unlike Sir Harry, Plaatje is concerned with the global disparities of black people's socioeconomic status. His capitalized *Native* terminology constitutes an effective nationalist tactic, emphasizing British responsibility for injustice against black South Africans. And as Sir Harry realizes, Plaatje's equation of *native* with *black* points to the black sovereignty that colonial settlement has violated. Sir Harry's backlash *Negro* terminology functions, in effect, as an imperialist alibi: it disguises the impact of colonial domination and racism on African peoples.[4]

If, for Sir Harry, black people last contributed to world history 100,000 years ago, for Plaatje the contributions are rather more recent. His novel *Mhudi* is set in the early nineteenth century, its opening ironically observing of its South African protagonists: "These peasants were content to live their monotonous lives, and thought nought of their overseas kinsmen who were making history on the plantations and harbours of Virginia and Mississippi at that time."[5] This history is equally economic *and* political, comprising both the slaves' labor and their resistance to slavery. The South Africans soon join their diasporic relatives as modern history makers, but these communities' dispossession and resistance is not identical. The novel's opening establishes a Black Atlantic framework to underscore both the relatedness and the distinctiveness of the continental and diasporic experiences.[6] The national divisions separating black experience call forth a comparative perspective.

This comparative framework was nowhere evident when, sixteen years later, a South African teenager published an autobiographical poem titled "Negro Youth."[7] The title choice proves particularly significant because this author, Peter Abrahams, was not "native" but "colored." Abrahams's identification emerged from reading New Negro writers of the United States; as his autobiography explains, this was to isolate him from his family: "My mother came from Vrededorp that night and we had a little family party. I told them about . . . my discovery of American Negro literature. I tried to tell them what it meant to me. But they were not really interested. America and Harlem were at the other end of the world. And in Coloured terminology Negroes were black people whom both whites and Coloureds called Natives in their polite moments."[8]

Abrahams was not simply choosing blackness over coloredness: his father was Ethiopian. Since Ethiopia operated then, as now, so intensely as a black political, spiritual, and cultural symbol, Abrahams's preference for an Americanized "Negro" identity assumes more significance still. Indeed, Abrahams published "A Negro Youth" during Ethiopia's struggle to preserve sovereignty against fascist Italy. Other black South Africans were fighting for Ethiopia—and so identifying as figurative Ethiopians.[9]

These two thinkers articulate very different political perspectives. Plaatje's racial and nationalist identifications are reciprocal; his approach to race is political and economic and based on a comparative historical understanding. Plaatje was among the nationalists who founded the African National Congress (ANC) in 1912; he also founded several black South African newspapers.

Cultural preservation and innovation constituted complementary components of his nationalism: he collected Setswana folk culture and published the first black South African novel in English.[10] Abrahams, in contrast, embraces an exclusively modern racial identity at the expense of national and nationalist identity; his transnational blackness operates as an existential rather than a historical category. A writer of fiction, essays, and autobiography, he left South Africa in 1939 and, after traveling the world and living in England for a time, in 1956 moved to Jamaica. His fiction moved from the South African concerns of *Mine Boy* (1946) to West African neocolonialism in *Wreath for Udomo* (1956). It proceeded to the quandaries of Caribbean postcoloniality in *This Island, Now* (1966) and thence to a global exploration, in *The View from Coyaba* (1985), of black Africa and the Americas. His first autobiography, *Tell Freedom: Memories of Africa*, was published in 1954; in 2001, he published another: *The Black Experience in the Twentieth Century: An Autobiography and Meditation.*

I am going to explore the black ideological currents that cause a Sol Plaatje to choose to express himself as a native and a Peter Abrahams as a Negro. It is important to undertake this for two reasons. For one, both Plaatje and Abrahams are major twentieth-century literary intellectuals, shockingly neglected by all but specialists in South African literature. Metropolitan postcolonial and Black Atlantic studies frequently ignore their work, as it tends to ignore African writing that precedes the midcentury Chinua Achebe, routinely identified as the "father" of modern African letters. Indeed, the metropole sanctions only a very few African intellectuals as the bearers of valuable knowledge, and black South Africans generally do not feature in that list. Furthermore, the concerns of blackness, the category of race itself, and the specifically racial elements of colonial experience that these writers foreground have yet to make their way into the horizon of hegemonic US postcolonial study other than in the form of Frantz Fanon's psychoanalytic *Black Skin, White Masks*.[11]

The other reason for my topic is that Abrahams and Plaatje, and the differences between them, point to the importance of expanding and sharpening the conceptual foundations of postcolonial and Black Atlantic studies. Paul Gilroy's *The Black Atlantic* generated two divergent academic directions:[12] One centers on intellectual and cultural traffic between Europe and the United States, tending to valorize transcultural or transracial "hybridity."[13] The other, racially exclusive direction focuses on black countercultures of modernity; it tends to view the black diaspora as the apex of black modernity to which Africa aspires.[14] Neither of these developments, together or in isolation, can properly illuminate the Black Atlanticism at work in the South African intellectuals under discussion here.

My critical agenda is animated by the concern that current critical hege-mony liberates the transnational analysis of intellectuals and cultures not only from the restraints of the nation-state but from rigorous critical frame-works as well. Transnationalism effectively becomes its own context and its own end, blocking from view the existence of conditions that mediate or de-termine cross-national flows. To exclude consideration of the material insti-tutions and political structures through and against which intellectuals such as Plaatje and Abrahams operated impairs our ability to grasp the meaning and significance of their transnationalism itself.

The category of the nation demands to be recentered as the only effec-tive means for interpreting the category of transnationality. And the theory and practice of anticolonial nationalism urgently need critical rehabilita-tion. Antinationalist opinion heavily predominates in postcolonial and Black Atlantic studies. It is responsible for such unsupported contentions as "Na-tionalist movements have an in-built tendency towards extremism and xeno-phobia, towards self-righteousness on the one hand and demonising the enemy on the other."[15] Such a characterization cannot explain the national-ism of Plaatje's ANC, to take but one example.[16] Elsewhere I analyze the prob-lematic relationship between postcolonial studies and nationalism;[17] here, I want simply to question the theoretical programming that renders all nation-alism as "oppressive" and all transnationalism as "liberatory." The relation-ship between these two practices should also not be reduced to a formu-laic antinomy: Plaatje's transnationalism works to support his nationalism; Abrahams's works against nationalism. Yet Abrahams's antithesis consti-tutes a historical choice, not the expression of a categorical law.

Some Versions of the English Metropole

Yekutiel Gershoni suggests that following South African union in 1910, South African blacks gradually turned away from the British metropolitan axis, investing their energy and imagination instead in the United States.[18] Gershoni overlooks the political and cultural importance that Britain con-tinued to have for black South Africans. Thus Peter Abrahams concludes *Tell Freedom* with the decision to move to England to pursue his vocation: "My mind was divided. The call of Harlem, Negro colleges, and the 'new Negro' writers, was compelling. But Charles Lamb, John Keats, Shelley and the glorious host they led made a counter call. And my mind's eye saw a peace-ful land that offered peace to a poet. . . . I decided . . . I would go to England first . . . my going there would be in the nature of a pilgrimage."[19] Abrahams associates England with "peace" and an aesthetic refuge from political ac-tivity. Plaatje, instead, rhetorically turns England into a self-contradictory war zone, using it as an intellectual, political, and cultural resource for his African nationalism. Plaatje's England has become a country of national degeneration; Abrahams's England is a place of personal regeneration.

There are historical reasons for these differences. For the young Plaatje, English liberalism—and its political expression in the nonracial franchise—was hegemonic. The fall came in 1910, when British and Afrikaner provinces united to form South Africa and usher in racist legislation to dispossess rural black South Africans.[20] To Plaatje, then, white nationalist racism was an emergent ideology rapidly becoming dominant through the political collusion of "liberal" colonial and metropolitan English people. *Native Life* records the ANC's attempts to repeal the hideous 1913 Natives' Land Act through delegations to British parliament.[21] In the book, Plaatje revisits British political culture, using English aesthetic icons to confront the supposedly liberal metropole with its betrayal of African people. Shakespeare, for Plaatje, accordingly becomes a protean resource in his battles against antiblack racism. Thus, for instance, he freely adapts Shylock's *Merchant of Venice* speech for a chapter epigraph: "He hath disgraced me and laughed at my losses, mocked at my gains, scorned my nation, thwarted my bargains, cooled my friends, heated mine enemies; and what is his reason? I am a Kaffir. . . . Hath not a Kaffir eyes? Hath not a Kaffir hands, organs, dimensions."[22] *Native Life* also borrows King Lear's speech on the heath; through it, Plaatje voices a revolutionary rage against the very white populations to whom his official narrative appeals.

As this suggests, Plaatje indigenizes English aesthetic culture to nativist politics. And also to African culture. His "Homage to Shakespeare" establishes him as the agent of indigenization among his African peers: "At the age of 18, I . . . went to see *Hamlet* in the Kimberley Theatre. The performance made me curious to know more about Shakespeare and his works. *Intelligence in Africa is still carried from mouth to mouth by means of conversations after working hours, and, reading a number of Shakespeare's works, I always had a fresh story to tell.*"[23] Plaatje goes on to depict a Shakespeare thoroughly absorbed into demotic expression and rendered an anonymous auxiliary for the production of African orality: "All this gave me an appetite for more Shakespeare, and I found that many of the current quotations used by educated natives to embellish their speeches, which I had always taken for English proverbs, were culled from Shakespeare's works."[24]

Peter Abrahams, some forty years younger than Plaatje, emerges from a radically different moment. Born nine years after the union of South Africa to an Afrikaans-speaking family, he was brought up in a Johannesburg slum as the son of a miner who died early, leaving a family that survived in acute poverty. It was an already impoverished, and urban, space that structured his childhood. This markedly contrasts with Plaatje's account, in *Native Life*, of his own childhood of agrarian plenitude. Where the emergent subject of Plaatje's *Native Life* is state racism, that of Abrahams's *Tell Freedom* is his own literary subjectivity. For Abrahams, racial injustice has no historical origin, but instead provides his narrative's matrix. Plaatje's project critically explores the English icons of his colonial childhood; Abrahams affirms English romanticism as a means to create free human subjects.

Even Abrahams's own relationship with Shakespeare is filtered through his nineteenth-century romantic code. The Shakespeare that begins Abrahams's literary awakening is in fact Charles Lamb's *Tales from Shakespeare*, a "free rendition" of Shakespeare's narratives for children. Abrahams's ten-year-old subjectivity is, he contends, reborn when the Lamb book is read aloud to him: "With Shakespeare and poetry, a new world was born. New dreams, new desires, a new self-consciousness, were born."[25]

While the youthful Plaatje actively disseminates metropolitan culture, Abrahams passively receives it. The English culture that helps Plaatje to reinforce black community instead helps Abrahams to separate absolutely from that community. Abrahams's departure for England constitutes the culmination of a series of refusals. In his determination to pursue his vocation as a writer, he refuses to be a teacher, and, most significantly, he refuses to join a political party. His account of Cape Town's 1938 anti-Hertzog protest march reveals his personal discomfort with organized struggle. Though Abrahams had in fact functioned as one of the march's organizers, he seems compelled to mock the march: "The procession formed. The toughs of District Six flanked their leaders. I strayed out of the tight little group. A huge giant grabbed me and lifted me bodily. He pushed his fierce face close to mine. 'Damn you! Stay there! You're a damn leader now!' My laughter angered him so much, I thought he was going to swipe me into kingdom come."[26] England ultimately functions as an expression of Abrahams's aestheticism, undergirding his categorical distinction between the spheres of professional artistry and political activism.

Homi Bhabha's conceptions of "ambivalence" and "mimicry" do not get us very far in understanding either Plaatje's or Abrahams's relationship to English culture.[27] The terms fail to differentiate between Plaatje's dehegemonizing and Abrahams's self-developmental engagement. Edward Said, writing of early-twentieth-century anticolonial intellectuals C. L. R. James and George Antonius, gets closer to capturing the dynamics of Plaatje here. He writes that James and Antonius "addressed their work to a world they considered their own, even if that very European world of power and colonial domination excluded, to some degree subjugated, and deeply disappointed them. They addressed that world from within it, and on cultural grounds they disputed and challenged its authority by presenting alternative versions of it, dramatically, argumentatively, and intimately."[28] As with mimicry, however, the articulation locks the anticolonial intellectual into a cultural and epistemological terrain that is exclusively European. It thus cannot register the persistence of African cultural and social values in Plaatje's anticolonial formation.

Souls of Du Bois

It is not only South Africa's relation to the imperial metropole that calls for critical revision. So does the intellectual relationship between South Africa and black America. In general, black South Africans have been seen as uncritical in their absorption and adaptation of African American thought and culture.[29] Ntongela Masilela, for example, in his study of new African cultural modernity, argues "in the literary field . . . the transAtlantic relation between United States and South Africa has been transacted without any traces of resistance, opposition or subterfuge."[30] That the transaction proved more complex is evident in even as unambitious a poem as the 1933 "Bantu Lament," by Simon Lekhela, which exhorts black South Africans to take up the racial uplift practiced in black America. The poem singles out as exemplary practitioners George Washington Carver of Booker T. Washington's Tuskegee Institute, Marcus Garvey, and W. E. B. Du Bois. These three men participated respectively in accommodationist, separatist, and social-democratic black emancipatory movements famously in conflict with one another. The poem refuses to privilege any one of these ideological directions, suggesting:

> But to endeavours let us turn
> Which give our race what it most needs,
> And by them we will surely earn
> A history of worldly deeds.

> For inspiration we may reach
> Beyond the seas to Negro soil
> In schools our children let us teach
> Of Carver, Garvey and Dubois [sic].[31]

Such rhetorical eclecticism should alert us to the dangers of reducing Black Atlanticism to a process in which South Africans simply took up and reiterated the ideological and cultural dynamics of black America. I want to go further and argue that there existed a strong if utterly neglected strain of critique on the South African–black American axis. Black South Africans subtly interrogated black American thought and culture, exposing its failure to advance an egalitarian political vision.

Clearly, black American modernity greatly impressed Plaatje and Abrahams. They both saw the United States of the 1920s and 1930s as a place of black educational, cultural, and economic opportunity that was completely lacking in South Africa. The United States seemed to provide both a black national community and black inclusion in a multiracial nation. Their iconic construction of black America did not, however, prevent Plaatje and Abrahams from serious criticism of black American intellectuals, including Du Bois. Du Bois's 1903 *Souls of Black Folk* served as a major influence on both Plaatje's *Native Life* and Abrahams's *Tell Freedom*. However, their engagement with him was highly selective.[32] Neither is remotely interested in Du Bois's formulation of double consciousness, on which so much contemporary black diaspora studies focuses. And both writers are troubled by Du Bois's Talented Tenth elitism. But their similarities end there, as the two versions of Du Bois Plaatje and Abrahams chose to construct from *Souls* prove almost diametrically opposed. For Plaatje, Du Bois is an empirical sociologist who gives a materialist history of black America. For Abrahams, Du Bois embodies, on the contrary, a visionary idealist who supplies an existential account of racial unfreedom.

As Plaatje sees it, he and Du Bois aim at evenhanded objectivity in documenting the damaging socioeconomic consequences of antiblack legislation. Du Bois's arguments are immaterial; what matters is his methodology. Plaatje's prologue concludes with a quotation that underscores Du Bois's methodological significance for his project: "Finally, I would say as Professor Du Bois says in his book *The Souls of Black Folk*, on the relations between the sons of master and man, 'I have not glossed over matters for policy's sake, for I fear we have already gone too far in that sort of thing. On the other hand I have sincerely sought to let no unfair exaggerations creep in. I do not doubt that in some communities conditions are better than those I have indicated; while I am no less certain that in other communities they are far worse.' "[33] Borrowing Du Bois's first-person voice allows Plaatje to underscore his own authority and sociological good faith. At the same time, it posits Du Bois as an intellectual brother. Such kinship subsequently allows Plaatje, as I have argued elsewhere, to question the adequacy of Du Bois's political leadership on the grounds of his class privilege.[34]

Abrahams's Du Bois is instead a poet-priest; he is not an intellectual brother, but a spiritual midwife. His voice does not preface the book, as it does for Plaatje, but functions as a pivotal narrative event. The discovery of *Souls* triggers an epiphany:

> I reached up and took out a fat black book. *The Souls of Black Folk*, by W. E. B. Du Bois. I turned the pages. It spoke about a people in a valley. And they were black, and dispossessed, and denied. I skimmed through the pages, anxious to take it all in. I read: "For this much all men know: despite compromise, war, struggle, the Negro is not free." . . . Now, having read the words, I knew that I had known this all along. But until now I had had no words to voice that knowledge. Du Bois's words had the impact of a revelation.[35]

Indebted though he is to Du Bois for this racial insight, Abrahams nonetheless proceeds to criticize the patrician elements of Du Bois's thought. This occurs through *Tell Freedom*'s account of Harlem, which critically responds to Du Bois's more famous vision of black cultural attainment. Du Bois's is a Talented Tenth fantasy of attaining to a "high" and exclusively European culture, featured as a space in whose halls men and women move: "I sit with Shakespeare and he winces not. Across the color line I move arm in arm with Balzac and Dumas, where smiling men and welcoming women glide in gilded halls. From out the caves of evening that swing between the strong-limbed earth and the tracery of the stars, I summon Aristotle and Aurelius and what soul I will, and they come all graciously with no scorn nor condescension. So, wed with Truth, I dwell above the Veil. Is this the life you grudge us, O knightly America?"[36]

Abrahams's Harlem vision of cultural community comprises, instead, black writers who mix "high" and popular cultural forms. Abrahams has already informed his readers that "the great Paul Robeson" lives in England; now, he suddenly appears as a resident of Harlem, as does the, long dead, Russian Aleksandr Pushkin, all of which suggests that symbolism is paramount here. Instead of Du Bois's cultural house where men and women "glide" in "gilded halls," Abrahams's vision pointedly takes the form of a street along which people walk and which, by implication, any black person can join. Furthermore, Abrahams's space is one of open-ended dialogue; his "truth" is contingent, collective, and it evolves through conversation. As such it contrasts sharply with the absolute Truth that Du Bois associates with Shakespeare and company: "A Negro city! Imagine Countee Cullen walking down a street and meeting Langston Hughes! And then imagine Paul Robeson joining them! And Du Bois! And Stirling [*sic*] Brown . . . Go on! Chuck in Pushkin too! And then let them talk! Imagine."[37] It is worth recalling the other fantasy cultural space earlier articulated by Abrahams, that of England: "Men now dead had once crossed its heaths and walked its lanes, quietly, unhurriedly, and had sung with such beauty that their songs had pierced the heart of a black boy." [38] It is as public spaces, as unenclosed walkways, that Abrahams imagines both England and Harlem. The spatiality of the articulation derives from Abrahams's profoundly spatialized sensibility, which has its foundation in his lifelong experience of racist segregation. The figurative rebuttal of this physical unfreedom, he seems to suggest, does not lie in Du Bois's contained, static, and privatized space of the manor house, repeating as it does all the hierarchical exclusivity of the segregationism it challenges. Instead, Abrahams implies, cultural emancipation is best imaged through figures of open space. Thus he provides a terrestrial, public, and mobile vision of cultural freedom to counter Du Bois's transcendental and circumscribed vision.

Struggling through Space

Different though Du Bois and Abrahams may be in their figurative projections of black cultural freedom, they nonetheless share an investment in geographical space and its metaphors as privileged literary vehicles. This distinguishes them from Plaatje, for whom systematic spatial segregation is only beginning to become the object of national law; it is its emergence — through land dispossession and the expansion of so-called native reserves and influx controls (the pass system) — that his writing targets. Space is, effectively, the end of Plaatje's political concern, rather than an imaginative means. The imaginative source of his literary strategies is, instead, the voice itself. Thus, one borrows the voice of Du Bois or Shakespeare, as we have seen, quoting them to authorize one's own project.

For Du Bois, Abrahams and, of course, the distinguished mid-twentieth-century anticolonialist Frantz Fanon also, however, segregation has become so integral to racism and colonialism that their imagination is profoundly conditioned by spatial ideology. This demands a radical examination of Abrahams's professed "pilgrimage" to England, the land that spawned the romantic poets. As we know, through his initial encounter with Shakespeare and the romantics, "New dreams, new desires, a new self-consciousness, were born." [39] The English writers make possible a new subjectivity that includes aesthetic, ontological, and epistemological dimensions. Yet they paradoxically control the new subject they have helped to produce. As Abrahams continues, "I desired to know myself in terms of the new standards set by these books." [40]

This establishes an ambiguous status for Shakespeare and his kin, as simultaneously liberating and dominating, that is swiftly pushed into open contradiction through Abrahams's traversal of segregated city space. His account, published seven years before Fanon's "Concerning Violence," proves remarkably similar.[41] As with Fanon, Abrahams's account of the Manichaean division between "the settlers' town" and "the native town"—"this world divided into compartments"—produces envy among the colonized, and a muscular anger.[42] But where these authors differ is that Abrahams emphasizes "sharp and painful inferiority" in his list of Manichaean affects, suggesting that he has internalized the racist value system that justifies this segregation. Furthermore, he contends, it is his three British books that have "fed" this sense of inferiority, even as they also feed the anger, envy, and desire that contest it:

> Impelled by something I could not explain, I went, night after night, on long, lonely walks into the white areas of Johannesburg. . . . Really, these streets and trees, almost the clean air I breathed here, were
>
> RESERVED FOR EUROPEANS ONLY
>
> . . .
>
> I longed for what the white folk had. I envied them their superior, European lot.
>
> The familiar mood that awaits the sensitive young who are poor and dispossessed is *a mood of sharp and painful inferiority, of violently angry tensions, of desperate and overwhelming longings. On these nightly walks, that mood took possession of me. My three books fed it.*[43]

Abrahams's ambivalence toward British literature advances to negativity when he is initiated into the literature of the Harlem Renaissance: "These poems and stories were written by Negroes! Something burst deep inside me. The world could never again belong to white people only! Never again!"[44] The emancipatory new world of aesthetic subjectivity initiated by Shakespeare has now become retroactively implicated in white worlding—and inseparable from the racism that physically delimits black freedom.

This is the context in which Abrahams's pilgrimage to England needs to be analyzed. In fact, Abrahams's move to England amounts less to a pilgrimage than to what Edward Said terms "the voyage in," a reverse colonization of a world coded as white, "reserved for Europeans only."[45] Even the passage that affirms England's raceless freedom contains a reversal. Abrahams's encounter with British literature had engendered a desire "to know myself in terms of the new standards set by these books." Now, however, it is not white books, but the spoken words of a black man that supply the instrument of measurement, and it is not the black self but the white country that has become the object of evaluation. Abrahams is about to make a voyage in that will subject England, as a society and as a physical landmass, to black judgment, conquest, and occupation:

> Rathebe talked fascinatingly about his travels. He had been to England and America. And we never tired of hearing him tell of his experiences. In England he had lived in the homes of white people, had sat at table with them! England had no colour bar. A man could go where he pleased when he pleased. A man was just a man. Of course, people had looked. He was different. But there was no colour bar. . . . But Harlem! Harlem . . . the city of Negroes. A city within a city: not a suburb, not a location, not a slum area, a city. . . . Rathebe's words gave us some slight yardstick with which to attempt an understanding of the meaning of freedom.[46]

Abrahams's spatial imagination is so thoroughly racialized, and Manichaean, in its perceptions that his rhetorical representation of England as a nonracist zone may be little more than a sales pitch to white metropolitan readers. *Tell Freedom* was, after all, written and published in England. Two years after its publication, the Notting Hill riots made impossible even the pretense of British nonracism, and Abrahams left England for Jamaica.

Abrahams's reverse colonization is sexual as well as social. It is not until his recent autobiography *The Black Experience* that Abrahams details his involvements with white English women, but these are anticipated in *Tell Freedom* through his dangerous liaison with a white South African woman, followed by a friend's prediction that "you're not likely to find a woman as developed as yourself among your own people."[47] (Indeed, the very first of Charles Lamb's stories to captivate the young Abrahams is, tellingly, Othello.)[48] *Tell Freedom* ends with Abrahams setting out for England, explaining his departure as an urgent matter of masculinity: "I needed, not friends, not gestures, but my manhood. And the need was desperate."[49] This sexual imperative resembles that of Fanon's "native" who wants to "sleep with the settler's wife" to "take the place of the settler."[50] Rather than replacing South Africa's Manichaean world, then, England may be its continuation; the place where Abrahams can, paradoxically, fully come into his own blackness through walking on white streets and sleeping with white women. In other words, for Abrahams, the bodies of English white women are analogous to the body of the English land: he views both as territory to be occupied in the furtherment of his black power.

It needs to be pointed out that the spatial politics of Fanon and Abrahams differ as much as they overlap. Abrahams lacks Fanon's activist dialectical vision, which construes sexual-territorial desire as leading to a collective political struggle that seeks ultimately to abolish Manichaean polarities altogether. Abrahams's individualism makes a goal of personal gratification; it seeks simply to reverse, not abolish, Manichaean power dynamics.

Black Transnationalism versus African Nationalism

Hegemonic postcolonial and Black Atlantic studies converge in viewing anticolonial nationalism as an epistemology that inevitably repeats the dominatory and elitist perspective of the imperialism it opposes. Black Atlanticism has promoted transnational black culture as nationalism's emancipatory opposite; Paul Gilroy contends that the political imaginations of nationalism and of the Black Atlantic are mutually exclusive. But the examples of Plaatje and Abrahams invite different conclusions. Plaatje's anticolonial nationalism (which I analyze in detail elsewhere) is neither incompatible with his Black Atlanticism nor inherently dominatory.[51] Abrahams, on the other hand, follows Gilroy in presenting nationalist and transnationalist affiliations as irreconcilable belief systems and identifications.

But his adoption of modern diasporic blackness as the basis of his racial identity is hardly the unqualified progressive gesture that Gilroy alleges. The politics of transnationalism are specific to their historical and geographical situation. In the context of 1930s South Africa, Abrahams's transnationalism, and his corollary rejection of African nationalism, invite rather more skepticism than affirmation. Gayatri Spivak is illuminating here. She construes both imperialism and nationalism to operate through the production of "self-consolidating others": the colonized, in imperialism, and the subaltern, in nationalism.[52] Abrahams's subject formation somewhat upholds her formulation, but with a crucial difference: it is his *transnationalism* that performs the very exclusionism Spivak so questionably ascribes to nationalism. His "self-consolidating others" are black Africans and nationalism.

Abrahams, however, also succeeds in presenting a progressive critique of elitist black nationalism. The object of his critique—Ethiopia—was and continues to be an important rallying point for black diasporans. Even as Abrahams aligns himself with diasporic blackness, that is, he contests its hegemonic global vision. Abrahams presents his readers with two versions of black African community: Zulu and Ethiopian. Near the opening of *Tell Freedom*, Abrahams casually remarks that his Ethiopian father "was the son of landowners and slave-owners."[53] His paternal lineage only becomes meaningful when the young Abrahams is befriended by Joseph, who introduces him to Zulu genealogy, telling "tales of black kings who lived in days before the white man."[54] On learning that there were no colored kings before the white man, Joseph "comforted me and said: 'It is of no moment. You are my brother. Now my kings will be your kings.'"[55] Peter's mother, however, assures him that he, too, has black royal connections, reminding him of his father's Abyssinian heritage. Peter consequently imagines telling Joseph "I am Lee of the Abyshinins! My kings were before the days of the white man, and my kings are still kings today!' How he would envy me! If only he were here! . . . I would lend my kings to him."[56]

Abrahams the youth continues with his hypermasculine fantasy: "I was far, far away, in a merry land called Abyshina. There black kings strode the earth in all their majesty. And I was a great warrior of Abyshina, serving my kings. I was the strongest, the bravest, the most daring of all the warriors in that glorious land called Abyshina."[57] Abrahams the adult criticizes this fantasy by reducing it to an infantile parody of Joseph's original Zulu narrative.[58] And at the same time he also heightens the contrast between the two versions of national identity. Unlike Joseph, who offers to share his kings with his "brother" Peter, Peter thinks only of lending his kings. Such exclusivity reflects the origins of Ethiopian history in property ownership. At the root of Abrahams's critique lies Ethiopia's history as a slave-owning country. This is, as Abrahams amplifies in *The Black Experience*, the reason for his father's choice of exile: "Ethiopia had its own troubles with Italy and with convincing others that it was not black like the rest of us (or if it was, it was a special kind of blackness which came down from the line of Solomon and Sheba). My own father had been one of a group of young Ethiopians who would not tolerate this mindset nor the brutal conditions of near-serfdom of the low-caste majority, so some were driven, and some chose to go, into exile."[59] Thus, for Abrahams, Ethiopia's elitist nationalism is insupportable—and highly inappropriate as a symbol of black global identity. Abrahams implies that there is more political inclusivity and positive potential in Zulu versions of nationhood. Through Joseph he presents Zuluness as a generous collective open to membership by non-Zulu "natives." By extension, Joseph's narrative supplies a version of African national and nationalist community available for adoption by colored South Africans like Abrahams. Yet Abrahams ultimately refuses to join this community, opting instead for an Americanized blackness that effectively excludes both black and colored South Africans.

Abrahams's egalitarianism may prevent him from embracing Ethiopia, but it does not overcome his territorialism. He does not want, as he sees it, to borrow someone else's kings, nor does he want to belong to a community with a precolonial historical foundation that precedes him. His imagination cannot stretch to a vision of inclusive anticolonialist collectivity, in which he takes his place alongside historically African people. Such nationalist associations existed in the 1930s, in the form of the All-African Convention.[60] Abrahams's poetry of this period—largely preoccupied with questions of racial and political identity—supports my argument here. Two autobiographical poems dedicated to Abrahams's blackness, "Negro Youth" and "Heritage," each feature blackness as a solitary condition. "Negro Youth" opens with "He stood alone, / A Negro Youth,"[61] while "Heritage" ends with

> But O, for the fair dark negro maids,
> With swaying hips and flow'ry braids;
> The tom-tom, the rushing long canoe!
> These I claim as my heritage too—
> In the dark and alone—![62]

Ironically, Abrahams is indebted to Harlem Renaissance poetry for these hackneyed African tropes. In "Freedom's Child," Abrahams attempts to articulate socialist third world internationalism, but he cannot imagine collective resistance in South Africa. His South African "slaves" give way to the image of an erupting volcano:

> I am segregation and the pass-law;
> I'm eight million slaves . . .
> But somewhere, too,
> I nurture a volcano,
> And out of love
> I shall cause a wild eruption.[63]

The poem's portrait of India, however, does imagine human political resistance both in the form of named leaders (Jawaharlal Nehru and Anand) and the body of the people:

> My body grows
> Bigger!
> BIGGER!
> Now there's room for me only here—
> No kings or princes.[64]

"Spring in a Coloured Woman" articulates coloredness as a supremely creative condition. But the poem's focus on the "bastard wench" precludes any engagement with the category of blackness: the "Negro" terminology and heritage claimed by his other poetry remains strikingly absent in this poem.[65] Blackness and coloredness exist, then, across Abrahams's poetic oeuvre as irreconcilable categories. That Abrahams cannot envision his own blackness except as a solitary individual, or envision a South African blackness that includes coloredness, points to a failure of social vision. This proves, ultimately, also the failure of his political vision: he cannot envision black collectivity as a creative nationalist force.

In such a context, Abrahams's election of literary black America as the basis for his identity emerges as the deliberate, and limiting, choice of an existential (over a politicized) blackness. For all the generality of the words *black* and *Negro*, it is clear that Abrahams's usage is exclusively diasporic and cannot contain African national or continental inflections. His usage is also exclusively modern; it leaves no room for a blackness connected to a precolonial existence. Black Atlantic affiliation becomes another, and negative, expression of a profoundly segregated subjectivity.

Conclusion

Many years before Paul Gilroy's celebratory *The Black Atlantic*, South African literary scholar Tim Couzens published a refreshingly unromantic evaluation of Black Atlantic cultural currents.[66] In "Moralizing Leisure Time," Couzens analyzes the determination of 1920s and 1930s South African white liberals to avert the real threat of black socialist militancy. The leisure of black workers and city dwellers was, accordingly, diverted from political mobilization by the introduction of social centers, film clubs, "Non-European" libraries, and debating societies. Aesthetic culture, in other words, was promoted in order to contain black opposition. Through these institutional means (funded, in part, by the US Carnegie Corporation), literature and music of black Americans was systematically introduced to and promoted in South Africa. The Johannesburg Bantu Men's Social Centre, where the young Peter Abrahams had his first encounter with Paul Robeson, the Harlem Renaissance, and Du Bois, was one such institution.

The calculated risk taken by white liberalism in disseminating racially uplifting black American culture seems to have paid off. Abrahams's encounter with American literary blackness influenced his decision to pursue a professional vocation as a writer. He openly rejected both Marxism and party political affiliation in the process. His embrace of a black diasporic identity came, indeed, at the expense both of black nationalism and socialism. Abrahams's case should alert us to the dangers of culturalist and intellectualist criticism. To examine the work of black intellectuals only from within the space of an ocean is to abandon mechanisms for analyzing their authority or representativeness. To look at cultural expressions as if they are self-contained—or are superior political articulations to those voiced by organized struggles—is to affirm an aestheticism that should stand in tension with the tenor of postcolonial and Black Atlantic studies. Elsewhere I have explored how Paul Gilroy's work surrenders to an aestheticism at odds with his own arguments about the holistic political, philosophical, and aesthetic foundation of Black Atlanticism.[67] As Plaatje's materialism and Abrahams's aestheticism suggest, there are various ways to formulate and to analyze this counterculture to modernity.

At the same time, however, it is important to register what Black Atlantic culture itself might gain through recognizing Abrahams's contribution, for Abrahams's affiliation to black American identity involved his critical interrogation of black American political and cultural norms. His egalitarian beliefs provide an important counterbalance to Afrocentric veneration of Ethiopia and to Du Bois's elitist vision of cultural attainment. The bias toward black diasporic communities that dominates in Black Atlantic studies makes it unlikely that Abrahams's and Plaatje's dissident African voices will be heard within this transnational arena. The very elitism and vanguardism that Plaatje and Abrahams criticize may effectively silence them.

The examples of Plaatje and Abrahams also indicate that the category of space itself needs more conceptual attention in the analysis of colonized and anticolonial subjectivity. Plaatje wrote before racial segregationism had become completely enshrined in South African law; Abrahams wrote from within a thoroughly segregated society, and this seems to have produced a correspondingly spatialized subjectivity. Abrahams not only polarizes race and nation but also polarizes politics and art as "spaces" that cannot be occupied at the same time. Fanon's equally spatial metaphors yield to dialectical reasoning; Abrahams's do not. The origins and the consequences of these different spatial logics require further investigation.

The political unevenness of Abrahams's project demands the abandonment of critical beliefs in transnationalism as an unconditional good and nationalism as an unconditional evil. Plaatje's liberal nationalism easily refutes the allegations of "inherent extremism and xenophobia" routinely made by postcolonial critics. So do the more radical nationalisms that followed his. Rather than blaming anticolonial nationalism for the problems of contemporary globalization, postcolonial studies should look at the responsibility of multinational capitalism. For that we need not a transnational but an international perspective.

Notes

1. Sir Harry Johnston to Sol Plaatje, June 4, 1915, Colenso Papers, Natal Archives Depot, Pietermaritzburg, South Africa. I am grateful to Brian Willan for sharing Johnston's letter with me.

2. Plaatje, *Native Life in South Africa before and since the European War and the Boer Rebellion.*

3. Solomon T. Plaatje, "Address to Pan-African Congress, Paris, 1921," in Plaatje, *Sol Plaatje: Selected Writings*, 265.

4. In 1925, the African National Congress passed a resolution that replaced the term *native* with *African*. See Kemp, *"Up from Slavery* and Other Narratives," xi.

5. Plaatje, *Mhudi*, 27.

6. For a discussion of black Americana in Plaatje, see Boehmer, *Empire, the National, and the Postcolonial*; and Chennells, "Plotting South African History." See Frederickson, *Black Liberation*, for an illuminating comparative historical study.

7. Peter Abrahams, "Negro Youth," in Couzens and Patel, *The Return of the Amasi Bird*, 85.

8. Abrahams, *Tell Freedom*, 230–31.

9. For contemporary South African literary support, see S. M. Stanley Silwana, "I Sing of Africa," in Couzens and Patel, *The Return of the Amasi Bird*, 82–83. George S. Schuyler's 1930s *Ethiopian Stories* provide an African American literary example. See Von Eschen, *Race against Empire*, for a historical study of black American anticolonialism. See also Adeleke, *UnAfrican Americans*; and Jacobs, *The African Nexus*.

10. See Willan, *Sol Plaatje*, for details.

11. An exception is Cooppan, "W(h)ither Post-Colonial Studies"; Fanon, *White Skin, Black Masks*.

12. Gilroy, *The Black Atlantic*.

13. See, for example, Brody, *Impossible Purities*.

14. See, for example, Diawara, *In Search of Africa*.

15. Avi Shlaim, "Dogged by Destiny," *The Guardian Review* (London), February 29, 2003.

16. See Walshe, *The Rise of African Nationalism in South Africa*. See also Jusdanis, *The Necessary Nation*, and Young, *Postcolonialism*, for useful reappraisals of nationalism.

17. Chrisman, "Nationalism and Postcolonial Studies."

18. Gershoni, *Africans on African-Americans*, 145–75.

19. Abrahams, *Tell Freedom*, 234.

20. See Magubane, *The Making of Racist State*.

21. For details see chapters 7 and 8 of Willan, *Sol Plaatje*.

22. Plaatje, *Native Life*, 136.

23. Sol Plaatje, "A South African's Homage," in Plaatje, *Sol Plaatje: Selected Writings*, 210; emphasis *mine*.

24. Ibid.

25. Abrahams, *Tell Freedom*, 189.

26. Ibid., 334.

27. Bhabha, *The Location of Culture*.

28. Said, *Culture and Imperialism*, 299.

29. See Kemp, *"Up from Slavery* and Other Narratives"; Masilela, "TransAtlantic Connections"; Masilela, "The 'Black Atlantic' and African Modernity in South Africa"; and Nixon, *Homelands, Harlem, and Hollywood*. While these studies insightfully discuss black South African applications of black American culture, they do not explore the possibility of a critical dimension in their South African material.

30. Masilela, "TransAtlantic Connections," 85.

31. Simon Lekhela, "A Bantu Lament," in Couzens and Patel, *The Return of the Amasi Bird*, 72.

32. On Du Bois of this period, as well as the Talented Tenth theory, see Lewis, *W. E. B. Du Bois*; and Reed, *W. E. B. Du Bois and American Political Thought*. See also Gaines, *Uplifting the Race*.

33. Plaatje, *Native Life*, 20.

34. Chrisman, "Rethinking Black Atlanticism," expanded as "Black Atlantic Nationalism: Sol Plaatje and W. E. B. Du Bois," in Chrisman, *Postcolonial Contraventions*, 89–106.

35. Abrahams, *Tell Freedom*, 224–25.

36. Du Bois, *The Souls of Black Folk*, 90.

37. Abrahams, *Tell Freedom*, 234.

38. Ibid.

39. Ibid., 189.

40. Ibid.

41. Frantz Fanon, "Concerning Violence," in Fanon, *The Wretched of the Earth*, 35–106.

42. Ibid., 39.

43. Abrahams, *Tell Freedom*, 192–93; emphasis mine.

44. Ibid., 226.

45. Edward W. Said, "The Voyage In and the Emergence of Opposition," in Said, *Culture and Imperialism*, 288–315.

46. Abrahams, *Tell Freedom*, 232.

47. Ibid., 302.

48. Ibid., 172.

49. Ibid., 370.

50. Fanon, "Concerning Violence," 39.

51. Chrisman, *Rereading the Imperial Romance*.

52. Spivak, *A Critique of Postcolonial Reason*.

53. Abrahams, *Tell Freedom*, 5.

54. Ibid., 47.

55. Ibid.

56. Ibid., 66.

57. Ibid., 67.

58. For a different reading of this episode, see Chiwengo, "Exile, Knowledge, and Self."

59. Abrahams, *The Black Experience in the Twentieth Century*, 11.

60. See Drew, *South Africa's Radical Tradition*.

61. Abrahams, "Negro Youth," in Couzens and Patel, *The Return of the Amasi Bird*, 85.

62. Peter Abrahams, "Heritage," in Couzens and Patel, *The Return of the Amasi Bird*, 100–101.

63. Peter Abrahams, "Freedom's Child," in Couzens and Patel, *The Return of the Amasi Bird*, 112.

64. Ibid.

65. Peter Abrahams, "Spring in a Coloured Woman," in Couzens and Patel, *The Return of the Amasi Bird*, 115–16.

66. Couzens, " 'Moralizing Leisure Time.' "

67. Chrisman, "Journeying to Death."

Pathways to Postcolonial Nationhood:

The Democratization of Difference in

Contemporary Latin America

ø ø ø

FLORENCIA E. MALLON

This essay is an attempt to work through, for the case of Latin America, my own ambivalent positioning in relation to the theoretical frameworks and methodologies that might loosely be grouped under the category of *postcolonialism*.[1] Over the past decade, I have become increasingly aware of an uncomfortable lack of fit between the postcolonial critique of modernism's intellectual assumptions, in both its Marxist and liberal registers — a critique with which I largely agree — and more subtle disciplinary and regional readings of postindependence history in Latin America. At the core of this incongruity lies, I think, the tension between the difficulty of postcolonialism as an approach to move outside its origins in twentieth-century British and French processes of decolonization and the emergence of postcolonialism as a body of critical thought. For the parts of the world that experienced decolonization in the twentieth century, postcolonialism as a historical condition — that is, the end of formal colonial rule — occurred more or less concurrently with the emergence of postcolonialism as an intellectual and political approach. In Latin America, by contrast, with the exception of the Caribbean, postcolonialism as a historical condition predated postcolonialism as a theoretical perspective by nearly two centuries. Despite the rich possibilities contained within the broad postcolonial critique, this complicates the adoption of postcolonial theory for the Latin American case, and I will explore below some of the ways in which this tension has manifested itself in recent years. At the same time, I believe we can most productively examine the complex responses to postcolonialism in Latin America by reading them against some of postcolonialism's more general ambiguities. Given limitations of space, I cannot do more than begin this process here.

A promising place to start this reflection might be with some reminders as to the powerful potential creativity and promise of a postcolonial perspective. "Postcolonial perspectives," wrote Homi Bhabha in 1994, "emerge from the colonial testimony of Third World countries and the discourses of 'minorities' within the geopolitical divisions of East and West, North and South. They intervene in those ideological discourses of modernity that attempt to give a hegemonic 'normality' to the uneven development and the differential, often disadvantaged, histories of nations, races, communities, peoples."[2] From a historian's point of view, Gyan Prakash noted a similar potential creativity in what he termed "the dynamic and double sense of the colonial aftermath," where "at stake is not simply the issue as to whether or not former colonies have become free from domination, but also the question as to how the history of colonialism and colonialism's disciplining of history can be shaken loose from the domination of categories and ideas it produced—colonizer and colonized; white, black, and brown; civilized and uncivilized; modern and archaic; cultural identity; tribe and nation."[3]

This idea of the "shaking loose" of colonial categories, of the disturbance of linear narratives by opening them to alternative periodizations and points of view, of the subversive fragmentation of history through the intrusion of the subaltern and the dominated, lies at the core of the attraction of postcolonialism. Dipesh Chakrabarty has taken the revolutionary implication of fragmentation to its ultimate conclusion, I think, when he wonders if it is possible to think of history as fragmentary not "in the sense of fragments that refer to an implicit whole but fragments that challenge not only the idea of wholeness but the very idea of the 'fragment' itself."[4] Yet almost at that very same moment, Chakrabarty retreats from the possibility: "What will history produced in this mode look like? I cannot say, for one cannot write this history in a pure form."[5] What is left, then, is the desire for full or complete subversion, next to the knowledge of its impossibility; the complex negotiation of the many modern and postmodern, colonial and postcolonial ways of seeing and knowing. Herein lies, I think, both the promise and the discontent of postcolonialism.

One especially dense knot of discontent can be found, it seems to me, in the friction between postcolonialism and Marxism that lies at the heart of many debates within postcolonial theory. Sometimes this friction is read as a dispute between those who continue to demand a sense of historicity and seek more systemic theoretical explanations, and those who eschew such goals as inevitably naive or authoritarian. It has also been read as a conflict between theory and politics. It is in this context, Leela Gandhi has suggested that "postcolonial studies critics are left to ponder the apparent chasm between the poststructuralist insistence on the impossibility of a universal human nature and the opposing Marxist verdict on the impossibility of a politics which lacks the principle of 'solidarity.' "[6]

At other times, the discussion has centered on different potential genealogies for postcolonialism itself, with some analysts linking foundational postcolonial texts, especially those by Edward Said and Gayatri Spivak, directly to postmodern and poststructural theorists and thus attributing the tension with Marxism to the ambiguity and ambivalence inherited from the other "posts." Those theorists who wish to contribute to postcolonial debates from a more historical materialist standpoint, however, tend to highlight the more revolutionary and liberationist origins of postcolonialism in the anticolonial struggles and texts associated with activist intellectuals such as Amilcar Cabral, Aimé Césaire, Frantz Fanon, or C. L. R. James. Thus Neil Lazarus approvingly quoted a 1995 essay by Edward Said where, after pointedly separating early postcolonial thinkers such as James, Anwar Abdel Malek, and Samir Amin from the postmodernism of Jean-François Lyotard, Said went on to emphasize that "this crucial difference between the urgent historical and political imperatives of post-colonialism and postmodernism's relative detachments makes for altogether different approaches and results."[7]

Ultimately, as Gregory Castle has written in the introduction to his recent anthology, these theoretical and genealogical questions are most profitably explored in "specific geographical, social and historical conditions."[8] And it is here, then, that Latin America can most fruitfully enter the discussion. Because the history of Latin America as a region, as well as the history of Latin American studies as a field, belongs with the story of Europe's first colonialism, most Latin American countries were already independent entities when the desire for autonomous national development took hold of a good part of the world between the 1880s and the 1960s. In contrast to those parts of the world targeted by Europe's second colonialism, and therefore in the throes of direct foreign domination precisely during a good part of those years, Latin Americans participated passionately if distinctively in that era's yearning for transformation. Since the postcolonial critique emerged precisely from the contradiction between this modernist yearning and the effects of modern industrial colonial rule, Latin America's divergent history thus prevented it from participating in this initial emergence.[9]

Indeed, by the time Europe's second colonialism was in bloom, toward the end of the nineteenth and beginning of the twentieth century, most of Latin

America, with the exception of the Caribbean, had already been independent from the Iberian powers for nearly a century. After World War II, when decolonization in Asia and Africa reached its peak, Latin America was hitting the culmination of what I call its national-popular period—that is, the time when activist and development-oriented states attempted a more recognizable national-democratic project, complete with broader social, economic, and political inclusion for oppressed groups. If, in a US or Western European context, the promise of national-democratic inclusion had been and was lived in a politically liberal register, in Latin America the nature of economic dependency made any project of redistribution, development, and economic growth take on characteristics of "national liberation." In contrast to the newly decolonizing regions of the so-called third world, however, national liberation in Latin America tended to occur under the guidance of populist or interventionist states, often in the guise of government programs of industrialization behind tariff barriers.[10] Despite the relative moderation of these attempts at reform, however, the United States, emerging from the Second World War as a world power on the rise and bound into an intensifying confrontation with the Soviet Union, would see the Latin American search for reform, redistribution, and development as a cold war challenge to its hemispheric strategic interests.

It is in this sense that Latin American studies, as a field whose contours first emerged in the United States, is often seen as a child of the cold war. From the very beginning of this period, there was pressure to take sides, politically speaking, in the discursive and intellectual struggles associated with the world balance of power. The first generation of Latin Americanists that emerged after World War II attempted to claim an intellectually independent, professional, and academically responsible intermediate ground that steered clear of both sides of this conflict, whether through the development of apparently value-free demographic or quantitative methods or through social-scientific models eschewing "ideology."[11] Yet at the same time, as Charles Hale remembered, they did not operate with full information, since they did not have access to any alternative data on the role of the US government and the CIA in the 1954 Guatemalan coup, for example. In part, of course, this resulted from the intensity of cold war ideology and of McCarthyism in the United States throughout the 1950s. This climate could not help but place important limits on the professional independence and daring of specialists whose field had been defined as the backyard of the United States.

A major watershed occurred, first in Latin America itself and then spreading to the United States and Europe, between the Guatemalan coup of 1954 and the Cuban Revolution of 1959. From the perspective of Latin America, the Cuban Revolution transformed both political and academic debates about contemporary reality and future expectations in the region. Politically, a so-called New Left supporting direct action, guerrilla struggle, and immediate revolution emerged from and challenged the more reformist-minded leftist and populist parties of the era. Academically, the older, more culturally based analyses of Latin American society were challenged by a new, more politically engaged generation of intellectuals who came of age in the 1960s. Marxism and dependency theory emerged, in this context, as vital, dynamic, and innovative Latin American traditions that then influenced debates in other parts of the world.[12]

By the 1960s and 1970s, then, as my generation came of age in the United States and Latin America, schooled in about equal parts by Cuba, 1968, Vietnam, and the cultural and youth revolutions, many of us chose a different path from those academics and intellectuals who had gone before. We were convinced that we faced an unavoidable choice between solidarity with popular, anti-imperialist, social-justice struggles in Latin America, on the one hand, and complicity with hemispheric repressive forces, on the other. Many of us based in the United States who then went into the field for research in the 1970s felt pressed to prove, through our actions of intellectual solidarity, that we were *not* CIA agents. The experiences of activism and solidarity we sought out in the midst of intellectual work would also mark our entry point into the US academy on our return.[13]

Between 1945 and the mid-1980s, therefore, Latin American studies became a dynamic field through the conflictual evolution of two distinct approaches to Latin American reality. The first was based in cold war training and debate—mainly within the United States, although some Latin Americans also participated—and it encouraged intellectuals to construct an "objective" and academically oriented field with a generally anticommunist perspective. The second approach foregrounded engagé research by establishing a dialogue between academia and the pressing problems of the day, thus forging a space of solidarity for like-minded radical scholars from both North and South America. It was in this second space that creative appropriations and rethinkings of Marxism and dependency theory continued to take shape across the 1970s and 1980s, and where a fresh and revolutionary pan-Latin Americanism was opposed to the cold war Latin Americanism of the US-based field.

Especially after the Cuban Revolution and guerrilla options took shape in the 1960s, cold war and leftist scholars of Latin America squared off against each other intellectually and politically. In most Latin American university settings, it proved hard for an intellectual or a scholar, whether resident or visiting, not to face questions about the contemporary relevance of his or her research. While this may have been a commonplace in post-1968 classrooms throughout the world, in Latin America, a direct connection was often drawn to socialist struggles for liberation. Indeed, throughout the region, it was commonplace for conference papers to either begin or end with a statement about the heroic struggles of Latin American peoples. Plenary sessions at the Latin American Studies Association became heated intellectual boxing matches where younger leftists confronted more established, modernization theory–oriented scholars.[14] Yet at the same time, I believe the two camps also upheld an implicit sharing, a sharing that ironically made their confrontations all the more intense and passionate: a bedrock belief in the democratic narrative of inclusion and development emerging with capitalism. As the human rights emergencies of the authoritarian period (late 1960s to the 1980s) took shape in Latin America, they intensified this sharing even further and postponed a reckoning on the limitations of the national-democratic promise that had already begun to emerge after an earlier September 11, in 1973, brought an end to Salvador Allende's democratic-socialist experiment in Chile.

As in the rest of the world, the promises of socialist inclusion finally fell apart in Latin America in the second half of the 1980s and during the 1990s. New social movements challenged the prescriptions for change and inclusion offered by socialism and the exclusionary practices of the nation-state. Feminist, indigenous, environmentalist, urban shantytown, and human rights movements all began to claim new spaces and new styles in the Latin American political arena, moving from the older socialist-Marxist emphasis on imperialism, class domination, and class struggle to a focus on subaltern agency and so-called identity politics. With resistance to authoritarianism and the resulting democratic transitions, it became more possible to focus on social complexity and contradiction, and at least briefly to hear new voices and see other forms of hierarchy and oppression. Latin American feminists, many of them emerging from the Left, interrogated the content of earlier narratives of liberation and pointed to leftist silences around the specificities of women's oppression. In some cases as well, the collapse of state-centered models of development and investment seemed to open up new styles and ways of thinking, especially in countries where state-controlled political party systems had discouraged strong critiques of the existing order or status quo.

The anger, the sense of betrayal, with which these changes have been received by some Latin American radical theorists emerges nowhere more

clearly than in the work of Peruvian scholar Aníbal Quijano, earlier one
of the strongest proponents of Marxism and dependency theory. Quijano
now deploys antinationalist versions of postcolonial theory to argue that for
two hundred years, Latin Americans have been chasing a mirage in their
attempts to build autonomous nation-states. This holds true, he argues, because independence in the region did not lead to true decolonization—by
which he means the democratization of relations among Europeans and non-
Europeans—but instead to "a rearticulation of the coloniality of power upon
a new set of institutions."[15] Using as his benchmark the cases of France and
the United States, which he accepts as effective and democratic nation-states
precisely because they did not face the inclusion of majority non-European
populations, he finds all cases of nation-state formation in Latin America
(with the possible exception of Chile) to be failures. And he concludes that
"it is time to learn to liberate ourselves from the Eurocentric mirror in which
our reflection will always and necessarily be distorted. It's time, in the end,
to stop being what we are not."[16]

While Quijano's foregrounding of racism and colonialism in a reconsideration of Latin American narratives of nation is most welcome, his emphasis
on the comparative demographics of non-European populations in order to
distinguish between unsuccessful and successful models of the nation may
not tell the whole story. Of course, to be fair, in his analysis of the southern cone societies of Argentina and Chile, where a policy of extermination
toward indigenous peoples and a relatively small presence of populations of
African descent would suggest the possibility of successful nation-states, he
adds to the mix the problem of land distribution and the prevalence of the
large landed estate. Still, the critiques of the national-popular model coming
from Latin America's indigenous peoples suggest that a model of colonial
domination, be it with reference to a majority or a minority population,
would still have the same long-term effects. And indeed, this would seem to
be the case in the United States as well, if we read more recent revisionist
versions of Western history that have questioned the validity of notions of
US exceptionalism.[17]

An important contributing factor to many of these intellectual rethinkings
has been the worldwide movement of First Peoples nurtured in the United
Nations, world religious organizations, and other international forums,
which since the 1970s has been challenging older models of inclusion and
economic development throughout the globe. In Latin America, indigenous
revitalization movements have emerged as part of this broader trend and
have highlighted the continuous history of marginalization experienced by
Native peoples in both colonial and postindependence periods, demand-

ing new forms of accountability from nation-states.[18] Indigenous intellectuals have found it relatively easy to perceive the commonalities between the situation of their own people—whose colonial domination had continued unchecked through all the permutations of the national-democratic narrative, whether capitalist or socialist—and the vision offered by postcolonial theorists that emphasized the nonemancipatory aspects of decolonization, thus challenging the very concept of the nation as it had been lived in Latin America.[19]

Indeed, we have an important lesson to learn from some of Latin America's indigenous intellectuals, who have begun to articulate a relationship between postcolonial theory and the more sophisticated forms of dependency theory from the 1970s and 1980s, especially the concept of internal colonialism. For these intellectuals, an engagement between postcolonial and anti-imperialist critiques has proven central to the formulation of a postcolonial perspective that resonates with their region's history and politics. And in this same vein, Aymara intellectuals in Bolivia have recently helped lead a project to translate key works by scholars in the India-based collective of Subaltern Studies, making a crucial contribution to Spanish-language debates over postcolonialism and helping to bridge the divide between the experiences of the first and second colonialisms.[20]

These innovative interventions by Native intellectuals suggest that recent Latin American events and practices have provided us with a series of potential sites for the creative fusion of previous radical experience with more recent postcolonial and postsocialist critiques and sensibilities. Such a fusion must begin, I believe, from a historical understanding of how earlier popular yearnings and visions were inscribed into, and often silenced by, postindependence experiments in national-popular inclusion. Especially if we wish to go beyond the deconstruction of popular agency to envision potentially new forms of community and equality, we must take seriously the existence of earlier experiments and discussions, no matter how partial or limited their effects may have been. While a postcolonial intellectual lens may bring the limitations of the national-popular more clearly into focus, it should also allow us to pay attention, ironically enough, to the national-popular yearnings, experiments, and discourses of the very people marginalized by the nation-state, whether in its capitalist or its socialist incarnations. In the remainder of this essay, I explore the tensions between the failure of national-popular experiments and the ongoing desire for national-popular inclusion and democracy across a series of quite distinct Latin American regional histories. My goal is to demonstrate, through specific historical reconstructions, how a creative fusion of earlier radical experience with contemporary "post" sensibilities, even if inspired by a broader, global need to resist new forms of imperialism and colonialism in the twenty-first century, must pass through concrete regional and local knowledges and practices.

Given the large shadow it has thrown across the last half century of history in the Americas, the Cuban Revolution—self-consciously an extension of the late-nineteenth-century anticolonial wars on the island—provides an especially good place to start. Interestingly, the Cuban Revolution of 1959 occurred in the region of the Western hemisphere where the notion of postcolonialism was the most applicable. Spain had held onto its Caribbean colonies throughout the nineteenth century, only to lose them in the 1898 Spanish-American War to a new and more vibrant imperial power. For Cuba and Puerto Rico, therefore, independence from Spain came attached to a new and more complex dependence on the United States.

Ada Ferrer has recently pointed out that a crucial motivation for US intervention in Cuba in 1898 was the nature of the island's thirty-year struggle against Spain, which culminated at that very moment. "In an age of ascendant racism, as scientists weighed skulls and as white mobs in the U.S. South lynched blacks," Ferrer writes, "Cuba's rebel leaders denied the existence of race, and a powerful multiracial army waged anticolonial war."[21] Ferrer goes on to argue that the complex nature of Cuba's independence struggle has remained in the shadows of historical consciousness, not only because there has been little interest in exploring the deeper racial and colonial motives of US intervention in the United States but also because Cuba's post-1959 regime based its revolutionary nationalism on the claim that it had successfully completed the unfinished independence sought nearly a century before. "Thirty years of conspiracies organized and betrayed," Ferrer concludes, "of alliances made and broken, of courses altered and modified, became simply an abstract—though admittedly rousing—tale of a People's struggle for a Nation. Thus the obscurity around anticolonial insurgency, imposed initially by the contempt and arrogance of empire, remains in many ways unchallenged by the romance and teleology of nationalist narratives."[22] The connection Ferrer draws between the silences of US imperialism, on the one hand, and of Cuban revolutionary nationalism, on the other, is tantalizing. It makes even more sense if we view these shared silences as part and parcel of a particular kind of national project, the "one-size-fits-all" concept of citizenship first elaborated in eighteenth-century Europe during the age of revolution, at least in part as a reaction against the deep and threatening diversity of the world uncovered by the first colonialism. Not only in its first elaboration but also in its attempted extensions in Latin America across the nineteenth century, this notion of citizenship, and of the nation, was challenged by difference. Rather than understanding variation as the medium for democratic negotiation, such a notion saw diversity as a challenge to unity and thus to viability.[23]

Immediate postwar events in Cuba seem to have provided precisely this kind of challenge or threat to unity. As Aline Helg has shown, the establishment of a government under US supervision marginalized Afro-Cuban leaders and veterans. When these individuals mobilized to demand participation and inclusion and established the Partido Independiente de Color (Independent Party of Color), their efforts were met with bloody repression in the so-called Race War of 1912.[24] The massacre of approximately three thousand people of African descent, most of them sugar workers, created a labor shortage then filled by the importation of migrant laborers from neighboring Haiti and Jamaica. According to Aviva Chomsky, this influx of black West Indian migrants led to an upswing and reorganization of racism on the island, in which mainly white Cubans hastened to construct the outsiders as "barbarian," distinguishing black Cubans as more "civilized."[25]

Following up on this moment of racial reorganization, Chomsky proposes that beginning in the 1920s, the emerging tendency among Cuban intellectuals to associate the sugar industry with foreign domination and dependence, and the tobacco industry with Cubanness and national autonomy, also had a racialized dimension. Tobacco, she suggests, was described as a smallholder-based system of cultivation, and the smallholding peasantry associated with it was coded as white. Sugar, on the other hand, as a foreign-dominated large plantation economy, was not only coded black but also coded "migrant labor" and therefore socially "backward" and "un-Cuban." Anti-imperialism's articulation to a critique of sugar, therefore, would not only involve denouncing dependence on the United States but also constructing a peculiarly Cuban form of antimigrant racism. If this is the case, as Chomsky's argument suggests, then the apparent racelessness of Cuban revolutionary nationalism in the twentieth century becomes a great deal less transparent.

And indeed, Cuba's conflictual attempts to create a multiracial national community have a long and contradictory history in which questions of race have been articulated in complex ways to questions of nationality. In the context of anticolonial war, a popular concept of racelessness—perhaps best represented in the phrase of the famous mulatto general Antonio Maceo, "no whites, nor blacks, but only Cubans"[26]—might well have inspired all to fight shoulder to shoulder and to build a sense of fraternity and equality in a multiracial embrace on the battlefield. Things proved different in peacetime, however, when racelessness meant that Cubans of color had no reason to complain about their situation on the basis of race. This was especially the case once black West Indian migrants dramatized, through their own extreme difference, that Afro-Cubans might have more in common with nonblack members of their own national community. Yet as many Cubans of color noticed, this provided little comfort because it then allowed for the construction of blackness as foreignness, reintroducing, through the back door, racialized concepts of inferiority. And their fears proved to be right. Chomsky writes: "Cuban blacks' appeals for racial justice were either ignored, or attributed to 'contamination' by Haitian immigrants. Black Cubans responded by resurrecting the contribution of the struggle for racial justice to the struggle for independence, and arguing that black racial consciousness was the guarantor of, rather than a threat to, Cuban sovereignty."[27]

Given the deep historical discord and contradiction contained in the relationship between race and nationality in Cuba, it perhaps comes as no surprise that such questions remained unresolved by the 1959 revolution. In a similar way to the anticolonial struggles of the late nineteenth century, the Twenty-Sixth of July Movement built an inclusive image of multiracial harmony and solidarity in the struggle for socialism. The citizen in the post-1959 revolutionary nation, therefore, was constructed in a similarly one-size-fits all fashion: ongoing inequalities were the fault of hostile foreign powers, symbolized by the US blockade. Any objections to the 1970s campaigns against Afro-Cuban religions, for example, or to the ongoing scarcity of Cubans of color among the top revolutionary leadership, could in this context be dismissed as unpatriotic.

Given the Cuban Revolution's sizable accomplishments, for a long time it was relatively easy for Cubans as well as foreign supporters to believe that in the long run, the promises of full national inclusion would be realized. As the first country in the Americas to successfully hold off US invasion and military pressure, 1960s revolutionary Cuba took on a dual and contradictory presence in the Latin American imaginary. On the one hand, it was seen as proof that the national-democratic narrative could reach a successful conclusion in Latin America through radical reform and socialism. By the end of the 1960s, the Cuban revolutionary leadership discursively marked this success by honoring the twin martyrs to Cuban nationality: José Martí as the intellectual leader of the 1895 revolution and its most radically antiracist white theorist; and Ernesto "Che" Guevara, the worldwide symbol of guerrilla struggle and personal revolutionary sacrifice. Yet if we build on the best in Cuba's nineteenth- and early twentieth-century revolutionary tradition and place the issue of race at the very center of any attempt to assess the accomplishments of Cuban revolutionary inclusion, in the past half century, the record appears much more mixed. And perhaps unsurprisingly, the lack of full and equal participation by Cubans of color has been matched by barriers that continue to exist for women and for lesbians and gays, as well as by the increasing closure of internal debate within Cuban society. Of course, the high hopes and idealistic yearnings for socialist inclusion attached to the Cuban image by radicals throughout the Americas have prompted many supporters of the revolution to justify these problems by pointing to the US blockade of the island, or suggesting that criteria developed in the assessment of bourgeois electoral democracies cannot be applied to a society where "real" democracy emerges from "the people" and from below. In the end, however, the arguments first advanced by Afro-Cubans in the early twentieth century—that full equality based on race must be at the center of any attempt at social justice and national sovereignty—continue to resonate today. The increasing centralization of power within the revolutionary elite—justified by the need to defend the revolution and the unity of the nation-state against its enemies, whether international or domestic—has instead assured that the democratic side of the national-democratic promise has remained unfulfilled.

It would be in the 1990s that the national side of the same promise also came unraveled. The breakup of the Soviet Union, and the consequent deep economic crisis in Cuba, uncovered, even for those who had previously refused to see, the deep dependence of the island's economy. Even if supporters of the revolution had previously argued that the Soviet subvention of Cuba signaled solidarity rather than imperialism, the economic free fall that followed the end of "solidarity," with its effective dismantling of a good part of Cuba's social-justice safety net, decisively uncovered Cuba's—and by implication Latin America's—postcolonial feet of clay. The twin promises of national autonomy and democratic inclusion, so much trumpeted in the glory days of the 1960s and 1970s, lay tattered at those very feet.

Perhaps it is only when these powerful promises are truly tattered and tarnished that the exclusionary side of the one-size-fits-all nation can come to the fore. Certainly, this has also been the case in Mexico, the other postrevolutionary regime able to survive the twentieth century in Latin America. When he was elected president in 2000, center-right candidate Vicente Fox ended the more than seventy years of uninterrupted rule by Mexico's institutionalized revolution,[28] yet only after the Partido Revolucionario Institucional (Institutional Revolutionary Party, PRI), under president Carlos Salinas de Gortari (1988–94), had already purged the constitution of most remaining revolutionary traces. Fox also inherited a seven-year insurgency in the southern state of Chiapas that by subscribing to the most radical and least incorporated elements of the country's revolutionary traditions, had challenged the official revolutionary party to live up to its own twentieth-century promises of redistribution and inclusion. Such has been the power of the national-democratic imaginary in Mexico that although Ejército Zapatista de Liberación Nacional (Zapatista Army of National Liberation, EZLN) cadres had been organizing and preparing in Chiapas for a number of years, the organization rose up and became public only after Salinas had himself abolished the last vestiges of the Mexican revolution's historic promises of national autonomy and democratic inclusion by instituting NAFTA and ending the agrarian reform.

In some ways, the EZLN seems a hopelessly hybrid construction. Composed in part of old *guevarista* guerrilla foco revolutionaries, it never had the least chance, militarily speaking, of taking the presidential palace. In contrast to earlier guerrilla movements in Latin America, therefore, the EZLN was unable to subjugate its political process and aims to its military arm. This made it more accessible to a broader population, attracting a substantial number of excluded and impoverished Maya peasants who have, by most accounts, had an important effect on the internal structure and goals of the organization. At the same time, however, this mix of leftist revolutionary project and internal participatory democracy—symbolized by the insistence that the military leaders such as Marcos be only *subcomandantes* (sub-commanders), while the indigenous political leadership in the communities be considered *comandantes* (commanders)—has also led to uneasy negotiations with the more patriarchal and gerontocratic elements of traditional indigenous *costumbre* (custom) as it is used to govern indigenous communities. An especially dramatic example of this uneasiness can be found in the debates around the Revolutionary Women's Law that, by granting women equal political status and individual reproductive rights, can be seen as challenging the authority of community elders and heads of household. In all, it seems that this new *zapatismo* seeks to challenge, through a project of radical decentralization based on the gathering of disparate traditions of indigenous communal democracy and liberation theology, the centralized form taken by the Mexican postrevolutionary nation-state. Instead of challenging the overall project of national-democratic inclusion, it aims instead to extend and deepen its nature through the construction of a decentralized, multiethnic polity.[29]

A third variation on the failure of the national-popular model comes in the case of Chile. From 1938 to 1973, with many ups and downs, Chile was governed by a series of Popular Front or coalition governments, many of which included left and center parties and that in one way or another advanced agendas of social inclusion and of responsibility toward the poor. Especially between 1965 and 1973, Christian Democratic and Popular Unity governments pushed forward strong reformist agendas that included economic nationalism, agrarian reform, unionization, and the redistribution of income. Under the military dictatorship installed in 1973, however, and in the midst of gross violations of human and civil rights, these social gains were reversed and a model of free-market reforms instituted from the top down. In 1979, with the national-popular model lying in tatters all around him and in keeping with the overall marketizing trend, General Augusto Pinochet signed a decree providing for the subdivision and privatization of Mapuche indigenous lands and the abolition of Mapuche communities. Only at this point did Mapuche urban activists organize a cultural revitalization movement that combined a reawakening of cultural and religious customs with the first concerted mass resistance to the dictatorship. As in Mexico, the power of the national-popular imaginary was so great that those who had been excluded from it all along began to take matters into their own hands only when it was finally and radically denied them.[30]

While present-day indigenous peoples' movements across the Latin American region do not face the extreme threats of ethnocide some experienced in the 1970s and 1980s, and most do not experiment with forms of armed action along the lines of the EZLN, many have developed projects of cultural and territorial autonomy with which to challenge the centralization of nation-states. In part, these projects build on long-standing yearnings for both inclusion and autonomy, and on desires for the construction of national communities that honor indigenous traditions. Indigenous peoples have, since independence from Spain, argued that nations built on justice and participation cannot begin from a one-size-fits-all notion of citizen. And yet, especially during the national-popular period (1930 to roughly 1979), the powerful social promises of developmentally oriented states tended to silence most dissonant voices, as all were urged to accept a common popular identity in the interests of national unity.[31]

Once again, it has been the unraveling of the national-popular model that has brought alternative voices and perspectives to the fore. Some of them, inspired by the expanded discourse of human rights that indigenous activists themselves helped formulate in the United Nations (UN) and the International Labor Organization (ILO) over the past twenty-five years, are presenting their desires for autonomy as radical *extensions* of, rather than major *challenges* to, the national-democratic project. This holds especially true since the UN documents and ILO conventions—especially ILO Convention 169 on Indigenous and Tribal Peoples—still begin from the assumed existence of a nation-state and cannot be deemed in force in a country until approved by the government.

We can find an especially interesting example of how radical an extension of, or engagement with, the nation-state can become in indigenous political discourse in present-day Bolivia. After nearly a generation of mobilization, during which the Aymara-led Katarista movement has deeply altered the consciousness and political presence of indigenous peoples in the country and even shared power at the national level, many indigenous activists now view the existing nation-state as irretrievable. They thus have proposed an alternative, a constitutional convention to refound the Bolivian nation on principles friendlier to true equality in diversity. In keeping with this alternative, some indigenous intellectuals are now rethinking earlier indigenous movements in the context of present-day demands for autonomy and decentralized participation.[32]

These attempts at dialogue coexist uneasily with a more radical critique of the nation that has emerged in many indigenous movements over the past generation and that calls into question apparently obvious and often deeply held periodizations and narratives of "the national." In Guatemala, for example, some Maya intellectuals have suggested that the thirty-year civil war, prompted by the 1954 overthrow of democratically elected president Jacobo Arbenz and extended through two guerrilla insurgencies that aimed to install a new popular government, was not only a heroic struggle of the Guatemalan people against repression but also, to a large degree, an ethnocidal struggle in which Maya peasants served as cannon fodder by both sides. In Chile, Mapuche activists and intellectuals have not only called the question on Chile's recent neoliberal success story by mobilizing against the destructive human and ecological impacts of transnational lumber companies and megadevelopment projects such as hydroelectric dams; they have also suggested that the military coup of 1973 did not constitute as radical a rupture between democracy and repression for the Mapuche as it did for the non-indigenous population.[33]

Until the present moment, however, the only people suggesting that indigenous critiques could lead to possible secession from the nation-state are those who oppose indigenous movements in the first place. Even the most radical among indigenous organizations, such as the Chilean Consejo de Todas las Tierras (All Lands' Council), have involved themselves in dialogue with the state and tend to see projects for autonomy as viable only within some form of existing structure, even if radically reformed. In the end, therefore, demands for autonomy are proposals for radical reconstruction, rather than destruction, and can perhaps best be understood in the context of the diverse indigenous experiments with national construction ongoing since the end of colonial rule.

Across two hundred years of postcolonial history, indigenous peoples in Latin America have elaborated and defended hybrid and democratizing visions of what citizenship based on diversity might look like. If, in the end, the category *indigenous* was created by colonialism, it should not surprise us that the concept of indigenous peoples or "first nations" should emerge with postcolonialism, as did the conflictual politics of indigenous inclusion in the notion of *citizen*. For the First Nations of Latin America, the project of citizenship is still a work in progress. Throughout the postcolonial period, indigenous struggles over land, political participation, and cultural identity have of necessity engaged the nation-state; but national "civilizing" projects have all but buried this creative and defiant presence. Generations of leaders, indigenous and not, committed to the national-popular option have also helped bury the alternatives brought forward by indigenous activists. It is in this new postcolonial, postnational, and international conjuncture, with all of its complex and tragic consequences, that we can turn a different eye on indigenous narratives of the nation. Although they have been there, in one form or another, for a long time, they have an important and very relevant lesson to teach us in today's world. Democracy, they say, is constructed through the negotiation of differences—of opinion, custom, history, and worldview.

And this brings me back to where I began in an effort to negotiate the difficult and contradictory fit between postcolonialism, as an approach emerging from a critique of the second colonialism, and the experience of Latin America, with a long and seductive, if ultimately extremely frustrating, national-popular period. Even if today we tend to dismiss this period and its promises as hollow and unfulfilled, it is still true that subaltern experimentations with and creative reconstructions of the national narrative, whether coming from Latin Americans of African descent, indigenous peoples, or other groups, have a deep resonance for the political crises and quandaries of our contemporary world. Nations, at least in the version offered by elites, have historically been forged through unity-in-integration, through what I have called the one-size-fits-all definition of citizenship. In such a version, diversity becomes marked as a threat to national unity, to the viability of the national community as a whole. As the viability of such nations breaks down in many parts of the world, however, along with their promises of development, autonomy, and participation, is there anything that might take their place? Tracing subaltern practices and alternative discourses across the past two centuries in Latin America would seem to suggest that there is, and contemporary indigenous movements have begun to demand it. Hybridity, difference, and decentralization, which for so long have been seen as impediments to national unification, turn out to be, in reality, key to national democratization. With all of its inevitable contradictions and limitations, might this notion still offer a potential pathway into a postcolonial nationhood?

Of course, a reengagement with issues of social justice and liberation, even more pressing now than before the second September 11 of the Americas, must not tempt us to simply reinvent the wheel, taking up older Marxisms or romanticizations of the popular—in whatever guise they may present themselves—without the benefit of intervening decades of experience and critical reflection. Yet it is precisely today's enduring and ever more urgent need for a politics of solidarity that challenges us to take seriously, from a postcolonial perspective, the deep yearning that so many common folk across the world have had for the promises of national autonomy and development. Even as we must deepen our criticism of national and capitalist metanarratives, and of why they have not worked for so many of the peoples of the world, we must also reconsider why national-popular yearnings have persistently proven such a powerful force in the lives of so many diverse groups, whether indigenous leaders, Pentecostal preachers, or leftist guerrillas, suicide bombers, shantytown organizers, or human rights activists.

In such a context, it is perhaps fitting to conclude by invoking Frantz Fanon, whose hunger for a decolonized, humanistic solidarity among peoples has been the subject of so much postcolonialist debate. In my reading of *The Wretched of the Earth*, Fanon explores the dialectical relationship between the nationalism of the native intellectual—circumscribed by a degree of privilege and complicity handed out to the urban and educated groups under colonialism—and the cultural and political energy and creativity of the colonized masses. It is in this energy and creativity that the radical native intellectual must find, in Fanon's estimation, the secret for turning what we might call "flag independence" into true decolonization. And the medium through which that transformation would occur was, for Fanon, violence. Of course, we now know, with a generation's additional hindsight, that violence in and of itself does not possess the qualities of alchemy. And yet, if we reread Fanon's exploration of how the colonized masses—not the workers by themselves, and not the political parties or urban organizations—must in a colonial situation hold the key to creativity and new forms of national and political transformation, his thoughts seem remarkably current in today's world. For the struggle to remake solidarity through the reincorporation of already existing, yet buried, subaltern practices and alternative discourses still constitutes a crucial task for the future. "Without that struggle," Fanon wrote in 1961, "without that knowledge of the practice of action, there's nothing but a fancy-dress parade and the blare of trumpets. There's nothing save a minimum of readaptation, a few reforms at the top, a flag waving: and down there at the bottom an undivided mass, still living in the middle ages, endlessly marking time."[34]

Notes

1. An earlier draft of this essay was presented at a special panel organized to honor Thomas Skidmore as the recipient of the Latin American Studies Association's Kalman Silvert Award for Lifetime Service to Latin American Studies. I am grateful to the other participants on the panel—Tom Skidmore himself, Simon Collier, Peter Smith, and Steve J. Stern—for their comments on the earlier version, as well as to Charles A. Hale who, as a member of the audience and a part of the generation trained at Columbia University in the 1950s, provided me with well-focused comments on my treatment of that period. I also thank Steve J. Stern for his careful reading of a later draft.

2. Bhabha, *The Location of Culture*, 171.

3. Prakash, introduction to Prakash, *After Colonialism*, 5.

4. Chakrabarty, "Radical Histories and the Question of Enlightenment Rationalism," 274.

5. Ibid., 276.

6. Gandhi, *Postcolonial Theory*, 28.

7. One example of a postmodern and poststructuralist genealogy can be found in ibid., 25–28. Neil Lazarus's quotation of Said can be found in Lazarus, *Nationalism and Cultural Practice*, 10. In the same book, Lazarus also provides an impressive general example of the more historical materialist genealogy. The two genealogies are also profitably commented on and discussed, as well as explored, in the following two anthologies: in Williams and Chrisman, *Colonial Discourse and Post-colonial Theory*; and Castle, *Postcolonial Discourses*.

8. Gregory Castle, "Editor's Introduction," in Castle, *Postcolonial Discourses*, xiv.

9. For some of the issues relating to the emergence of postcolonial critiques, see, in addition to the sources quoted in previous footnotes, Said, *Orientalism*; Chatterjee, *Nationalist Thought and the Colonial World*; Chatterjee, *The Nation and Its Fragments*; and McClintock, *Imperial Leather*. Comments on the absence of Latin America from postcolonial studies can be found in Coronil, "Del eurocentrismo al globocentrismo," esp. 119–20; and Robert J. C. Young, "Colonialism and the Desiring Machine," excerpted from his *Colonial Desire* and reproduced in Castle, *Postcolonial Discourses*, 74–98, esp. 79. Young attributes this absence to the nature of disciplinary boundaries in the British academy. Although disciplinary and academic issues are, of course, part of the explanation, I hope to show in this essay that the issue is actually quite a bit larger and more complex than that.

10. Examples of the most successful of these interventionist projects would in-

clude the Mexican postrevolutionary state, 1930–80, and the Chilean Popular Front governments between 1938 and 1973. For particularly perceptive histories of the promises and limitations of these projects for the case of Chile, see Rosemblatt, *Gendered Compromises*; Tinsman, *Partners in Conflict*; and Klubock, *Contested Communities*.

11. A particularly prestigious example of a "demographic school" from this period took shape at Berkeley under the leadership of Woodrow Borah and Sherburne F. Cook. See, for example, Borah, *New Spain's Century of Depression*; and their classic coauthored volumes: Borah and Cook, *The Aboriginal Population of Central Mexico*; and Borah and Cook, *The Population of the Mixteca Alta*. For a valuable summary of the development of the social-science literature during these years, see Jiménez, "The Elision of the Middle Classes and Beyond," esp. 211–15.

12. On these issues, see the essays by Steve J. Stern, William Roseberry, and Florencia E. Mallon in Cooper, *Confronting Historical Paradigms*, 23–83, 318–68, and 371–401, respectively. It is particularly interesting to note, in this context, that the origins of core-periphery and dependency perspectives are often attributed to anti-colonial writers in Africa who wrote after the first theories of this kind emerged in Latin America. I take this as evidence of the deep chasm and lack of interaction that long existed between Latin America and the rest of the so-called third world and that continues to mark the field of postcolonialism to this day.

13. The complex interactions of politics and theory, of activism, field experiences, and intellectual commitment are dynamically explored for members of this generation in Steve J. Stern, "Between Tragedy and Promise: The Politics of Writing Latin American History in the Late Twentieth Century," in Joseph, *Reclaiming the Political*, 32–77.

14. An excellent example of the modernization-oriented tendency can be found in the career and work of John J. Johnson, sympathetically summarized by Jiménez, "The Elision of the Middle Classes and Beyond," esp. 211–12, 282–83 nn. 18–21. As president of the Latin American Studies Association, Johnson also confronted the younger leftists in a heated exchange during a plenary remembered by Tom Skidmore.

15. Quijano, "Colonialidad del poder," 335; translations mine.

16. Ibid., 344.

17. See, for example, Cronon, Miles, and Gitlin, *Under an Open Sky*; Grossman, *The Frontier in American Culture*; Limerick, Milner, and Rankin, *Trails*; and Limerick, *The Legacy of Conquest*.

18. For accounts of this process, see Menchú, *Crossing Borders*; and Ewen, *Voice of Indigenous Peoples*.

19. This is not to say that earlier critical and radical theorists had not criticized colonialism or the enduring quality of imperialism and dependency. The difference was that the earlier critiques took place in an intellectual and political context that still considered a solution possible through socialism, and thus through the radical extension of the national-popular narrative. This was, of course, no longer deemed possible by the end of the 1980s and the beginning of the 1990s.

20. On internal colonialism in Bolivia, see Qayum, "Nationalism, Internal Colonialism and the Spatial Imagination." On recent Bolivian engagements with subaltern studies, see Cusicanqui and Barragán, *Debates post coloniales*.

21. Ferrer, *Insurgent Cuba*, 1.

22. Ibid., 7.

23. This is one of my main conclusions in Mallon, *Peasant and Nation*.

24. Helg, *Our Rightful Share*. See also Guerra, "Crucibles of Liberation in Cuba."

25. Chomsky, " 'Barbados or Canada?' " On the issue of race in twentieth-century Cuba, see also Fuente, *A Nation for All*.

26. Quoted in Ferrer, *Insurgent Cuba*, 7.

27. Chomsky, " 'Barbados or Canada?' " 421.

28. I have marked 1938 as the beginning of the institutionalized revolution because this is when the recognizable precursor to the Partido Revolucionario Institucional (PRI), the Partido Revolucionario Mexicano (PRM), was created by President Lázaro Cárdenas. The PRI itself, however, did not emerge until 1946.

29. The literature on the EZLN has become a veritable cottage industry. Some of the works that have influenced me the most include Collier with Quaratiello, *Basta!*; Collier and Stephen, "Ethnicity, Identity, and Citizenship in the Wake of the Zapatista Rebellion"; Harvey, *The Chiapas Rebellion*; and Stephen, *¡Zapata Lives!*

30. For the case of Chile see, in addition to the sources cited in note 7, Mallon, "Land, Morality, and Exploitation in Southern Chile." For the rise of the Mapuche movement, see Paillalef, *When a Flower Is Reborn*. A reliable overall summary of the breakdown of the national-popular state under the Pinochet dictatorship can be found in Constable and Valenzuela, *A Nation of Enemies*.

31. Several historians have examined early experiments by indigenous peoples with concepts of citizenship and republicanism, as well as their attempts to develop more complex and hybrid practices that engaged emerging nation-states. See, for example, Grandin, *The Blood of Guatemala*; Thurner, *From Two Republics to One Divided*; Walker, *Smoldering Ashes*; Ducey, "Village, Nation, and Constitution"; Rugeley, *Yucatán's Maya Peasantry*; and Annino, "Soberanías en lucha." There were, of course, powerful attractions to the national-popular call, especially since indigenous elites did not always keep the best interests of poor indigenous peasants foremost in their minds. For some discussions of this contradictory period, see Grandin, *The Blood of Guatemala*; Mallon, "Decoding the Parchments of the Latin American Nation-State"; and Mallon, *Peasant and Nation*.

32. Esteban Ticona, "Participación, autonomía y asamblea constituyente: La larga lucha indígena en los Andes bolivianos," paper presented at the "Race, Culture, and Power: From Purity of Blood to Indigenous Social Movements in Latin America" conference, University of Iowa, Iowa City, October 25–27, 2002.

33. On Guatemala, see Montejo, *Testimony*; Warren, *Indigenous Movements and Their Critics*; and Cuxil, "The Politics of Maya Revindication." On Chile, see José A. Mariman, "Cuestión mapuche: Decentralización del estado y autonomía regional" (1990), available at www.xs4all.nl/~rehue/art/jmar1.html; and José A Mariman, "Movimiento mapuche y propuestas de autonomía en la década post dictadura" (1997), available at www.xs4all.nl/~rehue/art/jmar4a.html; Pedro Cayuqueo, "La autodeterminación mapuche en el marco de un estado multinacional" (1999), available at mapuche.info.scorpionshops.com; Mallon, "Cuando la amnesia se impone con sangre"; and Mallon, *Courage Tastes of Blood: The Mapuche Community of Nicolás Ailío and the Chilean State, 1906–2001* (Durham: Duke University Press, forthcoming).

34. Frantz Fanon, "Spontaneity: Its Strength and Weakness," in Fanon, *The Wretched of the Earth*, 147. Despite the fact that the phrase "still living in the middle ages" is to me representative of the worst evolutionary thinking of the time, I leave it in to remind us of the historical contradictions of radicalism in general, but also as a marker of how, in today's world, the staggering disparities between rich and poor may indeed make the phrase more descriptive of reality than it has ever been before.

Traveling Multiculturalism:

A Trinational Debate in Translation

✧ ✧ ✧

ROBERT STAM AND ELLA SHOHAT

Challenged and debated from both Right and Left, terms such as *multiculturalism* and *postcolonialism* have become subject to the political force fields of the so-called culture wars, in some ways turning into sliding signifiers onto which diverse desires and anxieties are projected. While the term *multiculturalism* has been visible both inside and outside of the academy, *postcolonialism* maintains a strong academic institutional aura. While multiculturalism is commonly associated with ongoing debates over race, slavery, and colonialism within single countries, the postcolonial remains more associated with debates over colonialism and diaspora within Europe's ex-colonized geographies. Yet despite differences in emphasis, both movements share a critique of Eurocentrism, racism, and colonial discourse. Both form part of a loose constellation of interdisciplinary research initiatives and political projects that cover a wide range of theories, discourses, and areas of inquiry. That constellation includes such overlapping discourses as revisionist "bottom-up" history, diasporic indigenous studies, Afro-diasporic studies, critical race theory, transnational feminism, whiteness studies, antiracist pedagogy, media critique, postmodern geography, counter-Enlightenment philosophy, border theory, antiglobalization theory, and many other forms of adversarial knowledge.

What interests us in our current project, however, is how cultural debates travel across borders, notably in the cases of the United States, France, and Brazil.[1] The three countries were not chosen arbitrarily, since the triad consists of one paradigmatic European country with enormous cultural influence, along with the two most populous and powerful countries in the Americas. Furthermore, the three countries have been historically connected since the beginning, sometimes in surprising ways. To mention just a few, France was involved in colonizing efforts in both North and South America, French revolutionary ideas circulated widely among revolutionaries in both Brazil and the United States, and the French and the American Revolutions at first regarded each other as *républiques soeurs*. The 1824 charter in Brazil included a truncated version of the French Declaration of the Rights of Man. The fears triggered in official France by the success of the Haitian Revolution indirectly led to the hasty Louisiana Purchase, which vastly increased U.S. territory.[2] In Brazil, it was Napoleon's invasion of Iberia that led to the displacement of the Portuguese court to the South American country, and thus indirectly to Brazilian independence. And back in the days when New York was called New Amsterdam, enslaved Afro-Brazilians who came from Africa via Recife figured among the first blacks to come to North America. For complex reasons, the Dutch administration freed the slaves, with the result that men with names like Simao Congo and Paulo d'Angola came to be the proprietors of farms in what are now Greenwich Village and Soho in lower Manhattan.

In the context of this trilateral comparison, we will ask such questions as the following: What happens in the movement of debates from one geographical space and cultural semantics to another? Under what rubrics and keywords is multicultural or postcolonial work performed in these sites? How do the terms themselves shift political and epistemological valence? What happens when multiculturalism and postcolonialism are seen through other national grids or enter other intellectual fields? How are seemingly out-of-place ideas reinvoiced, recontextualized, transvocalized? How do debates get grafted onto other neighboring or preexisting debates? In what ways do so-called debates about debates in one nation-state allegorize debates about debates in another? What are the grids, prisms, and even funhouse mirrors through which the debates are seen? What is the role of the media in disseminating ideas and perspectives drawn from these debates? What is the role of national exceptionalisms and narcissisms? What myths of origin are operative in terms of the past, and which teleologies in terms of the future? What anxieties, utopias, and projections come into play? How do ideas travel along lines of force dictated both by particular national histories, but also by present-day global economic alignments? What is the role of the asymmetries of power in knowledge production and dissemination? Although we can only gesture toward answering these questions here, it seems to us that such questions are clearly worth asking, especially in the age of globalization. It is essential, we will argue, to think through cultural and political questions in terms that transcend the narrow confines of the nation-state.

When debates travel, a problem of translation often exists in a very literal sense, resulting in a collision of in some ways incommensurable vocabularies. Some of the terms common to both French and US political discourse, for example, have similar connotations, but others make for ideological *faux amis* (false friends). Whereas in the United States *Republicans* and *Democrats* refer to the two political parties, in France *republican* refers to the French Revolution and its ideas of citizenship, while *democrat* often refers to a society made up of communities. Indeed, the concept of multiculturalism is sometimes translated as *communautarisme* (communitarianism), which is seen in France as a descent from the lofty abstract neutrality of republican citizenship into embodied ethnic identities and communities. While *liberal* in the United States often appears as a synonym for *Left*, in France it means "neoliberal and capitalist," and therefore "Right." And whereas in the United States words like *identity* and *difference* evoke oppressed "minorities," in French discourse, *identity*, *identitarian*, and *differentialism* may just as likely refer to right-wing anti-immigrant movements, Islamic fundamentalism, and even US-style feminism. In terms of Brazil, too, the same words have very different connotations due to different histories. In Brazil, the word *Negro* is a term of pride for blacks who wear T-shirts saying "100 percent Negro," while *black* (*preto*) is seen as offensive. In the United States, meanwhile, the term *Negro* evokes Uncle Tom–style passivity and has been discarded in favor of *black* and *African American*. The term *miscegenation*, similarly, comes in the United States with a strong whiff of lynching and anti–race-mixing laws, while *miscegenacao* in Portuguese has positive connotations, so that Bahian carnival, in 1999, could officially celebrate "450 years of miscegenation."

France, Brazil, and the United States are all multicultural countries, but it is important to distinguish between the multicultural "fact" and the multiculturalist "project."[3] The former term references the obvious fact that virtually all countries in the world are multicultural: India is riotously plural in language and religion, the Americas generally mingle many constellations of cultures, and so forth. What provokes polemics in the United States, France, and Brazil, however, is not the indisputable fact of cultural difference, but rather the multiculturalist project. That project unleashed—and to some extent still unleashes—virulent polemics because it calls for decisive changes in the way we write history, think about society, teach literature, hire professors, curate art, program films, organize conferences, distribute cultural resources, and, last but not least, do cultural studies.

The concept of multiculturalism, admittedly, polysemically offers itself up to various interpretations. In Jamesonian terms, multiculturalism can be seen as a master code within which competing discourses fight it out. Rather than a discourse, multiculturalism constitutes a constellation of discourses, which is why it is misleading to make sweeping generalizations about it as in such phrases as "multiculturalism promises," "multiculturalism claims," or similar statements. Multiculturalism is above all protean, plural, conjunctural, and it exists in shifting relation to various institutions, discourses, disciplines, communities, and nation-states. As a "situated utterance,"[4] it can be top-down or bottom-up, hegemonic or resistant, or both at the same time. It all depends on who is multiculturalizing whom, from what social position, in response to what hegemonies, to whose benefit, as part of what political project, using what means, deploying which discourses, and so forth. And that is why it has become essential to specify exactly which current within multiculturalism one is speaking about—whence qualifiers such as "critical," "radical," "polycentric," and "antiracist" to delineate our kind of multiculturalism from "corporate," "co-optive," and "liberal" multiculturalism.

In other national contexts, *multiculturalism* alters its valence. In countries like Canada and Australia the term designates official government programs designed to both placate and to some extent empower "minorities" through a modicum of representation—a form of multiculturalism challenged by some radicals as too co-optive and assimilationist. In Mexico, the word designates the official encouragement of the autonomous identity of indigenous groups. In Brazil, it connotes both a taken-for-granted quality of Brazilian society and serves as the name for what is seen as a North American project, one regarded with ambivalence. Like their colleagues elsewhere, Brazilian intellectuals do critical work on colonialism and race, but the Right worries about "political correctness," while the Left worries about a new "multiculturalized neo-imperialism" whereby terms specific to US debates are "exported" to Brazil. And in France, both the Right and Left tend to denounce multiculturalism, in contradictory terms and usually on the basis of minimal actual knowledge. For the Center/Right (Alain Finkelkraut, Pascal Bruckner), multiculturalism constitutes a recycling of 1960s third worldist radicalism, while for the Left (Pierre Bourdieu/ Loic Wacquant) it represents a cunningly disguised form of American imperialism. Needless to say, it is less than clear how it could be both at the same time. Occasionally, however, some French writers call for a "multiculturalism à la française."

These debates, in our view, are but the surface manifestations of a deeper seismological shift: the decolonization of Eurocentric power structures and epistemologies. For us, issues of multiculturalism must be articulated together with issues of colonial history and Eurocentric discourse, or run the risk of being inoffensively pluralist and politically irrelevant. The term *Eurocentrism*, for us, points to the ideological substratum common to colonialist, imperialist, and racist discourse, one which still undergirds, permeates, and structures many contemporary discourses, practices, and representations in all three of the countries under discussion, even after the formal end of colonialism. While colonialist discourse explicitly justifies colonialist practices, Eurocentric discourse embeds, takes for granted, and normalizes the hierarchical power relations generated by colonialism and imperialism, without necessarily even thematizing those issues directly. Eurocentrism's links to the colonizing process are obscured within a buried epistemology.

Within Eurocentrism, Europe—and here we mean Europe in the broad sense to refer not to the continent of Europe but rather to Euro-American hegemony around the world—is seen as the world's center of gravity, as the originary fountain from which all good things flow. From the time of Europe's "civilizing mission" and the "white man's burden" to the time of "globalization" and the "new world order," Eurocentric discourse has been diffusionist; it assumes that democracy, science, progress, and prosperity all emanate outward from a Euro-American source. Eurocentric discourse projects a linear historical trajectory leading from classical Greece (anachronistically constructed as "Western") to imperial Rome and then to the metropolitan capitals of Europe and the United States. It renders history as a north-by-northwest sequence of empires: Pax Romana, Pax Hispanica, Pax Britannica, Pax Americana. Indeed, the contemporary partisans of Pax Americana shamelessly resurrect the term *imperial* as a positively connoted sign, as evidenced in a recent *New York Times* magazine cover article entitled "The American Empire: Get Used to It."[5]

Although Eurocentric discourse is complex, contradictory, and historically unstable, its composite portrait as a mode of thought might see it as engaging in a number of mutually reinforcing intellectual operations:

(1)   Eurocentrism attributes to the West an inherent trajectory toward democratic institutions (Tomás de Torquemada, King Leopold, Benito Mussolini, Adolph Hitler, Henri Petain, and other European despots are mere "aberrations" within an amnesiac logic of selective legitimation);

(2)   Eurocentrism elides non-Western democratic traditions, while obscuring the manipulations embedded in Western formal democracy and masking the West's part in subverting democracies abroad;

(3)   Eurocentrism regards the West's oppressive practices—colonialism, slave trading, imperialism—as contingent "accidents" that do not point to oppressive historical patterns in Europe's relation to those it has dominated;

(4)   Eurocentrism appropriates the cultural and material production of the non-West, while denying both the non-West's achievements and its own appropriation, thus consolidating its sense of self and glorifying its own cultural anthropophagy;

(5)   Eurocentrism adopts a systematic policy of nonreciprocity—it demands of others what it refuses to offer itself; it places the West as the arbiter of a morality that it does not itself practice.

In sum, Eurocentrism rigs the historical balance sheet; it sanitizes Western history while patronizing and even demonizing the non-West; it thinks of itself in terms of its noblest achievements—science, progress, humanism— but of the non-West in terms of its deficiencies, real or imagined. The double processes of self-idealization and Other-demonization adapted by the Bush regime's foreign policy rhetoric, which places the US corporate/military elite as judge, jury, and policeman of global offenses, can only be understood against the backdrop of the long history of colonialism and imperialism. Indeed, George W. Bush's ultimatums against Iraq resonate with five hundred years of colonial ultimatums, going all the way back to the Spanish *requerimiento*, the document which the conquistadores read (in Spanish) to uncomprehending indigenous people and which told them, in sum, that they would have to give up their land, religion, and language, and that if they did not do so forthwith, the Spanish would burn their houses and rape their women, and that it would all be their own fault.[6]

Issues of multiculturalism, in our view, must always be interarticulated with issues of colonialism, postcoloniality, and Eurocentrism. Unfortunately, multiculturalism has not succeeded in defining itself. It has largely been defined by its critics, whether by a Marxising Left, which finds it too culturalist and co-optable, or by an anti-Marxist Right, which finds it too radical and revolutionary. For the Right, multiculturalism represents 1960s revolutionary radicalism in a new guise, while for a certain class-based Left, it manifests a divisive detour into "identity politics," a form of cultural narcissism distracting from "real" struggles over class and power.

Multiculturalism has in a sense suffered the same fate as socialism earlier, dismissed by the far Left as too soft and co-optive and denounced by the Right as too radical and incendiary. But while the right-wing critique of multiculturalism remains completely useless because it is so blind and uninformed, the left-wing critique proves helpful because it reminds multiculturalists to both pay attention to political economy and support activism, so as not to confuse academic posturing with social change. Yet many versions of radical multiculturalism already do pay attention to political economy

and do support activism. And many of the Left's critiques of multiculturalism, in our view, have been premised on false dichotomies that would have
us choose between political economy or culture, race or class, activism or
scholarship. Multiculturalism, meanwhile, addresses a useful critique to the
Marxising Left, reminding it to recall the Eurocentric limitations of Marxism itself; to pay attention to culture as a constitutive element of power, including economic power, in the globalized postmodern world; and to not
forget the role of colonialism, slavery, and imperialism in shaping contemporary power stratifications both within and between cultures and societies.

What often gets lost in these debates is the actual scholarly work concerning multiculturalism, what might be called the "multicultural corpus." The
work is practiced under diverse names and rubrics and performed by hundreds of scholars in many countries, including the three countries on which
we have placed our focus here.[7] Work that critiques colonialism would in
France simply go under the name of history, as has happened with the work
of Yves Benot on colonial massacres or that of Benjamin Stora on the elision
of the Algerian War from French media and pedagogy.[8] Although some of
this work might not be performed under the multiculturalist banner per se,
and while tensions may exist between and even within their diverse modes
of critique, they all share a key element: a radically critical and multidisciplinary engagement with the legacies of colonialism, slavery, imperialism,
and racism.

But it is difficult to posit a precise term to evoke this kind of work. Phrases
like *polycentric multiculturalism* or *radical multiculturalism* are in some ways
more likely to evoke such thinking and writing than most of the alternative terms, each of which brings with it both advantages and disadvan-
tages. Despite the various attacks on *multiculturalism*, the term does have
certain advantages and originally proved strategically useful for a number
of reasons: (1) its very inclusiveness called for a broad progressive coalition, something lacking in terms like *black liberation*, which applied only to
one band on the radical spectrum; (2) the term's strategic vagueness made it
useful for prodding institutions—for example, university administrations—
into making progressive gestures, such as doing more "minority" hiring in
the name of "diversity"; (3) both constitutive elements of the term seemed
strategically helpful—the *multi-* called for a constitutive heterogeneity based
on multiple issues, multiple axes of identification, and multiple strategies,
while the word *culture* addressed a silent rebuke to those Marxists who remained blind to the importance of culture and race alongside that of class.
Furthermore, the term embedded, encoded in its DNA, as it were, two of its
historically interrelated source movements: the decolonizing independence

struggles in what used to be called the third world (aka the South), and minority community struggles of the so-called internal colonies of the first world (aka the North). The linguistic performative of putting *multi-* and *cultural* together verbally enacted a coalitionary strategy that implicitly transcended the binarism of race-relations discourse. Qualifiers like *critical, radical, counterhegemonic*, and *polycentric*, meanwhile, both warned against and provided an antidote to the eventual co-optability of the two constituent terms. At the same time, the *ism* in *multiculturalism* perhaps claimed too much by placing itself in the same paradigm as other isms, such as those referring to explanatory grids (Marxism), epochs (postmodernism), systems of production (capitalism), and ideologies (socialism).

While the term *multiculturalism* in some ways proves problematic, so do many of the alternative terms: *Revisionist history* focuses too narrowly on a single subfield of one discipline. *Antiracist studies* seems too negative, too locked into the same paradigm as the one being combated. *Postcolonial studies*, apart from its exclusive location in academia, has all the problems often highlighted about a *post-* not yet really "post" within a metanarrative that paradoxically recenters that which is presumably being transcended. *Critical race theory* remains too tied up with the legal discipline and excludes other axes of oppression like class and sexuality. *Whiteness studies*, while having the advantage of exnominating or outing whiteness, runs the risk of recentering it as well. *Identity politics* has come to emerge as the preferred term for the enemies of multiculturalism because it carries with it a hint of personal and cultural narcissism, of a philosophy autocentered on "my" identity. *Transnational studies*, given its partial congruency with transnational corporations, is just as politically tainted as *multiculturalism* and risks eliding forms of oppression that are national or infranational. In other words, each term, while problematic, also casts some light on a very complex subject. The point is to deploy all the concepts in a differential, contingent, and relational manner. It is not that one conceptual frame is "wrong" and the other "right," but rather that each frame only partially illuminates the issues. We can use all the terms as part of a more mobile set of grids, a more flexible set of disciplinary and cross-cultural lenses adequate to the complex politics of contemporary location, while simultaneously maintaining openings for agency and resistance.

With all that by way of background, we would like to address the traveling debates about race and multiculturalism. A preliminary point to make is that debates about multiculturalism, at least in the three countries under discussion here, have circulated more widely than debates about postcolonialism. In France, *postcolonial* tends to function merely as a synonym for *postindependence* in the formerly colonized world. In Brazil, the idea of post-coloniality tends to evoke the response, "What's new about that? We've been hybrid and postcolonial since the early nineteenth century." Also, although ideas and debates have in a sense always traveled—the Enlightenment, for example, was clearly a transnational movement—in a globalized world, the very production of ideas is itself transnational, with multiple locations and points of departure. The US debates about race and multiculturalism have circulated around much of the world, partly thanks to the global reach of the English language and of US power. Yet it would be misleading to say these movements originated in the United States and then traveled elsewhere. As a result of colonial karma, many ideas and people had already traveled back and forth between the United States and other geographies to mould US multiculturalism, just as traveling ideas shaped analogous movements elsewhere. The so-called voyages of discovery in the New World turned the indigenous peoples of the Americas into internal exiles and Africans into forced émigrés, generating a multitude of crisscrossing diasporas. Later developments—US imperialist policies, military interventions, expulsions, immigration, and what has come to be called the brain drain—brought a hybridized mix of peoples and ideas, all of which helped mould multiculturalism as both fact and project. The multiculturalist movement itself was impacted by many movements from elsewhere, by anticolonialist discourse (Aimé Césaire, Frantz Fanon, Albert Memmi, and Amílcar Cabral, all associated with the decolonizing third world), by poststructuralism (associated with France), by subaltern studies (associated with India), by hegemony theory (associated with Antonio Gramsci and Italy), and by dependency theory (associated with Latin America).[9]

The debates about race and multiculturalism resonate in various sites, in sum, not so much because they have been exported, but rather because they are historically relevant to those other sites and have often already been debated there, although not necessarily under the same keywords. This holds especially true of such debates resonating around the Black Atlantic. Indeed, all three countries discussed in our text can properly be called multicultural nation-states—Will Kymlicka might call them multination states[10]—diversely implicated in European conquest and slavery, whether as conqueror or conquered or both, as enslaver or enslaved or both. One thinks of the British conquest of North America, or of the Portuguese conquest of Brazil, or of the French role in the Caribbean and Canada, Africa and Southeast Asia, as well as of the resistance to all those conquests. Nor was it an accident that all three countries faced demands for reparations for colonialism and slavery at the United Nations World Conference against Racism in Durban. The race/multiculturalism/colonialism debates, in this sense, provide important indices of the historical legacies of colonialism.

Let us begin, however, with the two countries from the Americas. Both Brazil and the United States are colonial settler states, in which conquest, slavery, and racial difference form constitutive elements of the nation from the outset. Both countries began as colonies of European nation-states, and in both there ensued a conquest of vast territories that involved the near-genocidal subjugation of native peoples. Both countries massively imported Africans as slaves, and both abolished the institution of slavery in the nineteenth century, the United States in 1863 and Brazil in 1888. Both countries received waves of immigration from all over the world, ultimately forming pluriethnic multination states with substantial indigenous, African, European, Japanese, Jewish, and Arab communities. But while the United States and Brazil share their status as colonial settler states, the former has added another oppressive dimension to this relationship by becoming the neo-imperial hegemon of the hemisphere, while Brazil has ended up as a victim of that hegemony and of a US-led globalization disproportionately harming the nation-states of what was formerly known as the third world.[11]

Although Brazil is often thought to be a "young" country, its colonization actually began almost a century before that of the United States. While Jamestown was founded in 1607, São Vicente, the first Portuguese settlement, was founded in 1532. In their political history, both countries sought independence from Europe. In 1820, Thomas Jefferson even contemplated the idea of pan-American unity based on the convergence of aspirations and interests.[12] The literary histories of both countries are also marked by a parallel struggle for cultural independence from Europe. Ralph Waldo Emerson's "The American Scholar" address of 1836, which Oliver Wendell Holmes thought of as our intellectual declaration of independence, came a year after a similar declaration by Brazilian poet Goncalves de Magalhaes. We find many of the same literary movements and genres in both countries, for example, religious literature (Padre Vieira in Brazil and Jonathan Edwards in the United States) and abolitionist literature (Joaquim Nabuco in Brazil; William Garrison in the United States). Some literary movements are shared between France, Brazil, and the United States: romantic Indianism (Jose de Alencar in Brazil, François-René de Chateaubriand in France, and James Fenimore Cooper in the United States.); naturalism (Julio Ribeiro in Brazil, Émile Zola in France, and Frank Norris in the United States.); and modernism (Oswald de Andrade in Brazil, Alfred Jarry in France, and Ezra Pound in the United States).

Some readers might be surprised to find France included as part of the

Black Atlantic, but although metropolitan France on one level represents the very paradigm of a "normal" European nation, with a common language and an originary territory and population, on another level its history is deeply implicated in colonialism and slavery.[13] France participated in the slave trade and in slavery in Africa and the Caribbean, and was shaped, informed, and enriched by its extensive colonial involvements. By the late 1780s, France's Caribbean colonies produced more than two-fifths of the Western world's sugar and coffee, leading to a contradiction between France's economic dependence on colonial slavery and its (later) celebration of liberty. And, contrary to myth, there were slaves in France itself.[14] Yet the country supported no plantation system as did Brazil or the United States, so that slavery in France was largely practiced externally. France, too, is ethnically diverse and multicultural, but hardly in the same way as Brazil and the United States. Both Brazil and the United States have native populations—either unmixed on reservations (like the Xingu or the Onandoga) or mixed with other ethnicities such as African Americans (e.g., the Seminoles in Florida) or with Europeans (e.g., the Mamelucos in Brazil). Most of the African-descended people in France today are there as the long-term result of transatlantic slavery and colonialism; they represent a form of colonial karma, the return of the historically repressed. The United States, France, and Brazil, then, all represent distinct conjunctural formations within the larger configurations of the Black Atlantic.

Another common feature of our three countries lies in their deep roots in the Enlightenment, as expressed in the American Revolution in 1776, the French Revolution in 1789, and the Brazilian Republic in 1889. Many of the central conflicts in the histories of these countries revolve around this ambiguous heritage. How were Enlightenment values such as representative government and freedom and equality before the law to be reconciled with the actual practices of colonialism, genocide, slavery, and imperialism, which constituted the very antithesis of such values? Nothing is more revelatory of these contradictions than the way the three nations wrestled with the question of slavery. In the United States, at the Constitutional Convention in 1787, some of the delegates personally abhorred slavery, but they accepted it as part of a compromise favoring a stronger federal government. Jefferson occasionally pondered the possibility of abolishing slavery, but he decided not to. In Brazil, those eighteenth-century revolutionaries who wanted independence from Portugal also feared slave rebellions and the loss of their privileges. Tiradentes, the leader of an abortive eighteenth-century rebellion again Portuguese colonialism also thought of abolishing slavery, but like Jefferson, he thought better of it. And while France abolished slavery during the revolution, it reestablished the institution a few years later. In this sense, all three nation-states constitute that political oxymoron called "master race democracy." All three have tried to reconcile liberal Enlightenment principles of political democracy and social equality with the dumb historical inertia of colonialism and slavery; the US republic, where "all men are created equal," also allowed for slavery. The same men who penned revolutionary words owned slaves and dispossessed indigenous peoples of their lands.

Another vexed question dealt with the relationship between republics and empires. France became an imperial power, while the United States not only colonized Native American land but also indulged in occasional imperialist binges. (Even Brazil nominally constituted an empire during much of the nineteenth century, although hardly as aggressive a one as France or the United States.) Currently, the United States is engaged in what threatens to become a neo-imperialist binge with global claims. While American neo-imperialism in some ways does not resemble the old colonialisms and imperialisms—it does not aim at conquering territories, but "only" at achieving military, economic, and political hegemony—in another sense it forms a kind of historical synthesis of all previous colonialisms and imperialisms. In the discourses of the hawks of the Bush administration, the government claims to exercise a kind of benevolent world domination; in this sense it does not differ from earlier colonialisms, all of which claimed to be rescuing the benighted peoples of the world from despotism to bring them the benefits of civilization.

Both the French and American Revolutions, as the political arm of the Enlightenment, defined a falsely universalist set of values while posing as defending the "rights of man." The French model does not recognize *race* as a valid conceptual or institutional category. Yet the invocation of abstract republican principles can sometimes lead us to forget that the republic of *liberté, égalité, fraternité* did install and encode an ethnic and racial order. The canonical triad liberty, equality, and fraternity was undercut by the *nos ancêtres les Gaulois* (our ancestors, the Gauls) of the colonial history books, which taught the Martinicans, the Senegalese, and the Vietnamese that "our ancestors, the Gauls, had blue eyes and blond hair." In a similar fashion, the American constitution—by speaking as if all Americans were equal and free when slaves were in chains, Native Americans were suffering dispossession, and women were excluded from political representation—submerged the existence of African Americans, and Amerindians, and women, while simultaneously veiling white masculinist domination in falsely universalist language. The constitution, that "lovely piece of paper," in the words of Gil Scott Heron's song "Writer in America," forms a classic example of Walter Benjamin's "document of civilization" that hides a "document of barbarism." The constitution neutralized the whiteness of the dominant group by leaving it unnamed, while simultaneously hiding the red and the black and the female through euphemism or omission.[15]

While denouncing slavery abstractly, Enlightenment philosophers were often complicit with it practically. Slavery, as Susan Buck-Morss puts it, "came to underwrite the entire economic system of the West, paradoxically facilitating the global spread of the very Enlightenment ideas that were in such fundamental contradiction to it."[16] The exploitation of colonial slave laborers was accepted as a given by the very thinkers who proclaimed freedom as a natural human state and an inalienable right. All the countries around the Black Atlantic, all those countries somehow involved in the slave trade, wrestled with these dilemmas. When the Brazilian emperor granted the constitutional charter in 1824, there was no mention of slaves, and although article 179 of the charter defined freedom and equality as inalienable rights, millions of blacks continued to endure enslavement.[17]

In some respects, the Enlightenment, or certain elements of it, proved profoundly liberating for certain strata within Europe, and even for some outside it (for Haitian revolutionary Toussaint-Louverture, for example). One *avant la lettre* "multiculturalist," to our mind, was the Enlightenment philosopher Denis Diderot, who in his writings inverted the colonialist metonym of beast and savage, advising the African "Hottentots" that the ferocious beasts living in their forests were "less frightening than the monsters of the empire under which you are about to fall." More important, Diderot defended the right of the oppressed to revolt, and even fantasized about himself (as early as 1781) as a kind of anticolonialist guerilla: "Barbarous Europeans! The brilliance of your enterprises does not impress me. Their success does not hide their injustice. In my imagination I have often embarked in those ships which bring you to distant countries, but once on land, and witness of your misdeeds, I separate myself from you and I join your enemies, taking arms against you, bathing my hands in your blood."[18] Thus Diderot anticipated later radical renegades (e.g., the Jean-Paul Sartre of the preface to the 1948 *Orphée Noir* collection of African Negritude poetry and to Fanon's 1961 *The Wretched of the Earth*)[19] as a European intellectual who identifies with the colonized against European colonialism.

On the other hand, another less revolutionary Enlightenment justified the "progressive" subjugation of those who stood in Reason's way. Contemporaneous with Europe's rise to world power, the Enlightenment perpetuated, along with its progressive and libratory "overside," an imperialist, diffusionist, hierarchical underside. The social contract delineated by such philosophers as John Locke, Jean-Jacques Rousseau, and John Stuart Mill was doubled by what Y. N. Kly calls the "anti-social contract" in which the idea of "equality among equals" came to entail an equal opportunity to disappropriate and dispossess.[20] Charles W. Mills, in *The Racial Contract*, argues that white supremacy is the "unnamed political system that has made the modern world what it is today."[21] He traces this system back to the Enlightenment and a "racial contract," found in the work of Locke as well as in Rousseau's *Discourse on Inequality* (1755), that "naturalizes" inequality. "Race," although it goes unnamed, for Mills does not constitute an "afterthought" or "deviation" from "ostensibly raceless Western ideals, but rather a central shaping constituent of those ideals."[22]

The French Revolution defined an abstract, theoretical universalism materially embodied by institutions that ensured socialization (state schools), order (justice, police), and defense mechanisms (the republican army). But the republic violated its own abstract principles when it participated in the colonial enterprise of conquering indigenous populations and enslaving Africans. Louis Sala-Molins has looked at Enlightenment thought by focusing on the so-called Code Noir, the French royal decree regulating relations between masters and slaves in all the colonies, drawn up in 1685 and not definitely eradicated until 1848. Along with legalizing slavery in general, the code authorized the torture, mutilation, and killing of slaves, as well as the chasing away of any Jews who had "established residences from our isles." Enlightenment thinkers, according to Sola-Molins, denounced slavery in theory while ignoring it or indirectly condoning it in practice. Slavery became a metaphor that concerned intra-European relations. The silence of Rousseau, one of the patron saints of the French Revolution, Sola-Molins calls "racist" and "revolting."[23] Montesquieu, the philosopher to whom some French intellectuals would have us return for a model of correct thinking about contemporary cultural and political issues, justified slavery on pragmatic, climatic, and racist grounds and complained that "weak minds exaggerate too much the injustice done to Africans" by colonial slavery.[24] One aspect of radical multiculturalism, in our view, is the critique of the racist dimension of the Enlightenment apparent in the work of thinkers as diverse as Montesquieu, Locke, David Hume, Immanuel Kant, and Georg Wilhelm Friedrich Hegel. It is not for us a question of a blanket rejection—we need not throw out a certain legacy of human rights and civil liberties, for example—but rather of calling attention to the Herrenvolk aspects of Enlightenment thought, to the ways it was complicit with Europe's colonizing power.

Although intellectuals in all three of our countries engage in progressive, adversarial scholarship with regard to the questions outlined above, they (we) too often operate within intellectual boundaries dictated by the nation-state. We speak as if French imperialism had nothing to do with American imperialism, or as if US slavery remained completely separate from Brazilian slavery. Yet Portuguese, French, and US colonialisms are all connected by links both real and metonymical, comparative and metaphorical. It is a question of family resemblances around what Robert Farris Thompson has called "Black Atlantic civilization" and what Paul Gilroy later called the Black Atlantic.[25] France colonized and imperialized vast swaths of Asia, Africa, and the Caribbean. While the United States does not like to think of itself as a colonial power, it must recognize that long before its imperial binge at the turn of the twentieth century, it had already colonized, first of all the North American continent, through the genocidal policies of what was referred to as Manifest Destiny, and then it had pursued imperial domination of the hemisphere through the so-called Monroe Doctrine.

At first glance, Brazil remains innocent of the colonial/imperial charge; rather, it itself experienced colonization by France, the Netherlands, and Portugal, and later it became economically dominated by Great Britain and the United States. But from another perspective, as a colonial settler state, Brazil is, as Paulo Emilio Salles Gomes put it, both "occupier" and "occupied." The third world/first world binarism, in this sense, obscures subterranean affinities and commonalities between certain countries. Like the United States, Brazil, too, dispossessed its native peoples, with equally genocidal consequences. It, too, enslaved Africans on a massive scale. Indeed, slavery in Brazil existed before it did in the United States and lasted much longer, until 1888. Nor are the two slaveries unconnected. The very word *Negro*, in English, came from Portuguese, as did the word *pickaninny* (from Portuguese *pequininho* for "black child"). And while some historical comparatists argued that Brazilian slavery was somehow more "humane," the current scholarly consensus sees both forms of slavery—the (largely) Anglo-segregationist North American model and the Latin assimilationist Brazilian model—as unspeakably cruel and exploitative. In any case, the very posing of the question about which form of slavery was more humane is itself obscene and rather resembles comparing the creature comforts of Auschwitz and Treblinka.

As a result of all these partially converging histories, there is a family resemblance—if not an identity—between the contemporary social situations in all three countries, whence we find the present-day ghettos of the United States, the favelas of Brazil, and the *banlieux* of France. In all three settings, euphemisms—the *inner city*, *os bairros perigosos* (the dangerous neighborhoods), and *les quartiers sensibles* (the sensitive quarters)—disguise the transparent reality that in each one impoverished, dark-skinned people suffer political and economic disenfranchisement, negative stereotyping, and police brutality. Clearly, nuances exist in each case, but the patterns are similar. It is no accident, in a sense, that rap music and hip hop culture in general have become a kind of cultural lingua franca in all three settings, where rappers, initially inspired by black American musical performance but infusing new ideas and cultural energies into that performance, denounce racialized urban oppression in its various forms. Meanwhile, hip hop–inflected films — *Do the Right Thing* in the United States, *La haine* in France, and *City of God* in Brazil[26] — give cinematic expression to resistance to these same realities.

Our point is not to simplistically equate these different situations, but to point to historical relationalities across time and space. Just as contemporary police brutality against blacks in US cities can be seen in relation to chattel slavery, police brutality against Maghrebians in France, or against social "marginals" in Brazil, can all be at least partially traced to the legacies of colonialism and slavery. Indeed, it is fascinating to compare the latter-day tensions inherent in so-called master race democracy as they played themselves out in a single historical period—the 1950s and early 1960s—in all three countries. In Brazil in 1951, the congress, provoked by an incident in which African American dancer Katherine Dunham was refused entry to a São Paulo hotel, passed the Afonso Arinos law prohibiting racial discrimination in Brazil. Two years later, UNESCO, in the erroneous belief that Brazil had found a workable formula for racial togetherness, sponsored a series of studies of race relations in Brazil. Work by Brazilian and international social scientists, including later president Fernando Henrique Cardoso, compiled massive evidence that white Brazilians were prejudiced, that blacks may not have faced legal segregation but that they were "naturally" and informally segregated, and that most of the black population remained at the bottom of society with little chances for social mobility. As a result, the social scientists were accused of "inventing a racial problem that did not exist in Brazil."[27]

In the southern United States, African Americans were at the same time struggling against US-style apartheid, and specifically for the right to vote. In Algeria, then, in a sense, the "south" of France, Algerians were fighting for independence and equality. In the United States, the struggle revolved around whether the country would be a democracy for all its citizens or a master race democracy for white people alone. Yet a similar tension played itself out in North Africa. Although Algeria had been an integral part of France for over 130 years, supposedly an integral part of *la république, une et indivisible* (the republic, one and indivisible), the majority of Muslim Algerians were still second-class citizens, circumscribed by a series of discriminatory laws and decrees. The ordinances of 1944, and the statute of 1947, had established the right to vote, but within a so-called double college system, in which one European vote equaled eight Algerian votes, much in the same way as slaves in the United States were once considered three-fifths of a man. Within France itself, meanwhile, Algerians supposedly held full French citizenship, yet there, too, surveillance and all sorts of special laws restricted them. Such are the contradictions of Herrenvolk democracy.[28]

In France, the links between colonialism and racism, and, for that matter, anti-Semitism, become terribly manifest in the person of Maurice Papon, who organized deportations of Jews under the Vichy regime in the 1940s, served in the French colonial administration of the 1950s, and who in his function as Paris chief of police presided over a veritable pogrom against Algerians on October 17, 1961. After a peaceful protest march by thousands of Algerians, police fired machine guns into the crowd and then drove demonstrators into the Seine to drown. Six thousand Algerians were herded into a sports stadium, where many died in police custody. Over two hundred people were known to have died, hundreds were reported missing, and corpses appeared all along the Seine. According to some witnesses, Papon had several dozen Algerians clubbed to death in front of his eyes in the courtyard of the police prefecture.[29] The official police-led cover-up and the mainstream press had it that the Algerians opened fire and that the police had to restore "law and order."[30]

What is clear, and what the recent French election demonstrates, is that any coherent multicultural or even democratic movement needs to understand that "race matters." As in the United States, race in France is sometimes spoken in code. Two of the key words in the last French election—*immigration* and *crime (securité)*—both encode and euphemize race since the immigrants referred to are clearly not white immigrants from northern Europe, but rather olive-skinned immigrants from North Africa, and the "crime" referred to is not that taking place on the Left Bank, but rather that occurring in the North Africanized *banlieu*. Like "poor whites" and "Reagan democrats," the *petits blancs* of France were expressing a racialized backlash. In France, too, race is sometimes the modality by which class is lived, as we can see in the working-class drift from the Communist Party to the National Front. The electoral strength of Jean-Marie Le Pen, for its part, was intimately linked to the ressentiments provoked by the Algerian War, and the French press during the election was full of reports that Le Pen had personally tortured Algerians during what became known as the Battle of Algiers. Le Pen, for his part, does not speak in code: he defends "white Christian civilization" and denounces Jews and Arabs alike.

At times, the debate over race becomes a kind of triangular trade of ideas crisscrossing France, Brazil, and the United States. In a widely disseminated essay entitled "On the Cunning of Imperialist Reason," French sociologists Pierre Bourdieu and Loic Wacquant single out African American political theorist Michael Hanchard, and specifically his 1994 book *Orpheus and Power* concerning "black consciousness movements" in Brazil, as an example of the "cunning" of imperial reason.[31] In the contemporary period, according to Bourdieu and Wacquant, US imperialism uses people of color such as Hanchard, presumably "above suspicion" because of their race, to promulgate multiculturalism and the "Mcdonaldization" of thought. The targeting of Hanchard is ironic in that he writes from a densely theoretical and historical perspective, informed by the thought of Fanon, Gramsci, and many others. Hanchard addresses the intersection of class, race, and ideology in undermining black Brazilian efforts to form a strong resistance movement to Brazilian-style racism. But for the two French sociologists, Hanchard unilaterally exports the US "folk concept of race" into a society substantially without racism. In shrill and hyperbolic language, they call Hanchard's work "ethnocentric poison" and a "brutal ethnocentric intrusion."

The Bourdieu/Wacquant essay demonstrates the perils of drawing overly bold lines between nation-states, so that even generally progressive thinkers like Bourdieu and Wacquant fail to see the common racial patterns that bind the countries of the Black Atlantic. The two sociologists construct a viral approach to the circulation of ideas in a manner entirely out of keeping with the drift of Bourdieu's own work on "cultural fields." Their essay offers a broad and undifferentiated caricature of US intellectual trends—they equate multiculturalism with imperialism, make naive misstatements about the current state of scholarship on race in Brazil, and formulate an agenda-driven idealization of the Brazilian racial situation.[32] In "La nouvelle vulgate planetaire," Bourdieu and Wacquant evoke the possibility, as an example of the absurd, of a book called *Racist Brazil*, on the analogy of a French book by Michel Wieviorka entitled *La France raciste*. In fact, however, many books have already been written, mostly by Brazilians, books whose titles, if not precisely "Racist Brazil," carry exactly that same charge. Abdias do Nascimento's *O genocidio do negro brasileiro* (*The Genocide of Brazilian Blacks*) provides one example of such a book, but then perhaps Bourdieu and Wacquant might argue that Abdias drank "ethnocentric poison" during his stay as visiting professor at State University of New York at Buffalo when he fled the Brazilian dictatorship in the 1970s. Indeed, black Brazilians, like black US citizens, have been denouncing racism since the country's beginnings, and in the Brazilian case, going back to the seventeenth-century maroon republic of Palmares. Blind to broader patterns in the nations formed by colonialism and slavery, Bourdieu and Wacquant basically argue that only one of the three countries under discussion here is racist: the United States. Resurrecting discredited Luso-tropicalist notions, they argue that Hanchard injects US dichotomous thinking into Brazil's putative "racial democracy." But in fact, the critique of racism is common in Brazil—it animates scholarship, activism, journalism, and popular culture.[33] Therefore the notion that the race-obsessed Hanchard brought "ethnocentric poison" into Brazil gets the causality backward: Hanchard went to Brazil to study the black movement because that movement was already denouncing Brazilian-style racism. In their rescue narrative of Brazil from the (black) gringo, the two French sociologists have silenced not only the intellectual agency of the African American Left but also that of Brazilian intellectuals.

For many years, indeed, the scholarly/intellectual consensus has been that Brazilian racism tends to be covert and even "cordial," with less obvious or explicit hostility, but with equally disempowering effects. While Brazil has rarely had an officially declared "color line," black intellectuals like Abdias de Nascimento claim that Brazil has procured all the advantages of apartheid, for its white elite, while avoiding the racial tensions that accompany apartheid per se. Many analysts, furthermore, point to a kind of convergence, as the United States moves from black-white polarity to a more multipolar system, while Brazil moves toward the politicization of racial identities.

As long as one speaks of epidermic appearances ("We are all mixed.") or of atmospherics (the apparent lack of tensions and hostilities marked as directly racial), the Brazilian situation seems more "livable," at least for whites. But as soon as one poses the crucial question of economic, political, and institutional power, the Brazilian model seems far less appealing. (Hopefully, the election of a progressive coalition led by Luiz Inacio Lula da Silva, "Lula," will begin to remedy the situation.) It is no longer possible to confuse the absence of racial tension with the presence of equality and justice. It is of course true that certain features of Brazilian life and society do lend a humane face to what is in structural terms a racist society. Unlike the United States and South Africa under apartheid, Brazilian history has not been marked by ghettos, segregation, lynching, racialized rioting, or Ku Klux Klan–style white supremacist groups. But Brazilian-style racism in this sense more closely resembles the assimilationist Portuguese and French colonial models, which allowed for a minuscule colonized elite into the charmed circle of inclusion, than the Anglo-segregationist model. For us, it is not a question of better or worse, but rather one of two modalities of Euro-domination, one rooted in

Anglo-segregationist racism, the other in Latin assimilationist racism. While one offers a slap in the face, the other offers a suffocating, paternalistic embrace, along with an occasional slap in the face. Both ultimately work to reproduce white domination.

Yet if racism is a uniquely American problem, as Bourdieu and Wacquant seem to imply, why is it that the black, mulatto, and mestizo majority of Brazilians remains so vastly underrepresented in positions of prestige and projection in Brazil, including in the media? Why are blacks virtually nonexistent in the higher echelons of the military, the diplomatic corps, and the government? And why are blacks underrepresented in the universities and the congress, but overrepresented in the favelas, the prisons, and in the ranks of the unemployed? Of the 50,000 students at the University of São Paulo, only 500 are black, a ratio of 1:100 in a society that is half black and mestizo. It is precisely such discrimination that has provoked the current interest in forms of affirmative action in Brazil. Race, in Brazil, comes commingled with class: it is both a kind of salt rubbed into the wounds of class and a wound in itself. Indeed, the cliché that blacks are discriminated against only because they are poor, forgets that neither do the nonblack poor carry the specific stigma generated by racialized slavery and white supremacist ideology, nor that the perception of blackness as an index of poverty (and thus powerlessness) is itself an oppressive burden to bear in a stratified society. Another irony is that the kinds of social problems that Bourdieu and Wacquant see as plaguing the United States—police brutality, disproportionate incarceration, corrupted democracy, and so forth—hold equally true in Brazil, yet in the Brazilian case they provoke no outrage in the two authors. Thus an official report by the government of the state of São Paulo reveals that in the year 2000, the police killed over a thousand people in the state, that most of the victims were innocent or merely suspects, and that over half were shot in the back.

So what explains Bourdieu and Wacquant's desire to make Brazil as a nation innocent, if not a desire to make the United States uniquely guilty? Admittedly, the United States has contributed to Brazil's social problems— through support for the dictatorship, the dictatorship's militarization of the police, and through the devastating social effects of a US-led globalization. But Brazilians themselves also bear responsibility for the class and racial injustices of their society. US imperialism does not explain native Brazilian ethnocide, the present-day disempowerment of black Brazilians or a slavery that began before the United States existed and lasted long after it had expired in the northern country.

Despite the apparent absence of racially motivated violence, a barely concealed racial subtext clearly lurks behind the everyday inequities of Brazilian social life, for example in the aforementioned para-police and police murder of so-called marginals, most of whom are black or of mixed race. What is confusing in the Brazilian case is the fact that those who kill the marginals might also include people of color. Historically, the major confrontations of Brazilian history—the Portuguese against the Indians, Palmares, and Canudos—have not simply opposed white against black; there have always been people of color on both sides, but always within the larger trajectory of white domination and the ideology of "whitening." The situation lacks the stark clarity of a Rodney King/white police confrontation. Indeed, the recent Rodney King–like case in the São Paulo favela Diadema in 1997, in which a man with a camcorder registered the police abuse and murder of some favela residents, in this sense proved revealing. Although the perpetrators, the police, tended to be lighter and their victims darker, both sides were arguably "integrated." But is this kind of "integration" to be cheered, just because some black police also kill and some whites also fall victim to the killings? The world was horrified by the police murder of Amadou Diallo in New York, but it is important to remember that the police in cities like Rio de Janeiro and São Paulo murder at a rate roughly thirty times that of New York. Both race and class are lived differently in Brazil and the United States. In Brazil, it is often said, class hides race, whereas in the United States, race hides class. But it would be wrong to construe this difference as "better."

The debate around Hanchard's work provides a good example of the ways debates travel within transnational power formations, resulting in recombinations and recontextualizations as the work becomes filtered through (and clashes with) other historically conditioned schemata, prisms, and grids. Here we have tried to interrogate intellectual encounters as historically shaped and socially situated forms of interlocution, all within a transnational Black Atlantic context. The mapping of intellectual work should not be enclosed within clearly demarcated nation-state boundaries, with overly bold lines between native and foreign, points of origin and reception. What is needed, rather, is a sense of overlapping chronotopes, of crisscrossing messages and multidirectional channels, as part of the global configuration of power shaped by centuries of a Euro-colonial hegemony not yet quite "post." Indeed, in our view, all cultural studies should be transformed into multicultural and international studies, precisely because no national culture, especially in the age of the globalized mass media, comes pure and uncontaminated by the cultures of close or distant neighbors.

Our tale of traveling multiculturalism in three countries reveals a partly phantasmatic encounter, often with right- and left-wing versions, between various nationalisms, narcissisms, and exceptionalisms, each projecting its heroes and villains. In the US case, ethnocentrism has become armed and dangerous as the Bush regime pursues the preemptive strikes of hyperpower imperialism. But even on the liberal Left, a submerged American ethnocentrism has sometimes given us what we think of as "star-striped multiculturalism," "nationalism with a tan," "rainbow nationalism," or "nationalism in drag." Educational institutions concerned about "diversity" often glimpse multiculturalism through a largely unconscious national-exceptionalist lens that celebrates difference but that does not necessarily deconstruct the nationalist paradigm. But for us, "multiculturedness" is not a US monopoly, nor is multiculturalism the "handmaiden" of US identity politics. And while we have no quarrel with the idea of US uniqueness, we do quarrel with the idea that uniqueness is unique to the United States. We do not quarrel with *l'exception francaise*, either, yet we do not assume that France is uniquely exceptional. All nations have a palimpsest-like complexity and uniqueness of their own; and along with that common uniqueness, we find historical parallels and global links between and across different national formations, especially between nations implicated in broad historical processes like colonialism and slavery. The tacit nationalism of some forms of multiculturalism leads us to miss numerous opportunities for a relational, cross-disciplinary, and transnational analysis. Yet some international critiques of multiculturalism can also encode a covert nationalist agenda premised on a reified ethnonationalist conceptualization of the nation. A truly radical and polycentric multiculturalism, we have tried to suggest here, would call attention to, and try to dismantle, the vestiges of master race democracy wherever they appear.

   This situation calls not only for a reflexivity about national narcissism but also for a transnational examination of the linked modes of institutional racism within diverse spaces in the era of globalization, all seen as rooted in international, historically linked, and contrapuntally imaginable histories. Throughout this essay, we have assumed that we should move beyond the invisible traps of nation-state thinking. Rather than draw clear scholarly lines between nation-states as if they were impenetrable fortresses, any in-depth discussion of the multicultural and postcolonial debates must place often-ghettoized geographies in productive relation. Rather than segregate historical periods and geographical regions and nations into neatly fenced-off areas of expertise, we must assert their interconnectedness. Rather than speak of cultural, racial, and national groups in isolation, we must speak of them in relation, without ever suggesting that their positionings are identical. Histories, geographies, and communities exist not as hermetically sealed entities, but rather as part of a permeable, interwoven relationality, particularly in a transnational age typified by the global travel of images, sounds, goods, and populations. Given the global syncretization of ideas, it is imperative to interrogate the fixed lines drawn between "inside" and "outside," or between one national discourse and another. To draw such lines too rigidly not only proves historically invalid, we have tried to suggest, but also theoretically, methodologically, and even politically debilitating.

Notes

1. The book project, to be entitled "Traveling Multiculturalism," has been contracted by New York University Press. It involves research in France, Brazil, and the United States about the circulation of these debates. We plan to contact leading scholars in the three sites in order to gather, and cite, their views on the key questions discussed in this essay.

2. See Stam, *Tropical Multiculturalism*, 26–27.

3. See Shohat and Stam, *Unthinking Eurocentrism*.

4. For a discussion of this term, see V. N. Voloshinov, *Marxism and the Philosophy of Language*.

5. Michael Ignatieff, "The American Empire."

6. Spanish priest Bartolome de las Casas famously said of the *requerimiento* that it was hard to know whether to laugh or cry at its absurdity.

7. We do not have an umbrella term that might capture the spirit of the work of such diverse figures as—to mention only a minuscule portion of the scholars working out of the three countries under discussion—Gloria Anzaldúa, Joel Zito Araujo, Yves Benot, J. M. Blaut, Alfredo Bosi, Kamau Brathwaite, Jean-Lu Einaudi, Arturo Escobar, Jean Franco, Edouard Glissant, David Theo Goldberg, Lelia Gonzales, Donald Grinde, Carlos Hasenbalg, Robin Kelly, George Lipsitz, Manning Marable, Leda Martins, Abdelwahab Meddeb, Charles Mills, Chandra Mohanty, Clovis Moura, Rosa Amelia Plumelle-Uribe, Mary Louise Pratt, Joao Reis, Joel Ramon, David Roediger, Joel Rufino dos Santos, Edward Said, Louis Sala-Molins, Roberto Schwarz, Ngugi wa Thiongo, Ronaldo Vainfas, Françoise Verges, Emila Viotti da Costa, Patricia Williams, George Yudice, and countless others.

8. Benot, *Massacres Coloniaux*; Stora, *La gangrene et l'oubli*.

9. Caren Kaplan has usefully pointed out the limitations of the "travel" metaphor, which conflates very different forms of travel: forced migration, modernist artistic exile, the imperial grand tour, and so forth. In their passage across borders, some ideas traveled in the holds of ships, while others traveled in first-class cabins. See Kaplan, *Questions of Travel*.

10. Kymlicka, *Multicultural Citizenship*.

11. For an extended comparison of race and multiculturalism in Brazil and the United States, see Stam, *Tropical Multiculturalism*.

12. See Pike, *The United States and Latin America*.

13. Interestingly, France is the only one of the three countries that defines itself ethnically as the "country of the French," or which specifies a national language. Both the United States of America and the United States of Brazil include no such definitions or restrictions.

14. See Peabody, *"There Are No Slaves in France."*

15. Indeed, it strikes us that many commentators on US history, including French

commentators, are sometimes overly generous to the United States. François Furet, for example, in his contribution to Pierre Nora's *Lieux de mémoire* (*Realms of Memory*), recapitulates a common view that contrasts the French Revolution, haunted by the ghost of the repressed ancien régime, with the tabula rasa, void of an aristocracy, of the American Revolution, without acknowledging that the American Revolution, by dispossessing Native Americans and enslaving Africans, also created a new democratic nobility, new hierarchies, and new "tops" and "bottoms."

16. See, for an elaboration of this argument, Buck-Morss, "Hegel and Haiti."

17. See Viotti da Costa, *The Brazilian Empire*, 57.

18. Quoted in Benot, *Diderot*, 172.

19. Sartre, "Orphée Noir"; Fanon, *The Wretched of the Earth*.

20. Kly, *The Anti-Social Contract*.

21. Mills, *The Racial Contract*, 1; Roussea, *A Discourse on Inequality*.

22. Ibid., 14.

23. Quoted in Buck-Morss, "Hegel and Haiti."

24. Quoted in ibid., 828.

25. Thompson, *Flash of the Spirit*; Gilroy, *The Black Atlantic*.

26. *Do the Right Thing* (directed by Spike Lee, 1989); *La haine* (directed by Mathieu Kassovitz, 1995); *Cidade de Deus* (*City of God*; directed by Kátia Lund and Fernando Meirelles, 2002).

27. See Viotti da Costa, *The Brazilian Empire*, 234–35.

28. See Stora, *La gangrène et l'oubli*.

29. Vidal-Naquet, *Mémoire*, 150.

30. The history of these events is recorded in scrupulous and painful detail in Einaudi, *La Bataille de Paris*. Interestingly, the press accounts of Papon's trial, imprisonment, and subsequent release tend only to mention the incidents involving anti-Semitism, not the official massacre of hundreds of Algerians.

31. Bourdieu and Wacquant, "The Cunning of Imperial Reason"; Hanchard, *Orpheus and Power*.

32. We will not try here to undo all the folded misrepresentations in this second Bourdieu/Wacquant essay, "La nouvelle vulgate planetaire," *Le Monde Diplomatique*, May 2000. Indeed, John French, in an essay entitled "The Missteps of Anti-imperialist Reason," has already written a careful but devastating critique of the Bourdieu/Wacquant argument. French points out the innumerable errors of evaluation in their text. French, "Passos em falso da razao antiimperialista."

33. At the time of the centennial of the abolition of slavery in 1988, protest manifestos and position statements bore such titles as "One Hundred Years of Lies" and "Discommemoration," while a persistent editorial leitmotif was the idea that "slavery has not really ended." In 1988, even the samba school pageants protested the "farce of abolition." (The theme of slavery not having ended also functions as a major leitmotif in Brazilian rap music.) Even the popular newspaper *Folha de São Paulo* recognized the fact of a generalized racism in a 1995 special investigative report entitled "Cordial Racism" (in a play on Sergio Buarque de Holanda's celebrated description of the Brazilian as "cordial man").

The Ballad of the Sad Café: Israeli Leisure,

Palestinian Terror, and the Post/colonial Question

✪ ✪ ✪

REBECCA L. STEIN

Long after the arguments in Edward Said's *Orientalism* (1978) have acquired both academic and popular currency, the degree to which Said's *The Question of Palestine* (1979) remains a bold intervention into dominant US discourse on the Middle East seems remarkable. At the most rudimentary level, Said's text aimed to establish the very existence of Palestine and the Palestinian people, and to trace the genealogy of their displacement—both materially from their land and figuratively from the landscape of both Israeli and US history and collective memory. No less pressing, at the time of the text's publication, was the relatively uncharted work of systematically inserting Zionism into the history of European imperialism. In 1979, at a time when the signifier *Palestine* still resounded with insurgence for many US audiences, *The Question of Palestine* was both a courageous project and, as Said noted in the text's introduction, a rather lonely one—the loneliness of one who articulates the heretofore unsaid.[1] While the existence of the Palestinian people is no longer in question in the present, an aura of insurgence still haunts Said's colonial claim. Indeed, it is only very recently that academics, journalists, and activists in the United States have been authorized to speak openly about the coloniality of the Zionist project without the threat of sanction, without the need to defend against the charge of anti-Semitism—and, for Jewish critics, that highly problematic label of "self-hater," which has long done the work of disciplining Jewish dissent and delimiting the terms of intelligible Jewish identity.

Yet the parameters of permissible discourse about Zionism and the Jewish state have indeed shifted in the last few decades—and quite markedly at the turn of the millennium alone. The genesis of this shift has been multiple.

Certainly, it has been enabled by the success with which the Palestinian national movement and resistance struggle of the 1980s and early 1990s managed to export its historical claims, demands, and images of defiance into the US arena. The Oslo Accords of 1993, for all their flaws, bestowed international legitimacy on the Palestinian struggle for self-determination in relatively unprecedented ways. So, too, must one credit the World Conference against Racism of 2001, with its popularization of an anticolonial critique of the Zionist project. But it is certainly the magnitude of Israeli violence and repression in the years following the dissolution of the (so-called) peace process that enabled—indeed, required—this vocabulary to emerge in new ways and with new force. The spring of 2002 constitutes a dramatic case in point: amid the largest and most brutal Israeli incursion into the Occupied Palestinian Territories since the 1967 war, US audiences bore witness to a significant change in the texture of popular discourse. What exploded onto the screens of televisions, and in the pages of newspapers, was not merely the language of "military occupation" and (to a lesser degree) "colonialism" but also word of "war crimes," "ethnic cleansing," and even "genocide"—language deployed, particularly in the aftermath of the Israeli incursion into Jenin, as a way to name and make sense of Israel's military presence in the West Bank and the Gaza Strip. Certainly, some of these terms proved much more accurate than others. Nonetheless, what merits attention is the fact of their collective emergence within a discursive landscape that had long been fiercely policed for anything that smacked of anti-Israeli sentiment.

All of this does not mean to suggest the wholesale radicalization of US discourse and politics on Palestine during the period under discussion. In the spring of 2002, as Israeli fatalities mounted from a campaign of Palestinian militarism inside the state's 1967 borders, US audiences also witnessed a frightening return to classic Zionist rhetorics, and racist defenses of the Jewish state, particularly from within the mainstream Jewish American community. Of course, Israel's official discourse on the need for self-defense in the face of Arab terror proved a newly persuasive one for a US public still stinging from the pain and affront of September 11, 2001. What one witnessed was a polyphonic discursive sphere in which the language of Zionist coloniality and Palestinian terror competed for space and audibility within the mainstream media in relatively unprecedented ways. These complications—and, at times, contradictions—were exemplified in the language of President Bush, who lent his support to the Israeli administration in their battle against "terror" even as he experimentally deployed the term *Palestine*—a term bearing the marks of the Palestinian struggle for self-determination.

Taking my cue from this moment of discursive ambivalence and possibility in the US media, and building on the tradition of (post)colonial criticism that we have inherited from Said and others, this essay investigates the ways in which mainstream Israeli print media responded to this same moment—that is, the moment of heightened Palestinian militarism and escalating Israeli violence in the Occupied Territories in the spring of 2002. I am interested in a rather unlikely narrative that circulated in Hebrew- and English-language newspapers of this period.[2] As Israel's occupation grew in intensity, violence, and scope, and as Israelis were faced with a virtually unprecedented wave of Palestinian "suicide bombings" against civilian targets inside the state,[3] Israeli newspapers began to talk a lot about *leisure*. In order to dramatize and render intelligible the Israeli experience of Palestinian militarism, and the radical ways in which it had transformed daily life, the mainstream media told a story of Jewish leisure practices, and consumer patterns more generally, under attack.[4] At the center of this discourse stood the café or the coffeehouse, a central institution of Israeli bourgeois public life (and arguably of colonial metropolitan culture in broader terms),[5] now targeted by Palestinian militants in relatively unprecedented ways.

Yet the Israeli investment in the café as an index of Palestinian violence far exceeded its material status as terror's target. In the Israeli media, cafés as signs became heavily burdened with symbolic meaning—configured as superlative instances and indices of Israel in a time of crisis. Cafés were asked to carry a metonymic charge: to stand in for the Jewish nation-state and its fragility. The story of cafés under attack thus did the work of representing and managing popular anxiety about the mounting threat of Palestinian terror. Cafés also performed the labor of deflection; by telling the story of the current moment through an account of Israeli leisure institutions under attack, the café discourse elided not merely the concurrent Israeli violence against Palestinians in the West Bank and Gaza, where the toll on daily life was much more severe, but the histories of Israeli aggression and dispossession of which the current crisis was constitutive. The grossly myopic focus on Israeli loss in the face of enormous violence and devastation in the West Bank certainly constituted the narrative's greatest offense.

When one reads the café as metonym, a multiple set of story lines emerges in the Israeli media. Some are unsurprising—such as the stories of good citizenship and patriotism that respond to this moment of national threat by enunciating through a discourse on leisure-based consumption. One also sees a set of restorative narratives that take the café as their occasion to re-embed the dominant (and fictional) terms of Israeli nationness. This essay pays particular attention to the moment at which Israeli violence returns to the narrative from which it had been expunged. I will argue that the press's account of leisure under attack was haunted by precisely that which it sought to refuse—namely, the historic and enduring injustices of the Israeli settler-national project. To read the leisure narrative thus is by no means to refuse the very real and lasting trauma with which cafés have been associated in the lives of many Israelis. Rather, it is to consider how cafés—both as institutions and as signs—have been asked to carry the burden of this trauma and, in tandem, of the Israeli aggression and vitriol of this political moment, as well as the histories with which they resonate.

This essay draws heavily on postcolonial theory, particularly the (in)-famous textual strategies and analytics of Homi Bhabha and his project of reading the texts of Western imperialism against their grain with an eye to their ambivalences, indeterminacies, and double-sessions. For Bhabha, "ambivalence" was a way to name the "conflictual economy of colonial discourse," the perpetual slippages of its authority (epistemological and otherwise), the impossibility of a seamless disavowal of its violence.[6] In adapting Bhabha's reading strategy for my study of Israeli political culture, I want to tell a rather different story of ambivalence—its locations, histories, and subjects. Rather than resting on the conflictual economy of the psyche or the sign, the forms of ambivalence that I am tracing within the mainstream texts of Israeli settler-nationalism are highly situated and historical. My aim is not to position the café narrative—or the print media, by extension—as a superlative site of ambivalence/resistance. Rather, it is to suggest that it functions as a quotidian instance of a broader political field, that what haunted the pages of Israeli newspapers in the spring of 2002 were precisely those instabilities/aporias at issue in other, more explicitly political narratives, spaces, and institutions (e.g., on the floor of the Israeli parliament; in the official policies and rationales of Israeli politicians, demographers, and military strategists; in the texts of state-sponsored history books). In the broadest terms, then, I deploy postcolonial analytics to document the ways in which dominant Israeli discourse at the turn of the twenty-first century has made sense of the enduring coloniality of the Israeli national project—that is, the forms of coloniality that remain at play within the Occupied Territories and within the state itself, and the histories of coloniality on which these forms build and with which they resonate.

Reading the Café

To understand the leisure narrative, one must first grasp the political landscape out of which it emerged. The narrative took shape in the Israeli media during the spring of 2002, at a time when violence was erupting in new forms, and with new intensity, in Palestine and Israel. The second Palestinian uprising, a response to the failures of the Oslo process and the growing poverty and unemployment in the Occupied Territories, was in its second year. Unlike the first uprising (1988–93), this second one was growing increasingly militarized. Beginning in the winter of 2001, in a response to the Palestinian uprising, the Israeli Defense Forces (IDF) had gone on the offensive in the West Bank, shelling and demolishing houses, razing orchards and crops. In tandem, the Israeli government (now under the leadership of prime minister Ariel Sharon, elected in February 2001) was continuing to expand the settlement infrastructure and to fortify the military closure of the West Bank, effectively restricting Palestinian movement both in and out of Israel, and between towns and villages in the West Bank. Extrajudicial killings by the state of (so-called) wanted Palestinians were also on the rise. By the end of February 2002, Israeli forces had killed more than one thousand Palestinians by these and other means. In response to the Israeli offensive, armed Palestinian groups and individuals escalated their attacks against Israeli installations in the Occupied Territories and began to move their struggle increasingly inside the Green Line. By February of 2002, some 250 Israelis, the vast majority of them civilians, had been killed.[7] Inside the state, the rising death toll and growing fear of random violence profoundly altered daily life and popular politics, fueling the political shift to the right. Many Israeli Jews spoke of the need for self-defense at all costs.

The café discourse emerged most powerfully in the wake of March 9, 2002, after a young Palestinian bomber detonated his charge in a crowded café (Café Moment) in an affluent West Jerusalem neighborhood. The blast proved strong and deadly, killing eleven men and women and injuring some fifty others. In the days that followed the bombing, the café became a shrine of sorts, a place of secular homage.[8] Neighborhood mourners decked the sidewalk and the demolished storefront with flowers and memorial candles, and young girls gathered to recite psalms for the dead, their bodies draped in the Israeli flag—scenes which harkened back to the popular acts of public memorialization (therein, performative acts of citizenship) that followed the 1995 assassination of prime minister Yitzhak Rabin. Israel had experienced attacks like these before, most recently during the wave of bus bombings of the mid-1990s—a response to the Hebron massacre of 1994, the assassination of a prominent Hamas leader by Mossad agents in 1996, and to the (so-called) peace process more generally.[9] Yet in the winter and spring of 2002, the scope and form of Palestinian militarism began to change. Now, bombings became far more frequent, and they struck new kinds of targets. Bombers began to set their sights on places of middle-class consumption and leisure in the very heart of the Israeli metropole — including a pizzeria, a hotel lobby, a supermarket, a disco, and a number of cafés. While cafés were not unprecedented targets, they were becoming more frequent ones in the spring of 2002 — a change that many Israelis understood as a concerted shift in Palestinian strategy. In addition to the bombing of Café Moment, the month of March 2002 alone witnessed a bombing at a Tel Aviv coffeehouse (claiming far fewer lives) and word of a thwarted attack at another Jerusalem venue, prevented by a vigilant waiter. Nonetheless, the greatest number of attacks, and subsequent lives lost, from Palestinian bombings occurred at the more traditional sites of dense working-class assembly, such as army and settler installations in the Occupied Territories and inside Israel, open-air markets, and public buses — the latter remaining the favored site of militarism, as it had been for nearly a decade.

Yet in the mainstream Israeli media, the perception of Palestinian militarism and its preferred targets was otherwise. As the death toll from bombings mounted in March and early April, the Israeli press turned its attention to the café as the locus of Palestinian terror. The image of the Jewish state under fire was illustrated through a story of leisure and its loss — the loss of the café as a space of daily, ritualized consumption. The popularity of this narrative reached its peak in the weeks prior to the most brutal phase of the Israeli incursion, which began on March 29, 2002. Nonetheless, the narrative circulated at a time of disproportionate violence, when Israeli aggression in the West Bank was exacting a much greater toll on the daily lives of Palestinians.

Consider an article from *Ha'aretz* newspaper — the Hebrew daily of the Israeli intelligentsia. On March 10, the day following the Café Moment bombing, the newspaper broke from its standard idiom of reportage to decry in highly personalized form both the cost in human life and the violence afflicted on the Israeli way of life, with the café at its center: "This is our café," began the article, which was featured prominently on the first page of the newspaper, just below its masthead: "We came here in the morning for an espresso and a croissant. We came here in the evening for a [beer]. To grasp what is left of normalcy, of our secular sanity. To grasp at what is left of our way of life." [10] From the vantage of an intimate eyewitness, the paragraphs that followed surveyed the scene of death and destruction in the immediate aftermath of the blast. In blunt staccato prose, the article narrated the landscape of carnage: "the smell of burning," the "charred human flesh," fragments of human bodies amid the shattered glass, the screams of the evacuated survivors, the stillness of the dead. In turn, it offered a forceful political critique, lambasting the Left for naming settlement building and military occupation as the cause of the current political crisis. The author disagreed, telling his alternative political narrative through the figure of the café: "When the police sappers walk among the dead youth, searching for another explosive device, it does not seem to be so [a War for the Peace of the Settlements].[11] It seems very, very different. Maybe the War for Moment [Café]? Maybe the War for a chance of a Western society to survive in the Middle East? . . . [W]e can no longer keep fooling ourselves. This is a war about the morning's coffee and croissant. About the beer in the evening. About our very lives."

That a piece like this—in its highly editorial prose, in its lyrical eulogy—should appear on the front page was indeed unusual for a newspaper committed to the serious reporting of the *New York Times* variety.[12] Yet this was only the most dramatic instance of a discourse becoming ubiquitous in Israeli media of this moment, one that recurred with an almost absurd repetitiveness, returning to the same tropes and story lines. Print media and talk shows alike decried the sacrifice of cafés to Palestinian terror. In melancholic tones, they chronicled the "chilling quiet" that had befallen café districts in Tel Aviv and Jerusalem. In defiance, they spoke of the ad hoc efforts of residents to "take back the cafés" in their neighborhoods,[13] and hailed victims of café bombings as exemplary Israeli citizens, as the "Everyman, [as] mainstream Israel." In turn, the figure of the coffeehouse was used to narrate the decline of the peace process and thus to tell the story of the current political moment: "[The] Oslo peace agreement meant that we should be able to have a cup of coffee in Baghdad. Instead it has turned out that we cannot even have a cup of coffee in Tel Aviv."[14] So ubiquitous was the café discourse that it became the subject of Israeli bumper stickers, made its way into the political rhetoric of the Israeli housing minister,[15] appeared in Ariel Sharon's national address from the Knesset floor,[16] and was exported into the US media, where it circulated in similar—although less pervasive—ways. The café narrative acquired a complicated performative status; its very citation seemed to produce the effects of a pledge of allegiance—marking the speaker as in and of the Israeli nation-state.

Many of these accounts, particularly those appearing in the English-language media, borrowed from the post–September 11 narrative of defiance through consumerism, whereby the abnegation of normal consumptive patterns was deemed a victory for terrorists (as in, "If we don't go out for drinks, then 'they' win").[17] Die-hard customers were portrayed as heroes who persevered in the face of Palestinian terror—evidence of the lasting power of the Israeli people in the face of this assault on their existence. "If you want to understand [the state of Israel], come to Caffit [café] for breakfast," read an Israeli editorial from early April. "This is a people that aren't going away. They are not even going to stop drinking coffee."[18] Several daily papers interviewed the dedicated patrons that returned to their favorite coffee bars in the face of the current crisis: "Just about the most patriotic thing you can do now is go out and have a drink."[19] Burdened with new symbolic import, those cafés that remained open for table service became privileged sites for the performance of national allegiance. One's very presence in a café was rendered a superlative act of loyalty to the state in its battle against terror. Consumption itself became an act of defiance, and the consumer, the defiant citizen.

More than leisure practices were at issue. Also under fire was the possibility of public assemblage in café spaces. It was thus with considerable shock that West Jerusalemites learned of local plans to convert coffeehouses into take-out only facilities. Consider the following testimony of a Jewish Jerusalem resident, published as a personal essay on the crisis in a weekly Israeli magazine: "While [picking up] my son [after school] . . . I [ran] into [a] neighbor, who told me that the Aroma Café . . . had moved all its tables and chairs so customers could no longer sit there. At first I didn't really understand what she was saying, and she had to repeat herself before I let the reality of that statement sink in: Aroma had become a take-out place."[20] As the ones mentioned before, this story was a rather pervasive one. The emergence of café take-out became a matter of national importance that was covered by all major Israeli daily newspapers, as it reflected a radical shift in the landscape of civil society.[21] True to Habermas's telling, take-out threatened the space and possibility of social intercourse itself. The Israeli public feared an erosion of the public sphere—the loss of those spaces in which, through consumption, disparate patrons were rendered social equals and consumer-subjects became citizens.

While the loss of cafés threatened with a loss of citizenship and its practices, the threat of violence in café spaces (and the discourse that attended it) also inaugurated a new set of national subject positions. Not only consumers but also workers in the café sector were being called to duty for the nation-state in new ways. The Israeli press was particularly attentive, in this regard, to the case of a young West Jerusalem waiter who detected a Palestinian man armed with explosives at the entrance of a crowded coffeehouse ("Hero of the day," he was hailed by one popular Hebrew daily).[22] As the labor of racial profiling—of discerning terrorist from tourist—increasingly became the domain of café employees, labor in this leisure sector was increasingly marked with the semiotics of patriotic citizenship. Indeed, as the café acquired the status of a battleground,[23] the difference between waiters and armed guards began to blur; all were being conscripted into this war, all were being hailed not merely as citizens but as citizen-*soldiers* in new ways.

Thus it was that cafés became a kind of staging ground for many of the larger political questions and issues of the moment. One such issue was the problem of the border. At this moment, much of the Jewish Israeli public appeared united on the need to enclose the nation-state, to fortify and render it insular, not merely with armed checkpoints and border police, or with military closures and visa restrictions to keep Palestinians out, but with heavily fortified walls that would demarcate and protect (or so the story went) the edges of the nation-state.[24] Campaigns of Palestinian militancy inside the 1967 borders generated the desire for such enclosures even as they betrayed them as impossible fantasies. It was both in partial recognition of this fantasy and of the desire to preserve it that borders began to proliferate and move inward, to the heart of the public sphere—becoming "borders" of restaurants, shopping malls, and cafés. Now, waiters performed not merely as soldiers but as border guards of sorts. The café and its thresholds began to function as a kind of national enclosure writ small.

Cafés and Zionist Fantasy

As I have noted, cafés were not the only institutions targeted by Palestinian militants over the course of the last decade. In strictly numeric terms, both regarding attacks and lives lost, the public bus had long constituted the favored locus of Palestinian violence. The choice of buses as targets began in earnest in the mid-1990s as Palestinian militants worked to disrupt the initial workings of the Oslo peace process.[25] Yet as an institution, the bus failed to capture the Israeli imagination, to acquire symbolic value, to become mobilized as national instance. This is not to suggest an Israeli failure to take buses seriously as loci of terror. After each attack, conversation about the need to avoid bus travel would invariably proliferate in the Israeli media, and the number of users would precipitously decline (at least among populations with the means to travel otherwise). And at times of political extremity or during an election period, buses have been called into service as mobile billboards (in 1994, after the assassination of Rabin, calling on the Jewish Israeli public to preserve "tolerance" and say no to violence; in 2002, calling on the public to reelect Ariel Sharon). Yet buses have not been burdened with a set of national meanings exceeding their functional status. They could serve as *messengers* of meaning, but they did not themselves become inscribed, as signs, with meaning—they were not hailed as placeholders of the nation-state.

Why, then, the café? As an institution, it has long enjoyed a privileged place in the history and mythology of the Israeli nation-state.²⁶ Cafés, which proliferated in Tel Aviv from the very inception of the city in the early 1900s, were both a staple of the urban landscape (installed in large numbers along the city's main boulevards) and proved crucial in producing the space and geographical imagination of Tel Aviv as an explicitly *Western* city, that is, a city made in the likeness of Western European cosmopolitan centers and defined against the supposed premodernity of its urban neighbor, the Palestinian city of Jaffa.²⁷ In collective Ashkenazi memory, the story of Zionist cultural and intellectual life of the 1940s and 1950s remains intimately tied to café society (where, "sitting cheek by jowl, would be authors, architects, artists, public figures, actors and all the rest of the intelligentsia").²⁸ The labors of some of Israel's most important cultural figures (famously, poet Natan Alterman) is popularly traced back to particular Tel Aviv coffeehouses (e.g., Café Cassit). In turn, select Jerusalem cafés (e.g., Café Atara) are celebrated for their service to the early Zionist militias.²⁹ At issue is the importance of the café in the history of the Jewish state and the fabric of secular, Zionist modernity.³⁰

Cafés continue to do important symbolic national work in the present. The European-style café remains a defining feature of Tel Aviv's urban, Ashkenazi centers, continuing the process of demarcating and safeguarding the Western character of Israeli cosmopolitanism—a character growing increasingly phantasmatic in the face of the ever expanding nonwhite, and non-Israeli, working-class peripheries. Moreover, the mainstream Israeli and Jewish-diasporic imaginations of the city and its subjects remain linked to this leisure institution ("This is a city in which you are what your Friday café is," wrote the *Jerusalem Post* in 1989).³¹ In West Jerusalem, where coffeehouses have historically been less plentiful, cafés have been asked to do a different kind of work in the late twentieth and early twenty-first century: not merely to demarcate an explicitly Western form of cosmopolitanism but to preserve a *secular* Israeli geography within a city increasingly dominated by religious interests and communities. In recent decades, those cafés that have remained open on Saturday, in violation of religious dictates to the contrary, have become privileged fronts in the battle between the city's secular and religious populations—occasional targets of religious violence and, in turn, icons of secular defiance.

What these histories and discourses share with the leisure narrative of 2002 is the story of the café as an explicitly Western form of cosmopolitan modernity. The coffeehouse memorialized by the press in 2002 was always a European space and institution, a purveyor not merely of coffee per se but of espresso and croissant, a locus not merely of popular Israeli congress but of bourgeois Western society and taste.[32] In highly literal terms, such representations proved accurate: the cafés that received foremost media attention—and, indeed, those that bore the brunt of Palestinian violence during this period—were located in affluent Ashkenazi neighborhoods heretofore outside the daily circuits of the conflict and its violences. But at issue, again, is the way in which the story of European cafés was asked to function metonymically. The fiction of the metonym was twofold. First, it worked to obscure the historic and iconic status of the coffeehouse in the Arab world and the multiple kinds of Arab coffeehouses (both Palestinian and Mizrahi) that marked the Israeli landscape in the present.[33] But more pointedly, the fiction cohered in the ways in which the café as Euro-Jewish institution was installed to tell the story of the character and composition of a nation-state that, given both its Palestinian and Mizrahi histories, had never been. In the year 2002—as Israeli demographers continued to warn of rising Arab birthrates, the growing community of foreign workers, and the magnitude of the Russian Christian immigration inside the state—this proved a particularly fragile fiction that required vigilant making and remaking in the face of its dissolution.

Empty Landscapes

Perhaps the most ubiquitous trope in this discursive regime was that of *emptiness*—a trope that appeared with remarkable frequency in the Israeli press of this period. In this moment of random and frequent public violence and pervasive fear, the trope certainly told the truth of Israeli public space: in the aftermath of the March 9 bombing, cafés remained empty, as, indeed, did most places of leisure. Numerous articles began their accounts of the current political crisis with a visual sweep of the depopulated urban landscape.[34] They spoke of half-empty cinemas and dwindling numbers of consumers in shopping malls; of restaurants, pubs, and clubs, all suffering from lack of customers. They chronicled the new ease of barhopping on a Saturday night, as a popular route that once took several hours could now be covered in fifteen minutes—due to deserted venues and plentiful parking.[35] Articles noted the "chilling quiet [that had] taken control of [Israeli cities]," and the large number of armed guards outside cafés and restaurants, "watching empty places."[36] They spoke of popular bohemian neighborhoods, where parking was usually at premium, in which now "only a few hardy souls are out wandering the streets."[37]

I do not question the "truth" of these accounts. At issue, again, is their very ubiquity—the fact that the Israeli media invested so heavily in these desolate scapes as a way to enunciate the national crisis.[38] To begin with, the story of emptiness did the work of substitution; it functioned to obscure other landscapes of desolation and other kinds of empty scapes, particularly urban ones, coming into being at this political moment. Perhaps most striking in this regard, and largely ignored by the press, was the sudden absence from Israeli urban centers of Palestinian Arabs, who stayed away in fear of racial profiling by police and armed security guards and of the mounting anti-Arab rage of the Jewish population. Equally apparent, particularly in West Jerusalem, were the declining numbers of Arab residents using public transportation and entering Jewish neighborhoods or shopping districts, deterred by the racist slogans posted outside downtown businesses: "We do not employ Arabs." Or, "Enemies should not be offered livelihood."[39] These other modalities of emptiness, and these fantasies of a city stripped clean of Arabs, went largely unrecorded in the mainstream media, trumped by images of Jewish suffering and absence.

Yet the trope of emptiness also drew on a long discursive history, borrowing from, and resonating with, that most freighted of narratives about the history of the Jewish state, and that most classic of colonial tropes: the myth of "empty land." Empty land represents one of the founding narratives of the early Zionist movement as propagated in the work of Theodore Herzl, Hayyim Nahman Bialik, Max Mandelstamm, and others.[40] As in the larger colonial archive on which this narrative relied, "emptiness" marked the premodern: the sign of a place outside time and history, waiting, indeed beckoning, for Western intervention and development.[41] The founding of Tel Aviv was narrated through this story—that of a European city born out of sand—"an outpost of civilization against barbarism," in Herzl's famous words.[42] Of course, Jaffa was a thriving seaport at the time of Zionist settlement, as Jewish settlers were quick to discover. And much of the rural landscape of Palestine—imagined as uncultivated and sparsely populated—was densely settled by Palestinian Arabs, distributed throughout most of the fertile and cultivable regions.[43] As Zachery Lockman reminds us, early Zionist accounts of emptiness in the Palestine context should also be read metaphorically: not merely as testimonies of a place without people (for this fiction was easily discounted by a tour of the environs) but of a place without "a people," without the recognizable makings of a modern nation(-state).[44] Nonetheless, much of the violence that both preceded and followed Israeli state formation has turned on efforts to repair the gap between this fantasy and its countervailing reality—the effort to produce emptiness where there was none, both through the material dispossession of Palestinians and the more symbolic efforts to remove their traces from the landscape.

In much the same way did the trope resonate with the fantasies of emptiness articulated and enacted in contemporaneous Israeli policy—through new tactics and strategies of dispossession and the reinvigoration of old ones. More pointedly, it gestured toward the reemergence, in Israeli political culture of 2002, of the concept of mass population transfer of the Palestinian population as a means of political solution.[45] As some Israeli analysts argued, the violence and inhumanity of the Israeli incursion into the Palestinian territories seemed motivated by a proximate goal. On this issue, far-right members of the Israeli parliament were clear; should Palestinian violence escalate into a regional war, they warned, Palestinians should anticipate another 1948, another massive expulsion from their homes and lands.[46] Nor were Palestinians from the Occupied Territories the only population identified in such fantasies of ethnic cleansing; rather, in a radical revision of the transfer ideology as it had circulated in the Jewish Israeli political imagination heretofore, Israeli Jews were beginning to imagine the same for the Palestinian citizens of the state.[47]

I want to take seriously the ways in which the story of the empty leisure landscape, as told and retold in the Israeli media, resonated with these histories and contemporary fantasies of Palestinian dispossession. There is an uncanniness here, a way in which the ubiquitous narrative of the empty city both recalled and rehearsed, almost feverishly, the aftermath of such a dispossession—the strange scene of a once inhabited landscape rendered desolate. And yet, there is a crucial reversal at work: Jews, not Palestinian Arabs, were the ones missing from cafés, the once crowded pubs, and restaurants. Such a reversal functioned, perhaps, in recognition of the ways in which another war of dispossession would necessarily rebound into the Jewish state with untold violence.

This narrative transposition deserves careful consideration.[48] Borrowing rather loosely from Gayatri Spivak and her work in reading the British imperial archive against its grain, one can construct the *manifest* terms of the café narrative in terms of a single sentence: "They [the Palestinians] have emptied our cafés."[49] As did Spivak's formulation,[50] I aim to illustrate the kinds of displacements at work here—the "ideological dissimulation of imperialist political economy" at play in Israeli political culture of this period, and the shapes that such dissimulations take through the story of leisure.[51] When one reads the café narrative against its grain, in articulation with the political landscape from which it emerged, it appears that the sentence requires a transposition that returns to the referent for which *café* functions as metonym: "We [the Israelis] have emptied their nation." Read thusly, the story of leisure seems to function not only as a site of deflection and nation making, but also as confession for the past and fantasy about the future.

Postcolonialities and Palestine/Israel

My aim in this essay is, in part, to foster the relatively incipient conversation between theory and the case(s) of Palestine and Israel. To point to the incipient nature of this conversation is not to deny the generations of activists and scholars (including those in Israel) who have boldly insisted on the coloniality of the Zionist project—both on the historic links between the modern project and other European colonial endeavors and the colonial nature of the Israeli state and its occupation in the present.[52] Rather, it is to note the enduring reluctance of most Palestine/Israel scholars, a handful of important exceptions notwithstanding,[53] to take up the postcolonial theoretical rubric. At issue, in part, is the general theoretical conservatism of Middle East studies—a by-product, in part, of its cold war legacy. Yet the logics of postcoloniality as theoretical/historical rubric are also to blame—notably, the well-remarked vagaries of the key term and the ways in which much early postcolonial scholarship failed to adequately heterogenize "the postcolonial" as temporal, historical, and/or geographical index. As many scholars have noted, one product of this failure was a blurring of the differences between nation-states that had undergone decolonization, and those that had transformed into territorialized settler nation-states—states that now enjoyed independence, even as they remained on settled territory and maintained many forms of colonial privilege over conquered populations.[54]

It is for these and other reasons that the notion of a "postcolonial Israel" fails to tell a clear historical narrative—failing to account, for example, for the tensions between Israel's declaration of independent statehood in 1948 and the ways in which Palestinians who remained in the area of the emergent state continued to, as Joseph Massad has noted, "inhabit these spaces as colonial spaces." Of course, since 1967, the problem has become more difficult still.[55] At issue are both settler-nation and military occupation—two different and yet concurrent forms of coloniality, distinct and yet intimately imbricated. In addition, Israeli modalities of coloniality do not only take shape at the fault lines of "Arab versus Jew." As the work of Ella Shohat and Smadar Lavie teaches us,[56] a historically nuanced postcoloniality would also need to consider the ways that Arab Jews (or Mizrahim) were made to live as second-class citizens within a state founded on the notion of Euro-Jewish normativity. What this suggests, as Massad notes, are the ways in which the singularity of the term *postcolonial* radically fails to illustrate the complexities and multiple forms of coloniality (or its postness) in Palestine/Israel in any given time and space.

Interestingly, the historical problems of bringing postcoloniality to the Palestine/Israel context were reinforced by the ways in which Palestine and Palestinians became referenced within postcolonial literature of the early 1990s—the moment of the ascendance of this rubric within the humanities. What one sees at this time, particularly in the work of Homi Bhabha, are highly parenthetical detours through the Palestine/Israel case as a way to tell the story of postcoloniality writ large. In such detours, "the Palestinian" is offered up as a seemingly self-evident instance of displacement, homelessness, or abjection. While "the Israeli" is denied a similarly metonymic status in such literature, it is the absent present that makes such examples possible—implicitly marked as the selfsame locus of power/dominance against which the abject of "the Palestinian" (in its supposed singularity) takes shape. Consider, for example, the conclusion of *Location of Culture*, where Bhabha reflects on Frantz Fanon's story of "the Dirty Nigger": "Whenever these words are said in anger or in hate, whether of the Jew in the estaminet in Antwerp, or of *the Palestinian on the West Bank*, or the Zairian student eking out a wretched existence selling fake fetishes on the Left Bank . . . whenever and wherever I am when I hear a racist, or catch his look, I am reminded of Fanon's evocative essay 'The Fact of Blackness' and its unforgettable opening lines."[57] What is being offered here, as Amit Rai has argued, is a chain of subalternity that threatens to flatten the play of difference: "[Bhabha's] equation of all liminal and dominated groups and subjectivities also risks collapsing their social identities into an ontological correspondence which reduces their distinct struggles into analogous experiences of marginalization."[58] Of course, it is the availability of "the Palestinian on the West Bank" to appear in this list that interests me. This figure—simultaneously situated ("on the West Bank") and legible as a generality (an instance of "the Palestinian people")—takes its place amid the "whenever and wherever" of racism, illustrating a case with generalizable effects. The very legibility of "Palestinian" as parenthetical instance depends on the presumption of a singular referent, bearing radically circumscribed meaning.[59] Invisible in this and other similar asides are the forms of Palestinian history that do not conform to such a story of abjection, the histories and daily ways of being Palestinian that are cosmopolitan, located, enfranchised. Invisible, in turn, are the subaltern subjects and histories that cannot be mapped as easily onto the binary terms of occupier/occupied (e.g., Palestinians with Israeli citizenship,

Arab Jews, Palestinian refugees). My point here is not to protect the cosmopolitan Palestinian subject, but to open up a more varied and internally conflictual landscape of power and identity in the Palestine/Israel case, to make conceptual space for those communities, histories, and subjects who have been rendered invisible by the work of "the exemplar" and its presumed singularity.

In the light of such critiques, why take recourse to postcolonial theory as a way to study Palestine/Israel? In methodological terms, the poststructural theories of power/knowledge on which postcolonial theory builds force a productive rethinking of the normative paradigm of so-called conflict studies with its static story of power/resistance and politics. They offer, instead, an account of the political that radically multiplies both the sites of power and the places and technologies of its refusal. Perhaps most crucially, the mapping of Israel/Palestine onto the global and diachronic geography of the postcolonial refuses to abide by the terms of Israeli exceptionalism. The kind of colonial comparativism in which postcolonial theory engages mounts an important challenge to this most recalcitrant of Israeli state and popular discourses — an argument with at least a half century of violent effects. To insist on situating Israel/Palestine within this broader colonial geography is not only to enable a tracing of legacies of similitude (in terms of colonial violence, institutions, and cultural logics) but also to imagine the possibility of a decolonized future.

Notes

Thanks to editors of this volume for their sharp engagements with successive formulations. A shorter version of this essay was presented at Amherst College in 2002 and appeared in *Theory and Event* 6, no. 3 (2003), available at http://muse.jhu.edu/journals/tae/v006/6.3stein.html. Thanks also to Joel Beinin, Tom Dumm, Judith Frank, Andrew Janiak, Andrew Parker, and Shira Robinson for their critical readings.

1. Said writes: "To the West, which is where I live, to be a Palestinian is in political terms to be an outlaw of sorts, or at any rate very much an outsider. But that is a reality, and I mention it today only as a way of indicating the peculiar loneliness of my undertaking in this book." Said, *The Question of Palestine*, xviii.

2. This essay focuses on a variety of different Israeli newspapers, both Hebrew- and English-language, including *Ha'aretz* (the newspaper of the Israeli intelligentsia, often likened to the *New York Times*), *Yedi'ot Aharonot*, *Ma'ariv* (Israel's largest circulating Hebrew dailies), and the *Jerusalem Post* (an English-language daily with a considerably smaller circulation). All of these newspapers have a national rather than regional or city-specific identity, meaning both that they are consumed across Israel and speak in the idiom of the national, rather than that of the regional.

3. My quotes are meant to signal the ideological nature of this phrase, replete with a story of Islamic and/or Arab fanaticism and its disavowal of the value of human life.

4. Innumerable thanks to Shira Robinson, with whom I discussed the political economy of leisure. See Robinson, "My Hairdresser Is a Sniper."

5. I am particularly thinking of the place of the café in the battles for decolonization in the Algerian and Irish contexts. Gillo Pontecorvo's *Battle of Algiers* (1965) stages this battle most graphically.

6. Homi K. Bhabha, *The Location of Culture*, 85. Note that many scholars, among them Robert Young, argue that the problem with Bhabha's "ambivalence" rests in the story of "agency" it tells, whereby the postcolonial reader is inscribed as the primary agent of struggle in a seeming refusal of material acts of resistance (or, in Young's telling, "resistance by colonized peoples"). I take issue with such objections, whereby "real" politics is thought to rest beyond textual politics. See Young, *White Mythologies*, 149.

7. Amnesty International, *Israel and the Occupied Territories*.

8. Etgar Lefkowitz, "Hundreds Turn Bombed Café into Shrine," *Jerusalem Post*, March 11, 2002.

9. I am referring to the Baruch Goldstein massacre at the Ibrahimi Mosque in February of 1994 and the assassination of Yahya Ayyash in Khan Yunis in January of 1996.

10. In the following, all unmarked translations from the Hebrew are mine.

11. This was a central slogan of the Israeli Left during 2002, one which blamed settlement building and the military occupation for the wave of violence. The slogan punned on the state name for the Lebanon war ("War for the Peace of Galilee").

12. Despite the ubiquity of this narrative, it had its critics, some of whom were published in the Israeli press. For a critical response to this article, see Roman Bronfman, "The Terrorist Ruined His Morning Coffee," *Ha'aretz*, March 13, 2002.

13. Kelly Hartog, "Taking Back the Cafés," *Jerusalem Post*, March 29, 2002.

14. This quote from an Israeli soldier patrolling the streets of Bethlehem appeared in the foreign press: Peter Beaumont, " 'I Don't Want to Be Here . . . But What Would You Do?" *Observer*, April 7, 2002.

15. Natan (Anatoly) Sharansky, "An Open Letter," *Israel Resource Review*, April 9, 2002.

16. In a speech on April 8, 2002, before a special session of the Israeli parliament, Sharon said: "The murderous gangs have a leader, a purpose, and a directing hand. They have one mission: to chase us out of here, from everywhere, from our home in Elon Moreh, and from the supermarket in Jerusalem, *from the café in Tel Aviv* and the restaurant in Haifa." *New York Times*, April 9, 2002; emphasis mine.

17. This imported September 11 logic became particularly apparent in the Israeli English-language media of this moment. For example, a *Jerusalem Post* article quoted a Jewish Israeli mother and son on the merits of eating out: "We can't stop living our normal lives. That's what they [the Palestinian bombers] [*sic*] want us to do. *If we change what we do, then they win*." Ruth Mason, "Personal Lessons in Coping," *Jerusalem Post*, March 20, 2002; emphasis mine.

18. Hirsh Goodman, "Blood, Sweat, and Cappuccino," *Jerusalem Post*, April 8, 2002.

19. Lefkovitz, "Hundreds Turn Café into Shrine."

20. Ruth Mason, "Personal Lessons in Coping."

21. See Shirli Golan-Meiri, "Aroma Branches in Jerusalem Forbid Sitting in Their Spaces" [in Hebrew], *Yedi'ot Aharonot*, March 11, 2002; Lili Galili, "Jerusalem Becomes a City of Take-Out" [in Hebrew], *Ha'aretz*, March 11, 2002; and Efrat Weiss, "It's Impossible to Stop This Moment" [in Hebrew], *Yedi'ot Aharonot*, March 10, 2002.

22. See Efrat Weiss and Sharon Ropa, "Suicide Bomber Detained on Emek Rafayim Street in Jerusalem" [in Hebrew], *Yedi'ot Aharonot*, March 7, 2002; and Etgar Lefkovitz, "Waiter Foils Jerusalem Café Bombing," *Jerusalem Post*, March 8, 2002.

23. *Ha'aretz* put it this way: "People's fear is totally rational; if there are about 30 recreation venues in Jerusalem, and each week one explodes, then going out to recreate is really going out to the front lines." Yoash Foldesh, "Certain Half-Deserted Streets," *Ha'aretz English Edition*, March 17, 2002.

24. For a discussion of the fence in the Israeli press of 2002, see Haim Ramon, "Should a Security Fence Be Built between Israel and the West Bank?" *Jerusalem Report*, February 25, 2002; and Miriam Shaviv, "The Siege of Jerusalem," *Jerusalem Post*, February 1, 2002.

25. It should be noted that buses became targets as early as the 1950s and then reemerged in the 1970s. But it was only in the 1990s that they turned into popular and repeat targets.

26. The iconic status of the café has spawned two recent plays about Israeli history that take the café as their organizing principle: *And Off We Went to Cassit Café* [in Hebrew], by Hanna Marron (performed at the Herzilya Theater Ensemble in the winter of 2002), and *Let's Dance*, by Eldad Lidor, with choreography by Gaby Aldor, (performed at the Hebrew-Arabic Theater of Jaffa).

27. LeVine, *Overthrowing Geography*.

28. Helen Kaye, "Ghosts of the Past," *Jerusalem Post*, February 5, 2002.

29. Herb Keinon, "Culture in a Cup," *Jerusalem Post*, July 28, 2000; Greer Fay Cashman, "Jerusalem's Downtown Café Atara Closing for Good," *Jerusalem Post*, December 22, 2000.

30. For an instance of the iconic status of the café, see, Matan Shiram et al., "Over a Cup of Coffee" [in Hebrew] (Jerusalem: Shiram CMA Ltd., 2000).

31. David Louison, "A Café Society," *Jerusalem Post*, January 6, 1989.

32. For discussion of the cultural politics of Ashkenazi dominance, see Shohat, "Sephardim in Israel."

33. Hattox, *Coffee and Coffeehouses*.

34. Avirama Golan, "The City Turns Its Back" [in Hebrew], *Ha'aretz*, March 10, 2001; and Galili, "Jerusalem Becomes a City of Take-Out."

35. Shira Ben-Simon, "Nightlife Is Dying" [in Hebrew], *Ma'ariv*, April 4, 2002; Noam Vind, "Nowhere to Run" [in Hebrew], *Ma'ariv*, April 4, 2002; Hartog, "Taking Back the Cafés"; Mouin Khalbi, "Here, the Best in the World" [in Hebrew], *Ma'ariv*, April 10, 2002; and Yoash Foldesh, "Certain Half-Deserted Streets."

36. Galili, "Jerusalem Becomes a City of Take-Out."

37. Hartog, "Taking Back the Cafés."

38. Additional references to emptiness include the following: Yair Etinger and Anshel Pepper, "From Day to Day, the Residents Say, the City Is Being Erased" [in Hebrew], *Ha'aretz*, March 22, 2002; Hagit Almakis and Shirli Menzley, "Spot-check

Finds: Large Number of Restaurants and Cafés in Holon and Bat Yam Are Empty and Unprotected" [in Hebrew], *Ma'ariv*, April 4, 2002; Etgar Lefkovitz, "Attacks Leave Capital's Restaurants, Cafés Empty," *Jerusalem Post*, March 12, 2002; and Ilan Shahar, "Whoever Doesn't Have to, Doesn't Go Downtown" [in Hebrew], *Ha'aretz*, March 22, 2002.

39. Neve Gordon, "Where Are the Peaceniks?" *Nation*, April 29, 2002, 4–5.

40. For a recent discussion of the contours of this classic Zionist trope, see Piterberg, "Erasures." Also see Raz-Krakotzkin, "Exile within Sovereignty"; and Raz-Krakotzkin, "Exile within Sovereignty (Continued)."

41. Pratt, "Scratches on the Face of the Country."

42. Herzl, *The Jewish State*, 96.

43. Khaldi, *Palestinian Identity*, 101.

44. Lockman, *Comrades and Enemies*, 26–31.

45. See Blecher, "Living on the Edge." A poll taken by the Jaffee Center for Strategic Studies in the fall of 2001 reported that some 46 percent of Israel's Jewish citizens favored transferring Palestinians out of the territories. See Amnon Barzilai, "More Israeli Jews Favor Transfer of Palestinians, Israeli Arab Poll Finds" [in Hebrew], *Ha'artez*, September 17, 2001.

46. Such were promises made by far-right Knesset member Effi Eytan who, in 2002, openly supported Palestinian mass population transfer. See Ari Shavit, "Dear God, This is Effi," *Ha'aretz Internet Edition*, March 23, 2002, available at http://middleeastinfo.org/article290.html.

47. The Jaffee Center Poll also reported that some 31 percent of Jewish Israelis favored transferring Arabs with Israeli citizenship out of the country. Ibid. Barzilai, "More Israeli Jews Favor Transfer of Palestinians."

48. Thanks to Matti Bunzl and Jed Esty for pushing me in this direction.

49. I am building on Gayatri Spivak's "Can the Subaltern Speak?"

50. For example, "White men are saving brown women from brown men." Spivak, "Can the Subaltern Speak?," 296.

51. Ibid., 297.

52. An early Jewish Israeli critic of the colonial nature of the Zionist movement was Mazpen, an Israeli socialist organization, which emerged in the 1960s. A 1972 treatise argued that "the Israeli Jews constitute a society of settler-colonialists, and the Zionist state is the instrument that procures benefits for them based on the denial of these benefits to Palestinians." Bober, *The Other Israel*, 192. Quoted in Silberstein, *The Postzionism Debates*, 85.

53. The foundational work of Edward Said has been crucial in enabling such scholarship, as has the work of Ella Shohat, Smadar Lavie, and Joseph Massad.

54. See, for example, McClintock, "The Angel of Progress"; and Shohat, "Notes on the Postcolonial."

55. Massad, "The 'Post-colonial' Colony."

56. For example, Lavie, "Blow-Ups in the Borderzone"; Shohat, "The Invention of the Mizrahim"; and Shohat, "Sephardim in Israel."

57. Bhabha, *Location of Culture*, 236; emphasis mine.

58. Rai, " 'Thus Spoke the Subaltern . . .'," 167.

59. A similar logic informs McClintock's parenthetical list of "abject zones (*the Israeli Occupied Territories*, prisons, battered women's shelters)." McClintock, *Im-*

perial Leather, 72; emphasis mine. Marianna Torgovnick refers to the "art-world equivalent of the Palestinians" (an artistic form perpetually "wandering the globe"). Torgovnick, *Primitive Passions*. And John Gillis makes a gesture toward "those, *like the Palestinians* . . . [who] are forced to contend with multiple identities and multiple memories, as they are moved from place to place, time after time." Gillis, *Commemorations*, 16; emphasis mine.

FOUR ☉ Postcolonial Studies and the
Disciplines in Transformation

Hybridity and Heresy:

Apartheid Comparative Religion

in Late Antiquity

ᘒ ᘒ ᘒ

DANIEL BOYARIN

For Jacques Derrida, in memoriam

Jacques Derrida has written of the frontier between speech and writing as "the limit separating two opposed places. Like Czechoslovakia and Poland, [they] resemble each other, regard each other; separated nonetheless by a frontier all the more mysterious . . . because it is abstract, legal, ideal."[1] Derrida's metaphor could be extended into an allegory of the historical situation of Judaism and Christianity in the second, third, and fourth centuries, as the borderlines between them were being drawn. Like Czechoslovakia and Poland, ancient Judaism and Christianity resembled each other and regarded each other, and eventually came to be separated by a frontier that was abstract, legal, and ideal.

Heresiology, the "science" of heresies, inscribes these borderlines, and heresiologists are the religious customs' inspectors. Authorities on both sides tried to establish a border, a line that when crossed, meant that someone had definitively left one group for another. However, as Paul de Man has written, drawing out Derrida's metaphor, there is "no way of defining, of policing, the boundaries that separate the name of one entity from the name of another; tropes are not just travelers, they tend to be smugglers and probably smugglers of stolen goods at that."[2] Ancient heresiologists tried to police the boundaries so as to identify and interdict those who respected no borders, those smugglers of ideas and practices newly declared to be contraband, nomads who would not recognize the efforts to institute limits, to posit a separation between "two opposed places" and thus to clearly establish who was and who was not a "Christian," a "Jew."[3] They named such folk "Judaizers" or "minim," respectively, and attempted to declare their beliefs and practices, their very identities, as out of bounds.

Groups made different in various ways by class, ethnicity, and other forms of social differentiation become transformed into "religions" in large part, I would suggest, through discourses of orthodoxy/heresy.[4] Early Christian heresiology, whatever else it is, largely constitutes the work of those who wished to eradicate the fuzziness of the borders, semantic and social, between Jews and Christians and thus produce Judaism and Christianity as fully separate (and opposed) entities—as religions, at least in the eyes of Christianity.[5]

For nearly two decades now, scholars of early Christianity have been building up a major revision of the history of Christian heresiology. Working within a Foucauldian paradigm, Alain Le Boulluec has proven central in this shift in research strategy.[6] Aside from his specific historical achievements and insights, Le Boulluec's most important move was to shift the scholarly conversation away from the question of orthodoxy and heresy, understood as essences (even constructed ones),[7] and to move the discussion in the direction of a history of the representation of orthodoxy and heresy, the discourse that we know of as heresiology, the history of the idea of heresy itself. The Greek term *hairesis*, as is well known, earlier meant just a "choice," that is, an affinity group joined by common ideas, theories, and practices, without any pejorative overtones at all. Le Boulluec found Justin Martyr to be a crucial figure (if not *the* crucial figure) in the Christian shift from understanding *hairesis* as a "group of people, a party or sect marked by common ideas and aims" to "a party or sect that stands outside established or recognized tradition, a heretical group that propounds false doctrine in the form of a heresy."[8] As Le Boulluec himself puts it, the result of his research is that "il revient à Justin d'avoir inventé l'hérésie (Justin gets the credit for having invented [the concept of] heresy)."[9] Le Boulluec has been, perhaps, at somewhat more of a loss in attempting to explain the causes and functions of this invention, largely attributing them to the influence of "Judaism" and the challenge of "Gnosticism," neither of which turn out, on balance, to be very compelling explanations.[10] J. Rebecca Lyman has, therefore, taken Le Boulluec's ideas further, exploring in depth the politico-cultural position of a figure like Justin in the context of postcolonial theory and thus adumbrating, at any rate, a sharper explanation of these developments.[11]

Building on both Le Boulluec's and Lyman's insights, I theorize that at least a significant part of the function of heresiology, if not its proximate cause, was to define Christian identity as such, that is, not only to produce the Christian as neither Jew nor Greek but also to construct the whatness of what Christianity would be, not finally a third race or *genos* but something new entirely, a religion. When we look at heresiology as these scholars have taught us to do — not for its doctrine but as a discourse — possible historical answers emerge where there had not even been the questions before. It is no accident, I will suggest, that the alleged inventor of heresy is also the author of "one of the earliest texts ["The Dialogue"] which reflects a self-consciously independent Christianity," [12] or, as I would prefer to put the same point, one of the earliest texts self-consciously engaged in the production of an independent Christianity.

Extending Derrida's border conceit and invoking a well-known joke might help to make clearer the shift that I'm talking about here: [13] Every day for thirty years a man drove a wheelbarrow full of sand over the Tijuana border crossing. The customs inspector dug through the sand each morning, but could not discover any contraband. He remained, of course, convinced that he was dealing with a smuggler. On the day of his retirement from the service, he asked the smuggler to reveal what it is he was smuggling and how he had been doing the smuggling. The answer, of course, was that he was smuggling wheelbarrows. Where until now, it might be said, scholarship has been looking for what is hidden in the sand (with more success than the customs inspector), I prefer to look at smuggled wheelbarrows as the vehicles of language within which identities are formed and differences made. [14] Of course, not only modern scholars searched for the contraband but also the ancient heresiologists themselves. Little did they suspect, I warrant, that in struggling so hard to define who was in and who was out, who was Jewish and who was Christian, what was Christianity and what was Judaism, it was they themselves who were smuggling the wheelbarrows, the very discourses of heresiology and of religion as identity. Adopting such a perspective — a perspective that refuses itself the option of seeing Christian and Jew, Christianity and Judaism, as fully formed, bounded, separate entities and identities in late antiquity — will help us, I hope, to perceive more fully the very work of those early Christian and Jewish writers as they were making the difference.

Hybrids and Heretics

Homi Bhabha has written that cultures interact not on the basis of "the exoticism of multiculturalism or the *diversity* of cultures, but on the inscription

and articulation of culture's *hybridity*." Bhabha concludes, "it is the 'inter'—
the cutting edge of translation and negotiation, the *in-between* space—that
carries the burden of the meaning of culture."[15] A recent writer on the history of comparative religion, David Chidester, has utilized Bhabha's work in
developing a notion of an "apartheid comparative religion." By this (working
out of the Southern African situation as a model for theorization), Chidester
means a system "committed to identifying and reifying the many languages,
cultures, peoples, and religions of the world as if they were separate and
distinct regions."[16] The point of such a knowledge/power regime is that
"each religion has to be understood as a separate, hermetically sealed compartment into which human beings can be classified and divided." Following Chidester's descriptions, I want to suggest that the heresiologists of antiquity were performing a very similar function to that of the students of
comparative religion of modernity, conceptually organizing "human diversity into rigid, static categories [as] one strategy for simplifying, and thereby
achieving some cognitive control over, the bewildering complexity of a frontier zone."[17] Heresiology is, I might say, a form of apartheid comparative
religion.

Generally, the orthodox topos that describes Christian heretics as "Jews"
or "Judaizers" is seen as a sort of sideshow to the real heresiological concern, the search for the Christian doctrine of God, to put it in R. C. Hanson's
terms.[18] According to this view, heresiology is primarily an artefact of the
contact between biblical Christian language and Greek philosophical categories forcing ever more detailed and refined definitions of godhead, especially, in the early centuries, in the face of the overly abstract or philosophical
approaches of the Gnostics. Such an account treats the naming of heretics as
Jews or Judaizers as a nearly vacant form of reprobation for reprobation's
sake. Without denying that interpretation's validity for the history of Christian theology itself, I nonetheless hypothesize that it is not epiphenomenal
that so often heresy is designated as Judaism and Judaizing in Christian discourse of this time,[19] nor that a certain veritable obsession with varieties of
"Jewish-Christianity" (Nazoreans, Ebionites) became so prominent in some
quarters precisely at the moment when Nicene orthodoxy was consolidating.
Furthermore, it is not a necessary outcome for even a very refined theological discourse and controversy on such issues as the relations of the persons
of the trinity to produce a structure of orthodoxy and heresy without some
other cause or function intervening. At least one major impetus for the formation of the discourse of heresiology, on my reading, is the construction
of a Christianity that would not be Judaism. The "Jews" (i.e., for this context, heretics so named), the Judaizers, and the Jewish-Christians—whether

they existed and to what extent is irrelevant in this context—thus mark a space of threatening hybridity that it is the task of the religion-police to do away with.

Note that these religion-police, the border guards, operated on both sides: hybridity proved as threatening to a "pure" rabbinic Judaism as it did to an orthodox Christianity. An elegant example is the fair of Elone Mamre, which, according to the church historian Sozomen, attracted Jews, Christians, and pagans who each commemorated the angelic theophany to Abraham in their own way: the Jews celebrating Abraham, the Christians the appearance of the Logos, and the pagans, Hermes.[20] Here is, perhaps, the very parade instance of Bhabhan "interstitial" spaces that bear the meaning of culture. The rabbis prohibited Jews from attending at all,[21] thus reinscribing the hybridity as something like what would later be called syncretism and banishing it from their orthodoxy. We will see that this is an oft-repeated phenomenon at this particular time.[22]

One of the most important themes of postcolonial theorizing, as we have already seen, has been its emphasis on the hybridity of cultural identifications and the instability of dominating cultural paradigms, thus necessitating the latter's constant reproduction, and assertion of naturalness while marking hybridity as unnatural, monstrous.[23] It is the instability of the colonial discourse that makes possible the subaltern's voice, colonizing, in turn, the discourse of the colonizer. As Bhabha has put it, "in the very practice of domination the language of the master becomes hybrid—neither the one thing nor the other."[24] Robert Young glosses Bhabha's words: "Bhabha shows that [the decentering of colonial discourse from its position of authority] occurs when authority becomes hybridized when placed in a colonial context and finds itself layered against other cultures, very often through the exploitation by the colonized themselves of its evident equivocations and contradictions."[25] Bhabha focuses on the fault lines, on the border situations and thresholds, as sites where identities are performed and contested.[26] Borders are also places where people are strip-searched, detained, imprisoned, and sometimes shot. Borders themselves are not given but constructed by power to mask hybridity, to occlude and disown it. The localization of hybridity in some others—called the hybrids, the heretics—serves that purpose.

I thus argue that hybridity is double-edged. On the one hand, the hybrids "represent . . . a difference 'within,' a subject that inhabits the rim of an 'in-between' reality,"[27] but on the other hand, the literal ascription of hybridity on the part of hegemonic discourses to one group of people, one set of practices, disavows the very difference within by externalizing it. Hybridity itself is the disowned other. It is this very disowned hybridity that supports the notion of purity. Talal Asad clarifies this operation:

> The claim of many radical critics that hegemonic power necessarily suppresses difference in favor of unity is quite mistaken. Just as mistaken is their claim that power always abhors ambiguity. To secure its unity—to make its own history— dominant power has worked best through differentiating and classifying practices. . . . In this context power is constructive, not repressive. Furthermore, its ability to select (or construct) the differences that serve its purposes has depended on its exploiting the dangers and opportunities contained in ambiguous situations.[28]

Following this mode of analysis, the commonplace that orthodoxy needs heresy for its self-definition can be nuanced and further specified. Heresy is marked not only as the space of the not-true in religion but also as the space of the syncretistic, the difference that enables unity itself. A similar point has been made in another historical context by Robert Young who writes, "The idea of race here shows itself to be profoundly dialectical: it only works when defined against potential intermixture, which also threatens to undo its calculations altogether."[29] Young helps us see that it is not only that "white" is defined as that which is "not-black" but that the very system of race itself, the very division into white and black as races, depends on the production of an idea of hybridity over against which the notion of the "natural," pure races comes into discourse. This way of thinking about hybridity in the classification of humans into races can be mobilized in thinking about heresy and the classification of people and doctrines into religions as well. This provides a certain corrective, then, to those versions of a postcolonial theory that would seem to presuppose pure essences, afterwards "hybridized," thus buying into the very activity of an apartheid they would seek to subvert.[30]

Thinking Hybridity in Language

In my 1999 work, *Dying for God*, I suggested that we might think of Christianity and Judaism in the second and third centuries as points on a continuum from, on one end, the Marcionites—who followed the second-century Marcion in believing that the Hebrew Bible had been written by an inferior God and had no standing for Christians and who completely denied the "Jewishness" of Christianity—to many Jews on the other end for whom Jesus meant nothing. In the middle, however, there existed many gradations that provided social and cultural progression across this spectrum. In other words, to use a linguistic metaphor, I proffered a wave-theory account of

Christian-Jewish history in which innovations disseminate and interact like waves caused by stones thrown in a pond, an account in which convergence proved as possible as divergence and which ran in opposition to the traditional *Stammbaum* or family tree model, within which virtually only divergence was possible—after 70 AD in some versions, or after 135 AD in others. I argued the case via a close analysis of Christian and Jewish texts about martyrdom produced in the second, third, and fourth centuries and proposed that the best way to account for many features of these texts was the assumption of shared cultural and religious innovations flowing in both directions, providing social contiguity and contact and even cultural continuity between the two religious groups in formation.[31] To put the same point in terms drawn from postcolonial studies, we must imagine, I think, a "contact zone," a space of "transculturation," where, as Mary Louise Pratt defines it, "disparate cultures meet, clash, grapple with each other, often in highly asymmetrical relations of domination and subordination."[32] The advantage of the wave theory model for my purposes here is that it does not presuppose an originary separateness of the two cultures in question, which the colonial description tends to do.

The religious dialect map is a hybridized one, and the point is that that hybridity extends even to those religious groups that would consider themselves "purely" Jewish or "purely" Christian in their self-understanding. This shift in model proves significant not only for purely scholarly reasons, by which I mean that it provides a better, "truer" description of "facts," but also because it represents a shift in fundamental understandings of human difference and its meanings. Writing in an analogous context, Robert Young has said: "We may note here the insistently genetic emphasis on the metaphor of 'families' of languages, and the oft-charted language 'trees' which were to determine the whole basis of phylogenetic racial theories of conquest, absorption and decline—designed to deny the more obvious possibilities of mixture, fusion and creolization."[33] It is, then, no minor matter to revise our basic metaphors for understanding how religions—Christianity, Judaism, and paganism—came into being.

The wave theory analogy can be productively extended in ways that I hope will clarify my approach to modeling the hybridity of the late ancient religious world and narrating the history of the emergence of Judaism and Christianity in late antiquity. Jonathan M. Hall has undertaken a critical rethinking of the use of ancient genealogical texts for the reconstruction of archaic Greek history.[34] Among the other issues and methods that Hall has employed in his investigation are linguistic ones, in particular *Stammbaum* versus wave theory. Traditional historiography of Greek ethnicity has assumed that the various Greek groups, as well as their dialects—Ionian, Dorian, and so forth—derived from a once unified proto-Greek. Assuming this original unity and subsequent divergence has enabled historians to construct narratives of tribal migrations and invasions in the prearchaic period. Hall mounts a critique of this methodology, although his argument could have been enhanced by a sharper articulation of wave theory itself. Clarifying the difference between his and my understanding may prove an effective way for me to propose a first rough draft of the theory that I am developing in my work. Hall believes that wave theory, just as much as *Stammbaum* theory, presupposes primal linguistic (cultural) uniformity and merely explains the differences between dialects as owing to diffusion of innovations over various parts of the language area.[35] However, it is the virtue of wave theory, as usually understood by historical linguists, that it does *not* presuppose a unified protolanguage at any point in time and imagines dialects in contiguous geographical areas becoming more like each other than previously, not less, and thus producing dialect groups. Wave theory is, thus, more akin to the situation that Hall himself imagines as the historical origin of groupings such as Dorian in archaic Greece, where once unrelated groups became more like each other, linguistically and otherwise, and agglomerated into the so-called ethnic groups known from the archaic period.

This is a model to which I appeal as well. I am not claiming an undifferentiated Judaism that formed itself into Judaism and Christianity through the "borrowing" of various religious traits, but rather an assortment of religious "dialects" throughout the Jewish world that gradually developed structure as clusters through diffusion and eventually became organized as "languages" (religions) through processes very much analogous to those by which national languages such as French and Italian were also formed. In other words, I am not denying that in the second, third, and fourth centuries there existed religious groups that were more Christian than others (I shall immediately below be talking about what this comparative might mean), nor that there existed groups that were not Christian at all, but rather that the various Christian groups formed a dialect cluster within the overall assortment of dialects that constituted Judaism (or perhaps better Judaeo-Christianity) at the time.

Hall himself argues that "the clustering of dialects within dialect groups is 'a scholars' heuristic fiction.'" Linguist William Labov has also written: "But in regard to geographical dialects, it has long been argued that such gradient models are characteristic of the diffusion of linguistic features across a territory and the challenge has been to establish that boundaries between dialects are anything but arbitrary." Yet Labov goes on to state: "Nevertheless, even in dialect geography, most investigators agree that properties do bundle, and that it is possible to show boundaries of varying degrees of clarity even when all variable features are superimposed upon a single map."[36] In other words, one can model a situation in which there will be persons or groups who will clearly be "Christian" or "non-Christian Jewish," that is, persons or groups that form definable clusters of religious features, while the boundaries between the two categories will remain undefinable. The eventual triumph (or even partial triumph) of orthodoxies in defining a separate identity for the two religions much resembles the formation of national languages. Remarking on the fact that many dialects of Italian are more understandable by French speakers than by other Italians and other similar phenomena, Hall writes: "What allows for this at first sight surprising phenomenon is the fact that a 'national language' is seldom a higher order linguistic category which embraces and subsumes its constituent dialects. It is, rather, an invention which rarely precedes the nineteenth century and which owes its existence to reasons 'that are as much political, geographical, historical, sociological and cultural as linguistic.' From a linguistic point of view, there is little or no difference between a standardised national language and a dialect in terms of their hierarchical ranking within the historical structure of a language."[37] Adding only the proviso, following Labov, that dialects do group eventually into dialect clusters, analogous to Judaism and Christianity in formation, I suggest, once more, that this provides a powerful analogy for thinking about the history of these nascent religions. Not via a separation, a parting of the ways, but by a political partitioning through a series of choices made by different groups of different specific indicia of identity[38] and the diffusion and clustering of such indicia (such as, eventually, noncompliance with the law—hardly an essential "Christian" trait) groups gradually congealed into Christianity and Judaism. Yet it was only with the mobilizations of temporal power (via Ideological State Apparatuses and Repressive State Apparatuses[39]) in the fourth century that the process can be said to have formed religions, and even then only lopsidedly, as I shall try to show further on. One might say that Judaism and Christianity were invented in order to explain the fact that there were Jews and Christians.

In suggesting that Judaism and Christianity were not separate entities until very late in late antiquity, I am, accordingly, *not* claiming that it is impossible to discern separate social groups that are in important senses Christian/not-Jewish or Jewish/not-Christian from fairly early on (by which I mean the mid-second century). In order to make the opposite claim, even if I believed it, I would have to do a very different kind of historical research from what

I am doing here. Indeed, although I do not know quite how one would show this, such "separatist" groups may have been statistically dominant much earlier than the fifth century. Thus I cannot answer empirical questions such as "How much were Christian and other Jewish congregations mixed at any given time or place?"; or, "What was the social status of Jewish-Christian groups? Were they accepted as Jews, as Christians (by whom?), or neither at any given time?"

Instead, the question that I pose is a theoretical one, or at least an interpretative one: Even if we grant the statistical dominance (and perhaps a certain power dominance, although, once more, I do not know how we would show or know this) of the separatists, in terms of the semantics of the cultural language, the discourse of the time, are there sets of features that absolutely define who is a Jew and who is a Christian in such ways that the two categories will not seriously overlap irrespective of the numbers of members of the blurring sets? I think not.

The perspective adopted here is not unlike that of Mary Beard, John North, and S. R. F. Price, who write: "Our last section in this chapter does investigate the degrees of religious continuity in these cults traceable across the Roman world. By and large, however, in discussing the religions of the empire we have tried to avoid thinking in terms of uniformity, or in terms of a central core 'orthodox' tradition with its peripheral 'variants'; we have preferred to think rather in terms of different religions as clusters of ideas, people and rituals, sharing some common identity across time and place, but at the same time inevitably invested with different meanings in their different contexts."[40]

Discourse is a concept of recurring importance for me. This, here somewhat eclectic, notion has provided me one means—at least provisional—to the solution of a seemingly intractable theoretical problem, the relationship of the language games that I have been describing until now to anything other than words. Although I have hinted at my approach to this issue, that language is itself social practice and material, I would like to be a bit—just a bit—more expansive at this point.[41] The social theory with which I work best could be roughly defined as Western neo-Marxism. It is Marxist in that it mobilizes a hermeneutics of suspicion, assuming that texts and other linguistic practices are not innocent; they have designs on people, seeking to promote an ideology, by which I mean a set of understandings of the world, of social relations, taken to be simply "natural" but which can be historicized and thus exposed as having served the needs of a particular group of people or class. It is "neo" in that these needs and classes are not thought of as exclusively economic ones.

The interests served by the ideological text (by ideological nonstate apparatuses, to adapt Althusser) can be investments in other sorts of power and satisfaction for elites of various types within a given social formation. The discourses of orthodoxy/heresy, and thus, I will argue, of religious difference, do not necessarily serve the interests of an economic class (it would be hard to describe the rabbis of late Roman Palestine or Sassanid Babylonia or the bishops of Nicaea as an economic class), but they do serve in the production of ideology, of hegemony, in the consent of a dominated group to be ruled by an elite (hence *consensual orthodoxy*, that marvelous mystification). This makes an enormous difference, for it leads to the Althusserian notion of ideology as having its own material existence in that it "always exists in an apparatus, and its practice, or practices."[42] Ania Loomba's statement of the current theoretical position that "no human utterance could be seen as innocent," that, indeed, "any set of words could be analysed to reveal not just an individual but a historical consciousness at work,"[43] is crucial for me, for it is this postulate that enables my work as historian. This set of notions, to which I can more or less only allude in this context, does not quite dissolve completely (as sometimes charged), but surely renders much more permeable any boundary between linguistic (or textual) practice and the "real" conditions of life within a given historical moment and society, thus empowering the study of texts not as reflective of social realities, but as social apparatuses understood to be complexly tied to other apparatuses via the notion of a discourse or a *dispositif*.[44]

The problem, then, of how my texts relate to reality, that is, the methodological problem of how one moves from the legendary and legal texts of the Talmud to some understanding of the lives of Jews in late antiquity is, in a sense, solved by revealing it as an instance of a theoretical problem of the relation of language in general to social practice in general. "Discourse in this sense is a whole field or domain within which language is used in particular ways. The domain is rooted (as is Gramsci's or Althusser's notion of ideology) in human practices, institutions and actions."[45] Analysis of discourse in this sense, whatever its other theoretical and political virtues and defects, is ideally situated for constructing the past with greater complexity, depth, and nuance than might otherwise be attempted or thought possible, since, precisely, to adapt Loomba, "it seeks to widen the scope of studies [of religious history] by examining the intersection of ideas and institutions, knowledge and power."[46] I propose that there is a real dissymmetry between a reading of difference from within Christianity and from within Judaism. While Christianity finally configures Judaism as a different religion, Judaism itself, I suggest, in the end refuses that call, so that, seen from that perspective, the difference between Christianity and Judaism is not so much a difference between two religions as a difference between a religion and an entity that refuses to be one.

In Western languages one habitually speaks, in both the scholarly and the quotidian registers, of Judaism and Christianity—and, for that matter, of Islam, Buddhism, and Hinduism—as members of a single semiotic paradigm or of Judaism and Christianity as two members of a single category: (names of) religions, or, sometimes even, faiths. Various quarters have, however, hitherto recognized that this denomination leaves much to be desired, that it is, indeed, the reproduction of a Christian worldview, a Christian model imposed on peoples and practices that do not quite fit or do not even wish to fit its understanding of the world. Indeed, speaking for Judaism, it seems highly significant that there is no word in premodern Jewish parlance that means *Judaism*. When the term *Ioudaismos* appears in Jewish writing, to my knowledge only in 2 Maccabees and in Paul, it does not mean Judaism, the religion, and after that, is only used as the name of the Jewish religion by writers who do not identify themselves with and by that name, until, it would seem, well into the nineteenth century. It might appear, then, that Judaism has not, until some time in modernity, existed at all, that whatever moderns might be tempted to abstract out, to disembed from the culture of Jews and call their religion, was not so disembedded nor ascribed particular status by Jews until very recently.

Until our present moment, it could be defensibly argued, Judaism both is and is not a religion. On the one hand, for many purposes it, like Hinduism, operates as a religion within multireligious societies. Jews claim for their religion a semantic, cultural status parallel to that of Christianity in the West. We study Judaism in programs of religious studies, claim religious freedom, have sections of Judaism at the American Academy of Religion, and in general function as members of a faith—or system of ultimate meaning, or whatever—among other faiths. On the other hand, there are many ways that we continue to be uncomfortable and express our discomfort with this very definition. For both Zionists and many non-Zionist Jews (including me), versions of description or practice with respect to Judaism that treat it as a faith that can be separated from ethnicity, nationality, language, and shared history have felt false. Precisely that very position of Judaism at the American Academy of Religion has been experienced by us, sometimes, as in itself a form of ambivalently capitulating behavior (which is not, I hasten to add, altogether unpleasurable). Something about the difference between Judaism and Christianity is captured precisely by insisting on the ways that

Judaism does not constitute a religion. This ambivalence has deep historical roots.

The theory of interpellation, inter alia, the calling of names, is relevant here but itself needs some extension. As Judith Butler has remarked, "To be called a name is one of the first forms of linguistic injury that one learns. But not all name-calling is injurious. Being called a name is also one of the conditions by which a subject is constituted in language; indeed, it is one of the examples Althusser supplies for an understanding of 'interpellation.'" Butler goes further than this, however. She discerns that the injurious and the noninjurious moments of name-calling can be one and the same. Hailing is recognition. "In being called an injurious name, one is derogated and demeaned. But the name holds out another possibility as well: by being called a name, one is also, paradoxically, given a certain possibility for social existence, initiated into a temporal life of language that exceeds the prior purposes that animate that call."[47] As a surprising instance of this phenomenon, one might refer to the apparent invention of the term *rhetoric* by Plato as a term of reproach, "as part of an effort to limit the scope and popularity of Sophistic teaching, particularly that of his rival Isocrates." The term, however, quickly became an empowering one "for organizing thought and effort around a specific set of problems—those of being a persuasive *rhetor*." Indeed, "Plato may have helped to empower a discipline that his philosophical outlook found repugnant,"[48] thus exemplifying the rabbinic topos of one who came intending to curse and in the end blessed against her will, as it were.

Recently Virginia Burrus has mobilized the Althusser/Butler theory as a way of articulating the possible effect of one Christian heresiologist, Athanasius, on Jewish history. Burrus argues that Athanasius's "hate-speech," although directed at "Arians" and not Jews and, therefore, seemingly having nothing to do with Jews, is nevertheless well worth attending to, indeed, may be supremely relevant for the history of Judaism because "injurious address may, in the very act of inflicting pain, give rise to an 'other' agency within language, summon a [Jewish] subject into existence."[49] Once again, as Butler has put it: "If to be addressed is to be interpellated, then the offensive call runs the risk of inaugurating a subject in speech who comes to use language to counter the offensive call."[50] If, then, for example, to be called the name, *queer* in a powerful sense is not only to be injured but also to be called into being, then to be called *Jew, heretic*, is similarly so to be interpellated. Indeed, as David Brakke has shown, at the time that Athanasius was active, there a kind of Jewish revival occurred in Alexandria itself.[51]

A historically close analogy may prove useful. A leading historian of Christianity in late antiquity, Robert Markus, has argued (partially following Arnaldo Momigliano) that paganism also became a religion through the discourses of Christian orthodoxy:

> The image of a society neatly divided into "Christian" and "pagan" is the creation of late fourth-century Christians, and has been too readily taken at its face value by modern historians. Unlike Christianity, with its growing world-wide cohesiveness, "paganism" was a varied group of cults and observances. It never constituted a single coherent religious movement analogous to either Christianity or Judaism. It existed only in the minds, and, increasingly *the speech habits* of Christians. In so far as a particular section of Roman paganism acquired some sort of homogeneous identity—as did that of some groups of Roman aristocrats in the last decades of the fourth century—it was a response to the growing self-confidence and assertiveness of a Christian establishment.[52]

The hailing of the pagan subject via the hate speech of the Christian thus produced this subject and her religion.

What about Jews and Judaism? Did the hailing of Judaism as religion call forth a response similar to that of the pagans, those upper-class Romans of whom Markus speaks who adopted this name as a name for a religion? I suggest it did not. That Judaism is both interpellated as a religion and partly accepts and partly evades that position is perhaps, to start with, an artifact of the Christian invention of religion. According to Rowan Williams, orthodoxy is a way that a religion, separated from the locativity of ethnic or geocultural self-definition as Christianity was, asks itself: "How, if at all, is one to identify the 'centre' of [our] religious tradition? At what point and why do we start speaking about 'a' religion?"[53] I choose to understand these questions as historical rather than methodological ones, temporal rather than spatially located queries. At what point in history and why did *they* begin speaking about a religion, an orthodoxy, a heresiology? As it happens, and as I shall attempt to show, heresiology plays a powerful role within Judaism precisely during the period of mutual differentiation, yet once that border is (more or less) firmly inscribed, heresiology virtually drops out of Judaism entirely, leaving too, in its wake, this equivocal status. It is not a trivial, but, indeed, a very interesting fact that as history moved on, heresiology remained a living, vital, and central part of Christianity, while in rabbinic Judaism, eventually Judaism tout court, heresiology was to wither and (almost) die out,[54] leaving in its wake the ambiguity that marks Judaism till this day, sometimes a religion, sometimes not.[55]

I seek to locate the roots of this ambiguity in a time long before the present moment. The ambivalence about being a religion can be interpreted by means of an understanding of the "postcolonial" situation of Judaism at the time of the invention of religion. It has become a virtual truism that religion in its modern sense is an invention of Christians. Several theoreticians/historians have made this argument, notably Wilfred Cantwell Smith and Talal Asad.[56] These scholars have claimed that religion in the sense in which we use the term today is a post-Enlightenment concept and category produced within Protestant Christianity.[57] Other scholars locate the "invention of religion," not in the Enlightenment but much further back during the time of the very formation of Christianity itself at the dawn of late antiquity. This historical production does not belong to the eighteenth century, but was in process from nearly the beginnings of certain parts of the Jesus movement and largely complete—whatever that might mean precisely—by the beginning of the fifth century. Supporting the notion of a late ancient epistemic shift that we might call the invention of religion, Maurice Sachot has argued that the term *religio*, in the sense in which we use it, is entirely the product of Christianity.[58] This view has been maintained as well by historian of late ancient Judaism Seth Schwartz, who has phrased this point strikingly by referring to "Christianization, and what is in social-historical terms its sibling, the emergence of religion as a discrete category of human experience—religion's *disembedding*."[59] Schwartz is claiming that the production of Christianity is, itself, the invention of religion as such, as a discrete category of human experience. The production of this category does not imply that many elements of what would form religions did not exist before this time, but rather that the particular aggregation of verbal and other practices that would be named now as constituting a religion only came into being as a discrete category at the same time as Christianization itself.[60] In this sense, one cannot speak of Judaism as existing before Christianity, but only as part of the process of the invention of Christianity. "Religion," as pointed out recently by Denis Guénon, "is constituted as the difference between religions."[61] Christianity, in its constitution as a religion, therefore needed religious difference, Judaism, to be its other, the religion that is false.

The argument is that there was no Christianity before religion nor religion before Christianity, but that the historical form that Christianity ultimately took was part and parcel of its being invented as a religion, of the invention of religion itself. This invention had the effect of producing Judaism as a religion—although not necessarily for the Jews—as well. The technology for this production was heresiology. The self-definition by certain Christians of Christianity over against Judaism and the self-definition of orthodoxy as opposed to heresy are closely linked, for much of that which goes under the name of heresy in these early Christian centuries consists of one variety or another of Judaizing, or alternatively, of straying too far from Jewish roots. The rise to power of the rabbis, I will suggest, is deeply dependent on the impact of the very notion of orthodoxy on rabbinic Jewish discourse, that is, the autonomy brought by the self-definition of an orthodox Judaism vis-à-vis an orthodox Christianity, or Judaism as a religion.

Seth Schwartz has written that the disembedding of religion that constitutes the very invention of religion "had a direct impact on the Jewish culture of late antiquity because the Jewish communities *appropriated* much from the Christian society around them."[62] In other words, when Christianity separated religious belief and practice from *Romanitas*, cult from culture, Judaism as a religion came into the world as well. The rabbis articulated their own sense of identity and definition in part through "appropriation," not, of course, at this period owing to any power or dominance that Christianity—even if it made sense to claim the existence of such an entity—possessed, but owing to the compelling force of the question of identity asked by at least some early Christians. The partial (not parodic, but partial and in some sense strategic) appropriation referred to by Schwartz is not, then, on the interpretation to be offered here, a mimesis or the product of the influence of Christianity on Judaism. It should be read, I will argue, as a kind of mimicry (in the technical postcolonial sense) and thus as an act of resistance in the sense articulated by Bhabha: "Resistance is not necessarily an oppositional act of political intention, nor is it the simple negation or exclusion of the 'content' of another culture, as a difference once perceived. It is the effect of an ambivalence produced within the rules of recognition of dominating discourses as they articulate the signs of cultural difference and reimplicate them within the deferential relations of colonial power—hierarchy, normalization, marginalization and so forth."[63]

In the end—at least in the end of late antiquity—, I argue, rabbinic Judaism refused the option of becoming a religion, another species of the kind that Christianity offered. At the final stage of the development of classical rabbinism, a reassertion of the "locative" of identity as given and not as achieved—or lost—came to be emblematic of Judaism. One might say, adopting the language of Schwartz, that what made Judaism and Christianity different in the end, different products of the history of post-Israelite religious culture, was precisely the reembedding of the former, a final sub/mergence of religion as a discrete category of human experience, the refusal by the Jews of their interpellation as a religion.

In fine, it is not the case that Christianity and Judaism are two separate or different religions, but that they are two different kinds of things altogether.

From the point of view of the church's category formation, Judaism and Christianity (and Hinduism later on) are examples of the category *religion*, one a bad example and the other a very good one, indeed the only prototype; but from the point of view of the rabbis' categorization, Christianity is a religion while Judaism is not. Judaism remains a religion for the church, because, I suggest, it is a necessary moment in the construction of Christian orthodoxy, thus Christian religion, while occasional and partial Jewish appropriations of the name and status of religion are strategic, mimetic, and contingent. Like the layerings of the unconscious or the interpenetrating stratifications of Roman material culture that so inspired Freud, however, the vaunted ambivalence of Judaism is, I suggest, a product of that history, of that partial acceptance and then almost total refusal of the option of orthodoxy and heresy as the Jews' mode of self-definition, the refusal, that is, finally to become or be a religion.

Notes

This text is drawn from the introduction to my *Border Lines*.

1. Derrida, *Glas*, 189. It only underlines Derrida's point to observe that since his writing that very border has taken on entirely different meanings, not least because Czechoslovakia no longer exists.

2. Paul de Man, "The Epistemology of Metaphor," 17.

3. See Boyarin, *Dying for God*, 93–130, in which an argument is made for people attending both synagogue and church in third-century Caesarea as the "smugglers" who transported discourses of martyrology in both directions across the "abstract, legal, and ideal" frontier between Judaism and Christianity. I would add here "Jewish Christian" communities, such as that of the pseudo-Clementine productions.

4. I do not, of course, claim that terms such as *ethnicity* or *class* are unhistorical givens either; I just use these terms as convenient shorthand for various modes of group identity making.

5. Karen King has made the point that for early Christian writers, heresy was always defined with respect to Judaism: too much Judaism, and you became a Judaizer, too little, a Gnostic. King, *Making Heresy*.

6. Le Boulluec, *La notion d'hérésie*. See especially, building on Le Boulluec, Burrus, *The Making of a Heretic*; and Lyman, "The Making of a Heretic."

7. As had understood them Walter Bauer before him. See Bauer, Krodel, and Kraft, *Orthodoxy and Heresy in Earliest Christianity*.

8. This lucid summary of Le Boulluec's thesis is given by Runia, "Philo of Alexandria and the Greek *Hairesis*-Model," 118.

9. Le Boulluec, *La notion d'hérésie*, 110.

10. With respect to Gnosticism, falsely so called, see Pagels, "Irenaeus, the 'Canon of Truth,' and the *Gospel of John*"; and esp. Lyman, "The Politics of Passing," who interprets *Gnosticism* itself as a "polemical invention" of Justin and friends. See also Markschies, *Valentinus Gnosticus?*

11. Lyman, "The Politics of Passing."

12. Horner, *Listening to Trypho*, 8.

13. The joke was suggested to me for this context by Ishay Rosen-Zvi.

14. See also, partially anticipating Le Boulluec, Altendorf, "Zum Stichwort."

15. Bhabha, *The Location of Culture*, 38–39, and see Chidester, *Savage Systems*, xv.

16. Chidester, *Savage Systems*, 4.

17. Ibid., 22–23.

18. Hanson, *The Search for the Christian Doctrine of God*.

19. Lorenz, *Arius judaizans?* For a notable example of this discursive phenomenon, see Gregory of Nyssa's Life of Moses: Gregory, *The Life of Moses*, 184 n. 294.

20. Kofsky, "Mamre."

21. *Talmud Palestinensis Avoda Zara*, ch. 1, para. 5, p. 39, col. d.

22. This is not to assert, of course, that it is unknown or even atypical of other times.

23. For the persistence of the so-called monster as modern trope for human hybrids, see Rudyard Kipling and Thomas Carlyle as quoted in Young, *Colonial Desire*, 3, 5, respectively.

24. Bhabha, *The Location of Culture*, 33.

25. Young, *Colonial Desire*, 161.

26. I have adopted this language from the otherwise nearly scurrilous Marjorie Perloff, "Cultural Liminality/Aesthetic Closure? The 'Interstitial Perspective' of Homi Bhabha." Available at the Electronic Poetry Center Web site at the State University of New York, Buffalo, wings.buffalo.edu/epc/authors/perloff/bhabha/html.

27. Bhabha, *The Location of Culture*, 13.

28. Asad, *Genealogies of Religion*, 17.

29. Young, *Colonial Desire*, 19.

30. For other versions of problematization of "pure precolonial" selves as projected by certain forms of postcolonial analyses, see Loomba, *Colonialism/Postcolonialism*, 181–82. See, too, King, *Orientalism and Religion*, who writes, "Bhabha's notion of 'hybridity' implies that the colonial space involves the interaction of two originally 'pure' cultures (the British/European and the native) that are only rendered ambivalent once they are brought into direct contact with each other" (204). While I am somewhat doubtful as to whether this critique is properly applied to Bhabha, it does seem relevant to me in considering the postcolonial model for reading Judaism and Christianity in antiquity, which are surely always already hybridized with respect to each other.

31. It should be emphasized that wave theory is the historical or diachronic complement of dialect geography. For discussion of the latter and the fuzzy boundaries that it indicates between dialects, see Labov, "The Boundaries of Words and Their Meanings," 344–47.

32. Pratt, *Imperial Eyes*.

33. Young, *Colonial Desire*, 65.

34. Hall, *Ethnic Identity in Greek Antiquity*.

35. To be sure, he is careful to ascribe this version of wave theory to a single scholar, W. F. Wyatt (ibid., 166).

36. Hall, *Ethnic Identity in Greek Antiquity*, 172; Labov, "Boundaries of Words and Their Meanings," 347.

37. Hall, *Ethnic Identity in Greek Antiquity*, 172.

38. "What an ethnic group does is actively and consciously to select *certain arte-facts from within the overall material cultural repertoire* which then act as emblemic indicia of ethnic boundaries. In the words of Catherine Morgan, 'ethnic behaviour affects only those categories of artefact selected to carry social or political mean-ing under particular circumstances, rather than the totality of a society's material culture' " (Hall, *Ethnic Identity in Greek Antiquity*, 135). In this case, religious ideas and practices are the equivalent of artifacts. One example of this point that is very important to the further discussion of this issue in my *Border Lines* is the identifi-cation of modalism and its opposite as variation within Judaeo-Christian theology that was eventually chosen to be among the most significant of indicia for Christian and Jewish separate religious identities.

39. For this distinction, see Althusser, "Ideology and Ideological State Appara-tuses."

40. Beard, North, and Price, *Religions of Rome*, 249.

41. I have found Loomba, *Colonialism/Postcolonialism*, esp. 33–43, most helpful in articulating the basic theoretical apparatus with which I have been working for quite some time. Several formulations in these paragraphs are indebted to hers.

42. Althusser, "Ideology and Ideological State Apparatuses," 166.

43. Loomba, *Colonialism/Postcolonialism*, 37.

44. Following Dreyfus and Robinow (*Michel Foucault: Beyond Structuralism and Hermeneutics*, 121), I use the term *dispositif* to indicate a range of practices and in-stitutions that, in their relation to each other and to discourse, call for genealogical analysis.

45. Ibid., 38–39.

46. Ibid., 54.

47. Butler, *Excitable Speech*, 2.

48. Schiappa, *The Beginnings of Rhetorical Theory in Classical Greece*, 28–29.

49. Burrus, "Hailing Zenobia."

50. Butler, *Excitable Speech*, 2.

51. Brakke, "Jewish Flesh and Christian Spirit."

52. Markus, *The End of Ancient Christianity*, 28.

53. Williams, "Does It Make Sense to Speak of Pre-Nicene Orthodoxy?" 3.

54. See also Tropper, "*Tractate Avot* and Early Christian Succession Lists," for a convincing articulation of difference in the roles of heresiology within Christian proto-orthodox and rabbinic circles from nearly the very beginning.

55. We sometimes attempt in our language to naturalize this ambiguity, to reduce the shape-shifting quality of Judaism by drawing a distinction between Judaism and Jewishness—exploited to good effect in Cohen, *The Beginnings of Jewishness*—but it needs to be emphasized that this, to the best of my knowledge, parallels no distinc-tion made from within any traditional Jewish discourse at least, once again, until the nineteenth century.

56. Smith, *The Meaning and End of Religion*; Asad, *Genealogies of Religion*.

57. See, too, Limberis, " 'Religion' as the Cipher for Identity."

58. Sachot, "Comment le christianisme est-il devenu *religio*?"; Sachot, "*Religio/Superstitio*."

59. Schwartz, *Imperialism and Jewish Society*, 179.

60. For a similar argument with respect to the emergence of sexuality as such a discrete category, see Halperin, "How to Do the History of Male Homosexuality." This must be distinguished, however, from the concept of the precursor.

61. Guénoun, *Hypothèses sur l'Europe*, 117.

62. Schwartz, *Imperialism and Jewish Society*, 179.

63. Bhabha, *The Location of Culture*, 110–11.

Eugenic Woman, Semicolonialism, and Colonial Modernity as Problems for Postcolonial Theory

⊘ ⊘ ⊘

TANI E. BARLOW

If colonialism remained a historical and legal factor, this legacy did not necessarily turn Shanghai into a colony.
—LEO O. LEE, "Shanghai Modern: Reflections on Urban Culture in China in the 1930s"

If modernity and modernism describe how ideology formed and me-diated the emergent capitalist global order, then it seems right, as Dipesh Chakrabarty proposed in his 1983 "Conditions for Knowledge of Working Class Conditions," to focus historical attention on the content of modernist ideas and the conditions of thinking that inhere as residue in them.[1] This has been H. D. Harootunian's long-term project.[2] Yet two points remain out-standing for modern China historians: first, how are local articulations of modernity enmeshed, inextricably, with colonialism, and second, is it pos-sible that a feature of modernism—one that sweeps across all the various "singularities and universalism," in Timothy Mitchell's formula[3]—was the event of women?

Here, what concerns me specifically is eugenic woman. The effects of a bargain struck conclusively in the 1920s, eugenic woman proves significant not just in the Chinese national tradition but in national and international lineages of feminist liberation thinking to this day.[4] A significant center-piece of women's liberation discourse and key element of enlightened Chi-nese social theory in general, this female subject is legitimated in relation to the eugenic argument that natural selection and sexual selection work best in human populations where female procreators select their own sexual partners.[5]

The question is what sort of colonialism we are talking about in relation to eugenic woman, as well as what sort of modernity. As Kathy Le Mons Walker has shown, Chinese semicolonialism "can be viewed both as a historical moment—specified in relation to . . . international capitalist political, economic, and cultural projects in the modern era—and as a trope for domination, violation, and resistance," but "dominance in semicolonial China was doubly articulated," meaning that colonial capital eroded state hegemony and empowered new modernizing native elites who notably also could not establish popular hegemony.[6] Elite consumers and producers of so-called cosmopolitan ideas like eugenics showed the marks of this dominance and its limitations in a treaty port system that, like other such systems, played the role of a historically enabling constraint. Thus eugenic feminism cannot be described as a "derivative discourse" since it is not clear what sort of original it might be derivative of: Margaret Sanger in the United States depended as heavily on the population "problem" that China or India represented as Se Lu or Gao Xian did on Sanger in their intellectual homage to eugenic liberation theory.[7] Nonetheless, eugenic woman was probably not an indigenous Chinese phenomenon. Foundational Chinese social science in the 1920s, where women appeared most pointedly (particularly in the popular social contract theories of vernacular sociology), amalgamated European human sciences, Japanese pioneer social science, and the work of US sociologists like Lester Ward, Charlotte Perkins Gilman, Lester Wood, and Charles Elwood. Their thickly argued scholarly conventions are characteristic of contemporary international sociology, as well as feminist and socialist discourses.[8]

Because of what it is *not*—that is, a postcolonial entity, a colonial subject in the classic Anglo-Indian frame, a derivative discourse, a local or nativist signifier of authenticity—eugenic woman as a concept helps in the effort to understand current debates on Chinese modernism and to suggest possible ways out of some current methodological impasses. Shu-mei Shih's point that Chinese modernism or semicolonialism was not symptomatically Manichaean and recent historical studies demonstrating that Chinese intellectuals established prolonged, sometimes imaginary interlocutory relations with theorists in many parts of the colonial world (for example, Rabindranath Tagore, Ho Chi-min, Phan Boi Chao, Havelock Ellis, Ellen Key), indeed, in most metropolitan cores (Tokyo, London, Moscow, New York, Chicago, Paris), raise the question of how best to characterize colonial modernity in China in the twenties and thirties.[9] A small contribution to that effort, this essay begins (1) with a discussion of a feminist anomaly, (2) moves to a review of influential historical models structuring how specialist historians look at Chinese modernity, (3) measures China field historiography against the influence of postcolonial theory, and (4) concludes with a brief argument for why colonial modernity may be a useful way to think about Chinese republican governmentality.

Eugenic Woman

Mainstream feminist ideas emerged in Chinese treaty ports and new urban centers, largely in the twenties and early thirties, in the context of broadly accepted eugenic views of human reproduction and human will. This eugenic feminism held that Chinese men were responsible for securing Chinese women the social right to choose their own sexual partners because sex selection, the social/biological guarantee of racial vitality, required agency on the part of women. Organized patrilineal descent prostituted women, made men into pimps, and debilitated the race, according to major social theorists. This kind of evolutionary theory circuited through widely popular vernacular sociological ideologies to become a form of social biology and progressive Chinese feminism that served as a foundationally optimistic desire for social engineering in right- and left-wing social theory alike.[10]

Across the spectrum of social theory, a central preoccupation of Chinese intellectuals lay with the life sciences and the project of advancing a new, revolutionary, cleansed population. Hygiene, as Ruth Rogaski has pointed out in her brilliant short article "Hygienic Modernity in Tianjin," constituted the touchstone of Chinese colonial modern urbanity.[11] In Tianjin (a treaty port) and Taiwan (a Japanese colony), Japanese colonial institutions made sepsis the boundary line separating advanced Japanese and backward Chinese populations when colonizer and colonized occupied the same urban space.[12] The point is not simply that the colonizer/colonized distinction shifted from a scale of racial differentiation—difficult to sustain when both populations shared a common phenotype and superficial "racial" features—to an attention to hygienic practices. This landscape proves significant because of how the institutionalization of sepsis as social ideal linked up with related assumptions structuring social theory and the sort of residue these conditions left in the content of eugenic thinking. A key preoccupation on that score was the idea canonized in the 1920s that women's liberation was a eugenic necessity in modernizing societies.[13]

In the early twentieth century, modern Chinese scholarship predicated, that is, it proposed in theory, a subject defined by its alleged sexual essence. The project of consolidating and sexing this new woman unfolded in a contemporary, universalizing, eugenic, and progressive evolutionary theory that had, as does all evolutionary theory, sexual reproduction as its natural foundation. The discourse of evolutionary eugenics is what I call a colonial modernist discourse because it rested on a social theory that drew its legitimacy from observations about the lives of non-European peoples as a means of generalizing about sexuality as such. (In Mitchell's terms, it combined singularities with the universal in staging modernity.) In other words, the content of the ideology—its rationale and the subjects justifying its truths—prove as central to it as the generalization that it forwards. Elite male thinkers took up the question of the sexing of the modern female subject for the following reasons: First, the woman question played a central role in international social theory because theorists were preoccupied with social evolution and the dynamic role that human reproductive strategies played in it. Second, geopolitically, women had become a signifier of civilization and modernity in the international state system. Third, granting the implications of Darwinian social theory, it appears that progressive opinion sided with the notion that human and race evolution would accelerate when women had the freedom to express their instinctive heterosexual desires and freely select the best man for social reproduction.

One archival basis for my suggestion is a multivolume collection of pamphlets published by the Shanghai New Culture Press (Shanghai xin wenhua shushe) between 1923 and 1934. I exploit this resource because its editor, Mei Sheng, redacted and thus logically ordered theories of liberation when he selected and canonized key documents from what was in fact a huge universe of contemporary writing published in commercial journals and other new venues during that same period. The subject of Chinese feminism was always international, it turns out when one scans Mei Sheng's enormous reservoir of essays, and because of the way the arguments were framed in the decade when procreative or heterosexual or eugenic woman played a central role in grounding general social theory, she always manifested as an effect of the eugenic imagination.[14]

Cutting across Mei Sheng's complex analytic categories are a series of general arguments common to the entire collection. The most significant of these common arguments are:

(1)   The idea that Chinese women are socially deficient because while they should be taking an agential role in race improvement, their social conditioning prevents them from acting in accordance with their true nature. Women thus emerge as eugenically significant but socially insignificant because, in the dark reaches of time, men brutally suppressed them.

(2)   Chinese women are ethically deficient because men's alleged suppres-

sion of them imposes a normative handicap on women. (Gao Xian, Li Renjie, Y. D. [Li Rongdi], Zhou Zuoren, Zhou Jianren, Shi Heng, and many other critics address this alleged problem.)

(3) Because of this historical oppression, which had in effect stalled social evolution, the question of women's subjectivity (*renge*) is at issue. Only when family reform enabled women to live in small, "natural," middle-class procreative families could this question of ethical, social, and evolutionary personality formation be properly addressed. (This element of the debate had particular pertinence to class formation.)

(4) Women are a corporate entity with a "natural" social life (social forms that truly reflect underlying natural processes) when the coercive dead hand of the old civilization is removed from their throats.

The theoretical project that Mei Sheng's compendium represents is related to work produced in theory communities elsewhere in the world at around the same time. Between 1860 and 1930, social theory in Europe was particularly concerned with questions of sexual organization. By the 1920s, two poles of speculation existed. One theorized that social revolution originated in promiscuous, maternal communism, which only gradually gave way to male property-rights claims. This is the mother-right argument of Lewis Henry Morgan, Johann Jakob Bachofen, and John McLennan.[15] The other theorized paternal family formation as natural, originary, and universally normative and saw no historical, presocial, maternal bond cementing primeval social relations. This is Sir Henry James Sumner Maine's patriarchal theory, famously expressed in *Ancient Law*. Freud, as we know from the work of Zhang Jingyuan, traveled a slightly different theory network in China, contributing the notion of phylogenesis linking subject to society, and there is evidence that many social theorists found this argument useful as well.

My point in reiterating my findings (which appear in lengthy detail elsewhere) here is to suggest that eugenic presuppositions structured debates in Chinese modernist circles just as they saturated key modernist terms in other theory projects elsewhere. Furthermore, liberation theories like progressive Chinese feminism incorporate eugenic science. At stake in these discussions in Chinese treaty ports, as well as in sociological theories and feminism developing in the United States and Europe at the same time, is heterosexuality as a theoretical concept, naturalized fact, and social institution. Yi Jiayue, Zhou Jianren, Xi Leng, Feng Fei, Wang Qingni, and many others concurred that the evolutionary imperative of heterosexual eros needed renovation and that family reform should be a central vehicle of racial and national progress.[16] When heterosexuality as a progressive social expression became socially and ideologically institutionalized it promised to (1) revitalize the Chinese as a race and as a nation; (2) lend social and ethical legitimacy to social actors who engaged in the progressive struggle for a better, more hygienic future; (3) make social subjectivity available for women on the grounds of their heterosexual responsibility; and (4) consolidate the subject of women by fusing female will and emotions in the voluntary expression of erotic love in human reproduction. This ideology clearly had important implications for the reordering of social class hierarchy (as Wen-hsin Yeh and others have made clear). But that is not my present concern.

Two points are germane here. First, inside what I will describe later in this essay as a colonial modernist matrix, eugenic theory explicitly addressed what women's liberation was supposed to achieve, what women would be liberated to do. In this theory, the liberation of women in China would lead eugenically to a strengthening of a proud but debilitated race. The fusion of social Darwinian ideas and feminist liberation is therefore never the parochial concern of women, but always the central concern of all people. Second, the emphatic linking of hygienic and eugenics theories was the fruit of what appears to be an international, perhaps largely Japanese, colonial figuration of eugenic racialism and its suggestion that degenerate civilization in China was the mark of a degenerate population. In other words, eugenic feminism and its female subject are not simply a hygienist's version of modernism—they constitute colonial formations. Eugenic feminism appears at this level to participate in colonial logics of the same order as those that Ann Stoler and Warwick Anderson have argued were working in other colonial contexts.[17]

The Colonial Question in China Studies

An important development in the historiography of China, Japan, Korea, and the various former tributaries of the disintegrated Chinese imperium is the reassertion in the last decade of the colonial question. Many factors have contributed to this resurgence of interest. In East Asian studies, postcolonial theory has certainly emerged as one provocation, though it has proven more influential in cultural studies and literary criticism than history in any explicit sense. An older stream of scholarship had already described the complex control system involved particularly in Japan's economic colonization of the Chinese mainland and the seizure from the late Qing (1644–1911) government of Taiwan, Korea, and Manchuria as formal colonies when, in the early 1990s, the current debate over colonial modernity resurfaced.[18] Building on this older tradition and at the instigation of postcolonial studies, a newly relevant scholarship has been able to skip the traces of exclusively nation-based research and focus instead on Japanese colonial policy in dynamic relation to all affected regions;[19] on the homeland populations in Japan, Japanese colonies, and China; in a surge of important cultural studies research, on Manchuria, occupied Shanghai, and Taiwan; and on the intellectual history of colonial modernist speculation in Chinese and Japanese political discourse and critical theory.[20]

The historiographic point that colonialism is a modernist phenomenon has consequently been well established in most China-based studies. While not all disputants would agree with me that colonialism forms a constituting element of global modernity, even those who prefer, as Leo O. Lee does, to demur on the subject of colonization in China in the end confront the dilemma that colonialism poses. While it feels wrong to call Shanghai a true colony, Lee argues in his brief for what he calls "Shanghai modern" that the question of "internal colonization" may hold relevance. How else can egregious anomalies like Freudianism, social science, language reform, palladian banks, eugenic feminism, and so on be considered? Lee can, if he wishes, say that he *prefers* not to deal with the colonial question, as he does when he asserts that "on the basis of my research I am not fully prepared" to go down the colonialism road. But he cannot fully shake the feeling that what he chooses to name a worldly cosmopolitanism might, in the last instance, be a colonial modernist phenomenon as well.[21] Lee's loving evocation of Shanghai, recognizing and resisting recognition of an event that both resembles and yet does not resemble the "classic" England-to-India format means that, for him, Shanghai becomes a singular object, one outside the matrix of colonial history.

In the current specialist debates about region and colonialism, however, I also value the position that downright denies any purchase whatever to colonialism in any relation to Chinese modernity. While I obviously do not subscribe to this argument, it proves useful for three general reasons. First, because it is unconcerned with definitions of colonialism or semicolonialism per se, it does not rest its case on Chinese characteristics, does not build an abstract model on the alleged singularity of a particular colonial experience, and does not replicate the frequent reifications of "India" that some scholars find objectionable in postcolonial criticism. Second, it sets up a hostile, imaginary opposition between postcolonial studies and Chinese Marxist theory. This tactic sacrifices nuance and subtlety, but it helps to sharpen and delimit the point of theoretical work generally. Third, and a reason wholly related to my own arguments, the necessary theoreticism or special privileging of theoretical logics usefully throw into relief what is not available in arguments that engage yet disavow the colonial problem. The stringent argument that makes Chinese modernity the very antithesis of postcoloniality thus helps me to address my own questions, including, "What is colonial about Chinese colonial modernity?"

Liu Kang's important but undervalued *Aesthetics and Marxism: Chinese Aesthetic Marxists and Their Western Contemporaries* argues that modernity proves meaningless on a national scale because modernity is a global phenomenon and is furthermore the effect of ongoing revolutions.²² A student of Fredric Jameson, Liu Kang is concerned with the ways that cultural logics are extricable and meaningful or broadly useful in appropriate Marxist theoretical projects. The truest and most effective Marxism for adequately grasping the immediate Chinese past and for negotiating the international present and future is in fact an alternative to the Marxism canonized in cultural studies and postcolonial studies (as he understands them): Chinese aesthetic Marxism. To make his case, Liu Kang needs to demonstrate why aesthetics constitutes the primary signifier or exemplary modern quality in modernist thinking internationally, and specifically why it had such central purchase for Chinese intellectuals. Why it is, in other words, that aesthetics defines modernity wherever one finds it. In addition, Liu Kang takes on the task of justifying why the alternate, aesthetic, Marxist Chinese tradition is superior to the canonical European figures of Walter Benjamin, Theodor Adorno, Antonio Gramsci, and Louis Althusser.

Liu Kang's book argues that "the aesthetic . . . became the focal point in the history of Chinese revolution and modernity" because aesthetics fully apprehends and delivers a critique of modern experience.²³ Even non-Marxist giants like Wang Guowei (most commonly classified as a late Confucian thinker), Liang Qichao (usually considered a political philosopher), and Cai Yuanpei (a preeminent liberal social and institutional modernist), in other words, shared a passion for aesthetics with the Chinese Marxist tradition in thought. Lu Xun (father of Chinese modern fiction), Qu Qiubai (Chinese Communist Party leader, strategist, and martyr), and Mao Zedong were all Marxist modernists who shared the same moment with Wang Guowei, Liang Qichao, Cai Yuanpei, and, for that matter, Benjamin, Adorno, Gramsci, and Althusser. All belonged to the same conceptual set—modernist philosophers—because the contradictory, immanently fragmented, and nonidentitarian quality of modernity globally is precisely the quality that each modernist theorist, Marxist or liberal, sought to establish through his thinking. So because modernity is globally "coeval" (i.e., it temporally unfolds all at the same time), it is not surprising that the theoretical debates of Zhu Guangqian and Li Zehou resemble in many details the Althusserian revolution in European Marxism. Nor that Qu Qiubai's critique of the May Fourth era

(1919–27) ideology and his deepening concern for the elite domination of popular language and culture is the functional equivalent of Gramsci's theories on hegemony, which the latter developed during roughly the same era.

Liu Kang does something in his book that I find debatable yet valuable. He situates his Chinese alternate Marxist theoretical tradition in opposition to what he calls "today's postcolonialist academicians in the United States."²⁴ These postcolonial practitioners, he alleges, not only enfeeble and sap whatever vitality is left in university radicalism but they also impoverish Marxism generally speaking because they enshrine an antirevolutionary strain of theory. This postcolonial canon cannot draw on the energy that the genuine relation of theory to praxis—a truly revolutionary Marxism—can offer. The Chinese alternative aesthetic Marxism, in other words, offers to the international movement of Marxist scholars potentially canonical figures who are invaluable not just because they are modernists and aesthetic Marxists but because their revolutionary experiences have infused their thinking with a grave realism lacking in the writing of theorists who work in less unsettled conditions. So two reasons exist why Chinese thinkers are superior to those glamorized in current postcolonial theory: Unlike the canonical Europeans, the Chinese figures have actual firsthand experience of revolution because their objective was to create and institutionalize a socialist modernity. Liu Kang's position differs from the more typical criticism that postcolonialism is the effluvia of expatriate, elite theorists who constitute nothing less than a comprador class whose moral failings are dooming the international proletarian revolution. But it is also interesting that the dangers Liu Kang has vested in postcolonial criticism do not trouble Harootunian's critical histories of Japanese fascist modernity. While Liu Kang shares much with Harootunian's position, the latter's "vast field of unevenness" over which modernist discourses as ideological formations roam in their paranoid effort to repress difference (including colonial ones) simply presumes the colonial project without stress.

Another place where the question of colonialism has proven an explicit concern are China-oriented studies that presume the alleged paradox of "imperialism after [or without] empire" and the thesis of "informal" colonialism. Indeed, the informal empire and accidental colonies theses prove more influential in China scholarship than ever before. Recall that Ronald Robinson and John Gallagher, who originated the thesis of informal colonialism, began from the insight that imperialism and colonialism are not spatially isomorphic. Colonies, even formal ones, had taken different administrative and economic shapes depending on the time, place, and the colonizing states in question. Robinson and Gallagher challenged earlier, stricter, definitions of colonial structures based on the model of England to India. Their insight into the India-England paradigm rested on two more ambiguous cases, the so-called informal American empire and so-called Chinese semicolonialism.[25] Modeling the China case, and the theoretical vagueness of the conceptual apparatus, gave "informal colonialism" purchase in US East Asia studies; conservative scholars in East Asian studies fields, seeking a way to understand Japanese imperialism and the impact of Japanese occupation of territory on the China mainland, incorporated the model into research.[26]

This theory stream has recently reemerged in work borrowing its framework from Jürgen Osterhammel's "Semi-colonialism and Informal Empire in Twentieth-Century China: Towards a Framework of Analysis."[27] Osterhammel's key essay directly addresses the main complaint of many China specialists—that China was never really colonized—and suggests that a special case be made for China on the basis of a national essence argument.[28] In the early 1980s, Osterhammel set out a typology around the alleged China anomaly. It was an unusual focus since, as I have suggested above, China is ordinarily left out of globalized discussions or considered, along with the United States, as the exception to all rules. Osterhammel seems actually to be reinforcing—and he formalized this insight into an analytic model—a preexisting and enduring notion that China had the capacity to resist colonization because it had retained titular political sovereignty and because it, unlike India or Africa, indeed, perhaps alone among so-called traditional societies, had possessed a traditional culture ipso facto resistant to change from the outside. Colonialism and imperialism had left China relatively untouched in Osterhammel's reckoning because of its cultural integrity or traditional essence. On these grounds Osterhammel proposed three alternative models—Marxist, modernist, and marginal. The ideal typical case for the marginal model was China because somehow a modern China had developed outside (i.e., on the margin of) global imperialism and without real colonization; being singular or singularly marginal, China fit Osterhammel's general objective, which was apparently to apply the thesis of informal empire globally. He could then claim to augment a general theory with a "subtypology of the various forms of informal empire." China became "a model on an intermediate level of abstraction that takes important features from the ideal type of informal empire but, at the same time already incorporates basic characteristics of the Chinese situation."[29] The Osterhammel model is formalist. It rests on typologies invented using empirical details its author selected for their importance in relation to his larger abstractions about laissez-faire markets and liberalizing political power. I raise Osterhammel's influence not to launch objections or even because his influence among specialist scholars has been so pervasive, but rather because in addressing the colonial matter directly, Osterhammel's work tends to inoculate China historiography against postcolonial theoretical speculation.

The one significant debate that social science and cultural analyses share is the question of whether semicolonialism is singular and, if so, whether it is singularly Chinese. *Semicolonialism* is a Leninist term, half of the Maoist characterization of modern China as a semifeudal, semicolonial nation. Since one objection of historians to the postcolonial theory stream has been that such theorists do not respect the isomorphism of ideas to nation, some important writing has directly addressed the Chineseness of semicolonialism. Scholarship on the Osterhammel model has tended to exploit the partiality or incompleteness of semicolonial controls, for instance.[30] Thus Shumei Shih's *Lure of the Modern: Writing Modernism in Semicolonial China, 1917–1937* (which like Walker's *Chinese Modernity* draws on Ranajit Guha's thesis of domination without hegemony) has been influential in reworking some of the positions that the informal empire group stakes out.[31] Shih's argument turns the emphasis from incompletion to the multiplicity of colonialisms. She rests her study of literary and popular culture on the thesis that semicolonialism was a *"political* formation of layered domination by multiple foreign powers who competed and cooperated with each other in pursuit of their own individual economic and political agendas" and, consequently, mutually "prevented the constitution of a unified colonial state with well-coordinated policies of control."[32] Multiple and overlapping colonial oppressions meant that Japan, the United States, and the European powers dominated the modern sector of the economy. They also enforced juridical fragmentation. Because Chinese cultural modernists lost control over political sovereignty, a Chinese semicolonialism resulted. That semicolonialism had the following key characteristics: it was urban but non-Manichaean, given that a multitude of colonial powers left open no single stable target; it proved seductive to comprador intellectuals since the colonial powers never "impose[d] a colonial epistemology by force";[33] and it could be described as modernist since it was the brainchild of colonizers and collaborators alike. Enlightened native intellectuals abandoned "culture" as the terrain of anticolonial resistance and opted instead for what Shih calls the colonial modernist ideology of "cosmopolitanism."[34]

Postcolonialism and Its Worldly Expression

Clearly, the specter haunting this essay is "China." So far I have raised the question as to why it is useful to characterize the so-called republican period

(1911–49) around modernist anomalies like eugenic social theory and eugenic female subjects and indicated that some singular debates in the field of China studies either disregard or dispute postcolonial theory and attempted to explain why. Some general characteristics of postcolonial theory turn out to be tangential to China historiography even when semicolonialism is accepted as one common expression of monopoly capitalism and the system of global colonialism (to use L. S. Stavrianos's serviceable formula), and even when the fact of postcolonial theory's influence on topics and emphases is fully credited.[35]

Scholars like me do have a certain stake in postcolonial speculations, despite the fact that China's history of compulsory globalization and its singularity as a national formation in international systems probably exceed the current capacity of postcolonial theory to address. But that is not because China was "never colonized" or because semicolonialism is a poor cousin of "real colonialism." The lack of fit between postcolonial theory and the historiographic preoccupations of China scholars engaged in examining regional forms of colonial modernity is due as much to inherited frames of reference that condition historical conventions among specialists as to the centrality of Japanese imperialism within larger patterns of colonial activity over the last two centuries.

The more manageable question is what in postcolonial studies has contributed to the way I have staged and addressed my own problematics. I apologize for using shorthand to set out what I understand to be key debates in the field of postcolonialism pertinent to me and to indicate where, were I better educated in that discipline, I might be positioned by its advocates. First, I accept Gayatri Spivak's view that US postcolonialism is a discipline that "developed rather haphazardly in response to a felt need among minority groups" to consider our cultures and identities. It is consequently an outgrowth of literary and cultural studies; it does not fare equally well in disciplines of history and the social sciences.[36] Second, I take R. Radhakrishnan's point that "postcoloniality is always already marked by ambivalence and that the task is to politicize this given ambivalence and produce it agentially." (This also puts me in substantial agreement with Kalpana Seshadri-Crooks's insight that the value of postcolonial studies is its critique of the discourses of modernity and that that very critique lays postcolonial studies open to criticism of culturalism and apoliticism—despite the fact that self-appointed critics Aijaz Ahmed and Arif Dirlik, are themselves postcolonial Marxists who have made entire careers of thinking about margins, subjectivities, cultural criticism, disciplinary policing, and so on.)[37] Third, I agree with Sumit Sarkar, who draws attention back to the fact that Subaltern

Studies was originally (and in interesting ways remains) a Maoist project.[38] The question of what is Maoist about subaltern studies (e.g., its preoccupation with mass subjects, peasant revolution, rural society, landlordism, popular culture, cultural revolution, and so on) is a question in the history of Marxism since Maoism is properly, which is to say genealogically, a mediated Marxism. Like cultural Marxists elsewhere, Maoists have posed questions of social relations of production, alienation and oppression, aesthetics, ideology, and popular agency. Maoism participates, even in its genuinely catastrophic forms, in the global effort to establish viable analytic categories that are at once economic and cultural (or conversely, are neither economistic nor culturalist). Another way of thinking this point is to underscore the fact that no simple line can demarcate "postcolonialism" from "Chinese Marxism."[39]

Let us set aside for the moment postcolonial theory's Maoist roots and ask instead what relations obtain between a subdiscipline, postcolonial studies, that is, in Seshadri-Crook's phrase, distinguished from "other area studies . . . [in that it] *has no identifiable object*,"[40] and studies that begin (as mine does) from the assumption that notions of Chinese modernity cannot afford to overlook colonialism. Twentieth-century Chinese intellectual history is not comprehensible without considering key historical events—such as the event of woman in eugenic feminism—and these events are invisible until the colonial roots of modernity are brought into focus.

Since this proposition has proven contentious, it is useful to indicate elements that appear to be structuring specialist China research and are traceable to postcolonialism's generalities. This is an agonistic relationship since all sides appear peripherally aware of the others yet remain reluctant to admit the full implications of their interchanges. First, practitioners of postcolonial theory seem to imagine that China and its study is either terra incognita or an empiricist wasteland that has so far resisted incorporation into the postcolonial framework.[41] Certainly researchers in China studies are accused, with good reason, of hypostatizing the "China thing," or conversely, of collapsing all of Asia into the signifier China. But saying so does not alter the fact that current postcolonial theoreticians remain largely indifferent to histories of colonial configurations outside the South Asia canon, and this rigidity limits the flexibility and usefulness of postcolonial methods. Second, inversely, because postcolonial scholarship in the United States and Britain insists on reifying the India-England model, the colonial question in Chinese modern history can be infinitely dismissed on the grounds that China was never colonized. Third, China historians in the United States are split over an imaginary opposition that is held to distinguish "colonial modernity" from "revolutionary modernity." As Lin Chun has recently pointed out, it is increasingly clear that this distinction is an artifact of inadequate attention to questions of periodization and of an unwillingness in current China scholarship to appreciate the singularity of Chinese developmental theory (its "pathway," in Lin Chun's terms) as such, given that revolution is concurrent with colonization.[42] Fourth, in responding to questions raised in postcolonial studies (and the debate over postmodernity instigated by Jameson and his expatriate People's Republic of China students), studies of Chinese modernity or modernism have reignited.[43] Finally, less reflexive "applications" of postcolonial theory to the Chinese historical record keep the colonial question a sore point among specialist scholars. This situation of high ambiguity or lack of fit between history studies and postcolonial protestations is actually quite useful (as the work of Shu-mei Shih, Kathy Walker, and others has suggested). But alongside questions debated in Chinese history circles, the signifier *China* constitutes a useful reminder to historians and postcolonial theorists of the extent of colonial heterogeneity. Perhaps with time and patience the implicit relation of model to theory—India and England, colony to colonial, politics to culture—that the subaltern studies paradigm has entrenched will eventually erode sufficiently to allow for its own displacement.

Colonial Modernity

Let me forward in this final discussion reasons why it makes sense to develop the thesis of colonial modernity a bit further.[44] The term itself, *colonial modernity*, evokes Harootunian's thesis on modernity as the ideologization of an uneven field alongside Maoist-inspired subaltern studies critiques such as those of Spivak and the early Dipesh Chakrabarty. These are theoretical debts. The priorities now are historical. William Schaefer's reworking of familiar modernist tropes of primitivity through Shanghainese reflections on racialized "barbarians" in popular pictorial magazines of the twenties and thirties provides a good example.[45] Gennifer Weisenfeld's "Visual Cultures of Japanese Imperialism," an edited journal volume spotlighting how Japanese collectors' museum classifications of Korean artifacts became a foundation of colonial modern aesthetics, also provides a concrete application of colonial modernity as a temporal concept to an East Asian setting.[46] And Andrew Jones's concept of "phonographic realism," which I will take up momentarily, explicitly names the era of investigation as "colonial modernity."[47] Many other social historical and cultural investigations show a similar profile.

The value of these detailed studies lies in the fact that what counts in them is not the coeval quality of colonial modernity, but the systematic inequalities promoted by modernist ideologies. Because they involve distribution systems and commodities (often cultural commodities), they point to a cultural logic of colonial capitalism and its commercial relations. Feminist research has demonstrated that colonial modernist Chinese feminism unfolded with other national traditions of women's liberation, but simultaneity is only part of the picture. For instance, Jones's study of phonographic realism centers on the technologies of the phonograph and the photograph, the multinational corporations that collaborated with comprador music innovators, and mass or popular music consumption in the treaty port sectors. Jones explicitly addresses the question of colonial modernism. After the Opium War of 1839–42, European music spread from the imperial Chinese court to the popular masses through Protestant missionary, military, and academic conduits. This pattern, Jones notes, was "by no means unique to China. It played itself out on a global scale, irrespective of different degrees of territorial colonization. The introduction of Western music in Japan (which was not territorially colonized) and China (which was partially colonized by several of the colonial powers) was strikingly similar."[48] But Jones's primary point is that production capacity was owned by transnational capital, including US-, British-, and Japanese-based corporations and the Shanghai production studio Pathé (which distributed music to the Vietnamese, Burmese, Laotian, Indonesian, Malayan, and Philippine markets).[49] In this respect, music markets exemplify the commodification process that (Greg Blue argues) structured the opium trade in the nineteenth century. Like opium, music emerged in an "institutional nexus" and "cohesive trade structure" more collaborative than oppositional, though, as Blue stresses, the relation was from the outset agonistic.[50]

A similar argument has recently been made about the history of the institutionalization of the US social sciences as intellectual commodities in key Chinese universities. Jones's argument that phonographic realism was simultaneously domestic and international is echoed in Yung-chen Chiang's case study, which shows definitively that the social sciences emerged simultaneously in China, the United States, and Western Europe at a key point in the alignment of geopolitics (the relation of Japan and the United States) and in the history of US progressive imperialism. In his *Social Engineering and the Social Sciences in China, 1919–1949*, Chiang argues that the technocratic and statist quality of social science methods and their social objectives easily account for the similarity apparent in their content and timing.[51] The Rockefeller Foundation's role in founding departments of sociology and social science in China's treaty port cities and the generally uncritical adoption of an American social science curriculum both help explain colonial modernist epistemologies in the 1920s.[52]

At the top of Chiang's agenda in this argument, however, is to suggest that the amounts of money at stake in the founding projects shaped academic politics in compromising ways. The proliferation of eugenic feminist theories in the 1920s and 1930s rested to a great degree on the new media and on the epistemologies that Chiang uncovers. My initial point that it is only in light of colonial modernist frameworks that an anomaly like the subject of eugenic feminism emerges into intelligibility therefore rests on a series of specialist research projects.[53] Nonetheless, the logic in play proves similar in each case—opium, music, social science—and I will suggest here that it is useful to generalize this commodity logic because it underlies the modern system of commercial exchange that colonial incursions initiated. For a useful illustration I turn to the discussion of British American Tobacco's (BAT) cigarette manufacture, corporatization, and commodification and the relationship that BAT established between the development of the market and the commodification of tobacco.

Howard Cox's *The Global Cigarette* includes a lengthy chapter on BAT in China.[54] It focuses on the quotidian struggle of the tobacco industry: BAT, in a dominant position, facing constant competition with US, Japanese, and local Chinese manufacturers to keep its machine-made cigarettes profitable. In the early twentieth century, in response to the collapse of the central authority of the Qing state in 1911 and escalating competition from Japanese and other competing colonial states and corporations, BAT executives undertook campaigns to create markets for their machine-made cigarettes. They sought to build distribution networks that would adhere to the letter of the unequal treaties but violate Chinese intentions to contain foreign capital in the treaty ports and invented liability-sharing schemes that would include Chinese marketers and joint ventures in relations of inequality. By the 1920s, this involved 10,000 employees, 20 percent of whom were foreign, and a honeycomb system of locally registered holding companies (registered under amended British companies ordinances) that sought to claim immunity from Chinese laws but autonomy from the colonial authorities. British American Tobacco's innovating regional distribution system of carefully segmented markets resulted from the company's willingness to increase the involvement of native merchants (who stimulated already existing networks of dealers) while retaining majority control at the level of the corporation.

My interest in this commercial capitalist industry lies with the fact, as Cox argues, that the trade revolved around a commodity, machine-made cigarettes. But because the commodity form of tobacco cost more than other ways of smoking, "a pricing strategy needed to be developed which both encouraged consumers to adopt this form of smoking and allowed dealers a reasonable profit margin. . . . [The consequent] approach to pricing cigarettes, both in China and in India, was to offer them for sale at a price which was convenient in terms of the local currency."[55] In other words, although the commodity form of tobacco was "an article of mass production," selling it involved strenuous efforts; consumers willing to purchase the article had to be nurtured and deals with the various colonial shareholders on the China mainland had to be struck—in short, markets for commodity tobacco had to be created. The strategies for doing so involved, for instance, hiring sales representatives from US tobacco-producing regions, sending them out into the China mainland "as missionaries for the new project," plastering visual advertising in potential markets, giving out advertisements by hand, distributing sample product, relaying back to the sales department all commercial intelligence on the ground, and consequently creating, in Cox's words, "a system through which conditions in the different markets could be recorded . . . [setting] out prevailing conditions for each town" down to details like exchange rates and income levels.[56]

However, Cox's argument is not primarily concerned with the commodification of the tobacco market in China or in any of the other national, colonial, subnational, or regional markets that he describes in patient detail. His general argument concerns the reciprocal relation obtaining between the commodity and the creation of modern markets. The strategies that BAT and other colonial or transnational corporations developed to market their newly commodified tobacco had the effect of globalizing the commodity itself. Only in relation to the information that local missionaries or BAT (US-born) tobacco sales representatives gathered in a systematic way could the commodity itself prove its power. The profit that BAT extracted and the tax revenue that it provided to successive Chinese governments depended on both market-savvy distribution networks and the added value of branded cigarettes.

The marketing of cigarettes internationally—the global cigarette—established a dynamic relationship between the commodity and the market in which machine-made smokes only became preferable through marketing, and the market testing happened not in the countries of corporate origin, but in the colonial markets. Cigarette marketing tested itself in "the gorges of the Yangtze, across the Mongolian desert to Urga (Ulaan Baator) and to faraway Langchow (Lanzhou) in Kansu (Gansu)," as Cox cites J. A. Thomas, chief architect of the innovative BAT strategy.[57] In this the cigarette commodity resembles eugenic woman and eugenicist theories, which are colonial modernist formations because they posit a modernity heavily indebted to the underdeveloped or premodern peoples that it alleged to represent. This is only to say that although they are relatively autonomous cultural forms and theories, they are mediated through the complex circuitry of capitalist production and consumer relations. Perhaps the era of colonial modernity was precisely that moment when social ideologies and cultural representations fed back into the circuit of production and consumption, and were, in turn, affected by the global circulation of commodities. What the marketing of cigarettes, the acceptance of eugenic and Chinese social science theory (not to restrict this event to China, but taking it as a case in point) reveal is that social cultural representation feeds back into the emerging circuit of production and consumption as it spreads into colonizing contexts and is tested out beyond the territorial precincts of the United States and Europe.

Conclusion

In a gesture to Edward Said's orientalism debates, tacking the word *colonial* onto the ideologically charged word *modernity* underlines the constitutional doubleness of discourses of modernity and shifts away from Said's preoccupation with hegemonic representation to consider conditions of modernity actually obtaining in colonies, subcolonies, indirect colonies, and semicolonies, all under the overlapping rubrics of *modernity, modernism,* or *modernization.*[58] Colonial modernity consequently accentuates the political and ideological dependency, or intellectual interrelatedness, of colonizing powers and colonial regimes. The commodity economies—for example, opium, tea, sugar, or tobacco—that integrated international trade during the imperialists' efforts to regulate colonial domains of various kinds also, thus, reshaped political, administrative, governmental, ideological, and intellectual lines of power. In Britain, India, and China, the integration of the opium industry not only fed Japanese colonial and capital accumulation; it also altered Qing styles of governmentality, reorganized the relation of Chinese state and population, affected semicolonial styles of modern urbanization, and (to a degree) structured the diasporic movements of Chinese capital and labor into Southeast Asia. Often obscured or denied in modernity studies are precisely these colonial commodities (e.g., opium, tea, labor), trade routes, reordered styles of governmentality, juridical norms (e.g., international laws and treaties), administrative innovations (e.g., customs, extraterritoriality, treaty ports), and colonial trade in ideas that characterize colonizers as well as colonial regimes.[59]

Colonial modernity is therefore cumulative. The colonial storehouse of policy and strategy could be and routinely was raided and its contents recycled. The relationship even between a colonizer and a directly colonized people is not exactly bilateral. Even a directly bilateral treaty rests on administrative techniques and policy that draw on past experience. Thus, for instance, the primary colonizing strategy of the treaty port system was not initiated in China, but rather redeployed after having been tested first against the Ottomon Empire.[60] In other words, the European consolidation of Shanghai and Hong Kong, the so-called US open-door policies, and Japan's indirect colonies in Manchuria and subsequent colonial empire in Manchukuo, Taiwan, and the Korean peninsula had historical precedents. Each drew on older techniques developed over long periods of time in the unequal relationship between Britain and India, Britain and Kenya, Spain and Mexico, Portugal and Brazil, and so on. The fact of multiple imperialist adventures in China, leading to the term *semicolonialism*, should not distract attention away from the fact that already well-established colonial knowledge informed the Great Powers' experiments and contributed to "development" in their "spheres of influence."[61]

Colonial modernity is, consequently, more a planar or spatial term than a temporal one. There is no direct line of teleological development connecting British, Dutch, or Spanish colonial occupation with the various overlapping semicolonial projects of the Great Powers in China two centuries later. That is because by the nineteenth and twentieth centuries, most of the vast plane of the earth's surface had been colonized or partly colonized, and because of this spatial extension of the colonial project, colonial knowledge circulated through the colonial capitals. By the late nineteenth century, the colonial agent was no longer necessarily the imperial navy or policy maker. As they scattered over the globe, laissez-faire business agents, entrepreneurial prostitutes, joint-venture media capitalists, anthropologists and sociologists, opium traders, and missionaries all brought with them the assumptions and techniques that disseminated colonial knowledge without necessitating direct colonization.[62]

Colonial modernity, with its ambiguous, multiple, or planar quality, offers a useful platform for thinking about the singularity of Chinese enlightened theories, including what I call progressive Chinese feminism and its theories of feminine subjectivity. Progressive Chinese feminist thinking rested on orientalist anthropologies, in the Saidian sense, or grossly disciplinary representations of primitive social relations. Without arcane colonial knowledge about "Hindoos" and Iroquois, matriarchal societies and social evolutionary reproductive instincts, Mohammedans, their harem and social pathologies, the great theorists of colonial modernity from James Frazer and Charles Darwin to Gao Xian, Zhou Jianren, Pan Guangdan, Sun Benwen, and their Japanese or US counterparts could not have developed their ideological projects. Enlightenment social sciences of sociology, anthropology, and political science in Cambridge or Beijing, Tokyo or London, centered and authorized themselves with reference to these other places and times. Enlightenment (in this essay, as in my recent work generally, feminism stands in a metonymic relation to enlightened thinking) seems to not require an other that is passive, amorphous, or incommensurate. That is likely because it can and does focus its powers of reason and social logics on immediate terrains.[63]

The duality—both modern and colonial—of enlightened thinking frees historical writing from the burden of comparison. Chinese Enlightenment thinking was neither derivative nor not derivative. It was the line on which new intellectuals crafted policy, ideology, social and scholarly critique, strategy, and all the practical theoretical projects of intellectual modernity. The question shifts: it is not "What is a colony," but rather, given the colonial roots of modernity per se even in Europe, "What is singular about the way modernity was thought in China?"[64] Theorists, then, in the disciplines of comparative anatomy, sociology, cultural anthropology, and sex theory, are responsible for engineering sexed identity, not just in semicolonies like China's treaty ports but, as Nancy Armstrong and Mary Poovey, Robert Young and Dipesh Chakrabarty have made very clear, in London and Lancashire too. The subjects that emerged out of the conditions of knowledge in Chinese treaty ports were, as Tomiyama Ichiro has shown for the subject "islanders" in Japanese colonial discourses, specifically and irreducibly themselves.[65] Like the Japanese body, these scientized, biologized, evolutionized identities of woman and man constitute core elements of colonial modernity. But each modernist subject, like each new factory producing commodities coded in terms of capitalist value, is recast within a semiotic political economy that can be read back into the conditions of its formation as knowledge.

Notes

It is a pleasure to thank Antoinette Burton, Jed Esty, and Matti Bunzl for skilled editorial consideration and all the editors of this volume for including a noncanonical scholar like me in their project. My most exacting critic Donald M. Lowe contributed a final reading and refinement. My grateful thanks to Yingjing Zhang for generously sharing his important review of 1990s modernity studies among largely expatriate China-born China specialists, "Five Faces/Phases of Modernity in China: Towards a Typology/Genealogy in Literary and Cultural History, "an unpublished manuscript. Excepting Andrew Jones, *Yellow Music*, China scholars have not generally raised the problem of colonial modernity, and hence the debate continues to work the ground "between China and the West." See Barlow, *Formations of Colonial Modernity in East Asia*; and Shin and Robinson, *Colonial Modernity in Korea* for scholars who focus on colonial modernity.

1. Chakrabarty, "Conditions for Knowledge of Working Class Conditions."

2. Harootunian, *Overcome by Modernity*, defines modernity historically. Aesthetic is not the primary or exclusive stake because modernity and modernism are a "broad signifier that includes art and literature . . . but also philosophy, religion and social and political thought. . . . I am . . . using modernism as an ideologization of the process of capitalist modernization and transformation Japanese were experiencing and trying to grasp," Harootunian states. "Although Japanese modernism conformed to the broader global conjuncture, it also decisively inflected it into patterns of difference that marked, as elsewhere, the distinct place where a regional past co-existed with industrialism. . . . *modernism in Japan's interwar period was produced in a conjuncture that prompted the recognition of a vast field of economic and cultural unevenness that it sought to resolve, overcome, and even repress*" (xx–xxi).

3. Timothy Mitchell, introduction to Mitchell, *Questions of Modernity*, xii–xiii.

4. Very likely in the US nationalist tradition of racialized white feminism, as current scholarly preoccupation with Margaret Sanger in the United States is beginning to suggest. See Ordover, *American Eugenics*, 137–59.

5. Barlow, *The Question of Women in Chinese Feminism*, ch. 3.

6. Walker, *Chinese Modernity and the Peasant Path*, 13. She profitably follows Ranajit Guha's thesis of dominance without hegemony to argue that neither colonial capital nor the empowerment of ruling class fragments successfully hegemonized the rising peasantry.

7. *Funüzazhi*, June 1922. An example of the complex relation of indebtedness and inequality that characterizes Chinese colonial modernity is the Margaret Sanger special issue of the mainstream journal *Funüzazhi*—in it are Qiu Shiying and Se Lu's essays on eugenic sex and Sangerism, but also Japanese- and English-authored thought pieces that explicitly link the discourses of civilization to notions of birth limitation and race improvement, as well as the usual, international nod in the direction of Sanger's so-called neo-Malthusianism. The international character of Chinese colonial modernity's foundational discourses is usefully illustrated in the focus on women's right to choose for race improvement.

8. Barlow, "Wanting Some: Natural Science, Social Science and Colonial Modernity."

9. See Edwards, "The Shadow of Shadows"; and Mullen, "Du Bois, Dark Princess, and the Afro-Asian International." Also see Karl, *Staging the World*.

10. Sakamoto Hiroko has established the centrality of similar ideas in the thinking of major Chinese social philosophers (including some of the figures cited as aesthetic Marxists by Liu Kang; see below). Sumiko Otsubo, Fa-ti Fan, and Yuehtsen Juliette Chung are clarifying the context in which eugenic philosophy came into mainstream thinking in Beijing and Shanghai in the 1920s from Japan. The Japan-filtered concern with sepsis and modern antiseptic reproductive strategies was then a preoccupation with liberation theories among Chinese intellectuals and US social purity advocates. Sakamoto periodizes the trend as probably originating in Britain in 1883,

taken up a year later in Japan in 1884, and emerging with force in Chinese intellectual circles only five years later in the influential thinking of Yan Fu. The latter infused these ideas to Kang Youwei and Liang Qichao in the early years of the first decade of the twentieth century. Sakamoto Hiroko, "China and Eugenic Thought," China Program Seminar, Jackson School of International Relations, March 7, 2002.

11. Rogaski, "Hygienic Modernity in Tianjin." Rogaski draws on Ann Stoler, Paul Rabinow and Gwen Wright, Brenda Yeo, and others who have demonstrated that metropolitan notions of hygiene were premised on the need of Europeans and North Americans to meet the challenge they confronted in their own colonial projects. As Rogaski argues, "hygienic modernity altered the built environment and the human landscape" in Tianjin, which she describes as the "ultimate treaty port" (30) and, alternately, as a "hyper-colony," meaning that the population as a whole was under the gaze and control of multiple imperial powers, dividing the native population into zones and providing native administration with limited self-governance. However, after the 1895 Qing defeat in the Sino-Japanese War, Japanese theory and practice of scientific, modern hygiene, "the product of Euro-American administration, European laboratories, and Japanese bureaucrats," as Rogaski puts it, became a mark of the colonist superiority and the increasingly medicalized and thus racialized inferiority of the Chinese elites and masses (38–39). Because "Japanese experience with hygienic modernity had" such a "profound impact on the development of health technologies" in the Japanese concessions as well as in the colony of Taiwan, it is difficult not to classify this modernity as a colonial one.

12. Sakamoto Hiroko, "China and Eugenic Thought."

13. Although Yuetsen Juliett Chung emphasizes the process through which eugenic vocabulary and key ideas were stabilized in Chinese mainstream thinking via Japanese intellectual categories, she also makes the important point that eugenics in China became a counterdiscourse to the prevailing idea that the Chinese were a degenerate (sub-Japanese) population. The primary effect of eugenic philosophy was the emergence of a full-fledged theory of race and the scientific racialization of national populations. It is also clear that, as Chung writes, debates on race purity were "both Lamarckian (hygienic) and Mendelian (eugenic)," and yet she describes "Larmarckism as a cultural logic playing [out] in the Japanese context" (29–30). Sumiko Otsubo's work on eugenic theories of the female body and race improvement in the 1880s through the 1920s focuses particularly on the relation between Osawa Kenji (1852–1927) and Hiratsuka Raicho (1886–1971), a founding figure in Japanese female feminism. Sumiko Otsubo, "Medicalization of Race Improvement Theory and the Female Body: Osawa Kenji and Eugenic Thought in Meiji Japan," 1999, unpublished; and Otsubo, "Engendering Eugenics."

14. Barlow, *The Question of Women*, chapter 3.

15. Morgan, *Ancient Society*; Bachofen, *Myth, Religion, and Mother Right*; and McLennan, *Primitive Marriage*.

16. For a discussion of Yi Jiayue, see Glosser, *Chinese Visions of Family and State*.

17. Stoler, *Race and the Education of Desire*; and Anderson, "Leprosy and Citizenship."

18. See, for instance, Myers and Peattie, *The Japanese Colonial Empire*. A recent follow-up volume is Duus, Myers, and Peattie, *The Japanese Wartime Empire*.

19. See, for instance, Coble, *Chinese Capitalists in Japan's New Order*, esp. 52–

66. This is the latest of a series of detailed studies Coble began in 1986 that focused on the agent of the new capitalist class, the emergent Chinese state, and Japanese colonialism. Coble's argument is that Japanese policy favored "creation of a colonial regime" except when exigencies of war forced the country to engage in a more collaborative relation to Chinese capitalists. His point revises the notion that Chinese "puppet governments" were collaborative in nature and thus cannot be considered outright colonization projects.

20. Young, *Japan's Total Empire*. "In all colonizing societies," she argues, "forces of modernity propelled imperial expansion. This point is of considerable significance for the interpretation of Japanese history, since it runs against the idea that the excesses of the wartime empire were the product of an incomplete modernization. . . . The evidence on Manchukuo suggests, to the contrary, that it was not the leftovers from the old Tokugawa regime but institutions developed after the Meiji Restoration—modern industry, mass culture, political pluralism, and new social organizations—that were the real forces behind the new imperialism. Thus the maturation of modern institutions, and not their stunting, led to the burst of expansionism of the 1930s" (435). Karl, *Staging the World*, usefully pushes back colonial modernist theory to the 1895–1911 era.

21. Lee, "Shanghai Modern," 102. A similar conclusion is drawn by Duara, *Sovereignty and Authenticity*, 246–47.

22. Kang, *Aesthetics and Marxism*.

23. Ibid., 34.

24. Ibid., 67.

25. One can argue that the US empire is not that informal and that semicolonialism is not an exclusively Chinese phenomenon but a generic category, since it characterized the Ottoman Empire as well. See Stavrianos, *Global Rift*, 256–77.

26. Mommsen and Osterhammel, *Imperialism and After*, 290–313. For an example of the use of "informal empire" in an East Asian area discussion, see Duus, Myers, and Peattie, *The Japanese Informal Empire in China*.

27. Jürgen Osterhammel, "Semi-colonialism and Informal Empire in Twentieth-Century China: Toward a Framework of Analysis," in Mommsen and Osterhammel, *Imperialism and After*, 290–314.

28. Ronald Robinson, "The Excentric Idea of Imperialism, with or without Empire," in Mommsen and Osterhammel, *Imperialism and After*, 267, 280. "And so, retreating in some places, advancing in others, imperialism sprawled its roving variances from Latin America to Australia, from China to Africa, changing degree and shape between formality and informality with endless flexibility. But did the various cases have anything in common? They all show the same international connections at work to a greater or lesser degree imperialistically" (280). See Wolfe, "History and Imperialism, for an evaluation of Robinson and Gallagher's position within theories of imperialism generally.

29. Osterhammel, "Semi-colonialism," 299. Peter Duus, "Introduction: Japan's Informal Empire in China, 1895–1937; An Overview," in Duus, Myers, and Peattie, *The Japanese Informal Empire in China*, gives a discussion of the strengths as weaknesses of the wholesale use of the informal empire metaphor to the case of Japanese aggression. He confronts an "irony" that is once again resolved with reference to the alleged ability of Chinese culture to withstand aggression (xxiv, xxviii). Also, see

Osterhammel's recent publication, *Colonialism.* In this book, Osterhammel acknowl-
edges the influential critiques of the twenty-year notion of informal empire (specifically Hind, "The Internal Colonial Concept") and revises his early formula on China
using the new notion of "quasi-colonial control" (20). Although I am interested in
Osterhammel simply because of the impact his metaphor has had in thinking about
Chinese colonial modernity, I do find it fascinating that the entire reworking of the
quasi-colonial control case is based on the alleged Chinese experience. Thus quasi-
colonial control is characterized by weakened independent policy, a mixture of foreign and indigenous administration, unequal treaties, gunboat diplomacy, extraterritoriality, resident diplomats and advisors, a collaborative elite, economic advantages
to the quasi-colonizing power that semioccupies the terrain, and, finally, the possibility of multiple colonial powers or "multiple quasi-colonial controls" (20-21). For
an example of up-to-date research that rests its case soundly on the Osterhammel
thesis, see Goodman, "Improvisations on a Semicolonial Theme."

30. Walker, *Chinese Modernity and the Peasant Path*, usefully distinguishes incomplete control from her own thesis of containment.

31. Shih, *Lure of the Modern.*

32. Ibid., 371; emphasis mine.

33. Ibid., 373.

34. Ibid., 272-76. One could argue that in this general characterization, Shih did
not consider Maoism to be about Chinese culture and did not consider the rural revolution as an anticolonial effort. Each of these most definitely took "culture" as the
terrain of struggle, and each in its way would qualify as a nativist use of culture.

35. Stavrianos, *Global Rift*, 169-77.

36. Spivak, "The New Subaltern," 331. "The Subaltern Studies collective," Spivak
confirmed recently while interviewing herself, "is certainly related to South Asian
history, as Gramsci was related to Italy." Then she adds, "One major difference [be-
tween Subaltern Studies and postcolonial theory] is that the disciplinary connection
of post-colonial studies is to literary criticism rather than history and the social sciences."

37. Radhakrishnan, "Postmodernism and the Rest of the World," 37; and
Seshadri-Crooks, "At the Margins of Postcolonial Studies," 7.

38. Sarkar, "The Decline of the Subaltern in *Subaltern Studies.*" Given the Maoist
roots of the project, I found myself questioning Dipesh Chakrabarty's positions in
"Postcoloniality and the Artifice of History," which unfold within an airless embrace
of imperial England and colonial India with no overt recognition of the colonial experiences elsewhere. Chakrabarty, *Provincializing Europe*, ch. 1.

39. The relationship between Maoist projects in China and elsewhere and the centrality of cultural critique globally in the Left is a central question. This is certainly
the case in the development of feminist theories in many parts of the world in the
seventies and eighties. See Kannabiran and Kannabiran, "Looking at Ourselves,"
for instance. Also Prazniak, "Mao and the Woman Question." As the editors and
contributors to *Critical Perspectives* point out, Maoist themes have structured neo-
Marxism in Europe and the United States through Althusser. See Kang, "The Legacy
of Mao and Althusser." I agree in large part with Liu Kang, whose *Aesthetics and
Marxism* argues that "culture and cultural revolution are inextricably related to the
Marxist projects of critiquing capitalist modernity and constructing an alternative

modernity. . . . In this respect the diverse practices and designs of Chinese Marxism are similar to those of Western Marxism, or an equally distinct variety of Euro-American Marxist intellectual enterprises" (x).

40. Seshadri-Crooks, "At the Margins of Postcolonial Studies," 19; emphasis mine.

41. An exception is Seth's "Interpreting Revolutionary Excess."

42. Chun, "The Transformation of Chinese Socialism: A Critical Commentary."

43. Zhang, "Five Faces/Phases."

44. See Barlow, *Formations of Colonial Modernity*, 6.

45. Schaefer, "Shanghai Savage."

46. Weisenfeld, "Visual Cultures of Japanese Imperialism." Weisenfeld's recent monograph, *Mavo*, shows the originary internationalism of a Japanese avant-garde that sought from the outset to integrate art into everyday modern life.

47. Jones, *Yellow Music*.

48. Ibid., 30.

49. Ibid., 61–64. As the corporate capacity to market recordings expanded into the Asian market, corporate management and production strategies coalesced. The production matrix for the phonograph was the multinational corporation, which created and distributed the technology and the commodity. In China, this was Pathé-EMI, which opened its Shanghai factory in 1916 and merged with the London-based company Columbia Gramophone in 1926, which annexed Columbia Phonograph USA and the German corporation Lindström (and its subsidiaries, Beka-Record and Odeon). In 1931, the conglomerate became Pathé-EMI. Shanghai, a major production and distribution node in the originary globalization of the gramophone, was from the outset colonial modern in character.

50. Blue, "Opium for China," 46–47.

51. Chiang, *Social Engineering and the Social Sciences in China*. Under this relationship, which would have far-reaching importance even after 1949, US-educated scholars and US foundations, especially the Rockefeller Foundation, institutionalized the social science disciplines in the modern universities. Even the radical wing of Chinese social science scholarship, which drained necessary funding for its Comintern activities and links with party-building and socialist scholarship in the USSR, relied on US financing for institutional growth. Of course, what Chiang does not follow out in any detail is the repatriation of this colonial knowledge back to the United States after 1949, when Chinese social scientists like Fei Shaotong, Chu Tongzu, K. C. Hsiao, and others became mainstays of the United States–China field. The importance of Chinese "data" on the development of US social science remains to be researched. The centrality of US concerns, US visions of China's importance as a market, and, foremost, the importance that US donor agencies saw in the project of training comprador intellectuals is indisputable. Also see Kai-wing Chow, "Narrating Nation, Race, and National Culture: Imagining the Hanzu Identity in Modern China, in Chow, Doak, and Fu, *Constructing Nationhood in Modern East Asia*, 47–83, for social science and scientific racist categories in China in the 1910s.

52. See Pollak, *Une identité blessée*, 381–92, for the activities of the Rockefeller Foundation in US colonial social sciences.

53. The discussion is indebted to Uta Poiger, member of the Modern Girl around the World research cluster at the University of Washington. The research group con-

sists of Tani E. Barlow, Madeleine Yue Dong, Uta Poiger, Lynn Thomas, and Alys Weinbaum. Its objective is to address the question of why the "modern girl" or commodified female consumer subject appeared in so many venues globally and how that subject can be agentially claimed. My thanks to Poiger for raising this issue of conditions of historical intelligibility in our discussion of the "modern girl." The research group does not share my concern with colonial modernism and does not accept these findings as generally applicable in all of its members' contexts.

54. Cox, *The Global Cigarette.*

55. Ibid., 160.

56. Ibid., 160–61.

57. J. A. Thomas, *A Pioneer Tobacco Merchant in the Orient* (1928), quoted in ibid., 160 n. 25.

58. A longer version of this summary appears in Barlow, *The Question of Women.*

59. See Brook and Wakabayashi, *Opium Regimes,* 1–30, for the trade's economic centrality, and Tagliacozzo, review of *Opium Regimes,* for a discussion of supporting monographs reinforcing this position.

60. Stavrianos, *Global Rift,* 132–40.

61. Ibid.

62. Goodman, "Improvisations on a Semicolonial Theme." Goodman argues that semicolonialism is not a historically adequate term because "throughout the modern period China never in fact became a subject nation, but retained sovereignty over nearly all of its territory and was recognized as a sovereign nation by international law" (889).

63. Modernity is colonial not because China resembles India, but because colonial strategies infused political, social, developmental, and economic thinking about the China trade and settlement projects.

64. Brook and Wakabayashi, *Opium Regimes.* See particularly their introduction, which lays out the commodification of opium as a vehicle of capital accumulation and the impact of this commodity on governmentality. When that question is posed, the underlying problematic becomes just how modernity and colonialism are historically related on a global scale. The contribution of the Subaltern Studies initiative broadly speaking, and the specific projects of Sara Suleri, Dipesh Chakrabarty, Ranajit Guha, and others, is to establish, contra Michel Foucault, the colonial roots of modernity. This mutuality holds as true for codifying and standardizing the English language as it does when we consider the transformative effect of colonialism on standard Chinese in the twentieth century, or the financing of the Industrial Revolution from the proceeds of the Atlantic triangle trade. Indeed, if research by Timothy Brook, Bob Wakabayashi, R. Bin Wong, and Judith Wyman in *Opium Regimes* holds up, modernity in China may be directly connected to the larger colonial economy through the Pacific opium trade.

65. See many of the excellent articles in Chaudhuri and Strobel's useful collection *Western Women and Imperialism.* The human sciences generally, and not just the modernist history narrative, established woman as a proper subject of and vehicle for describing racial, ethnic, social, national and sexual difference. See Ichiro, "Colonialism and the Sciences of the Tropical Zone."

The Social Construction of Postcolonial Studies

Ø   Ø   Ø

DAVID SCOTT

Don't ask for the meaning, ask what's the point.
—IAN HACKING

In a book published a few years ago—a book provocatively entitled *The Social Construction of What?*—Ian Hacking gave voice to some disquiet about the social constructionism that has become so ready-made a staple especially of work in the humanities and social sciences in the past two decades or so.[1] Hacking, as ever the measured and charitable critic, is neither merely antagonistic toward, nor simply dismissive of, this now prominent strategy of investigation. Rather, being the exploratory thinker he is, he is concerned to inquire into the ways in which social constructionist claims are established, to determine their coherence, and to judge their usefulness and salience.[2] Of course, Hacking has his doubts about these claims, and these doubts are inspired by the principle that occurs appropriately early in his book and that I have used as my epigraph: "Don't ask for the meaning, ask what's the point" (5). This disarmingly simple pragmatist (and Wittgensteinian) advice proves eminently salutary whatever the field of investigation. As we shall see, it comports well with a good deal of what I want to concern myself with, and I mean to follow out some of its implications in the course of raising some doubts of my own—doubts about the contemporary *point* of what is called postcolonial studies.

My purposes here are fairly limited and circumscribed, and it may be as well to state them as explicitly as I can at the outset, so as to avoid confusion and misunderstanding. My general concern is with the career of a critical strategy, the occupational life, so to speak, of its purchase. In my view, a critical strategy—which comprehends, among other features, the kinds of questions taken up and pursued, the target confronted and engaged, and the

stakes claimed—is a historical formation inasmuch as it is always assembled
and set to work within a distinctive conceptual and ideological conjuncture
or problem space. A critical strategy, in other words, always answers (however adequate this is judged to be) a discursively constituted demand. In my
view, therefore, it is always important for a critic to inquire, at any given
conjuncture, into the ways in which a critical strategy conceives its demands,
its ends, its yield, and its limits—how it conceives the operational field, so
to put it, of its practical action. In particular, however, I am interested in
that moment in the life of a strategy at which it solidifies and hardens into a
disciplined and cumulative research apparatus; this is the moment at which,
having arrived at a sort of plateau of maturity, it begins to slide from criticism toward method, or in Thomas Kuhn's memorable idiom, from a revolutionary paradigm toward a normal one.[3] This is arguably a very paradoxi-
cal moment in the career of any critical strategy, since the conditions of its
normative institutionalization, the conditions of its scholarly regularization
and canonization, constitute, invariably, the conditions of its loss of critical force.

Certainly this is my sense of the career, such as it has been, of postcolonial studies as a strategy for investigating the trace of colonial effects in our
postcolonial time. In what follows, my aim is to explore some aspects of
this suspicion. I hope it will be appreciated, however, that I do not aim to
make out a case for a fresh approach to, or a new model of, postcolonial
studies. It is by no means clear to me that there is any such case to be made.
But it should be clear that this is not the same as saying that we ought no
longer to inquire critically into the diverse ways in which the colonial past
weighs on the postcolonial present. Such a preoccupation remains a matter
of considerable, and sometimes urgent, importance.

In *The Social Construction of What?* Hacking seems to be making at least two
sorts of arguments about social constructionism. Both prove germane to my
concerns here with postcolonial studies, though one more so than the other.
The first argument is that in social constructionist work, there often appears
to be some confusion, or at least some ambiguity, regarding exactly *what*
is supposed to be socially constructed. The title of his book draws its force
from this preoccupation. It is frequently unclear, Hacking argues, whether
what is thought to be socially constructed is the action itself, or the classificatory ideas about the action. Hacking knows, of course, that every human
action (insofar as it is recognizable as an action as such) takes place under
some description. He writes: "All our acts are under description, and the
acts that are open to us depend, in a purely formal way, on the descriptions

available to us" (31). But this, Hacking urges, does not make the actions and their description indistinguishable from each other. Take, for example (using one of his own illustrations), the idea that women refugees are socially constructed. It is obvious, he says, that individual women who become refugees do so in consequence of social and political events or conditions of one sort or another. It is trivial or redundant (Hacking's word is "foolish") to make this fact into a specifically *theoretical* point (although it would not be trivial or redundant to describe these conditions in their specific detail). What is *relevantly* socially constructed, therefore, is not the individual people, the women refugees, but rather the classification *women refugees*. In short, he says, what is in question is women refugees as *kinds* of persons; what is in question, in other words, is "the classification itself, and the matrix within which the classification works" (11).

It is not irrelevant to note that part of Hacking's interest in this distinction derives from his long-standing and ongoing preoccupation with the subject-forming (or subject-transforming) propensities of authoritative classifications—what he calls in more recent work the "dynamic of classification."[4] Unlike things, people interact, more or less self-consciously, with "kinds," and this interaction produces effects. Individual women classified as women refugees, Hacking says, sometimes find that this particular classification alters their experiences of themselves: "A woman refugee may learn that she is a certain kind of person and act accordingly. Quarks do not learn that they are a certain kind of entity and act accordingly" (32). Hacking devotes his remarkable book on psychopathological classification and "memoro-politics," *Rewriting the Soul*, to this theme.[5] People are (partially at least) "made up" by the dominant categories that authoritatively classify them as people of a certain sort. Hacking famously calls this phenomenon the "looping effect of human kinds," or now, more simply, the problem of "interactive kinds."[6]

The second argument I take Hacking to be making focuses more on the (conceptual, rhetorical, ideological) *work* that the metaphor of social construction performs. "Social construction," he says in the preface, "has in many contexts been a truly liberating idea, but that which on first hearing has liberated some has made all too many others smug, comfortable, and trendy in ways that have become merely orthodox. The phrase has become a code. If you use it favorably, you deem yourself rather radical. If you trash the phrase, you declare that you are rational, reasonable, and respectable" (vii). The idea here is that there was a moment in its career at which social constructionism produced a useful labor of criticism, when it offered a valuable contrast effect with existing strategies of investigation. This is when it was libratory. But this moment has passed (or at least is passing)—partly because social constructionism has itself contributed to reorganizing the conditions of inquiry in such a way as to make its distinctiveness more the background to be assumed than the foreground to be gained: the contrast effect has given way to platitudes. As Hacking says: "The metaphor of social construction once had excellent shock value, but now it has become tired." And later: "An all-encompassing constructionist approach has become rather dull—in both senses of that word, boring and blunt" (11). Whereas social constructionism emerged in the late 1970s and 1980s as a (self-consciously) critical strategy, it is not clear whether it continues to command the same critical purchase or provide the same critical bite now as it did then. Part of the so-called linguistic turn (and thus the turn to meaning) in the humanities and social sciences, social constructionism sought to demonstrate the falsehood in the assumption that human affairs are naturally as we find them, are necessarily described in the way they are. Far from being given, such practices of description come into being at particular historical moments and under certain social and cultural circumstances.

The social constructionist, in short, is principally a critic of inevitability, a skeptic, an unmasker, an anti-essentialist. Hacking has his doubts about this radical pose. He delights in showing the Kantian roots of the constructionist metaphor. As he says, somewhat mischievously: "Although social constructionists bask in the sun they call postmodernism, they are really very old-fashioned" (49). I think that at least part of what Hacking is saying is that this strategy of critical interpretation (especially when the burden of the argument is made to rest on its shoulders) only has purchase if your opponent thinks otherwise than you do, if, that is, he or she is an essentialist (in the appropriate sense). However, if we are all largely constructionists now, if we all subscribe more or less to the view that human action always takes place under a description and that such descriptions are as historical (and therefore as located in social, institutional, and material circumstances) as the actions they describe, little critical point may obtain in staging a constructionist confrontation. Social constructionism, in short, may well have lost the contrast effect that once gave it critical bite.

This is the argument that especially interests me, because it connects with some ideas that I have been trying to develop recently about the practice of criticism generally, but postcolonial criticism more specifically.[7] Postcolonial studies (or discourse or theory or criticism or whatever) is, after all, a subspecies of social and cultural constructionism. It grew up in the 1980s in the very heyday of the culture wars in which Hacking locates constructionism's breeding ground. It drew its identity from the (largely Foucauldian) program of unmasking Eurocentric essentialisms at work in the West's representations of non-European ideas and behaviors. Like Hacking, I, too, wonder whether this venture in postcolonial social constructionism has not now exhausted, spent, itself, whether we have not arrived at a sort of threshold of normalization at which it no longer produces a useful contrast effect.

I have two quibbles with Hacking, however. They bear remarking, though neither, I think, should lead us to dismiss the argument he advances. The first is that Hacking's own trafficking in the borderlands of the postcolonial has proven less than inspiring. Clearly this provides one instance of the general rule that insight rarely travels well across adjacent disciplines and scholarly fields. In his discussion of the so-called debate between anthropologists Gananath Obeyesekere and Marshall Sahlins on the question of the death of the South Pacific explorer James Cook on Hawai'i in 1779, he misses virtually everything worth talking about, even though almost everything worth talking about turns precisely on the social constructionism in which both anthropologists participate. Hacking is quite right, of course, that the rash of enthusiasm that gathered around Obeyesekere's book, *The Apotheosis of Captain Cook*, and Sahlins's reply to it, *How "Natives" Think*, has to be situated in relation to the culture wars of the 1980s and 1990s. But, oddly, he does not, in fact, explore any of the complexity of that debate, especially as it pertains to the humanities and social sciences.[8] (The story of that complexity is partly the story of the so-called cultural turn of the 1970s that solidifies and takes hold in the 1980s and that constitutes one dimension of the conceptual context in which these culture wars take place.)[9] Instead, Hacking takes curious refuge in the uncharacteristically unnuanced view that "based on the evidence presented," "Sahlins is right about the so-called apotheosis of Captain Cook" (212).

The second quibble (the more important one for my immediate concern) is one I derive from R. G. Collingwood and Quentin Skinner. There is sometimes a strong sense in Hacking, I think (perhaps a strong antirelativist sense), that social constructionism has *always* been conceptually vacant (as he says, he has himself never been a constructionist). For him, it sometimes appears, the fact that social constructionism no longer produces an interesting contrast effect only underscores what ought all along to have been suspected, namely, that its understanding of the relation between concepts and action was really misconceived from the beginning. I am not entirely persuaded by this line of argument. If what is at stake for Hacking is whether social constructionism is or is not conceptually confused (or just plain wrong), then one has two options: one can either agree with the assessment and write off social constructionism as a coherent strategy of critical inquiry; or one can dispute the assessment and show where Hacking himself is mistaken. Neither option appeals to me, however. Evading both, I want to pursue the more historicist line of discussion that Hacking gestures at, and take more seriously than I think he does his own recognition that social constructionism *once* had, but has *now* lost, critical bite.

As I have already indicated, I am interested in this kind of shift as a general problem in the life of any practice of criticism, and as a specific problem in the life of postcolonial criticism. If we claim that the principal target of our criticism is the comprehension of the present we inhabit, as I would, then gauging whether our critical practices are in fact addressing this present's predicaments is not irrelevant. For some years now, I have been urging that the English Hegelian philosopher R. G. Collingwood offers an instructive way of negotiating this problem. Collingwood, of course, is best known for his doctrine (famously elaborated in *The Idea of History*) that history should be understood as the reenactment of past thought or past experience in the mind of the historian. But Collingwood also formulated a distinctive dialectical strategy of investigation (most succinctly expressed in *An Autobiography*), what he called the "logic" of "question and answer." In describing this activity, Collingwood writes: "I began by observing that you cannot find out what a man means by simply studying his spoken or written statements, even though he has spoken or written with perfect command of language and perfect truthful intention. In order to find out his meaning you must also know what the question was (a question in his own mind, and presumed by him to be in yours) to which the thing he has said or written was meant as an answer." [10] Propositions always form part of question-answer complexes; and therefore to understand any proposition, it is necessary to read it not for its internal cognitive consistency, but for the question to which it purports to be an answer.

Not many people have taken up and pursued this suggestive formulation, but one philosophically inclined historian who has is Quentin Skinner. Working less through Hegel than through the pragmatic language philosophy of John Austin, John R. Searle, and Ludwig Wittgenstein, Skinner has very usefully elaborated Collingwood's question-answer principle in a speech-act direction. In thinking about statements, Skinner urges, we should be more concerned with the dimension of linguistic action than the dimension of linguistic meaning. Words, as Wittgenstein said, are also deeds. In an act of linguistic communication, therefore, an author is not only meaning something in virtue of the semantic content of the words employed, but also doing something by virtue of "putting forward" the statement. And in consequence of this, Skinner suggests, propositions should be thought of as linguistic moves in an ongoing argument; and to understand what the author is doing in them, it is necessary to reconstruct the ideological and conceptual context into which they have been inserted.[11] It is not hard to see the connection between this and Hacking's "Don't ask for the meaning, ask what's the point." Both Skinner and Hacking are focused on the *import* of theoretical activity.

I have wanted to press this insight in the direction of a further implication, what I think of as a strategic one. I want to suggest that if the predicament of the present makes up the target of our critical practice (as, again, it seems to me it should be), the critic ought not only to be concerned with determining whether statements are consistent with the questions that can be shown to underlie them but also with determining whether these underlying questions *continue* to be questions worth having answers to in the present. Or to put this another way, if, as Skinner suggests, a proposition constitutes a move in an ongoing argument, then it is part of the task of the critic of the present to gauge, at any conjuncture, whether this move continues to be a move worth making. Consequently, from this point of view, it is perhaps less that the social constructionist or anti-essentialist propositions are now themselves demonstrably false or incoherent where they once appeared plausible (Hacking's point, so far as I can tell) as that the important or interesting or critical questions for our present have changed.[12]

This, anyway, is something of what I have been arguing about postcolonial criticism: the *demand* in the present has altered. In the 1980s, when postcolonial studies was becoming established as a going scholarly domain in the North Atlantic academy (what I call the moment of postcolonialism), its project was to criticize (in the hermeneutical language of the day, to *deconstruct*) colonial knowledge and its assumptions. Edward Said's *Orientalism* (1978) of course in many ways constituted the inaugural move in this enterprise. But the purchase it had on strategies of criticism was made possible not only by the changing global politics of the third world (the decline of national liberationism) but also by a cognitive shift (the cultural turn) exemplified in the work of three of Said's contemporaries, Clifford Geertz's *The Interpretation of Cultures*, Hayden White's *Metahistory* (both published in 1973), and Richard Rorty's *Philosophy and the Mirror of Nature* (published in 1978). Postcolonial social constructionism could claim a critical contrast effect with an older paradigm of discourse about colonialism (what I call the moment of anticolonialism) insofar as it enabled the recognition of a level of unproblematized assumptions governing it, teleological and essentialist assumptions largely, regarding history, politics, subjectivity, gender, race, and so on. As opposed to anticolonialism's description of the problem of colonialism in terms of the demand for political decolonization, postcolonialism commended its redescription as an epistemological problem, a problem about the politics of representation, about the relation between knowledge and power.

On this view, anticolonialism and postcolonialism are not progressively successive theoretical strategies, one providing better answers to questions addressed by the other. Contrary to the anti-essentialist dogma, postcolonialism's social constructionism is not better theory than anticolonialism's essentialism. Rather, to use Collingwood's terms, anticolonialism and postcolonialism should be understood as occupying different question-answer complexes; or as Skinner might put it, they are critical moves located in different arguments, interventions into different and differently constituted problem spaces. My concern, though, has been with whether the questions that have animated postcolonialism's genealogical critique of colonial knowledge continue to be questions worth having answers to. I wonder whether the historical context of problems that produced the postcolonial effect as a critical effect has not now altered such that the yield of these questions is no longer what it was. I wonder, in other words, whether postcolonialism has not lost its point and become normalized as a strategy for the mere accumulation of meaning.

It is a long time now (exactly four decades, in fact) since Thomas Kuhn's popularization of the idea of a "paradigm" in *The Structure of Scientific Revolutions*.[13] Readers of that memorable book will remember the brilliant illustration there of what happens when a "revolutionary" paradigm becomes a "normal" one. Kuhn would not have put it quite this way, but, essentially, criticism becomes method. Whereas "normal" scientific change occurs with the cumulative stockpiling of scientific knowledge, revolutionary change takes place by altering our conceptual lenses in such a way as to bring new objects into view. Once a scientific revolution occurs, Kuhn suggested, there is a more or less rapid emergence of an increasing array of rival methodological apparatuses for uncovering deeper and broader meanings and devising more and more complex explanations regarding the new object now brought under investigation. However, he maintained, this methodological expansion is accompanied by a steady loss of focus on the contrastive point of the exercise itself, the distinctive relevance of its new questions to the objects organized by the new classificatory field.[14] This constitutes the moment of normalization.

It may be noticed that Kuhn and Hacking (and indeed Collingwood and Skinner) have something important in common, namely, a distinctive way of conceiving the field of theoretical investigation. They are, all of them, reflexively self-conscious of what is at stake—what objective is being engaged—in the historical formation of the objects of theoretical investigation. None of them, in other words, take for granted the configuration of the conceptual problem space of inquiry, think of it as transparent, as merely the background to the investigation at hand, but rather as a constitutive part of it. Nor do they see one problem space as seamlessly connected in a continuously progressive series to successive ones. Rather, they see all problem spaces as discontinuous with each other and characterized by some degree of incommensurability. All would agree, therefore, that a certain amount of reconstruction is always necessary in order to make adjacent or successive theories intelligible to one another. Of course, they all share this angle of preoccupation with Michel Foucault, whose practice of criticism has proven so important for postcolonial studies. Foucault's genealogies were precisely modes of problematization. But Foucault, too, can be turned into the method of normal social science, as Hacking captures nicely in this passage: "Foucault carved numerous turns of phrase into ice sculptures, which had, for a moment, sharp contours. Then he walked away from them, insouciant, and let them melt, for he no longer needed them. His less gifted readers put the half-melted shapes back in the freezer and, without thinking, reproduce these figures as if they still glistened in the midnight sun and meant something."[15]

To my mind, normalization has been the fate of social constructionism generally, and of one of its principal branches, postcolonial studies, in particular. The great success of social constructionist postcolonial studies as a mode of inquiry is not only that it incisively and relentlessly demonstrated the essentialisms at work in older paradigms (that, for example, of anticolonialism) but that in institutionalizing this insight, it constituted a new field, colonial studies, and made vast swathes of new territory available for research. And of course, in the manner described by Kuhn, the growth and sustenance of this new territory of knowledge depended on the continuous expansion of its constitutive relations of meaning. And as it moved from being a strategy for levering open new conceptual space to being an institutionalizable research paradigm, the question of the distinctive demand in the postcolonial present addressed gave way to the multiplication of an increasing number and variety of studies of the colonial past, each making a contribution to the cumulative building up, stockpiling, and stabilization of a normal paradigm. The point, in short, gave way to the meaning; criticism gave way to method.

As an illustration of what I am getting at here—the transformation of postcolonial studies from criticism into method—let me take as an instance a line of argument for the revision and expansion of research on colonialism associated most prominently (in the United States at least) with the anthropologist Ann Stoler and the historian Frederick Cooper. Both distinguished scholars in their respective fields, they have been critical of what they describe as the "Manichaean conception" of colonialism that characterizes "colonial studies."[16] In this Manichaean conception, Stoler and Cooper argue, Europe and its colonies, the colonizer and the colonized, are taken to be discrete entities occupying separate frames of reference. Part of what disturbs them is that in this conception of the problem of colonialism, Europe tends to be excluded as a legitimate object of critical analysis inasmuch as the only line of determinable colonial effects runs in one direction, that is, from metropole to colony. In their view, we should have one all-embracing analytical frame of reference, namely, "empire," understood as a "shared but differentiated" space inclusive of both metropole and colony; for as they say, "Europe was made by its imperial projects, as much as colonial encounters were shaped by conflicts within Europe itself" ("Between Metropole and Colony," 1).

The Manichaean conception, Stoler and Cooper argue, is in the first place mistaken. The colonial world quite simply was not made up of discrete entities or one-way effects. As they say, colonial regimes "were neither monolithic not omnipotent"; closer and more discerning attention to the historical and ethnographic facts "reveals competing agendas for using power, competing strategies for maintaining control, and doubts about the legitimacy of the venture" (6). In support of this view of the heterogeneity and instability of the empire, Stoler and Cooper offer such illustrations as the following: "Paul Gilroy . . . has shown [in *The Black Atlantic*] that various expressions of popular culture as well as literary and philosophical productions coming out of the African diaspora—in Africa, the Americas, and Europe—evince a complex engagement with 'Western' culture entailing more than either its repudiation or an attempt to build an 'authentic' alternative" (8). Or again: "Sidney Mintz [in *Sweetness and Power*] has argued . . . that the demand in Europe for sugar produced in the colonies was crucial to European working-class formation" (9). The authors take these examples as evidence against the binary and unidirectional model of the colonial world. The empire was characterized by a good deal less coherence and a good deal more ambiguity, contingency, contestation, and negotiation than has usually been allowed. In short: "The Manichaean world of high colonialism that we have etched so deeply in our historiographies was thus nothing of the sort" (8).

But Stoler and Cooper's argument does not merely aim to demonstrate that the Manichaean conception of colonialism is, on the historical and ethnographic data, wrong. Their argument is the stronger one, namely, that the Manichaean conception is also misguided, indeed *ideologically* misguided. It is the colonial regimes, they say, that drew a sharp dichotomy between the colonizer and the colonized as a function of the requirements of rule. Consequently, for scholars of colonialism to deploy such a conception today is only to reproduce a colonial myth. Stoler and Cooper urge, therefore, that we ought to "think through not only the colonial history that appears as Manichaean but a historiography that has invested in that myth as well" (9).

There hovers about this view, to be sure, an atmosphere of palpable reasonableness—or anyway, social constructionist reasonableness. It seems quite indisputable that to think in a "binary" way—as in talk of the colonizer and the colonized as though they were separate portraits—is both theoretically crude, and more, simply wrong. After all, the historical and ethnographic evidence shows itself to be overwhelmingly in support of hybridity, complexity, contingency, ambiguity, and so on. It seems undeniable, moreover, that it is dominant power—rather than subaltern resistance to it—that produces conceptual and ideological divisions of this sort, and therefore that to reproduce them in the name of criticism is not only misguided but indeed complicit with that power. Consequently, it seems hard to deny that the concept of empire provides a more appropriate framing device for the study of colonialism. After all, Europe, too, was transformed by the colonial project; it was not merely the agent of changes in its colonies but also an object of changes coming from them. Therefore, Europe ought not in turn to be treated as if it were a space of essences. If it has been demonstrated that the colony constituted a space of socially constructed discourses and identities, a space of "invention," the same sort of anti-essentialist gaze should be directed at Europe.

I am not persuaded by this argument, however. It seems to me that reframing the question of colonialism in terms of empire on the grounds that it more fully captures the complex reality of the world made by colonialism is precisely the kind of argument that turns on asking for the meaning rather than the point of the investigation. Notice that this argument rests on at least one unexamined assumption, namely, the assumption of the epistemological equivalence of colony and metropole as objects of inquiry. Inasmuch as colony and metropole are equally socially constructed, that is, inasmuch as they are equally fields of ambiguity and heterogeneity, of contested and negotiated meanings, they are conceived as occupying an equivalent epistemological register as cognitive objects. However, this assumption overlooks a number of questions that seem to me of vital importance for a criticism of the present: if colony and metropole make for equivalent *epistemological* objects, are they necessarily thereby equal *ideological* objects, which is to say, are the moral-political stakes involved in the way they are constructed in a critical discourse the same? Or, for whom might this be the case, when, and in which agenda of criticism? Furthermore, how and by what theoretical operations are the epistemological and the ideological separated out in this conception of empire? Or, what is the connection between the meaning and the point of this exercise? It seems to me that to argue as social constructionists do that colony and metropole constitute epistemological equivalents without attention to these questions obscures the fact that earlier critics did not necessarily imagine colonialism in the binary way they are accused of doing out of naïveté or ignorance, but because their agenda of criticism depended on a particular—which is to say, a *different*—characterization of Europe. And therefore we might well ask: What is the moral-political demand that underlies the turn to empire in this particular way? What ideological history of the postcolonial present does its conceptualization comport with?

These are difficult questions. But to see their import, let us think for a moment about an earlier theorist of colonialism, Albert Memmi, whose *The Colonizer and the Colonized* is perhaps a classic instance of the sort of "Manichaean conception" of colonialism that Stoler and Cooper object to. Memmi was not, it is true, concerned about the academic business of "colonial studies," but his book surely constitutes one of the defining texts in any genealogy of the criticism of colonialism. In *The Colonizer and the Colonized*, Memmi presents a very memorable series of "portraits" of figures and situations in the colonial context.[17] Memmi's principal concern, remember, was to define a dialectically coconstitutive relationship between the colonizer and the colonized; he wanted to demonstrate that they were bound together in a reciprocal relationship of asymmetrical dependence, in which the privilege of one entailed the deprivation of the other. Neither the figures nor the situations are entirely self-contained, therefore, but they do have about them a slightly frozen or reified quality. This is because, as portraits, they are meant to *typify* kinds of individuals, not produce holistic images of them: from the opening figure of the colonialist in his Wellington boots leaning complacently against his shovel to the anguished insurgent native about to give in to an intoxication of violence, they are meant to pass before us not as idealizations, but as a succession of deliberately abstract typifications. Now, Memmi imagines the relationship between the colonizer and the colonized in this, if you like, "binary" way, *not* because he is unaccountably naive or ignorant of ambiguities, contingencies, hybridities, and other such subtleties commended by the social constructionist. To the contrary, ambivalence, uncertainty, instability, are what the portraits consistently draw our attention to, what they poignantly illuminate; and it is precisely to enable a phenomenological exploration of the intractable moral dilemma that constitutes certain plausible subject positions in the colonial situation that he assigns to them these dispositions and fixes them in these attitudes. It is enough to call to mind the dramatization of the irreconcilable dilemma of the "colonizer who refuses," who believes in the justness of the political cause of the oppressed, but is unable to form any sympathy for the way they live and is nauseated by the odor of their food and repelled by the sound of their music. (As Memmi writes: "To be a rightist or leftist is not merely a way of thinking but also—perhaps especially—a way of living.")[18]

Nor is Europe ignored in Memmi's account. The entire discussion is in fact framed by the anxious shadow of a European, and specifically French, Left that (in 1957) was still not committed to decolonization. Notably, however, Europe in *The Colonizer and the Colonized* does not merely emerge as one more socially constructed site in the differentiated field of "empire." Europe's opacity (if this is what it is) is not a mistake. It is not that Memmi has failed to appreciate Gilroy or Mintz; it is that Memmi's Europe is not theirs. His Europe is self-consciously constructed in such a way as to make vivid to the reader the moral ambiguity—even moral impossibility—of the colonial situation, and the political imperative of overthrowing colonial rule.[19]

I want to make clear that I am *not* suggesting that Memmi's anticolonial conception of the relation between the colonizer and colonized is one we should continue to endorse. Indeed, I believe we should not. I am suggesting, though, that the picture of colonialism drawn in analyses such as Memmi's, the epistemological status (or meaning) of colony and metropole they rest on, cannot be critically located (much less dismissed or overcome) outside of a genealogical redescription linking it to the ideological project in which its point is made. The problem with the formulation of the research agenda urged by Stoler and Cooper, therefore, is its narrow assumption that the idea of Europe required of any critical discussion of colonialism is stable, is known in advance of the project in which it is supposed to play a role; that the meaning of Europe one mobilizes and makes use of does not depend *strategically* on the nature of the question at stake or the point of the investigation one is carrying out. This is not to deny the complexity of Europe or the potential importance of making analytically visible the ways in which its colonial enterprise shaped it. It is to insist, however, that without specifying the distinctive question in the postcolonial present as to which empire appears as the analytical frame in which the answer is to be sought, this revision of colonial studies makes for little more than a methodological move within a normal paradigm. For the idea of a method, as I have noted, is in part the idea of an object settled enough into a normal paradigm of investigation so as to require only more and more nuanced knowledge of more and more of its dimensions and constituent elements. Where once postcolonial criticism might have been concerned with bringing a new cognitive field into existence, with reconstituting the relevant question about colonialism, it now is concerned merely with building in more and more object relations and widening the scope of the paradigm's reach. But as that arch-Manichaean theorist, Frantz Fanon, said many years ago, "There is a point at which methods devour themselves."[20]

In short, it seems to me that there is a labor of criticism that Stoler and Cooper's sort of argument has failed—fatally—to take into consideration: the labor of inquiring into what the point is (the *conceptual* no less than the *polemical* point) in constructing this particular picture of colonialism or Europe at this particular time; the labor of inquiring into the distinctive question to which this particular image of colonialism or Europe constitutes an answer; and the labor of inquiring into the argument in which this conception of colonialism or Europe is mobilized as part of a particular move.

In his recent inaugural lecture at the Collège de France, Ian Hacking returned to an idea he had urged some years ago and which he has worked with implicitly and explicitly for a long time, namely, the idea of "styles of reasoning" as the covering name for the object of his historical ontology. Hacking is a historian of (largely, scientific) styles of reasoning. A style of reasoning is an analytic ensemble that introduces a new domain of objects and a new way of finding out the truth about them, including the articulation of new conditions and criteria of proof and demonstration. Like Kuhn's paradigms, or Foucault's modes of problematization, a style of reasoning is "more than a group of techniques for bringing new kinds of fact into our awareness, into our living, mental, social world." Rather, as Hacking says, "it creates the very criteria of truth."[21] To think in terms of styles of reasoning, then, is precisely to think in terms of the point of an inquiry, what its particular mode of classification is meant to do, what particular question-and-answer complex it brings into being, what particular difference it makes.

In my view, postcolonial studies needs to be more self-conscious of the style of reasoning that characterizes it at any given moment and must make an effort to historicize itself in terms of a genealogy of styles of reasoning that have constituted the history of criticism of colonialism. Then perhaps those of us interested in the critical purchase of our work on colonialism for the varied postcolonial presents we inhabit might be urged to begin, not with proposals for new models of colonial study, but with attempts to identify the relevant features of the postcolonial problem space in which our investigation takes place. This will enable us to more adequately gauge whether our preoccupation with revising colonial history (a preoccupation I fully endorse) is meeting a salient demand or not. This is because colonialism is neither a stable nor a self-evident object: it is not merely there, in the past, awaiting better and better methodology in order to elicit deeper and deeper or more and more encompassing meanings. And therefore, how colonialism ought to be understood for the present we live in has always to be a question we formulate and argue out rather, than something we generate abstractly on the basis of theoretical inclusiveness or ethnographic broadmindedness. It seems to me that unless we persistently ask what the point is of our investigations of colonialism for the postcolonial present, what the question is to which we are fashioning an answer, what the argument is in which we are making a move and staking a claim, unless we systematically make this part of our strategy of inquiry, we are only too likely to slide from a criticism of the present to "normal" social science.

Notes

1. Hacking, *The Social Construction of What?* Further references to this book will be made parenthetically in the text.

2. See also, more recently, the essays collected in Hacking, *Historical Ontology*.

3. Kuhn, *The Structure of Scientific Revolutions*.

4. This is the subject of his recent inaugural lecture at the Collège de France: Hacking, "Inaugural Lecture."

5. Hacking, *Rewriting the Soul*.

6. Hacking, *The Social Construction of What?* 32; and Hacking, *Rewriting the Soul*, 21, 61. Hacking first wrote about this phenomenon much earlier in his essay, "The Looping Effect of Human Kinds."

7. See Scott, *Refashioning Futures*.

8. See Obeyesekere, *The Apotheosis of Captain Cook*; and Sahlins, *How "Natives" Think*. I have commented briefly on the dispute in Scott, "Colonialism."

9. See, usefully, Bonnell and Hunt, *Beyond the Cultural Turn*. For some ways in which this cultural turn has reconstituted the nature of disciplinary claims, see Scott, "Culture in Political Theory."

10. See Collingwood, *An Autobiography*, 31.

11. See Skinner, "Reply to my Critics," 274–75.

12. One should note that Hacking has in fact brought precisely this kind of problem to our attention, especially in his use of the idea (adapted from A. C. Crombie) of

"styles of reasoning." This idea is outlined in Hacking, "Language, Truth and Reason," and developed in his "'Style' for Historians and Philosophers."

13. Kuhn, *The Structure of Scientific Revolutions*.

14. For a useful statement of Kuhn's argument, see his reflective essay, "What Is a Scientific Revolution?"

15. Hacking, *Mad Travelers*, 85.

16. Perhaps the clearest statement of their objections to the state of affairs in colonial studies is set out in their programmatic essay, "Between Metropole and Colony: Rethinking a Research Agenda," which introduces and frames a volume of essays by various contributors on various aspects of colonialism, in Cooper and Stoler, *Tensions of Empire*, 1–56 (further references to this essay will be given parenthetically in the text). See also, Stoler, *Race and the Education of Desire*, which also makes out a case for a single analytic framework for studying empire.

17. Memmi, *The Colonizer and the Colonized*.

18. Ibid., 27.

19. Something similar could be said of the extraordinary image of Europe drawn by Aimé Césaire in *Discourse on Colonialism*. For Césaire, the problem of colonialism had to do not simply with the effects of its barbarisms in the colonies but with the effects in the metropole as well. In some very memorable passages, he describes colonialism as a disorder rotting away the heart of the European soul, distorting its civilization, and perverting its humanism. A particular "Europe," therefore, occupies the center of his theoretical gaze, but not the one offered by Stoler and Cooper.

20. Fanon, *Black Skin, White Masks*, 12.

21. Hacking, "Inaugural Lecture," 4.

Postcolonial Studies and the Study of History

✺ ✺ ✺

FREDERICK COOPER

By the 1970s, the historical study of colonial empires had become one of the deadest of dead fields within the discipline of history. Students interested in pushing the frontiers of historical research looked to Africa, Asia, or Latin America, or they sought to look at Europe and North America "from the bottom up." The revival of interest in the colonial world a generation later reflects the influence of literature and anthropology, and, more important, wider intellectual currents that threw into question the most basic narratives and the most fundamental ways in which knowledge is configured. Historians had to face the fact that the new challenges were not simply to add an African or Asian component to a previously Europe-centered curriculum but to rethink what it meant to study a continent called Europe and to examine the position of the researcher in the production of historical scholarship.[1]

But perhaps it is now the interdisciplinary domain of postcolonial studies that needs a shot in the arm, particularly a more rigorous historical practice. Postcolonial studies has brought before a large and transcontinental public the place of colonialism in world history, yet it has tended to obscure the very history whose importance it has highlighted. A generic colonialism— located somewhere between 1492 and the 1970s—has been given the decisive role in shaping a postcolonial moment, in which intellectuals can condemn the continuation of invidious distinctions and exploitation and celebrate the proliferation of cultural hybridities and the fracturing of cultural boundaries. This essay will develop a critique of ahistorical tendencies in colonial studies and argue for approaches that give more weight to the specificity of colonial situations and the importance of struggles in colonies, in metropoles, and between the two.[2]

History, as a discipline, has itself become the object of critique. Ashis

Nandy argues that history is inseparable from its imperialist origins, that it necessarily imposes the imperialist's understanding of a people's past over their own. To some scholars, history confines the zigzags of time into linear pathways, privileges state building over other forms of human connection, and tells a story of progress that inevitably leaves Africans or Asians on the side, lacking some crucial characteristic necessary to attain what is otherwise universal.[3] Such arguments constitute valid criticisms of many histories, but do they amount to an indictment of the study of history itself? In fact, the indictment of history is itself historical. To trace history to imperialism is to give power to a phenomenon that is historically located. If there is some truth in Nicholas Dirks's assertion of the "irrevocable link between History and the Nation-State," the evidence that the nation-state is not so universal makes for another sort of history that documents more varied sorts of political imagination.[4] The question is whether one can be satisfied with the simple *naming* of imperialism or colonialism as the dark side of universality, progress, or modernity, or whether we need to know something more about imperialism and colonialism.

Here, the virtues and the weaknesses of recent scholarship run close together. If any intervention shook up historians' complacency, it was Edward Said's *Orientalism* (1978). Said showed how certain visions of Asiatic societies were deeply woven into canonical European literature. Colonization no longer resided out there, in exotic places, but in the heart of European culture. Said soon faced criticism for presenting a view of the colonized as Other so tight that no room remained for alternative constructions, including those by Arabs, Africans, or South Asians. In a subsequent book, *Culture and Imperialism*, Said tried to restore balance by emphasizing not the stark separation of European and indigenous discourses but the efforts of colonized intellectuals to work between them and to develop cross-cutting languages of liberation.[5] Such an argument necessarily proves a historical one.

To some postcolonial theorists, the goal has been no less than to overthrow the place of reason and progress as the beacons of humanity, insisting that the claims to universality that emerged from the Enlightenment occlude the way colonialism imposed not just its exploitative power but its ability to determine the terms—democracy, liberalism, rationality—by which political life the world over would from then on be conducted. By holding this universalizing modernity against the ugly particularity of colonialism, postcolonial theorists attack head-on a metanarrative of a history that shows Europe step by step repudiating the oppressiveness of its own past and making itself into a model to the rest of the world. Some hope to persuade us to "give up the seemingly powerful corollary *presumption* that liberalism and indeed democracy (even a purportedly radical one) have any *particular* privilege among ways of organizing the political forms of our collective lives."[6]

Critics—and even some scholars who identify themselves with postcolonial studies—at times worry that the repudiation of Enlightenment may have gone too far and brought aid and comfort to political forces—such as the Hindu Right in India—whose rejection of liberal democratic values does not serve to enhance respect for the values of different communities. Some fear that the critique of so-called foundational concepts in Western thought, particularly those of Marxist theory, disarms social scientists of the tools they need to understand the all-too-real power of global capitalism.[7]

These arguments are not what concerns me here. My focus is the double occlusion that results from turning the centuries of European colonization overseas into a critique of the Enlightenment, democracy, or modernity. First is the occlusion of European history, for the counterpart of the charge of reducing non-Western history to the lack of what the West had is the assumption that the West actually had it itself, that the metanarrative of European progress is more relevant than the messy and uneven history of post-1789 Europe. Second is the occlusion of the history of the people who lived in what became colonies. What is lost in telling nineteenth- and twentieth-century colonialism as the story of the coming ashore "of the terrible storm called progress" or as "the politico-ethical project of producing subjects and governing their conduct," or as the production of "colonial modernities through the regulation of cultural difference" is the range of experiences and actions among people who confronted colonial rule.[8] One misses the crudeness and the excess of violence of much of nineteenth-century colonization, as well as the ways in which colonized people sought—not entirely without success— to build lives in the crevices of colonial power and to deflect, appropriate, or reinterpret the teachings and preachings thrust on them. The line of argument mentioned above may celebrate "resistance," but the idea that struggle actually had effects on the course of colonization is lost in the timelessness of colonial modernity. The Haitian Revolution—and especially the possibility that the Haitian Revolution actually affected the meanings of citizenship or freedom in Europe and the Americas—remains as strikingly absent in prominent postcolonial texts as in conventional narratives of European progress.[9]

For some, the occlusion is explicit, as in this formulation of Robert J. C. Young: "The postcolonial does not privilege the colonial. It is concerned with colonial history only to the extent that history has determined the configurations of power structures of the present, to the extent that much of the world still lives in the violent disruptions of its wake, and to the extent that the anti-colonial liberation movements remain the source and inspiration of

its politics."[10] How one would be able to judge "the extent" without studying the history is not obvious, but that is beside the point: the "colonial"
that is relevant here is the generic one, a singular colonialism, spatially un-
defined and temporally spread out over four centuries, whose contours are
exempted from examination, yet whose power still determines the present.[11]
But might not this generic colonial history produce an equally generic postcolonial present?

My argument is not with the postcolonial critic's insistence that the evils
of nineteenth- and twentieth-century colonialism lie firmly within the political structures, values, and understandings of its era; colonialism should
not be reduced to an atavistic holdover from the past. It is with a juxtaposition of a supposed post-Enlightenment universality and colonial particularity frozen in time, isolated from the dynamics ensuing from the tensions
within any ideological formation and the tensions produced by efforts of
empires to install real administrations over real people. What such an approach privileges is the stance of the critic who decodes this transhistorical
phenomenon, hence the label Gyan Prakash and others have attached to their
project, "colonial critique."[12]

Such a critique has had its value, above all in forcing historians—like anthropologists or other social scientists—to question their own epistemological positions and to think long and hard about how historical sources, as
much as interpretations, are produced. But critique is no substitute for historical or ethnographic research, and the question is how one understands
and moves beyond the limits inherent to the stance of the critic.[13] Let me
turn now to a brief analysis of modes of writing that can be called ahistorical history, which purport to address the relationship of past to present but
which do so without interrogating the way processes unfold over time. I will
mention three modes of looking at history ahistorically: story plucking, leapfrogging legacies, and time flattening. My goal in doing so is not to dismiss
certain critical strategies, but to suggest limitations that can be transcended.
It is not to issue a blanket criticism of "postcolonial studies" (a category
containing much variety and debate), but to point to the insufficiency and
imprecision of certain concepts and certain ways of framing issues. And it
is not to defend one discipline or condemn another, for some of the most
searching historical questions have been asked by literary critics or anthropologists, and historians, including some who have stimulated the study of
colonial questions, have also contributed to the tendency to take colonialism
out of a historical framework.[14]

First, story plucking. Here I mean extracting tidbits from different times
and places and treating them as a body independent of their historical re-

lationship, context, or countervailing tendencies. Postcolonial writers from Homi Bhabha to Walter Mignolo to Dipesh Chakrabarty write with little apparent misgivings about a phenomenon labeled colonial, appearing in many places and times.[15] Implicitly or explicitly, "coloniality," or its related form "postcoloniality," can be abstracted from context and process. The weighty *-ity* attached to the colonial implies that there exists an essence of being colonized, independent of what anybody did in a colony. One can pluck a text or a narrative from Spanish America in the sixteenth century, or from the slave colonies of the West Indies in the eighteenth century, or from a moderately prosperous twentieth-century cocoa planter in the Gold Coast, and derive a lesson that conveys a generalizable meaning. What gets lost here is that colonial power, like any other, is the object of struggle, a struggle that depends on the specific resources of those involved, and that colonizer and colonized themselves constitute far from immutable categories, categories that must be reproduced by specific institutions, institutions that themselves change historically. People did not just sit around contemplating what it meant to be colonized, and examining repressive power is not the same as assuming that it alone characterized a particular situation; the extremes of colonial violence may well reflect the limits of routinized power. Traders, peasants, religious converts, and others might seize spaces that colonial authorities could not understand or bend an institution in a new direction, or else Creole elites might replicate metropolitan institutions while attacking imperial rule. Different forms of exploitation, from compulsory production on plantations to taxation of the exports of peasants whose farms and families were largely ignored, could have very different social and cultural implications. A concept like coloniality is either so dilute that it carries little meaning, or so essentializing that it becomes deeply misleading.[16] Naming the colonial says little about how people confronted the forms of power they faced, about the social and cultural resources they brought to the confrontation, or about the dynamics of interaction and struggle.

Second, leapfrogging legacies. Here I refer to claims that something at time A caused something in time C without considering time B. Students of race in the United States have encountered a striking instance of this fallacy: the Moynihan report done during Nixon's presidency, which blamed the dislocation of African American families on the legacy of slavery. The causes of dislocation were placed in the safely distant past, skipping over anything that happened between 1863 and 1963, notably the effects of industrialization and urbanization on African Americans. Colonial legacy arguments exhibit the same flaw. African political scientist Mahmood Mamdani, in his book *Citizen and Subject: Contemporary Africa and the Legacy of Late*

Colonialism,[17] draws a direct causal connection between a colonial policy, arguably important in the 1920s and 1930s, of ruling through "decentralized despotisms," African chiefdoms given authority under colonial auspices, and the brittle politics of authoritarianism and ethnicity in Africa in the 1980s and 1990s. Like Moynihan, Mamdani has a point at either end of his leap-frog, but he misses everything in between. His book says almost nothing about the 1950s and 1960s, and thus misses the alternative explanation for Africa's malaise: that there was indeed effective mobilization in those years that cut across ethnic divisions and urban/rural distinctions, through which Africans made strong claims to citizenship, which African politicians used against colonial regimes. But once in power, such leaders understood all too well the danger such claims represented. The explosion of citizenship in the final years of colonial rule appears nowhere in Mamdani's book, and he thus misses not only the sequence of processes in the decolonization era but the tragedy of recent African history, people's heightened sense of pos-sibility, and the thwarting of their hopes. This book does not stand alone in finding a too-ready explanation of the postcolonial by invoking the colo-nial, leapfrogging over precisely the period and the processes that most need examination.[18]

Third, time flattening. This refers to an assumption that a certain essence characterizes a long period of time, passing over the conflict and change within it. This constitutes an old vice of history departments, notably in course listings that divide modern and premodern, distinctions bad enough in European history, but often extended elsewhere. Era labeling has been given a new interdisciplinary lease on life, in part through the work of Michel Foucault that locates modern governmentality in a space amorphous in time and amorphous in agency and causality, but that provides a blueprint for a wide range of scholars to attribute practices and discourses to the fact of modernity, often elided with post-Enlightenment rationalism, bourgeois equality, and liberalism.

Let me take the most persuasive version of this argument, from historian Dipesh Chakrabarty.[19] He justly criticizes versions of Indian history—colo-nialist, nationalist, or Marxist—that measure the colonized by how well they did at class formation and state building—where Europe supposedly led the way—and attribute their failures to certain "lacks" on their part (of a proper working class, of a proper bourgeoisie). Chakrabarty instead calls for the "provincialization" of Europe, its history seen as particular rather than as a universal model.

But then he proceeds to do the opposite. What he variously calls post-Enlightenment rationality, bourgeois equality, modernity, or liberalism become not provincial ideologies, but a grid of knowledge and power forcing people to see the nation-state as the only political model and obliging them to give up diverse understandings of community in favor of a one-to-one relationship of the unmarked individual and the nation-state, at best seeking "alternatives" to a modernity decidedly singular and decidedly European.

The pleasant irony of this argument is that Europeans become the people without history, a tag formerly reserved for the victims of their colonial endeavors.[20] European history, from Denis Diderot to Jacques Derrida, is flattened into a single post-Enlightenment era. A reference to Georg Wilhelm Friedrich Hegel stands in for a European history reduced to the claim of progress.[21] The problem, of course, is that Europeans—like the people they conquered—had a history that does not fit in boxes like this. Nineteenth-century Europe was immersed in struggles within and among many parochialisms and many universalities. Secularism was more often beleaguered than triumphant, anciens régimes and aristocracies did not die out on the guillotine. One would not know from Chakrabarty's account how intense the struggles have been over what the Enlightenment meant and what political deductions to draw from this. The balancing of the universalized, rights-bearing individual against questions of difference, constituted, as gender historian Dena Goodman argues, a vital debate *within* Enlightenment thinking. Critiques of post-Enlightenment thinking, as David Hollinger notes, have "evacuated" the history of "modernism" in the era 1890 to 1930, with its "revolt against the positivism, rationalism, realism, and liberalism," in order to create a stark—and profoundly ahistorical—opposition between the Enlightenment and the posts- in vogue today.[22]

Instead of provincializing Europe, Chakrabarty seems to be saying that Europe cannot be provincialized. He assumes not only that the Enlightenment won a complete ideological victory after 1789 over the defenders of aristocratic, Catholic, and monarchic social orders but that modernity constituted a kind of lived experience in contrast to that of India.[23] What is lost when one takes Europe out of its history is not only how badly the tale of progress fits the political, intellectual, and cultural history of this continent but the extent to which even such constructs dismissed as bourgeois equality were not some essence of "the West," but products of struggle. The English citizen, for example, far from constituting an unmarked individual in direct relation to the state, emerged from a vision of community centered around the idea of a jury of one's peers.[24] The ascension of a liberal idea of a rights-bearing individual over the equally liberal idea of rights as earned by the civilized behavior of a collectivity reflected the labors not only of a Frederick Douglass but of unnamed ex-slaves, dependent laborers, and colonized peasants who revealed the limits of colonial power and defined alternative modes of living and working in the crevices of authority.[25]

One antidote to writing history as the rise of the nation-state could focus on alternative readings of European history itself. Postrevolutionary France, for example, proved a peculiar combination of so-called old colonies, especially in the Caribbean, and a European France whose boundaries and degrees of "Frenchness" were far from clear even a century later. Precisely because Saint Domingue (later Haiti) formed part of an imperial space, the question of whether the rights of man and the citizen applied there was argued over in both Saint Domingue and Paris. The Haitian Revolution of 1791 stands alongside the French in opening questions of slavery and citizenship, of cultural difference and universal rights, to wider debate, the long-term relevance of which C. L. R. James made clear in 1938.[26] Napoleon's conquests in Europe and Egypt extended even further the fact of France as a differentiated territory, establishing a differentiation that did not neatly line up in a self-Other dichotomy.[27] That ex-slaves of African descent in the old colonies became citizens in 1848 while the large Muslim population taken in by the conquest of Algeria in 1830 were defined as subjects points to the difficulties of producing a stable theory of imperial difference. Most important, the range of distinctions within the French empire meant that people of any given status knew of the other possibilities, and just as in Haiti white planters, mulatto planters, and slaves had all used the citizenship concept to make claims, the efforts of France to define an imperial space produced a succession of claims to reconfigure citizenship, especially in moments of uncertainty like 1848, the beginnings of the Third Republic in the 1870s, and the world wars. If one wants to rethink France from its colonies, one might even argue that France itself only became a nation-state in 1962, when it finally gave up its hold on Algeria and tried for a time to define itself as a singular citizenry in a single territory.[28]

In the colonies, meanwhile, flattening nineteenth-century history into the imposition of colonial governmentality or colonial modernity produces, to an African historian at least, something unrecognizable. Certainly, one can point to efforts of geographers, explorers, and scholarly minded colonial officials in the aftermath of conquests of the 1870s to slot African cultures into schemas of scientific knowledge, but any study of knowledge and power must also recognize the deliberate ignorance of early-twentieth-century colonial states: there was no need to know the laborer whom one was going to use and discard. If advocates of so-called free labor hoped to extract a market-responsive individual from the confines of both slavery and community, colonial officials soon realized that the West Indian ex-slave or the

African ex-peasant was not following the script, and rather than make individual subjects, a powerful colonial lobby advocated new forms of coerced labor and the alteration of community structures to provide collective discipline. Religious conversion and education had their proponents, who wished to colonize minds, but until the 1940s, the detractors were more centrally placed in African administrations, and British, French, and German colonial regimes spent very little money to realize whatever civilizing missions they professed. In French and British Africa, a patchwork of early colonial projects to remake the African largely gave way after World War I, in the face of the inability of regimes to impose their will, to a more custodial version of colonialism, to acceptance of working through the indigenous elites once labeled primitive and tyrannical, and to a refusal to spend metropolitan funds on "development" until confronted with a new wave of challenges in the late 1930s and 1940s. For an African living in a colony, fluctuations or variants in colonial policy could have an enormous impact: between the forced laborer on a Mozambican sugar farm and the relatively autonomous coffee farmer in the southern Gold Coast, between the teacher trained at the École William Ponty in Senegal and the Algerian victimized by land alienation and labor exploitation, a great deal hung in the balance. And the kinds of politics for which such people could be mobilized varied accordingly, in place and in time. African historians since the 1970s have shed a good deal of light on such phenomena, and the specific trajectories of struggle deserve a place in the pantheon of colonial and postcolonial studies.

Doing history historically, as these examples suggest, does more to challenge the supposedly dominant narratives of nation building and development than an approach to the past based on story plucking, leapfrogging legacies, or time flattening. Criticisms of many historians for writing everything into a linear history of human progress are often accurate and appropriate, but an understanding of different forms of temporality is not assisted by positing a Western temporality divided into premodern, modern, and postmodern epochs or by focusing on an era of modernity in which European ascendancy is juxtaposed against but unaffected by the actions and ideas of colonized populations. A more dynamic view of the exercise of power, of the limits of power, and the contestations of power constitutes a fundamentally historical endeavor, demanding methodologies both rigorous and self-aware.

Colonial studies has by and large been so intent on taking apart the narrative of Western progress that it has remained rather uncurious about exploring the implications of looking backwards in time or toward the variety of forms of state power that shared the temporal field of modernity. Scholars of early modern Europe—Peter Hulme stands out in this regard—have gone further to engage postcolonial theory than have scholars of later colonization and decolonization to extend their own temporal bounds.[29] My coedited book *Tensions of Empire* proves no exception to this orientation toward Western Europe in the nineteenth and twentieth centuries.[30] The focus risks reproducing Eurocentrism by all but ignoring other empires—the Ottoman, the Habsburg, the Chinese, the Japanese, and the Russian—and initiatives to compare the Soviet empire of 1917–89 to empires of Britain and France in the twentieth century have come almost entirely from the side of scholars of the Soviet Union. Nineteen eighty-nine is not celebrated here as a milestone of decolonization: Central Asian Muslims conquered by the czars and subjected to the violent modernizing project of the Soviets are not the object of analogous moral and political attention as North African Muslims colonized by the French.

The narrowing of the range is based on certain assumptions: that these empires are different sorts of animals, that they are not really colonial, and, above all, that with the exception of the Soviet case, they were not "modern." The latter argument is actually a bit of whig history, reading backwards the collapse of the Ottoman, Habsburg, and Russian empires in 1917–23 into a thesis of the inevitable transition from empire to nation-state. Recent scholarship has shown that far from being beleaguered holdouts against claims to the nation, these empires produced a strong empire-centered imagination that captured the minds of many self-conscious opponents of imperial power until the time of World War I. Ottomanism constituted a compelling ideology, even among Young Turks whose national focus to a large extent postdated the demolition of the empire rather than inspired it. Likewise, the critics of Habsburg conservatism included many who saw the imperial unit as a possibility offering something to reform-minded intellectuals, Jews, and others who sought a bigger field than what became national units. Yet these empires were not quaint repositories of aristocratic cosmopolitanism. If difference is the hallmark of colonialism, they articulated and reproduced difference aplenty—and did not lack for repression either, but not in the same way as Britain or France.[31] And what passes for "modern governmentalities" in nineteenth-century Europe—cadastral surveys, the enumeration of imperial subjects—was a thousand years old in China.[32] Like the empires of nineteenth-century Western Europe, these empires had both universalizing and particularizing tendencies and illustrate a stunning range of possibilities for examining their relation.

Broadening the range of oppositional movements as well as empires should underscore the point made earlier: the dangers of the backward projection of the post-1960s world of nation-states into a nineteenth-century path of inevitability. One can fruitfully put in relation to each other the saliency of Ottomanism in the late nineteenth century, the rise of pan-Arab and pan-Slavic movements in the same era, and the long history of pan-Africanism, all of which put political affinity into a nonterritorial framework. Many scholars quote the same passage from Aimé Césaire in which he eloquently depicts the horrors of colonial rule, but not everybody remembers that his vision of decolonization was not limited to forging independent nation-states, but stressed remaking France itself to eliminate the invidious inequality among the component parts of this supranational unit and recreating a capitalist world order.[33] The possibilities that the political imagination of Césaire opened up—and the ways in which those possibilities were constrained—require a historical analysis more attuned to different voices than the assumption of a course from empire to nation-state set at the time of the French Revolution.

My own thinking has been shaped by reading old trade union pamphlets and colonial archives from French Africa in the late 1940s, where one finds workers' organizations telling officials: you want to talk about civilizing us, but what we want to talk about is equal pay for equal work, about piped water in our neighborhood, about schools for our children.[34] Such demands in their own way proved as threatening as the efforts of a Ho Chi Minh to throw France out of Southeast Asia, for they promised to turn the very premises of postwar imperial ideology into a series of expensive demands whose refusal would be ideologically as well as politically dangerous. Multiplied by many mobilizing efforts throughout the French empire, such demands not only won concrete benefits for many people—the forty-hour week for wage workers, for example—but the fact of insisting that such measures should apply to Africans as much as anybody else profoundly affected the meaning of citizenship and social distinction. They provoked doubts in Paris about the entire doctrine of postwar French colonialism, whose insistence that Greater France was the only unit of political possibility implied that the French standard of living was a legitimate reference point for colonial social movements. Political mobilization around imperial citizenship also injected a self-confidence into social movements themselves—and above all a socially focused, activist notion of citizenship—that proved threatening to postindependence regimes as well.

The efforts of trade unions, farmers' organizations, traders' organizations, and groups of teachers and students to challenge modernizing colonial regimes for both material benefits and political voice risk being lost if one privileges the Manichaean version of studying colonialism and anticolonialism.[35] But more is lost than the stories of a generation of activists in the 1940s and 1950s and the important but bounded accomplishments they achieved. The very claim of the "victors" of the politics of the 1950s and 1960s to represent a true anticolonialism and their contempt for the more diverse politics that had made the 1950s such a volatile era provided a rationale for the labeling of challengers to the new regimes as imperialist stooges or enemies of the people and the purging of the opposition from the political spectrum. The cultivation of heroic anticolonialism became part of postcolonial repression. Rather than contrast an era of pure anticolonialism, built around iconicized heroes, against a sordid picture of postcolonial corruption and venality, one can gain a more thorough understanding of the possibilities and tragedies of decolonization by examining the political space people opened for themselves, with its limitations and their compromises, provisional victories, and powerful disappointments.[36]

To some postcolonial theorists, those Africans who insisted (or who today insist) that the real issue is water, schools, or wages did not have it right. What is "important for the present," writes David Scott, is "a critical interrogation of the practices, modalities, and projects through which modernity inserted itself into and altered the lives of the colonized." Well, yes, but what about the water pipe, the health clinic, and the farmers' cooperative? Is there not a danger that we, as scholars, project onto people who lived at a certain time and in a certain place a metahistorical perspective that crowds out the question of how people, in a particular conjuncture, phrased their demands and organized themselves?[37]

The issues raised here are not mere exercises in historical refinement. History, as such, does not offer any lessons (although historians offer plenty), but to think through a historical process is to observe the relationship of action and its consequences. That is why I keep insisting on the importance of looking at the way in which specific actions by states or political movements reconfigured concepts and possibilities. If we are to do more than lament the passing of an era of true radicalism or to assume that colonialism's opponents could only follow a script written by colonizers themselves, we need to do more careful research into social and political movements at all levels, from the people trying to put together a local cooperative to transterritorial movements of intellectuals who fought to make colonialism an anathema. We cannot read that history off a text by Fanon.

There is a danger that ahistorical history encourages an apolitical politics. To take a stance against the Enlightenment, to hold modernity responsible for racial and class hierarchy, offers little account of the responsibility of elites for their words and actions and little insight into how people facing the possibilities and constraints of particular colonial situations acted. We lose the power of their example to remind us that our own moral and political choices, made in the face of the ambivalences and complications of our present situation, will have consequences in the future. As politically attuned a writer as Chakrabarty separates his politics from his critique, conceding that the liberal order and Enlightenment ideals he criticizes may be the best means for defending the position of the subaltern.[38] A more dynamic view of history would make the separation of colonial critique in the academy from politics in South Asia less artificial.

The antislavery movement, the anticolonial movement, and the antiapartheid movement have been subjected to relentless irony, for their humanistic claims can be set off against the exclusions and hierarchies they reinscribed and the whiggishness that narrating their history seems to imply.[39] But such movements were not simply entrapped in a framework of European beliefs; they profoundly changed what Europeans thought they believed. The Haitian Revolution, the Jamaican slave revolt of 1830, the Martinique slave revolt of 1848, the countless escapes and small acts of defiance of slaves in the southern United States—all formed part of the process that made slavery, a very normal part of very normal empires, into something first questioned and then attacked. That colonialism became the object of attack in Hanoi or Paris in the 1930s the way slavery did a century earlier reflects not the opposition of an abstracted "colonial subject" against a colonizer, but the coming together of specific forms of struggle in a particular conjuncture. At critical moments, the intersection of locally or regionally rooted mobilizations with movements deploying a liberal-democratic ideology, with attempts at articulating a Christian universalism, with the mobilization of Islamic networks, with the linkages of anti-imperialist movements in different continents, with trade union internationalism helped to shape and reshape the terrain of contestation. Such interactive mobilizations have hardly eliminated exploitation or invidious distinction, and they have had to contend with powerful forces seeking to confine challenges to carefully bounded domains, but incremental changes and systemic shifts are nonetheless part of the history of the present.[40]

One can readily agree with Uday Mehta when he writes, "I do not claim that liberalism *must be* imperialistic, only that the urge is *internal* to it."[41] One could just as easily write, "I do not claim that liberalism *must be* anti-imperialist, only that the urge is *internal* to it." As in the case of nineteenth-century English liberalism, the crucial questions about arguments for liberation and democratization today are not resolvable by epistemological critique alone, but turn on the concrete possibilities that our political, economic, and social conjuncture permits and the political choices that people make. Which liberalism? Whose Enlightenment? What kind of development? Which vision of an Islamic *umma* (community)? Whose community? Which network of connections across linguistic or cultural divisions?

If such an argument is valid, the question of how one finds evidence and constructs an argument about moments of possibility and moments of constraint proves crucial. The stance of the critic has been useful in reminding scholars in dusty archives of the impossibility of seeing themselves in a position of neutral judges outside of the history about which they write. Historians are warned of the dangers of imposing a notion of "objective truth" without probing the truth regime that gives weight to certain evidence and denies it to others; of missing the "temporal heterogeneity," the diverse ways people understand time and their relation to it, and of the need to get inside religious or other forms of understanding that deviate from secular, rationalist visions of how people make choices and act.[42] But it would be unfortunate if these issues were reduced to the imposition of modern reason on a recalcitrant nonmodern past; they prove fundamental to understanding *any* past. How regimes of truth are constructed in a particular context has been the subject of important analyses, and the efforts (notably among African historians since the 1960s) to build a more inclusive notion of the archive and to analyze the production of history—how the telling or writing of history is itself part of a history—have helped to make history writing a more examined and debated process.[43] A critical stance need not reproduce the modern/nonmodern dichotomy it pretends to deconstruct or to which it claims to provide alternatives.

Postcolonial studies has a strong stake in not carrying the contextualization of truth claims into a dismissal of truth as just another Western conceit. The moral force of the insertion of colonialism into world history depends on the reader's conviction that the slaves on a Jamaican sugar plantation actually felt the whip and that the Toussaint-Louvertures of the colonial world— and the unnamed peasants who frustrated the plans of colonial agents— are more than archetypes. The colonial apologist's tale of colonialism as the bringing of schools and hospitals to hapless natives might be seen as the expression by a group with its own cultural criteria, its own regime of truth, equivalent to but different from the cultural criteria and truth regimes of other groups. If all versions are to be seen as alternative fictions, each associated with a specific identity category, then there is no basis, other than an already specified position (race, gender, ethnicity) for anybody to convince anybody of anything.[44]

The historian's insistence on referring to the archive—oral, written, or whatever—pushes debate toward consideration of the time and the context in which a process occurs and makes it imaginable that a historian from, say, South Asia, might convince a reader in Great Britain to question a received truth. That the ground on which contestation takes place is not even, and that the historical or any other profession may resist the reconstitution of its canons, does not negate the importance of such debate. To foster the material and political conditions that extend the range of discussion outside of academic venues in which it has become accepted is no easy task, but the importance of extending intellectual debate derives from it being more than the juxtaposition of preconstituted stances.

One of the achievements of scholars who consider themselves postcolonial is to bring the colonial question out of the colonies and into Europe and North America. Here, too, there is a danger of the power of this insight becoming diffuse, of explaining generalized difference in the cities of England via reference to an undifferentiated colonial past stretching back to Columbus. One cannot understand the Le Pen phenomenon in France without understanding Algeria, but one cannot understand Le Pen by reducing him to Algeria. The terms in which Le Pen–style xenophobia is articulated also comes out of a line of right-wing Catholicism that has been anti-Semitic and anti-Protestant, loudly proclaiming itself "French" while at the same time opposing the republican notions of civic virtue that others consider the basis of Frenchness.[45] The problems of immigrants from ex-colonies or other regions outside of Western Europe will not be solved by juxtaposing a postcoloniality that is filled with hybridity and multiculturalism against an all-containing colonial modernity.

Tejumola Olaniyan writes that "even the most unforgiving critics of the *term* [postcolonial] do not deny that a lot of relevant work is being done in its name."[46] He is certainly correct, and the most important question is how to go about continuing the work. Stuart Hall has given historians, among others, plenty of employment when he describes the domain of postcolonial studies as "the whole process of expansion, exploration, conquest, colonisation and imperial hegemonisation which constituted the 'outer face,' the constitutive outside, of European and their Western capitalist modernity after 1492."[47] This agenda will, and should be, pursued by scholars using a variety of theoretical frameworks, in useful conversation with the conceptual critiques that postcolonial theory has encouraged. But the metaclaim that the unit in question is "Western capitalist modernity since 1492" can easily become a shortcut of just such an examination, an evocation of a past flattened into a blunt tool useful for showing the ugly flip side of European progress, but not for building up other ways of narrating and explaining a complex history. If the kind of inquiry I am advocating is consistent with the goals of many who consider themselves postcolonial theorists, some of the concepts deployed within such a framework contribute more to the flattening than to the examination, and I have suggested that coloniality, colonial modernity, post-Enlightenment rationality, and colonial legacy are among them. Similarly, Homi Bhabha and others have brought into wide usage notions like hybridity, aporia, and fragmentation, and they have provoked a useful debate against other theorists who see discourses in colonial spaces in more Manichaean terms, but there are risks in deploying such concepts generically and at a high level of abstraction, for they may say too little (about the different forms in which hybridity appears) or not enough (about the specific conjunctures in which hybridity or dualism gain ascendancy).[48]

Let us, in short, *really* provincialize Europe. To do that is not to invert the narrative of progress to expose its underbelly, but to examine the limits as well as the power of European domination, the unevenness and conflict within Europe itself; it is to study systems of power and representation in interaction with each other, neither presuming the centrality of modern Europe as a reference point nor shying away from analysis of power as it actually was exercised.

Enlarging the field should not dilute the importance of European colonization in its earliest or most recent manifestations, but rather produce a more compelling account of its mechanisms and its limits, including the mechanisms and limits of modes of representation. It is worth thinking about how far one can generalize about a phenomenon called colonialism, about the degree to which different historical trajectories are linked by the shared experience of coercive and cultural subjugation. One can recognize that all colonizing systems—from Rome's universal empire to Islamic universalism to the civilizing mission of twentieth-century France—created a tension between the incorporation of conquered peoples into a singular imperial system and the maintaining lines of distinction that marked the center's unique role in the system. Such a tension, and the conflicts it provoked, was built into the institutions of empires, given their geographic dispersion, extended chains of command, incorporation of regional economic circuits, local systems of authority and patronage, and often the presence of religious or ideological affinities embodied in the values not just of a subjugated community but of an alternative version of universality. Generalization can homogenize too far (as in abstracting coloniality from the lived experience of people in colonies) and demarcation can be misleading (separating modern empires from those prior or contemporaneous to those of nineteenth-century Western Europe). But comprehensive historical analysis might help sketch out likely fields of struggle, might help to look for conjunctures where power relations were most vulnerable and to probe limits of power beneath the claims to dominance. The analytical challenge consists of both comparing and studying connections, of examining changes in the imaginable and the possible across time and space.

The analytical challenge cannot be separated from a political one, for one should neither avoid the specific trajectories of Western European expansion nor fetishize them. At the same time, one loses a great deal by using *colonial* as a mere metaphor for extremes of power, for that is to give up a differentiated vocabulary with which to discuss the spatial, institutional, and cultural patternings of colonial systems. I agree with Stuart Hall that one should not shy away from using *postcolonial* in an epochal sense, for the decolonization movements of the decades after World War II did in fact remove colonization from the political repertoire, and from then onward the institutionalization and representation of transnational power had to take forms other than that of a colonial empire.[49] Once again, one can try to name or invoke a "postcolonial moment" as if it had a distinguishing essence, or one can use the concept as the point of departure for a methodologically diverse examination of different trajectories of power, of its mechanisms and limits, as well as of the changing ways in which such forms of power were contested.[50]

We are not faced with a dichotomous choice of practicing history in one way only or rejecting historical scholarship altogether, between reducing colonization to a sideshow of European progress or assuming it represented a single, coherent project; between romanticizing anticolonial movements in their moment of triumph or treating colonial history as if the actions of the colonized never changed its course; between making clear the colonial histories' continued effects today or accepting that anticolonial movements have succeeded in eliminating colonial rule as a normal part of world politics. Far from having to choose between examining the complexities of a colonial past and broadening our sense of the opportunities and constraints of the future, a critical and sensitive historical practice can help us retain our focus on the possibilities of political imagination and on the importance of accountability for the consequences of our actions.

Notes

1. Most notable is the recognition within the historical profession achieved by scholars whose work crosses the colony/metropole divide: Alice Conklin and Julia Clancy-Smith in "French" history; Antoinette Burton, Catherine Hall, and Susan Thorne in "British" history; Lora Wildenthal in "German" history; and Christopher

Schmidt-Nowara in "Spanish" history, to name a few. And if my generation of historians of Africa (early 1970s) tended to think that colonial topics were not African enough, subsequent generations have if anything tilted in the opposite direction. The establishment of journal *American Historical Review* has recently given colonial questions a prominent place; note also the proliferation of journals like *Postcolonial Studies, Journal of Colonialism and Colonial History*, and *Interventions: International Journal of Postcolonial Studies*.

2. Some of the critiques and analyses suggested in this essay are developed at greater length in my *Colonialism in Question: Theory, Knowledge, History* (Berkeley: University of California Press, forthcoming).

3. Nandy, "History's Forgotten Doubles."

4. Dirks, "History as a Sign of the Modern," 25.

5. Said, *Orientalism*; and Said, *Culture and Imperialism*. For a recent reassessment of Said's contribution by historians, see Rotter, Fleming, and Biddick, "Orientalism Twenty Years On."

6. Scott, *Refashioning Futures*, 156.

7. For sympathetic critiques, see Spivak, *A Critique of Postcolonial Reason*; and Dirks, "Postcolonialism and Its Discontents," 244, 246. For hostile ones, see Sumit Sarkar, "The Fascism of the Sangh Parivar," *Economic and Political Weekly*, January 20, 1993, 164–65; and Dirlik, "The Postcolonial Aura." For an illuminating debate on foundational concepts, see Prakash, "Writing Post-orientalist Histories of the Third World"; O'Hanlon and Washbrook, "After Orientalism"; and Prakash, "Can the 'Subaltern' Ride?"

8. Dirks, "Postcolonialism and Its Discontents," 246; Scott, *Refashioning Futures*, 52; Burton, introduction to *Gender, Sexuality, and Colonial Modernities*, 2.

9. Thus Dipesh Chakrabarty, for whom the post-Enlightenment is a crucial category, makes no mention of the post-Enlightenment of the Haitian revolutionaries. Chakrabarty, *Provincializing Europe*; Scott does not mention Haiti either in *Refashioning Futures*. Young, *Postcolonialism*, cites Haiti as a slave revolt, not as a revolt that shaped debates on emancipation. It is the very "unpost" C. L. R. James who appreciated the significance of this event (*The Black Jacobins*).

10. Young, *Postcolonialism*, 4.

11. For Stuart Hall, the relevant unit of analysis is "European and then Western capitalist modernity after 1492." Hall, "When Was 'the Postcolonial,'" 249.

12. Prakash, "Subaltern Studies as Postcolonial Criticism."

13. Young defines postcolonialism as a stance, as an assumption of the mantle of anticolonial liberation movements in a changed situation. He posits a singular intellectual-political lineage going from Marxism to analyses of the subjective affects of colonialism. Denying any particular interest in colonial history, his postcolonialism nevertheless assumes "a common political and moral consensus towards the history and legacy of western colonialism" (*Postcolonialism*, 5). He dismisses the historians' potential concern about the variety of colonial experiences with a rhetorical flourish: "Postcolonial critique . . . identifies with the subject position of anti-colonial activists," while the "empiricist" historian presumably does not (19). The problem with defining a mode of inquiry by a stance is not merely its cavalier attitude toward human experience but that any political thinking or forms of mobilization that do not fit the singular narrative are excluded from the start. Yet Young's dismissive com-

ments are contradicted by his often context-sensitive text, and even by his subtitle, *An Historical Introduction*.

14. Any criticism of work coming out of Subaltern Studies must acknowledge that no group has done more, by exhortation and practice, to stimulate research on colonial history. Fruitful debate is also animated by Indian historians outside the Subaltern Studies fold, such as Chandavarkar, *Imperial Power and Popular Politics*; and Bose and Jalal, *Modern South Asia*.

15. Bhabha, "Of Mimicry and Man"; Mignolo, *Local Histories/Global Designs*; Chakrabarty, *Provincializing Europe*.

16. This dilution is the basic problem with using *coloniality* to express extremes of power and extremes of differentiations—but without regard to institutions—and with treating a wide range of experiences of subordination as the consequences of a generic "centuries of Western colonial expansion," rather than specific trajectories, as in Grosfoguel and Georas, " 'Coloniality of Power.' "

17. Mamdani, *Citizen and Subject*. Daniel Patrick Moynihan's report was entitled "The Negro Family: The Case for National Action," and the controversy it provoked can be examined in Rainwater and Yancey, *The Moynihan Report and the Politics of Controversy*.

18. For another example of the leapfrogging fallacy, see Price, *The Convict and the Colonial*. This book is constructed around the ironic juxtaposition of a violent confrontation of police and demonstrators on the French island of Martinique in 1925 and the trivializing of the memory of colonization in the period of Price's fieldwork, when the people of Martinique were caught up in the peculiarities of the tourist business and the French welfare state. By omitting the history in between, Price occludes the seriousness of political mobilization in the 1930s and 1940s, when a strong Caribbean movement pressed the French government to accord this colony the status of a French department and thereby could lay claim to French educational and social resources equivalent to those claimed by other French citizens. One would not know from Price's account that this movement succeeded in 1946, that the victims of the 1925 conflict did not die in vain, or that the noted writer/activist whose authority Price invokes in indicting French colonialism, Aimé Césaire, was the main leader of the departmentalization movement. The missing middle contains the politics.

19. Chakrabarty, *Provincializing Europe*. If in some of his writing, Chakrabarty has engaged the difficulties of using Marxist theory in colonial situations by focusing on the specific modes in which economic, political, and social power operates; other writing goes in the opposite direction, toward abstraction and away from context. See his *Habitations of Modernity*.

20. The allusion here is to Wolf, *Europe and the People without History*.

21. Chakrabarty, *Provincializing Europe*, 237; Prakash, *Another Reason*, 8, 118; Dirks, *Castes of Mind*, 52.

22. Goodman, "Difference"; and Hollinger, "The Enlightenment and the Genealogy of Cultural Conflict in the United States," 11–12.

23. Similarly, Prakash places a valuable reading of the variety of ways in which South Asians engaged in science against a singular notion of European "reason." Prakash, *Another Reason*.

24. Somers, "Rights, Relationality, and Membership."

25. On the role of slaves in redefining the meanings of freedom, see Blackburn, *The*

Overthrow of Colonial Slavery; Fredrickson, *Black Liberation*; and Holt, *The Problem of Freedom*.

26. James, *The Black Jacobins*. See also Dubois, *Les esclaves de la République*.

27. Curiously, arguments about post-Enlightenment colonialism have not led to a reexamination of Napoleon's empire. This maps poorly onto a modern/nonmodern distinction, for Napoleon combined the deployment of "scientific" principles of geography and rationalized organization with a symbolic orientation toward Rome (and Caesar's Rome more than republican Rome); he restored slavery (abolished in 1794) and was close to some elites of the ancien régime. Most important was that Napoleon's France was more complicated than a "nation" subjecting others: his conquests incorporated some territories into the departmental system and ruled others through local monarchs or elites, or else through relatives or clients, and sometimes with the support of local republican elements. An attempt to rethink part of this story was a colloquium at the University of Paris VIII–Saint Denis, held in June 2002, entitled "Rétablissement de l'esclavage dans les colonies françaises: Ruptures et continuités de la politique coloniale française: 1802, 1804, 1825, 1830." See also Woolf, "French Civilization and Ethnicity in the Napoleonic Empire."

28. For the switches in direction in policy toward citizenship and nationality, see Weil, *Qu'est-ce qu'un Français?*; and Conklin, *A Mission to Civilize*.

29. Hulme, *Colonial Encounters*; Pagden, *Spanish Imperialism and the Political Imagination*; and Schwartz, *Implicit Understanding*. As Florencia Mallon notes in this volume, many Latin Americanists feel that postcolonialism does not apply to them.

30. Cooper and Stoler, *Tensions of Empire*.

31. Judson, *Exclusive Revolutionaries*; Deringil, *The Well-Protected Domains*; Duus, *The Abacus and the Sword*; and Barkey and von Hagen, *After Empire*.

32. Wong, *China Transformed*.

33. Césaire, *Discourse on Colonialism*, 21. A notable effort to bring a transnational perspective to studying such questions is Gilroy, *The Black Atlantic*. One wishes that Africa had more of a place in his Black Atlantic.

34. Cooper, *Decolonization and African Society*.

35. Hence the argument that Ann Stoler and I made claiming that understanding Manichaean tendencies within colonial ideologies should not imply taking a Manichaean position oneself. Cooper and Stoler, "Between Metropole and Colony: Rethinking a Research Agenda," in *Tensions of Empire*, 1–56.

36. My argument differs from David Scott's stage theory that develops from "anticoloniality" to "postcoloniality" to "after postcoloniality." Even more striking than Scott's willingness to reduce the politics of the 1950s to its icons is the absence in his book of consideration of a liberation movement that does not fit his anticolonial stage, the struggle in South Africa against apartheid in the 1980s and 1990s. Scott, *Refashioning Futures*, 10–14, 16, 45, 199. Achille Mbembe vividly evokes the atmosphere of politics after independence, but lets the category of the postcolonial do the work that a historical analysis would do much better. Mbembe, *On the Postcolony*.

37. Scott, *Refashioning Futures*, 17. See also James Ferguson's essay in this volume. Modernity-bashing is by no means limited to postcolonial studies. A considerable literature criticizes "development" by focusing on its rhetoric (with less to say about the material stakes). See Escobar, *Encountering Development*; and Sachs, *The Development Dictionary*.

38. Chakrabarty, "Modernity and Ethnicity in India," 3374.

39. A more satisfying approach is Catherine Hall's contextualized analysis of debates among antislavery advocates, which brings out the openings as well as the closures of their different discourses. Hall, *Civilising Subjects*.

40. I have argued elsewhere that anticolonial movements, as well as colonialism itself, have been transnational and transcontinental and that—contrary to those who write about globalization as a phenomenon of the present—both processes have a very long history. Cooper, "What Is the Concept of Globalization Good For?"

41. Mehta, *Liberalism and Empire*, 20; emphasis original.

42. Chakrabarty, *Provincializing Europe*, 243; see also 99–113, 237–55. Chakrabarty notes that today's historian of the European Middle Ages, not just the historian of India, uses secular reason to dissect a religious framework (110–12). But so, too, will an American scholar exploring the relationship of fundamentalist Christianity to the Republican Party under the Bush administration, and such a scholar needs both to understand the religiosity of his/her subjects *and* not be limited to interpreting politics in the administration's terms. Discussion of the problematic nature of truth claims goes back, indeed, to the Enlightenment, and becomes clear in "modernist" texts like Mannheim, *Ideology and Utopia*. For the debate over objectivity among historians, see Novick, *That Noble Dream*; and Appleby, Hunt, and Jacob, *Telling the Truth about History*.

43. Guha, "The Prose of Counterinsurgency"; and Stoler, "In Cold Blood." For pioneering and innovative work on sources in African history, see Vansina, *Oral Tradition*. For more recent interventions, see Hunt, *A Colonial Lexicon*; Desai, *Subject to Colonialism*; and Cohen and Odhiambo, *Burying SM*.

44. Guarav Desai astutely uses a text written by Akiga Sai, a mission-educated, colonial-era Nigerian, to show how an African could subtly insert his views into the "colonial library." But Desai's comments about the need to "nuance" truth made in relation to a story illustrating the falsity of certain representations of the truth miss the point that the power of Sai's text lies in that he has already convinced the reader that one version of the story is in fact true. Desai's comments on truth depend on a stark separation of a "modern" conception and an indigenous one, which is what Sai's text refuses. See Desai, *Subject to Colonialism*, 131–36, 144, 148. See also Chakrabarty, *Provincializing Europe*, 99–100.

45. For the complexities of questions of inclusion and nationality in both colonial and postcolonial European polities, see Weil, *Qu'est-ce qu'un Français*; Paul, *Whitewashing Britain*; and Tabili, *"We Ask for British Justice."*

46. Olaniyan, "On 'Post-colonial' Discourse," 745.

47. Hall, "When Was 'the Postcolonial,'" 249.

48. Bhabha, *The Location of Culture*, 2–4, 171. The view of colonialism as Manichaean, most powerfully articulated by Frantz Fanon, has been defended by, among others, JanMohamed, *Manichean Aesthetics*.

49. Hall, "When Was 'the Postcolonial,'" 246. This redefinition of the political repertoire provides a better way of distinguishing the postcolonial epoch than a distinction based on a binary coloniality and a hybrid postcoloniality. In arguing that *postcolonial* can be used in an epochal sense, but not in a substantive one (that postcolonial societies or polities have given characteristics), I am making the reverse argument of that which Bernard Yack makes about postmodernism: that one can identify

certain patterns of postmodern thought, but that such thought does not distinguish any particular era, including the present one. Although I am not convinced of a modern/postmodern divide in intellectual terms, Yack's antiepochal argument about the postmodern is not incompatible with my or Hall's epochal argument about postcolonialism. See Yack, *The Fetishism of Modernities*, esp. 4–5, 19, 29. It should also be noted that it is the recent decolonizations that extinguished colonialism as a legitimate political form, not earlier ones (the independence of Haiti, the United States, or Latin American countries).

50. For an extreme instance of the former, of an evocation without grounding in any kind of historical or institutional analysis (indeed, without even curiosity about the kind of information that might support one's assertions), see Hardt and Negri, *Empire*. For a critique of the way this and other works misuse the concept of empire in relation to the present conjuncture, see Cooper, "Empire Multiplied."

The Politics of Postcolonial Modernism

❧ ❧ ❧

NEIL LAZARUS

In recent years—since the mid-1990s, say—a more or less concerted materialist critique has arisen of the epistemological and ideological tendencies that have been predominant in postcolonial studies from the time of its initial consolidation as an academic field of inquiry in the universities of Europe and North America. While it would clearly be too much to claim at this point that this still-emerging critique has succeeded in overturning the ruling tenets and protocols of the field, it has nevertheless begun to exercise a discernibly widening influence there. The specific assumptions and investments predominant in the field from its inception are still predominant today, though not nearly as serenely as formerly. Among these assumptions and investments, I would list in particular the following: a constitutive anti-Marxism; an undifferentiating disavowal of all forms of nationalism and a corresponding exaltation of migrancy, liminality, hybridity, and multiculturality; a hostility toward "holistic forms of social explanation" (toward totality and systematic analysis);[1] an aversion to dialectics; and a refusal of an antagonistic or struggle-based model of politics. Where as recently as a decade ago, a theorist as authoritative as Homi K. Bhabha could characterize these investments quite unilaterally and unselfconsciously as representing "*the* postcolonial perspective,"[2] those speaking for the prevailing positions today tend to look over their shoulders while doing so, hedging their bets and introducing all kinds of qualification into what had previously been a relatively unconditional discourse.

I do not plan, in this essay, to rehearse the arguments that have been adduced by the materialist critics in postcolonial studies—the best-known of which (those of Aijaz Ahmad, Tim Brennan, Arif Dirlik, Biodun Jeyifo, Neil Larsen, Benita Parry, and E. San Juan Jr., for example), will in any event be familiar to interested readers.[3] What I want to do, instead, is to take up some properly disciplinary questions deriving from the materialist critique and concerning so-called postcolonial literatures. Joining a discussion already underway in recent work by such very diverse critics as Simon Gikandi, Nicholas Harrison, Patrick Colm Hogan, Graham Huggan, David Murphy, and Kelwyn Sole,[4] I want to argue, very broadly, that because of the tendentiousness and partiality of the theoretical assumptions that have structured postcolonial studies hitherto, literary scholars working in the field have tended to write with reference to a woefully restricted and attenuated corpus of works. On the one hand, a great many works that ought—by the most routine and uncontroversial of criteria such as representativeness or aesthetic significance—to have been taken into consideration have been ignored entirely; on the other hand, the relatively few works that postcolonial critics *have* considered have typically been read in the most leadenly reductive of ways. I am tempted to overstate the case, for purposes of illustration, and declare that there is in a strict sense only one author in the postcolonial literary canon. That author is Salman Rushdie, whose novels—especially *Midnight's Children* and *The Satanic Verses*—are endlessly and fatuously cited in the critical literature as testifying to the imagined-ness—that is to say, ideality— of nationhood, the ungeneralizable subjectivism of memory and experience, the instability of social identity, the volatility of truth, the narratorial constructedness of history, and so on.[5]

I am sure I am not alone among scholars who read and teach postcolonial literature as well as postcolonial theory in deploring both the sheer opportunism of so many of the critical readings currently produced and also the narrowness of the research base or range of works typically canvassed for this production. To read across postcolonial literary studies is to find, to an extraordinary degree, the same questions asked, the same methods, techniques, and conventions used, the same concepts mobilized, the same conclusions drawn—about the work of a remarkably small number of writers (who are actually much more varied, even so, than one would ever discover from the existing critical discussion). For some scholars in the field, evidently, all that is required of the postcolonial literary texts evoked is that they permit—which is to say, not actively disallow—a certain, very specific and very restricted kind of reading to be staged through reference to them. Thus, it seems to me, the profuse critical discussions of nationalism as imagined community, with their talismanic and utterly formulaic evocations of *Midnight's Children* or Ben Okri's *The Famished Road* or Amitav Ghosh's *The Shadow Lines*; and thus also the busy commentaries on history as a master narrative intrinsically complicit with domination, which authoritatively summon Assia Djebar or Patrick Chamoiseau or Gabriel García Márquez to the bar, as though the texts by these novelists were not themselves militantly historicist in conception. So widespread and routine have such critical readings become that they have even begun to spawn a literary practice in their image. As Timothy Brennan has pointed out in a powerful critique of what he terms "new cosmopolitan writing," today a new literary genre is emerging of works that give the impression of having been produced precisely with an eye to their postcolonialist reception. "Several younger writers," Brennan writes, "have entered a genre of third world metropolitan fiction whose conventions have given their novels the unfortunate feel of ready-mades."[6] It is difficult to read at least some of the work by such writers as Jessica Hagedorn, Raj Kamal Jha, Cristina Garcia, and Caryl Phillips in terms other than these.

Let me illustrate the general point I am trying to make here through reference to a book published about a decade ago, coedited by Feroza Jussawalla and Reed Way Dasenbrock and entitled *Interviews with Writers of the Postcolonial World*.[7] It is a fine book in many ways, certainly one of the more engaging collections of interviews in the postcolonial studies field to have been published to date, noteworthy for its range and theoretical sophistication. Fourteen writers are interviewed: Chinua Achebe, Rudolfo Anaya, Sandra Cisneros, Anita Desai, Buchi Emecheta, Nuruddin Farah, Zulfikar Ghose, Roy Heath, Rolando Hinojosa, Witi Ihimaera, Ngugi wa Thiong'o, Raja Rao, Sam Selvon, and Bapsi Sidhwa. I shall refer only in passing to the obvious problems posed by this collocation of names. What thematic concerns, historical conditions, or existential predicaments can plausibly be said to license the inclusion of such authors as Ngugi, Ghose, and Ihimaera under any shared rubric, let alone that of "postcoloniality"? Does it make sense to extrapolate the work of US-based Latino writers like Anaya, Cisneros, and Hinojosa to the postcolonial?

To do them credit, Jussawalla and Dasenbrock attempt to provide answers to these questions. They argue, thus, that the writers interviewed in the volume all share "a common heritage of colonialism and post-colonialism, a common heritage of multilingualism and multiculturalism, a common heritage of displacement and migration" (14). This, they suggest, not only makes it advisable to situate "minority" writers from Britain and North America in relation to "postcolonial" writers from Africa and Asia and the South Pacific; it also explodes the credibility of any nation-based approach to these writers. Jussawalla and Dasenbrock advocate instead a new variant of comparative literature, a "comparative literature within English" (14) that will be sensitive to the emergence of new traditions of writing while remaining alert to the degree to which these new traditions are being produced "in some respects against the grain and against the conventions of mainstream Anglo-American writing" (18–19).[8]

Such a standpoint has something to commend it, at least. Jussawalla and Dasenbrock's commitment to the aesthetics of so-called multiculturalism serves as a plausible platform from which to engage urbane and cosmopolitan writers like Ihimaera or Farah or Anaya in conversation. Unsurprisingly, therefore, these are among the most successful interviews in the volume. Certain of the other "postcolonial" writers interviewed, however, do not share the editors' cultural or intellectual commitments. With respect to these writers, Jussawalla and Dasenbrock's determination to place the problematics of hybridity and multiculturalism center stage is dogmatic, and it sometimes strangles conversation rather than facilitating it. Desai, Sidhwa, Heath, and Cisneros are all encouraged to reflect on their multiculturality, whether or not this seems in keeping with the general tone of the discussion. The interview with Rao quickly goes awry when Jussawalla and Dasenbrock refer in general terms to postcolonial writers' interest in cross-cultural communication. Rao responds both that he is an Indian and not any other kind of writer, and that he is "not interested in communicating across cultures" (143). But Jussawalla and Dasenbrock seem strangely incapable of grasping the thrust of this authentically conservative position. On the very next page we find them alluding to the "multiculturalism" of India, which draws from Rao the counterquestion: "Why are you so interested in multiculturality?" (144); and two pages later Rao is obliged to protest that "here again we are talking too much about internationalism and interculture" (146). The interview ends with the editors still not having taken the point: Jussawalla asks about "the accessibility of literature to the common reader," causing Rao to respond tartly that he is "not in the least interested in that" (154).

A similar pattern manifests itself in the interview with Zulfikar Ghose. Again, the editors sound their general themes of hybridity and multiculturalism, communication and accessibility; again, the writer being interviewed demurs from the line of questioning, indicating his commitment to an entirely different aesthetic ideology; and again, the editors seem obtusely incapable of recognizing the writer's standpoint—or perhaps they are disinclined to do so? Jussawalla asks how Ghose wants his reader to get at the "larger meanings" in his work. He answers, "I have no interest in the reader. I never think of the reader. I don't know who the reader is" (186). Jussawalla then asks what Ghose makes of his status as "a multicultural writer," to which Ghose's response is, "I'm not multicultural. I'm British. I'm really more Anglo-Saxon than the Anglo-Saxons" (187). It is a firm, if perverse, rejoinder, but the editors wholly disregard it. Within a few pages—as though

Ghose had said nothing—they are referring to him once more as a "multicultural" writer who embodies in his person "what's getting to be an increasingly multicultural world" (195). Ghose is compelled to reiterate that "this talk about the importance of the multicultural background that supposedly makes some Commonwealth writers so remarkable is utterly inconsequential. The only thing of consequence is the quality of the mind of the writer" (195-96). It is no wonder that Ghose seems generally testy, snapping back on one occasion that he is "not an intellectual at all" and that in fact "I refuse to have ideas. I despise ideas. Ideas have never helped mankind. Only *things* help. Things like penicillin and flushing toilets" (193).

The sheer appropriativeness of some of the readings regularly put forward in postcolonial studies can still make one gasp: as in the example just cited, where novelists like Ngugi and Heath and Rao are linked under the unlikely sign of multiculturalism, so elsewhere we encounter presentations of Wole Soyinka and Kamau Brathwaite as poets closely aligned, in their deepest convictions, with deconstruction; of Bessie Head as a "difference" feminist, less the Cape Gooseberry than the Southern African Hélène Cixous; of Assia Djebar, Ama Ata Aidoo, and Mahasweta Devi as principled opponents of nationalist discourse; and so on. But part of what I want to argue is that even the work of such writers as Rushdie, Vikram Chandra, Maryse Condé, Merle Hodge, Tahar Ben Jelloun, Abdelkebir Khatibi, B. Kojo Laing, or Derek Walcott—which undeniably lends itself to what we might call pomo-postcolonialist reading (*pomo* as in *postmodernist*)—is not necessarily best or most illuminatingly approached in these terms. There is no need to deny that the concepts, problematics, and methods generated within postcolonial studies have contributed decisively to the interpretation and elucidation of important literary works today called postcolonial. It is also obvious that elective affinities obtain between many such works and the distinctive concepts, problematics, and methods of postcolonial studies— between J. M. Coetzee's fiction and poststructuralist theories of difference, *différance*, alterity, and incommensurability, for instance; or between Ben Jelloun's work and contemporary theories of identity as a performative construct; or between Edouard Glissant's work and the critique of essentialist myths of origin. Even so, however, it seems to me that there is so much that we *fail* to attend to when we programmatically refer Coetzee's novels only to Jacques Lacan or Emmanuel Levinas; or Caribbean literature as a whole to the Deleuzean concepts of extraterritoriality and the rhizome; or the representation of home and belonging in Nuruddin Farah's *Maps* or the work of Bharati Mukherjee or Caryl Phillips only to the explicitly postnationalist debates on diaspora and hybridity.

Moreover, just as important as the fact that works like these are being read so unimaginatively is the fact that so many other extraordinary works, which are not really susceptible to analysis in terms of the received categories and conventions in the field, are being substantially neglected by postcolonialists, if indeed they are known at all. As a number of critics have pointed out, the field of postcolonial studies is structured in such a way that it is much more likely to register the presence of writing in English and, to a lesser extent, French or Spanish, than writing in such other languages as Chinese, Arabic, Yoruba, Zulu, Amharic, Malay, Urdu, Telugu, Bengali, Sinhala, Tagalog, or even in the metropolitan and formerly colonial languages of Dutch and Portuguese. Similarly, it is much more likely to register the presence of writers who adopt generic and modal conventions readily assimilable by Euro-American readers than of writers who root their work in other conventions. We should not be particularly surprised, under these circumstances—though we might still find it deplorable—that writers like Abdel Rahman al-Sharqawi, Ismat Chughtai, Mia Couto, Duong Thu Huong, Faiz Ahmed Faiz, Ebrahim Hussein, Hwang Sun-won, Clarice Lispector, Naguib Mahfouz, Gabriela Mistral, Odia Ofeimun, Pramoedya Ananta Toer, Lesego Rampolokeng, Trefossa, Nirmal Verma, and Xi Xi, remain pretty much completely unknown to a majority of scholars in postcolonial literary studies.[9] More unexpected, however, must be the fact that one could just as easily come up with an equally long list of equally consecrated Anglophone and Francophone writers who, despite their formal accessibility and their consecration, again command only slender prestige in the postcolonial field per se: Peter Abrahams, Mongo Beti, Ralph de Boissière, Dennis Brutus, Jan Carew, Anita Desai, Mohammed Dib, Nissim Ezekiel, Abdellatif Laâbi, Earl Lovelace, Jamal Mahjoub, Jack Mapanje, Timothy Mo, V. Y. Mudimbe (as a novelist, not as a theorist), Femi Osofisan, Ninotchka Rosca, Nayantara Sahgal, Shyam Selvadurai, Ahdaf Soueif, Véronique Tadjo, and Albert Wendt, to pluck some names almost at random from my own bookshelves.

Let me pause for a moment here to clarify what I mean. There are, of course, quite substantial critical literatures on at least some of the authors from each of the two lists I have just presented—dedicated books and many articles (perhaps even hundreds), for instance, on each of Desai, Lispector, Mahfouz, Mistral. This is precisely why I speak of these as *consecrated* writers. But my point is that their consecration has been bestowed in literary and critical fields other than that of postcolonial studies, even if, in abstract terms, abutting and intersecting it—fields such as "Indian" or "Nigerian" or "Latin American" or "Arabic" literature, where the principles of selection and hierarchization are demonstrably different from those operating in the postcolonial studies field. Among the questions that we then need to ask are: How is the relative neglect by literary postcolonialists of writers like these, *especially* when they are so well-regarded by scholars working in the adjacent and abutting critical fields, to be explained? And what conclusions ought we to draw about the adequacy of what scholars in postcolonial studies have been saying about postcoloniality or postcolonial literature when they so consistently fail to take writers like these into account?

In trying to answer these questions, I have found Raymond Williams's revisionary critique of literary modernism in his posthumously published book, *The Politics of Modernism*, immensely suggestive. Williams's argument is that modernism was the name of a specific and determinate intervention into the field of modern literary production in Europe at the beginning of the twentieth century. This intervention succeeded beyond its proponents' wildest expectations. Modernism displaced the received cultural formations of its time and consolidated itself at their expense. Not only did it succeed in establishing itself as the dominant aesthetic formation in its time and place; it construed its own particular dispositions—Williams lists exile and metropolitanism, for instance—as being uniquely responsive to modernity. It constructed its own historically, socially, and culturally specific protocols, procedures, and horizons as those of the modern as such. As Williams puts it, modernism recast, rewrote, and rearranged cultural history, producing a selective tradition whose selectivity remained invisible to it: the authors and "theoretic contours" usually addressed under the rubric of modernism constituted "a highly selected version of the modern which then offer[ed] to appropriate the whole of modernity." [10] The selective tradition that was modernism construed itself in universalistic terms as *the* literature of modernity. And because it emerged as the victor in the culture wars of its own time, modernism was able to ground its own definitions as the operative definitions in the fields in which it was active. It was able, to switch theoretical vocabularies for a moment (from that of Williams to that of Pierre Bourdieu), to establish for itself the monopoly of legitimacy in the cultural field, "the monopoly of the *power of consecration* of producers and products." [11] What this meant was, among other things, that all of the forms of cultural production displaced by modernism—those, that is, that were not modern*ist*— were pronounced pre*modern* and disparaged as such, as relics, mere anachronisms, forms whose time had definitively come and gone.

One can—and must, I think—contest the final adequacy of Williams's construction of modernism, which rather tends to write out of the modernist project its critical and even revolutionary dimensions, as evidenced in the intellectual and cultural practice of such figures as El Lissitsky and Sergei Eisenstein, Bertolt Brecht and Walter Benjamin, Federico García Lorca and Pablo Picasso, among literally dozens of others. The modernism that Williams critiques is in a sense a retrospective modernism, the modernism that would come into existence belatedly or after the fact, as it were—and as a result of what Fredric Jameson has termed the "canonization and academic institutionalization" of the modernist movement, "that can be traced to the late 1950s." Jameson records that the Victorian and post-Victorian bourgeoisies, at least, were under no illusions about the challenge or affront represented by modernist culture, whose "forms and ethos" they found "variously ugly, dissonant, obscure, scandalous, immoral, subversive, and generally 'antisocial.'" In undergoing incorporation, canonization, and institutionalization after 1945, however, modernist works lost their criticality, according to Jameson; their sting was drawn, their dissonance domesticated, their sheer oppositionality neutralized. Today, he writes, "not only are Picasso and Joyce no longer ugly; they now strike us, on the whole, as rather 'realistic.'"[12] (By "realistic" here, I take it, Jameson means mundane, routine, everyday, matter-of-fact. In the light of the brutal and lurid record of the twentieth century, the occasional extremism, grotesquerie, and excessiveness of modernist representation that had so offended its contemporary audience no longer seem particularly shocking or morbid.)

Jameson's periodizing commentary proves helpful in allowing us to qualify Williams's critique of modernism, which might otherwise seem undiscriminating. Williams is clearly too quick to generalize from that particular tendency within modernist literary practice that found consecration and academic institutionalization in the post-1945 period. His conceptualization of modernism is therefore susceptible to criticism on historical grounds. Conversely, however, I think we should also be wary of accepting without reflection Jameson's argument that modernism's criticality has become neutralized. We can readily concede that in today's world, what would once have seemed ugly now seems realistic. But to say this is not to say that what is thus represented is no longer disturbing or disquieting or unnerving. Consider for a moment Theodor W. Adorno's evocative claim (in an essay written as late as 1962, interestingly), that "anyone over whom Kafka's wheels have passed has lost both his sense of being at peace with the world and the possibility of being satisfied with the judgment that the course of the world is bad: the moment of confirmation inherent in a resigned acknowledgment of the superior power of evil has been eaten away."[13] Looking back at this formulation from our contemporary vantage point, forty years on from Adorno, we might indeed be inclined to follow Jameson's lead and declare that whatever truth it might initially have held (with respect to Kafka's own time, or perhaps even to Adorno's), it is no longer true. (Any teacher of literature who reads Adorno's words and—thinking of how astoundingly blasé today's students seem to have become—finds himself or herself saying wistfully, "if only," might be reckoned to be speaking in confirmation of Jameson's point.) For is it not in fact the case (our own deep investment, as literary scholars, in what Bourdieu has called the aesthetic *illusio* aside) that Kafka's wheels today pass over most of his readers without much consequence?[14] With rare exceptions, surely, Kafka's contemporary readers are *not* frozen in their tracks, rocked to their socks, by their encounter with him. Still less does the encounter leave them forever unconsoled, as Adorno would have hoped and even, indeed, expected.[15] The unassimilable Kafka, we might therefore be led to infer, has become the canonized, assimilated Kafka. Modernist writing has lost its erstwhile power of destabilizing or unnerving: on the one hand, the world has changed; on the other hand, in the restricted sphere of literary criticism, the meaning of *modernism*—skeletalized by New Criticism into a metaphysics and a technique—has changed too, and, along with it, the abilities, sensitivities and predilections of readers.

Jameson's arguments about the waning of "affect" and "criticality" are certainly challenging and thought-provoking. But I ultimately remain unpersuaded by them. My own position differs from both Williams's, on the one side, and Jameson's, on the other. For I want to insist, as neither of these theorists does, on the *ongoing* criticality of modernist literary practice. I am interested in work by contemporary writers (including "postcolonial" ones), which is (still), arguably, illuminated by recognizably modernist protocols and procedures. My suggestion is that, confronted by this work and these writers, we cannot proceed without a theory responsive simultaneously to the notional indispensability and the practical achievement of what, basing myself on Adorno's investigation of the "Kafka-effect" in the formulation cited above, I will call "disconsolation" in and through literature. Neither Williams nor Jameson seems to allow—if for different reasons—that there might be a modernist writing *after* the canonization of modernism—a writing, that is to say, that resists the accommodationism of what has been canonized as modernism and that does what at least some modernist work has done from the outset: namely, says "no"; refuses integration, resolution, consolation, comfort; protests and criticizes.

To say that there is only the shortest of distances between "In the Penal Colony" and Coetzee's *Waiting for the Barbarians*, or that the crazy lucidity of *The Trial* finds a compelling echo in Saadat Hasan Manto's "Toba Tek Singh," is not merely to talk truistically about Kafka's "influence" on

Coetzee and Manto but to begin to specify the conceptual underpinnings of a particular *kind* of writing, a particular *mode* of literary practice, common to all three authors. *Disconsolation* is the project of this writing, its deepest aesthetic (hence indirectly social) aspiration. I do not believe that this project has been exhausted over the course of the past fifty years, either as a result of the recuperation of modernism in academic discourse or as a result of more far-reaching changes in the social order. It is still within the compass of art, as Arundhati Roy (writing of the south Indian dance form of *kathakali*) puts it in two beautiful and profound sentences in *The God of Small Things*: to "reveal the nugget of sorrow that happiness contains. The hidden fish of shame in a sea of glory."[16]

I cannot resist mentioning Kazuo Ishiguro in this context, not least because the title of his fourth novel, *The Unconsoled*, so perfectly captures the essential gesture of modernist literary practice as I am presenting it here. Disconsolation is also the central aesthetic effect of Ishiguro's fiction, as it is of Kafka's. The sadness that suffuses Ishiguro's work is finally of the order of philosophy. His novels offer us intimate portraits of the wreckage of lives that have been lived wrongly, in the shadow or under the auspices of malign social, cultural, ideological, and familial dispensations. These lives themselves matter, of course—those of Etsuko and Sachiko, of Masuji Ono, of Stevens, for instance, in Ishiguro's first three novels (*A Pale View of Hills*, *An Artist of the Floating World*, and *The Remains of the Day*, respectively)—and the search in these novels for consolation, justification, and reconciliation is urgent and unceasing. But what seems to me to matter more in Ishiguro's fiction is that the acts and thoughts that *cannot* be forgiven or apologized for or reconciled be glimpsed in the light of a yearning for fellowship or collectivity—even though it is precisely these acts and thoughts that, in substantive terms, have made fellowship and collectivity impossible. "Chips of messianic time":[17] a frail light from utopia shines on, or rather, through, the unseeing eyes and unknowing thoughts of Ishiguro's characters. It is this transcendental implication that engenders disconsolation in us as readers and that enables us to register Ishiguro's work as modernist in its thrust and tendency.

I have been suggesting that Williams's construction of modernism can be faulted both for its relative lack of internal discrimination and for its relative insensitivity to modernism's (ongoing) critical dimension. Even so, it seems to me that his critique of modernism retains a striking cogency by analogy in the analysis and critique of postcolonial studies. The key point here is that in postcolonial studies, as in modernism on Williams's reading of it, a certain limited optic on the world, a selective tradition, has been imagined as a universal. Like Williams's modernists, postcolonial critics have also been disposed to construe their own particular dispositions—their own particular situations, their own specific locations in the social order, their own specific views onto the world—as cultural universals. (A slippage, or disjuncture, in the analogy must then immediately be noted. The selectivity of the "tradition" represented by what Gary Pearce helpfully terms "conscious modernism" was at least partially the product of such modernist writers as T. S. Eliot, Ezra Pound, and Virginia Woolf themselves [aided, of course, and especially after 1945, by New Criticism in the United States and the Scrutiny project in Britain and the Commonwealth territories].[18] In the case of postcolonial studies, by contrast, the attenuated or selective tradition is almost exclusively the product of critical discourse. With notable and important exceptions—Coetzee, Condé, Antonio Benítez-Rojo, for instance—very few so-called postcolonial writers have been involved in the conscious delimitation of postcolonial studies.)

In "The Postcolonial and the Postmodern," an essay in which he tries, as he puts it, "to rename the postmodern from the position of the postcolonial," Bhabha writes that

> the postcolonial perspective forces us to rethink the profound limitations of a consensual and collusive "liberal" sense of cultural community. It insists that cultural and political identity are constructed through a process of alterity. Questions of race and cultural difference overlay issues of sexuality and gender and overdetermine the social alliances of class and democratic socialism. The time for "assimilating" minorities to holistic and organic notions of cultural value has dramatically passed. The very language of cultural community needs to be rethought from a postcolonial perspective.[19]

I freely concede that the political claims lodged in this formulation are serious ones, even though Bhabha's politics are not at all mine. But the presumptive universalism of Bhabha's formulation is without empirical warrant.[20] It quickly collapses when subjected to critical scrutiny. For if the predicates that Bhabha lays out here are what "the postcolonial perspective" mandates (and he does, after all, say "*forces* us to rethink"), then we are obliged to conclude—on the basis of any representative sampling—that most of the writers who write from locations in the various different postcolonial states today, as well as most of those who hail from such states but currently reside—temporarily or permanently—in the metropolitan societies of Europe and North America, are not in fact postcolonial writers at all, but must instead be considered somehow "pre-postcolonial." For most such writers simply do not write from the perspective that Bhabha spells out for us—and which he himself clearly believes is uniquely responsive to the social and histori-

cal condition of postcoloniality. And in the case of a significant number of
these writers, at least, they do not fail to write from this perspective by omission or default, but on the basis of the strictest conviction. Put baldly, their
assumptions about identity and community and cultural value and politics
differ quite markedly from those revealed in the passage just quoted. Think
of Ngugi's sustained commentary on the language question in African literature, for instance, where an emphatically identitarian and unisonant notion
of cultural community is presented in order to ground the novelist's opposition to Europhone-languages as being in a fundamental sense "alien" to
Africa.[21] Think also of Ngugi's late novels, *Petals of Blood*, *Devil on the Cross*,
and *Matigari*, with their rigorous insistence on the class basis of social identity in Kenya and Africa. Or think, in quite a different register, of Sahgal,
whose writing over half a century now, fictional and nonfictional—from
Prison and Chocolate Cake to *A Time to Be Happy* to *Rich Like Us* to *Mistaken
Identity*—has consistently ratified the very "consensual," "liberal" notion of
"cultural community" (her own version of Nehruvianism) that Bhabha describes as being profoundly limited and as needing to be rethought. Or, again
changing register radically, think of Mo's willfully perverse and provocatively essentialist evocation of "oriental fatalism"—the term he himself uses
in *Renegade or Halo*—as "something real, not the invention of the West."[22]

I cite Ngugi and Sahgal and Mo—in one respect they merely stand in for
literally hundreds of novelists, poets, and dramatists who could have been
mentioned here to make the same point—because there is almost nothing
that they have in common as writers and thinkers except, ironically, the
fact that they are not remotely spoken for by "the postcolonial perspective."
(Ngugi is a Marxist, Sahgal a Nehruvian secular socialist—or perhaps, as
Rushdie's Vasco Miranda in *The Moor's Last Sigh* would have it, a "circular
sexualist"[23]—Mo a quirky conservative whose encomium—"This is one of
those rare books . . . which will shape the times as well as reflect them"—
adorns the back page of the British edition of Samuel Huntington's *The Clash
of Civilizations* and keeps company there with Henry Kissinger, Zbigniew
Brzezinski, and Francis Fukuyama.) Yet it seems obvious to me that any
attempt to theorize "postcolonial literature" or even "postcoloniality" will
need to come to terms with them, or with writers like them—to contextualize them, assess them, situate them alongside a teeming and heterogeneous
(but not for this reason unsystematizable) multiplicity of other writers, *including* pomo-postcolonialist ones. What such a theory cannot afford to do,
however, without abandoning its claims to validity, is to follow the example
of the pomo-postcolonialist critics and misdiagnose a restricted mode of

practice as a cultural universal. It ill behooves a theory professing a commitment (however vague and ill defined) to the critique of imperialism, to mistake a discrete cultural tendency—even if it is held to be a cultural dominant—for the only game in town.

In *The Politics of Modernism*, Williams proposes a double-sided counterpractice to literary modernism. It involves, on the one hand, exploring modernism

> with something of its own sense of strangeness and distance, rather than with the comfortable and now internally accommodated forms of its incorporation and naturalization. This means, above all, seeing the imperial and capitalist metropolis as a specific historical form, at different stages: Paris, London, Berlin, New York. It involves looking, from time to time, from outside the metropolis: from the deprived hinterlands, where different forces are moving, and from the poor world which has always been peripheral to the metropolitan systems. This need involve no reduction of the importance of the major artistic and literary works which were shaped within metropolitan perceptions. But one level has certainly to be challenged: the metropolitan interpretation of its own processes as universals. (47)

In the analogous context of postcolonial studies, this kind of work is already well underway. Dozens of scholars have recently undertaken to situate postcolonial studies in sociological and historical terms—both as an intellectual formation and in wider institutional and ideological terms; and they have effectively described and challenged the premises and conclusions of its leading proponents. But Williams also calls for another kind of work, which is equally important in challenging the hegemony of modernism. "If we are to break out of the non-historical fixity of *post*-modernism," he writes, "then we must search out and counterpose an alternative tradition taken from the neglected works left in the wide margin of the century, a tradition which may address itself not to this by now exploitable because quite inhuman rewriting of the past but, for all our sakes, to a modern future in which community may be imagined again" (35).

My sense is that if we take up this injunction in the postcolonial context, we will find no single "alternative tradition," but rather any number of them. Nevertheless, the injunction is absolutely worth taking up. For while an immanent critique of the so-called postcolonial perspective is both possible and necessary, it is only on the basis of a transcendental critique—that is to say, on the basis of the production of an alternative theory—that it can be definitively superseded. It is to this task, I believe—of formulating a new theory of postcolonial literature—that we in postcolonial studies are now especially enjoined, and we should not shrink from it.

Notes

Earlier versions of this essay were given as talks at the "Postcolonial Studies and Beyond" conference at the University of Illinois at Urbana-Champaign (April 2002), the "Postcolonial Interventions" conference at Oxford University (June 2002), the "Postcolonial Conversations: Africa and the Caribbean" conference at Wellesley College (October 2002), and to the English department at the University of Newcastle (May 2002). I would like to thank the organizers of those events (Suvir Kaul and Ania Loomba, Robert Young and Rajeswari Sunder Rajan, Selwyn Cudjoe, and Kate Chedgzoy and Michael Rossington, respectively) for their encouragement; and also Tim Brennan, Tim Cribb, Jed Esty, Keya Ganguly, Priyamvada Gopal, Benita Parry, Ellen Rooney, Kelwyn Sole, and Khachig Tölölyan, from whom I received especially valuable feedback and criticism. An earlier version of this article has been published in *The European Legacy* 7, no. 6 (2002): 771–82, in a special issue entitled "Europe in Post-colonial Narratives," guest-edited by Rajeev Patke.

1. The phrase is Homi K. Bhabha's. See "The Postcolonial and the Postmodern: The Question of Agency," in Bhabha, *The Location of Culture*, 173.

2. Ibid; emphasis mine.

3. See, for instance, Ahmad, *In Theory*; Ahmad, "The Politics of Literary Postcoloniality"; Brennan, *At Home in the World*; Brennan, "Cosmopolitanism and Internationalism"; Brennan, "The Illusion of a Future"; Brennan, "Antonio Gramsci and Post-colonial Theory"; Dirlik, "The Postcolonial Aura"; Dirlik, "Is There History after Eurocentrism?"; Jeyifo, "The Nature of Things"; Larsen, *Determinations*; Larsen, "Imperialism, Colonialism, Postcolonialism"; Parry, "Problems in Current Theories of Colonial Discourse"; Parry, "Directions and Dead Ends in Postcolonial Studies"; Parry, "The Marxist Legacy in Cultural and Postcolonial Studies"; San Juan, *Beyond Postcolonial Theory*; and San Juan, *Hegemony and Strategies of Transgression*. See also the essays by Brennan, Larsen, Parry, and San Juan (among others) in Bartolovich and Lazarus, *Marxism, Modernity, and Postcolonial Studies*.

4. See, for instance, Gikandi, *Ngugi wa Thiong'o*; Gikandi, "Cultural Translation and the African Self"; Gikandi, "Theory, Literature, and Moral Considerations"; Harrison, *Postcolonial Criticism*; Hogan, *Colonialism and Cultural Identity*; Huggan, *The Post-colonial Exotic*; Murphy, "De-centering French Studies"; Sole, "South Africa Passes the Posts"; Sole, "Political Fiction, Representation, and the Canon"; and Sole, "The Witness of Poetry."

5. A notable exception to such readings is Brennan's *Salman Rushdie and the Third World*, in fact the first study of Rushdie to have been published, which stands almost alone in the critical literature in its attempt to *situate* the mode of representation in Rushdie, and not simply to abstract it as an epistemology.

6. Brennan, *At Home in the World*, 203.

7. Jussawalla and Dasenbrock, *Interviews with Writers of the Postcolonial World*. Further references to this work will be given parenthetically in the body of the text.

8. Jussawalla's and Dasenbrock's conceptualization of the status and tendency of

these new traditions of writing has much in common with Wlad Godzich's theorization of "emergent literature." See his "Emergent Literature in the Field of Comparative Literature," in Godzich, *The Culture of Literacy*, 274–92.

9. One needs to reemphasise here the *metropolitan* contexts within which postcolonial literary studies has, for the most part, been developed. As Graham Huggan, among others, has pointed out in *The Post-colonial Exotic*, the "politics of cultural value" in postcolonial studies are clearly Eurocentric in their constitution. Between the writing of a work and its reading lie the channelizing, selecting, and censoring social processes of publishing, distributing, and marketing. One notes, thus, that "postcolonial" writers' residency in the West (or frequent appearances in it) clearly facilitates the marketing of their works, and that their relative assimilability to contemporary Euro-American ideological programs does so too. Concerning this assimilability, it is not that postcolonial writers need—like V. S. Naipaul, for instance—to pander shamelessly to the prevailing Euro-American perspectives. On the contrary, the liberal discourse of multiculturalism—under which postcolonial literature is promoted and thrives—expects and wants to be presented with cultural difference. But while difference—and even dissidence—will be tolerated, outright oppositionality will likely be afforded rougher treatment.

10. Williams, *The Politics of Modernism*, 33. Further references to this work will be given parenthetically in the body of the text.

11. Bourdieu, *The Rules of Art*, 224.

12. Jameson, *Postmodernism*, 4.

13. Adorno, "Commitment," 90.

14. Bourdieu, *The Rules of Art*, esp. 227–31, 331–36.

15. I am referring here to the wording in a second English translation of Adorno's "Commitment" essay. Francis McDonagh translates the sentence we are considering as follows: "He over whom Kafka's wheels have passed, has lost forever both any peace with the world and any chance of consoling himself with the judgement that the way of the world is bad." Adorno, "Commitment," 315.

16. Roy, *The God of Small Things*, 219.

17. The reference is of course to Walter Benjamin's "Theses on the Philosophy of History," in Benjamin, *Illuminations*, 263.

18. See Pearce, "Margins and Modernism."

19. Bhabha, "The Postcolonial and the Postmodern," 175.

20. In a suggestive and thought-provoking argument, in fact, Shalini Puri proposes that we construe Bhabha's writings under the generic sign of the manifesto rather than as thetic discourse. Viewed thus, they are able to emerge as utopian texts, exemplifying an "intense nostalgia for the poetic word." See Puri, *The Caribbean Postcolonial*.

21. "I was born into a large peasant family: father, four wives and about twenty-eight children. I also belonged, as we all did in those days, to a wider extended family and to the community as a whole.

We spoke Gikuyu as we worked in the fields. We spoke Gikuyu in and outside the home. I can vividly recall those evenings of story-telling around the fireside. It was mostly the grown-ups telling the children but everybody was interested and involved. . . . We . . . learnt to value words for their meaning and nuances. Language was not a mere string of words. It had a suggestive power well beyond the immediate and lexical meaning . . . the language, through images and symbols, gave us a view of the world. . . . The home and the field were then our pre-primary school but what is important, for this discussion, is that the language of our evening teach-ins, and the language of our immediate and wider community, and the language of our work in the fields were one.

And then I went to school, a colonial school, and this harmony was broken. The language of my education was no longer the language of my culture." Thiong'o, *Decolonising the Mind*, 10–11.

22. Mo, *Renegade or Halo²*, 10.

23. Rushdie, *The Moor's Last Sigh*, 166.

Bibliography

Abrahams, Peter. *The Black Experience in the Twentieth Century: An Autobiography and Meditation.* Bloomington: Indiana University Press, 2000.

———. *Tell Freedom: Memories of Africa.* New York: Knopf, 1954.

Abu-Lughod, Janet. *Before European Hegemony: The World System A.D. 1250–1350.* Oxford: Oxford University Press, 1989.

Abu-Manneh, Bashir. "The Illusions of Empire." *Interventions* 5, no. 2 (2003): 159–77

Achebe, Chinua. *Things Fall Apart.* New York: Knopf, 1994.

Adeleke, Tunde. *UnAfrican Americans: Nineteenth-Century Black Nationalists and the Civilizing Mission.* Lexington: University Press of Kentucky, 1998.

Adelzadeh, Asghar. "From the RDP to GEAR: The Gradual Embracing of Neo-liberalism in Economic Policy." *Transformation* 31 (1996): 66–95.

Adorno, Theodor. "Commitment." In *Notes to Literature,* ed. Rolf Tiedemann, trans. Shierry Weber Nicholsen, 2: 76–96. New York: Columbia University Press, 1992.

Afzal-Khan, Fawzia, and Kalpana Seshadri-Crooks, eds. *The Pre-occupation of Post-colonial Studies.* Durham, NC: Duke University Press, 2000.

Agarwal, Purushottam. "Surat, Savarkar, and Draupadi: Legitimising Rape as a Political Weapon." In *Women and the Hindu Right: A Collection of Essays,* ed. Tanika Sarkar and Urvashi Butalia, 29–57. Delhi: Kali for Women, 1995.

Ahmad, Aijaz. *In Theory: Classes, Nations, Literatures.* London: Verso, 2002.

———. "The Politics of Literary Postcoloniality," *Race and Class* 36, no. 3 (1995): 1–20.

Ahmed, S. M. Faizan. "Men at Work: An Inquiry into the Survival Aspects of Men in Beauty Work." In *From Violence to Supportive Practice: Family, Gender, and Masculinities in India,* ed. Radhika Chopra, 81–88. Delhi: UNIFEM, 2002.

Alonso, Carlos. *The Burden of Modernity: The Rhetoric of Cultural Discourse in Spanish America.* New York: Oxford University Press, 1998.

Altendorf, H.-D. "Zum Stichwort: Rechtsgläubigkeit und Ketzerei im ältesten Christentum." *Zeitschrift für Kirchengeschichte* 80, no. 1 (1969): 61–74.

Althusser, Louis. "Ideology and Ideological State Apparatuses: Notes towards an Investigation." In *Lenin and Philosophy, and Other Essays,* trans. Ben Brewster, 127–86. London: New Left Books, 1971.

Amin, Samir. *Capitalism in the Age of Globalization: The Management of Contemporary Society.* London: Zed, 1997.

———. *Neo-colonialism in West Africa*. Harmondsworth, UK: Penguin, 1973.

Amnesty International, *Israel and the Occupied Territories: The Heavy Price of Israeli Incursions*. April 11, 2002. Archived at www.amnestyusa.org/countries/Israel_and _occupied_territories/reports.do.

Anderson, Lorraine, Scott Slovic, and John O'Grady, eds. *Literature and the Environment: A Reader on Nature and Culture*. New York: Longman, 1999.

Anderson, Warwick. "Leprosy and Citizenship." *positions* 6, 3 (1998): 707–30.

Annino, Antonio. "Soberanías en lucha." In *De los imperios a las naciones: Iberoamérica*, ed. Annino, Luis Castro Leiva, and Francois-Xavier Guerra. Saragossa: IberCaja, Obra Cultural, 1994.

Appadurai, Arjun. *Modernity at Large: Cultural Dimensions of Globalization*. Minneapolis: University of Minnesota Press, 1996.

———. "Patriotism and Its Futures." In *Modernity at Large: Cultural Dimensions of Globalization*, 158–79. Minneapolis: University of Minnesota Press, 1996.

———, ed. *The Social Life of Things: Commodities in Cultural Perspective*. Cambridge: Cambridge University Press, 1986.

Appiah, Kwame Anthony. "Is the Post-in Postmodernism the Post-in Postcolonial?" *Critical Inquiry* 20, no. 2 (1994): 336–57.

Appleby, Joyce, Lynn Hunt, and Margaret Jacob. *Telling the Truth about History*. New York: Norton, 1994.

Apter, Emily. *Continental Drift: From National Characters to Virtual Subjects*. Chicago: University of Chicago Press, 1999.

Armstrong, John. "Mobilized and Proletarian Diasporas." *American Political Science Review* 70 no. 2 (1976): 393–408.

Arnold, David, and Ramachandra Guha, eds. *Nature, Culture, Imperialism: Essays of the Environmental History of South Asia*. Delhi: Oxford University Press, 1995.

Arrighi, Giovanni. *The Long Twentieth Century: Money, Power and the Origins of Our Times*. London: Verso, 1994.

———. "Tracking Global Turbulence." *New Left Review* 20 (March/April 2003): 5–72.

Asad, Talal. *Genealogies of Religion: Discipline and Reasons of Power in Christianity and Islam*. Baltimore, MD: Johns Hopkins University Press, 1993.

Ashcroft, Bill, Gareth Griffiths, and Helen Tiffin, eds. *The Post-colonial Studies Reader*. London: Routledge, 1999.

Athanasiou, Tom. *Divided Planet: The Ecology of Rich and Poor*. Boston: Little, Brown, 1996.

Bachofen, Johann Jakob. *Myth, Religion, and Mother Right: Selected Writings*. Trans. Ralph Manheim. Princeton, NJ: Princeton University Press, 1967.

Bairoch, Paul. *Economics and World History: Myths and Paradoxes*. London: Harvester Wheatsheaf, 1993.

Baker, Davd, and Willy Maley, eds. *British Identities and English Renaissance Literature*. Cambridge: Cambridge University Press, 2002.

Gopal Balakrishnan, ed. *Debating Empire*. New York: Verso, 2003.

————. "Virgilian Visions." *New Left Review*, no. 5 (2000): 142–48.

Balibar, Etienne. "Is There a Neo-racism?" In *Race, Nation, Class: Ambiguous Identities*, ed. Balibar and Immanuel Wallerstein, 17–28. London: Verso, 1991.

————. "Subjection and Subjectivation." In *Supposing the Subject*, ed. Joan Copjec, 1–15. London: Verso, 1994.

Bank, Leslie. "The Social Life of Paraffin: Gender, Domesticity, and the Politics of Value in a South African Township." In *Culture and the Commonplace*, ed. P. McAllister, 157–79. Johannesburg: University of Witwatersrand Press, 1997.

Baran, Paul. *The Political Economy of Growth*. New York: Monthly Review Press, 1957.

Bardhan, Pranab. *The Political Economy of Development in India*. Delhi: Oxford University Press, 1984.

Barkey, Karen, and Mark von Hagen, eds. *After Empire: Multiethnic Societies and Nation-Building; The Soviet Union and Russian Ottoman, and Habsburg Empires*. Boulder, CO: Westview, 1997.

Barlow, Tani E., ed. *Formations of Colonial Modernity in East Asia*. Durham, NC: Duke University Press, 1997.

————. *The Question of Women in Chinese Feminism*. Durham, NC: Duke University Press, 2004.

————. "Wanting Some: Natural Science, Social Science, and Colonial Modernity." In *Women in Republican China*, ed. Mechthild Leutner and Nicola Spakowski. Münster: Lit Verlag, 2004.

Bartolovich, Crystal, and Neil Lazarus, eds. *Marxism, Modernity, and Postcolonial Studies*. Cambridge: Cambridge University Press, 2002.

Bataille, Georges. *The Accursed Share*. 3 vols. Trans. Robert Hurley. New York: Zone, 1988–91.

Bate, Jonathan. *The Song of the Earth*. Cambridge, MA: Harvard University Press, 2000.

Baudrillard, Jean. *For a Critique of the Political Economy of the Sign*. Trans. Charles Levin. Saint Louis: Telos, 1981.

Bauer, Walter. *Orthodoxy and Heresy in Earliest Christianity*. Ed. Robert A. Kraft and Gerhard Krodel. Philadelphia: Fortress Press, 1971.

Bauman, Zygmunt. *Globalization: The Human Consequences*. New York: Columbia University Press, 1998.

Bayet, Fabienne. "Overturning the Doctrine: Indigenous People and Wilderness—Being Aboriginal in the Environmental Movement." In *The Great New Wilderness Debate*, ed. J. Baird Callicott and Michael P. Nelson, 314–24. Athens: University of Georgia Press, 1998.

Beard, Mary, John A. North, and S. R. F. Price. *Religions of Rome*. Cambridge: Cambridge University Press, 1998.

Behdad, Ali. "INS and Outs: Producing Delinquency at the Border." *Aztlan: A Journal of Chicano Studies* 23, no. 1 (1998): 103–14.

Beinart, William, and Peter Coates. *Environment and History: The Taming of Nature in the USA and South Africa*. London: Routledge, 1995.

Benjamin, Walter. *Illuminations.* Ed. Hannah Arendt. Trans. Harry Zohn. New York: Harcourt, Brace, and World, 1968.

Bennett, Jane. "Enough Lip-Service! Hearing Post-colonial Experience of Gender-Based Violence." *Agenda,* no. 50 (2001): 88–96.

Benot, Yves. *Diderot: De l'athéisme à l'anticolonialisme.* Paris: Armand Colin, n.d.

———. *Massacres Coloniaux.* Paris: La Decouverte and Syros, 1994.

Bhabha, Homi K. *The Location of Culture.* London: Routledge, 1994.

———. "Of Mimicry and Man: The Ambivalence of Colonial Discourse." In *Tensions of Empire: Colonial Cultures in a Bourgeois World,* ed. Frederick Cooper and Ann Laura Stoler, 152–60. Berkeley: University of California Press, 1997.

———. "Statement for the Critical Inquiry Board Symposium." *Critical Inquiry* 30, no. 2 (2004): 345–48.

———, ed. *Nation and Narration.* New York: Routledge, 1990.

Bidwai, Praful, and Achin Vanaik. *South Asia on a Short Fuse: Nuclear Politics and the Future of Global Disarmament.* Delhi: Oxford University Press, 1999.

Black, P. "'Ordinary People Come through Here': Locating the Beauty Salon in Women's Lives." *Feminist Review,* no. 71 (2002): 2–17.

Black, P., and Ursula Sharma. "Men Are Real, Women Are Made Up: Beauty Therapy and the Construction of Femininity." *Sociological Review* 49, no. 1 (2001): 100–16.

Blackburn, Robin. *The Making of New World Slavery: From the Baroque to the Modern, 1492–1800.* London: Verso, 1997.

———. *The Overthrow of Colonial Slavery, 1776–1848.* London: Verso, 1988.

Blaut, James. *The Colonizer's Model of the World: Geographical Diffusionism and Eurocentric History.* New York: Guilford, 1993.

———. *Eight Eurocentric Historians.* London: Guilford, 2000.

Blecher, Robert. "Living on the Edge: The Threat of Transfer in Israel and Palestine." *Middle East Report* 225 (2002). Available at www.merip.org/mer225/225_blecher .html.

Blue, Gregory. "Opium for China: The British Connection." In *Opium Regimes: China, Britain, and Japan, 1839–1952,* ed. Timothy Brook and Bob Tadashi Wakabayashi, 31–54. Berkeley: University of California Press, 2000.

Bober, Arie. *The Other Israel: The Radical Case against Zionism.* New York: Anchor, 1972.

Boccaccio, Giovanni. "De Canaria et insulis reliquis." 1341. Vol. 1 of *Monumenta Henricina* (15 vols.). Coimbra: Atlântida, 1960.

Boehmer, Elleke. *Empire, the National, and the Postcolonial, 1890–1920.* Oxford: Oxford University Press, 2002.

Bond, Patrick. *Against Global Apartheid: South Africa Meets the World Bank,* IMF, *and International Finance.* Cape Town: University of Cape Town Press, 2001.

———. *Elite Transition.* Pietermaritzburg, South Africa: University of Natal Press, 2000.

Bonnell, Victoria E., and Lynn Hunt, eds. *Beyond the Cultural Turn: New Directions in the Study of Society and Culture.* Berkeley: University of California Press, 1999.

Borah, Woodrow. *New Spain's Century of Depression*. Berkeley: University of California Press, 1951.

Borah, Woodrow, and Sherburne Cook. *The Aboriginal Population of Central Mexico on the Eve of the Spanish Conquest*. Berkeley: University of California Press, 1963.

———. *Essays in Population History: Mexico and the Caribbean*. 3 vols. Berkeley: University of California Press, 1971–79.

———. *The Population of the Mixteca Alta, 1520–1960*. Berkeley: University of California Press, 1968.

Bordwell, David, Kristin Thompson, and Janet Staiger. *The Classical Hollywood Cinema: Film Style and Mode of Production to 1960*. New York: Columbia University Press, 1985.

Borges, Jorge Luis. *Collected Fictions*. Trans. Andrew Hurley. New York: Viking. 1998.

Bornstein, Erica. *The Spirit of Development: Protestant NGOs, Morality, and Economics in Zimbabwe*. New York: Routledge, 2003.

Bose, Sugata, and Ayesha Jalal. *Modern South Asia: History, Culture, Political Economy*. London: Routledge, 1998.

Bourdieu, Pierre. *The Rules of Art: Genesis and Structure of the Literary Field*. Trans. Susan Emanuel. Stanford, CA: Stanford University Press, 1995.

Bourdieu, Pierre, and Loic Wacquant. "The Cunning of Imperial Reason." *Theory, Culture, and Society* 16, no. 1 (1999): 41–58.

Bové, Paul. "Can American Studies Be Area Studies?" In *Learning Places: The Afterlives of Area Studies*, ed. Masao Miyoshi and H. D. Harootunian, 206–30. Durham, NC: Duke University Press, 2002.

Boyarin, Daniel. *Border Lines: The Partition of Judaeo-Christianity*. Philadelphia: University of Pennsylvania Press, 2004.

———. *Dying for God: Martyrdom and the Making of Christianity and Judaism*. Stanford, CA: Stanford University Press, 1999.

Brakke, David. "Jewish Flesh and Christian Spirit in Athanasius of Alexandria." *Journal of Early Christian Studies* 9, no. 4 (2001): 453–81.

Braudel, Fernand. *Civilization and Capitalism, Fifteenth to Eighteenth Centuries*. Trans. Siân Reynolds. New York: Harper and Row, 1981.

———. *The Mediterranean and the Mediterranean World in the Age of Philip II*. 2 vols. Trans. Siân Reynolds. New York: Harper and Row, 1976.

Brennan, Timothy. "Antonio Gramsci and Post-colonial Theory: 'Southernism.'" *Diaspora* 10, no. 2 (2001): 143–87.

———. *At Home in the World: Cosmopolitanism Now*. Cambridge, MA: Harvard University Press, 1997.

———. "Cosmopolitanism and Internationalism." *New Left Review*, no. 7 (2001): 75–84.

———. "The Empire's New Clothes." *Critical Inquiry* 29, no. 2 (2003): 337–67.

———. "From Development to Globalisation: Postcolonialism and Transnational Cultural Studies." In *The Cambridge Companion for Postcolonial Studies*, ed. Neil Lazarus, 120–38. Cambridge: Cambridge University Press, 2003.

———. "The Illusion of a Future: Orientalism as Traveling Theory." *Critical Inquiry* 26, no. 3 (2000): 558–83.

———. "The Magician's Wand: A Rejoinder to Hardt and Negri," *Critical Inquiry* 29, no. 2 (2003): 374–78.

———. *Salman Rushdie and the Third World*. Basingstoke, UK: Macmillan, 1989.

Brenner, Robert. "The Origins of Capitalist Development: A Critique of Neo-Smithian Marxism." *New Left Review*, no. 104 (1977): 25–92.

Brewer, John. *Party Ideology and Popular Politics at the Accession of George III*. Cambridge: Cambridge University Press, 1982.

Brody, Jennifer DeVere. *Impossible Purities: Blackness, Femininity, and Victorian Culture*. Durham, NC: Duke University Press, 1998.

Brook, Timothy, and Bob Tadashi Wakabayashi, eds. *Opium Regimes: China, Britain, and Japan, 1839–1952*. Berkeley: University of California Press, 2000.

Brotton, Jerry. "Terrestrial Globalism: Mapping the Globe in Early Modern Europe." In *Mappings*, ed. Denis Cosgrove, 71–89. London: Reaktion, 1999.

———. *Trading Territories: Mapping the Early Modern World*. London: Reaktion, 1997.

Brown, Lloyd Arnold. *The Story of Maps*. New York: Dover, 1977.

Brown, Nicholas, and Imre Szeman. "The Global Coliseum: On *Empire*." *Cultural Studies* 16, no. 2 (2002): 177–92.

Brown, Roger, and Albert Gilman. "Politeness Theory and Shakespeare's Four Major Tragedies." *Language in Society* 18, no. 2 (1989): 159–212.

———. "The Pronouns of Power and Solidarity." In *Style in Language*, ed. Thomas A. Sebeok, 253–76. Cambridge, MA: MIT Press, 1960.

Buck-Morss, Susan. "Hegel and Haiti." *Critical Inquiry* 26, no. 4 (2000): 821–65.

Buell, Lawrence. *The Environmental Imagination: Thoreau, Nature Writing, and the Formation of American Culture*. Cambridge, MA: Harvard University Press, 1996.

———. *Writing for an Endangered World: Literature, Culture, and Environment in the U.S. and Beyond*. Cambridge, MA: Harvard University Press, 2001.

Bunn, David. "The Insistence on Theory: Three Questions for Megan Vaughan." *Social Dynamics* 20, no. 1 (1994): 24–34.

Burnett, A. D. *The Engraved Title-Page of Bacon's "Instauratio Magna": An Icon and Paradigm of Science and Its Wider Implications*. Durham, UK: Thomas Harriot Seminar, 1998.

Burroughs, Peter, and A. J. Stockwell. *Managing the Business of Empire: Essays in Honour of David Fieldhouse*. London: Cass, 1998.

Burrus, Virginia. "Hailing Zenobia: Anti-Judaism, Trinitarianism, and John Henry Newman." *Culture and Religion* 3, no. 2 (2002): 163–77.

———. *The Making of a Heretic: Gender, Authority, and the Priscillianist Controversy*. Berkeley: University of California Press, 1995.

Burton, Antoinette, ed. *Gender, Sexuality, and Colonial Modernities*. London: Routledge, 1999.

Butler, Judith. *Excitable Speech: A Politics of the Performative*. New York: Routledge, 1997.

Cannadine, David. *Ornamentalism: How the British Saw Their Empire*. Oxford: Oxford University Press, 2001.

Casteel, Sarah Phillips. "New World Pastoral: The Caribbean Garden and Emplacement in Gisele Pineau and Shani Mootoo." *Interventions* 5, no. 1 (2003): 12–28.

Castells, Manuel. *End of Millennium*. 2d ed. London: Blackwell, 2000.

Castle, Gregory, ed. *Postcolonial Discourses: An Anthology*. Oxford: Blackwell, 2001.

Césaire, Aimé. *Discourse on Colonialism*. Trans. Joan Pinkham. New York: Monthly Review Press, 1972.

Chakrabarty, Dipesh. "Conditions for Knowledge of Working Class Conditions." In *Selected Subaltern Studies*, ed. Ranajit Guha et al., 179–232. New York: Oxford University Press, 1988.

———. *Habitations of Modernity: Essays in the Wake of Subaltern Studies*. Chicago: University of Chicago Press, 2002.

———. "Modernity and Ethnicity in India: A History for the Present." *Economic and Political Weekly* 30, no. 52 (1994): 3373–80.

———. *Provincializing Europe: Postcolonial Thought and Historical Difference*. Princeton, NJ: Princeton University Press, 2000.

———. "Radical Histories and the Question of Enlightenment Rationalism: Some Recent Critiques of *Subaltern Studies*." In *Mapping Subaltern Studies and the Postcolonial*, ed. Vinayak Chaturvedi, 256–80. London: Verso, 2000.

Chandavarkar, Rajnarayan. *Imperial Power and Popular Politics: Class, Resistance, and the State in India, c. 1850–1950*. Cambridge: Cambridge University Press, 1998.

Chatterjee, Partha. *Nationalist Thought and the Colonial World: A Derivative Discourse?* London: Zed, 1986.

———. *The Nation and Its Fragments: Colonial and Postcolonial Histories*. Princeton, NJ: Princeton University Press, 1993.

———. *A Possible India: Essays in Political Criticism*. Delhi: Oxford University Press, 1997.

Chaturvedi, Vinayak, ed. *Mapping Subaltern Studies and the Postcolonial*. London: Verso, 2000.

Chaudhuri, Nupur, and Margaret Strobel, eds. *Western Women and Imperialism: Complicity and Resistance*. Bloomington: Indiana University Press, 1992.

Chennells, Anthony. "Plotting South African History: Narrative in Sol Plaatje's *Mhudi*." *English in Africa* 24, no. 1 (1997): 37–58.

Chiang, Yung-chen. *Social Engineering and the Social Sciences in China, 1919–1949*. Cambridge: Cambridge University Press, 2001.

Chidester, David. *Savage Systems: Colonialism and Comparative Religion in Southern Africa*. Charlottesville: University Press of Virginia, 1996.

Chiwengo, Ngwarsungu. "Exile, Knowledge, and Self: Home in Peter Abrahams's Work." *South Atlantic Quarterly* 98, nos. 1–2 (1999): 163–76.

Chomsky, Aviva. " 'Barbados or Canada?' Race, Immigration, and Nation in Early-Twentieth-Century Cuba." *Hispanic American Historical Review* 80, no. 3 (2000): 415–62.

Chow, Kai-wing, Kevin M. Doak, and Pashek Fu, eds. *Constructing Nationhood in Modern East Asia*. Ann Arbor: University of Michigan Press, 2001.

Chrisman, Laura. "Journeying to Death: Paul Gilroy's *Black Atlantic*." *Race and Class* 39, no. 2 (1997): 51–64.

———. "Nationalism and Postcolonial Studies." In *The Cambridge Companion to Postcolonial Literary Studies*, ed. Neil Lazarus, 183–98. Cambridge: Cambridge University Press, 2004.

———. *Postcolonial Contraventions: Cultural Readings of Race, Imperialism, and Transnationalism*. Manchester: Manchester University Press, 2003.

———. *Rereading the Imperial Romance: British Imperialism and South African Resistance in Haggard, Schreiner, and Plaatje*. Oxford: Oxford University Press, 2000.

———. "Rethinking Black Atlanticism." *Black Scholar* 30, nos. 3–4 (2000): 12–17.

Chun, Lin. "The Transformation of Chinese Socialism: A Critical Commentary." Unpublished manuscript.

Clark, J. P. *All for Oil*. Lagos: Malthouse Press, 2000.

Clifford, James. *Routes: Travel and Translation in the Late Twentieth Century*. Cambridge, MA: Harvard University Press, 1997.

Clifford, James, and George E. Marcus, eds. *Writing Culture: The Poetics and Politics of Ethnography*. Berkeley: University of California Press, 1986.

Coble, Parks M. *Chinese Capitalists in Japan's New Order: The Occupied Lower Yangzi, 1937–1945*. Berkeley: University of California Press, 2003.

Cobley, Alan. "Does Social History Have a Future? The Ending of Apartheid and Recent Trends in South African Historiography." *Journal of Southern African Studies* 27, no. 3 (2001): 613–25.

Coetzee, J. M. *Life and Times of Michael K*. New York: Penguin, 1995.

———. *White Writing: On the Culture of Letters in South Africa*. New Haven, CT: Yale University Press, 1988.

Cohen, Coleen Ballerino, Richard Wilk, and Beverley Stoeltje, eds. *Beauty Queens on the Global Stage: Gender, Contests, and Power*. New York: Routledge, 1996.

Cohen, David William, and E. S. Atieno Odhiambo. *Burying SM: The Politics of Knowledge and the Sociology of Power in Africa*. Portsmouth, NH: Heinemann, 1992.

Cohen, Jeffrey Jerome, ed. *The Postcolonial Middle Ages*. Houndmills, UK: Macmillan, 2000.

Cohen, Shaye J. D. *The Beginnings of Jewishness: Boundaries, Varieties, Uncertainties*. Berkeley: University of California Press, 1998.

Cohen, Warren. *East Asia at the Center: Four Thousand Years of Engagement with the World*. New York: Columbia University Press, 2000.

Collier, George, with Elizabeth Lowery Quaratiello. *Basta! Land and the Zapatista Rebellion in Chiapas*. Oakland, CA: Institute for Food and Development Policy, 1994.

Collier, George, and Lynn Stephen, eds. "Ethnicity, Identity, and Citizenship in the Wake of the Zapatista Rebellion." Special issue, *Journal of Latin American Anthropology* 3, no. 1 (1997).

Collingwood, R. G. *An Autobiography.* Oxford: Oxford University Press, 1939.

Comaroff, Jean, and John Comaroff. "Alien-Nation: Zombies, Immigrants, and Global Capitalism." *CODESRIA Bulletin,* nos. 3–4 (1999): 17–28.

———. "Millennial Capitalism: First Thoughts on a Second Coming." In "Millennial Capitalism and the Culture of Neoliberalism," ed. Comaroff and Comaroff, special issue, *Public Culture* 12, no. 2 (2000): 291–343.

———. "Naturing the Nation: Aliens, Apocalypse, and the Postcolonial State." *Hagar: International Social Science Review* 1, no. 1 (2000): 7–40.

———, eds. *Modernity and Its Malcontents: Ritual and Power in Postcolonial Africa.* Chicago: University of Chicago Press, 1993.

Conklin, Alice. *A Mission to Civilize: The Republican Idea of Empire in France and West Africa, 1895–1930.* Stanford, CA: Stanford University Press, 1997.

Conrad, Joseph. *Heart of Darkness.* 1902. Ed. Robert Kimbrough. New York: Norton, 1988.

Constable, Pamela, and Arturo Valenzuela. *A Nation of Enemies: Chile under Pinochet.* New York: Norton, 1991.

Cooper, Frederick. *Colonialism in Question: Theory, Knowledge, History.* Berkeley: University of California Press, forthcoming.

———. *Decolonization and African Society: The Labor Question in French and British Africa.* New York: Cambridge University Press, 1996.

———. "Empire Multiplied." *Comparative Studies in Society and History* 46, no. 2 (2004): 247–72.

———. "Modernizing Bureaucrats, Backward Africans, and the Development Concept." In *International Development and the Social Sciences: Essays on the History and Politics of Knowledge,* ed. Cooper and Randall Packard, 64–92. Berkeley: University of California Press, 1997.

———. "What Is the Concept of Globalization Good For? An African Historian's Perspective." *African Affairs,* no. 100 (2001): 189–213.

Cooper, Frederick, and Ann Laura Stoler, eds. *Tensions of Empire: Colonial Cultures in a Bourgeois World.* Berkeley: University of California Press, 1997.

Cooper, Frederick, et al., *Confronting Historical Paradigms: Africa and Latin America in the World System.* Madison: University of Wisconsin Press, 1993.

Cooppan, Vilashini. "W(h)ither Post-colonial Studies: Toward the Transnational Study of Race and Nation." In *Postcolonial Theory and Criticism,* ed. Laura Chrisman and Benita Parry, 1–36. Cambridge: D. S. Brewer, 2000.

Cormack, Lesley. *Charting an Empire: Geography at the English Universities, 1580–1620.* Chicago: University of Chicago Press, 1997.

Coronil, Fernando. "Beyond Occidentalism: Toward Nonimperial Geohistorical Categories." *Cultural Anthropology* 11, no. 1 (1996): 51–87.

———. "Del eurocentrismo al globocentrismo: La naturaleza del poscolonialismo." In *La colonialidad del saber: Eurocentrismo y ciencias sociales; Perspectivas latinoamericanas,* ed. Edgardo Lander 119–53. Caracas: UNESCO, 2000.

———. "Listening to the Subaltern: Postcolonial Studies and the Neocolonial Poetics of Subaltern States." In *Postcolonial Theory and Criticism*, ed. Laura Chrisman and Benita Parry, 37–55. Cambridge: D. S. Brewer, 2000.

———. "Toward a Critique of Globalcentrism: Speculations on Capitalism's Nature." In *Millennial Capitalism and the Culture of Neoliberalism*, ed. Jean Comaroff and John L. Comaroff, 63–87. Durham, NC: Duke University Press, 2001.

Cosgrove, Denis. *Apollo's Eye: A Cartographic Genealogy of the Earth in the Western Imagination*. Baltimore, MD: Johns Hopkins University Press, 2001.

Couzens, Tim. "'Moralizing Leisure Time': The Transatlantic Connection and Black Johannesburg, 1918–1936." In *Industrialisation and Social Change in South Africa: African Class Formation, Culture and Consciousness, 1870–1930*, ed. Shula Marks and Richard Rathbone, 314–37. Harlow, UK: Longman, 1982.

Couzens, Tim, and Essop Patel, eds. *The Return of the Amasi Bird: Black South African Poetry, 1891–1981*. Braamfontein, South Africa: Ravan, 1982.

Cox, Howard. *The Global Cigarette: The Origins and Evolution of British American Tobacco, 1880–1945*. Oxford: Oxford University Press, 2000.

Cronon, William. "The Trouble with Wilderness; Or, Getting Back to the Wrong Nature." In *Uncommon Ground: Rethinking the Human Place in Nature*, ed. Cronon, 69–90. New York: Norton, 1996.

Cronon, William, George Miles, and Jay Gitlin, eds. *Under an Open Sky: Rethinking America's Western Past*. New York: Norton, 1992.

Cusicanqui, Silvia Rivera, and Rossana Barragán, eds. *Debates post coloniales: Una introducción a los estudios de la subalternidad*. La Paz: Editorial Historias, SEPHIS, Ayuwiyiri, 1997.

Cuxil, Demetrio Cojtí. "The Politics of Maya Revindication." In *Maya Cultural Activism in Guatemala*, ed. Edward F. Fischer and R. McKenna Brown, 19–50. Austin: University of Texas Press, 1996.

Dangor, Achmat. *Kafka's Curse: A Novella and Three Other Stories*. Roggebaai, South Africa: Kwela Books, 1997.

Davis, Mike. *Late Victorian Holocausts*. London: Verso, 2001.

Daymond, Margaret, ed. *South African Feminisms*. New York: Garland, 1996.

De Beauvoir, Simone. *The Ethics of Ambiguity*. Trans. Bernard Frechtman. New York: Citadel, 1976.

De Certeau, Michel. *The Practice of Everyday Life*. Trans. Steven Rendell. Berkeley: University of California Press, 1984.

De Cervantes, Miguel. *Don Quixote*. 1605. Trans. Charles Jervas. London: Oxford University Press, 1907.

Decker, Elly, and Peter van der Krogt. *Globes from the Western World*. London: Zwemmer, 1993.

De Kock, Leon. "The Pursuit of Smaller Stories: Reconsidering the Limits of Literary History in South Africa." In *Rethinking South African Literary History*, ed. J. Smit et al., 85–92. Durban, South Africa: Y Press, 1996.

De Kok, Ingrid. "Cracked Heirlooms: Memory on Exhibition." In *Negotiating the Past*, ed. S. Nuttall and C. Coetzee, 57–71. Cape Town: Oxford University Press. 1998.

De Man, Paul. "The Epistemology of Metaphor." In *On Metaphor*, ed. Sheldon Sacks, 11–28. Chicago: University of Chicago Press, 1979.

Dening, Greg. *Islands and Beaches: Discourses on a Silent Land, Marquesas, 1774–1880*. Melbourne: Melbourne University Press, 1980.

———. "Writing, Rewriting the Beach." *Rethinking History* 2 (1998): 143–72.

Deringil, Selim. *The Well-Protected Domains: Ideology and Legitimation of Power in the Ottoman Empire, 1876–1909*. London: Tauris, 1998.

Derrida, Jacques. *Glas*. Trans. John Leavey Jr. and Richard Rand. Lincoln: University of Nebraska Press, 1990.

———. *On Grammatology*. Trans. Gayatri Chakravorty Spivak. Baltimore: Johns Hopkins University Press, 1974.

Desai, Gaurav. *Subject to Colonialism: African Self-Fashioning and the Colonial Library*. Durham: Duke University Press, 2001.

DeShazer, Mary. *A Poetics of Resistance*. Ann Arbor: University of Michigan Press, 1994.

Devi, Mahasweta. *Imaginary Maps: Three Stories*. Trans. Gayatri Chakravorty Spivak. New York: Routledge, 1995.

Diawara, Manthia. *In Search of Africa*. Cambridge, MA: Harvard University Press, 1998.

Diouf, Mamadou. "The Senegalese Murid Trade Diaspora and the Making of a Vernacular Cosmopolitanism." *Public Culture* 12, no. 3 (2000): 679–702.

Dirks, Nicholas. *Castes of Mind: Colonialism and the Making of Modern India*. Princeton, NJ: Princeton University Press, 2001.

———. "History as a Sign of the Modern." *Public Culture* 2, no. 2 (1990): 25–32.

———. "Postcolonialism and Its Discontents: History, Anthropology, and Postcolonial Critique." In *Schools of Thought: Twenty-five Years of Interpretive Social Science*, ed. Joan W. Scott and Debra Keates, 227–51. Princeton, NJ: Princeton University Press, 2001.

———, ed. *In Near Ruins: Cultural Theory at the End of the Century*. Minneapolis: University of Minnesota Press, 1998.

Dirlik, Arif. "Empire?" *Interventions* 5, no. 2 (2003): 207–18.

———. "Is There History after Eurocentrism? Globalism, Postcolonialism, and the Disavowal of History." *Cultural Critique* 42 (1999): 1–34.

———. "The Postcolonial Aura: Third World Criticism in the Age of Global Capitalism." *Critical Inquiry* 20, no. 2 (1994): 328–56.

Dirlik, Arif, Paul Healy, and Nick Knight, eds. *Critical Perspectives on Mao Zedong's Thought*. Atlantic Highlands, NJ: Humanities Press International, 1997.

Dixon, Melvin. *Ride Out the Wilderness: Geography and Identity in Afro-American Literature*. Urbana: University of Illinois Press, 1987.

Donham, Donald. *Marxist Modern: An Ethnographic History of the Ethiopian Revolution*. Berkeley: University of California Press, 1999.

Donzelot, Jacques. *The Policing of Families*. Trans. Robert Hurley. New York: Pantheon, 1979.

Drayton, Richard. *Nature's Government: Science, Imperial Britain, and the "Improve-ment" of the World*. New Haven, CT: Yale University Press, 2000.

Drew, Allison, ed. *South Africa's Radical Tradition: A Documentary History*. Vol. 1, *1907-50*. Cape Town: University of Cape Town Press, 1996.

Dreyfus, Hubert L., and Paul Robinow. *Michel Foucault: Beyond Structuralism and Hermeneutics*. Chicago: University of Chicago Press, 1983.

Duara, Prasenjit. *Sovereignty and Authenticity: Manchukuo and the East Asian Mod-ern*. Lanham, MD: Rowman and Littlefield, 2003.

Dubois, Laurent. *Les esclaves de la République: L'histoire oubliée de la première éman-cipation 1789-1794*. Paris: Calmann-Lévy, 1998.

Du Bois, W. E. B. *The Souls of Black Folk*. 1903. New York: Penguin, 1989.

Duby, Georges. *The Knight, the Lady, and the Priest: The Making of Modern Marriage in Medieval France*. Trans. Barbara Bray. Chicago: University of Chicago, 1994.

Ducey, Michael. "Village, Nation, and Constitution: Insurgent Politics in Papantla, Veracruz, 1810-1821." *Hispanic American Historical Review* 79, no. 3 (1999): 463-93.

Dussel, Enrique D. "Beyond Eurocentrism: The World-System and the Limits of Modernity." In *The Cultures of Globalization*, ed. Fredric Jameson and Masao Miyoshi, 3-31. Durham, NC: Duke University Press, 1997.

———. "Eurocentrism and Modernity (Introduction to the Frankfurt Lectures)." In "The Postmodernism Debate in Latin America," ed. John Beverley and José Oviedo, special issue, *boundary 2* 20, no. 3 (1993): 65-76.

———. *The Invention of the Americas: Eclipse of "the Other" and the Myth of Moder-nity*. Trans. Michael D. Barber. New York: Continuum, 1995.

Duus, Peter. *The Abacus and the Sword: The Japanese Penetration of Korea, 1895-1910*. Berkeley: University of California Press, 1995.

Duus, Peter, Ramon Myers, and Mark Peattie, eds. *The Japanese Informal Empire in China, 1895-1937*. Princeton, NJ: Princeton University Press, 1989.

———. *The Japanese Wartime Empire, 1931-1945*. Princeton, NJ: Princeton Univer-sity Press, 1996.

Easterly, William. *The Elusive Quest for Growth: Economists' Adventures and Mis-adventures in the Tropics*. Cambridge, MA: MIT Press, 2001.

Eden, Richard. *The History of Trauayle in the West and East Indies*. London: Richarde Iugge, 1577.

Edney, Matthew. *Mapping an Empire: The Geographical Construction of British India, 1765-1843*. Chicago: University of Chicago Press, 1997.

Edwards, Brent Hayes. "The Shadow of Shadows." In "The Afro-Asian Century," ed. Andrew F. Jones and Nikhil Pal Singh, special issue, *positions: east asia cultures critique* 11, no. 1 (2003): 11-49.

Einaudi, Jean-Luc. *La Bataille de Paris: 17 octobre 1961*. Paris: Seuil, 1991.

El Guindi, Fadwa. *Veil: Modesty, Privacy, and Resistance*. Oxford: Berg, 1999.

Englund, Harri. "The Dead Hand of Human Rights: Contrasting Christianities in Post-transition Malawi." *Journal of Modern African Studies* 38, no. 4 (2000): 579-603.

————."Witchcraft, Modernity, and the Person: The Morality of Accumulation in Central Malawi." *Critique of Anthropology* 16, no. 3 (1996): 257–79.

Enloe, Cynthia. *Banana, Beaches, and Bases: Making Feminist Sense of International Politics.* Berkeley: University of California Press, 1990.

Eribon, Didier. *Michel Foucault.* Trans. Betsy Wing. Cambridge, MA: Harvard University Press, 1991.

Errington, Joseph. *Shifting Languages: Interaction and Identity in Javanese Indonesia.* Cambridge: Cambridge University Press, 1998.

Escobar, Arturo. *Encountering Development: The Making and Unmaking of the Third World.* Princeton, NJ: Princeton University Press, 1995.

Ewen, Alexander, ed. *Voice of Indigenous Peoples: Native People Address the United Nations.* Santa Fe, NM: Clear Light, 1994.

Fabian, Johannes. *Time and the Other: How Anthropology Makes Its Object.* New York: Columbia University Press, 1983.

Fanon, Frantz. *Black Skin, White Masks.* Trans. by Charles Lam Markmann. 1952. New York: Grove, 1967.

————. *The Wretched of the Earth.* Trans. Constance Farrington. 1961. New York: Grove, 1985.

Fast, Howard. *Being Red.* Boston: Houghton Mifflin, 1990.

Felski, Rita. "Introduction." *New Literary History* 33, no. 4 (2002): 607–22.

————. "The Invention of Everyday Life." *New Formations* 39 (1999–2000): 15–31.

Ferguson, James. "The Country and the City on the Copperbelt." In *Culture, Power, Place: Explorations in Critical Anthropology,* ed. Akhil Gupta and Ferguson, 137–54. Durham, NC: Duke University Press, 1997.

————. *Expectations of Modernity: Myths and Meanings of Urban Life on the Zambian Copperbelt.* Berkeley: University of California Press, 1999.

————. "Of Mimicry and Membership: Africans and the 'New World Society.'" *Cultural Anthropology* 17, no. 4 (2000): 551–69.

Ferguson, Niall. *Empire: The Rise and Demise of the British World Order and the Lessons for Global Power.* London: Basic Books, 2002.

Ferrer, Ada. *Insurgent Cuba: Race, Nation, and Revolution, 1868–1898.* Chapel Hill: University of North Carolina Press, 1999.

Fieldhouse, D. K. *The Colonial Empires: A Comparative Survey from the Eighteenth Century.* New York: Delacorte, 1966.

Forbes, Jack D. *Africans and Native Americans: The Language of Race and the Evolution of Red-Black Peoples.* 2d ed. Urbana: University of Illinois Press, 1993.

————. *Apache, Navaho, and Spaniard.* Norman: University of Oklahoma Press, 1963.

Forster, E. M. *Howard's End.* 1910. New York: Penguin, 1975.

Frank, Andre Gunder. *Capitalism and Underdevelopment in Latin America: Historical Studies of Chile and Brazil.* New York: Monthly Review Press, 1969.

————. *Re-orient: Global Economy in the Asian Age.* Berkeley: University of California Press, 1998.

Frankenberg, Ruth, and Lata Mani. "CrossCurrents, Crosstalk: Race, "Postcoloniality," and the Politics of Location." *Cultural Studies* 7, no. 2 (1993): 292–310.

Fredrickson, George. *Black Liberation: A Comparative History of Black Ideologies in the United States and South Africa*. New York: Oxford University Press, 1995.

Friedman, Thomas. *The Lexus and the Olive Tree: Understanding Globalization*. New York: Anchor Books, 2000.

French, John. "Passos em falso de Razao Antiimperialista: Bourdieu, Wacquant e o Orfeo e o Poder de Hanchard." *Estudos Afro-Asiaticos* 24, no. 1 (2002): 97–140.

Fuente, Alejandro, de la. *A Nation for All: Race, Inequality, and Politics in Twentieth-Century Cuba*. Chapel Hill: University of North Carolina Press, 2001.

Gaines, Kevin. *Uplifting the Race: Black Leadership, Politics, and Culture in the Twentieth Century*. Chapel Hill: University of North Carolina Press, 1996.

Gal, Susan. *Languages and Publics*. Manchester: St. Jerome's, 2001.

Gamble, Clive. "Archaeology, History, and the Uttermost Ends of the Earth: Tasmania, Tierra del Fuego, and the Cape." *Antiquity* 66 (1992): 712–20.

Gandhi, Leela. *Postcolonial Theory: A Critical Introduction*. New York: Columbia University Press, 1998.

Gaonkar, Dilip Parameshwar. *Alternative Modernities*. Durham, NC: Duke University Press, 2001.

Garcés, María Antonia. *Cervantes in Algiers: A Captive's Tale*. Nashville, TN: Vanderbilt University Press, 2002.

Gershoni, Yekutiel. *Africans on African-Americans: The Creation and Uses of an African-American Myth*. New York: New York University Press, 1997.

Geschiere, Peter. *The Modernity of Witchcraft: Politics and the Occult in Postcolonial Africa*. Charlottesville: University of Virginia Press, 1997.

Geschiere, Peter, and Michael Rowlands. "The Domestication of Modernity: Different Trajectories." *Africa* 66, no. 4 (1996): 552–54.

Giddens, Anthony. *The Consequences of Modernity*. London: Polity, 1991.

Gikandi, Simon. "Cultural Translation and the African Self: A Postcolonial Case Study." *Interventions* 3, no. 3 (2001): 355–75.

———. "Globalization and the Claims of Postcoloniality." *South Atlantic Quarterly* 100, no. 3 (2001): 627–58.

———. *Ngugi wa Thiong'o*. Cambridge: Cambridge University Press, 2000.

———. "Theory, Literature, and Moral Considerations." *Research in African Literatures* 32, no. 4 (2001): 1–18.

Gillis, John, ed. *Commemorations: The Politics of National Identity*. Princeton, NJ: Princeton University Press, 1994.

Gilpin, Robert. *The Challenge of Global Capitalism: The World Economy in the Twenty-First Century*. Princeton, NJ: Princeton University Press, 2000.

Gilroy, Paul. *The Black Atlantic: Modernity and Double Consciousness*. Cambridge, MA: Harvard University Press, 1993.

———. *"There Ain't No Black in the Union Jack": The Cultural Politics of Race and Nation*. London: Hutchinson, 1987.

Ginsburg, Faye, and Rayna Rapp, eds. *Conceiving the New World Order: The Global Stratification of Reproduction*. Berkeley: University of California Press, 1995.

Glosser, Susan. *Chinese Visions of Family and State, 1915-1953*. Berkeley: University of California Press, 2003.

Glotfelty, Cheryll, and Harold Fromm, eds. *The Ecocritical Reader: Landmarks in Literary Ecology*. Athens: University of Georgia Press, 1996.

Godzich, Wlad. *The Culture of Literacy*. Cambridge, MA: Harvard University Press, 1994.

Goffman, Erving. "Footing." *Semiotica* 25, nos. 1-2 (1979): 1-29.

Goodman, Bryna. "Improvisations on a Semicolonial Theme; Or, How to Read a Celebration of Transnational Urban Community." *Journal of Asian Studies* 59, no. 4 (2000): 889-926.

Goodman, Dena. "Difference: An Enlightenment Concept." In *What's Left of Enlightenment? A Postmodern Question*, ed. Keith Michael Baker and Peter Hanns Reill, 129-47. Stanford, CA: Stanford University Press, 2001.

Goody, Jack. *The Development of the Family and Marriage in Europe*. Cambridge: Cambridge University Press, 1983.

Gould, Stephen Jay. *The Mismeasure of Man*. Rev. ed. New York: Norton, 1996.

Grandin, Greg. *The Blood of Guatemala: A History of Race and Nation*. Durham, NC: Duke University Press, 2000.

Gregory of Nyssa, *The Life of Moses*. Trans. by Abraham J. Malherbe and Everett Ferguson. New York: Paulist Press, 1978.

Griffiths, Tom, and Libby Robin. *Ecology and Empire: Environmental History of Settler Societies*. Seattle: University of Washington Press, 1997.

Grosfoguel, Ramón, and Chloe S. Georas. " 'Coloniality of Power' and Racial Dynamics: Notes toward a Reinterpretation of Latino Caribbeans in New York City." *Identities: Global Studies in Culture and Power* 7 (2000): 85-126.

Grossman, James R., ed. *The Frontier in American Culture: An Exhibition at the Newberry Library*. Berkeley: University of California Press, 1994.

Grove, Richard. *Green Imperialism: Colonial Expansion, Tropical Island Edens, and the Origins of Environmentalism, 1600-1860*. Cambridge: Cambridge University Press, 1995.

Guénoun, Denis. *Hypothèses sur l'Europe: Un essai de philosophie*. Belfort, France: Circé, 2000.

Guerra, Lillian. "Crucibles of Liberation in Cuba: José Martí, Conflicting Nationalisms, and the Search for Social Unity." PhD diss., University of Wisconsin, 2000.

Guha, Ramachandra. "Radical American Environmentalism and Wilderness Preservation: A Third World Critique." *Environmental Ethics*, no. 11 (1989): 71-83.

Guha, Ranajit. *Elementary Aspects of Peasant Insurgency in Colonial India*. Delhi: Oxford University Press, 1983.

———. "The Prose of Counterinsurgency." In *Select Subaltern Studies*, ed. Guha and Gayatri Chakravorty Spivak, 48-88. New York: Oxford University Press, 1988.

Guillen, Mauro. "Is Globalization Civilizing, Destructive, or Feeble? A Critique of

Five Key Debates in the Social Science Literature." *Annual Review of Sociology*, no. 27 (2001): 235–60.

Gupta, Akhil. *Postcolonial Developments: Agriculture in the Making of Modern India.* Durham, NC: Duke University Press, 1998.

Gutmann, Amy, ed. *Multiculturalism: Examining the Politics of Recognition.* Princeton, NJ: Princeton University Press, 1994.

Habermas, Jürgen. *The Structural Transformation of the Public Sphere: An Inquiry into a Category of Bourgeois Society.* Trans. Thomas Burger, with Frederick Lawrence. Cambridge, MA: MIT Press, 1989.

———. "Struggles for Recognition in the Democratic Constitutional State." In *Multiculturalism: Examining the Politics of Recognition*, ed. Amy Gutmann, 107–48. Princeton, NJ: Princeton University Press, 1994.

Habib, Adam, et al. "South Africa and the Global Order: The Structural Conditioning of a Transition to Democracy." *Journal of Contemporary African Studies* 16, no. 1 (1998): 95–116.

Hacking, Ian. *Historical Ontology.* Cambridge, MA: Harvard University Press, 2002.

———. "Inaugural Lecture: Chair of Philosophy and History of Scientific Concepts at the College de France, 16 January 2001." *Economy and Society* 31, no. 1 (2002): 1–14.

———. "Language, Truth, and Reason." In *Rationality and Relativism*, ed. Martin Hollis and Steven Lukes, 48–66. Oxford: Blackwell, 1982.

———. "The Looping Effect of Human Kinds." In *Causal Cognition: A Multidisciplinary Approach*, ed. Dan Sperber, D. Premack and A. J. Premack, 351–94. Oxford: Clarendon, 1994.

———. *Mad Travelers: Reflections on the Reality of Mental Illness.* Charlottesville: University Press of Virginia, 1998.

———. *Rewriting the Soul: Multiple Personality and the Sciences of Memory.* Princeton, NJ: Princeton University Press, 1995.

———. *The Social Construction of What?* Cambridge, MA: Harvard University Press, 1999.

———. " 'Style' for Historians and Philosophers." *Studies in History and Philosophy of Science* 23, no. 1 (1992): 1–20.

Hall, Catherine. *Civilising Subjects: Metropole and Colony in the English Imagination, 1830–1867.* London: Polity, 2002.

Hall, Jonathan. *Ethnic Identity in Greek Antiquity.* Cambridge: Cambridge University Press, 1997.

Hall, Stuart. "Race, Articulation, and Societies Structured in Dominance." In *Sociological Theories, Race, and Colonialism*, 305–45. Paris: Unesco, 1980.

———. "When Was 'the Postcolonial'? Thinking at the Limit." In *The Post-Colonial Question: Common Skies, Divided Horizons*, ed. Iain Chambers and Lidia Curti, 242–60. New York: Routledge, 1996.

Halperin, David. "How to Do the History of Male Homosexuality." GLQ: *A Journal of Lesbian and Gay Studies* 6, no. 1 (2000): 87–123.

Hanchard, Michael George. *Orpheus and Power*. Princeton: Princeton University Press, 1994.

Hansen, Karen Tranberg. *Salaula: The World of Second-Hand Clothing and Zambia*. Chicago: University of Chicago Press, 2000.

Hansen, Miriam Bratu. "The Mass Production of the Senses: Classical Cinema as Vernacular Modernism." *Modernism/Modernity* 6, no. 2 (1999): 59–77.

Hanson, R. C. *The Search for the Christian Doctrine of God: The Arian Controversy 318–381 AD*. Edinburgh: Clark, 1988.

Harding, Jeremy. *The Uninvited: Refugees at the Rich Man's Gate*. London: Profile Books and the London Review of Books, 2000.

Hardt, Michael, and Antonio Negri. *Empire*. Cambridge, MA: Harvard University Press, 2000.

———. *Labor of Dionysus*. Minneapolis: University of Minnesota Press, 1994.

———. "The Rod of the Forest Warden: A Response to Timothy Brennan." *Critical Inquiry* 29, no. 2 (2003): 368–73.

Harley, J. Brian. "The Map and the Development of the History of Cartography." In *The History of Cartography*, ed. Harley and David Woodward, 1–42. Chicago: University of Chicago Press, 1987.

———. "Maps, Knowledge, and Power." In *The Iconography of Landscape: Essays on the Symbolic Representation, Design, and Use of Past Environments*, ed. Denis Cosgrove and Stephen Daniels, 277–312. Cambridge: Cambridge University Press, 1988.

———. *The New Nature of Maps: Essays in the History of Cartography*. Baltimore, MD: Johns Hopkins University Press, 2000.

Harootunian, H. D. *Overcome by Modernity: History, Culture, and Community in Interwar Japan*. Princeton, NJ: Princeton University Press, 2000.

Harrison, Nicholas. *Postcolonial Criticism: History, Theory, and the Work of Fiction*. Oxford: Polity, 2003.

Harvey, David. *The Condition of Postmodernity: An Enquiry into the Origins of Cultural Change*. Cambridge: Blackwell, 1989.

———. *The New Imperialism*. Oxford: Oxford University Press, 2003.

Harvey, Neil. *The Chiapas Rebellion: The Struggle for Land and Democracy*. Durham, NC: Duke University Press, 1998.

Hasseler, Terri, and Paula Krebs, "Losing Our Way after the Imperial Turn: Charting Academic Uses of the Postcolonial." In *After the Imperial Turn: Thinking with and through the Nation*, ed. Antoinette Burton, 90–101. Durham, NC: Duke University Press, 2003.

Hattox, Ralph S. *Coffee and Coffeehouses: The Origins of a Social Beverage in the Medieval Near East*. Seattle: University of Washington Press, 1985.

Haug, Fritz. *Communication and Class Struggle*. Vol. 2. New York: International General, 1983.

Head, Bessie. *Where Rain Clouds Gather*. New York: Heinemann, 1996.

Hegel, G. W. F. *The Phenomenology of Mind.* Trans. J. B. Baillie. New York: Harper and Row, 1967.

———. *The Philosophy of Right.* Trans. T. M. Knox. New York: Oxford University Press, 1952.

Held, David, et al. *Global Transformations: Politics, Economics, and Culture.* Stanford, CA: Stanford University Press, 1999.

Helg, Aline. *Our Rightful Share: The Afro-Cuban Struggle for Equality, 1886–1912.* Chapel Hill: University of North Carolina Press, 1995.

Hemsley, J., and R. Blumenthal, eds. *Of Money, Mandarins, and Peasants.* Johannesburg: SANGOCO, 2000.

Herzl, Theodore. *The Jewish State.* New York: Dover, 1988.

Hess, Andrew. "The Mediterranean and Shakespeare's Geopolitical Imagination." In *"The Tempest" and Its Travels,* ed. Peter Hulme and William H. Sherman, 121–31. London: Reaktion, 2000.

Hind, Robert. "The Internal Colonial Concept." *Comparative Studies in Society and History* 26, no. 3 (1984): 543–68.

Hirst, Paul, and Grahame Thomoson. *Globalization in Question: The International Economy and the Possibilities of Governance.* Cambridge: Polity, 1996.

Hobsbawm, Eric. *The Age of Revolution: 1789–1848.* New York: Vintage, 1962.

Hodgson, Dorothy. *Gendered Modernities: Ethnographic Perspectives.* New York: Palgrave, 2001.

Hofmeyr, Isabel. *'We Spend Our Years as a Tale That Is Told": Oral Historical Narrative in a South African Chiefdom.* Portsmouth, NH: Heinemann, 1993.

Hogan, Patrick Colm. *Colonialism and Cultural Identity: Crises of Tradition in the Anglophone Literatures of India, Africa, and the Caribbean.* Albany: State University of New York Press, 2000.

Hollinger, David. "The Enlightenment and the Genealogy of Cultural Conflict in the United States." In *What's Left of Enlightenment? A Postmodern Question,* ed. Keith Michael Baker and Peter Hanns Reill, 7–18. Stanford, CA: Stanford University Press, 2001.

Holsinger, Bruce. "Medieval Studies, Postcolonial Studies, and the Genealogies of Critique." *Speculum,* no. 77 (2002): 1195–27.

Holstun, James. *Ehud's Dagger.* London: Verso, 2000.

Holt, Thomas. *The Problem of Freedom: Race, Labor, and Politics in Jamaica and Britain, 1832–1938.* Baltimore, MD: Johns Hopkins University Press, 1992.

Horn, Peter. "A Radical Rethinking of the Art of Poetry in an Apartheid Society." *Journal of Commonwealth Literature* 29, no. 1 (1993): 97–113.

Horner, Timothy. *Listening to Trypho: Justin Martyr's Dialogue Reconsidered.* Leuven, Netherlands: Peeters, 2001.

Houlbrooke, R. A. *The English Family, 1450–1700.* London: Books Britain, 1984.

Huggan, Graham. *The Post-colonial Exotic: Marketing the Margins.* London: Routledge, 2001.

Hulme, Peter. "Cast Away: The Uttermost Parts of the Earth." In *Sea-Changes: His-*

toricizing the Ocean, ed. Bernhard Klein and Gesa Mackenthun, 187–201. London: Routledge, 2003.

———. *Colonial Encounters: Europe and the Native Caribbean, 1492–1797*. London: Methuen, 1986.

———. "Dire Straits: Ten Leagues Beyond." In *Native Texts and Contexts: Essays with Post-colonial Perspectives*, ed. Fadillah Merican and Ruzy Suliza Hashim, 29–40. Kebangsaan, Malaysia: Selangor Darul Ehsan Universiti, 2002.

———. "Including America." *Ariel* 26, no. 1 (1995): 117–23.

———. "Reading from Elsewhere: George Lamming and the Paradox of Exile." In *'The Tempest' and Its Travels*, ed. Peter Hulme and William H. Sherman, 220–35. London: Reaktion, 2000.

———. "Stormy Weather: Misreading the Postcolonial *Tempest*." *Early Modern Culture*, no. 3 (2003). Available at http://eserver.org/emc/default.html.

———. "Tales of Distinction: European Ethnography and the Caribbean." In *Implicit Understandings: Observing, Reporting, and Reflecting on the Encounters between Europeans and Other Peoples in the Early Modern Era*, ed. Stuart B. Schwartz, 157–97. Cambridge: Cambridge University Press, 1994.

———. "Voice from the Margins? Walter Mignolo's *The Darker Side of the Renaissance*." *Journal of Latin American Cultural Studies* 8, no. 2 (1999): 219–33.

Hume, David. *A Treatise of Human Nature*. Oxford: Oxford University Press, 1980.

Hunt, Nancy Rose. *A Colonial Lexicon of Birth Ritual, Medicalization, and Mobility in the Congo*. Durham, NC: Duke University Press, 1999.

Ichiro, Tomiyama. "Colonialism and the Sciences of the Tropical Zone: The Academic Analysis of Difference in 'the Island Peoples.'" *positions* 3, no. 2 (1995): 367–91.

Ignatieff, Michael. "The American Empire." *New York Times Magazine*, January 5, 2003, 22.

Ingham, Patricia Clare, and Michelle R. Warren, eds. *Postcolonial Moves: Medieval through Modern* London: Palgrave, 2003.

Irvine, Judith, and Susan Gal. "Language Ideology and Linguistic Differentiation." In *Regimes of Language*, ed. Paul V. Kroskrity, 35–83. Santa Fe, NM: School of American Research Press, 2000.

Iyer, Pico. *The Global Soul: Jet Lag, Shopping Malls, and the Search for Home*. New York: Vintage, 2000.

Jacobs, Sylvia. *The African Nexus: Black American Perspectives on the European Partitioning of Africa, 1880–1920*. Westport, CT: Greenwood, 1981.

Jacobson, Matthew Frye. *Barbarian Virtues: The United States Encounters Foreign Peoples at Home and Abroad*. New York: Hill and Wang, 2000.

James, C. L. R. *The Black Jacobins: Toussaint L'Ouverture and the San Domingo Revolution*. 1938. New York: Vintage, 1963.

Jameson, Fredric. *The Cultural Turn: Selected Writings on the Postmodern, 1983–1998*. London: Verso, 1998.

———. *The Geopolitical Aesthetic*. Bloomington: Indiana University Press, 1992.

————. "Globalization and Political Strategy." *New Left Review* 4 (2000): 49–68.

————. "Notes on Globalization as a Philosophical Issue." In *The Cultures of Globalization*, ed. Jameson and Masao Miyoshi, 54–77. Durham: Duke University Press, 1997.

————. *Postmodernism; Or, The Cultural Logic of Late Capitalism*. Durham, NC: Duke University Press, 1995.

————. "Postmodernism; Or, The Cultural Logic of Late Capitalism." *New Left Review* 1, no. 146 (1984): 53–92.

Jameson, Fredric, and Masao Miyoshi, eds. *The Cultures of Globalization*. Durham, NC: Duke University Press, 1998.

JanMohamed, Abdul. *Manichean Aesthetics: The Politics of Literature in Colonial Africa*. Amherst: University of Massachusetts Press, 1983.

Jeyifo, Biodun. "The Nature of Things: Arrested Decolonization and Critical Theory." *Research in African Literatures* 21, no. 1 (1990): 33–48.

Jiménez, Michael. "The Elision of the Middle Classes and Beyond: History, Politics, and Development Studies in Latin America's 'Short Twentieth Century.' " In *Colonial Legacies: The Problem of Persistence in Latin American History*, ed. Jeremy Adelman, 207–28. New York: Routledge, 1999.

Johnson, Chalmers. *Blowback: The Costs and Consequences of American Empire*. New York: Metropolitan, 2000.

Jones, Andrew. *Yellow Music: Media Culture and Colonial Modernity in the Chinese Jazz Age*. Durham, NC: Duke University Press, 2001.

Joseph, Gilbert, ed., *Reclaiming the Political in Latin American History: Essays from the North*. Durham, NC: Duke University Press, 2001.

Joyce, Patrick. "The End of Social History?" *Social History* 20, no. 1 (1995): 73–91.

Judson, Pieter. *Exclusive Revolutionaries: Liberal Politics, Social Experience, and National Identity in the Austrian Empire, 1848–1914*. Ann Arbor: University of Michigan Press, 1996.

Jusdanis, Gregory. *The Necessary Nation*. Princeton, NJ: Princeton University Press, 2001.

Jussawalla, Feroza, and Reed Way Dasenbrock, eds. *Interviews with Writers of the Postcolonial World*. Jackson: University Press of Mississippi, 1992.

Kabeer, Naila. *Bangladeshi Women Workers and Labour Market Decisions: The Power to Choose*. Delhi: Vistaar Publications, 2001.

Kane, Cheikh H. *Ambiguous Adventure*. Trans. Katherine Woods. New York: Heinemann, 1972.

Kane, Joe. *Savages*. New York: Knopf, 1995.

Kang, Liu. *Aesthetics and Marxism: Chinese Aesthetic Marxists and Their Western Contemporaries*. Durham, NC: Duke University Press, 2000.

Kannabiran, Vasanth, and Kalpana Kannabiran. "Looking at Ourselves: The Women's Movement in Hyderabad." In *Feminist Genealogies, Colonial Legacies, Democratic Futures*, ed. M. Jacqui Alexander and Chandra Talpade Mohanty, 213–58. New York: Routledge, 1997.

Kaplan, Alice, and Kristin Ross. "Introduction." *Yale French Studies*, no. 73 (1987): 1–4.

Kaplan, Caren. *Questions of Travel: Postmodern Discourses of Displacement*. Durham, NC: Duke University Press, 1996.

Kaplan, Robert. *The Coming Anarchy: Shattering the Dreams of the Post Cold War*. New York: Vintage, 2001.

———. *Warrior Politics: Why Leadership Demands a Pagan Ethos*. New York: Random House, 2001.

Karl, Rebecca. *Staging the World: Chinese Nationalism at the Turn of the Twentieth Century*. Durham, NC: Duke University Press, 2003.

Kaviraj, Sudipta. "Democracy and Development in India." In *Democracy and Development*, ed. Amiya Bagchi, 39–57. London: St. Martin's, 1995.

———."The Imaginary Institution of India." In *Subaltern Studies VII*, ed. Partha Chatterjee and Gyanendra Pande, 1–39. Delhi: Oxford University Press, 1992.

Keane, Webb. "Public Speaking: On Indonesian as the Language of the Nation." *Public Culture* 15, no. 3 (2003): 508–30.

Kemp, Amanda Denise. "*Up from Slavery* and Other Narratives: Black South African Performances of the American Negro (1920–1943)." PhD diss., Northwestern University, 1997.

Khaldi, Rashid. *Palestinian Identity: The Construction of Modern National Consciousness*. New York: Columbia University Press, 1997.

Kincaid, Jamaica. "Alien Soil." In *The Best American Essays*, ed. Tracy Kidder. Boston: Houghton Mifflin, 1994.

———. *My Garden*. New York: Farrar, Straus, Giroux, 2001.

———. *A Small Place*. New York: Farrar, Straus, Giroux, 1988.

King, Anthony D., ed. *Culture, Globalization, and the World-System: Contemporary Conditions for the Representation of Identity*. Binghamton: Department of Art and Art History, State University of New York at Binghamton, 1991.

King, Karen. *Making Heresy: Gnosticism in Twentieth-Century Historiography*. Cambridge, MA: Harvard University Press, 2003.

King, Richard. *Orientalism and Religion: Postcolonial Theory, India, and the Mystic East*. London: Routledge, 1999.

Klubock, Thomas Miller. *Contested Communities: Class, Gender, and Politics in Chile's El Teniente Copper Mine, 1905–1951*. Durham, NC: Duke University Press, 1998.

Kly, Y. H. *The Anti-Social Contract*. Atlanta: Clarity, 1997.

Kofsky, Arieh. "Mamre: A Case of a Regional Cult?" In *Sharing the Sacred: Religious Contacts and Conflicts in the Holy Land; First-Fifteenth Centuries CE*, ed. Guy G. Stroumsa and Kofsky, 19–30. Jerusalem: Yad Izhak Ben Zvi, 1998.

Kota, Nosipho. "Introduction: A Frank Poet." In *Timbila 2001*, ed. Vonani Bila, 35–36. Elim, South Africa: Timbila, 2001.

Kuhn, Thomas. *The Structure of Scientific Revolutions*. Chicago: University of Chicago Press, 1962.

―――. "What Is a Scientific Revolution?" In *The Probabilistic Revolution*, ed. Lorenz Kruger and Lorraine Daston, 1:7–22. Cambridge: Cambridge University Press, 1987.

Kumar, Amitava. *Passport Photos*. Berkeley: University of California Press, 2000.

Kumar, Radha. *The History of Doing*. Delhi: Kali for Women, 1993.

Kupchan, Charles. *The End of the American Era: U.S. Foreign Policy and the Geopolitics of the Twenty-First Century*. New York: Knopf, 2002.

Kymlicka, Will. *Multicultural Citizenship: A Liberal Theory of Minority Rights*. Oxford: Oxford University Press, 1995.

Labov, William. "The Boundaries of Words and Their Meanings." In *New Ways of Analyzing Variation in English*, ed. Charles-James N. Bailey and Roger. W. Shuy, 340–73. Washington, DC: Georgetown University Press, 1973.

Lamming, George. *The Pleasures of Exile*. 1960. London: Allison and Busby, 1984.

Langbauer, Laurie. "Cultural Studies and the Politics of the Everyday." *Diacritics* 22, no. 1 (1992): 47–65.

Larsen, Neil. *Determinations: Essays on Theory, Narrative, and Nation in the Americas*. London: Verso, 2001.

―――. "Imperialism, Colonialism, Postcolonialism." In *A Companion to Postcolonial Studies*, ed. Henry Schwarz and Sangeeta Ray, 23–52. Oxford: Blackwell, 2000.

Latour, Bruno. *We Have Never Been Modern*. Cambridge, MA: Harvard University Press, 1993.

Lavie, Smadar. "Blow-Ups in the Borderzone: Third World Israeli Authors' Gropings for Home." *New Formations*, no. 18 (1992): 84–105.

Laxman, Satya. *Cotton and Famine in Berar, 1850–1900*. Delhi: Munishiram Manoharal, 1997.

Lazarus, Neil. *Nationalism and Cultural Practice in the Postcolonial World*. Cambridge: Cambridge University Press, 1999.

Le Boulluec, Alain. *La notion d'hérésie dans la littérature grecque deuxième–troisième siècles*. Paris: Études Augustiniennes, 1985.

Lee, Benjamin. "Textuality, Mediation, and Public Discourse." In *Habermas and the Public Sphere*, ed. Craig Calhoun, 402–18. Cambridge, MA: MIT Press, 1993.

Lee, Leo Ou-fan. "Shanghai Modern: Reflections on Urban Culture in China in the 1930s." In *Alternative Modernities*, ed. Dilip Parameshwar Gaonkar, 86–122. Durham, NC: Duke University Press, 2001.

Lefebvre, Henri. "The Everyday and Everydayness." Trans. Christine Levich. *Yale French Studies*, no. 73 (1987): 7–11.

―――. *Everyday Life in the Modern World*. Trans. Sacha Rabinovitch. London: Penguin, 1971.

Lencek, Lena, and Gideon Bosker. *The Beach: The History of Paradise on Earth*. London: Secker and Warburg, 1998.

Leopold, Aldo. *Game Management*. 1933. Madison: University of Wisconsin Press, 1986.

Lester, Yami. *Yami: The Autobiography of Yami Lester*. New York: Iad, 2000.

LeVine, Mark. *Overthrowing Geography, Reimagining Identities: A History of Jaffa and Tel Aviv, 1880 to the Present*. Berkeley: University of California Press, 2005.

Lewis, David Levering. *W. E. B. Du Bois: Biography of a Race, 1868-1919*. New York: Henry Holt, 1993.

Lewis, Malcolm, ed. *Cartographic Encounters: Perspectives on Native American Mapmaking and Map Use*. Chicago: University of Chicago Press, 1998.

Lewis, Reina, and Sara Mills, eds. *Feminist Postcolonial Theory: A Reader*. Edinburgh: Edinburgh University Press, 2003.

Limberis, Vasiliki. " 'Religion' as the Cipher for Identity: The Cases of Emperor Julian, Libanius, and Gregory Nazianzus." *Harvard Theological Review* 93, no. 4 (2000): 373-400.

Limerick, Patricia Nelson. *The Legacy of Conquest: The Unbroken Past of the American West*. New York: Norton, 1987.

Limerick, Patricia Nelson, Clyde A. Milner II, and Charles E. Rankin, eds. *Trails: Toward a New Western History*. Lawrence: University of Kansas Press, 1991.

Linehan, Peter, and Janet L. Nelson, eds. *The Medieval World*. London: Routledge, 2001.

Lockman, Zachery. *Comrades and Enemies: Arab and Jewish Workers in Palestine, 1906-1948*. Berkeley: University of California Press, 1996.

Loomba, Ania. *Colonialism/ Postcolonialism*. London: Routledge, 1998.

Loomba, Ania, and Suvir Kaul, eds. "On India: Writing History, Culture, and Postcoloniality.

Lorenz, Rudolf. *Arius judaizans? Untersuchungen zur dogmengeschichtlichen Einordnung des Arius*. Göttingen, Germany: Vandenhoek und Ruprecht, 1979.

Lovejoy, Arthur O. *The Great Chain of Being: A Study of the History of an Idea*. Cambridge, MA: Harvard University Press, 1936.

Lucy, John, ed. *Reflexive Language: Reported Speech and Metapragmatics*. Cambridge: Cambridge University Press, 1993.

Ludden, David, ed. *Reading Subaltern Studies: Critical History, Contested Meaning, and the Globalization of South Asia*. Delhi: Permanent Black, 2001.

Lyman, J. Rebecca. "The Making of a Heretic: The Life of Origen in Epiphanius *Panarion* 64." *Studia Patristica*, no. 31 (1997): 445-51.

———. "The Politics of Passing: Justin Martyr, Mimicry, and the Origins of Christian 'Orthodoxy.' " In *Conversion in Late Antiquity and the Middle Ages*, ed. Anthony Grafton and Kenneth Milles, 36-60. Rochester, NY: University of Rochester Press, 2000.

Mabey, Richard. *Landlocked: In Pursuit of the Wild*. London: Sinclair Stevenson, 1994.

Macfarlane, Alan. *The Origins of English Individualism: The Family, Property, and Social Organization*. London: Blackwell, 1978.

Magogodi, Kgafela oa. *The Condom Come*. Amsterdam: New Leaf: 2000.

Magubane, Bernard. *The Making of a Racist State: British Imperialism and the Union of South Africa, 1875-1910*. Trenton, NJ: Africa World Press, 1996.

Mahan, A. T. *The Interest of America in Sea Power, Present and Future.* Boston: Little, Brown, 1897.

Mahendra, K. L. "A Protectionist Measure." In *Labour, Environment, and Globalization*, ed. J. John and Anuradha Chenoy, 40–59. Delhi: Centre for Education and Communication, 1996.

Mahmood, Saba. "Feminist Theory, Embodiment, and the Docile Agent: Some Reflections on the Egyptian Islamic Revival." *Cultural Anthropology* 16, no. 2 (2000): 202–36.

Malange, Nise, et al. "Albie Sachs Must Not Worry: Culture and Working Life's Response." In, *Spring Is Rebellious: Arguments about Cultural Freedom*, ed. Ingrid de Kok and Karen Press, 99–103. Cape Town: Buchu, 1990.

Malcomson, Scott. *Tuturani.* New York: Poseidon, 1990.

Mallon, Florencia. *Courage Tastes of Blood: The Mapuche Community of Nicolás Ailío and the Chilean State, 1906-2001.* Durham: Duke University Press, forthcoming.

———. "Cuando la amnesia se impone con sangre, el abuso se hace costumbre: El pueblo Mapuche y el estado chileno." In *El modelo chileno: Democracia y desarrollo en los noventa*, ed. Paul Drake and Iván Jaksic, 435–64. Santiago: LOM Editores, 1999.

———. "Decoding the Parchments of the Latin American Nation-State: Peru, Mexico, and Chile in Comparative Perspective." In *Studies in the Formation of the Nation-State in Latin America*, ed. James Dunkerley, 14–53. London: Institute of Latin American Studies, 2002.

———. "Land, Morality, and Exploitation in Southern Chile: Rural Conflict and the Discourses of Agrarian Reform in Cautín, 1928–1974." *Political Power and Social Theory*, 14, no. (2000): 141–193.

———. *Peasant and Nation: The Making of Postcolonial Mexico and Peru.* Berkeley: University of California Press, 1995.

Mamdani, Mahmood. *Citizen and Subject: Contemporary Africa and the Legacy of Late Colonialism.* Princeton, NJ: Princeton University Press, 1996.

Mani, Lata. "Contentious Traditions: The Debate on Sati in Colonial India." In *Recasting Women: Essays in Colonial History*, ed. Kumkum Sangari and Sudesh Vaid, 88–126. Delhi: Kali for Women, 1989.

Mannheim, Karl. *Ideology and Utopia: An Introduction to the Sociology of Knowledge.* 1936. Trans. Louis Wirth and Edward Shils. San Diego: Harcourt Brace Jovanovich, 1985.

Marais, Hein. *South Africa: Limits to Change.* Cape Town: University of Cape Town Press, 1998.

Marcus, George, and Michael Fischer. *Anthropology as Cultural Critique: An Experimental Moment in the Human Sciences.* Chicago: University Chicago Press, 1986.

Mariscal, George. "The Role of Spain in Contemporary Race Theory." *Arizona Journal of Hispanic Cultural Studies*, no. 2 (1998): 7–22.

Marks, Shula. "Rewriting South African History; Or, The Hunt for Hintsa's Head." In *Rethinking African History*, ed. S. McGrath et al. Edinburgh: University of Edinburgh Center for African Studies, 1996.

Markschies, Christoph. *Valentinus Gnosticus? Untersuchungen zur valentinianischen Gnosis mit einem Kommentar zu den Fragmenten Valentins.* Tübingen, Germany: Mohr, 1992.

Markus, Robert. *The End of Ancient Christianity.* Cambridge: Cambridge University Press, 1990.

Masilela, Ntongela. "The 'Black Atlantic' and African Modernity in South Africa." *Research in African Literatures,* no. 27 (1997): 88–96.

———. "The TransAtlantic Connections of the New African Movement." Unpublished manuscript.

Massad, Joseph. "The 'Post-colonial' Colony: Time, Space, and Bodies in Israel/ Palestine." In *The Pre-occupation of Postcolonial Studies,* ed. Fawzia Afzal-Khan and Kalpana Seshadri-Crooks, 311–46. Durham, NC: Duke University Press, 2000.

Massey, Doreen. *Space, Place, and Gender.* Cambridge: Polity, 1994.

Mayekiso, Mzwanele. *Township Politics: Civic Struggles for a New South Africa.* New York: Monthly Review Press, 1996.

Mbembe, Achille. "African Modes of Self-Writing." *Public Culture* 14, no. 1 (2002): 239–73.

———. *On the Postcolony.* Berkeley: University of California Press, 2001.

McAllister, P., ed. *Culture and the Commonplace.* Johannesburg: University of Witwatersrand Press, 1997.

McClintock, Anne. "The Angel of Progress: Pitfalls of the Term Postcolonial." *Social Text,* nos. 31–32 (1992): 84–98.

———. *Imperial Leather: Race, Gender, and Sexuality in the Colonial Contest.* New York: Routledge, 1995.

McClure, Kristie. "Difference, Diversity, and the Limits of Tolerance." *Political Theory* 18, no. 3 (1990): 361–91.

McGrath, S. M., et al., eds. *Rethinking South African History.* Edinburgh: Edinburgh University Press, 1996.

McLennan, John. *Primitive Marriage.* Edinburgh: Adam and Charles Black, 1865.

Meer, Shamim. "The Demobilisation of Civil Society: Struggling with New Questions." *Development Update,* no. 3 (1999): 109–118.

Mehta, Uday. *Liberalism and Empire: A Study in Nineteenth Century British Liberal Thought.* Chicago: University of Chicago Press, 1999.

Memmi, Albert. *The Colonizer and the Colonized.* 1957. Trans. Howard Greenfeld. New York: Orion, 1965.

Menchú, Rigoberta. *Crossing Borders.* Trans. Ann Wright. London: Verso, 1998.

Menocal, Maria Rosa. *The Arabic Role in Medieval Literary History: A Forgotten Heritage.* Philadelphia: University of Pennsylvania Press, 1987.

Menon, Nivedita. "Universalism without Foundations?" *Economy and Society* 31, no. 1 (2002): 152–69.

Menon, Nivedita, and Aditya Nigam. "The 'War' in Europe." *Economic and Political Weekly,* May 1, 1999, 1021–22.

Mernissi, Fatima. *The Veil and the Male Elite: A Feminist Interpretation of Women's Rights in Islam.* Trans. Mary Jo Lakeland. Rading, MA: Addison-Wesley, 1991.

Meyer, Birgit. *Translating the Devil: Religion and Modernity among the Ewe in Ghana.* Edinburgh: Edinburgh University Press, 1999.

Meyer, Birgit, and Peter Geschiere, eds. *Globalization and Identity: Dialectics of Flow and Closure.* Oxford: Blackwell, 1999.

Mignolo, Walter. *The Darker Side of the Renaissance: Literacy, Territoriality, and Colonization.* Ann Arbor: University of Michigan Press, 1995.

———. "I Am Where I Think: Epistemology and Cultural Difference." *Journal of Latin American Cultural Studies* 8, no. 3 (1999): 235–45.

———. *Local Histories/Global Designs: Coloniality, Subaltern Knowledges, and Border Thinking.* Princeton, NJ: Princeton University Press, 2000.

Miller, Toby, et al. *Global Hollywood.* London: British Film Institute, 2001.

Mills, Charles W. *The Racial Contract.* Ithaca, NY: Cornell University Press, 1997.

Mitchell, Timothy. *Colonising Egypt.* Berkeley: University of California Press, 1991.

———, ed. *Questions of Modernity.* Minneapolis: University of Minnesota Press, 2000.

Miyoshi, Masao. "A Borderless World? From Colonialism to Transnationalism and the Decline of the Nation-State." *Critical Inquiry* 19, no. 4 (1993): 726–51.

Miyoshi, Masao, and H. D. Harootunian, eds. *Learning Places: The Afterlives of Area Studies.* Durham, NC: Duke University Press, 2002.

Mo, Timothy. *Renegade or Halo².* London: Paddleless, 1999.

Mofokeng, Boitumelo. "Workshop on Black Women's Writing and Reading." *Current Writing,* no. 2 (1990): 71–89.

Molema, Silas Modiri. *The Bantu, Past and Present.* Edinburgh: Green, 1920.

———. *Chief Moroka: His Life, His Times, His Country, and His People.* Cape Town: Methodist Publishing House, 1951.

———. *Montshiwa, 1815–1896: Barolong Chief and Patriot.* Cape Town: Struik, 1966.

Mommsen, Wolfgang, and Jürgen Osterhammel. *Imperialism and After: Continuities and Discontinuities.* London: Allen and Unwin, 1986.

Montejo, Víctor. *Testimony: Death of a Guatemalan Village.* Trans. Victor Perera. Willimantic, CT: Curbstone, 1987.

Moreiras, Alberto. *The Exhaustion of Difference: The Politics of Latin American Cultural Studies.* Durham, NC: Duke University Press, 2001.

Morgan, Lewis Henry. *Ancient Society.* New York: Henry Holt, 1877.

Mosse, George. *Toward the Final Solution: A History of European Racism.* New York: Howard Fertig, 1978.

Mpe, Phaswane. Introduction to Kgafela oa Magogodi, *Thy Condom Come,* v–ix. Amsterdam: New Leaf, 2000.

Muldoon, James. *Popes, Lawyers, and Infidels: The Church and the Non-Christian World, 1250–1550.* Philadelphia: University of Pennsylvania Press, 1979.

Mullen, Bill. "Du Bois, Dark Princess, and the Afro-Asian International." In "The Afro-Asian Century," ed. Andrew F. Jones and Nikhil Pal Singh, special issue, *positions* 11, no. 1 (2003): 217–39.

"Multiple Modernities." Special issue, *Daedalus* 129, no. 1 (2000).

Mundy, Barbara. *The Mapping of New Spain: Indigenous Cartography and the Maps of the Relaciones Geográficas*. Chicago: University of Chicago Press, 1996.

Munif, Abdelrahman. *Cities of Salt*. Trans. Peter Theroux. New York: Vintage, 1987.

Murphy, David. "De-centering French Studies: Towards a Postcolonial Theory of Francophone Cultures." *French Cultural Studies*, no. 38 (2002): 165–85.

Murphy, Patrick. *Further Afield in the Study of Nature-Oriented Literature*. Charlottesville: University of Virginia Press, 2000.

———. *Literature of Nature: An International Sourcebook*. Chicago: Fitzroy Dearborn, 1998.

Myers, Fred. *The Empire of Things: Regimes of Value and Material Culture*. Santa Fe, NM: School of American Research Press, 2001.

Myers, Ramon, and Mark R. Peattie, eds. *The Japanese Colonial Empire, 1894-1945*. Princeton, NJ: Princeton University Press, 1984.

Mzamane, Mbulelo. "From Resistance to Reconstruction." *Ariel* 27, no. 1 (1996): 18.

Naipaul, V. S. *The Enigma of Arrival: A Novel*. New York: Knopf, 1987.

Nandy, Ashis. "History's Forgotten Doubles," *History and Theory* 34 (1995): 44–66.

Nascimento, Abdias do. *O Genocidio do Negro Brasileiro: Proesso de un Racismo Mascarado*. Rio de Janeiro: Achiamne, 1978.

Ndebele, Njabulo. *Rediscovery of the Ordinary: Essays on South African Literature and Culture*. Johannesburg: COSAW, 1991.

———. *South African Literature and Culture: Rediscovery of the Ordinary*. Manchester: Manchester University Press, 1994.

Nhlapo, Thandabantlu. "The African Customary Law of Marriage and the Rights Conundrum." In *Beyond Rights Talk and Culture Talk: Comparative Essays on the Politics of Rights and Culture*, ed. Mahmood Mamdani, 136–148. Claremont, South Africa: David Phillip, 2000.

Nigam, Aditya. "Radical Politics in the Times of Globalization." In *Democratic Governance in India: Challenges of Poverty, Development, and Identity*, ed Niraja Gopal Jayal and Sudha Pai. Delhi: Sage, 2001.

Nina, Daniel. "Beyond the Frontier: Civil Society Revisited." *Transformation*, no. 17 (1992): 61–73.

"Nise Malange." In *Exchanges*, ed. D. Brown and B. van Dyk, 41–45. Pietermaritzburg, South Africa: University of Natal Press, 1991.

Nixon, Rob. "Caribbean and African Appropriations of *The Tempest*." *Critical Inquiry* 13, no. 3 (1987): 557–78.

———. *Homelands, Harlem, and Hollywood: South African Culture and the World Beyond*. New York: Routledge, 1994.

———. "Pipedreams: Ken Saro-Wiwa, Environmental Justice, and Micro-Minority Rights." *Black Renaissance/Renaissance Noire* 1, no. 1 (1996): 39–55.

Novick, Peter. *That Noble Dream: The "Objectivity Question" and the American Historical Profession*. Cambridge: Cambridge University Press, 1988.

Noyes, John. "The Place of the Human." In *Senses of Culture: South African Cultural Studies*, ed. Sarah Nuttall and Cheryl-Ann Michael, 46–60. Oxford: Oxford University Press, 2000.

Nussbaum, Martha. *Women and Human Development: The Capabilities Approach.* Cambridge: Cambridge University Press, 2000.

Nuttall, Tim, and John Wright. "Exploring History with a Capital 'H,'" *Current Writing* 10, no. 2 (1998): 38–61.

Nye, Joseph. *The Paradox of American Power: Why the World's Only Superpower Can't Go It Alone.* Oxford: Oxford University Press, 2002.

Obeyesekere, Gananath. *The Apotheosis of Captain Cook: European Mythmaking in the Pacific.* Princeton, NY: Princeton University Press, 1992.

O'Brien, Anthony. *Against Normalization: Writing Radical Democracy in South Africa.* Durham, NC: Duke University Press, 2001.

O'Brien, Patrick. "The Costs and Benefits of British Imperialism, 1846–1914." *Past and Present*, no. 120 (1998): 163–200.

O'Brien, Susie, and Imre Szeman, "The Globalization of Fiction/The Fiction of Globalization." *South Atlantic Quarterly* 100, no. 3 (2001): 603–26.

Oelschlaeger, Max. *The Idea of Wilderness: From Prehistory to the Age of Ecology.* New Haven, CT: Yale University Press, 1991.

O'Gorman, Edmundo. *La invención de América: El universalismo de la cultura del occidente.* Mexico City: Fondo de Cultura Económica, 1958.

———. *The Invention of America: An Inquiry into the Historical Nature of the New World and the Meaning of its History.* Bloomington: Indiana University Press, 1961.

O'Hanlon, Rosalind. "Recovering the Subject: Subaltern Studies and Histories of Resistance in Colonial South Asia." *Modern Asian Studies* 22, no. 1 (1988): 189–224.

O'Hanlon, Rosalind, and David Washbrook. "After Orientalism: Culture, Criticism, and Politics in the Third World." *Comparative Studies in Society and History* 34, no. 1 (1992): 141–67.

Ohmae, Kenichi. *The End of the Nation-State: The Rise of Regional Economies.* New York: Free Press, 1995.

Olafioye, Tayo. *A Carnival of Looters: Poems.* Ibadan, Nigeria: Kraft, 2000.

Olaniyan, Tejumola. "On 'Post-colonial' Discourse: An Introduction," *Callaloo* 16, no. 4 (1993): 743–49.

Ong, Aiwha. *Flexible Citizenship: The Cultural Logics of Transnationality.* Durham, NC: Duke University Press, 1999.

———. "The Gender and Labor Politics of Postmodernity." *Annual Review of Anthropology*, no. 20 (1991): 279–310.

Oomen, Barbara. "Chiefs, Law, Power, and Culture in Contemporary South Africa." PhD diss., Van Vollenhoven Institute, Leiden University, 2002.

Ordover, Nancy. *American Eugenics: Race, Queer Anatomy, and the Science of Nationalism.* Minneapolis: Minnesota University Press, 2003.

Osterhammel, Jürgen. *Colonialism: A Theoretical Overview.* Trans. Shelley Frisch. Princeton, NJ: Markus Wiener, 1997.

Otsubo, Sumiko. "Engendering Eugenics: Feminists and Marriage Restriction Legislation in the 1920s." In *Gendering Modern Japanese History*, ed. Barbara Molony and Kathleen Uno. Cambridge, MA: Harvard University Council on East Asian Studies, forthcoming.

Owolabi, Kolawole. *Because of Our Future: The Imperative for an Environmental Ethic for Africa*. Ibadan: IFRA/African Book Builders, 1996.

Pagden, Anthony. *Spanish Imperialism and the Political Imagination: Studies in European and Spanish-American Social and Political Theory, 1513-1830*. New Haven, CT: Yale University Press, 1990.

Pagels, Elaine. "Irenaeus, the 'Canon of Truth,' and the *Gospel of John*: 'Making a Difference' through Hermeneutics and Ritual," *Vigiliae Christianae* 56, no. 4 (2002): 339-71.

Paillalef, Rosa Isolde Reuque. *When a Flower Is Reborn: The Life and Times of a Mapuche Feminist*. Trans. and ed. Florencia E. Mallon. Durham, NC: Duke University Press, 2002.

Parry, Benita. "Directions and Dead Ends in Postcolonial Studies." In *Relocating Postcolonialism*, ed. David Theo Goldberg and Ato Quayson, 66-81. Oxford: Blackwell, 2002.

———. "The Marxist Legacy in Cultural and Postcolonial Studies: A Return of the Repressed?" In *Common Ground: Crossovers between Cultural Studies and Postcolonial Studies*, ed. Bernhard Klein and Jürgen Kramer, 9-20. Trier, Germany: Wissenschaftlicher Verlag, 2001.

———. "The Postcolonial: Conceptual Category or Chimera?" In "The Politics of Postcolonial Criticism," special number, *Yearbook of English Studies*, 27 (1997): 3-21.

———. "Problems in Current Theories of Colonial Discourse." *Oxford Literary Review* 9, nos. 1-2 (1987): 27-58.

Passavant, Paul, and Jodi Dean, eds. *Empire's New Clothes: Reading Hardt and Negri*. New York: Routledge, 2004.

Pattullo, Polly. *Last Resorts: The Cost of Tourism in the Caribbean*. London: Cassell, 1996.

Paul, Kathleen. *Whitewashing Britain: Race and Citizenship in the Postwar Era*. Ithaca, NY: Cornell University Press, 1997.

Payne, Daniel G. *Voices in the Wilderness: American Nature Writing and Environmental Politics*. Hanover, NH: University Press of New England, 1996.

Peabody, Sue. *"There Are No Slaves in France": The Political Culture of Race and Slavery in the Ancien Régime*. New York: Oxford, 1996.

Pearce, Gary. "Margins and Modernism: Ireland and the Formation of Modern Literature." PhD diss., Monash University, 2002.

Pechey, Graham. Introduction to *South African Literature and Culture: Rediscovery of the Ordinary*, ed. Njabulo Ndebele, 1-16. Manchester: Manchester University Press, 1994.

———. "Post-apartheid Narratives." In *Colonial Discourse/Postcolonial Theory*, ed. F. Barker et al., 151-71. Manchester: Manchester University Press, 1994.

———. "The Post-apartheid Sublime: Rediscovering the Ordinary." In *Writing South*

Africa: Literature, Apartheid, and Democracy, 1970-1995, ed. Derek Attridge and Rosemary Jolly, 57-74. Cambridge: Cambridge University Press, 1998.

Peirce, Charles Sanders. "Pragmaticism." In *The Essential Peirce: Selected Philosophical Writings.* Vol. 2, *1893-1913*, ed. The Peirce Edition Project, 398-433. Bloomington: Indiana University Press, 1998.

Peters, Arno. *Compact Peters Atlas of the World.* Harlow, UK: Longman, 1991.

——. *The New Cartography.* New York: Friendship Press, 1984.

Petrarch. *The Life of Solitude.* Trans. Jacob Zeitlin. Chicago: University of Chicago Press, 1924.

Phillips, Anne. *The Enigma of Colonialism: British Policy in West Africa.* London: James Currey, 1989.

Pigafetta, Antonio. *The First Voyage around the World.* Ca. 1525. Ed. Theodore J. Cachey Jr. New York: Marsilio, 1995.

Pike, Fredrick B. *The United States and Latin America: Myths and Stereotypes of Civilization and Nature.* Austin: University of Texas Press, 1992.

Piot, Charles. *Remotely Global: Village Modernity in West Africa.* Chicago: University of Chicago Press, 1999.

Piper, Karen. *Cartographic Fictions: Maps, Race, and Identity.* New Brunswick, NJ: Rutgers University Press, 2002.

Piterberg, Gabriel. "Erasures." *New Left Review*, no. 10 (2001): 31-46.

Plaatje, Solomon Tshekisho. *The Diary of Sol T. Plaatje: An African at Mafikeng.* Ed. John L. Comaroff. London: Macmillan, 1973.

——. *Mhudi.* 1930. London: Heinemann, 1982.

——. *Native Life in South Africa.* Harlow, Essex: Longman, 1987.

——. *Native Life in South Africa before and since the European War and the Boer Rebellion.* 1916. Athens: Ohio University Press, 1991.

——. *Sol Plaatje: Selected Writings.* Ed. Brian Willan. Athens: Ohio University Press, 1996.

Pollak, Michael. *Une identité blessée: Études de sociologie et d'histoire.* Paris: Éditions Métailié, 1993.

Pomeranz, Kenneth. *The Great Divergence: China, Europe, and the Making of the Modern World Economy.* Princeton, NJ: Princeton University Press, 2000.

Porter, Bernand. *Critics of Empire: British Radical Attitudes to Colonialism in Africa, 1895-1914.* New York: St. Martin's, 1968.

Prakash, Gyan. *Another Reason: Science and the Imagination of Modern India.* Princeton: Princeton University Press, 1999.

——. "Can the 'Subaltern' Ride? A Reply to O'Hanlon and Washbrook." *Comparative Studies in Society and History* 34, no. 1 (1992): 168-84.

——. "Subaltern Studies as Postcolonial Criticism." *American Historical Review* 99, no. 5 (1994): 1475-90.

——. "Writing Post-orientalist Histories of the Third World: Perspectives from Indian Historiography." *Comparative Studies in Society and History* 32, no. 2 (1990): 383-408.

————, ed. *After Colonialism: Imperial Histories and Postcolonial Displacements*. Princeton, NJ: Princeton University Press, 1995.

Pratt, Mary Louise. *Imperial Eyes: Travel Writing and Transculturation*. London: Routledge, 1992.

————. "Modernity and Periphery: Towards a Global and Relational Analysis." In *Beyond Dichotomies: Histories, Identities, Cultures, and the Challenge of Globalization*, ed. Elisabeth Mudimbe-Boyi. Albany: State University of New York Press, 2002.

————. "Scratches on the Face of the Country; Or, What Mr. Barrows Saw in the Land of the Bushman." In *"Race," Writing, and Difference*, ed. Henry Louis Gates Jr., 138–62. Chicago: University of Chicago Press, 1985.

Prazniak, Roaxanne. "Mao and the Woman Question in an Age of Green Politics: Some Critical Reflections." In *Critical Perspectives on Mao Zedong's Thought*, ed. Arif Dirlik, Paul Healy, and Nick Knight, 23–58. Atlantic Highlands, NJ: Humanities Press International, 1997.

Price, Richard. *The Convict and the Colonial: A Story of Colonialism and Resistance in the Caribbean*. Boston: Beacon, 1998.

Ptolemy, Claudius. *Ptolemy's Geography: An Annotated Translation of the Theoretical Chapters*. Ed. J. Lennart Berggren and Alexander Jones. Princeton, NJ: Princeton University Press, 2000.

Puri, Shalini. *The Caribbean Postcolonial: Social Equality, Post/Nationalism, and Cultural Hybridity*. New York: Palgrave, 2003.

Qayum, Seemin. "Nationalism, Internal Colonialism, and the Spatial Imagination: The Geographic Society of La Paz in Turn-of-the-Century Bolivia." In *Studies in the Formation of the Nation-State in Latin America*, ed. James Dunkerley, 275–98. London: Institute of Latin American Studies, 2002.

Quayson, Ato. "Obverse Denominations: Africa?" *Public Culture* 14, no. 3 (2992): 585–88.

Quijano, Aníbal. "Colonialidad del poder, eurocentrismo y América Latina." In *La colonialidad del saber: Eurocentrismo y ciencias sociales; Perspectivas latinoamericanas*, ed. Edgardo Lander 281–348. Caracas: UNESCO, 2000.

Rabasa, José. *Inventing America: Spanish Historiography and the Formation of Eurocentrism*. Norman: University of Oklahoma Press, 1993.

Radhakrishnan, R. "Nationalism, Gender, and the Narrative of Identity." In *Nationalisms and Sexualities*, ed. Andrew Parker et al., 77–95. New York: Routledge, 1992.

————. "Postmodernism and the Rest of the World." In *The Pre-occupation of Postcolonial Studies*, ed. Fawzia Afzal-Khan and Kalpana Seshadri-Crooks, 37–70. Durham, NC: Duke University Press, 2000.

Rahnema, Majid, with Victoria Bawtree, eds. *The Post-development Reader*. London: Zed, 1997.

Rai, Amit. " 'Thus Spoke the Subaltern . . .': Postcolonial Criticism and the Scene of Desire." *Discourse* 19, no. 2 (1997): 163–93.

Rainwater, Lee, and William Yancey. *The Moynihan Report and the Politics of Controversy: A Trans-action Social Science and Public Policy Report*. Cambridge, MA: MIT Press, 1967.

Randles, W. G. L. *Geography, Cartography, and Nautical Science in the Renaissance: The Impact of the Great Discoveries*. Aldershot, UK: Ashgate, 2000.

Raspail, Jean. *The Camp of the Saints*. Trans. Norman Shapiro. Petoskey, MI: Social Contract Press, 1995.

Raz-Krakotzkin, Amnon. "Exile within Sovereignty" [in Hebrew]. *Theory and Criticism*, no. 4 (1993): 23–56.

———. "Exile within Sovereignty (Continued)" [in Hebrew]. *Theory and Criticism*, no. 5 (1994): 113–32.

Reed, Adolph L., Jr. *W. E. B. Du Bois and American Political Thought: Fabianism and the Color Line*. New York: Oxford University Press, 1997.

Retamar, Roberto Fernández. "Nuestra América y Occidente." 1961. In *Para el perfil definitivo del hombre*, 222–50. Havana: Editorial Letras Cubanas, 1995.

Rich, Paul. "Is South African Radical History Becoming Irrelevant?" *South African Historical Journal*, no. 31 (1994): 191–97.

Robbins, Bruce. *Feeling Global: Internationalism in Crisis*. New York: New York University Press, 1999.

Robinson, Marilynne. *Mother Country*. New York: Faber, 1989.

Robinson, Shira. "My Hairdresser Is a Sniper." *Middle East Report* 223 (2002). Available at www.merip.org/mer/mer223/223_robinson.html.

Rodriguez, Richard. *Days of Obligation: An Argument with My Mexican Father*. New York: Viking, 1992.

———. "True West." In *The Anchor Essay Annual: The Best of 1997*, ed. Phillip Lopate. New York, 1998.

Rogaski, Ruth. "Hygienic Modernity in Tianjin." In *Remaking the Chinese City: Modernity and National Identity, 1900-1950*, ed. Joseph W. Esherick, 30–46. Honolulu: University of Honolulu Press, 2000.

Rosemblatt, Karin Alejandra. *Gendered Compromises: Political Cultures and the State in Chile, 1920-1950*. Chapel Hill: University of North Carolina Press, 2000.

Rotter, Andrew, K. E. Fleming, and Kathleen Biddick. "Orientalism Twenty Years On." *American Historical Review* 105, no. 4 (2000): 1204–49.

Rouse, Roger. "Mexican Migration and the Social Space of Postmodernism." *Diaspora* 1, no. 1 (1991): 8–23.

Rousseau, Jean-Jacques. *A Discourse on Inequality*. Trans. Maurice Cranston. New York: Penguin, 1984.

Roy, Arundhati. *The Cost of Living*. London: Modern Library, 1999.

———. *The God of Small Things*. New York: Random House, 1997.

Rugeley, Terry. *Yucatán's Maya Peasantry and the Origins of the Caste War*. Austin: University of Texas Press, 1996.

Runia, David. "Philo of Alexandria and the Greek *Hairesis*-Model." *Vigiliae Christianae* 53, no. (1999): 117–47.

Rushdie, Salman. *The Moor's Last Sigh.* London: Vintage, 1996.

Sachot, Maurice. "Comment le christianisme est-il devenu *religio*?" *Revue des Sciences Religieuses*, no. 59 (1985): 95–118.

——. ' "*Religio/Superstitio*': Historique d'une subversion et d'un retournement." *Revue d'Histoire des Religions* 207, no. 4 (1991): 355–94.

Sachs, Wolfgang, ed. *The Development Dictionary: A Guide to Knowledge as Power.* London: Zed, 1992.

Sahlins, Marshall. *How "Natives" Think: About Captain Cook, for Example.* Chicago: University of Chicago Press, 1995.

Said, Edward W. *Culture and Imperialism.* New York: Knopf, 1993.

——. *Orientalism.* New York: Vintage, 1978.

——. *The Question of Palestine.* New York: Vintage, 1979.

Sangari, Kumkum. "New Patriotisms: The Beauty Queen and the Bomb." In *From Gender to Nation*, ed. Rada Ivekovic and Julie Mostov, 153–70. Ravenna: Longo Editore, 2002.

San Juan, E., Jr. *Beyond Postcolonial Theory.* New York: St. Martin's, 1998.

——. *Hegemony and Strategies of Transgression: Essays in Cultural Studies and Comparative Literature.* Albany: State University of New York Press, 1995.

Sarkar, Sumit. "The Decline of the Subaltern in *Subaltern Studies*." In *Reading Subaltern Studies: Critical History, Contested Meaning, and the Globalization of South Asia*, ed. David Ludden, 400–29. Delhi: Permanent Black, 2001.

Sarkar, Tanika. *Hindu Wife, Hindu Nation: Community, Religion, and Cultural Nationalism.* Bloomington: Indiana University Press, 2001.

Sarkar, Tanika, and Urvashi Butalia, eds. *Women and the Hindu Right: A Collection of Essays.* Delhi: Kali for Women, 1995.

Saro-Wiwa, Ken. *A Month and a Day: A Detention Diary.* London: Penguin, 1995.

——. *Nigeria: The Brink of Disaster.* Port Harcourt, Nigeria: Saros International Publishers, 1991.

Sartre, Jean-Paul. "Orphée Noir." 1948. In Léopold Sédar Senghor, *Anthologie de la Nouvelle Poésie Nègre et Malgache de Langue Française.* Paris: Presses Universitaires de France, 1969.

Sassen, Saskia. "Spatialities and Temporalities of the Global: Elements for a Theorization." *Public Culture* 12, no. 1 (2000): 215–35.

Sauer, Carl Ortwin. *The Early Spanish Main.* Berkeley: University of California Press, 1966.

——. *Sixteenth-Century North America: The Land and the People as Seen by the Europeans.* Berkeley: University of California Press, 1971.

Sawyer, Suzana. "The Politics of Petroleum: Indigenous Contestation of Multinational Oil Development in the Ecuadorian Amazon." MacArthur Consortium Occasional Papers Series. MacArthur Program, University of Minnesota, 1997.

Scarce, Rick. *Eco-warriors: Understanding the Radical Environmental Movement.* Chicago: Nobel, 1990.

Schaefer, William. "Shanghai Savage." In "The Afro-Asian Century," ed., Andrew F. Jones and Nikhil Pal Singh, special issue, *positions* 11, no. 1 (2003): 91–133.

Schiappa, Edward. *The Beginnings of Rhetorical Theory in Classical Greece.* New Haven, CT: Yale University Press, 1999.

Schiefflin, Bambi, Kathryn Woolard, and Paul Kroskrity, eds. *Language Ideologies: Practice and Theory.* Oxford: Oxford University Press, 1998

Schmitt, John. "Inequality and Globalization: Some Evidence from the United States." In *The Ends of Globalization: Bringing Society Back In,* ed. Don Kalb et al., 157–168. Lanham, MD: Rowman and Littlefield, 2000.

Schueller, Malini Johar. "Articulations of African-Americanism in South Asian Post-colonial Theory: Globalism, Localism, and the Question of Race." *Cultural Critique,* no. 55 (2003): 35–62.

Schuyler, George S. *Ethiopian Stories.* Comp. and ed. Robert A. Hill. Boston: Northeastern University Press, 1995.

Schwartz, Seth. *Imperialism and Jewish Society from 200 B.C.E. to 640 C.E.* Princeton, NJ: Princeton University Press, 2001.

Schwartz, Stuart, ed. *Implicit Understanding: Observing, Reporting, and Reflecting on the Encounters between Europeans and Other Peoples in the Early Modern Era.* Cambridge: Cambridge University Press, 1994.

Schwarz, Roberto. *A Master on the Periphery of Capitalism: Machado de Assis.* Trans. John Gledson. Durham, NC: Duke University Press, 2001.

Scott, David. "Colonialism." *International Social Science Journal,* no. 154 (1997): 517–526.

———. "Culture in Political Theory." *Political Theory* 31, no. 1 (2003): 93–116.

———. *Refashioning Futures: Criticism after Postcoloniality.* Princeton, NJ: Princeton University Press, 1999.

Seed, Patricia. *Ceremonies of Possession in European Conquests of the New World, 1492–1640.* Cambridge: Cambridge University Press, 1995.

Selverston, Melina. "The 1990 Indigenous Uprising in Ecuador: Politicized Ethnicity as Social Movement." Papers on Latin America, no. 32. New York: Columbia University Institute of Latin American and Iberian Studies, 1993.

Serote, Mongane. *Hyenas.* Florida Hills, South Africa: Vivlia, 2000.

Seshadri-Crooks, Kalpana. "At the Margins of Postcolonial Studies: Part 1." In *The Pre-occupation of Postcolonial Studies,* ed. Fawzia Afzal-Khan and Seshadri-Crooks, 1–23. Durham, NC: Duke University Press, 2000.

Seth, Sanjay. "Interpreting Revolutionary Excess: The Naxalite Movement in India, 1967–1971." In *New Asian Marxisms,* ed. Tani E. Barlow, 333–58. Durham, NC: Duke University Press, 2002.

Shakespeare, William. *The Tempest.* Ed. Stephen Orgel. 1611. Oxford: Oxford University Press, 1987.

Sharma, Sanjay. *Famine, Philanthropy, and the Colonial State.* Oxford: Oxford University Press, 2001.

Sharpe, Jenny. "Is the United States Postcolonial? Transnationalism, Immigration, and Race." In *Postcolonial America*, ed. C. Richard King, 103–21. Urbana: University of Illinois Press, 2000.

Shih, Shu-mei. *Lure of the Modern: Writing Modernism in Semicolonial China, 1917–1937*. Berkeley: University of California Press, 2001.

Shin, Gi-wook, and Michael Robinson, eds. *Colonial Modernity in Korea*. Cambridge, MA: Harvard University Press, 1999.

Shiva, Vandana. *Staying Alive: Women, Ecology, and Development*. Delhi: Kali for Women, 1988.

Shohat, Ella. "The Invention of the Mizrahim." *Journal of Palestine Studies* 29, no. 1 (1999): 5–20.

———. "Notes on the Postcolonial." *Social Text*, nos. 31–32 (1992): 99–113.

———. "Sephardim in Israel: Zionism from the Standpoint of Its Jewish Victims." *Social Text*, nos. 19–20 (1988): 1–35.

Shohat, Ella, and Robert Stam. *Unthinking Eurocentrism: Multiculturalism and the Media*. London: Routledge, 1994.

Siegel, James. *Solo in the New Order: Language and Hierarchy in an Indonesian City*. Princeton, NJ: Princeton University, 1986.

Silberstein, Lawrence J. *The Postzionism Debates: Knowledge and Power in Israeli Culture*. New York: Routledge, 1999.

Silko, Leslie Marmon. *"Yellow Woman" and "A Beauty of the Spirit."* New York: Simon and Schuster, 1996.

Silverstein, Michael. "Case Marking and the Nature of Language," *Australian Journal of Linguistics*, no. 1 (1981): 227–46.

———. "Hierarchy of Features and Ergativity." In *Grammatical Categories in Australian Languages*, ed. R. M. W. Dixon, 112–71. Canberra: Australian Institute of Aboriginal Studies, 1976.

Silverstein, Michael, and Greg Urban, eds. *Natural Histories of Discourse*. Chicago: University of Chicago Press, 1996.

Simmel, Georg. "The Metropolis and Mental Life." In *Simmel On Culture*, ed. David Frisby and Mike Featherstone. London: Sage, 1997.

———. *The Philosophy of Money*. Trans. Tom Bottomore and David Frisby. Boston: Routledge and Kegal Paul, 1978.

Sinclair, Upton. *Oil!* 1926. Berkeley: University of California Press, 1997.

Singh, Amritjit, and Peter Schmidt, eds. *Postcolonial Theory and the United States: Race, Ethnicity, and Literature*. Jackson: University Press of Mississippi, 2000.

Skinner, Quentin. "Reply to My Critics." In *Meaning and Context: Quentin Skinner and His Critics*, ed. James Tuly, 231–88. Cambridge: Cambridge University Press, 1988.

Slaymaker, William. "Echoing the Other(s): The Call of Global Green and Black African Responses." *PMLA* 116, no. 1 (2001): 129–44.

Slovic, Scott. "Forum on Literatures of the Environment." *PMLA* 116, no. 5 (1999): 1089–1106.

———. *Seeking Awareness in American Nature Writing: Henry Thoreau, Annie Dil-*

lard, *Edward Abbey, Wendell Berry, Barry Lopez*. Salt Lake City: University of Utah Press, 1992.

Smith, Neil. "Contours of a Spatialized Politics: Homeless Vehicles and the Production of Geographical Scale." *Social Text*, no. 22 (1992): 54–81.

———. "Scales of Terror and the Resort to Geography: September 11, October 7." *Environment and Planning D: Society and Space* 19, no. 6 (2001): 631–37.

Smith, Wilfred Cantwell. *The Meaning and End of Religion*. London: Society for the Propagation of Christian Knowledge, 1978.

Sole, Kelwyn. "Political Fiction, Representation, and the Canon: The Case of Mtutuzeli Matshoba." *English in Africa* 28, no. 2 (2001): 101–22.

———."South Africa Passes the Posts." *Alternation* 4, no. 1 (1997): 116–51.

———. "The Witness of Poetry: Economic Calculation, Civil Society, and the Limits of the Everyday in Post-liberation South Africa." *New Formations*, no. 45 (2002): 24–53.

Solnit, Rebecca. *Savage Dreams: A Journey into the Landscape Wars of the American West*. Berkeley: University of California Press, 1999.

Somers, Margaret. "Rights, Relationality, and Membership: Rethinking the Making and Meaning of Citizenship." *Law and Social Inquiry*, no. 19 (1994): 63–112.

Soyinka, Wole. *The Swamp Dwellers*. In *Collected Plays*. Oxford: Oxford University Press, 1973.

Spivak, Gayatri Chakravorty. "Attention: Postcolonialism!" *Journal of Caribbean Studies* 12, nos. 2–3 (1997–98): 159–79.

———. "Can the Subaltern Speak?" In *Marxism and the Interpretation of Culture*, ed. Cary Nelson and Lawrence Grossberg, 271–313. Urbana: University of Illinois Press, 1988.

———. *A Critique of Postcolonial Reason: Toward A History of the Vanishing Present*. Cambridge, MA: Harvard University Press, 1999.

———. "Cultural Talks in the Hot Peace: Revisiting the 'Global Village.'" In *Cosmopolitics: Thinking and Feeling beyond the Nation*, ed. Pheng Cheah and Bruce Robbins, 329–48. Minneapolis: University of Minnesota Press, 1998.

———. *In Other Worlds: Essays in Cultural Politics*. New York: Methuen, 1987.

———. "The New Subaltern: A Silent Interview." In *Mapping Subaltern Studies and the Postcolonial*, ed. Vinayak Chaturvedi, 324–40. London: Verso, 2000.

———. *The Post-colonial Critic: Interviews, Strategies, Dialogues*. New York: Routledge, 1990.

———. "Race before Racism: The Disappearance of the American." In *Edward Said and the Work of the Critic: Speaking Truth to Power*, ed. Paul A. Bové, 51–65. Durham, NC: Duke University Press, 2000.

———. "Scattered Speculations on the Question of Value." In *In Other Worlds: Essays on Cultural Politics*. New York: Methuen, 1987.

———. "Who Claims Alterity?" In *Remaking History*, ed. Barbara Kruger and Phil Mariani, 269–92. Seattle: Bay, 1989.

Stam, Robert. *Tropical Multiculturalism: A Comparative History of Race in Brazilian Cinema and Culture*. Durham, NC: Duke University Press, 1997.

Stavrianos, L. S. *Global Rift: The Third World Comes of Age*. New York: Morrow, 1981.

Stephen, Lynn. ¡*Zapata Lives! Histories and Cultural Politics in Southern Mexico*. Berkeley: University of California Press, 2002.

Stiglitz, Joseph. *Globalization and Its Discontents*. New York, Norton, 2002.

Stoler, Ann Laura. "Carnal Knowledge and Imperial Power: Gender, Race, and Morality in Colonial Asia." In *Gender at the Crossroads of Knowledge: Feminist Anthropology in the Postmodern Era*, ed. Micaela di Leonardo, 51–88. Berkeley: University of California Press, 1991.

———. "In Cold Blood: Hierarchies of Credibility and the Politics of Colonial Narratives." *Representations*, no. 37 (1992): 151–89.

———. *Race and the Education of Desire: Foucault's "History of Sexuality" and the Colonial Order of Things*. Durham, NC: Duke University Press, 1995.

Stone, Lawrence. *Uncertain Unions: Marriage in England, 1660-1753*. Oxford: Oxford University Press, 1992.

Stora, Benjamin. *La gangrène et l'oubli: La mémoire de la guerre d'Algérie*. Paris: La Découverte, 1998.

Tabb, William. "Capitalism and Globalization." In *Imperialism: Theoretical Directions*, ed. Ronald H. Chilcote, 315–22. Amherst, NY: Humanity Books, 2000.

Tabili, Laura. *"We Ask for British Justice": Workers and Racial Difference in Late Imperial Britain*. Ithaca, NY: Cornell University Press, 1994.

Tagliacozzo, Eric. Review of *Opium Regimes*. *Journal of Asian Studies* 60, no. 3 (August 2001): 819–820.

Thiong'o, Ngugi wa. *Decolonising the Mind: The Politics of Language in African Literature*. London: J. Currey, 1986.

———. *Grain of Wheat*. New York: Heinemann, 1994.

Thompson, E. P. *The Making of the English Working Class*. 1963. New York: Vintage, 1966.

Thompson, Robert Farris. *Flash of the Spirit: African and Afro-American Art and Philosophy*. New York: Random House, 1983.

Thurner, Mark. *From Two Republics to One Divided: Contradictions of Postcolonial Nationmaking in Andean Peru*. Durham, NC: Duke University Press, 1997.

Tinsman, Heidi. *Partners in Conflict: The Politics of Gender, Sexuality, and Labor in the Chilean Agrarian Reform, 1950-1973*. Durham, NC: Duke University Press, 2002.

Torgovnick, Marianna. *Primitive Passions: Men, Women, and the Quest for Ecstasy*. New York: Knopf, 1997.

Tropper, Amram. "*Tractate Avot* and Early Christian Succession Lists." In *The Ways That Never Parted*, ed. Peter Schaeffer, 159–88. Berlin: Mohr/Siebeck, 2002.

Urban, Greg. "The 'I' of Discourse in Shokleng." In *Semiotics, Self, and Society*, ed. Benjamin Lee and Urban, 27–51. Berlin: Mouton de Gruyter, 1989.

Vanderbilt, Tom. "The Advertised Life." In *Commodify Your Dissent: Salvos from the Baffler*, ed. Thomas Frank and Matt Weiland, 127–43. New York: Norton, 1997.

Van Dijk, Rijk. "Pentecostalism, Cultural Memory, and the State: Contested Representations of Time in Postcolonial Malawi." In *Memory and the Postcolony: African Anthropology and the Critique of Power*, ed. Richard Werbner, 155–82. London: Zed, 1999.

Vansina, Jan. *Oral Tradition: A Study in Historical Methodology*. Trans. H. M. Wright. 1961. Chicago: Aldine, 1965.

Vaughan, Megan. "Colonial Discourse Theory and African History; Or, Has Postmodernism Passed Us By?" *Social Dynamics* 20, no. 2 (1994): 1–23.

———. *Curing Their Ills: Colonial Power and African Illness*. Stanford, CA: Stanford University Press, 1991.

Vidal-Naquet, Pierre. *Mémoire*. Vol. 1, *La trouble et le mémoire, 1955–1998*. Paris: Seuil, 1998.

Viotti da Costa, Emilia. *The Brazilian Empire: Myths and Histories*. Chapel Hill: University of North Carolina Press, 1985.

Viswanathan, Gauri. *Masks of Conquest: Literary Study and British Rule in India*. New York: Columbia University Press, 1989.

———. *Outside the Fold: Conversion, Modernity, and Belief*. Princeton, NJ: Princeton University Press, 1998.

Voloshinov, V. N. *Marxism and the Philosophy of Language*. Trans. Ladislav Matejka and I. R. Titunik. Cambridge: Harvard University Press, 1986.

Von Eschen, Penny. *Race against Empire: Black Americans and Anticolonialism, 1937–1957*. Ithaca, NY: Cornell University Press, 1997.

Wales, Kathleen. "*Thou* and *You* in Early Modern English: Brown and Gilman Reappraised." *Studia Linguistica*, no. 37 (1983): 107–25.

Walker, Charles. *Smoldering Ashes: Cuzco and the Creation of Republican Peru, 1780–1840*. Durham, NC: Duke University Press, 1999.

Walker, Cherryl. "Conceptualising Motherhood in Twentieth-Century South Africa." *Journal of Southern African Studies* 21, no. 3 (1995): 417–37.

Walker, Kathy Le Mons. *Chinese Modernity and the Peasant Path: Semicolonialism in the Northern Yangzi Delta*. Stanford, CA: Stanford University Press, 1999.

Wallace, David. "Humanism, Slavery, and the Republic of Letters." In *The Public Intellectual*, ed. Helen Small, 62–88. Oxford: Blackwell, 2002.

Wallerstein, Immanuel. *The Decline of American Power: The U.S. in a Chaotic World*. New York: New Press, 2003.

———. *The Modern World-System: Capitalist Agriculture and the Origins of the European World-Economy in the Sixteenth Century*. New York: Academic, 1974.

Walshe, Peter. *The Rise of African Nationalism in South Africa: The African National Congress, 1912–1952*. Berkeley: University of California Press, 1971.

Warner, Michael. *Publics and Counterpublics*. New York: Zone, 2002.

Warren, Kay. *Indigenous Movements and Their Critics: Pan-Maya Activism in Guatemala*. Princeton, NJ: Princeton University Press, 1998.

Wasser, Frederick. "Is Hollywood America? The Trans-nationalization of the American Film Industry." *Critical Studies in Mass Communication*, no. 12 (1995): 423–37.

Watson, Tim. "An American Empire?" *Postcolonial Studies* 4, no. 3 (2001): 351–59.

Weber, Eugen. *Peasants into Frenchmen: The Modernization of Rural France, 1870–1914*. Stanford, CA: Stanford University Press, 1976.

Weber, Max. *The Protestant Ethic and the Spirit of Capitalism*. Trans. Talcott Parsons. London: Routledge, 1992.

Weil, Patrick. *Qu'est-ce qu'un Français? Histoire de la nationalité française depuis la Révolution*. Paris: Grasset, 2002.

Weisenfeld, Gennifer. *Mavo: Japanese Artists and the Avant-Garde, 1905–1931*. Berkeley: University of California Press, 2002.

———, ed. Special issue, *positions* 8, no. 3 (2000).

Werbner, Richard, and Terence Ranger, eds. *Postcolonial Identities in Africa*. London: Zed, 1996.

Whitmore, John. "The Opening of Southeast Asia: Trading Patterns through the Centuries." In *Economic Exchange and Social Interaction in Southeast Asia: Perspectives from Prehistory and Ethnography*, ed. Karl L. Hutterer, 139–53. Ann Arbor: University of Michigan Press, 1977.

Wieviorka, Michel. *La France Raciste*. Paris: Seuil, 1992.

Willan, Brian. *Sol Plaatje: South African Nationalist, 1876–1932*. Berkeley: University of California Press, 1984.

Williams, Patrick, and Laura Chrisman, eds. *Colonial Discourse and Post-colonial Theory: A Reader*. New York: Columbia University Press, 1994.

Williams, Raymond. *The Country and the City*. New York: Oxford University Press, 1973.

———. *Marxism and Literature*. New York: Oxford University Press, 1977.

———. *The Politics of Modernism: Against the New Conformists*. London: Verso, 1990.

———. *Towards 2000*. London: Chatto and Windus, 1983.

Williams, Rowan. "Does It Make Sense to Speak of Pre-Nicene Orthodoxy?" In *The Making of Orthodoxy: Essays in Honour of Henry Chadwick*, ed. Williams, 1–23. Cambridge: Cambridge University Press, 1989.

Wilson, Arthur. "The Enlightenment Came First to England." In *England's Rise to Greatness, 1660–1763*, ed. Stephen B. Baxter, 1–28. Berkeley: University of California Press, 1983.

Witz, Leslie. *Write Your Own History*. Johannesburg: Sached/Ravan, 1988.

Wolf, Eric. *Europe and the People without History*. Berkeley: University of California Press, 1982.

Wolf, Martin. "Will the Nation-State Survive Globalization?" *Foreign Affairs* 80, no. 1 (2001): 178–90.

Wolfe, Patrick. "History and Imperialism: A Century of Theory, from Marx to Postcolonialism." *American Historical Review*, no. 102 (1997): 388–420.

Wollstonecraft, Mary. *A Vindication of the Rights of Woman.* 1792. Ed. Sylvana Tomaselli. Cambridge: Cambridge University Press, 1995.

Wong, R. Bin. *China Transformed: Historical Change and the Limits of European Experience.* Ithaca, NY: Cornell University Press, 1997.

Wood, Gordon S. *The Radicalism of the American Revolution.* New York: Knopf, 1991.

Woodward, David. "Maps and the Rationalization of Geographic Space." In *Circa 1492: Art in the Age of Exploration,* ed. Jay A. Levenson, 83–87. New Haven, CT: Yale University Press, 1991.

Woodward, David, and G. Malcolm Lewis. Introduction to *The History of Cartography,* vol. 2, book 3. Ed. J. B. Harley and David Woodward. Chicago: University of Chicago Press, 1999.

Woolf, Stuart. "French Civilization and Ethnicity in the Napoleonic Empire." *Past and Present,* no. 124 (1989): 96–120.

Yack, Bernard. *The Fetishism of Modernities: Epochal Self-Consciousness in Contemporary Social and Political Thought.* Notre Dame, IN: University of Notre Dame Press, 1997.

Young, Louise. *Japan's Total Empire: Manchuria and the Culture of Wartime Imperialism.* Berkeley: University of California Press, 1998.

Young, Robert. *Colonial Desire: Hybridity in Theory, Culture, and Race.* London: Routledge, 1995.

———. *Postcolonialism: An Historical Introduction.* Oxford: Blackwell, 2001.

———. *White Mythologies: Writing History and the West.* London: Routledge, 1990.

Contributors

TANI E. BARLOW is a historian of modern China and teaches in women's studies at the University of Washington. Recent publications include *The Question of Women in Chinese Feminism* (2004), *Inter/national Feminism and China* (2003), and, as editor (with Jing Wang), *Cinema and Desire: The Cultural Politics of Feminist Marxist Dai Jinhua* (2002).

ALI BEHDAD is an associate professor of English and comparative literature at the University of California, Los Angeles. He is the author of *A Forgetful Nation: On Immigration and Cultural Identity in the United States* (forthcoming) and *Belated Travelers: Orientalism in the Age of Colonial Dissolution* (1994). He has also written many articles on such topics as nationalism, exile, immigration, orientalist photography, and travel literature.

DANIEL BOYARIN is Taubman Professor of Talmudic Culture and rhetoric, at the University of California, Berkeley. His books include *Intertextuality and the Reading of Midrash* (1990), *Carnal Israel: Reading Sex in Talmudic Culture* (1993), *A Radical Jew: Paul and the Politics of Identity* (1994), *Unheroic Conduct: The Rise of Heterosexuality and the Invention of the Jewish Man* (1997), and *Dying for God: Martyrdom and the Making of Christianity and Judaism* (1999). *Border Lines: Hybrids, Heretics, and the Partition of Judaeo-Christianity* will be published in 2004.

TIMOTHY BRENNAN is a professor of comparative literature, cultural studies, and English at the University of Minnesota, and director of the Humanities Institute there. He is the author of *At Home in the World: Cosmopolitanism Now* (1997), *Salman Rushdie and the Third World: Myths of the Nation* (1989), and has edited and introduced Alejo Carpentier's *Music in Cuba* (2001). He has just completed a book titled *Cultures of Belief*.

MATTI BUNZL is an associate professor of anthropology and history at the University of Illinois, Urbana-Champaign, where he also directs the Illinois Program for Research in the Humanities. He is the author of *Symptoms of Modernity: Jews and Queers in Late-Twentieth-Century Vienna* (2004) and the coeditor (with Glenn Penny) of *Worldly Provincialism: German Anthropology in the Age of Empire* (2003).

ANTOINETTE BURTON is a professor of history at the University of Illinois, Urbana-Champaign. Her recent publications include *Dwelling in the Archive: Women Writing House, Home, and History in Late Colonial India* (2003) and *After the Imperial Turn: Thinking with and through the Nation* (2003).

LAURA CHRISMAN teaches English at the University of York. Her latest book is entitled *Postcolonial Contraventions: Cultural Readings of Race, Imperialism, and Transnationalism* (2003). Other books include *The Rendez-Vous of Conquest: Rethinking Race and Nation* (2001), *Rereading the Imperial Romance: British Imperialism and South African Resistance in Haggard, Schreiner, and Plaatje* (2000), *Postcolonial Theory and Criticism,* coedited with Benita Parry (2000), and, with Patrick Williams, *Colonial Discourse and Postcolonial Theory: A Reader* (1994).

JEAN COMAROFF is the Bernard E. and Ellen C. Sunny Distinguished Service Professor of Anthropology at the University of Chicago. She has published widely on the intersection of anthropology and history, her most recent books being the two-volume *Of Revelation and Revolution* (1991/1997) and *Millennial Capitalism and the Culture of Neo-liberalism* (2001), both with John L. Comaroff.

FREDERICK COOPER is a professor of African history at New York University. His most recent books are *Africa since 1940: The Past of the Present* (2002), *Beyond Slavery: Explorations of Race, Labor, and Citizenship* (with Thomas Holt and Rebecca Scott, 2000), *Decolonization and African Society: The Labor Question in French and British Africa* (1996), and *Tensions of Empire: Colonial Cultures in a Bourgeois World* (coedited with Ann Stoler, 1997).

VILASHINI COOPPAN is an assistant professor in the Humanities Division at the University of California, Santa Cruz. She has published essays on postcolonial theory, psychoanalysis and Cuban literature, and new pedagogies of world literature, and has articles forthcoming on gender politics in the work of W. E. B. Du Bois and on the South African literature of transition. She is currently completing a book manuscript entitled "Inner Territories: Phantasms of the Nation in Post-Colonial Writing."

JED ESTY is an associate professor in the English department and the Unit for Criticism and Interpretive Theory at the University of Illinois, Urbana-Champaign. He is the author of *A Shrinking Island: Modernism and National Culture in England* (2003), as well as of several essays on British, Irish, and postcolonial literature.

JAMES FERGUSON is a professor of anthropology at Stanford University. His most recent book is *Expectations of Modernity: Myths and Meanings of Urban Life on the Zambian Copperbelt* (1999). He is now completing work on a book of essays exploring the meaning of the contemporary situation in Africa for current theories of globalization and modernity.

PETER HULME is a professor in literature at the University of Essex. His most recent books are *Remnants of Conquest: The Island Caribs and their Visitors, 1877–1998* (2000), *"The Tempest" and Its Travels*, coedited with William H. Sherman (2000), and the *Cambridge Companion to Travel Writing*, coedited with Tim Youngs (2002).

SUVIR KAUL is a professor of English at the University of Pennsylvania. He is the author of *Thomas Gray and Literary Authority* (1992) and *Poems of Nation, Anthems of Empire* (2000). He has also edited *The Partitions of Memory: The Afterlife of the Division of India* (2001).

NEIL LAZARUS is a professor of English and comparative literary studies at the University of Warwick. He is the author of *Resistance in Postcolonial African Fiction* (1990) and *Nationalism and Cultural Practice in the Postcolonial World* (1999), editor of *The Cambridge Companion to Postcolonial Literary Studies* (2004), and co-editor, with Crystal Bartolovich, of *Marxism, Modernity, and Postcolonial Studies* (2002).

ANIA LOOMBA is Catherine Bryson Professor of English at the University of Pennsylvania. She is the author of *Gender, Race, Renaissance Drama* (1989), *Colonialism/Postcolonialism* (1998), *Shakespeare, Race, and Colonialism* (2002), and has edited, with Martin Orkin, *Postcolonial Shakespeares* (1998).

FLORENCIA E. MALLON teaches Latin American history at the University of Wisconsin, Madison. In addition to *Peasant and Nation: The Making of Postcolonial Mexico and Peru* (1995), she has published extensively on social theory and on agrarian, political, and social history. She has edited and translated Rosa Isolde Reuque Paillalef, *When a Flower Is Reborn: The Life and Times of a Mapuche Feminist* (2002) and is completing a manuscript entitled "Courage Tastes of Blood: The Mapuche Indigenous Community of Nicolás Ailío and the Chilean State, 1906–2000."

NIVEDITA MENON, reader at the Department of Political Science, Delhi University, is the author of *Recovering Subversion: Feminist Politics beyond the Law* (2004). She has written on gender and politics for Indian and international journals and has edited *Gender and Politics in India* (1999).

ROB NIXON is Rachel Carson Professor of English at the University of Wisconsin, Madison. He is author of *London Calling: Homelands, Harlem, and Hollywood* (1992), and *Dreambirds: The Natural History of a Fantasy* (2000). His work has appeared in the *New Yorker*, the *Atlantic*, the *New York Times*, *Critical Inquiry*, and elsewhere.

ELIZABETH A. POVINELLI is a professor of anthropology at the University of Chicago. She is the author of two books, *Labor's Lot* (1994) and *The Cunning of Recognition* (2002), as well as the current editor of *Public Culture*. Her research and writing focuses on the semiotic mediation of power, transnational sexuality, and the politics of recognition.

DAVID SCOTT is a professor of anthropology at Columbia University. He is the author of *Formations of Ritual: Colonial and Anthropological Discourses on the Sinhala Yaktovil* (1994), *Refashioning Futures: Criticism after Postcoloniality* (1999), and *Conscripts of Modernity: The Tragedy of Colonial Enlightenment* (2004). He is also editor of the journal *Small Axe*.

ELLA SHOHAT is a professor of cultural studies in the Departments of Art and Public Policy, Middle Eastern Studies, and Comparative Literature at New York University. Her books include *Israeli Cinema: East/West and the Politics of Representation* (1989), *Unthinking Eurocentrism* (coauthored with Robert Stam, 1994), *Talking Visions: Multicultural Feminism in a Transnational Age* (1989), and *Forbidden Reminiscences* (forthcoming).

KELWYN SOLE is a professor in the English department at the University of Cape Town. He has published four volumes of poetry and numerous articles and polemics in books and journals, mainly on postcolonial theory, contemporary South African poetry, and the literature of black consciousness in South Africa.

ROBERT STAM is University Professor at New York University. He is the author of some fifteen books on the cinema and on cultural studies, most recently *Tropical Multiculturalism* (1997), *Film Theory: An Introduction* (2000), and (with Ella Shohat) *Multiculturalism, Postcoloniality, and Transnational Media* (2003). Three further books on literature and film are forthcoming.

REBECCA L. STEIN is an assistant professor of cultural anthropology at Duke University. She is on the editorial board of *Middle East Report*, and her writing on Israeli political culture has appeared in *Social Text*, *Public Culture*, and *Theory and Event*. She is the coeditor, with Ted Swedenburg, of *Palestine, Israel, and the Politics of Popular Culture* (2005), and, with Joel Beinin, of *The Struggle for Sovereignty in Palestine and Israel, 1993–2004* (forthcoming).

Index

ANIA LOOMBA is Catherine Bryson Professor of English at the University of Pennsylvania.

SUVIR KAUL is a professor of English at the University of Pennsylvania.

MATTI BUNZL is an associate professor of anthropology and history at the University of Illinois, Urbana-Champaign.

ANTOINETTE BURTON is a professor of history at the University of Illinois, Urbana-Champaign.

JED ESTY is an associate professor in the English department and the Unit for Criticism and Interpretive Theory at the University of Illinois, Urbana-Champaign.

Library of Congress Cataloging-in-Publication Data
Postcolonial studies and beyond / edited by Ania Loomba . . . [et al.].
p. cm.
Includes bibliographical references and index.
ISBN 0-8223-3511-5 (cloth : alk. paper) — ISBN 0-8223-3523-9 (pbk. : alk. paper)
1. Postcolonialism—Congresses. 2. Globalization—Congresses. 3. National state—Congresses. 4. Liberalism—Congresses. I. Loomba, Ania.
JV51.P652 2005
325'.3–dc22   2004028255